CompTIA® Linux+ / LPIC-1 Cert Guide

Ross Brunson
Sean Walberg

800 East 96th Street
Indianapolis, Indiana 46240 USA

CompTIA Linux+ / LPIC-1 Cert Guide
(Exams LX0-103 & LX0-104/101-400 & 102-400)

Ross Brunson

Sean Walberg

ISBN-13: 978-0-7897-5455-4

ISBN-10: 0-7897-5455-X

Library of Congress Control Number: 2015945796

Printed in the United States of America

3   17

Trademarks

All terms mentioned in this book that are known to be trademarks or service marks have been appropriately capitalized. Pearson cannot attest to the accuracy of this information. Use of a term in this book should not be regarded as affecting the validity of any trademark or service mark.

Warning and Disclaimer

This book is designed to provide information about Linux. Every effort has been made to make this book as complete and as accurate as possible, but no warranty or fitness is implied. The information is provided on an "as is" basis. The authors and publisher shall have neither liability nor responsibility to any person or entity with respect to any loss or damages arising from the information contained in this book or from the use of the DVD or programs that may accompany it. The opinions expressed in this book belong to the authors and are not necessarily those of Pearson IT Certification.

Special Sales

For information about buying this title in bulk quantities, or for special sales opportunities (which may include electronic versions; custom cover designs; and content particular to your business, training goals, marketing focus, or branding interests), please contact our corporate sales department at corpsales@pearsoned.com or (800) 382-3419.

For government sales inquiries, please contact governmentsales@pearsoned.com.

For questions about sales outside the U.S., please contact international@pearsoned.com.

Publisher
Paul Boger

Associate Publisher
Dave Dusthimer

Executive Editor
Mary Beth Ray

Development Editor
Eleanor C. Bru

Managing Editor
Sandra Schroeder

Project Editor
Seth Kerney

Copy Editor
Geneil Breeze

Indexer
Tim Wright

Proofreader
Brad Herriman

Technical Editors
Ted Jordan
William "Bo" Rothwell

Publishing Coordinator
Vanessa Evans

Multimedia Developer
Lisa Matthews

Interior Designer
Mark Shirar

Cover Designer
Alan Clements

Composition
Trina Wurst

Contents at a Glance

Contents

About the Authors

Ross Brunson has more than 20 years of experience as a Linux and Open Source trainer, training manager, and technologist and is author of the popular LPIC-1 Exam Cram (QUE Publishing).

Ross is currently senior training/certification engineer at SUSE and recently spent almost five years as the director of member services for the Linux Professional Institute, where he contributed to placing several LPI courses into the Cisco Networking Academy, conducted dozens of Train-the-Trainer sessions, and provided sales enablement support for the worldwide Master Affiliate network spanning more than 100 countries.

Ross holds a number of key IT certifications and is also author of several successful technical books and dozens of technical courses for major organizations (including the first LPI Certification Bootcamps). He is skilled at both contributing to and building community around IT products.

He lives in Paradise Valley, Montana, with his family and enjoys traveling far and wide, winter sports, and photography.

Sean Walberg has more than 20 years of experience as a Linux administrator, network engineer, and software developer. He has written extensively on Linux certification for IBM and NetDevGroup, and has contributed to other books both as an author and technical reviewer.

Sean currently works at Northfield IT and is responsible for infrastructure automation for a large professional sports league. Using tools like Ruby, shell scripts, and Chef, he automates the creation and maintenance of more than a thousand servers and the associated network infrastructure. Sean works closely with developers to scale applications to the demands of an internationally recognized series of web properties.

He lives in Northern Virginia with his wife and three sons.

About the Contributing Author

At the impressionable age of 14, **William "Bo" Rothwell** crossed paths with a TRS-80 Micro Computer System (affectionately known as a "Trash 80"). Soon after the adults responsible for Bo made the mistake of leaving him alone with the TRS-80. He immediately dismantled it and held his first computer class, showing his friends what made this "computer thing" work.

Since this experience, Bo's passion for understanding how computers work and sharing this knowledge with others has resulted in a rewarding career in IT training. His experience includes Linux, Unix, and programming languages such as Perl, Python, Tcl, and BASH. He is the founder and president of One Course Source, an IT training organization.

About the Technical Reviewer

Ted Jordan has more than 25 years of programming, administration, and training experience in UNIX, IRIX, Solaris, and Linux. His career spans from General Motors, Silicon Graphics, to SUN. He holds the LPIC, Linux+, and SUSE Linux certifications. He is the founder and president of two successful startups, the latest being Funutation Tech Camps where he teaches kids to code computer games.

Ted lives with his family near Worcester, Massachusetts, and enjoys tennis, golf, and karaoke.

Dedications

Ross Brunson: *To my good friends, Andres and Ken, we few, we happy few. With love and respect to my wife and daughter, for putting up with my being locked in my office writing and editing while the sun shone and breezes blew. To every student/attendee/customer I've ever taught a Linux topic to, it's really all for you.*

Sean Walberg: *To my amazingly beautiful and intelligent wife, Rebecca. The completion of this book happens to coincide with the start of our new adventure together, and I can think of no one else I'd like to share it with.*

Acknowledgments

Ross Brunson: To the ultimate nerd-herders, Ellie Bru and Mary Beth Ray; Ellie for her ability to take the peeping and muttering of technical geeks and make it something useful, workable, and often profound, and Mary Beth for believing in authors and technologists, even when we break her heart by blowing out deadlines and not doing what we say we will on time.

To my little brother, Leighton, who will make the most awesome history professor one day.

To Sean Walberg, who I have known and respected over several book projects, years of interactions in the LPI community, and all the way back to the Cramsession days with Qcumber and the gang.

To Bo Rothwell and Ted Jordan, awesome technical editors and great guys, as well as two of the best technical trainers it is my pleasure to know.

Sean Walberg: To the crew at Pearson, most notably Geneil, Ellie, and Mary Beth: This project is better because of your patience and input.

The technical editors, Ted and Bo, also deserve special mention. Not only did you fix my technical missteps, but your years of experience as trainers pointed out where I was using some words that were going to confuse new Linux users.

Finally, my knowledge of Linux wasn't earned alone. It came through long nights, hard work, and lots of arguing with people like Marc Caron, Hany Fahim, Patrick leMaistre, Daniel Little, Dave Rose, and of course, my co-author Ross Brunson who I'm happy to have known for more than 15 years.

We Want to Hear from You!

As the reader of this book, you are our most important critic and commentator. We value your opinion and want to know what we're doing right, what we could do better, what areas you'd like to see us publish in, and any other words of wisdom you're willing to pass our way.

We welcome your comments. You can email or write to let us know what you did or didn't like about this book—as well as what we can do to make our books better.

Please note that we cannot help you with technical problems related to the topic of this book.

When you write, please be sure to include this book's title and author as well as your name and email address. We will carefully review your comments and share them with the author and editors who worked on the book.

Email: feedback@pearsonitcertification.com
Mail: Pearson IT Certification
ATTN: Reader Feedback
800 East 96th Street
Indianapolis, IN 46240 USA

Reader Services

Register your copy of CompTIA Linux+ / LPIC-1 Cert Guide at www.pearsonit-certification.com for convenient access to downloads, updates, and corrections as they become available. To start the registration process, go to informit.com/register and log in or create an account. Enter the product ISBN (9780789754554) and click Submit. Once the process is complete, you will find any available bonus content under "Registered Products." Be sure to check the box that you would like to hear from us in order to receive exclusive discounts on future editions of this product.

Introduction

This book was written to help people learn to use Linux. Not just learning Linux by memorizing commands, but learning Linux by understanding how the parts are put together. Approaching Linux from this perspective means that you'll know where to look when you run up against something new and are better suited to handle problems as they come up. The authors of this book are experienced writers, but more importantly, are in the trenches every day.

The CompTIA Linux+ exams LX0-103 and LX0-104 and Linux Professional Institute LPIC Level 1 exams 101-400 and 102-400 (which are identical) encompass the knowledge necessary to become an entry level Linux administrator. There are certainly other books that cover this material, but this is the one that looks beyond the exam to preparing people for the Linux workforce.

You don't need to be taking either the Linux+ or LPIC exams to get use out of this book. Concepts such as filesystems, hardware, shell usage, and managing email systems are needed in the workforce, and we, as authors, have endeavored to produce a book that is just as helpful to all new Linux users.

Goals and Methods

The goal of this book is to provide a guided tour of the Linux operating system with an eye to achieving an entry-level certification at the completion of the book. Readers with no intention of writing an exam will still find this book helpful as the certification content, by design, closely maps to the skills required by a Linux administrator. The authors also hope that the examples and practical advice in this text prove valuable well after the reader is done with the book.

The Linux+ and LPIC Level 1 certification exams are broken into specific topics that build upon each other, and the book does its best to mirror those. Not only does this provide a natural progression to learning Linux, but for those who are taking the exam, allows them to focus on troublesome areas.

Linux commands and their output are interspersed with the text to provide concrete examples right next to the description. Examples, for the most part, are adaptations of real world usage rather than being contrived. And since no good Linux graybeard should take himself too seriously, the authors have done their best to inject some levity into the discussion.

Who Should Read This Book?

This book was written for people who want to learn Linux—people just getting into the information technical field, Windows administrators who want to branch out to Linux, or students looking to understand Linux. Even if you're not taking the Linux+ or LPIC Level 1 exams you'll find this book helpful.

The first half of the book focuses on concepts and basic command usage, while the second half turns the attention to applications found in a typical Linux environment. People looking to be more competent Linux users, as opposed to administrators, will find immense benefit in the first half of the book, but will still appreciate the view of what else can be done on Linux provided by the second half.

Managers looking for some Linux familiarity will also find this book helpful because of the abundant examples and real world applications that will help them to speak in the same language as their more technical reports.

This book was not meant just to be read and cast aside. Instead, it can be a reference for common command usage and some basic application administration.

How To Use This Book

The best way to learn Linux is to use Linux. There are many examples within the text, from simple one-line commands to reusable scripts. Find yourself a Linux distribution such as Fedora, Ubuntu, Debian, or openSUSE. They're free and run on most hardware.

If you don't have a spare computer on which to install Linux you can try a LiveCD, which is a bootable image that runs entirely in memory. Most distributions offer a LiveCD download. Alternatively, you can run Linux in a virtual machine with software like VirtualBox (http://www.virtualbox.org).

All the software shown in this book is available on the most basic of Linux distributions and does not need an extra download. However Chapter 13, "Basic SQL Management," offers a sample database that you can use to follow the examples. To install this, download the compressed attachment from http://www.pearsonitcertification.com/title/9780789754554. Inside the compressed file are two database files. The first, called **lpic_basic.sqlite3**, contains the data for the first part of the chapter. The second includes the additional data for the later examples. Instructions for using the databases are found in Chapter 13.

Above all, experiment with your Linux system. Try a couple of different distributions. Run the commands in this book and see whether you can come up with your own examples. Poke around in the configuration files and explore alternative uses for the commands in this book.

How This Book Is Organized

Although you could read this book cover-to-cover, it is designed to be flexible and allow you to easily move between chapters and sections of chapters to cover only the material you need. If you do intend to read them all, the order in which they are presented is an excellent sequence.

Chapter 1 through 21 cover the following topics:

- **Chapter 1, "Installing Linux":** This chapter teaches you the basics of how a Linux system is installed. Core topics like hard disk partitioning and dealing with hardware are the focus of this chapter.

- **Chapter 2, "Boot Process and Runlevels":** The Linux system has a specific order in which things happen both for starting up and shutting down. This chapter discusses the way these processes work and how to make changes so that you get the services that you need on your system.

- **Chapter 3, "Package Install and Management":** Finding, installing, and configuring software is a big part of the system administrator's job description. This chapter walks you through the usage of both the Debian and RedHat package systems.

- **Chapter 4, "Basic Command Line Usage":** This chapter takes you through the basics of working on the Linux command line, including running applications and some commands to orient yourself on a new system. The work here forms the basis of the next three chapters.

- **Chapter 5, "File Management":** This chapter delves into the commands that manipulate files. You create, delete, compress, move, and look at the files on disk and gain a solid understanding of how the Linux filesystems operate.

- **Chapter 6, "Text Processing/Advanced Command Line":** The Linux command line is a programming environment that lets you do complicated tasks with a few keystrokes. This chapter introduce you to the most powerful feature of the shell of all: chaining together individual commands into increasingly powerful command lines. Along the way you learn how to search through text using regular expressions.

- **Chapter 7, "Process Management":** Things that run on a Linux system are called processes, and this chapter teaches you how to manipulate these processes. You learn how to start and stop processes, run them in the background, and see which ones are taking the most resources from your computer.

- **Chapter 8, "Editing Text":** This chapter teaches you to be productive in the vim editor. Vim makes repetitive tasks a breeze and lets you perform powerful edits on text files without moving the mouse. As most configuration and programming on Linux is through a text file, an administrator who can wield a text editor with efficiency is one who has her work done on time.

- **Chapter 9, "Partitions and Filesystems":** This chapter takes a deep dive into how a Linux system uses disks. You learn how filesystems work and how to add and remove capacity from a Linux workstation.

- **Chapter 10, "Permissions and Ownership":** Linux was built as a multiuser system from the very beginning, so an understanding of how access to resources is granted and checked is important to maintain the security of your data and the sanity of your users. This chapter investigates the Linux permission model along with the commands used to check and set permissions.

- **Chapter 11, "Customizing Shell Environments":** This chapter explores ways that you can customize your command line, such as by making shorter versions of longer commands or adding your own functions to the command line. Here, we also look at the roles played by internationalization and localization, which are methods that let the shell adapt to different languages and countries without needing to maintain multiple installations.

- **Chapter 12, "Shell Scripting":** The Linux shell is actually a sophisticated programming environment and this chapter shows you the basics. You don't have to be a programmer to write shell scripts—this chapter starts with the most basic script and works from there.

- **Chapter 13, "Basic SQL Management":** The Structured Query Language is a way that databases query and manipulate data. This chapter, through real world examples, teaches you the basics of SQL so that you can more effectively help your users and answer questions about your own data.

- **Chapter 14, "Configuring User Interfaces and Desktops":** Linux isn't just a command line system—there are many graphical tools from word processors to video games. This chapter shows you how to use Linux in a graphical mode.

- **Chapter 15, "Managing Users and Groups":** Users and groups are the other half of the Linux permissions model that was started in Chapter 10. This chapter teaches the administrative tasks associated with managing the users on your system.

- **Chapter 16, "Schedule and Automate Tasks":** This chapter walks you through the various ways that Linux systems can run tasks without user intervention, such as to process statistics from logs while you're sleeping.

- **Chapter 17, "Configuring Print and Email Services":** This chapter looks at two basic services that Linux is often called to solve: printing and email. With printing, you learn how the Common Unix Printing System (CUPS) is put together and how it can be used to manage printing for a single system or a large enterprise. In the email half of the chapter you learn how email works and what software is used on Linux to perform the various roles in an Internet email system. You also see how to do basic account management in an email system.

- **Chapter 18, "Logging and Time Services":** Logs provide a detailed accounting of what happened when you weren't looking. This chapter explains the Linux logging systems and how to configure and use them. Additionally you learn how time is kept on a Linux system and how different Linux systems can talk to coordinate their time.

- **Chapter 19, "Networking Fundamentals":** A Linux system that provides network services is only as good as its network configuration. This chapter gives you the solid understanding of networking needed to determine whether Linux or the network is causing a problem. You also learn about the various services used to connect computers on a network.

- **Chapter 20, " System Security":** Security is all about assessing the risk to your machine and keeping the bad guys out. In this chapter you learn how to assess the security of your system, lock down services to only people you want, and encrypt your data from prying eyes.

- **Chapter 21, "Final Preparation":** In this final chapter you find exam questions that challenge your understanding of the material and provide a test that assesses your readiness to take either the LPIC 101 or Linux+ exams.

- **Glossary**: The glossary defines all terms that you were asked to define at the end of each chapter.

Each chapter follows the same format and incorporates the following tools to assist you by assessing your current knowledge and emphasizing specific areas of interest within the chapter:

- **"Do I Know This Already?" Quizzes:** Each chapter begins with a quiz to help you assess your current knowledge of the subject. The quiz is divided into specific areas of emphasis that enable you to best determine where to focus your efforts when working through the chapter.

- **Foundation Topics:** The foundation topics are the core sections of each chapter. They focus on the specific commands, concepts, or skills that you must master to successfully prepare for the examination.

- **Exam Preparation Tasks:** At the end of the foundation topics, the Exam Preparation Tasks highlight the key topics from the chapter and lists the pages where you can find them for quick review. This section also provides a list of key terms that you should be able to define in preparation for the exam. It is unlikely that you will be able to successfully complete the certification exam by just studying the key topics and key terms, although they are a good tool for last-minute preparation just before taking the exam. For a thorough understanding of how to prepare for the exam, see Chapter 21.

- **Review Questions:** Questions at the end of each chapter measure your understanding of the topics discussed in the chapter.

- **DVD-Based Practice Exam:** This book includes a DVD containing several interactive practice exams. It is recommended that you continue to test your knowledge and test-taking skills by using these exams. You will find that your test-taking skills improve by continued exposure to the test format. Remember that the potential range of exam questions is limitless. Therefore, your goal should not be to "know" every possible answer but to have a sufficient understanding of the subject matter so that you can figure out the correct answer with the information provided.

Pearson IT Certification Practice Test Engine and Questions on the DVD

The DVD in the back of the book includes the Pearson IT Certification Practice Test engine—software that displays and grades a set of exam-realistic multiple-choice questions. Using the Pearson IT Certification Practice Test engine, you can either study by going through the questions in Study Mode, or take a simulated exam that mimics real exam conditions. You can also serve up questions in a Flash Card Mode, which displays just the question and no answers, challenging you to state the answer in your own words before checking the actual answers to verify your work.

The installation process requires two major steps: installing the software and then activating the exam. The DVD in the back of this book has a recent copy of the Pearson IT Certification Practice Test engine. The practice exam (the database of exam questions) is not on the DVD.

Note The cardboard DVD case in the back of this book includes the DVD and a piece of paper. The paper lists the activation code for the practice exam associated with this book. Do not lose the activation code. On the opposite side of the paper from the activation code is a unique, one-time-use coupon code for the purchase of the Premium Edition eBook and Practice Test.

Install the Software from the DVD

The Pearson IT Certification Practice Test is a Windows-only desktop application. Unfortunately, you cannot easily run this .exe on a Linux machine. You can run it on a Mac using a Windows virtual machine, but it was built specifically for the PC platform. The minimum system requirements are as follows:

- Windows 10, Windows 8.1, Windows 7, or Vista (SP2)

- Microsoft .NET Framework 4.0 Client

- Pentium-class 1 GHz processor (or equivalent)

- 512 MB RAM

- 650 MB disk space plus 50 MB for each downloaded practice exam

- Access to the Internet to register and download exam databases

The software installation process is routine as compared with other software installation processes. If you have already installed the Pearson IT Certification Practice Test software from another Pearson product, there is no need for you to reinstall the software. Simply launch the software on your desktop and proceed to activate the practice exam from this book by using the activation code included in the DVD sleeve.

The following steps outline the installation process:

1. Insert the DVD into your PC.

2. The media interface that automatically runs allows you to access and use all DVD-based features, including the exam engine and sample content from other Cisco self-study products. From the main menu, click the Install the Exam Engine option.

3. Respond to windows prompts as with any typical software installation process.

The installation process gives you the option to activate your exam with the activation code supplied on the paper in the DVD sleeve. This process requires that you establish a Pearson website login. You need this login to activate the exam, so please do register when prompted. If you already have a Pearson website login, there is no need to register again. Just use your existing login.

Activate and Download the Practice Exam

Once the exam engine is installed, you should then activate the exam associated with this book (if you did not do so during the installation process) as follows:

1. Start the Pearson IT Certification Practice Test software from the Windows Start menu or from your desktop shortcut icon.

2. To activate and download the exam associated with this book, from the My Products or Tools tab, click the Activate Exam button.

3. At the next screen, enter the activation key from the paper inside the cardboard DVD holder in the back of the book. Once entered, click the Activate button.

4. The activation process downloads the practice exam. Click Next and then click Finish.

When the activation process completes, the My Products tab should list your new exam. If you do not see the exam, make sure that you have selected the My Products tab on the menu. At this point, the software and practice exam are ready to use. Simply select the exam and click the Open Exam button.

To update a particular exam you have already activated and downloaded, display the Tools tab and click the Update Products button. Updating your exams ensures that you have the latest changes and updates to the exam data.

If you want to check for updates to the Pearson Cert Practice Test exam engine software, display the Tools tab and click the Update Application button. You can then ensure that you are running the latest version of the software engine.

Activating Other Exams

The exam software installation process and the registration process, only have to happen once. Then, for each new exam, only a few steps are required. For instance, if you buy another Pearson IT Certification Cert Guide, extract the activation code from the DVD sleeve in the back of that book; you do not even need the DVD at this point. From there, all you have to do is start the exam engine (if not still up and running) and perform steps 2 through 4 from the previous list.

Certification Exam Topics and This Book

The questions for each certification exam are a closely guarded secret. However, we do know which topics you must know to successfully complete this exam. CompTIA and LPI publishes them as an exam blueprint.

Tables I.1 and I.2 list the exam topics for each exam.

Table I.1   CompTIA Linux+ (LX0-103) and LPIC-1 (101-400) Exam

Exam Topics for CompTIA Linux+ (LX0-103) and LPIC-1 (101-400) Exam
Topic 101: System Architecture
101.1 Determine and configure hardware settings
101.2 Boot the system
101.3 Change run levels/boot targets and shutdown or reboot system
Topic 102: Linux Installation and Package Management
102.1 Design hard disk layout
102.2 Install a boot manager
102.3 Manage shared libraries
102.4 Use Debian package management
102.5 Use RPM and YUM package management
Topic 103: GNU and Unix Commands
103.1 Work on the command line
103.2 Process text streams using filters
103.3 Perform basic file management
103.4 Use streams, pipes, and redirects
103.5 Create, monitor, and kill processes
103.6 Modify process execution priorities
103.7 Search text files using regular expressions
103.8 Perform basic file editing operations using vi
Topic 104: Devices, Linux Filesystems, Filesystem Hierarchy Standard
104.1 Create partitions and filesystems
104.2 Maintain the integrity of filesystems
104.3 Control mounting and unmounting of filesystems
104.4 Manage disk quotas
104.5 Manage file permissions and ownership
104.6 Create and change hard and symbolic links
104.7 Find system files and place files in the correct location

Table I-2   CompTIA Linux+ (LX0-104) and LPIC-1 (102-400)

Exam Topics for CompTIA Linux+ (LX0-104) and LPIC-1 (102-400)
Topic 105: Shells, Scripting, and Data Management
105.1 Customize and use the shell environment
105.2 Customize or write simple scripts
105.3 SQL data management
Topic 106: User Interfaces and Desktops
106.1 Install and configure X11
106.2 Set up a display manager
106.3 Accessibility
Topic 107: Administrative Tasks
107.1 Manage user and group accounts and related system files
107.2 Automate system administration tasks by scheduling jobs
107.3 Localization and internationalization
Topic 108: Essential System Services
108.1 Maintain system time
108.2 System logging
108.3 Mail Transfer Agent (MTA) basics
108.4 Manage printers and printing
Topic 109: Networking Fundamentals
109.1 Fundamentals of Internet protocols
109.2 Basic network configuration
109.3 Basic network troubleshooting
109.4 Configure client side DNS
Topic 110: Security
110.1 Perform security administration tasks
110.2 Set up host security
110.3 Securing data with encryption

Assessing Exam Readiness

Exam candidates never really know whether they are adequately prepared for the exam until they have completed about 30% of the questions. At that point, if you are not prepared, it is too late. The best way to determine your readiness is to work through the "Do I Know This Already?" quizzes at the beginning of each chapter and review the foundation and key topics presented in each chapter. It is best to work your way through the entire book unless you can complete each subject without having to do any research or look up any answers.

Exam Registration

For LPI exams, start at lpi.org to get a member ID and a link to pearsonvue.com/ lpi/ to schedule an exam. For the Linux+ variants, sign up directly from https://certification.comptia.org/certifications/linux.

Where Are the Companion Content Files?

Register this print version of *CompTIA Linux+ / LPIC-1 Cert Guide* to access the content from the DVD online.

This print version of this title comes with a disc of companion content. You have online access to these files by following these steps:

1. Go to www.pearsonITcertification.com/register and log in or create a new account.

2. Enter the ISBN: 9780789754554.

3. Answer the challenge question as proof of purchase.

4. Click on the Access Bonus Content link in the Registered Products section of your account page to be taken to the page where your downloadable content is available.

Please note that many of our companion content files can be very large, especially image and video files.

If you are unable to locate the files for this title by following these steps, please visit www.pearsonITcertification.com/ contact and select the Site Problems/Comments option. Our customer service representatives will assist you.

This chapter covers the following topics:

- Understanding Your Hardware
- Laying Out the Hard Drive
- Working with Boot Managers

The exam objectives covered in this chapter are

- Understanding your hardware: 101.1
- Laying out the hard drive: 102.1
- Working with boot managers: 102.2

## CHAPTER 1

Installing Linux

Becoming proficient with Linux starts with understanding the hardware that runs the operating system. Linux has a long and bumpy past with hardware support because it was originally written with no help from the manufacturers. Over time hardware support has become better and compatibility information is easier to find. This author remembers long nights poring over message boards to find someone else running the same video card! Thankfully these problems are becoming rarer.

In general you can expect excellent compatibility on server hardware and the last generation of desktop hardware. If you buy only the newest and most expensive desktop equipment, you may find that you're doing a bit of extra reading to get things to work.

The LPI exam isn't concerned with the exact procedure to install Linux as this varies between Linux distributions and is constantly changing. The exam is more focused on the topics that are consistent between different Linux installations such as the hardware, disk layout, and boot loaders.

"Do I Know This Already?" Quiz

The "Do I Know This Already?" quiz enables you to assess whether you should read this entire chapter or simply jump to the "Exam Preparation Tasks" section for review. If you are in doubt, read the entire chapter. Table 1-1 outlines the major headings in this chapter and the corresponding "Do I Know This Already?" quiz questions. You can find the answers in Appendix A, "Answers to the 'Do I Know This Already?' Quizzes and Review Questions."

Table 1-1 "Do I Know This Already?" Foundation Topics Section-to-Question Mapping

Foundation Topics Section	Questions Covered in This Section
Understanding Your Hardware	1-2
Laying Out the Hard Drive	3-5
Working with Boot Managers	6-7

1. Which one of the following is not used for peripherals to communicate with the CPU and other peripherals?

   a. IO ports

   b. Direct memory access channels

   c. Interrupt requests

   d. TCP/IP ports

2. Which command gives an overview of all the hardware and drivers in the system including the ports they use to talk to the CPU?

   a. **lspci**

   b. **lsdev**

   c. **lsusb**

   d. **sysinfo**

3. /dev/sda3 refers to a

   a. Partition

   b. Flash drive

   c. Filesystem

   d. Disk

4. Which LVM component would be formatted with a filesystem and mounted?

   a. Physical volume

   b. Volume group

   c. Physical extent

   d. Logical volume

5. Which of the following is not commonly placed on its own partition?

   a. /sbin

   b. /home

   c. /usr

   d. /tmp

6. The first stage of the boot manager is typically stored in

    a. The BIOS

    b. /boot

    c. The partition table

    d. The master boot record

7. The configuration file for GRUB2 is

    a. menu.lst

    b. grub.cfg

    c. grub.conf

    d. bootloader.conf

Foundation Topics

Understanding Your Hardware

Hardware refers to the entire computer your Linux operating system will run on while the *peripherals* are the hardware bits that are removable or otherwise talk with the world. Video cards can be part of the motherboard or separate cards, they're still considered peripherals. To get more technical the peripherals talk to the CPU over some kind of *bus*, which is what starts to complicate Linux support. Peripherals are also called devices.

An operating system refers to the system as a whole, including all the application software you use. Linux is an operating system. The kernel of an operating system is just the part that manages the interactions between the hardware and the applications. The Linux kernel runs on the CPU and memory that's on the motherboard. To write something to disk, display something on the screen, or talk to a web server in Brazil, the kernel must send messages over the bus that connects the CPU to the peripherals. Think of the kernel as an air traffic controller that coordinates all the airplanes, runways, and ground crew.

Every hardware manufacturer manipulates data differently, which makes support difficult for any operating system. The solution is to get the kernel to speak a common language and have the peripheral manufacturers provide a *driver* that allows their specific hardware to speak that common language. In the old days manufacturers didn't want to spend the time to write Linux drivers so this had to be done by the community. If the vendor didn't offer enough information for the Linux community to write a driver, the hardware would often go unsupported.

NOTE   Linux is not written by a single company; it's written by a community of people like you who want to make Linux better. People make fixes, called patches, and submit them for inclusion into the Linux kernel and associated utilities. Core members of the Linux project work with the submitter to make sure the patch follows the direction of the project and are of sufficient quality. Some of these people are hobbyists who like solving difficult problems, and some people are hired by companies that use Linux and want to contribute their improvements.

As Linux gains support, more and more hardware has Linux drivers provided directly by the manufacturer or as a result of an increasingly large community that's willing to spend the time to make things work.

Peripheral Compatibility

Your interest in peripheral compatibility will come in one of two forms:

- You need to buy some hardware and want to select gear that's Linux compatible

- You already have the hardware and need to get it to work.

The easiest way to find out what hardware is supported is to check your distribution's list of supported equipment and consult your favorite search engine to find out what other people have done. Not all distributions provide these hardware compatibility lists, especially for newer gear. Therefore you will find yourself most often looking at forums or trusting the vendor.

Most peripheral devices work in some capacity; what you are looking for is how to activate the advanced features. That expensive new 3D video card may boot and give you a decent display but without all the acceleration you paid for.

If you can boot a machine into Linux that has the hardware, even if it's through a Live DVD that runs Linux inside memory instead of overwriting the operating system, you can use some of the following techniques.

NOTE   Live DVDs are a way to use Linux without making any changes to your existing operating system. To use a Live DVD, you download an image that is burned to a DVD or USB stick and then boot your computer from that image. You get a full installation of Linux that runs out of your computer's memory without touching your existing operating system. If you like what you see you can usually jump into the installation process, or you can reboot your computer to get back to your old operating system.

All major Linux distributions have some kind of Live DVD image that can be downloaded. It's a low effort way to try a new distribution without the hassles of trying to boot multiple operating systems.

Enumerating Your Peripherals

Peripherals talk to the CPU and other peripherals on a shared resource called a *bus*. To uniquely identify hardware, the CPU needs to be able to address the peripheral through one or more of several means:

- **IO port**—An address, or range of addresses, identifying the device; e.g., 0080, 1000-107f.

- **IRQ**—Interrupt requests (IRQs) signal the processor that an event has happened and that the CPU is requested to come check on the resource. It a limited resource that can sometimes be shared.

- **DMA**—Direct memory access (DMA) allows a peripheral to access system memory directly rather than having the CPU intervene.

The two methods of viewing the current hardware list on a Linux system are

- Viewing the contents of the **/proc** filesystem
- Using one of the hardware listing tools

The Proc Filesystem

Unix has a philosophy that "everything is a file," and part of that means that hardware information and state information for both the system and processes are exposed on the filesystem. In Linux this started off as the procfs, which is usually mounted on **/proc**. In this directory you find that each process on the system has a directory containing information about itself. Features that must keep state to work, such as a firewall that tracks network connections being handled by the system, also expose their information through **/proc**.

Additionally, procfs contains details about the hardware in the system. Such files as **/proc/ioports**, /**proc/dma**, and **/proc/interrupts** can show the investigating user or sysadmin a lot of pertinent information about the system's configuration.

Incidentally, procfs is called a *pseudofilesystem*. It looks like a device but doesn't exist on any real hardware. It's simply a way of exposing kernel information to the user in a well-defined format.

When errors or conflicts occur, the following commands are essential to resolving the conflicts shown in the output. Viewing that information straight from the **/proc** directory is accomplished with the following commands:

```
cat /proc/interrupts
cat /proc/ioports
cat /proc/dma
cat /proc/usb
cat /proc/pci
```

There is also a series of commands beginning with **ls*** that gather the same information and present it in more human readable format.

The pertinent commands are

- **lsmod**—Shows the kernel modules loaded, along with any dependencies for those modules. Helpful for double checking that the driver is loaded for a peripheral. If the module is not present then use the **modprobe** command to load it, such as with **modprobe bluetooth**.

- **lscpu**—Provides details about your CPU, such as the number and speed of each socket and core.

- **lspci**—Shows a lot of information about your PCI bus and devices. This can identify devices on the bus that the kernel doesn't know about and provides addressing information for configuring them.

- **lsscsi**—Shows information about the SCSI devices on your system, if the system supports SCSI. This tells you if the system can see the disk.

- **lsdev**—Shows the devices recognized by your system.

- **lsraid**—Displays the Redundant Array of Inexpensive Disks (RAID) devices on the system.

- **lsusb**—Displays the USB information and devices for your system.

- **lsblk**—Displays the block devices (disks) attached to your system.

NOTE   Expect to get questions about the output of these programs, such as which one will show the most comprehensive information about your system's IO ports, DMA, and IRQs. The **lsdev** command shows the most definitive set of information in one stream of output.

Example 1-1 shows the **lsdev** command in action.

Example 1-1   lsdev Command

```
[root@bob ~]# lsdev
Device           DMA    IRQ   I/O Ports
------------------------------------------------
0000:00:1f.0                  1000-107f 1180-11bf
acpi                    9
cascade          4
e100                          2000-203f
eth0                   20
eth1                   16
[root@bob ~]# lspci | grep 00:1f.0
00:1f.0 ISA bridge: Intel Corporation 82801BA ISA Bridge (LPC) (rev 12)
```

In Example 1-1 you can see that the first device shown occupies two ranges of IO ports and has a numeric ID, which is a PCI address. The second command in the example searches for that address in the **lspci** command's output, showing that it's a bridge to the legacy ISA bus.

The next device is the advanced configuration and power interface (ACPI), which lets the hardware and software talk together for managing power usage. This communicates to the CPU with interrupt number 9.

Next is a DMA device called cascade, which is used by the hardware to let two DMA controllers talk to each other. It has DMA channel 4.

The last 3 entries are for the network peripherals. The first is the network driver, which has some IO ports reserved. The last two are for the cards, each has an IRQ.

Friends of procfs

procfs is the most popular way to expose kernel information to users, but there are more. The files under **/proc** are unstructured and contain both information about processes and devices. The goal of **sysfs** is to solve some of these shortcomings by migrating device data to /sys. Data still can exist on both, and the device tools such as **lspci** still use **/proc**.

udev is the Linux kernel's device manager. It manages the device files under /dev using information about the device from **sysfs**. Every accessible device on the system will have a corresponding device file under /dev. If a device is plugged in to the computer while it is running, **udev** can configure it and make it available to the system. Devices that support being plugged in at runtime are also called *hotplug* devices, as opposed to *coldplug* devices that require the computer to be rebooted for them to be used.

Another loosely related service is called D-Bus. This is a distributed software bus that lets desktop applications send messages to each other and receive messages from the kernel. The D-Bus could be used for an email client to notify the window manager that an email has been received so that it can display an icon. It could also be used by udev to notify the window manager when a DVD has been inserted into the system.

Dealing with Integrated Peripherals

Motherboards, the component that houses the CPU and RAM, often comes with *integrated peripherals*, which are peripherals built into the motherboard. Video cards and network adapters are the most frequent integrated peripherals, but sound cards, RAID adapters, or special external peripheral ports could also be present.

Manufacturers include the hardware drivers with the motherboard, but these drivers may not support Linux. To make matters worse, integrated peripherals often require software support from the operating system to work properly. For example, some motherboards duplicate data across multiple disks for redundancy using a feature called a *Redundant Array of Independent Disks (RAID)* by supplying an integrated RAID adapter. This adapter may do some of the necessary parity calculations on the computer's CPU instead of on the adapter to lower the price of the motherboard. This means that the Linux driver needs to support both the hardware and the software features.

If an integrated peripheral is not supported in Linux, your first step should be to see whether it works in a reduced capacity. A video card that shares memory with the system may not work in 3D accelerated mode but may work fine for regular use.

If the peripheral is not supported at all, your best course of action is to disable it entirely so that you can replace it with something that works. To do so

Step 1. Reboot your computer and enter BIOS setup mode. This involves pressing a special key while the computer boots. Your computer's BIOS displays a message such as "PRESS F12 TO ENTER BIOS SETUP."

Step 2. Navigate the setup menu to find the hardware section corresponding to the device you want to disable.

Step 3. Select the option to disable the peripheral.

Step 4. Exit the BIOS menu, making sure to select the option to save. This last part is important as the usual default is to discard all changes and reboot!

Laying Out the Hard Drive

Storage comes in many different flavors—hard drives, Universal Serial Bus (USB) flash drives, floppy and compact discs, DVDs, and network attached drives. Linux treats all these mass storage devices similarly and expects the administrator to fill in the details. This might mean entering a network or port address for a network file share, or identifying a particular hard drive. But to the user, these details are hidden from view.

Partitions and Devices

A single disk drive is divided up into one or more *partitions* that logically separate the disk. This logical separation allows you to assign space on the same drive for different uses. For example, a 3TB drive may be split up with the first 500GB for the operating system and applications, 1TB for database files, and 1.5TB for users' home directories.

A partition is then formatted with a *filesystem* that allows it to store files. The operating system uses the filesystem to map files to the actual blocks on disk and manage directories and permissions.

Partitioning allows you to limit the scope of disk problems and to tune according to the intended use. For example, you may not want to track the last time a file was looked at on system binaries and database files but track the time on users' files. Breaking out user files onto its own partition means you can use a different set of options for user files than you use for system binaries.

The problems encountered in an unexpected reboot are also reduced through partitioning. When a system is improperly shut down, files that were opened for writing may not have all their data persisted to disk. As the operating system files are rarely open for writing, that partition can usually survive an unclean shutdown. You can then get the computer up and running and tackle the problem of validating the consistency of user files in a separate action.

Linux uses device names to refer to the drives and partitions. The drives or devices are given a letter and a number is appended for the partition as follows:

- /dev/sda is the first hard drive (a) in the system.

- /dev/sda1 is the first partition (1) on the first hard drive (a) in the system.

- /dev/sdb3 is the third partition (3) on the second drive (b) in the system.

Caution: The first partition is partition 1, but in most other situations 0 (zero) is the first device. /dev/md0 is the first RAID volume and /dev/scd0 is the first CD drive.

The Root Filesystem

Linux has many differences from Microsoft operating systems, but the one that seems to stand out the most is the single filesystem. In Windows, if you have three disk drives, they will probably be called C:, D:, and E:. Add a DVD drive and that is called F:. In Linux, just like other Unixes, there's just one filesystem, and drives are grafted onto directories by mounting the filesystem at a particular point in the parent filesystem. The parent filesystem could be the root filesystem or it could be a descendant.

Figure 1-1 shows a typical configuration where directories are split among multiple drives and partitions.

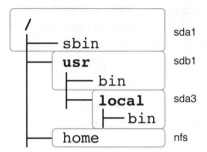

Figure 1-1   A typical set of mounted directories showing two hard-drive mounts and one network mount

In Unix, the system starts off with a single *root filesystem* called /. In Figure 1-1 this is on device sda1. The /usr partition is mounted from sdb1, and on top of that, sda3 is mounted on /usr/local. Given this system, these statements are all true:

- Directories with bolded names are *mount points*—their contents come from a different device than their parent.
- Files in / go on sda1; it is the root partition.
- Files in /sbin go on sda1; it is still part of the root filesystem.
- Files in /usr go on sdb1; it is mounted off the root filesystem on /usr.
- Files in /usr/bin go on sdb1; it is part of the same filesystem as /usr.
- Files in /usr/local go on sda3; it is mounted on /usr/local/.
- Files in /usr/local/bin go on sda3; the /usr/local/mount is more specific than the /usr mount.
- Files in /home go over a network file system (NFS) share and are stored on a completely different computer.

Each partition has a filesystem on it, and the operating system stitches everything together to look like one big filesystem even though it may span multiple devices or even separate computers.

The user of a Linux system doesn't have to worry about where one disk begins and another one ends—that's the unfortunate job of the administrator. This layer of abstraction means that disks can be moved around, resized, put on the network, or cloned without any changes. Think of what would happen in Windows if your D: drive suddenly became E:! This just doesn't happen in Linux.

The single filesystem also applies when accessing removable devices. When you plug in a USB flash drive you need to mount it somehow so that you can access the files stored on the drive. The software running your desktop environment may mount it for you or you may need to type commands, but in either case it's treated as if it were a fixed hard drive.

When deciding how to lay out your disks, a useful acronym to remember for real-world needs is PIBS:

- **Performance**—Performance increases if the system's heavy usage directory trees are put on another disk. Good candidates for a move to another disk are the /home directory or the swap partition.

- **Integrity**—Integrity improves by having critical files in their own partition. If disk resources become corrupted or damaged, such as from a sudden power outage, the computer can be down for hours to complete a filesystem check. Distancing risky partitions such as an FTP upload folder from the traditional root of the system is a good idea; otherwise, an FTP user that fills up the system partition would cause the system to crash.

- **Backup**—Separate partitions give you more control over backups. For example, you may only want to back up files that change often in /home and conduct less frequent backups for files that do not change often within /usr. The **tar** command is used to back up sets of files and directory trees. It can be used to back up an entire file system, but there are more efficient tools for backup up partitions and complete disks like **dump** or **dd**.

- **Security**—When placing partitions and directory trees on the system, be aware that it's much easier to isolate or jail a risky portion of your server if it's contained on a separate partition or disk. This is accomplished through options that are set at mount time, such as not allowing people to execute files with increased privilege or write to the filesystem. Mount options are discussed thoroughly in Chapter 9, "Partitions and Filesystems."

Logical Volume Manager (LVM)

Over time the shuffling of physical disk partitions to keep up with demand gets tiring. What happens if you need a /home drive that's bigger than a single disk? Do you just throw away your older disks when you add more space?

You could use the RAID system to create a virtual volume out of smaller disks, but that gets messy, especially if you want to use RAID's fault tolerance.

Enterprise Unixes solve this problem with something called *Logical Volume Management (LVM)*. Linux took ideas from enterprise Unixes and implemented the LVM feature. With LVM, system physical disks are combined into smaller sets of pools, and the partitions themselves are built from those pools.

Figure 1-2 shows the basic components of LVM and how they fit together.

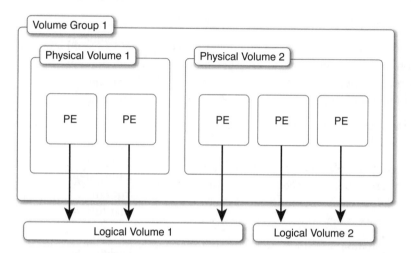

Figure 1-2   Logical volume concepts

The base unit of storage in LVM is the *physical volume (PV)*. A PV corresponds to a hard disk partition such as /dev/sda1 or some kind of block storage device coming from a dedicated storage system called a Storage Area Network (SAN). One or more physical volumes are combined to form a pool of storage called a *volume group (VG)*. Under the hood the physical volume is chopped up into a series of *physical extents (PE)* to make allocations easier.

The administrator then carves up the volume group into a series of *logical volumes (LV)*. Each logical volume holds a filesystem that is used by the operating system.

Many interesting things can happen now that the filesystem on the logical volume is thoroughly abstracted from the exact placement on disk. If you need more disk space on a logical volume you can take it from anywhere in the volume group. If the volume group is low on space simply add another physical volume to the volume group and the new physical extents are available to any logical volume.

Filesystems can be grown and shrunk by adjusting the size of their underlying logical volume as long as the filesystem supports it. The LVM system takes care of allocating the physical extents to the logical volume so you don't have to worry about shuffling around partitions on disk anymore.

Snapshotting is now possible in an LVM enhanced system. A snapshot takes a point in time copy of a logical volume and makes it available as another disk while still allowing writes to happen to the original filesystem. This allows you to back up the snapshot image without needing to take the files or database offline; you can continue to work and change the files for later backup.

Commonly Used Mounts

A filesystem can be mounted on almost any directory as needed. You could mount a filesystem on top of /usr and then another one onto /usr/local if you wanted. Just because you can do it doesn't mean you should, however. With experience, you'll find a few common ways for administrators to lay out their filesystems.

The first option is to put everything on a single root partition. With LVM and large hard drives this isn't a bad option.

The two most common places that a new partition is added is in /home and /var. Home is for the user's home directories, which includes their work in progress and saved files. In a larger environment this may even be a network file share so that all computers share a common home directory system.

The other common mount point on which to split off another filesystem is /var, which is typically used for system log and data files. A database may store its files in /var/lib/mysql, system logs usually go under /var/log, and so forth.

When considering whether to split a directory off to another partition think about the activity on the disk: Do you expect the use of the partition to grow over time? What is the balance of reads and writes? Does the partition contain important system files, including the utilities to mount other partitions?

Both /home and /var are good candidates for separate filesystems because they grow the most and have the most write activity. The flexibility offered through separate partitions, even if they are backed by the same LVM volume group, is usually worth the added complexity.

Other lesser candidates for separate partitions are /tmp and /usr. The former is used for temporary file storage and can often grow, or need to be supported by a faster disk, and the latter can grow over time or may be shared across multiple systems.

A final partition you may run into is /boot. This is a small partition used to contain files necessary for loading the kernel.

Swap Files

Most partitions you encounter store files. There is another kind of partition, called a *swap partition*, that stores memory instead of files.

The operating system uses *virtual memory*, which means that the kernel presents a contiguous memory space to each application but can store the bytes wherever it needs to. If an application isn't using all its memory, it doesn't really matter whether the bytes are in RAM or stored on disk. Thus the kernel can swap memory pages to disk as needed, allowing the system to behave as if it has more memory than it actually does.

Access to disk data is much slower than access to RAM data, so it's vital to avoid the need to constantly *swap* memory to and from disk or *thrashing* will happen. When your disks start to thrash, the system becomes painfully slow. Consider swap to be a safety net more than anything else.

Working with Boot Managers

The final piece of the installation puzzle is the *boot manager*. The boot manager's job is to take the computer from power up to a functioning Linux kernel.

When a computer boots up, it doesn't know how to talk to all its peripherals or load applications. But each computer has a *Basic Input-Output System (BIOS)* that gives it just enough intelligence to read and write to local disks and write some text to the screen.

Once the computer boots up it transfers control to the BIOS, which initializes the hardware and reads the first block—512 bytes—from the boot disk. This block contains the first part of the boot loader that loads the boot manager from disk and runs it. This special sector on the disk is called the *master boot record (MBR)*.

The Linux boot block can be placed in the first block of the Linux partition itself in cases where an existing operating system already occupies the MBR. In this case the first boot manager needs to be told to pass control over to the Linux boot manager. It's complicated, but this *multi-booting* allows two different operating systems to co-exist on the same computer.

The boot manager displays a menu offering different operating system choices. Usually a default is chosen if no input is received within a short period of time, which allows a computer to boot unattended. Boot managers can also pass parameters to the kernel such as to initialize hardware differently, disable problematic features, or alter the boot sequence.

Several boot managers are available though most distributions have standardized on the *Grand Unified Boot Loader (GRUB)*.

GRUB Legacy

In the early days of Linux the boot manager was simple. You would either boot a kernel from an existing Microsoft DOS system through LOADLIN.EXE or directly with the Linux Loader (LILO). The latter was fairly inflexible. While you had a basic menu system, any changes needed to be made by rewriting the boot manager to disk. Even the location of the kernel blocks on disk needed to be known beforehand! LILO would have to generate a list of blocks containing a kernel and write them to a known place so that it could piece the kernel back together on boot.

Eventually the GNU Foundation started work on GRUB. This boot manager is more flexible than others because it offers an interactive menu that can be easily change and adapt to boot many operating systems. GRUB understands different filesystems, which allows it to read the kernel from disk as if it were a file instead of needing to know where the individual blocks are.

GRUB uses a temporary boot volume, /boot by default, on which to store kernels and the GRUB configuration. Some BIOSes can't see the whole disk, so putting the boot manager in a safe area means that it can boot a kernel that has the functionality to read the entire disk.

GRUB2

GRUB2 is the version of GRUB currently in use. The software was rewritten to allow plugins and expand features available in the menu system. GRUB legacy and GRUB2 are otherwise fairly similar.

Installing GRUB2

The first step to getting GRUB2 installed is to have the tool write itself to the master boot record as follows:

```
[root@localhost ~]# grub2-install /dev/sda
Installing for i386-pc platform.
Installation finished. No error reported.
```

This copies the boot sector image to disk and the remaining files to /boot. If your bootable partition is not /boot you can override this default setting, such as /mnt/tmpboot in Example 1-2.

Example 1-2   Installing GRUB2 to an Alternate Location

```
[root@localhost ~]# grub2-install --boot-directory=/mnt/tmpboot /dev/
sda
Installing for i386-pc platform.
Installation finished. No error reported.
[root@localhost ~]# tree -d /mnt/tmpboot/
```

```
/mnt/tmpboot/
└── grub2
    ├── fonts
    ├── i386-pc
    └── locale
4 directories
```

In Example 1-2 the GRUB2 files are installed to /mnt/tmpboot and the **tree** command shows the directories created for the boot manager. The GRUB2 image and related modules are found inside the **i386-pc** directory.

This alternate boot disk option is most often used if you're making your own boot disks on an existing system, where you will have an image of the disk temporarily mounted.

Using the GRUB2 Command Line

Your first interaction with the GRUB2 command line is during the boot process. When you boot a computer you see the GRUB2 menu offering a list of kernels to boot and also an option to enter the "c" character to get to the command line. Pressing this gets you to a simple command prompt:

```
grub>
```

If you can't boot normally you can use the GRUB2 command line to inspect your running system and get a kernel booted. Look at the list of devices with the **ls** command:

```
grub> ls
(proc) (hd0) (hd0,msdos2) (hd0,msdos1)
```

The syntax of the partitions is similar to the Linux way of naming partitions. It's important to remember that disks are counted from zero, but partitions are counted from one. So the first partition on the first disk is hd0,msdos1, which corresponds to sda1 in Linux. It is often difficult to know which partition contains the files you want, so you can inspect each. The shell does not provide wildcards, though the TAB key can be used as a substitute:

```
grub> ls (hd0,msdos1)/vml<TAB>
```

Possible files are

```
vmlinuz-0-rescue-bc31f38de2ee4e2cab0ad674986cee12
vmlinuz-3.17.6-300.fc21.x86_64
```

If you are new to Linux, you may find these naming inconsistencies confusing. Linux tools are developed by different people with different ways of doing things. Devices in the Linux kernel are fairly consistently named, but GRUB is developed by a completely different set of people with a different set of goals. GRUB was designed to boot different operating systems so some concepts don't line up directly to the way it's done in Linux.

The Tab key looks for any files beginning with vml, which are kernel files, on the device. Two are shown here. Knowing that the second one is the kernel to boot because of the name, you can give GRUB enough information to boot it by supplying the name of the kernel and the name of the corresponding *initial RAM disk*. The initial RAM disk, abbreviated initrd, contains extra drivers necessary to boot the kernel on the specific hardware the kernel is running on.

```
grub> linux (hd0,msdos1)/vmlinuz-3.17.6-300.fc21.x86_64 root=/dev/
mapper/fedora-root ro
grub> initrd (hd0,msdos1)/initramfs-3.17.6-300.fc21.x86_64.img
grub> boot
```

While several parameters are involved in booting the kernel, they are already in the **grub.cfg** file, which can be viewed with the **cat** command or searched for on the Internet. The kernel can take many parameters, but it is important to pass the path to the root filesystem (**root=**) and that the filesystem should initially be booted read-only (**ro**).

In the early days of Linux a problem with your boot manager meant that you needed to find a CD or floppy disk that had Linux so that you could boot and begin recovery. GRUB2's command line means that you can still get into your system and fix it up more quickly.

Configuring GRUB2

GRUB2's configuration file is called **grub.cfg**. In this, you find the configuration that sets up the menus you see when the system boots.

NOTE   GRUB legacy uses menu.1st and grub.conf for configuration. The syntax changed between versions, and your distribution's default may look more like code than a configuration file.

Configuring GRUB2 has become more complicated than GRUB legacy (unnecessarily so in this author's humble opinion). While previously you would edit grub.conf and be done, the new grub.cfg is generated with a script so you must look to the scripts to see how to make your changes.

The **grub-mkconfig** command generates the configuration file for you, optionally receiving a path to the output file. If you don't specify a file, the output goes to your screen.

```
# grub-mkconfig -o /boot/grub/grub.cfg
Generating grub configuration file ...
Found linux image: /boot/vmlinuz-3.13.0-32-generic
Found initrd image: /boot/initrd.img-3.13.0-32-generic
Found memtest86+ image: /memtest86+.elf
Found memtest86+ image: /memtest86+.bin
done
```

The inputs to **grub-mkconfig** are /etc/default/grub and the files in /etc/grub.d/. The former sets various defaults; the latter is a series of shell scripts:

```
# ls /etc/grub.d/
00_header        20_linux_xen     30_uefi-firmware   README
05_debian_theme  20_memtest86+    40_custom
10_linux         30_os-prober     41_custom
```

Each one is run in order and their outputs are all concatenated into the master output. If you want to add a custom section to your boot manager menu, look at the files marked custom and either extend them or add your own.

Summary

In this chapter you learned how the Linux kernel interacts with hardware. Peripheral devices talk to the kernel through a combination of IO ports, direct memory access channels, and interrupt requests. Commands such as **lsdev** and **lspci** allow you to inspect the exact resources that the peripherals are using.

Block storage devices store permanent data for the system. Disks that attach to your system have a name, such as /dev/sda, and a partition number that is appended to that name such as /dev/sda1. A filesystem is applied to a partition so that the kernel knows how to place files on the disk blocks, and these filesystems are then mounted in a tree structure onto the root filesystem.

Finally, a boot loader is responsible for taking the computer from power on to a running kernel. The most common boot loader is the Grand Unified Boot Loader, which is split across two versions: GRUB Legacy and GRUB2.

Exam Preparation Tasks

As mentioned in the section "How to Use This Book" in the Introduction, you have a couple of choices for exam preparation: the exercises here, Chapter 21, "Final Preparation," and the practice exams on the DVD.

Review All Key Topics

Review the most important topics in this chapter, noted with the Key Topics icon in the outer margin of the page. Table 1-2 lists a reference of these key topics and the page numbers on which each is found.

Table 1-2   Key Topics for Chapter 1

Key Topic Element	Description	Page Number
List	How CPUs identify hardware	7
List	Using **/proc** commands	8
List	Key utilities to list information about your system	8
Paragraph	udev and /dev	10
Paragraph	Partitions and block devices	11
Paragraph	Naming of disks and partitions	12
Paragraph	Mounted directories	13
Paragraph	Mounting removable devices	14
Paragraph	Logical Volume Manager terms	15
Paragraph	Commonly mounted partitions	16
Paragraph	Virtual memory and swap	17
Paragraph	The importance of the boot sector	17
Paragraph	GRUB boot volume	18
Paragraph	GRUB configuration files	20

Define Key Terms

Define the following key terms from this chapter and check your answers in the glossary:

hardware, peripherals, bus, driver, pseudofilesystem, coldplug, hotplug, integrated peripherals, partitions, filesystem, root filesystem, mount points, Redundant Array of Independent Disks (RAID), Logical Volume Manager (LVM), physical volume (PV), volume group (VG), physical extents (PE), logical volumes (LV), swap partition, swap, thrashing, boot manager, Basic Input Output System (BIOS), master boot record (MBR), Grand Unified Boot Loader (GRUB), multi-booting, initial RAM disk, virtual memory

Review Questions

The answers to these review questions are in Appendix A.

1. Which acronym refers to a feature that allows a peripheral to access system memory without needing to use the CPU?

   a. IRQ

   b. DMA

   c. TCP

   d. MEMCP

2. What does the **lsdev** command do?

   a. Shows PCI devices

   b. Shows IO ports

   c. Shows DMA channels

   d. All of the above

3. How does a peripheral notify the CPU that there is an event that needs its attention?

   a. Contacts the CPU over an IO port

   b. Initiates a direct memory access channel

   c. Issues an interrupt request

   d. Modifies the program counter of the CPU to execute code on the device

4. A pseudo-filesystem containing information about the system is

   a. /dev

   b. /proc

   c. /usr

   d. /sbin

5. What subsystem manages entries under /dev?

   a. systemd

   b. init

   c. procfs

   d. udev

6. A hotplug device:

   a. Doesn't need a driver

   b. Can be inserted and removed without rebooting the system

   c. Can't be removed without rebooting the system

   d. Is another name for a hard drive

7. Which of the following are not mass storage devices?

   a. Network attached drive

   b. Flash drive

   c. RAM

   d. CD-ROM

8. /dev/sda2 is

   a. A hard drive

   b. A logical volume

   c. A network adapter

   d. A partition on a hard drive

9. A filesystem is applied to

   a. A hard drive

   b. A partition

   c. A physical volume

   d. A volume group

10. Your root volume is /dev/sda1. You mount /dev/sda2 on /usr and then /dev/sdb1 on /usr/local/. Files in /usr/bin are then stored on:

    a. /dev/sda2

    b. /dev/sdb1

    c. /dev/sda1

    d. You can't nest mounts.

11. When laying out hard drive partitions, which of the following is not a primary consideration?

    a. Performance

    b. Integration

    c. Backup

    d. Security

12. In the Logical Volume Manager, the hard drive partitions themselves are

    a. Logical volumes

    b. Volume groups

    c. Physical extents

    d. Physical volumes

13. The Logical Volume Manager lets you resize disks without rebooting:

    a. True

    b. False

14. When the kernel is under pressure to give memory to a process, and there is another process that hasn't used its memory in a while, the kernel will

    a. Swap the old memory to disk

    b. Give the memory to the new process knowing it's not being used

    c. Compress the memory pages and give the reclaimed space to the new process

    d. Refuse to give memory to the new process

15. The first block on the disk is called (the):

    a. GRUB

    b. Bootloader

    c. Master boot record

    d. Index

16. GRUB2's configuration file is called:

    a. /etc/grub2/menu.lst

    b. /etc/grub2/grub.conf

    c. /etc/grub2/grub2.conf

    d. /etc/grub2/grub.cfg

This chapter covers the following topics:

- The Linux Boot Process
- Boot Sequence from BIOS to Fully Running System
- systemd
- Shut Down and Reboot from the Command Line
- Properly Terminating Processes
- Logging Boot Events

This chapter covers the following objectives:

- Boot the system: 101.2
- Change runlevels/boot targets and shut down or reboot the system: 101.3

## CHAPTER 2

Boot Process and Runlevels

In this chapter we discuss the Linux boot process, runlevels, boot logging, and how to manage the boot process.

"Do I Know This Already?" Quiz

The "Do I Know This Already?" quiz enables you to assess whether you should read this entire chapter or simply jump to the "Exam Preparation Tasks" section for review. If you are in doubt, read the entire chapter. Table 2-1 outlines the major headings in this chapter and the corresponding "Do I Know This Already?" quiz questions. You can find the answers in Appendix A, "Answers to the 'Do I Know This Already?' Quizzes and Review Questions."

Table 2-1 "Do I Know This Already?" Foundation Topics Section-to-Question Mapping

Foundation Topics Section	Questions Covered in This Section
The Linux Boot Process	1-2
Boot Sequence from BIOS to Fully Running System	3
systemd	6
Shut Down and Reboot from the Command Line	5
Properly Terminating Processes	7
Logging Boot Events	4

1. Write on the following line the exact text to specify at the GRUB prompt to cause a default install of a Linux distribution to boot directly to runlevel 2 after system initialization:

_____

2. When using the GRUB boot loader, which of the answers describes the first logical partition on the first hard disk in a GRUB configuration?

   a. /dev/sda5

   b. (hd0,4)

   c. c:8000:6

   d. /dev/dsk/c0d0s3

3. Which of the following commands would allow you to make changes to parameters for a configured GRUB menu choice, before booting the system?

   a. c (change)

   b. b (boot menu)

   c. e (edit)

   d. a (alter)

4. Which of the following commands shows messages read from the kernel ring buffer to standard output?

   a. cat /var/log/messages/kernel

   b. dmesg

   c. kernring

   d. lastlog

5. Which of the following commands are symlinks to the **reboot** command? (Choose two.)

   a. shutdown

   b. halt

   c. poweroff

   d. init 6

6. Which of the following are a part of the systemd utilities or commands? (Choose all that apply.)

   a. servicectl

   b. haltd

   c. journald

   d. shutdownd

   e. systemctl

7. If you wanted to remove all running instances of the foobar application, which of the following commands would accomplish this?

    a. pskill foobar

    b. halt foobar

    c. kill foobar*

    d. killall foobar

    e. pstree foobar

Foundation Topics

The Linux Boot Process

Booting your Linux system isn't just a matter of turning on your system and having it eventually present you with a login prompt. It's more a set of events that results, if all goes well, in your being presented with that login prompt.

In this section we look at the boot process as a set of tasks performed to get the system to the point where it can enter the default runlevel, where things can become complex due to the various methods of configuring, starting, and managing system services or processes.

What Is the Boot Process?

The *boot process* for Linux is how a system progresses from the power-on of the hardware (or virtual hardware in some cases) until the chosen operating system is at the desired state of functionality. With the popularity of systemd, Upstart, and other initialization methods, a number of pathways to achieving a running system can be taken.

The Linux boot process can be broken up into four distinct stages. They are typically:

1. Boot loader phase

2. Kernel phase

3. Early user space

4. Init process

Boot Loaders

Before we run through the different possible scenarios for the available/tested system initialization choices, a quick note about *boot loaders* is necessary.

Historically, you would find systems that either ran LILO, the Linux Loader, or early versions of GRUB, the Grand Unified Boot Loader. In this and future decades you'll likely encounter GRUB Version 1 and increasingly GRUB Version 2 bootloaders on systems.

NOTE   The installation of GRUB and other boot loader topics are covered in Chapter 1, "Installing Linux."

Possible boot loaders include the following:

- **LILO**—A much older and less-configurable system for booting systems. LILO-booted machines still exist in some production environments, but LILO is definitely not the best or most up-to-date choice available.

- **GRUB**—Grand Unified Boot Loader is the default boot loader for nearly all production and almost all user instances of Linux these days. Its superior configurability, boot options for just about any desired action, and the capability to change the boot process while it's happening make it the boot loader of choice.

- **SYSLINUX**—Seldom seen on systems these days, SYSLINUX was primarily used for boot or rescue disk options, to boot Linux from live USB devices and other types of nontraditional Linux systems. In addition, SYSLinux was used extensively to load Linux systems from a FAT file system on a DOS or early Windows system.

- **Loadlin**—Another method of booting from a non-Linux system, Loadlin literally swaps out or replaces a running non-Linux operating system with a running version of Linux.

Key Topic

A Linux computer typically has the boot loader in one of two places: the master boot record (MBR) or the first sector of one of the Linux partitions. Because many other operating systems use the same methodology—particularly Windows claiming the exact same MBR location as Linux—conflicts can occur.

Dual-booting Linux and Windows can be a challenge, but if you install them in the correct order and use GRUB to manage the boot loader environment, it's not difficult. I recommend installing the Windows product first because it's pickier about the MBR. Then, after the final *reboot*, install the Linux system in the prepared free space, allowing GRUB to notice and configure the Windows partition in the boot loader setup.

NOTE When you install Windows, it typically uses the entire disk, so when installing a distribution of Linux as a dual-boot, be prepared to use the gparted or installation partitioning tool to shrink the Windows partition to allow for enough space for the Linux partitions.

Common Commands at Boot Time

When booting Linux, you often want to change an option at the beginning of the process, such as changing the default *runlevel*, disabling or enabling specific hardware capabilities, or setting a particular mode for hardware that allows Linux to load properly.

> **NOTE**   The parameters typed on the command prompt or boot options prompt are passed directly to the Kernel upon initialization. These prompts are typically at the beginning of the boot process and are the first opportunity to enter any parameters. Some distributions are configured to show a splash screen or logo, and you have to find out what keystroke allows for the entry of boot parameters.

Some common Linux boot options are

- **vga**—Allows the setting of the framebuffer's resolution to a given mode, such as "vga=2", historically used for difficult laptop LCDs

- **apm**—APM or Automated Power Management is on by default. Declaring **apm=off** or **noapm** at the beginning of the boot process enhances the system's compatibility. This should be done only when indicated by a vendor or FAQ from a distribution provider.

- **init**—Specifying **init** at the start causes the /sbin/init process to be the first process run on the system. This may not work properly on initialization schemes where **init** is not present.

- **panic=#seconds**—The kernel does not reboot by default after a panic error occurs, which can cause a system to sit disabled until a technician can reach it physically. If a panic occurs, the kernel waits the specified number of seconds and then reboots and attempts to load normally.

- **single or 1**—These options cause the system to skip a full initialization to a default runlevel, instead putting the system into a troubleshooting or simple root-level state, where you are the root user and have minimal processes running.

- **2,3,4,5**—These options when entered at the GRUB prompt cause the system to initialize and then move to the specified runlevel, or in the case of systemd, the specified target that matches the runlevel number indicated.

- **ro or rw**—The **ro** option causes the root filesystem to be mounted in a read-only mode so that fsck can be run on the root filesystem in the case of possible errors. The **rw** parameter is to make sure the root filesystem is mounted read-write, which is the default state.

- **mem=xxxxM**—This is an old chestnut of a system boot parameter, and it simply sets the amount of memory that can be accessed by the about-to-be-booted system. This is used when you suspect a memory bank is bad, or to test a system with a specific amount of memory, such as when testing a set-top box configuration or other limited-hardware device.

NOTE   You have to look at the boot parameter documentation for your given distribution and boot manager to find out exactly which ones are appropriate.

Boot Sequence from BIOS to Fully Running System

The Linux system's boot steps are relatively similar across distributions, except maybe for Slackware and the BSD variants. The following steps show the boot process if you are using the SysVinit system initialization method. systemd and Upstart are covered in the following sections.

SysVinit

The SysVinit bootup process is outlined in the following steps:

1. Turn on the system power.

2. The basic input/output system *(BIOS)* code loads and looks for a valid boot sector.

3. The BIOS loads the boot sector from a floppy disk, HD, or CD-ROM according to the seek order.

4. The master boot record (MBR) is read; it's contained in the first 512 bytes of the first sector of the first or active hard disk.

5. Any boot loader code found is executed.

6. GRUB or the installed boot loader starts.

7. The user selects or types in a choice, or the boot loader times out and begins to load the default entry.

8. If you select a Linux image/choice, the path to load the Linux kernel is read and the compressed kernel is executed.

9. When the Linux kernel is loading, it initializes the devices, loads any necessary modules, looks for the initial RAM disk (initrd), and loads that if necessary.

Then it mounts the root filesystem, as defined by the root=/dev/XXX information in the entry.

10. The /sbin/init program is loaded and becomes PID 1, the grandparent of all other processes on the system.

11. The *init process* then reads the /etc/inittab file and runs the /etc/init.d/rcS script for Debian systems and the /etc/rc.d/init.d/ rc.sysinit script for Red Hat systems.

12. The system initialization script loads the necessary modules, checks the root file system, mounts the local file systems, starts the network devices, and then mounts the remote file systems (if configured to do so).

13. The init process reads the /etc/inittab again and changes the system to the default runlevel by executing the scripts in the appropriate directory.

14. The runlevel scripts are executed, with the SXXservice scripts in the default runlevel directory being run in standard numeric sorting order. (This is easy to see in most boot situations because a long scrolling list of [OK] notations appear in green on the right of the system's screen indicating the service loaded properly.)

15. The mingetty sessions laid out in /etc/inittab are loaded, and the system (and login) shows the login prompt and waits for the user to log in.

systemd

systemd is both a new method of system initialization and one vaguely familiar to those who have historically used SysVinit as their initialization method.

systemd was specifically written to replace the SysVinit system, while keeping some connection to the methodology of SysVinit as well as some command compatibility.

Although controversial at its introduction, often predicted to increase the likelihood of broken system dependencies, and just generally hated-upon because, well, it's new, systemd has nonetheless become the default system initialization method for most modern distributions.

The hallmarks or major features of systemd are

- It's not SysVinit.

- It's considered more efficient and parallel in operation than SysVinit.

- It's less dependency-driven than other methods.

- It allows for more prioritization of what services start first and have precedence over system resources.

- It can dramatically reduce system startup times.

Similar to the init daemon from the SysVinit method, the systemd daemon is linked to by a symlink from /sbin/init. There are 60+ binaries included in the entire systemd suite, with the following being its core components:

- **systemd**—The systems and services manager for the operating system

- **systemctl**—The systemd state inspection and state controlling utility

- **systemd-analyze**—The utility that allows you to inspect performance statistics regarding system bootup as well as view trace and current state information

A number of additional daemons and libraries make up the core functionality of systemd; they include

- **journald**—The logging system for systemd by default. journald uses binary files for its logging, and it can be replaced by more traditional logging mechanisms such as rsyslog and syslog-ng.

- **consoled**—A console daemon for use as a user console, this replaces the more traditional virtual terminal system with what can be a more system-friendly component.

- **networkd**—The daemon that provides networking support for systemd's network access.

- **logind**—A daemon designed to replace Consolekit, logind supports X display managers, user logins, and so on.

Additional features that recommend systemd to administrators include

- **Logging capabilities**—The system's entire set of log messages are stored securely in systemd's journal, reducing message loss and increasing reliability of troubleshooting.

- **Service activation**—systemd's way of dealing with services frees them from a given runlevel and allows them to be more on-demand in nature, activated by a number of hardware and software events.

- **Component groups**—A Cgroup is similar in structure and function to the historical SysVinit runlevels in that they have a hierarchy of what starts when and before or after what other service. Cgroups help system memory space cleanliness dramatically by using a group tag for processes that allows the precise and total removal of groups of processes from memory.

- **System resource allocation**—Since you can determine exactly what Cgroup a service is associated with, it's possible to more precisely control what system resources a service or group of services can consume. Whereas before you could only control a runaway or hog process with nice/renice, systemd now allows the exact setting of a limited set of resources per service. An example of this would be an Apache server that gets hit by an extreme amount of visitors and would traditionally grow its processes to take over a majority of the system's resources. Now that service or group of services can be controlled exactly.

Units in systemd

When using systemd instead of SysVinit, you swap out the concept of "init scripts" and replace them with systemd "units." Effectively, a unit is a file that represents the configuration of a system service, much like the init scripts did in SysVinit.

systemd units come in a number of types, with the name of the service as the prefix of the filename, followed by a "." and then the type of service as the postfix of the filename, such as blahwoof.service.

systemd units are typically located in the following directories and have precedence over each other:

- **/usr/lib/systemd/system/**—Units that have been installed with the distribution

- **/run/systemd/system**—Units that have been created at runtime; may have precedence over non-runtime or installed units

- **/etc/systemd/system**—Units that are controlled by the sysadmin and have ultimate precedence over all the other units

Table 2-2 displays the type of service, lists the extension for the service, and describes the service.

Table 2-2   systemd Unit Types

Type of Service	Extension	Description
Service	.service	A given system service
Socket	.socket	An IPC (interprocess communication) socket
Target	.target	A grouping of units
Mount	.mount	A mount point on a file system
Automount	.automount	An automount point on a file system
Device	.device	A device file used by the kernel

Type of Service	Extension	Description
Scope	.scope	A process created externally
Timer	.timer	A timer
Path	.path	A file or directory on a file system
Slice	.slice	A grouping of units in a hierarchy; used to manage system processes
Snapshot	.snapshot	A saved instance of the state of the systemd manager
Swap	.swap	A swap file or a swap device

systemd Targets and Runlevels

In SysVinit systems, you had a defined but configurable set of runlevels numbered from 0 to 6. A runlevel is essentially a set of capabilities or running services that you can predefine and set the system to boot to so you have a predictable set of services.

In systemd, targets are the new runlevels. For example, the default.target file is typically a symbolic link to another target file such as the graphical.target file. Targets directly correspond to the SysVinit runlevels in that you can match them up as shown in Table 2-3.

Table 2-3 shows the correlation between runlevels, targets, and the files and describes what action occurs when that runlevel or target is initiated.

Table 2-3   What Happens When Runlevels and Targets Are Initiated

Runlevel	Target File	What It Does
0	poweroff.target	Shuts down and powers off the system
1	rescue.target	Configures a rescue shell session
2	multi-user.target	Sets the system to a nongraphical multiuser system, typically with no network services
3	multi-user.target	Sets up the system as a nongraphical multiuser system, with network services
4	multi-user.target	Same as 3
5	graphical.target	Sets up the system as a graphical multiuser system with network services
6	reboot.target	Shuts down and boots the system again

NOTE   The targets also have another designation, that of runlevel#.target where the "#" character would be 0-6. This is for compatibility.

Wants and Requires

The systemd procedure uses a set of options or requirements called "wants" and "requires" to indicate dependencies between units and groups of units.

For example, if you were to look at the typical contents of the graphical.target file, you might find the following lines:

```
Requires=multi-user.target
After=multi-user.target
Wants=display-manager.service
```

The Requires statement means that before the graphical.target can be processed, all the items listed in the multi-user.target must be started, which means that all the linked services in the /usr/lib/systemd/multi-user.target directory must be started.

Only after that requirement is met will the Wants statement be processed (which again means the starting of linked services in the appropriate directory, this time the /usr/lib/systemd/multi-user.target.wants directory), after which the graphical.target will be used.

Booting with systemd

When booting a system that uses systemd, the same set of steps outlined previously are true, except for when the system starts systemd/init from GRUB, there is a structure overlaid on the system reminiscent of SysVinit's init script structure.

The file that is read after the kernel and initramdisk is typically the default.target file. This file is simply a link to the multi-user.target file.

This is where it gets pretty strange, because while the boot process may look simple, like that shown in Example 2-1, it's not.

Example 2-1   Theoretical Hierarchy of the Boot Process

```
Kernel
  |
  V
multi-user.target
      |
      V
      graphical.target
```

The reality of the situation is that the graphical.target requires multi-user.target, which requires basic.target, which in turn requires the sysinit.target. All these must load their configured services successfully to move on to the other, so the real order of bootup is shown in Example 2-2.

Example 2-2   Actual Hierarchy of the Boot Process

```
                        local-fs-pre.target
                            |
                            V
sysinit.target    -- wants local-fs.target and swap.target
     |
     V
basic.target -- wants
     |
     V
multi-user.target -- wants
     |
     V
graphical.target -- wants
```

It takes a while to bend your consciousness around the way systemd works, but in practice, it's not that different from SysVinit and its dozens of links in multiple directories.

Upstart

Of particular note is the *Upstart* system initialization scheme, in that its design goals are simple:

- **Asynchronous operation**—Upstart handles the starting of services during boot and stopping of services during *shutdown*, as well as their running during normal system operations.

- **Ease of implementation**—Upstart is easy to transition to due to its compatibility with sysinit.

- **Backward compatibility**—Upstart runs unaltered sysvinit scripts and can perform well in a mixed system initialization environment.

- **Extensibility**—Upstart is eminently extensible to allow for more inputs, events, custom tasks and services, and much more.

Unfortunately for Upstart, the world of Linux distributions has been moving toward systemd as a rule, or staying with SysVinit, with the most public defection being Ubuntu, to maintain compatibility with the upstream Debian code bases and methodologies.

> **NOTE**   Chrome OS, from Google and the OS on Chromebooks features Upstart, so a growing base of systems take advantage of Upstart's features.

Managing System Runlevels

Being able to properly manage your system's runlevels means you will be able to predictably run the system in the appropriate mode with the correct services enabled and ready for use.

Determining the Default Runlevel

On a SysVinit system, determining the runlevel is simple: You execute the **runlevel** command and it returns the following command output:

```
N 2
```

The first column, (containing the character **N**) shows you that there was No previous runlevel, so the system has been booted and has arrived at Runlevel 2 (column 2 in the output) without any intervening steps such as Runlevel 1.

> **NOTE**   If you see a previous runlevel such as "1" and then the current runlevel, in this case "2," you should be certain that you or another valid sysadmin were responsible for taking that system to a single-user mode for a good reason, or else the system may have been tampered with.

In addition, you might be able to run the **who -r** command to get additional and more English-sentence-like output:

```
run-level 2  2015-03-01 10:14
```

On a running systemd system, you can use **systemctl get-default** to determine what the default target is. The output is the resolved name of the target that the symbolic link points to, such as

```
multi-user.target
```

> **NOTE**   Runlevels are exclusive, and targets are not. In other words, only a single run-level can be the current runlevel, whereas you can actually have multiple active targets.

To determine all the targets that are active, use the **systemctl list-units --type=target** command. The output is the names of the target files that are active, such as

```
multi-user.target
graphical.target
```

Setting the Default Runlevels

On a SysVinit system, setting the default runlevel is as simple as choosing what run-level you want and then editing the **/etc/inittab** file and changing **id:5:initdefault:** to reflect the number of the runlevel you want (replacing the number 5 with the desired number from 0-6).

On a systemd machine, you change the default runlevel by specifying a given target via a symlink. For example, to make your system default to the graphical.target run-level, you would create a symlink named default.target that points to the appropriate location of the graphical.target file.

```
ln -sf /usr/lib/systemd/system/graphical.target
/etc/systemd/system/default.target
```

Changing Runlevels

On a SysVinit system, changing the current runlevel involves two commands, either the **init** or **telinit** command.

> **NOTE**   The **/sbin/telinit** command is a symbolic link to the **/sbin/init** command, so they are not exactly two commands; **telinit** is there for historical purposes, or if you have a lot of old scripts that use it, anti-hysterical purposes, aka those who still use telinit, or have it in their scripts.

To set the current runlevel to 3, execute the command as root or using sudo:

```
init 3
```

On a systemd machine, you can set the current target(s) to a single target only by executing the command:

```
systemctl isolate runlevel5.target
```

or

```
systemctl isolate graphical.target
```

Shut Down and Reboot from the Command Line

Shutting down a system properly, without any unnecessary loss of unwritten data in filesystem buffers or corruption of disk is important. Current versions of Linux filesystems are much more flexible and forgiving than in decades past, but dropping the power on a running system is almost guaranteed to cause an issue or many issues.

On a SysVinit system, you can use several commands to shut down the system properly, starting with

```
halt -p
```

This halts the system and then powers it off using hardware calls.

Key Topic

The more common command to be used is the **shutdown** command, which offers multiple useful options:

- **-H, --halt**—Halts the machine, but doesn't power it off.

- **-P, --poweroff**—Halts and powers off the machine.

- **-r, --reboot**—Reboots the machine after shutting it down properly.

- **-k**—Does not power off, halt, or reboot, but just writes a wall message (otherwise known as -Kidding). This option is to hopefully scare the users off the system so critical tasks can be performed.

Shutting down a systemd machine can be done as outlined previously with the SysVinit commands and options, or you can use the **systemctl** command as follows:

- **systemctl halt**—Does exactly what it says: halts the system; doesn't power it off.

- **systemctl poweroff**—Shuts down the system (halts) and powers it off.

- **systemctl reboot**—Shuts down the system (halts) and then reboots the system.

> **NOTE**   On systems where you are not the root, or the root user account isn't used for normal administration, prefix the **systemctl** commands with the **sudo** command. The **sudo** command must be set up for your account to use, but once done, you can run the **systemcel** commands such as
>
> ```
> sudo systemctl reboot
> ```

Alerting Users

No section on powering off, halting, or rebooting systems can be complete without a discussion of how to notify users who will be affected by the change in the system's state.

Since a shutdown is by definition an orderly shutdown, there is ample warning to the system's processes that it's going down, but often users would appreciate a little more time and ability to wrap up their current work.

> **NOTE**   The **shutdown** command contains just about anything you need to properly notify users of the impending shutdown, including the ability to disable new user logins shortly before the shutdown commences.

For example, you can schedule a system shutdown for 7:00 p.m. of the current day with the absolute command:

```
shutdown 19:00
```

You can also use a relative notation to specify when to shut down the system, say 20 minutes in the future, with the command

```
shutdown +20
```

You can mix a time specification with a notice to all logged-in users (those logged in to a console, not a network share connection) with the command:

```
shutdown +30 "System going down in 30 minutes, save your work and log
off!"
```

> **NOTE**   The KDE desktop features a daemon to watch for system reboots for logged-in graphical user interface (GUI) users. All you need to do is issue the proper shutdown command, and the KDE system notifies users of the shutdown.

If you have scheduled a shutdown in the future, you can cancel it by issuing the **shutdown** command with the **-c** option:

```
shutdown -c
```

Properly Terminating Processes

Sysadmins frequently have to terminate processes that either can't or won't end properly or on demand from their parent processes. Being able to find the processes in the process table and kill them individually by the PID (process ID) or in groups based on the process name are critical.

 kill and killall

Controlling daemons can also include using the **kill** and **killall** commands, which work on the PID and command name, respectively.

kill and **killall** use the same signals; other than using PIDs and names, they are functionally similar. The **kill** command is simple, but you need to find the PID or Process ID of the process you want to kill first to find that out. To find the PID(s) of the smb processes on your system, run the command:

```
ps aux | grep smb
```

This returns the output shown here:

```
root 388 0.0 0.9 7324 2460 ? S 00:38 /usr/sbin/smbd -D
```

You then take the number from the second column, the PID, and supply it as the argument to the kill command:

```
kill 388
```

If the program doesn't respond, or it is the parent process of a zombie process (a process that is so far gone it can't respond to a valid **kill** or **SIGTERM** command), use an absolute kill or the **kill** command with a **-9** option to send the SIGKILL signal, such as

```
kill -9 388
```

The **killall** command works similarly. You can name the runaway or undesired processes by the actual command that is running, which is the last column of the **ps** output.

To kill all running instances of the Mozilla browser on your machine, as root you enter

```
killall mozilla-bin
```

If, for some reason, the browser doesn't respond, use the **kill** command with the **-9** option to send a SIGKILL or absolute kill, like so:

```
killall -9 mozilla-bin
```

This forcibly removes the processes from memory without even allowing them time to clean up memory and disk processes. So be aware that using the **kill** and **killall** commands to abruptly terminate processes can cause issues with memory usage over time and can even cause you to spend some quality time with fsck.

Reloading or "Hanging Up" Processes

When you are running a server with many system services active and providing multiple clients with access to resources, it's not always possible to reboot the system to make sure all the changes to configuration files are taken into account.

A convenient way to restart a system process, such as Apache, Samba, or Syslog and make it reload its configuration file is to use the SIGHUP signal. Essentially, this signal causes the process to simply reload its configuration file as a result, thereby making any new configuration options active without any interruption in connections or client access.

Sending a process the SIGHUP signal looks like this:

```
kill -HUP 2112
```

Additionally, you can also use the -1 numeric signal to accomplish the same reloading of the process's configuration file.

Logging Boot Events

When you are running a SysVinit system, the *boot logging* is relatively simple: You can use the **dmesg** command to see the output from the last system's boot. This output will also be mixed in with the other entries in the main system's log, typically /var/log/messages or /var/log/syslog.

When you are using the **dmesg** command, what you are really viewing isn't a log file, but the messages generated by the kernel ring buffer, a section of the running kernel.

NOTE   On some distributions, initialization scripts may send these kernel ring buffer messages to the configured logging system and log files such as /var/log/messages.

By contrast, a systemd machine keeps all the logging information in the systemd/journald binary log journal. To view a particular boot log, you can use the **journalctl** command and specify the boot you want.

For example, to list out the boot logs available under systemd, issue the following command:

```
journalctl --list-boots
```

This returns a number of logs or "journals" that you can choose from, with the format as follows:

```
-1 cadadcadadffldkljadlalwdkfjpadlk  Tue 2015-03-22  MDT-Tue 12:12:37
2015-03-22 12:13:01 MDT
0 aekdaldkadslufadmfadadwwetsdasgad  Tue 2015-03-23  MDT-Tue 08:00:22
2015-03-23 08:01:13 MDT
```

The log that starts with the reference ID of 0 is the current boot of the system; the previous one is notated with a -1, and so on. If there were 34 previous boots, there would be the 0 entry and -1 to -34 entries listed.

To view the previous system boot log, you would use the command:

```
journalctl  --boot=cadadcadaffldkljadlalwdkfjpadlk
```

Exam Preparation Tasks

As mentioned in the section "How to Use This Book" in the Introduction, you have a few choices for exam preparation: the exercises here, Chapter 21, "Final Preparation," and the practice exams on the DVD.

Review All Key Topics

Review the most important topics in this chapter, noted with the Key Topics icon in the outer margin of the page. Table 2-4 lists a reference of these key topics and the page numbers on which each is found.

Table 2-4 Key Topics for Chapter 2

Key Topic Element	Description	Page Number
Paragraph	Linux boot loader	31
List	Common Linux boot options	32
List	Core components of the systemd suite	35
List	Directories where systemd units are typically located	36
Paragraph	Targets are the new runlevels	37
Paragraph	Multi-user.target files	38
Paragraph	Using the **runlevel** command to determine the default runlevel	40

Key Topic Element	Description	Page Number
Paragraph	Using **systemctl get-default** command to determine the default runlevel	40
Section	Setting the default runlevels	41
List	**shutdown** commands	42
Paragraph	Time specifications and notices	43
Section	**kill** and **killall**	44
Section	Reloading or "hanging up" processes	45
Paragraph	**dmesg** command	45

Define Key Terms

Define the following key terms from this chapter and check your answers in the glossary:

boot process, BIOS, boot loader, init process, systemd, Upstart, boot logging, runlevels, shut down, reboot

Review Questions

The answers to these review questions are in Appendix A.

1. When attempting to boot your Linux system, you see an error message and the system will not complete a normal boot. Which of the following could you type at the GRUB menu to enter a system administrator mode for trouble-shooting? Choose all that apply.

    a. 1

    b. 2

    c. 5

    d. s

    e. S

2. In which of the following locations are you most likely to find the boot loader code on a Linux system?

    a. Master boot record

    b. /boot/vmlinuz

    c. /dev/d0/s0

     d. First sector of partition

     e. /grub/boot.msg

3. Which feature listed below helps in the orderly removal of processes and groups of processes when the system is using the systemd initialization process?

     a. /etc/group

     b. group tag

     c. groupmod

     d. gkill

4. Which of the follow commands simulate a shutdown event on the system, but do not actually take the system down?

     a. shutdown -h

     b. shutdown -k

     c. shutdown -r

     d. shutdown -c

5. You have edited the configuration file of the service named daemon1 and need that service to reread the configuration and continue serving its attached client processes. Which of the following will accomplish this? Choose all that apply.

     a. kill –s SIGHUP daemon1

     b. kill -15 daemon1

     c. kill -9 daemon1

     d. kill –HUP daemon1

     e. kill -1 daemon1

6. During your last system boot, you noticed several error messages that quickly scrolled off the screen and could not be viewed. You are not sure which system initialization scheme is in place. Which of the following commands will likely show you just the messages from the most recent system boot? (Choose three.)

     a. systemctl --viewboot

     b. journalctl -b

     c. syslog --boot

     d. dmesg

     e. cat /var/log/boot.msg

This chapter covers the following topics:

- Software in a Linux System
- Debian Package Management
- RPM and YUM Package Management

The exam objectives covered in this chapter are

- Manage shared libraries: 102.3
- Use Debian package management: 102.4
- Use RPM and YUM package management: 102.5

## CHAPTER 3

Package Install and Management

The purpose of a Linux system should be to do something useful such as reading email, browsing the Web, or being some kind of application server. The Linux kernel is great, but by itself it doesn't do much—for that you need software.

A lot of software is available for Linux; you just need to install it. You can install software in a few ways depending on your distribution and how the software was packaged.

At one point software was distributed in *source format*, which needed to be compiled into something that could run on the computer. That's still around, but as a community we've moved on to distributing *binary packages* that are much easier to install. Not only do the binary packages avoid the compilation step, but also dependencies, libraries, configuration, and documentation are automatically managed. There are a few different formats of these packages, but for the most part two are most prevalent: Debian style and Red Hat style.

In the past the LPIC exam was offered in two flavors, corresponding to Debian and Red Hat. Now you're expected to know both. The concepts are the same; the commands differ.

"Do I Know This Already?" Quiz

The "Do I Know This Already?" quiz enables you to assess whether you should read this entire chapter or simply jump to the "Exam Preparation Tasks" section for review. If you are in doubt, read the entire chapter. Table 3-1 outlines the major headings in this chapter and the corresponding "Do I Know This Already?" quiz questions. You can find the answers in Appendix A, "Answers to the 'Do I Know This Already?' Quizzes and Review Questions."

Table 3-1 "Do I Know This Already?" Foundation Topics Section-to-Question Mapping

Foundation Topics Section	Questions Covered in This Section
Software in a Linux System	1-2
Debian Package Management	3-6
RPM and YUM Package Management	7-9

1. libjpg.so.8.0.3 is probably a

   a. Static library

   b. Shared library

   c. Binary

   d. Shell script

2. The dynamic linker is called _____ and is configured in _____.

   a. ld.so, /etc/ld.so.conf

   b. so.linux, /etc/ld.so.conf

   c. ld.so, /etc/so.linux.conf

   d. so.linux, /etc/so.linux.conf

3. How would you install a package called foo-1.2.3.deb?

   a. **yum install foo-1.2.3.deb**

   b. **rpm -i foo-1.2.3.deb**

   c. **dpkg --install foo-1.2.3.deb**

   d. **apt-get install foo-1.2.3.deb**

4. How would you query your Debian system to see whether the bulldozer package was installed?

   a. **dpkg --info bulldozer**

   b. **apt-cache search bulldozer**

   c. **rpm -q bulldozer**

   d. **dpkg --list bulldozer**

5. After updating your list of remote Debian repository files you should run:

   a. **dpkg update**

   b. **apt-cache fetch**

   c. **apt-cache update**

   d. **apt-get update**

6. If you want to install a local Debian package and ignore any dependency errors, what do you need to do?

   a. Nothing, this is the default.

   b. Add **--force-depends (dpkg -i pkg.deb --force-depends)**

   c. Add **--force-conflicts (dpkg -i pkg.deb --force-conflicts)**

   d. Add **--force-reinstreq (dpkg -i pkg.deb --force-reinstreq)**

7. An RPM package's long name does not contain:

   a. Name of the package

   b. Version

   c. Distribution version

   d. Architecture

8. To check the signatures on a directory full of RPM files, use

   a. **rpm -K ***

   b. **rpm -qk ***

   c. **rpm --check-sig ***

   d. **rpm-sig ***

9. How would you check for the presence of an installed package called foobar?

   a. **rpm -qV foobar**

   b. **rpm -qVp foobar**

   c. **rpm -q foobar**

   d. **rpm -qp foobar**

Foundation Topics

Software in a Linux System

A typical piece of software is comprised of five pieces:

- Binaries

- Libraries

- Configuration

- Documentation

- Data

Binaries are the things that you run like programs or applications. The kernel loads them into memory and starts running the instructions. Libraries are shared components such as methods to read files from a disk or display a certain graphical widget. Configuration is usually in the form of one or more files that direct the application to behave properly. Documentation provides instructions on how to use the software, and the data stores your information.

These five pieces may be spread about your filesystem according to the Filesystem Hierarchy Standard (FHS). If you want to upgrade your software you generally have to reinstall the new version on top of the old one, but this can leave older versions of some files lying around. Eventually you end up with several outdated pieces that you're not sure whether you can delete and your system gets messy. The same problem happened if you needed to delete some software.

The FHS describes where particular types of files are to be placed, which helps maintain consistency across different distributions. The FHS is covered in Chapter 5, "File Management."

Package managers were invented to solve these types of problems. A package manager keeps track of which files belong to which package, which packages depend on which other packages, and where the different types of files are stored. All modern distributions of Linux use package managers in some fashion.

Shared Libraries

Much of what a software developer needs to do has already been done. Writing files to disk, displaying windows, even talking over the network—Linux has *libraries* that handle all of these. Libraries are reusable components that a software developer can *link* to an application so that the library's functionality can be used. Applications themselves may offer libraries for other applications to use, such as a database providing code for other applications to query it.

A library can either be statically or dynamically linked to an application. In the *static linking* process, a copy of the library is placed into the resulting application. With *dynamic linking*, the application only needs a series of stubs that later point to a systemwide copy of the library.

Figure 3-1 shows this concept in more detail.

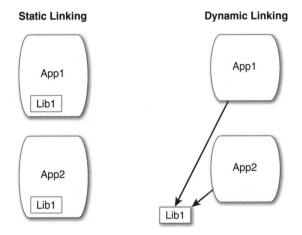

Static Linking   **Dynamic Linking**

Figure 3-1   The difference between a statically linked application and a dynamically linked application

Figure 3-1 shows two applications, App1 and App2; both use a library called Lib1. The statically linked versions have a copy of Lib1 inside each application, while the dynamically linked versions point to a common Lib1 and are therefore smaller.

With static linking you don't need to worry whether the system has the library installed because the library is built into the application. As a result the files are much bigger. Dynamic linking results in smaller applications, but the appropriate shared libraries must be present.

The best reason for dynamic linking is ease of upgrades. Every application with a built-in static library needs to be recompiled and linked if you need to upgrade the library. With dynamic linking, one update works across all the binaries.

Dynamic linking is used in almost all cases because it saves disk space and eases upgrades.

Working with Shared Libraries

An application that needs to use a shared library asks a service called *ld.so*, otherwise known as the *dynamic linker*. The dynamic linker knows where all the shared libraries are stored and loads the library for the application.

Libraries are typically stored in /lib or /usr/lib for 32-bit libraries, and /lib64 or /usr/lib64 for 64-bit binaries. A 64-bit system can load 32-bit applications, so you will likely see both. A 64-bit system relies on newer hardware that supports more memory, while 32-bit is for older hardware. Even though 64-bit machines have been around since the early 2000s, 32-bit code is still widely used.

Distributions are free to store application-specific shared libraries anywhere, so you may find /lib is just a link to /usr/lib and that particular applications may store its libraries in a separate directory.

You can recognize a shared library because it ends with or contains a **.so** extension, short for *shared object*. The files usually have a version number in them like so:

```
[sean@localhost lib64]$ ls -l libcrypt*
-rwxr-xr-x 1 root root    36752 Sep 27 11:48 libcrypt-2.20.so
lrwxrwxrwx 1 root root       25 Sep 27 11:45 libcrypt.so -> libcrypt.
so.1
lrwxrwxrwx 1 root root       16 Sep 27 11:45 libcrypt.so.1 ->
libcrypt-2.20.so
```

You can see in this example that the actual library file is libcrypt-2.20.so and that there are two symbolic links: libcrypt.so points to libcrypt.so.1, which itself is a link to libcrypt-2.20.so. Each one of these files represents a version number, depending on who or what is asking, but all go to the same file. This allows multiple incompatible versions of a shared library to exist on the same system. Applications simply need to ask for the version they were originally linked with.

The dynamic loader is taking care of this linking for you. It does this by querying the binaries as they are run.

Determining Required Libraries

When you find a program and want to know whether the libraries it relies on are present, either run it and see what breaks (the unsafe way) or query the program for the necessary libraries with the **ldd** command:

```
$ ldd /usr/bin/passwd
       ...
       libc.so.6 => /lib64/libc.so.6 (0x00007fa7a3bae000)
       libcrypt.so.1 => /lib64/libcrypt.so.1 (0x00007fa7a3773000)
       /lib64/ld-linux-x86-64.so.2 (0x00007fa7a55be000)
```

The output tells you that the **passwd** command needs access to `libc` (the C library, which is a basic set of functionality for all applications), the `libcrypt`, and a peculiarly named shared library that's actually the dynamic linker itself.

Looking for Libraries in Other Places

Some library files might not have enough header or internal information to be correctly identified by the linker when it builds the links in the library directories.

The **ldconfig** program reads the headers of all the libraries in the **/lib** and **/usr/lib** directories and any directories noted in the **/etc/ld.so.conf** file. From those headers and the filenames of the libraries, **ldconfig** makes the proper links to the libraries.

> **NOTE**   ld.so.conf might include a line similar to **ld.so.conf.d/*.conf**. In this case, the files specified there are also read and processed by **ldconfig**. This system lets packages drop in the locations of their libraries without having to edit a shared file.

The **ldconfig** program also builds the **/etc/ld.so.cache** file, a binary file that is an ordered list of the libraries on the system. This file is not readable as text but is used as a quick reference by the system linker **ld.so**.

Libraries must be accessible to the dynamic linker or added into in a variable called **LD_LIBRARY_PATH**, which contains the library path(s) separated by colons (:). This provides a hint to the dynamic linker that it should look in a place other than what it was told about earlier.

To set the **LD_LIBRARY_PATH** variable, you can declare it on the command line, like so:

```
export LD_LIBRARY_PATH=/some/path/name
```

Or, you can edit the **/etc/profile** or **~/.bash_profile** file and copy the same command there. Chapter 11, "Customizing Shell Environments," investigates these files in more depth.

> **CAUTION**   Although this must be known for the exam, the **LD_LIBRARY_PATH** is considered to be a security risk because it might allow unauthorized programs access to system libraries accidentally or otherwise expose system library paths to unauthorized users.

Debian Package Management

Debian, and Debian derived systems such as Ubuntu, have a powerful package management system that provides a way for administrators to find, install, query, and remove packages. The package tracks the parts of an application and helps you figure out which other packages are needed to install a given package, and if any packages rely on another.

The basic unit of Debian package management is a file with a .deb extension, for example, application.deb. This is a Debian package: It contains the application, any default configuration files and documentation, instructions to the system on how to install and remove it, and a list of any dependencies the package has.

You install, remove, and query packages with the **dpkg** tool. But that only works if you have the package, so the *Advanced Package Tool (APT)* contains a series of utilities that help you find the packages on remote servers. The apt-* tools download a package you want along with any dependencies and then install them all using **dpkg**.

Graphical and text-based interfaces such as **aptitude** and **synaptic** are layered on top of the APT tools. These give you a nicer interface to use instead of having to remember commands.

So, to recap: Local packages are .deb files and are installed with **dpkg**. APT handles searching remote package repositories and downloading packages. Aptitude and the like provide a graphical interface to APT.

Managing Local Debian Packages

The **dpkg** tool manipulates packages on your system and can process the .deb packages you may download. If you have a package on your system, you can find out what's inside it with the **--info** option as shown in Example 3-1.

Example 3-1   Finding Out What's Inside a .deb File

```
# dpkg --info acct_6.5.5-1_amd64.deb
 new debian package, version 2.0.
 size 120424 bytes: control archive=1899 bytes.
      79 bytes,     4 lines      conffiles
     746 bytes,    18 lines      control
    1766 bytes,    27 lines      md5sums
     507 bytes,    30 lines    * postinst           #!/bin/sh
     370 bytes,    26 lines    * postrm             #!/bin/sh
     163 bytes,     7 lines    * prerm              #!/bin/sh
 Package: acct
```

```
Version: 6.5.5-1
Architecture: amd64
Maintainer: Mathieu Trudel-Lapierre <mathieu.tl@gmail.com>
Installed-Size: 380
Depends: dpkg (>= 1.15.4) | install-info, libc6 (>= 2.3)
Section: admin
Priority: optional
Homepage: http://www.gnu.org/software/acct/
Description: The GNU Accounting utilities for process and login
accounting
  ...
```

The information about the package is contained inside the .deb file; the **dpkg** command is just displaying it nicely for you. The top section describes the control files that provide the metadata for **dpkg** to use. The file itself is 120424 bytes and inside it is an archive of control files totaling 1899 bytes. Inside that archive are

- **conffiles**—A list of files used to configure the package after it's installed. These are treated differently than other files in the package; for example, they are not removed when the package is removed.

- **control**—The file containing all the metadata about the packages such as dependencies.

- **md5sums**—A list of files and a checksum so that you can verify the file hasn't changed at any point.

- **postinst**—A shell script that is run after (post) the installation.

- **postrm**—A shell script that is run after the removal of the package.

- **prerm**—A shell script that is run just before the package is removed.

After the control information you see various pieces of information about the package, such as the name, version, which hardware it is meant to go on, and the dependencies.

Installing Packages with dpkg

The most common way to install packages is using the command line from the current directory using one of the following commands:

```
dpkg --install gcc-4.7-base_4.7.2-5_amd64.deb
dpkg -i gcc-4.7-base_4.7.2-5_amd64.deb
```

This returns output similar to the following:

```
Selecting previously unselected package gcc-4.7-base:amd64.
(Reading database ... 142987 files and directories currently
installed.)
Unpacking gcc-4.7-base:amd64 (from gcc-4.7-base_4.7.2-5_amd64.deb) ...
Setting up gcc-4.7-base:amd64 (4.7.2-5) ...
```

Sometimes you need to install dependencies for a package. Either install the dependency first or specify all the necessary packages on the same command line. The command for the latter option looks like this:

```
dpkg -i gcc-4.7-base_4.7.2-5_amd64.deb libgcc1_1%3a4.7.2-5_amd64.deb
```

Removing Packages

When you need to remove a package with the **dpkg** command, you can use one of two methods: remove or purge. The **-r** or **--remove** option removes the package's files but leaves any configuration files intact on the disk. The other option for getting rid of packages is the **-P** or **--purge** option, which removes all the package's files, including any configuration files.

To remove a package but leave its configuration files in place, use one of the following:

```
dpkg --remove package_name
dpkg -r package_name
```

To purge a package, including its configuration files, use one of the following:

```
dpkg --purge package_name
dpkg -P package_name
```

When a package is installed, any configuration files are noted in the conffiles file. This is used to determine which files are left in place during a remove action and which files should also be purged in a purge action.

Dependency Issues

When you are working with packages, a desired package installation often finds entries in the package database that conflict with the files it is attempting to install. Also, sometimes during a removal, a package has a file that other packages depend on.

In keeping with the sturdy and less-than-verbose nature of Debian, using the package tools **--force** option can lead to some truly unpleasant circumstances for your machine. Take great care when removing packages that have dependencies, and read in detail the man page for **dpkg**'s **force** section. For the exam, you need to know how to force an action, but not all the 20 or so forcing options.

To force the removal of a broken package marked in the database as requiring reinstallation, use the following:

```
dpkg --force-reinstreq packagename
```

The **--force-reinstreq** is used on packages marked as requiring reinstallation, and it allows **dpkg** to remove that package.

Additionally, you can use the **--force-depends** option after **--install** to turn all those nasty error messages into dire warnings, but the tool then allows you to do whatever inadvisable action you're about to perform. Here's an example:

```
dpkg --install --force-depends packagename
```

Finally, you can also use the **--force-remove-essential** option. Be warned, however, overriding the dependency recommendations might leave your system in a broken state.

If you positively must (usually on direction from the vendor or a nearby Debian guru), you can force the installation of a package, regardless of the conflicts generated with the command and options, like so:

```
dpkg --install new_pkg.deb --force-conflicts
```

If you have problems with the package or other packages after forcing past any conflicts, remember that you were warned.

Querying Packages

Packages currently installed can be queried for a plethora of information. In particular, you can list the existence, version, name, and a description of the package by using the **-l** or **--list** option:

```
dpkg --list krb*
dpkg -l krb*
```

You can use either a singular package name, such as krb5-user for the Kerberos-related package, or use the previous filename to see the listing shown in the following output.

```
# dpkg --list krb*
Desired=Unknown/Install/Remove/Purge/Hold
| Status=Not/Inst/Conf-files/Unpacked/halF-conf/Half-inst/trig-aWait/
Trig-pend
|/ Err?=(none)/Reinst-required (Status,Err: uppercase=bad)
||/ Name              Version         Architecture    Description
+++-================-================-================-
=============================
```

```
un  krb5-doc          <none>                   (no description
available)
ii  krb5-locales       1.10.1+dfsg-5+d all Internationalization support
for MIT Kerberos
un  krb5-user          <none>                   (no description
available)
```

After some headers, the output shows that there are three packages starting with krb5. Two of them, with lines beginning with the string **un** are uninstalled, while krb5-locales is installed as version 1.10.1. The Debian package system shows you packages previously installed in your system, which is different from other systems.

You can check the status of a particular package or packages by using the **-s** or **--status** option:

```
dpkg --status krdc
```

The output returned is an abbreviated version of the **--info** option.

You can see the files that were installed by a package by using the **-L** or **--listfiles** option:

```
dpkg --listfiles coreutils
```

This results in output similar to that shown in the following output (output truncated to fit):

```
/.
/bin
/bin/cat
/bin/chgrp
/bin/chmod
/bin/chown
```

The use of either the **-S** or **--search** option lets you search the installed files on disk via the package database, such as

```
dpkg -S apt.conf
```

The following output contains the various places an apt.conf file was found from the database entries:

```
apt: /etc/apt/apt.conf.d/01autoremove
unattended-upgrades: /etc/apt/apt.conf.d/50unattended-upgrades
apt: /usr/share/man/ja/man5/apt.conf.5.gz
apt: /usr/share/man/pt/man5/apt.conf.5.gz
apt: /usr/share/doc/apt/examples/apt.conf
apt-listchanges: /etc/apt/apt.conf.d/20listchanges
```

```
aptdaemon: /etc/apt/apt.conf.d/20dbus
aptdaemon: /etc/dbus-1/system.d/org.debian.apt.conf
```

The output lists all the packages that contain a file with apt.conf in the name. The package name is on the left and the filename is on the right. Note that the search string can happen anywhere within the filename, even if it's a directory name.

Reconfiguring Packages

Some packages include a configuration tool executed when you install the package. This tool makes it easy to set the initial setup of the software you are installing. If a package includes such a configuration tool you can run that utility again with the **dpkg-reconfigure** command followed by the name of the package.

Figure 3-2 shows the output of running the Postfix mail server configuration with this command:

```
dpkg-reconfigure postfix
```

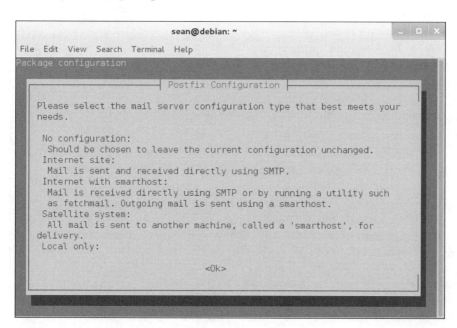

Figure 3-2   Reconfiguring Postfix with dpkg-reconfigure

Using Remote Repositories

Downloading packages before installing them gets tiresome especially when you forget a dependency and have to go back and download more packages. The Debian project made apt—the Advanced Package Tool—to help out. APT is a series of tools that build on **dpkg** to add more features. The two utilities that are important for the exam are **apt-get** and **apt-cache**.

Installing Remote Packages

The **apt-get** utility is responsible for most remote software installation operations. Every **apt-get** invocation is followed by a command that indicates what to do. Use the **install** command to install a package, as shown in Example 3-2.

Example 3-2   Installing a Remote Package

```
# apt-get install nginx-light
Reading package lists... Done
Building dependency tree
Reading state information... Done
The following extra packages will be installed:
  nginx-common
The following NEW packages will be installed:
  nginx-common nginx-light
0 upgraded, 2 newly installed, 0 to remove and 63 not upgraded.
Need to get 392 kB of archives.
After this operation, 863 kB of additional disk space will be used.
Do you want to continue [Y/n]? y
Get:1 http://cdn.debian.net/debian/ wheezy/main nginx-common all
1.2.1-2.2+wheezy3 [72.8 kB]
Get:2 http://cdn.debian.net/debian/ wheezy/main nginx-light amd64
1.2.1-2.2+wheezy3 [320 kB]
Fetched 392 kB in 1s (373 kB/s)
Selecting previously unselected package nginx-common.
(Reading database ... 156200 files and directories currently installed.)
Unpacking nginx-common (from .../nginx-common_1.2.1-2.2+wheezy3_all.
deb) ...
Selecting previously unselected package nginx-light.
Unpacking nginx-light (from .../nginx-light_1.2.1-2.2+wheezy3_amd64.
deb) ...
Processing triggers for man-db ...
Setting up nginx-common (1.2.1-2.2+wheezy3) ...
Setting up nginx-light (1.2.1-2.2+wheezy3) ...
```

Example 3-2 installs the `nginx-light` package through **apt-get install nginx-light**. The program determines that the nginx-common package is also required, so both are downloaded and installed. Any setup scripts, including the **dpkg-reconfigure**, are run at this time too.

Finally, pay attention to the differences between the **apt-get** and **dpkg** commands, especially with regards to the first option. **apt-get** commands do not have a leading dash or dashes, while **dpkg** does. For example, **dpkg -i** installs a local package, but **apt-get install** installs a remote package. Don't get tripped up on any questions that try to conflate the two, such as with **apt-get --install pkgname**.

Working with the Cache

The apt tools work by maintaining a local cache of what packages are available on remote servers including the dependencies. You can then search your local cache much more quickly than if you had to query remote servers.

The list of remote package repositories is stored in **/etc/apt/sources.list** and in individual files under **/etc/apt/sources.list.d**. Each line represents one repository.

A `sources.list` file may look like that shown in Example 3-3.

Example 3-3 A Default Sources List File

```
deb http://cdn.debian.net/debian/ wheezy main
deb-src http://cdn.debian.net/debian/ wheezy main

deb http://security.debian.org/ wheezy/updates main
deb-src http://security.debian.org/ wheezy/updates main

# wheezy-updates, previously known as 'volatile'
deb http://cdn.debian.net/debian/ wheezy-updates main
deb-src http://cdn.debian.net/debian/ wheezy-updates main
```

The first field is either deb or deb-src, representing binary and source package installations, respectively. Next is a path to the repository of packages to be installed, which can be a local file, a CD-ROM, or a remote server on the Internet. After the location is the name of the distribution, which is named after the version of Debian that you are running, and sometimes an indicator such as testing or stable. Finally, the line has one or more components. The final column, main, refers to these packages as being part of the core Debian distribution rather than a third-party repository.

You must update the package cache after modifying sources.list or to fetch any up-stream changes. This is done by running **apt-get update**.

Now that the APT cache is up to date you can investigate packages with the **apt-cache** command.

- **apt-cache search** *term*—Searches for packages matching the term

- **apt-cache show** *packagename*—Shows information about a given package name including a description and dependencies

- **apt-cache showpkg** *packagename*—Shows more technical details about the package such as what depends on it, what it depends on, and what services it provides

Upgrading the System

Your system has many packages installed—hundreds, if not thousands. Each one of these packages may have updates at some point in time. Updates take the form of

- Security updates that fix problems in a package that could lead to bad guys do-ing bad things on your machine

- Bug fixes to correct problems in software that cause it to perform incorrectly, crash, or even lose data

- Feature improvements by updating to the latest version of some software

To update a specific package you reinstall that package, as shown in the following output:

```
# apt-get install cpio
Reading package lists... Done
Building dependency tree
Reading state information... Done
Suggested packages:
  libarchive1
The following packages will be upgraded:
  cpio
```

The last two lines of the output show that **apt-get** upgrades the package rather than installs it fresh. If **cpio** weren't installed, it would be installed. If it's important that the package is not installed if it is missing, add the **--only-upgrade** long option.

Updating package by package is tedious. You can run **apt-get dist-upgrade** to upgrade all the packages on your system at once. If you are running a more conservative system, **apt-get upgrade** is a safer choice. The difference between the two upgrade options is the **dist-upgrade** may remove some minor packages to handle dependency problems while the upgrade would rather fail than remove a package.

Removing Packages

The time will come when you want to get rid of a package entirely. The **apt-get** command has two options: **remove** and **purge**. The difference is that **remove** leaves configuration files behind, while **purge** gets rid of them entirely.

Graphical Managers

Even the grayest of beards among us sometimes long for an interface where we can look at packages graphically instead of working on a command line.

Debian offers two graphical package managers: aptitude and synaptic. They both are front ends to the APT tools. Aptitude has a text mode interface while synaptic is fully graphical. Figure 3-3 shows the two next to each other. Synaptic is running on the left, and aptitude is running inside a terminal window on the right.

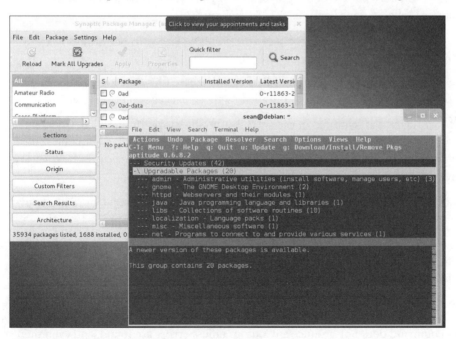

Figure 3-3   A look at graphical package managers

RPM and YUM Package Management

RPM refers not only to the package format, but the **rpm** command and the RPM database. The components of the RPM package management style are

- **The RPM database**—A collection of files that manage the RPMs on a system
- **Package files**—The packages in RPM format that are distributed with the .rpm extension
- **The rpm command**—Used for all package installation, removal, and query tasks

Graphical package management tools such as gnorpm or the RPM-handling routines built in to the various file managers (Nautilus and Konqueror) are typically just a front end to the text-mode **rpm** command and provide a friendly interface for installing packages.

Incidentally, RPM originally stood for Red Hat Package Manager before it became more widely used in other distributions. Referring to the system as RPM Package Manager will draw the ire of the graybeards in your office, almost as if you called an automated teller at your bank an "ATM machine."

The RPM Database

The RPM database is a collection of Berkeley database files that together make up the database of packages and files installed by those packages on the system.

The RPM database is located in the /var/lib/rpm directory. In that directory are many files in a binary format that are used by the **rpm** command. Thankfully, you don't need to know all the files in the directory and their purposes, just that they are there and exist in an uncorrupted state.

Modifications to the RPM database are restricted to the root user. Unprivileged users can query and verify installed packages against this database.

The RPM database can become outdated or corrupted with heavy usage and needs to be rebuilt. To rebuild the database from the installed package's headers, you use the following command as the root user:

```
rpm --rebuilddb
```

This command does not produce any output unless errors are found, and even then the errors are purely informational and not of much use for fixing the problem.

Only one user can use the database at a time. This prevents corruption of the data itself and also prevents two people from installing software on top of each other. If you accidentally try to run two **rpm** commands while one has the database locked, you see the following:

```
warning: waiting for transaction lock on /var/lib/rpm/.rpm.lock
```

This message simply conveys that the database is in use and cannot be locked for additional tasks at this time. This keeps multiple sysadmins from causing corruption by performing incompatible tasks simultaneously.

RPM Package Files

RPM packages come in two types: source and binary. A binary RPM file is a discrete package that, when installed, copies the compiled binary files, other associated files such as documentation and configuration, along with any other files needed to run that package to specified locations.

A *source RPM* file is a collection of the source files needed for installing the package, plus some instructions for building the binary RPM from the source.

An important distinction must be made between installed packages and uninstalled package files. Information about an installed package comes from the RPM database, whereas information about an uninstalled package comes from the RPM file itself. After an RPM file has been installed, the original RPM is no longer required.

RPM packages contain a set of files and configuration scripts that comprise a software program or application in most instances. Notable exceptions are packages strictly for placing text configuration files, such as files in the /etc directory. RPM packages should contain at least the following:

- Compressed binary application files
- The name and version of the package's software
- The build date and host on which it was built
- A description of the package and its purpose
- The checksums and dependencies required

Package Name Conventions

Installed packages are known by a short name, although some operations require the long names be used. Typically, long package names are needed for deletions when multiple packages whose short names match exist.

Here's an example of a short package name:

```
wireshark
```

Here's an example of a long package name:

```
wireshark-1.12.2-2.fc31
```

An example of two packages installed with different versions of the same software is as follows:

```
rpm -q kernel
```

This returns the output:

```
# rpm -q kernel
kernel-3.17.7-300.fc21.x86_64
kernel-3.17.8-300.fc21.x86_64
```

This makes viewing a particular package's information difficult if you use the **-l** and **-i** options for file listings and info pages. This is fine if you want to compare the differences, but it's maddening when you really need to see just the latest version's information. You need to use the long name (**kernel-3.17.7-300.fc21**) to get just that package's information.

The rpm Command

The text-mode `.rpm` package tool is used to perform all operations on packages on the system, either installed and in the RPM database, or uninstalled and on disk.

Common operations that use the **rpm** command include

- Installing packages
- Upgrading packages
- Removing and uninstalling packages
- Querying the RPM database for information
- Verifying the package file
- Checking installed files

The **rpm** command keywords and options come in several formats. The common options are short and use a single letter—for example, **-i** is the installation option. There are almost always long options that match, and some options occur only in the long format.

NOTE   On the exam you might see long options in several locations, either right after a short option or on the end of the entire command. The important thing is to have tried the long options and to know that you can tack them on the end, as long as something else doesn't depend on that option's placement.

Validation of Packages

For purposes of security it's important that you validate or check the signatures of packages that are downloaded from any source other than the distribution vendor's site; otherwise, you could be installing malware. RPM has two checks it uses to ensure the integrity of a package: MD5 and PGP (which might also be seen by its open source variant, GPG).

The MD5 acts as a checksum to make sure that the package contents have not changed since the package was created. The PGP or GPG signature is tied to a particular person or organization and indicates that the person or organization created the package.

Validating packages typically takes place when the package is accessed or installed, although it can be triggered explicitly. To check the MD5 checksum and GPG signatures for the **R** statistics environment you use the following command:

```
rpm -K R-3.1.2-1.fc22.x86_64.rpm
```

This returns the following output:

```
R-3.1.2-1.fc22.x86_64.rpm: RSA sha1 ((MD5) PGP) md5 NOT OK (MISSING
KEYS: (MD5) PGP#8e1431d5)
```

The presence of NOT OK shows that the signatures could not be verified. Importing the key from the distribution site fixes the problem. For example, if you are working on a Fedora system you could execute:

```
# rpm --import https://getfedora.org/static/8E1431D5.txt
# rpm -K R-3.1.2-1.fc22.x86_64.rpm
R-3.1.2-1.fc22.x86_64.rpm: rsa sha1 (md5) pgp md5 OK
```

Knowing that signatures come in md5 and gpg varieties, plus the **--checksig** and **-K** options, is plenty for the exam. The key is to be sure that the package you have is the original from the maintainer, not one full of Trojan horses and rootkits.

Installation of Packages

Installing software via packages requires root access, the **rpm** command, and a package(s). Prior to installation, the **rpm** command checks the following:

- That enough free disk space exists for the package
- That existing files will not be overwritten
- That all dependencies listed in the package are met

You install packages with at least the **-i** option, (or the **--install** long option), often including other options that improve the experience. To install the **R** package, get a progress bar (consisting of hash marks printed onscreen) and verbose messages on the installation; then use the command:

```
# rpm -ivh R-3.1.2-1.fc21.x86_64.rpm
Preparing...                           ##############################
## [100%]
Updating / installing...
   1:R-3.1.2-1.fc21                     ##############################
## [100%]
```

These options work well for installing groups of packages, too. Instead of specifying a singular package as shown previously, specify a file glob instead:

```
rpm -ivh *.rpm
```

Wildcards can be used for installing and upgrading but not removing packages because the glob operator, *****, expands to match files in the current directory, not packages in the RPM database. Wildcards are more thoroughly described in Chapter 5, but for now understand that ***.rpm** means "any file that ends in **.rpm**".

Additional Installation Options

Whenever you install RPM packages, keep in mind that there will be extenuating circumstances such as files that exist on the system that RPM doesn't know about but that will be overwritten by a package's contents. Sometimes this happens when someone installs software manually or if a previous package operation fails.

These can be handled with the **--replacefiles** or **--force** options. (The **force** option overrides a variety of these safeguards, including **replacefiles**, which just overrides the duplicate file safeguard.) For example, if you try to install a package named tar-foo-1.2-3.i386.rpm and it finds a file on the system that will be overwritten by a file in the package, you get an error message stating so and the installation fails:

```
rpm -ivh tarfoo-1.2-3.i386.rpm
tarfoo     /etc/tarfoo.conf conflicts with file from snafu-1.1
```

The solution is to check the offending file and either remove it if it's unnecessary or use this command to force it:

```
rpm -ivh --force tarfoo-1.2-3.i386.rpm
```

If the package won't install due to unresolved dependencies, you can (somewhat foolishly!) use the **--nodeps** option to have the **rpm** command ignore dependencies. Using **--nodeps** without a clear fix in mind or an understanding of where the dependencies will come from will almost certainly cause problems when you try to use the software that the package provides.

For example, if you try to install the pebkac package and it has dependency issues, it might look like this:

```
rpm -ivh R-3.1.2-1.fc22.x86_64.rpm
```

This returns output such as

```
error: Failed dependencies:
    R-devel = 3.1.2-1.fc22 is needed by R-3.1.2-1.fc22.x86_64
    R-java = 3.1.2-1.fc22 is needed by R-3.1.2-1.fc22.x86_64
    libRmath-devel = 3.1.2-1.fc22 is needed by R-3.1.2-1.fc22.x86_64
```

You have the possibility of seriously munging your system if you use the **--nodeps** option outside a recommendation from the distribution vendor or a support professional. You might so severely damage the software that a full reinstall is the only option.

Verifying a Package's Integrity

There may be situations where you need to verify that the package is working properly. For example, if users are complaining about problems with running the software that came with the package, or you suspect that someone has been tampering with your computer, you may want to verify the package.

Verify an installed RPM with the **-V** option (or **--verify**) like so:

```
# rpm -V logrotate
S.5....T.  c /etc/logrotate.conf
```

The status of the package is returned as a series of nine characters indicating the results of nine different tests:

- **S**—The file size differs.
- **M**—The mode differs (permissions or type of file).
- **5**—The MD5 sum differs; this is also seen by **--checksig**.

- **D**—The device's major/minor number doesn't match.

- **L**—A readLink(2) path problem exists.

- **U**—The user ownership was altered.

- **G**—The group ownership was altered.

- **T**—The modification time is different from the original.

- **P**—The capabilities set on the file differs.

Following the nine tests is an attribute marker that helps you understand if the file should change as part of normal operations. The most common option is a configuration file, indicated by the letter **c**.

The output shown indicates that **/etc/logrotate.conf** is a configuration file that has changed in size, content, and modification time, since the RPM was installed.

Change is not always a bad thing. Configuration files change often because the defaults provided by the distribution may not line up with your needs. Email configurations, log cleanup policies, and web server configurations are all things that get customized frequently and therefore show up as changes. If you expect them to change, you can ignore the output, which is why configuration files have the separate attribute marker. If you see a change to binaries, such as **/bin/ls**, you should be suspicious.

To verify the state of all the packages on the system, you add an **-a** instead of specifying a package name, as such:

```
# rpm -Va
```

If you want to log the state of your configuration files for comparison against a future date, you can check the condition of every configuration file on the system and write it to a file with this command:

```
rpm -Vac > /root/somelog.txt
```

Freshening Versus Upgrading

The daily maintenance of your newly installed system will likely involve updates and fixes downloaded as package updates. Properly applying these to the system takes some finesse, particularly when you have a system that must stay as stable as possible or not have new software added to it without strict testing.

The **-U** and **--upgrade** options are designed to install or upgrade versions of packages to the latest version. An interesting side effect of these options is the removal of all other versions of the targeted package, leaving just the latest version installed.

As an example, the following command upgrades the system to the latest version of the RPMs in a particular directory of patches and fixes downloaded from the distribution vendor:

```
rpm -U *.rpm
```

The **-U** and **--upgrade** options upgrade packages that are already installed and install packages that aren't.

Freshening your system is different in one important aspect: If a package isn't installed and you try to freshen it with a new RPM, the installation will be skipped. If the package is installed already, freshening behaves the same as upgrading.

As an example, you use the following to apply a directory full of .rpm files that contains security patches and fixes to a firewall or other security server:

```
rpm -Fvh *.rpm
```

This feature is useful for local package cache updates, where you've downloaded the latest patches and fixes to a local network resource and want to run scripts on your machines to update them to the latest security releases.

Removing Packages

Removing a package or set of packages consists of using the **-e** or **--erase** option and requires root access. Removal of packages can be even more fraught with dependency problems than installation because a package can be deeply buried in a tree of dependencies over time.

Removing a package without dependencies is easy. To remove the `tarfoo` package, you use the following command:

```
rpm -e tarfoo
```

There's usually no output, the package is removed, and the system returns to the prompt.

The trouble begins when you have multiple packages that all have the same short name, such as a kernel. With two versions of the kernel package on a system, querying the database for the package as shown here returns both packages' long format names:

```
# rpm -q kernel
kernel-3.17.7-300.fc21.x86_64
kernel-3.17.8-300.fc21.x86_64
```

If you attempt to remove the package by its short name, you get this error:

```
# rpm -e kernel
error: "kernel" specifies multiple packages:
  kernel-3.17.7-300.fc21.x86_64
  kernel-3.17.8-300.fc21.x86_64
```

Instead, use the long name of the package:

```
# rpm -e kernel-3.17.7-300.fc21
```

To remove both packages with one command, you use

```
rpm -e kernel --allmatches
```

No output is returned if all is successful; you just get a return to the prompt. If you don't want to remove both of the packages, the only choice is to specify the long package name of the package you want to remove.

Other Removal Options

At times you need to force the removal of a package or remove one regardless of the broken dependencies. A good example of this is fixing a broken package by forcibly removing it and reinstalling it to refresh the files and links that were broken. This usually takes place on the recommendation of support professionals, not some thread you found on a six-year-old forum!

To remove a package that has other packages depending on it, use the following command:

```
rpm -e foobar --nodeps
```

Be careful removing packages you can't replace or don't have the original package file to reinstall from. You need to find the original package or rebuild it from source. If you remove a package that is depended on by other packages, those packages will not be able to run.

Removing packages can also leave behind altered or customized configuration files. For example, if you alter a package's main configuration file and then remove the package, the configuration file is saved with its original name suffixed with .rpmsave. This configuration file can be archived for future use or, if the package is to be upgraded with the **-U** option, a complex set of algorithms goes into play to ensure the configuration is properly applied.

Querying Packages

Querying for package data is only one of the steps that take place when you manage packages, although it has arguably the most options of all the tasks RPM performs.

It's important that you understand the difference between packages installed on the system (that appear in the RPM database) and packages that exist simply as files on the disk or other resource. The chief difference in the **rpm** command's usage is the addition of the **-p** option to specify that the package being acted on is a file on disk.

The most basic of all queries is to check to see whether a particular package is installed:

```
# rpm -q cogl
cogl-1.18.2-9.fc21.x86_64
```

Simply by adding a few modifier characters to this query, you can gather much more information about any package. The first modifier I usually recommend is to get information on the package, as shown in Example 3-4.

Example 3-4   Querying a Package for Information

```
# rpm -qi cogl
Name        : cogl
Version     : 1.18.2
Release     : 9.fc21
Architecture: x86_64
Install Date: Wed 03 Dec 2014 02:38:45 PM CST
Group       : Development/Libraries
Size        : 1404466
License     : LGPLv2+
Signature   : RSA/SHA256, Mon 17 Nov 2014 06:11:24 PM CST, Key ID
89ad4e8795a43f54
Source RPM  : cogl-1.18.2-9.fc21.src.rpm
Build Date  : Sun 16 Nov 2014 10:36:50 AM CST
Build Host  : buildvm-19.phx2.fedoraproject.org
Relocations : (not relocatable)
Packager    : Fedora Project
Vendor      : Fedora Project
URL         : http://www.clutter-project.org/
Summary     : A library for using 3D graphics hardware to draw pretty
pictures
Description :
Cogl is a small open source library for using 3D graphics hardware to
draw
```

```
pretty pictures. The API departs from the flat state machine style of
OpenGL and is designed to make it easy to write orthogonal components
that
can render without stepping on each others toes.
As well aiming for a nice API, we think having a single library as
opposed
to an API specification like OpenGL has a few advantages too; like
being
able to paper over the inconsistencies/bugs of different OpenGL
implementations in a centralized place, not to mention the myriad of
OpenGL
extensions. It also means we are in a better position to provide
utility
APIs that help software developers since they only need to be
implemented
once and there is no risk of inconsistency between implementations.


Having other backends, besides OpenGL, such as drm, Gallium or D3D are
options we are interested in for the future.
```

To get information about a package's files, use both the **-q** (query) option and the **-l** (file listing) option, as shown in the following output:

```
# rpm -ql cogl
...
/usr/lib64/libcogl-path.so.20
/usr/lib64/libcogl-path.so.20.2.0
/usr/lib64/libcogl.so.20
/usr/lib64/libcogl.so.20.2.0
/usr/share/doc/cogl
/usr/share/doc/cogl/COPYING
```

When you get questions about listing package files or information, remember the difference between listing the contents of a package in the database and doing the same for a package on disk:

- **rpm -qil package_name**—Used for installed packages by specifying a short or long name

- **rpm -qilp package_name.rpm**—Used for uninstalled packages by specifying a file

In addition, remember that you can specify these options in any order, as long as they are all there. In effect, **rpm -qipl**, **rpm -qlip**, and **rpm -pliq** all work.

To see a revision history or changelog for the package, use the command shown in the following output:

```
# rpm -q --changelog cogl
* Sun Nov 16 2014 Kalev Lember <kalevlember@gmail.com> - 1.18.2-9
- Obsolete compat-cogl116 from rhughes-f20-gnome-3-12 copr

* Thu Nov 13 2014 Kalev Lember <kalevlember@gmail.com> - 1.18.2-8
- Disable cogl-gst as long as we don't have clutter-gst3 (#1158676)
```

This output is similar to the release notes found in most software package source code repositories describing the history of the package's changes.

This is the sort of thing that LPI loves to put on the exam. If you've never used rpm to this level, the questions will get the best of you. Don't forget that you must use the **-q** and **--changelog** options together; otherwise, you get a syntax error.

To find all the configuration files for a package, you use the query and config options like that shown in Example 3-5.

Example 3-5   Finding a Package's Configuration Files

```
# rpm -qc postfix
/etc/pam.d/smtp.postfix
/etc/postfix/access
/etc/postfix/canonical
/etc/postfix/generic
/etc/postfix/header_checks
/etc/postfix/main.cf
/etc/postfix/master.cf
/etc/postfix/relocated
/etc/postfix/transport
/etc/postfix/virtual
/etc/sasl2/smtpd.conf
```

This shows only the files marked by the package as configuration files. If you want the whole list of files inside the package, you need **rpm -ql**.

To see other capabilities or package dependencies use the **--requires** or **-R** option (remember it's a package on disk, so use **-p**), as shown in Example 3-6.

Example 3-6 Querying the Dependencies of a Package File

```
# rpm -qRp tree-1.7.0-3.fc21.x86_64.rpm
libc.so.6()(64bit)
libc.so.6(GLIBC_2.14)(64bit)
libc.so.6(GLIBC_2.2.5)(64bit)
libc.so.6(GLIBC_2.3)(64bit)
libc.so.6(GLIBC_2.3.4)(64bit)
libc.so.6(GLIBC_2.4)(64bit)
rpmlib(CompressedFileNames) <= 3.0.4-1
rpmlib(FileDigests) <= 4.6.0-1
rpmlib(PayloadFilesHavePrefix) <= 4.0-1
rtld(GNU_HASH)
```

This method of finding the dependencies tells you which files or packages are needed without having to install the package. You can track the dependencies back to a package, such as to find out which package provides the libc.so.6 file required by **tree**.

```
# rpm -qf /usr/lib64/libc.so.6
glibc-2.20-8.fc21.x86_64
```

What about the problem of finding the package from which a particular file was installed? For example, if the /etc/krb.conf file were somehow damaged, you could find the package it came from with this command:

```
# rpm -qf /etc/krb5.conf
krb5-libs-1.12.2-9.fc21.x86_64
```

Package Management with YUM

YUM, the Yellowdog Updater Modified, is a front end to RPM. Just like the apt-* series of tools makes working with **dpkg** and remote repositories easier, YUM brings **rpm** and remote repositories together for you and packages it in an interface with far fewer options to remember.

Installing Packages

Install a package, such as the R statistical language, with **yum install**, as shown in Example 3-7.

Example 3-7   Installing a Package from a Remote Repository

```
# yum install R
Loaded plugins: langpacks
Resolving Dependencies
--> Running transaction check
---> Package R.x86_64 0:3.1.2-1.fc21 will be installed
--> Processing Dependency: R-devel = 3.1.2-1.fc21 for package: R-3.1.2-
1.fc21.x86_64
--> Running transaction check
---> Package R-devel.x86_64 0:3.1.2-1.fc21 will be installed
--> Processing Dependency: R-core-devel = 3.1.2-1.fc21 for package:
R-devel-3.1.2-1.fc21.x86_64
--> Running transaction check
---> Package R-core-devel.x86_64 0:3.1.2-1.fc21 will be installed
--> Processing Dependency: R-core = 3.1.2-1.fc21 for package: R-core-
devel-3.1.2-1.fc21.x86_64
--> Running transaction check
---> Package R-core.x86_64 0:3.1.2-1.fc21 will be installed
--> Finished Dependency Resolution


Dependencies Resolved


=======================================================================
==============
 Package              Arch           Version             Repository
Size
=======================================================================
==============
Installing:
 R                    x86_64         3.1.2-1.fc21        updates
27 k
Installing for dependencies:
 R-core               x86_64         3.1.2-1.fc21        updates
48 M
 R-core-devel         x86_64         3.1.2-1.fc21        updates
99 k
 R-devel              x86_64         3.1.2-1.fc21        updates
26 k


Transaction Summary
=======================================================================
==============
Install  1 Package (+3 Dependent packages)
```

```
Total size: 48 M
Total download size: 48 M
Installed size: 74 M
Is this ok [y/d/N]: y
Downloading packages:
Running transaction check
Running transaction test
Transaction test succeeded
Running transaction (shutdown inhibited)
Warning: RPMDB altered outside of yum.
  Installing : R-core-3.1.2-1.fc21.x86_ 64
  Installing : R-core-devel-3.1.2-1.fc21.x86_64
  Installing : R-devel-3.1.2-1.fc21.x86_64
  Installing : R-3.1.2-1.fc21.x86_64
  Verifying  : R-devel-3.1.2-1.fc21.x86_64
  Verifying  : R-3.1.2-1.fc21.x86_64
  Verifying  : R-core-devel-3.1.2-1.fc21.x86_64
  Verifying  : R-core-3.1.2-1.fc21.x86_64

Installed:
  R.x86_64 0:3.1.2-1.fc21

Dependency Installed:
  R-core.x86_64 0:3.1.2-1.fc21      R-core-devel.x86_64 0:3.1.2-1.fc21
  R-devel.x86_64 0:3.1.2-1.fc21

Complete!
```

The command in Example 3-7 shows that **yum** calculated the dependencies, downloaded all needed packages, and installed them.

yum commands do not take dashes or double dashes; the **rpm** commands do. Use **yum install**, **rpm -i**, or **rpm --install**, but don't mix them up on the exam!

If you want to skip the step where you confirm the installation, simply add **-y** such as **yum -y install foo.**

It is possible to just download the packages instead of installing them. There are several ways to accomplish this:

- At the y/d/N prompt above, answer **d** (download) instead of **y** (yes).

- Use **yum install --downloadonly** instead of the plain **yum install**.

- Use **yumdownloader** instead of **yum**.

The **yumdownloader** command behaves similarly to **yum install** except that you have a few more options available to you:

- **--source** downloads the source RPM instead of binary RPMs.

- **--urls** display the URLs of the files instead of downloading them.

- **--resolve** modifies the command to also include any missing dependencies.

- **--destdir** specifies the location the files will be stored.

Fetching Updates

YUM knows where to get new packages and what's currently on your system, so it can also calculate which packages are out of date. Upgrading a package is just **yum update packagename**, so **yum update tcpdump** updates the tcpdump package along with any dependencies.

You can check for any out-of-date packages with **yum check-update** and upgrade the whole system with **yum update** all by itself.

Finding Packages to Install

You can search remote repositories in different ways. If you know the name of the package you can use **yum list**:

```
# yum list tomcat
Loaded plugins: langpacks
Available Packages
tomcat.noarch                      7.0.54-3.fc21                fedora
```

Packages that can be split into separate components are usually distributed as separate packages sharing a common prefix. Suppose you want to see what components you could add to Tomcat. You could use a wildcard operator with the previous command, as shown in Example 3-8.

Example 3-8   Listing Packages That Match a Wildcard

```
# yum list tomcat*
Loaded plugins: langpacks
Available Packages
tomcat.noarch                      7.0.54-3.fc21                fedora
tomcat-admin-webapps.noarch        7.0.54-3.fc21                fedora
tomcat-docs-webapp.noarch          7.0.54-3.fc21                fedora
```

tomcat-el-2.2-api.noarch	7.0.54-3.fc21	fedora
tomcat-javadoc.noarch	7.0.54-3.fc21	fedora
tomcat-jsp-2.2-api.noarch	7.0.54-3.fc21	fedora
tomcat-jsvc.noarch	7.0.54-3.fc21	fedora

Finally, if you knew you needed a web server but weren't sure what to pick, a general search is available, as shown in Example 3-9.

Example 3-9   Searching YUM Repositories for Packages That Match a Concept

```
# yum search "web server"
Loaded plugins: langpacks
================= N/S matched: web server =================
boa.x86_64 : Single-tasking HTTP server
mongoose.x86_64 : An easy-to-use self-sufficient web server
rubygem-thin.x86_64 : A thin and fast web server
tlssled.noarch : An evaluation tool for SSL/TLS (HTTPS) web server
implementations
undertow.noarch : Java web server using non-blocking IO
xsp.x86_64 : A small web server that hosts ASP.NET
Spawning.noarch : A HTTP server for hosting WSGI python web
applications
apache-rat.noarch : Apache Release Audit Tool (RAT)
apache-scout.noarch : JSR 93 (JAXR) implementation
aws.i686 : Ada Web Server
... output omitted ...
```

Configuring Yum

The main configuration file for **yum** is /etc/yum.conf. In it are the global options for **yum** and some defaults for all the repositories. You will rarely have to edit this file, but it does contain helpful information if you're trying to figure out where files are kept. Example 3-10 shows a default Fedora configuration.

Example 3-10   A Default yum.conf Configuration for Fedora

```
 [main]
cachedir=/var/cache/yum/$basearch/$releasever
keepcache=0
debuglevel=2
logfile=/var/log/yum.log
```

```
exactarch=1
obsoletes=1
gpgcheck=1
plugins=1
installonly_limit=3
```

From the example you can see that all the cached files are stored under **/var/cache/ yum**, and the log file is **/var/log/yum.log**. A full list of the options is in the man page for yum.conf.

The repository configuration files are stored in **/etc/yum.repos.d**. Each file may contain multiple repositories though you will find that the repositories are grouped according to function. For example, the main distribution repository is in one file along with the repository for the source packages and a repository for the debugging symbols. Another file contains the repositories for the updates, source for the up- dates, and the debugging symbols for the updates.

A single repository configuration looks like that shown in Example 3-11.

Example 3-11   An Individual Repository's Configuration from Fedora

```
[updates]
name=Fedora $releasever - $basearch - Updates
failovermethod=priority
#baseurl=http://download.fedoraproject.org/pub/fedora/linux/
updates/$releasever/$basearch/
metalink=https://mirrors.fedoraproject.org/metalink?repo=updates-
released-f$releasever&arch=$basearch
enabled=1
metadata_expire=6h
gpgcheck=1
gpgkey=file:///etc/pki/rpm-gpg/RPM-GPG-KEY-fedora-$releasever-$basearch
skip_if_unavailable=False
```

You may have noticed several options starting with a dollar sign ($). These are placeholders that are expanded when **yum** is invoked. The $releasever becomes the Fedora version, and the $basearch becomes the hardware architecture such as x86_64.

The name of the repository in Example 3-11 is updates. A repository either has a baseurl, which is a link to the repository, or it has a metalink, which returns a list of mirrors for the repository. (A mirror spreads the load across many different serv- ers hosted by different companies.)

An important directive in the configuration is `enabled`. When you run a **yum** command only the enabled repositories are searched. You can enable a repository in a **yum** command by adding **--enablerepo reponame**.

Hiding repositories is helpful because it gives you access to a wider variety of packages without needing to configure the repository. You can use this to hide the debugging symbol repository unless you actually need debugging symbols, such as when trying to track down crashes. You can also have access to bleeding edge software when you need it, but install more trusted software by default.

Summary

In this chapter you learned about Red Hat (RPM) and Debian packages. Packages solve the problem of needing to compile software before using it, provide for easier uninstallation and upgrading, and maintain lists of dependencies.

The Debian **dpkg** series of tools operate only on local packages. You can layer on **apt-get** and **apt-cache**, whose job is to connect to remote repositories and download necessary packages. In the RPM world you use **rpm** for local packages and **yum** for remote packages.

Each tool has its own command line parameters that involve you passing a command to the tool, such as to indicate an installation or deletion. **dpkg** and **rpm** expect the commands to be in dashed or double dashed format, such as **-i** or **--install**. **yum** and **apt-get** use commands that are bare words such as **install**.

Exam Preparation Tasks

As mentioned in the section "How to Use This Book" in the Introduction, you have a couple of choices for exam preparation: the exercises here, Chapter 21, "Final Preparation," and the practice exams on the DVD.

Review All Key Topics

Review the most important topics in this chapter, noted with the Key Topics icon in the outer margin of the page. Table 3-2 lists a reference of these key topics and the page numbers on which each is found.

Table 3-2   Key Topics for Chapter 3

Key Topic Element	Description	Page Number
Paragraph	Static versus dynamic linking	55
Paragraph	How to recognize a shared library	56
Paragraph	Determining required libraries with ldd	56
Paragraph	ldconfig	57
Paragraph	Using LD_LIBRARY_PATH	57
Paragraph	Local versus remote packages with Debian	58
Paragraph	Installing a local package	59
Paragraph	Purging versus removing packages	60
Paragraph	Forcing actions with **dpkg**	61
Figure 3-2	Reconfiguring postfix with **dpkg-reconfigure**	63
Paragraph	**apt-get** installs remote packages	64
Paragraph	sources.list	65
Paragraph	Location of the RPM database	68
Paragraph	RPM database rebuilding	68
Paragraph	Source versus binary RPMs	69
Paragraph	Validating an RPM's signature and checksum	71
Paragraph	RPM and querying local versus installed packages	78

Define Key Terms

Define the following key terms from this chapter and check your answers in the glossary:

Source format, binary packages, package managers, libraries, link, static linking, dynamic linking, dynamic linker (ld.so), shared object, Advanced Package Tool (APT), source RPM

Review Questions

The answers to these review questions are in Appendix A.

1. Which of the following commands shows the revision history for a software application from the package file on disk?

   a. **rpm --revision tree-1.2-7.i386.rpm**

   b. **rpm -qp tree-1.2-7.i386.rpm --changelog**

   c. **rpm -qc tree-1.2-7.i386.rpm**

   d. **rpm -qlp tree-1.2-7.i386.rpm --showrev**

2. Which of the following identifies the file produced by the ldconfig program after it is run and has processed all the library files on the machine:

   a. /etc/ld.so.conf

   b. /etc/ld.so.cache

   c. /var/cache/ld.so.cache

   d. /etc/ld.cache.d

3. What is the purpose of running the **ldd** program?

   a. Rebuilding links to library files

   b. Creating a link to a library file

   c. Displaying a program's required libraries

   d. Reading a program's library capabilities

4. Which environment variable is used to provide additional library support and is also considered to be a security risk?

   a. LIBC_EXTRA

   b. LD_SO_ETC

   c. LD_LIBRARY

   d. LD_LIBRARY_PATH

5. Which of the following is a valid cause to receive the error message? (Choose all that apply.)

   ```
   error: cannot get exclusive lock on /var/lib/rpm/Packages?
   ```

   a. Attempting an **rpm install** command as non-root

   b. Performing multiple **remove** commands simultaneously

   c. Performing multiple **verification** commands simultaneously

   d. Performing multiple **install** commands simultaneously

6. You need to remove all instances of the package woohoo, regardless of the version, with a single command. Which of the following accomplishes this task? (Choose all that apply.)

    a. rpm -e woohoo*

    b. rpm -ea woohoo

    c. rpm -a woohoo --remove

    d. rpm -e woohoo --allmatches

7. You are the system administrator of two firewalls and want to apply updates from a set of packages in the current directory, but you don't want to install any new packages on the systems. Which command will do this?

    a. rpm -F *.rpm

    b. rpm -Uvh *.rpm

    c. rpm -qp *.rpm

    d. rpm -Fp *.rpm

8. To view the list of required capabilities that a package needs to function properly, which command and options display this for an installed package?

    a. rpm -qi

    b. rpm -qR

    c. rpm --whatrequires

    d. rpm -qa

9. How would you see whether you have installed the iceweasel package?

    a. apt-cache search iceweasel

    b. apt-get --list iceweasel

    c. dpkg --info iceweasel

    d. dpkg --list iceweasel

10. How would you upgrade the iceweasel package to the latest version?

    a. apt-get install iceweasel

    b. apt-get update iceweasel

    c. apt-get upgrade iceweasel

    d. dpkg --install --upgrade iceweasel

This chapter covers the following topics:

- What Is a Shell?
- Global and User Settings
- Using the Command Line
- Controlling Command Execution
- Environment Variables and Settings
- Setting Options in Bash

This chapter covers the following objectives:

- Work on the command line: 103.1

## CHAPTER 4

Basic Command Line Usage

One of the things that shocks newbies to the Linux command line environment is that nearly everything they see is text—command output, errors, data of all kinds, logs, and even emails are just simple text files.

Having the ability to properly manipulate and process large volumes of text is one of the most important attributes of a system administrator; without it you are just continually surrounded by meaningless data.

"Do I Know This Already?" Quiz

The "Do I Know This Already?" quiz enables you to assess whether you should read this entire chapter or simply jump to the "Exam Preparation Tasks" section for review. If you are in doubt, read the entire chapter. Table 4-1 outlines the major headings in this chapter and the corresponding "Do I Know This Already?" quiz questions. You can find the answers in Appendix A, "Answers to the 'Do I Know This Already?' Quizzes and Review Questions."

Table 4-1 "Do I Know This Already?" Foundation Topics Section-to-Question Mapping

Foundation Topics Section	Questions Covered in This Section
What Is a Shell?	1
Global and User Settings	2
Using the Command Line	3
Controlling Command Execution	4
Environment Variables and Settings	5
Setting Options in Bash	6

1. Which of the following words best describes what the Bash shell does with what we type into it?

    a. Extrapolates

    b. Interprets

    c. Expresses

    d. Translates

2. Which of the following files are executed upon a user's terminal login?

   a. /etc/profile

   b. ~/.profile

   c. ~/.bashrc

   d. None of the above

3. You want to navigate from wherever you currently are on the system to the directory named .h, which is a subdirectory of the test directory in the currently logged-on user's home directory. Which of the following will do this?

   a. cd /home/{user}/test/.h

   b. cd ../home/$USER/test/.h

   c. cd ~/test/.h

   d. None of the above

4. While monitoring your backup success and failure, you notice that at times your sole backup scheme is failing. As it's a simple command typed at the command line, what character(s) could you use to separate the main command from an alternate command to ensure that if the first command fails, the secondary or alternative command will run, but only then?

   a. **

   b. ||

   c. &&

   d. !=

5. What is the simplest method of viewing all the variables in your execution environment?

   a. env

   b. getent

   c. for * in $; echo

   d. show all

6. You want to remove an option in the Bash Shell, which of the following would accomplish that? (Choose two.)

   a. shoptout

   b. undel

   c. set +o

   d. optdel

   e. unset

Foundation Topics

What Is a Shell?

A *shell* is a program designed to interpret the commands users type, parse for expansions and wildcards, and then produce instructions to the computer to accomplish those tasks.

Unless you change the defaults, the Linux shell is normally the bash shell. Of course, many other shells exist.

A partial list is shown in Table 4-2.

Table 4-2   Common Shells

	ash	bash	C-shell	PD-ksh	T-shell	Zsh
Binary	ash	bash	csh	pdksh	tcsh	zsh
Job control	N	Y	Y	Y	Y	Y
Aliases	N	Y	Y	Y	Y	Y
Functions	Y	Y	N	Y	N	Y
Redirection	Y	Y	Y	Y	Y	Y
History	N	Y	Y	Y	Y	Y
Editing	N	Y	N	Y	Y	Y
Completion	N	Y	Y	Y	Y	Y

Among other pieces of information, the user's default shell is specified in the **/etc/passwd** entry for that user. If the shell specified does not exist, the user gets the bash shell by default.

Special shells can be specified, such as **/bin/false** (which returns a nonzero error code, effectively blocking access by a user attempting to log in) or **/etc/nologin** (which is used to block logins for accounts and echo a message that login is denied).

NOTE   The **/etc/nologin** file should not normally exist on systems, as it disables logins. If your system suddenly doesn't allow logins after you study this chapter, you know what you did!

Global and User Settings

When users log in to the system, either from a remote shell session or via the console, their environment is made up of information from various ASCII text files that are sourced or read to make up the user's environment. Different distributions handle these differently, but to actually understand what happens on most systems, we focus on the Red Hat and Debian methods, which are outlined next.

Sourcing Versus Executing

It is critical to your development as a systems administrator to know the difference between "executing" a script and "sourcing" it.

Executing a Script

When you execute a script, Bash causes a new level of shell to be entered, and then the contents of the script file to be executed one by one as if they were entered on the command line by you.

While you are executing the script, and are in that new lower level of shell, all the *variables* and settings that are set are active in that level of shell and possibly below if *exported*.

When you exit the lower level of shell, for example, when the script is finished executing, then all the variables and settings that were acted upon are wiped out as the shell is exited.

Example of executing a script

```
# ./script1
```

Sourcing a Script

Sourcing a script is slightly but importantly different from executing it. Whereas in an executed script you are opening a new lower shell and then the commands are executed, a sourced script executes the lines of the script into the environment of the current shell.

With the number of environment configuration files that a user must "source" while logging in to a system, without sourcing, there would be three to five nested instances of the shell by the time the user gets to a shell prompt and can interact with the system.

With sourcing, the user is put into the shell, and the contents of the "sourced" configuration files are loaded into the current shell, making up the user's environment.

You can source a script either of two ways:

```
# source script1
# . script1
```

A Login Shell Session

A login shell is one that is executed when logging in to the system. In other words, a login shell is one where either the user approaches the physical system and logs normally as a user, or does so across the network, and gets the full benefit of the contents of the files that make up the user's environment.

The **/etc/profile** is the global configuration file that affects all users' environments if they use the bash shell. It's sourced (read) every time a user performs a login shell. This file is a script and is sourced right before the user's profile script is sourced.

The user's **~/.bash_profile** script, if it exists, is the next script sourced. This file contains variables, code, and settings that directly affect that user's—and only that user's—environment. This script calls, or sources, the next script, which is **~/.bashrc.**

> **NOTE**   The ~/.bash_profile script can also be referred to or named as the .bash_login or .profile script. If all three exist, the ~/.bash_profile is sourced alone; otherwise, if it doesn't exist, the .bash_login is sourced. Finally, if the first two are nonexistent, the .profile script is sourced. This functionality is used almost entirely by Bourne shell users upgrading to a bash system as a way to keep their settings in the same .profile file.

The **~/.bashrc** file is called by the **~/.bash_profile** or one of the profile's aliases and is used to set various shell settings and options, set the prompt, and define aliases and functions for command-line execution.

The last script sourced during a user's login session is the **.bash_logout** file. This file is used to issue the **clear** command, so text from any previous command is not left on the user's screen after he logs out.

> **NOTE**   Be careful on the exam because a lot of test-takers do not pick the .bash_logout file as part of the user's login session. It's definitely one of the more missed elements in the shell section.

An example of the user's login session might be the following:

1. The user logs in with a username and password.

2. The **/etc/profile** is sourced.

3. The user's **~/.bash_profile** is sourced.

4. The user's **~/.bashrc** is sourced from within the **~/.bash_profile**.

5. The user conducts his or her business.

6. The user initiates a logout with the **logout** or **exit** command or by pressing **Ctrl+D**.

7. The user's **.bash_logout** script is sourced.

A Non-Login Shell Session

Non-login shell sessions are typically the root user using the **su** command to temporarily become another user or a sysadmin using **su** to become the root user without loading the entire environment of the root or other user.

When a user executes a non-login session, the only file sourced is the target account's **~/.bashrc** file. (On Red Hat machines, the first action in the **~/.bashrc** is to source the **/etc/bashrc** file if it exists.)

Upon exiting that account's login, no logout files or scripts are sourced, nor are the source account's scripts run again.

On a Red Hat machine of the 7.3/AS 2.1 vintage, if the target user's .bashrc file is not present, the /etc/bashrc file does not automatically get sourced. This can easily be tested if you rename the target user's .bashrc file, put a variable in the /etc/bashrc, log in as that user, and attempt to echo the variable. Doing this causes the variable to not be there.

Table 4-3 shows each file and when it's sourced.

Table 4-3   Order of Precedence for Configuration Files

Global	/etc/profile	/etc/bashrc
Local	~/.bash_profile	
	~/.bashrc	
	~/.profile (optional)	
	~/.bash_login (optional)	
	~/.bash_logout	

Using the Command Line

Perhaps one of the most common and important tasks a sysadmin can perform and learn is to be competent with the command line or in the shell. Most of Linux demands good shell skills, and many server implementations don't even load or use the GUI (XFree86) tools, so neglecting the shell is almost criminal negligence.

NOTE LPI exams focus heavily on the commands, their options, and how they work together. If you're not familiar or competent with the command line, passing the exams (and being a good sysadmin, for that matter) is virtually impossible. Almost 20 questions of the exam center on the command line/shell and, of those, at least 3 to 4 will be fill-in-the-blanks, so this is a critical area.

There Are Commands and, Well, Commands

At its simplest, a command is just that, a command. Though what might appear to be an actual binary or script on disk sometimes is not.

The following list shows the various types of commands:

- **Actual commands**—These are binaries installed via a package or compiled and installed manually.

- **Scripts**—These are text files that contain a set of commands and are set to be executable via the permissions.

- **Built-in commands**—These are what appear to be commands and are actually resident in memory because they are a part of the code of the Bash shell.

- **Aliases**—These are little macros that reside in the user's environment. A typical one might be to alias the **ls –l** command so that you can just type "ll" and get the same results.

- **Functions**—A more complex feature than just aliases, functions can do repetitive and recursive actions, be formatted more clearly, and essentially are scripts contained in system memory.

NOTE Aliases and functions are covered in a later chapter, so the limited understanding you have from the previous definition is enough for this section.

Structuring Commands

For the most part, commands take the following form:

```
command options arguments
```

An example of a simple command is

```
ls
```

A more complex example would be a command with an option:

```
ls -l
```

A command can also just be suffixed with an *argument*:

```
ls /etc
```

Adding on an argument to the command makes it more functional:

```
ls -l /etc
```

While most commands follow the preceding conventions, the positions of some of the options are flexible. Often, if you type a long command string, having to arrow or hotkey back to a certain position is just too much work, so some options can be tacked onto the end, like so:

```
ls /etc/profiles -R
```

The rule I recommend is to not tack on to the end of the command any options that require an argument. Likewise, if the **-f** option specifies a file, you can't unhook the **-f filename** pairing and expect it to work.

Breaking Long Command Lines

When constructing a long command string, it's often useful to break it up onscreen to make it easier to understand or more visually pleasing. The backslash (\) character is used to turn the Enter key into a line feed, not a carriage return. The backslash is for causing *special characters* to be taken literally.

The following example is confusing because it breaks when it wraps onscreen:

```
rpm -ql package1.1.1.rpm | xargs file | grep -i LSB | nl | pr | tac
```

You could break it like the following and still produce the same results:

```
rpm -ql package-1.1.1.i386.rpm \
>| xargs file \
>| grep -i LSB \
```

```
>| nl \
>| pr \
>| tac
```

 Command Completion

The nicest option for the command line by far is the capability to have a <TAB> complete either a portion of a directory or filename or the command if it's in the path.

For example, when you're trying to find out which commands in the /usr/bin directory start with the letters ls, you can use the following:

```
/usr/bin/ls <TAB>

lsattr       lsb_release  lsdev        lsdiff       lskat
lskatproc
lspgpot
```

It also works well when changing from one directory to the other. You just need to insert a recognizably unique portion of the next element and press the Tab key to have it complete the directory name:

```
cd /home/rb <TAB>
cd /home/rbrunson/Des <TAB>
cd /home/rbrunson/Desktop/Se <TAB>
cd /home/rbrunson/Desktop/Settings <Enter>
```

Using <TAB> immediately after the rb characters completes the /home/rbrunson directory. Adding a slash (/) to that and typing **Des** and then <TAB> completes the Desktop directory. Finally, adding **/Se** to the end and then <TAB> completes the full path for the target directory.

> **NOTE**   Tab completion is not just for speed; it's for accuracy as well. Many a systems administrator has not deleted an entire filesystem by using Tab completion with the **rm** command.

Special Characters in the Shell

Numerous characters have special meaning to the shell; a smattering of which are defined in Table 4-4.

Table 4-4   Common Special Characters

Character	Purpose	Example
~	Shorthand for the current user's home directory	vi ~/.bashrc
\	Ignore next character (esc character)	echo $PRD is \\$5
/	Directory separator	cd /home/rbrunson
$	Variable, precedes any var	echo $VAR
?	Single-character wildcard	ls *.t?t
'	Single (absolute) quotation mark	echo 'Cost: $100'
`	Back tick, used for substitution	echo `date`
"	Double (soft) quotation marks	echo "Cost: $VAR"
*	None-to-many wildcard	ls dar*.*
&	Background a job in shell	mozilla &
&&	If cmd1 exits 0 (Success), then do cmd2	cmd1 && cmd2
|	Pipe output to a program	ls –l | pr
||	If cmd1 exits 1 (Fails), then do cmd2	cmd1 || cmd2
;	Execute multiple commands	cmd1 ; cmd2
[]	Ranges of letters/numbers	ls file[0-9]
>	Redirect output to a file	prog1 > file
<	Redirect input to a program	prog1 < file

Controlling Command Execution

When commands are executed, an exit status is always returned but not always displayed. To display the exit status, you must use the **echo** command and the string **$?.**

Possible Exit Statuses

The following executes a command that's guaranteed to work, showing all files in the current user's home directory:

```
ls –a ~
.acrobat  .adobe  .bash_history  .bashrc  .dvipsrc
```

Next, the command is run again with a special character and a special variable to return the exit status:

```
ls -a ~ ; echo $?
.acrobat  .adobe  .bash_history  .bashrc  .dvipsrc
0
```

0 is the exit status of the command, as **echo**ed back by the **$?** variable.

Now, a command that is fake or you know won't work is run (my favorite is **farg**). You must suffix it like the previous code with the **$?** variable; the exit status is something like 1 or 127—anything but 0:

```
farg ; echo $?
-bash: farg: command not found
127
```

To sum this up, either a program executes with no errors (successfully) and returns an exit status of 0 or it has a failure and returns an exit status that is a nonzero value, usually 1 or 127.

NOTE   One of my training class attendees long ago summed up exit statuses like this: "I feel like the system's using sign language with me. If the command executed all right, it's making an 'OK' sign. If there is an error, it's using a different digit to show me that something didn't work."

Environment Variables and Settings

The parent process of all processes on a Linux machine is the init process, with a process ID (PID) of 1. The init process executable is /sbin/init, and its environment is inherited by all child processes.

Hard-coded into init is a default set of paths that are the basis for all paths added by the environment files. This default or set of base paths is shown here:

```
/usr/local/sbin:/sbin:/bin:/usr/sbin:/usr/bin
```

Viewing the system's environment variables in a pure state is difficult because viewing them requires the user to log in and execute the same scripts he is viewing.

To view your environment, use **env** to show environment variables but not shell settings or shell-oriented variables; you can use the **set** command or the **shopt** command to see those.

The Path

The path is a colon-separated list of directories that are searched for executables. It's normally used to locate commands not in the current directory, although Linux does not run a command in the current directory unless that directory is in the path.

You can always refer to an executable in your current directory with one of two methods:

- **Absolute pathname**—/home/ulogin/command
- **Relative pathname**—; ./command

> **NOTE**   So, if you see topics on the exam about how a user tried to execute a file in the current directory but couldn't, you know that the directory isn't in the path. The user should refer to the file with the full path from the root (/) or prefix the filename with ./ for the shortest method.

The path is usually set in the /etc/profile for all users or the ~/.bash_profile for an individual user. It's easy to alter the current path and add a directory without disrupting the previous path definitions. The following example shows how:

1. Edit /etc/profile or .bash_profile.
2. Navigate to the bottom of the file with the keystroke G.
3. Open a new line for editing with the keystroke o.
4. Add the following line, replacing yournewpath with the path that's correct for your system:

```
export PATH=$PATH:yournewpath
```

Getting $HOME

Some shortcuts and variables point to the user's home directory, and several utilities can take the user there quickly.

The HOME variable is read from the user's home directory entry in the /etc/passwd file. This variable's value is the full path to the current user's home directory:

```
cd $HOME - takes you to /home/username
```

Another method is using the **cd** command alone. This takes the user back home with the least number of keystrokes.

Finally, you can refer to the user's home directory with the tilde (~) character, so typing **cd ~** gets the user home as well.

NOTE   The exam tests your ability to understand how a user can get home and what certain characters do for you. One of the most missed and misunderstood areas is the use of the ~username combination. Here's an example:

Your system has a user named tarfoo, and you logged in as the root user. There is a directory named /root/tarfoo on the system. Running the command **cd ~tarfoo** takes you to the tarfoo user's home directory, whereas running the command **cd ~/tarfoo** takes you to the /root/tarfoo directory.

---

bash's History Feature

The **history** command shows the stack of previously executed commands.

bash's history function depends on a variable called HISTFILE, normally set to the current user's .bash_history file (located in the user's home directory). When echoed, it returns the full path and name of the user's history file, like so:

```
echo $HISTFILE
/home/rbrunson/.bash_history
```

When a user logs in with either a login or interactive/non-login shell, the user's .bash_history file is opened. Normally, the history stack is not written to the .bash_history file until the user logs out of that shell session. In the case of a user logging in and then executing a bash subshell to the login shell, the subshell reads the parent shell's history file and writes to it upon exit. You can see this happen if you do the following steps:

1. Log in to a machine as a user.

2. Execute the following command:

   ```
   echo "this is the main shell history"
   ```

3. Then start a new shell:

   ```
   bash
   ```

4. In the new shell, execute the following:

   ```
   history
   ```

5. Execute these commands:

   ```
   echo "this is the subshell history"
   history
   ```

6. Exit the subshell with the following command:

```
exit
```

7. View your history stack with the following:

```
history
```

8. View the last 10 lines of the existing .bash_history file with the following:

```
tail $HISTFILE
```

Important History Variables

Variables are used to control bash's use of history files. The following are common
history variables that are initialized when the shell is started:

- **HISTFILE**—Defaults to **~/.bash_history** and is set in the environment at
  login.

- **HISTCMD**—The history or index number of the current command, so **echo
  $HISTCMD** shows the number for that command.

- **HISTCONTROL**—If it's set to **ignorespace**, lines that start with a space are
  not added to the history file. If it's set to **ignoredups**, a line that duplicates the
  previous line is ignored regardless of the times it's repeated.

- **HISTFILESIZE**—The amount of lines used for the history stack when it's
  written to the history file. If the resulting stack is larger than the size indicated, it is truncated from the front of the file to match the correct size. The
  default is 500.

Setting Options in bash

bash uses the built-in command **set** to turn on or off options for the shell. New in
bash version 2.0 and higher is the **shopt** command, which encompasses the functionality of the **set** command. LPI exams focus on the **set** command:

```
set -o option (sets the option to on)
set +o option (sets the option to off)
```

The **set** command uses a **–o** option specifier when setting options to on; conversely,
it uses a **+o** specifier to turn options to off.

Important bash Options

Bash has a set of options you should know about for the exam and for use in real life.
The most common options are shown in the following list:

- **emacs or vi**—These set the keymap style for editing the command line.

- **history**—This option is on by default. The value of the variable HISTFILE is read to determine the history file.

- **hashall**—On by default, this option enables a hash table of requested commands and their locations for repeated use of the command.

- **monitor**—This option causes job control to make background processes run in a separate group and notify the console when they are ended or completed.

- **noclobber**—This option is off by default; when it's on, it disallows the overwriting of an existing file by a redirect symbol (>). A syntax error occurs if this is attempted. The use of double redirects (to append the file) is recommended.

- **noexec**—A dry run for script files when turned on. Interactive shells ignore it, but a script syntax-checks all commands without executing them.

- **notify**—Reports terminated jobs to the console immediately, instead of waiting until the next execution of the **jobs** command.

- **verbose**—This option echoes or prints to the screen any commands before they are executed. It's useful for the visually impaired users and as a check of the executed string.

Expect to see questions about how to toggle options with the **set** and **unset** commands. Remember that setting an option is accomplished with the **set –o** option syntax, whereas unsetting or removing an option requires the **set +o** option syntax. Expect to see such options as **noclobber**, **history**, **vi**, and **emacs**.

Exam Preparation Tasks

As mentioned in the section "How to Use This Book" in the Introduction, you have a few choices for exam preparation: the exercises here, Chapter 21, "Final Preparation," and the practice exams on the DVD.

Review All Key Topics

Review the most important topics in this chapter, noted with the Key Topics icon in the outer margin of the page. Table 4-5 lists a reference of these key topics and the page numbers on which each is found.

Table 4-5   Key Topics for Chapter 4

Key Topic Element	Description	Page Number
Paragraph	Definition of a shell	93
Section	Sourcing versus executing	94
Section	A login shell session	95
Section	Structuring commands	98
Section	Command completion	99
Table 4-4	Common special characters	100
Section	Possible exit statuses	100
Section	The path	102
Section	Important history variables	104

Define Key Terms

Define the following key terms from this chapter and check your answers in the glossary:

argument, export, history, option, shell, special characters, variables

Review Questions

The answers to these review questions are in Appendix A.

1. Which of the following shell does not support inline editing of the command line?

    a. Bash

    b. Ash

    c. pdKsh

    d. csh

2. Read the following phrase: _____ is the process of reading the contents of a configuration script and loading the results of the commands in the current shell environment.

    Which of the following words correctly completes the above statement?

    a. Substituting

    b. Transliterating

    c. Loading

    d. Parsing

    e. Sourcing

3. While attempting to execute a command utility with a long name, you cannot remember the last several characters. After typing what you are sure of, what character or characters can you typically type next to find out the rest of the command?

    a. ESC

    b. Ctrl-Enter

    c. Tab Tab

    d. \~

4. After executing a command, you don't see an error message, but the behavior of the command and its output are different. What could you type on the command line immediately afterward to see whether there was an error?

    a. echo $#

    b. echo $?

    c. echo $

    d. echo $|

5. Which of the following when executed on the command line immediately returns you to your home directory? (Choose all that apply.)

    a. cd $HOME

    b. cd `

    c. cd ~

    d. cd

    e. cd /home

6. Which command can be used to show only the last 10 lines of your History file?

    a. tail –f /var/log/history

    b. history | tail

    c. cat +10 $HISTFILE

    d. lasthist

This chapter covers the following topics:

- Filesystem Overview
- File Management Commands
- Where Are Those Files?
- Backup Commands

This chapter covers the following objectives:

- Perform basic file management: 103.3
- Create and change hard and symbolic links: 104.6
- Find system files and place files in the correct location: 104.7

## CHAPTER 5

File Management

Most of what you do on a Linux machine involves manipulating files in some manner. You have to know where certain files go, such as binaries, configuration, and user data. You also need to be able to manipulate files from the command line rather than a GUI.

"Do I Know This Already?" Quiz

The "Do I Know This Already?" quiz enables you to assess whether you should read this entire chapter or simply jump to the "Exam Preparation Tasks" section for review. If you are in doubt, read the entire chapter. Table 5-1 outlines the major headings in this chapter and the corresponding "Do I Know This Already?" quiz questions. You can find the answers in Appendix A, "Answers to the 'Do I Know This Already?' Quizzes and Review Questions."

Table 5-1 "Do I Know This Already?" Foundation Topics Section-to-Question Mapping

Foundation Topics Section	Questions Covered in This Section
Filesystem Overview	1, 3
File Management Commands	2, 4-6
Where Are Those Files?	7-8
Backup Commands	9-11

1. Files that change often should go under:
    a. /usr
    b. /proc
    c. /root
    d. /var

2. Your shell is in /usr/local. You type **cd ../bin**. Which directory is shown when you type **pwd**?

   a. /bin

   b. /usr/bin

   c. /usr/local/bin

   d. Nothing, this command returns an error.

3. Which of the following directories should be on the same partition as the root?

   a. /boot

   b. /usr

   c. /home

   d. /sbin

4. You happen across a file in a directory called **foo**. What is a good way to find out what the file is or does?

   a. **file foo**

   b. **/foo**

   c. **cat foo**

   d. **which foo**

5. What command would be used to update the date on a file?

   a. **tar**

   b. **file**

   c. **date**

   d. **touch**

6. You are trying to create a new series of nested directories: /a/b/c/d/. What is the fastest way to create this nested directory set?

   a. **mkdir /a; mkdir /a/b; mkdir /a/b/c; mkdir /a/b/c/d**

   b. **mkdir /a/b/c/d**

   c. **mkdir -p /a/b/c/d**

   d. **md /a/b/c/d**

7. You know that you have multiple copies of the **doit** command on your system. How do you find which one you will run if you type **doit** at the command line?

   a. whereis doit

   b. locate doit

   c. find doit

   d. which doit

8. You know that you downloaded a file called backup.tar.gz this morning but can't remember where you put it. Which is the most appropriate command to find the file?

   a. find / -name backup.tar.gz

   b. find backup.tar.gz

   c. locate backup.tar.gz

   d. whereis backup.tar.gz

9. You want to package up Fred's home directory on a USB stick to send with him as he's leaving your company. Which command is the best? Hurry, because there's cake!

   a. find /home/fred | tar -czf > /media/removable/fred.tar.gz

   b. tar -czf /home/fred > /media/removable/fred.tar.gz

   c. cd /home/; tar -cjf /media/removable/fred.tar.bz2 fred

   d. cd /home/fred tar -cjf /media/removable/fred.tar.bz2 *

10. What does the command **tar -tf archive.tar etc/pine.conf** do?

   a. Makes a new archive called archive.tar containing /etc/pine.conf

   b. Adds etc/pine.conf to archive.tar

   c. Checks to see whether etc/pine.conf is inside the archive

   d. Extracts etc/pine.conf from archive.tar

11. Which compression utility offers the highest level of compression?

   a. bzip2

   b. gzip

   c. compress

   d. cpio

Filesystem Overview

The filesystem's structure starts with the root of the filesystem, which is denoted by the forward slash character (/). Every item on the filesystem is accessible by a single unique path from the root of the system, such as /usr/local/bin/foobar, no matter which device that file is stored on.

Unix evolved its own set of traditions as to where certain files would go. The fragmentation of the commercial and academic Unixes led to differences in conventions depending on which flavor of Unix you were using.

Linux borrows practices from many different Unixes and has fragmentation of its own in the form of different distributions. The community started working on a standard for filesystem layout called the *File System Hierarchy Standard (FHS)* to make it easier for both people and software to know where files can be found.

The latest FHS is always found at http://www.pathname.com/fhs/.

LPI bases the exam questions about the directory structure from the FHS 2.3. The FHS isn't really a standard but a firm set of suggestions that most, but not all, distribution vendors obey. A good number of questions on the exams reference the FHS.

What Belongs Where

The exams make somewhat of a big deal about what the proper directories and locations are for Linux files, but few things are more vexing than to be asked what should positively be in the root (/) directory, or what can be elsewhere.

The Root of the System

Starting in the root (/) directory, the Table 5-2 lists common top-level directories and includes a short explanation for each:

Table 5-2 Common Directories

Directory	Description
bin	Binaries for all users
boot	Kernel, system map, boot files
dev	Device files
etc	Configuration files for the host

Directory	Description
home	Home directories for users
lib	Necessary shared libraries/modules
lost+found	Storage directory for unlinked files (found with fsck)
media	Mount points for removable media
mnt	Temporary mount point for the sysadmin
opt	Third-party application software
proc	Kernel and process information
root	The root user's home directory
sbin	System binaries needed for boot
tmp	Temporary data
usr	Sharable, read-only data and programs, no host-specific data
var	Variable data, logs, Web, FTP, and so on

The exam makes a big deal out of what's optional and required in the **root** (**/**) directory. If you read the FHS 2.3 (highly recommended), you see that the word "optional" appears next to the **/root** and **/home** directories. It is possible that the computer is some kind of application server where users are not expected to log in. This is key because you'll be asked questions about which directories are optional in the root filesystem.

The FHS documentation states, "The contents of the root filesystem must be adequate to boot, restore, recover, and/or repair the system. To boot a system, enough must be present on the root partition to mount other filesystems. This includes utilities, configuration, boot loader information, and other essential start-up data. / usr, /opt, and /var are designed such that they may be located on other partitions or filesystems."

From this statement you can understand which of the preceding directories need to be on the root partition and which can be moved to other partitions.

Classifying Data

FHS makes distinctions between data that changes and data that is static, and data that can be shared versus data that's local to the computer. Data of different categories should be separated into different directories.

Because of the way the FHS is laid out, with the root filesystem being described in section 3 and **/usr** and **/var** happening later, it's easy to misunderstand what is really supposed to be on the root filesystem as opposed to another device that's mounted after boot.

The relationship between **/usr** and **/var** is that, long ago in Unix times, **/usr** used to contain all types of data. The FHS tried to extract the data that changes and is non-sharable to **/var**, leaving **/usr** with just static, sharable data.

Where Programs Live

The FHS does not allow programs to create their individual named directories in the **/usr** section. The subdirectories allowed to exist directly under the **/usr** directory are

- **bin**—Contains user commands
- **include**—Contains header files for C programs
- **lib**—Contains libraries
- **local**—Contains local/sharable programs
- **sbin**—Contains nonessential system binaries
- **share**—Contains data/programs for multiple architectures

The **/usr** section has a location for programs named **/usr/local**. This is for the sys-admin to install software in a place that won't conflict with the distribution files. Programs in the **/usr/local** path are also allowed for sharing among groups of hosts.

For example, say your developers have come up with a program to calculate loans and you want to install it on the workgroup server for other systems to remotely mount and use. Because this is a third-party or custom application, the logical place for it is in **/usr/local/appname**, possibly with a link to the program binary in the **/usr/local/bin** directory (because that's where local binaries are expected to be found).

If given a choice between putting the software package BIGPROG in the /usr/local/ BIGPROG section and the /opt/BIGPROG section, it's hard to choose. Read any relevant exam question closely—the main difference being that the /opt section is not considered to be sharable, whereas the /usr section is often shared and mounted by client systems.

File Management Commands

A major section of the 101 exam is dedicated to how to run commands properly with the right options and arguments. As a good sysadmin, you are expected to know how to create, delete, edit, set permissions, display, move, copy, and determine the type of files and programs.

Tips for Working with Linux Files

Because most users and sysadmins come from a Windows or other OS background, a quick set of recommendations for the less-experienced can be of help here:

- **Hidden files aren't really hidden**—They just begin with a ., such as the **.bashrc** and **.bash_profile** files. They are normally not visible unless you explicitly ask for them to be displayed and aren't deleted by commands such as **rm –f *.***.

- **Filenames can contain multiple periods or no period characters**—The filenames **this.is.a.long.file** and **thisisalongfile** are perfectly reasonable and possible.

- **Spaces in filenames look nice, but are a pain to type**—Use an _ or a - instead of spaces because it's neater and easier than prefixing all spaces with a \. (To display a space in a filename, the system shows a space prefixed with a backslash.)

- **File extensions aren't mandatory**—But they are useful for sorting, selection, and copy/move/delete commands, as well as for quickly identifying a file's type.

Basic Navigation

The command to change the current working directory, **cd**, is used frequently and knowing how to move around the filesystem is a main focus of the exams.

The following command simply moves you from wherever you are to the **/etc** directory. This type of move uses absolute pathnames and can be used from within any directory:

```
cd /etc
```

The path is called *absolute* because it defines a path starting at the root of the filesystem. The easy way to tell whether the path is absolute is that it starts with a slash (/).

Moving relatively from the current directory to a subdirectory is quick and easy, such as if you are in the **/etc/** directory and want to change into the **/etc/samba** directory. Here's how:

```
cd samba
```

This is referred to as a *relative path* because the option you pass to the **cd** command is relative to the current directory. You are in **/etc** and moving to **samba** gets you in **/etc/samba**. If you were in **/home** and ran **cd samba** it would not work unless **/home/samba** also existed.

If you get confused as to where you currently are, use the **pwd** command to print the working (current) directory:

```
# pwd
/etc/samba
```

By itself, the **cd** command takes you back to your home directory, wherever you happen to be. The tilde (~) also means "home directory," so **cd ~** takes you to your home directory and **cd ~sean** takes you to Sean's home directory.

Advanced Navigation

It's good to get experience with some complex relative path situations. For example, if you were in the directory **/home1/user1** and wanted to move into the directory **/home2/user2**, which command could be used?

```
$ tree /

/
|-- home1
|    `-- user1
`-- home2
     `-- user2
```

Remember, you aren't using absolute pathnames, just relative pathnames.

The answer is

```
# cd ../../home2/user2
```

Each of the **..** pairs takes you up one level: The first takes you to **/home1** and the second puts you at the root. From there it's relative pathnames. Practice this method, and remember that going up one level in this exercise only got you to the **/home1** directory. This is a relative path because the path does not start with a /. The directory in which you end up depends on where you started.

Though this example of relative and absolute pathnames was used to look at changing directories, it applies to any situation where you're prompted for a filename.

Listing Files and Directories

The ls command is used for listing directories or files, or both.

If you use the **ls** command to see a multicolumn output of the current directory, only the file or directory names are shown, not other details about the file:

```
ls
file1  file2  file3  file4
```

Use the **–l** long listing option to see all the details of a particular file or directory, or set of files or directories in a single column, like so:

```
$ ls -l
total 0
-rw-r--r--   1 root      root         0 Jan 24 18:55 file1
-rw-r--r--   1 root      root         0 Jan 24 18:55 file2
-rw-r--r--   1 root      root         0 Jan 24 18:55 file3
-rw-r--r--   1 root      root         0 Jan 24 18:55 file4
```

The **–l** long listing style is the only way to use the **ls** command and see the permissions, ownership, and link counts for objects. The only other command that can give such information is the **stat** command, which shows a single filesystem object at a time.

Other examples of using the **ls** command include

- **ls /home/user**—Shows a plain listing of that directory.

- **ls –a**—Lists all files, including hidden . files.

- **ls –d foo**—Lists just the directory called foo, not the contents.

- **ls –i**—Lists the inode number for the targetfile or directory. Inodes are the way Linux represents a file on disk and are discussed later in the section "Copying Files and Directories."

- **ls –l**—Shows permissions; links; and date, group, and owner information. Permissions dictate who can access the file and are discussed in detail in Chapter 10, "Permissions."

- **ls –lh**—Shows human-readable output of file sizes, in KB, MB, and GB, along with file details.

Chaining the options together produces useful results. For example, if you needed to see all the files (including hidden ones) in the current directory, their permissions, and their inode numbers, you would use the following command:

```
# ls -lai
290305 drwxr-x---  13 root    root     4096 Jan 24 18:55  .
     2 drwxr-xr-x  20 root    root     4096 Jan 24 17:56  ..
292606 -rw-r--r--   1 root    root     1354 Jan 21 00:23  anaconda-ks.
cfg
```

```
292748  -rw-------    1 root    root        3470 Jan 24 18:16 .bash_history
290485  -rw-r--r--    1 root    root          24 Jun 10  2000 .bash_logout
290486  -rw-r--r--    1 root    root         234 Jul  5  2001 .bash_profile
290487  -rw-r--r--    1 root    root         176 Aug 23  1995 .bashrc
290488  -rw-r--r--    1 root    root         210 Jun 10  2000 .cshrc
```

Determining File Types

With no requirement for extensions on Linux files, a tool for easily determining file types is essential. The **file** command can be used to read the file's headers and match that data against a known set of types.

The **file** command uses several possible sources, including the **stat** system call, the magic number file (**/usr/share/magic**), and a table of character sets including ASCII and EBCDIC. Finally, if the file is text and contains recognizable strings from a given programming or other language, it is used to identify the file.

The output can be used, manipulated, and filtered to show you useful things.

For example, simply using the **file** command on a given file shows the type:

```
$ file file1
file1: ASCII text
```

Running the **file** command against a known binary shows various elements about the architecture and layout of the file, such as shown here:

```
$ file /bin/ls
/bin/ls: ELF 32-bit LSB executable, Intel 80386, version 1 (SYSV),
dynamically linked (uses shared libs), for GNU/Linux 2.6.32, stripped
```

Running the **file** command against a directory full of files is useful for viewing the possible types, but the real gold lies in filtering the output using the pipe operator (|) and the **grep** command, showing only the results that contain the word "empty":

```
$ file /etc/* | grep empty
/etc/dumpdates:                      empty
/etc/exports:                        empty
/etc/fstab.REVOKE:                   empty
/etc/motd:                           empty
/etc/printconf.local:                empty
```

This is one way of finding empty files that are littering your system. They are probably required in the **/etc** directory but only clutter temporary directories such as **/tmp**.

> **NOTE** The asterisk (*) in the previous command is known as a glob. A *glob* is a wild-card operator that matches some number of files based on a pattern. /etc/* matches all files in the /etc directory such as /etc/foo, /etc/bar, but not /etc/foo/bar!

One thing that's distinct about Linux (and all Unixes) is that the shell is responsible for expanding the glob to the list of files it matches. If you type **ls /tmp/thing*** and there are two files that start with thing such as **thing1** and **thing2**, it's the same thing as if you typed **ls /tmp/thing1 /tmp/thing2**:

```
$ ls thing*
thing1    thing2
```

This globbing feature is why renaming a group of files is harder. In Windows you could type **ren *.foo *.bar** and any file with an extension of foo would then have an extension of bar. In Linux, typing **mv *.foo *.bar** would expand the globs to the list of files matched—***.foo** would match the files you want to rename and ***.bar** would match nothing. This is different from what you might expect! The following output shows this problem.

```
$ ls *.foo *.bar
ls: *.bar: No such file or directory
file1.foo      file2.foo
$ echo mv *.foo *.bar
mv file1.foo file2.foo *.bar
$ mv *.foo *.bar
mv: target `*.bar' is not a directory
```

In the output, the first command shows there are two files with an extension of **foo** and none of **bar**. The **echo** command displays the output that follows it, such that it shows what would be executed if you ran the **mv** command by itself. The *.bar glob shows up because there are no files that match it. The error happens because there is no such directory called ***.bar**.

There are other glob operators. Example 5-1 shows some uses of file globs.

Example 5-1 Examples Using a Glob

```
$ ls
file  file1  file10  file11  file2
$ ls file*
file  file1  file10  file11  file2
$ ls file?
file1  file2
```

```
$ ls *1
file1   file11
$ ls file[123]
file1   file2
```

Example 5-1 starts by listing all the files in the directory. The same list of files is also available with **file***, which matches the word "file" followed by anything, or nothing at all. Note how it includes the bare name "file". Next the **file?** glob matches anything starting with the word "file" and followed by one character. Both "file" and the files with two-digit numbers in their names are excluded.

Globs don't have to appear at the end of a filename. ***1** matches anything ending in the number "1". Finally, **file[123]** uses the square bracket operator that means "any one character from the set". This matches file1 and file2.

Touching Files

The **touch** command seems odd at first, but it comes in handy often. You give it the name of one or more files, and it creates the files if they don't exist or updates their timestamps if they do.

There are various reasons to use the **touch** command, such as creating a new blank log file or updating a file's modification time to use as a reference such as to know the last time a job was run.

To create a new file, you can use the relative pathname for creating one in the current directory:

```
touch filename
```

Or, you can use absolute pathname to create the file, such as shown here:

```
touch /home/rossb/filename
```

Expect to see **touch** on the exams for log file creation, along with using a reference file to mark the last backup. In other words, if a log file is created from a successful backup, that file can be used as a date and time reference file because it occurred at a desirable time.

When you use **touch** on an existing file, the default action is to update all three of the file's times:

- **access**—The last time a file was written/read from

- **change**—The last time the contents of the file were changed, or that the file's metadata (owner, permission, inode number) was changed
- **modify**—The last time the file's contents were changed

A programmer preparing a new release of a software package would use the **touch** command to ensure that all files have the exact same date and times. Therefore, the release could be referred to by the file date, given multiple revisions.

Setting a file's date is relatively easy; the following command sets **file1**'s date to a particular date and time:

```
touch -t 201501010830 file1
```

The time format used is represented by yyyymmddhhmm, or a four-digit year, two-digit month, two-digit day, two-digit hour, and two-digit minutes.

Reference files are useful, particularly when you just want to have a file or set of files updated to a particular date/time, not the current one. You could use

```
touch -r reffile file2update
```

The date and time of **reffile** is applied to the **file2update** file date and time.

Copying Files and Directories

One aspect of copying an object is that the act creates a new file with a separate inode. This means that the operating system sees the new file as separate from the old one. Contrast this to a move operation where it's the same file with a new name.

When you create an object in a filesystem, it gets its own permissions. **cp** doesn't always copy the permissions over to the new file. This can be done, but it requires the use of the **-p** option to preserve the permissions and ownership. The root user is the only user that can change the ownership of a file; therefore, regular users using this option always own the copied files no matter who the original owner was.

A normal copy is simple to perform. You're essentially causing the file to be replicated to the new location:

```
cp file1 /dir1/file2
```

A few options that make life easier for copying files include

- **-d**—Doesn't follow symbolic links; copies the link instead. Links point one file to another and are explored later in the "Linking Files" section.
- **-f**—Force overwriting existing files.
- **-i**—Interactively asks before overwriting.

- **-l**—Creates a hard link to the source file.

- **-r** or **–R**—Recursively traverses directories (copying everything).

- **-s**—Creates a symlink to the source file.

- **-u**—Only updates the copy when the source is newer than the target or the target doesn't exist.

- **–x**—Doesn't traverse to filesystems mounted from other devices.

Copying an existing directory to a new one is simple:

```
# cp -r dir1 dir2
```

The **-r** option is necessary because the **cp** command doesn't process directories by default. As long as the target directory does not exist, the previous command makes an identical copy of the source and all subordinate files and directories in the target directory.

Copying a source directory to an existing target directory doesn't attempt an overwrite; it makes the source directory into a new subdirectory of the target.

For example, if you are in the **/test** directory and have the structure shown in the following, you might assume that issuing a **cp –r dir1 dir2** would overwrite **dir2**, or at least prompt you to see whether you wanted to:

```
$ tree .
|-- dir1
|   |-- file1
|   `-- subdir1
`-- dir2
```

When you issue the **cp –r dir1 dir2** command, the filesystem (along with the **cp** command) notices the existing **dir2** entry and automatically drops the source directory into **dir2** as a subdirectory, like this:

```
|-- dir1
|   |-- file1
|   `-- subdir1
`-- dir2
    `-- dir1
        |-- file1
        `-- subdir1
```

The correct way to copy the contents of **dir1** into **dir2**, thereby mirroring **dir1** exactly, is to focus on the word "contents." By suffixing the source (**dir1**) with a forward slash and an asterisk (**dir1/***), you tell the **cp** command to ignore the directory entry and focus on the filenames inside the directory.

With the same initial setup, if you issue the command **cp –r dir1/* dir2**, you get the correct results:

```
$ tree .
|-- dir1
|   |-- file1
|   `-- subdir1
`-- dir2
    |-- file1
    `-- subdir1
```

The inability to properly copy a directory or its contents will come back to haunt you on the exam. In addition, if you see a source directory with only a trailing forward slash (dir1/) but no asterisk, it's identical to using (dir1). In other words, to copy just the contents of a directory, you have to address them specifically with the forward slash and asterisk (dir1/*).

Two special characters used in relative directory naming are often used when copying files. The current directory is represented by a single period (.) and the parent directory by two periods (..).

For example, if you are currently in the **/home/rossb** directory and want to copy a set of files from the **/home/lukec** directory, you can avoid typing the full path of the current directory with the (.) character. Both of these commands perform the same action:

```
cp /home/lukec/*.mp3 .
cp /home/lukec/*.mp3 /home/rossb
```

Moving Objects

Where the **cp** command copies a file by creating a new file, inode, and data, the **mv** command simply changes which directory file contains the file or directory entry or alters the entry in the file if it stays in the same directory. By changing just the metadata that points to the file, moving a file on the same device is quick. If the file move happens across two devices, the file is copied to the new device and deleted from the old one.

Create a file named **file1**; then run the **stat** command on it to check the details, as shown in Example 5-2.

Example 5-2 Running the **stat** Command on **file1**

```
$ touch file1
$ stat file1
  File: `file1'
  Size: 0         Blocks: 0         IO Block: 4096    regular empty
file
Device: fd00h/64768d         Inode: 2261179      Links: 1
Access: (0664/-rw-rw-r--) Uid: (500/sean)     Gid: (500/sean)
Access: 2015-02-03 21:47:46.000000000 -0600
Modify: 2015-02-03 21:47:46.000000000 -0600
Change: 2015-02-03 21:47:46.000000000 -0600
 Birth: -
```

Now move the file to a new name with the **mv** command, as shown in Example 5-3.

Example 5-3 Moving Files to a New Name

```
$ mv file1 file2
$ stat file2
  File: `file2'
  Size: 0         Blocks: 0         IO Block: 4096    regular empty
file
Device: fd00h/64768d         Inode: 2261179      Links: 1
Access: (0664/-rw-rw-r--) Uid: (500/sean)     Gid: (500/sean)
Access: 2015-02-03 21:47:46.000000000 -0600
Modify: 2015-02-03 21:47:46.000000000 -0600
Change: 2015-02-03 21:48:41.000000000 -0600
 Birth: -
```

Because the device and inode stayed the same you know this is the same file as before. The change time was modified to reflect the fact that the file was renamed.

When you move a file, the **mv** command overwrites the destination if it exists. This command supports an option, **-i**, that first checks the target to see whether it exists. If it does, **mv** asks whether you want to overwrite the target. Some distributions make **-i** a default option with a shell alias. Chapter 11, "Customizing Shell Environments," discusses shell aliases in more detail.

Another quirk of the command is the lack of an **-r**, or recursive, option. This is because when you move a directory or a file you're just changing the directory entry for the file. The directory continues to point to the same files so there is no need to move the files themselves.

You can avoid the overwriting of newer target files or directories with the **-u** option, preserving the latest copy of an object.

Examples of moving files and directories include moving a single directory to another directory name, as shown here:

```
mv -f dir1 dir2
```

This merely changes the directory entry **dir1** to the new name **dir2**. It also removes the "are-you-sure" prompt with the **-f** option.

Just like the **cp** command, moving directory contents requires a correctly formed command; otherwise, you'll move a directory not to the new name, but to a subdirectory of the existing directory.

For example, consider the **/test** directory again, with its structure similar to the following:

```
$ tree .
|-- dir1
|   |-- file1
|   `-- subdir1
`-- dir2
```

If you were a Windows administrator, it would make sense to run the following command to move **dir1** to **dir2**:

```
mv dir1 dir2
```

If you do this on a Linux system and then run the **tree** command, you see the following output:

```
$ tree .
`-- dir2
    `-- dir1
        |-- file1
        `-- subdir1
```

This moves **dir1** under **dir2** because **dir2** already existed. To properly move the contents of the source **dir1** to the target **dir2**, you don't need to use the nonexistent **-r** option (exam trick). You can just use a forward slash and an asterisk to refer to the files underneath **dir1**, like this:

```
mv dir1/* dir2
```

> **NOTE**   The * wildcard operator won't match hidden files because they begin with a period. Handling this case is actually quite complicated and outside the scope of the exam.

If you run the **tree** command, you see the following output:

```
$ tree .
|-- dir1
`-- dir2
    |-- file1
    `-- subdir1
```

Finally, the directories you pass to the **mv** command don't always have to be underneath your current directory. You can use absolute pathnames, such as **mv /dir1 .** to move **dir1**, which is off the root directory into the current directory. You can also run **mv /dir1 /tmp** from anywhere in the system to move that same directory into the temporary directory.

Transforming Data Formats

The **dd** command is useful for a variety of tasks, not the least of which is creating backup images, called ISO files, of CD or DVDs. The two main formats **dd** interacts with are the raw device file and the full path of a file or object on the system.

For example, when creating a new boot disk, the **.img** binary file is read block by block from the CD-ROM (as a file) and written to a USB disk raw device as a set of blocks:

```
dd if=/mnt/cdrom/images/boot.img of=/dev/sdb
```

Creating an image of a CD-ROM involves reading the raw USB device block by block and creating a file on the filesystem that contains all those blocks:

```
dd if=/dev/sdb of=/root/usb.img
```

To duplicate a USB device named sdb to another USB device named sdc, the command is

```
dd if=/dev/sdc of=/dev/sdc
```

The **if** keyword means input file and the **of** keyword means output file. The exact order is unimportant, but as you can imagine, mixing up the in and out files can cause you to do terrible things such as overwriting parts of your hard drive!

dd, unlike most other Unix utilities, does not use dashes for its options. Options are specified in the format of **option=value**.

The **dd** command is also often used to duplicate a drive or partition of a drive to another like object.

For example, to copy the first partition from the /dev/sda disk to the same location on the second hard drive on the system, you would use the following command:

```
dd if=/dev/sda1 of=/dev/sdb1
```

You can also copy an entire disk device to another on the system by leaving off the partition numbers:

```
dd if=/dev/sda of=/dev/sdb
```

This works only if the second device is as large as or larger than the first; otherwise, you get truncated and worthless partitions on the second one.

Backing up the MBR is another trick that **dd** does well. Remember that the master boot record contains the indexes of all the partitions on that drive, and thus is very important. To create a disk file that contains only the first 512 bytes of the first hard drive in the system, use this command:

```
dd if=/dev/sda of=/root/MBR.img count=1 bs=512
```

The **count** keyword sets the number of reads from the input file you want to retrieve, and the **bs** keyword sets the block size.

If you don't set the count and block size on this command to back up the MBR, you'll be copying the entire device's blocks to the filesystem—a snake-eating-its-own-tail operation that is guaranteed to fill up the partition quickly and crash the system.

The restoration procedure is just the opposite:

```
dd if=/root/MBR.img of=/dev/sda count=1 bs=512
```

Creating and Removing Directories

A basic task of file management is to be able to create and remove directories, sometimes creating or removing whole trees at once. To create a directory named **dir1**, you use **mkdir dir1**. To create a directory named **subdir1** in the **dir1** directory, you use **mkdir dir1/subdir1**.

Always think of the last segment of any directory path as the object being created or removed, and think of the rest as supporting or parent objects. The **mkdir** and **rmdir** commands are similar in features and options, including the capability of **mkdir** to create a deep subdirectory tree from scratch in a single command:

```
mkdir -p /dir1/dir2/dir3/dir4
```

One of the quirks about the **rmdir** command is that it cannot remove anything but an empty directory. For example, the last directory of the chain **/dir1/dir2/dir3/ dir4** is the real target for this command, and only if that directory is empty (no regular or directory files) can it be removed.

```
rmdir -p /dir1/dir2/dir3/dir4
```

One option to the **rmdir** command does allow it to remove directories that have files and so on in them. It's called **--ignore-fail-on-non-empty** and is the longest option I know of in Linux. I'd rather type **rm –rf targetdir** 20 times than this beast.

Removing Objects

It follows that you'll want to remove objects after creating or copying them, and this is done with the **rm** command for most objects. **rmdir** can also be used.

Deleting files with the **rm** command is a matter of choosing the target to be removed and the options that work best.

If you want to remove a particular file and never be prompted by confirmation messages, the command is **rm –f target**.

To remove a directory and all its contents, and never get a confirmation message, the command is **rm –rf /full/path/to/target**.

Where Are Those Files?

Having a mechanism for finding or locating files on a Linux system is essential because the sheer amount of directories and files makes searching manually nearly impossible.

There are two methods for accomplishing this task—quick and dirty or slow and methodical. Most people try the quick **locate** command before resorting to the plodding **find** command.

Locating Files with Locate

The quickest way to find a file or set of files is to use the **locate** command. It's fast, database-driven, and secure. When you run the **locate** command you are searching a database instead of the filesystem, and only files that you have access to are shown. The downside of the database is that it's updated nightly and is therefore unaware of any changes that have happened since the last update.

locate has a quirky way of showing results. You would probably expect that using **locate** for a file named **readme** would locate only files named **readme**, but that's not quite true. It finds anything that has a filename of **readme**, including regular files and any part of the path.

For example, while attempting to locate the **readme** file, you run the following command:

```
locate readme
```

This finds both of the following entries, one with the string **readme** as a part of the filename and the other a directory:

```
/readme
/usr/src/linux-2.4.20-8/drivers/net/wan/8253x/readme.txt
```

Use the **locate** command to find items you know are on the disk, or that you know existed before the last **locate** database update. The database that **locate** uses is updated nightly when the system runs its maintenance routines, or on demand. If you don't have permissions to the object, it isn't shown in the **locate** output.

Use **locate** with the **-i** option to ignore the case (upper or lower) and return anything that matches your search string using a case-insensitive match:

```
locate -i string
```

The **locate** database needs to be updated regularly to ensure good results. Your distribution probably puts it in the list of nightly jobs to be run. For more details on the nightly jobs, see Chapter 16, "Schedule and Automate Tasks." Updating the database can take a long time, and it is frustrating having to wait for the updates to finish when you need to search.

The **update** commands must be run as **root**, and either one will do the job:

```
updatedb
```

Sometimes you want to exclude files or directories from the **locate** database because they either are inappropriate or simply take too long to index without any apparent benefit. This is configurable in the **/etc/updatedb.conf** file. This file is read and the variables are used by the updating commands.

The two main methods of excluding objects in the configuration file are either by filesystem type or path. The following output is an example of a working **/etc/updatedb.conf** file:

```
PRUNEFS="devpts NFS nfs afs sfs proc smbfs autofs auto iso9660"
PRUNEPATHS="/tmp /usr/tmp /var/tmp /afs /net /sfs"
export PRUNEFS
export PRUNEPATHS
```

The **PRUNEFS** keyword is for filesystem types you want excluded from the **locate** database update; as you might expect, the **PRUNEPATHS** keyword is for directory trees you want excluded. Notice that most of the paths are temporary data locations or exotic file locations.

Remember for the exam that **locate** returns results for the search string in any portion of the path or filename it finds the string in. There will be questions that **locate** is right for, and some that really want the **whereis** command.

Finding Files

The **find** command is the most accurate but time-consuming method for searching the system for file objects because it crawls the list of files in real time versus the **locate** indexed database. The command consists of several (sometimes confusing) sections. But, if it's learned properly, it can be a powerhouse for the busy sysadmin.

The structure of a **find** command is

```
find startpath -options arguments
```

To make sense of this jumble of sections, let's take a look at a useful **find** command and match up the sections:

```
# find /home -iname *.mp3
/home/snuffy/g3 - red house.mp3
```

The previous command sets the start path to the **/home** directory and then looks for any instance of the string **mp3** as a file extension, or after the last **.** in the filename. It finds a file in the user **snuffy**'s home directory and returns the full path for that file.

Options for **find** include

- **group**—Based on files belonging to the specified group
- **newer**—Based on files more recent than the specified file
- **name**—Based on files with names matching a case-sensitive string
- **iname**—Based on files with names matching a non-case-sensitive string
- **user**—Searches for files belonging to the specified user
- **mtime**—The modify time; used for finding files x days old
- **atime**—Based on the number of days since last accessed
- **ctime**—Based on the number of days since the directory entry was last changed

A useful feature of the **find** command is its capability to execute another command or script on each and every entry normally returned to standard output.

For example, to find all MP3 files in the user's home directories and archive a copy into the root user's home directory, you could use this command:

```
find /home –iname *.mp3 –exec cp –f {} .\;
```

This command uses the **-exec** option, which accepts every line returned to standard output one by one and inserts the full path and filename between the curly brackets ({}). When each line of output is parsed and the command is executed, it reaches the \; at the end of the line and goes back to standard input for the next line. The last line of output is the last one with a command executed on it; it doesn't just keep going and error out.

Running multiple operators in a single command is possible, too. Just be sure not to get the values for one operator mixed up in the next. You could look for all MP3 files owned by a given user with the following command:

```
find /home –iname *.mp3 –user snuffy
/home/snuffy/bls – all for you.mp3
```

The **find** command is complex, and rather than bore you with more possible options, I've worked out a number of examples of how to use **find**:

To find a file and execute **cat** on it, use

```
find /etc –iname fstab –exec cat {} \;
```

To delete all **core** files older than seven days, use the following:

```
find /home –mtime +7 -iname core -exec rm -f {} \;
```

To find all files on the system owned by **bob** and change the ownership to **root**, use

```
find / -user bob –exec chown root {} \;
```

To find all files by user tjordan and change his group, use this command:

```
find /data -user tjordan -exec chGRP users {} \;
```

For safety you can use **-ok** instead of **-exec** to be prompted for confirmation each time the command runs.

```
find /data -user tjordan -ok chgrp users {} \;
```

To find all inodes related to a hard link, use the command find **/ -inum 123456**.

The **find** command's operators and the capability to execute commands on the search results will be covered on the exam. Practice all the examples you see here and get inventive with the possibilities. Particularly watch out for the use of **-mtime** and its cousins: **-atime** and **-ctime**.

Which Command Will Run?

With the plethora of commands and executable scripts offered on a Linux machine, you need to know which of the possible commands will run when you type the name of it on the command line. This all depends on the contents of the **PATH** variable. This variable's contents are used as a sequentially read set of locations to search for executable objects.

The **which** command is used to determine the full path of commands that are queried from the **PATH** variable. To determine which command is indeed executed just by typing the name, run the following command:

```
which ls
alias ls='ls --color=tty'
        /bin/ls
```

As you can see, two entries were found that contain the **ls** command. The first is an alias, one that sets some color functions to the **ls** command; the other is the real command binary in **/bin/ls**.

When you execute a command, it finds the first available match, which might not be the one you wanted, as is the case with the **ls** command. To make it execute a physical binary and ignore any aliases that have been set, preface the command with a backslash (\), like so:

```
\ls
```

Try it again on a command that has two executables on the system, the **gawk** command:

```
which gawk
/bin/gawk
```

This returns a single entry, but there are multiple **gawk** commands on a Linux box. The first matching command found is returned by default, and only if you use the proper switch does it find all possibilities:

```
which -a gawk
/bin/gawk
/usr/bin/gawk
```

Researching a Command

When you need more information about a command than just which one will execute, try **whereis**. This command shows up to three possible bits of information, including its binary files, the man page path, and any source files that exist for it. Here's its syntax:

```
$ whereis ls
ls: /bin/ls /usr/man/man1/ls.1.gz
```

Options for **whereis** include

- **-b**—Searches for binaries
- **-m**—Searches for manual entries
- **-s**—Searches for sources
- **-u**—Finds unusual or improperly documented entries

To find a file by name but not get all the entries that contain the name in the path, use the **whereis** command—not the **locate** command—because it finds the string in all elements of the path.

In Chapter 11, Customizing Shell Environments, you will learn how to extend the shell to make common tasks even easier. The **type** command will tell you if a command has been extended. To check what happens when you type **ps**:

```
$ type ps
ps is /bin/ps
```

The output of the **type** command above indicates that the **/bin/ps** application will be run if you type **ps**.

The **ls** command is often extended to show common options, such as to add color to the output:

```
$ type ls
ls is aliased to `ls --color=auto'
```

The output above shows that when you run **ls**, you actually get **ls --color=auto**. You can see all the possible variants of **ls** by using **type**'s **-a** option:

```
$ type -a ls
ls is aliased to `ls --color=auto'
ls is /bin/ls
```

The **-a** option shows that the shell knows about both an alias and a file on disk.

Linking Files

Links come in two varieties: symbolic and hard. (Symbolic links are often known as soft links.) Each has its own set of advantages and disadvantages. Sysadmins use links for a multitude of purposes; chief among them is the need to make shortcuts on the system for users to access data without having to navigate multiple directory levels.

If you have users on your Linux systems, you need to have a single mount point accessible to multiple users. The options include having users navigate to the **/mnt/somemount** directory to save data or putting a link to that mount point in their home directories. You're much better off using a link for this task.

Symbolic Links

Symbolic links are used primarily to make a shortcut from one object to another. A symbolic link creates a tiny file with its own inode and a path to the linked file. Symlinks can span across filesystems and drives, primarily because a symlink has its own inode. Figure 5-1 shows the relationship between a symlink and the target file.

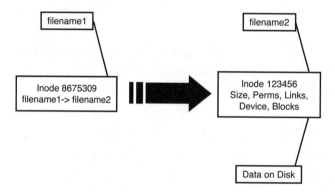

Figure 5-1   Symbolic link detail

For example, you might mount an external disk on the **/mnt/projdata** mount point and want each user to be able to access that remote share from her own home directory. You simply have to issue the following command in each user's home directory to accomplish this:

```
ln -s /mnt/projdata projdata
ls -l projdata
lrwxrwxrwx    1 root    root    13 Jan 26 12:09 projdata -> /mnt/
projdata
```

Notice that the listing for the new symlink shows exactly where the link points, and the permissions are set to the maximum so as to not interfere with the permissions on the target object.

Symbolic links always look like they have the same permissions, but don't try to change them. Changing permissions on a symlink changes the permissions on the target permissions instead.

Hard Links

A *hard link* is normally used to make a file appear in another place. A hard link is simply an additional name in a directory that points to the exact same inode and shares every aspect of the original file except the actual name (although the filename could be identical if in a different directory). Figure 5-2 shows the relationship between a hard link and the target file.

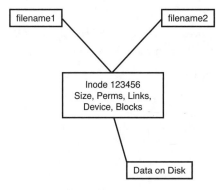

Figure 5-2   Hard link detail

For an example of using a hard link, consider the need to ensure that a frequently deleted file is easily restorable for a given user. The user, Jaime, travels a lot, but when he's in the office he seems to delete things a lot or claims the system has eaten his files. When Jaime is flying, you don't have any issues, so the problem must be the user's actions.

To anchor or back up an important file such as the company contact list in Jaime's home directory, you first must create a backup directory, something like **/backup**.

Then, you create a hard link from Jaime's **ccontactlist.txt** file to a file in the **/backup** directory, like so:

```
cd ~jaime
ln ccontactlist.txt /backup/home_jaime_ccontactlist.txt
ls -l ccontactlist.txt
-rw-r--r--    2 jaime    users    0 Jan 26 13:08 ccontactlist.txt
```

Notice that the file appears normal, but the number **2** for the link count lets you know that another name entry for this file exists somewhere.

Also notice that the listing for the new hard link doesn't show the target file or seem to refer to it in any way. Running the **stat** command on this file won't show you the other filename or seem to be aware of it outside the higher link count.

The name and location of a file are the only things about the file not stored in the inode. This appears on the exam in questions for this set of objectives.

Hard links can't be created if the target is on another filesystem, disk, or remote object. The need to associate multiple names to the same inode makes this impossible.

Be careful when changing the permissions and ownership on the hard-linked files because all name entries point to exactly the same inode. Thus, any changes are instantly made to what would appear to be multiple files but what, in reality, are only filenames.

To delete a file that has multiple hard links requires the removal of every hard link or the multiple names. To find all the links for a file, run the following command:

```
ls -i ccontactlist.txt
17392 ccontactlist.txt
find / -inum 17392
/home/jaime/ccontactlist.txt
/backup/home_jaime_ccontactlist.txt
```

NOTE   On the exam, remember that a symlink is another actual file with its own inode. A large number of symlinks can therefore cause a problem for a filesystem, such as one that contains users' home directories. Too many inodes used can restrict you from using the storage space available. Run the **df –i** command to see what the statistics are.

Backup Commands

As an administrator you often are called upon to deal with file archives, which are one or more files that have been packaged into one file and optionally compressed.

There are several uses for archives:

- You want to send a few files to someone or copy them to another server and want to package and compress them.

- You need to back up a partition to other media in case a disk fails or the file is otherwise lost.

- You want to make a temporary copy of something before you make a change so you can restore it quickly if needed.

- You need to keep files around but in compressed format, such as for archiving old logs.

A number of backup options are available for Linux systems. Some are more useful than others, and some act on files, whereas others work best on partitions or disks as a unit.

Backup commands on the exams include the following:

- **cpio**

- **tar**

- **gzip** and **gunzip**

- **bzip2** and **bunzip2**

- **xz**

Using tar

The **tar** command is the workhorse of the archival world. The name comes from the term tape archive and goes back to the time when most backup was done to a local tape drive. You can think of **tar** as a pipeline that takes in a series of files and outputs a single file that is meant to be streamed to tape, but this output could be sent to a file on disk as well.

On the way through the pipeline you can do some transformations on the files such as chop up the output onto something that fits across multiple tapes, exclude files that weren't recently changed, or rewrite the directory names stored in the archive.

tar also provides the extraction options. You take a **.tar** file, also called a *tarball*, and run it through **tar** to get back a copy of the original files. It is possible to extract only certain files and manipulate the filenames.

The **tar** command also can use various compression commands, particularly the **gzip/gunzip** and **bzip2/bunzip2** commands by the use of special option characters. This has the effect of creating a compressed archive file, typically named **.tar.gz** for **gzip**-compressed files and **.tar.bz2** for **bzip2**-compressed files.

tar commands have an unusual syntax. The command is **tar**, followed by a dash (-), and then all the options concatenated together such as **xvjf**. After this is a list of zero or more filenames; the meanings depend on the options you chose.

The **tar** command has three main methods that act on files or **tar** archives; each has a corresponding letter that must be the first letter in the list of options:

- **c**—Creates an archive
- **t**—Tells you the contents of an archive
- **x**—Extracts files from an archive

The rest of the command can be optional, but some typical options are

- **v**—Be verbose by giving a list of files as they are processed.
- **j** or **z**—Compress or decompress with **bzip2** or **gzip**, respectively.
- **f**—The next word is the name of the file to operate on.

Figure 5-3 shows your choices graphically. We look at examples of each.

Figure 5-3   Picturing the tar options

When you're creating an archive with **tar**, you should think about what you want to archive, where you want the resulting archive to be created, and what compression if any you want to use.

To create a simple **tar** archive, the options you need are as follows:

```
tar -cf archive.tar /foo
```

In this example, the **-c** option signals **tar** to create the file specified after the **-f** option and specifies the directory you are archiving, which is the **/foo** directory. Note that you have to add the .tar suffix. By default the operation is recursive.

To create the same archive with **gzip** compression, you simply insert a **-z** option and use the letters .gz as the filename suffix:

```
tar -czf archive.tar.gz /foo
```

This creates a compressed archive file that uses the **gzip** compression algorithms. If you want slightly higher compression, use the **-j** option (instead of the **-z** option) for **bzip2** compression and create your archive with a suffix of .bz or.bz2.

You will likely see questions on the exam that test your knowledge of which compression command has the highest compression. For example, using **bzip2** generally results in a smaller archive file at the expense of more CPU cycles to compress and uncompress. The **gzip** package is almost always part of the default installation of Linux while **bzip2** may not be.

To create a **tar** archive and see the filenames as they are processed use the **-v** option:

```
tar -cvf archive.tar /foo
```

This produces the following output:

```
tar: Removing leading `/' from member names
foo/
foo/install.log
foo/install.log.syslog
foo/.bash_logout
```

If given an absolute directory name to archive, **tar** strips the leading **/** from the full path of the objects in the archive. It would not be good if you could overwrite files in your **/usr** directory by extracting a file in an unrelated directory!

You may pass more than one directory or file to **tar**. For example, **tar –cf foo.tar bin var** creates an archive called **foo.tar** containing both the **bin** and **var** directories.

Taking Pity on the Unarchiver

It's considered proper and elegant to create **tar** archives by specifying a directory that contains the files to be archived, not just a bunch of files that are in the current directory. This means that when the files are untarred they show up in a single directory instead of in the current directory.

For example, create an archive of the **/etc** directory contents with the following command:

```
tar -cf etc.tar /etc
```

When you unarchive the **tar** file, by default it creates an **etc** directory in the current directory, which contains the entirety of the **/etc** directory you archived.

Contrast this with the nightmare that happens when you navigate to the **/etc** directory and create the archive from there with this command:

```
tar -cf /root/badetc.tar *
```

This archive file contains the same files as the previous one, except they aren't contained in a top-level **etc** directory—everything is in the top level of the archive.

Imagine what will happen to your system when you unarchive this file in the root user's home directory. You will have spewed approximately 2,400 files directly into the root user's home directory!

It really does matter where you are in the filesystem and which path options you use when you create or expand an archive file. It's best practice to use absolute pathnames.

To solve the problem of 2,400 files polluting your root user's home directory, use the following command, where **badetc.tar** is the offending archive file:

tar -tf badetc.tar | xargs rm -rf

This command produces a list of the paths and filenames of files in the archive and uses the **xargs** command to feed each line of output as a filename specification to the **rm -rf** command, removing all the files and directories expanded from the **badetc. tar** file.

Useful Creation Options

A number of other options can be used for creating **tar** archives. Here is a list of the more useful and testable ones:

- **-b**—Sets the block size to fit the media to which you are archiving. This is necessary for some tape devices.

- **-M**—This specifies multiple archive targets or spreads a large archive across multiple tapes or media.

- **-g**—Creates a new format incremental backup (only those that have changed since the last full or incremental).

- **-l**—Stays on the local filesystem; it's used to keep from backing up the entire NFS network by accident.

- **-L**—This is followed by a number that reflects 1024 bytes, so **-L 500** equals 500KB. (It's used for setting the tape length so multiple tapes can be used for an archive.)

- **--remove-files**—This is dangerous because the specified files are removed from the filesystem after they have been added to the archive!

Listing Archive Files

An underrated option, listing is something that typically is used after you don't get the results you want or realize what you've just done and want to confirm how hard it is going to be to clean up.

To tell you the contents of a **tar** archive, use the following command:

```
tar -tf archive.tar
```

This produces the output shown here:

```
etc/
etc/sysconfig/
etc/sysconfig/network-scripts/
etc/sysconfig/network-scripts/ifup-aliases
etc/sysconfig/network-scripts/ifcfg-lo
```

To list an archive that uses compression, simply insert the necessary letter between the **-t** and the **-f** options, such as the **bzip2 -j** option shown here:

```
tar -tjf archive.tar.bz2
```

This produces the following output:

```
etc/
etc/sysconfig/
etc/sysconfig/network-scripts/
etc/sysconfig/network-scripts/ifup-aliases
etc/sysconfig/network-scripts/ifcfg-lo
```

To list an archive and see the file details for its contents, you add the **-v** option to the existing command to see an output of the details:

```
tar -tvjf archive.tar.bz2
```

This returns output similar to the following:

```
drwxr-xr-x root/root          0 2015-02-10 03:46 etc/
drwxr-xr-x root/root          0 2015-01-31 10:09 etc/sysconfig/
drwxr-xr-x root/root          0 2014-11-10 22:13 etc/sysconfig/network-
scripts/
```

When you create an archive with the **-v** option, a list of the files being archived is shown onscreen. When you unarchive an archive with the **-v** option, it shows a similar list of the files being unarchived.

It's only when you list an archive with the **-v** option that you get the type of output that approximates an **ls -l** command being run on the archive contents. This is an exam topic, so be ready for it.

Using cpio

The **cpio** command appears extensively in the Level 2 LPI objectives. This level of the exam might ask you about the **cpio** command at only the simplest levels, such as knowing that it exists, how it works in general terms, and whether it can be used to back up a Linux system.

The **cpio** command actions all treat the filesystem as the home base. If you are copying out, it's from the filesystem out to another file. The same is true with copying in—it's from a file into the filesystem.

The **cpio** command has three options for acting on files and filesystems:

- **-o** or **--create**—This copies files to an archive using a list of files typically created by the **find** command.

- **-i** or **--extract**—This copies files into the filesystem from an archive or a list of the archive contents.

- **-p** or **--pass-through**—This copies files from one directory tree to another without the use of an archive, essentially performing the same function as the **cp -r** command.

The **cpio** command accepts a list of files in a one-file-per-line format and uses this list to send the archived files to either the standard output or an archive file you specify.

cpio supports a variety of archive formats, including binary, ASCII, crc, and tar, to name the most relevant.

An example of creating a cpio archive from the files in the current directory is shown here:

```
find . "*" | cpio -o > archive.cpio
```

This outputs the list of files found by this particular **find** command, with the **cpio** command taking the entirety of the files and sending them to the **archive.cpio** file by redirecting standard output to the file.

The **cpio** command doesn't accept a list of files to archive on the command line like the other utilities you've seen so far. Instead, it reads the names of the files from the standard input or console. So be aware that using either the **find** or **ls** command is necessary to feed **cpio** a list of filenames.

For example, if you needed to archive all the files that have an extension of .txt in the current directory to a **cpio** archive named txt.cpio, you would use the following command:

```
ls *.txt | cpio -o > txt.cpio
```

Notice that you're redirecting the output of cpio to a file rather than letting it write the file itself. Therefore the filename is up to you, and if you want a **cpio** file extension, you need to add it yourself.

Compression Utilities

Whereas the **tar** command is used to gather files and put them in a container, the **gzip**, and **bzip2** commands are used to compress that container. Used by themselves, they act on each file they find and replace that file with a compressed version that has an extension that indicates the file is compressed.

The **gzip** and **bzip2** compression utilities compress files and are similar in their functions and operations. The main difference is that **bzip2** offers slightly better compression than **gzip**, but **gzip** is much more widely used.

These commands replace the original file with a new file that has an additional extension, so don't delete the .gz or .bz2 files that you create. They are the original files in a compressed wrapper!

To compress all the files in the current directory with **gzip** or **bzip2**, use this command:

```
gzip *
```

This replaces all the regular files (not the directories or their contents) in the current directory with the original filenames plus a **.gz** extension. So, if you had two files named file1 and file2 in the directory, they would be replaced with

```
file1.gz
file2.gz
```

To uncompress these files, just do the exact opposite of the compression:

```
gunzip *
```

This restores the original files.

Using **bzip2** produces the same sort of results. You can issue the following command in the same directory:

```
bzip2 *
```

You would then have the following two files:

```
file1.bz2
file2.bz2
```

To uncompress these files, issue this command:

```
bunzip2 *
```

This restores the files to their original states.

xz is a third option for compressing files just like **bzip2** and **gzip**. It is newer, and in some cases has better performance than **bzip2** at a cost of more memory. Files are compressed with one of **xz**, **xz -z**, or **xz --compress**, and decompressed with one of **unxz**, **xz -d**, **xz --uncompress**, or **xz --decompress**.

The .xz file extension indicates that a file was compressed with **xz**. To uncompress **foo.xz** you would run **xz -d foo.xz**, and would be left with an uncompressed file called **foo**.

Watch for questions that ask about why you would use either **gzip** or **bzip2** for a particular compression task. **bzip2** offers slightly better compression at the expense of increased CPU cycles. **gzip2** is faster but doesn't compress as well. **gzip2** also has a recursive option (**-r**) that compresses all files in a directory.

Summary

In this chapter you learned about the Linux File System Hierarchy Standard (FHS) and what it means for laying out partitions. You also learned how to find files in real time with the **find** command, and through a database lookup with the **locate** command. This chapter also covered the **cp**, **mv**, and **touch** commands for copying, moving, and updating files, along with the proper use of file globs for matching files on the command line.

Finally you learned about the various archival and compression utilities that Linux makes available to you.

Exam Preparation Tasks

As mentioned in the section "How to Use This Book" in the Introduction, you have a couple of choices for exam preparation: the exercises here, Chapter 21, "Final Preparation," and the practice exams on the DVD.

Review All Key Topics

Review the most important topics in this chapter, noted with the Key Topics icon in the outer margin of the page. Table 5-3 lists a reference of these key topics and the page numbers on which each is found.

Table 5-3 Key Topics for Chapter 5

Key Topic Element	Description	Page Number
Paragraph	FHS documentation about what goes on the root volume	113
Paragraph	The use of the /usr and /usr/local/ directories	114
Paragraph	Relative pathnames and . (period character)	116
Paragraph	Long listing format (**-l**) to see permissions	117
Paragraph	Using the **touch** command	120
Paragraph	Using a glob to avoid copying into a directory incorrectly	122
Paragraph	**Locate** needs the database refreshed periodically	129
Paragraph	**Locate** searches whole names	130
Paragraph	Examples of **find** usage	131
Paragraph	When to use **whereis** versus **locate**	133
Paragraph	The filename is not stored in the inode	136
Note	Symlinks consume inodes	136
Paragraph	The order and function of **tar**'s options	138
Paragraph	Creating a **tar** archive	138
Paragraph	**bzip2** has the highest compression rate	138
Paragraph	The **-v** option to tar	141
Paragraph	**cpio** accepts its files from the standard input	142

Define Key Terms

Define the following key terms from this chapter and check your answers in the glossary:

File System Hierarchy Standard, relative path, absolute path, hard link

Review Questions

The answers to these review questions are in Appendix A.

1. You are installing a customized server and need to strip the root filesystem down to the essentials only. According to the FHS 2.3, which of the following are considered optional on the root (/) filesystem? (Choose two.)

    a. /root

    b. /usr

    c. /tmp

    d. /home

2. One of your programmers has produced an order entry system that will be shared among your users from a central file server. What is the appropriate directory to place this program and its associated files in?

    a. /usr/local/bin

    b. /usr/local

    c. /usr/share

    d. /opt

3. Which of the following is a true statement about files on a default Linux system? (Choose all that apply.)

    a. Filenames can start with a number.

    b. Filenames can contain multiple periods.

    c. Filenames can contain spaces.

    d. Filenames can contain ampersands.

    e. Filenames can contain backslashes.

4. You find a string in a shell script that contains the following command:

    ```
    cp /data/*.doc ~tarfoo
    ```

    What is the meaning of the characters ~tarfoo?

    a. A special function named tarfoo

    b. A directory named tarfoo in your home directory

    c. The tarfoo user's home directory

    d. The /data/tarfoo directory

5. You are currently in the directory /home1/user1/subdir1 and need to navigate to the directory /home12/user3. Which of the following commands will accomplish this?

   a. **cd home12/user3**

   b. **cd ~/user3**

   c. **cd ../../home12/user3**

   d. **cd ../../../home12/user3**

6. You have a directory named /dir1 that contains subdirectories and regular files. You want to replicate this directory structure exactly into an existing directory named /dir2. Which of the following commands accomplish this? (Choose all that apply.)

   a. **cp --contents dir1/ /dir2**

   b. **cp –r /dir1/* /dir2**

   c. **xcopy /dir1 /dir2**

   d. **cp –r /dir1 /dir2**

7. You are currently in the /bbb directory and want to move the contents from the /ccc directory to this one. What is the shortest command that will accomplish this?

   a. **mv /ccc/*.* .**

   b. **mv ../ccc/*.* .**

   c. **mv /ccc/* .**

   d. **mv /ccc/ /bbb**

8. Which option to the **mkdir** and **rmdir** commands allows you to create a nested subdirectory tree?

Example:

```
/dir1/dir2/dir3/dir4
```

   a. **-c**

   b. **-n**

   c. **-d**

   d. **-p**

9. You are the sysadmin of a busy server and need to save space on your /home partition. You need to remove all files named **core** that are older than seven days in the users' home directories, without receiving any prompts.

   a. **find /home –mtime +7 –name core –exec rm –f {} \;**

   b. **find ~ -mtime +7 -name core -exec rm -f {} \;**

   c. **find /home -mtime -7 -name core -exec rm -f {} \;**

   d. **find /home -older 7d -name core -exec rm -f {} \;**

10. Which of the following situations would prevent you from creating a hard link?

    a. The link spans filesystems.

    b. The source of the link is a hidden file.

    c. The source of the link is a device file.

    d. The source of the link is a directory.

    e. The destination contains special characters.

11. How would you back up Rebecca's home directory using the best compression available?

    a. **cd /home; tar -czf rebecca.tgz rebecca**

    b. **find ~rebecca | tar -cjf - > rebecca.tar.bz2**

    c. **tar -cjf rebecca.tar.bz2 ~rebecca**

    d. **tar -xjf rebecca.tar.bz2 ~rebecca**

This chapter covers the following topics:

- Working with Input/Output Streams
- Pipes
- Executing Multiple Commands
- Splitting and Processing Streams
- Filters
- Formatting Commands
- Using Regular Expressions and grep

This chapter covers the following objectives:

- Use streams, pipes, and redirects: 103.4
- Process text streams using filters: 103.2
- Search text files using regular expressions

## CHAPTER 6

Text Processing/Advanced Command Line

This chapter focuses on the concepts and practice of getting a lot done on the shell command line. Chief among the skills you gain from this chapter is the ability to choose commands and chain them together properly, and sometimes interestingly, to get your work done.

Unix and Linux have a toolset mentality that needs to be cultivated, and it must be learned to be successful in your sysadmin/programming work and on the exams.

Everything in the Linux command arena needs to do three things:

- It should do one thing very well.
- It should accept standard input.
- It should produce standard output.

With commands and the shell's constructs that help connect things together (pipes, redirection, and so on), it becomes possible to accomplish many things with just one command string of connected commands.

"Do I Know This Already?" Quiz

The "Do I Know This Already?" quiz enables you to assess whether you should read this entire chapter or simply jump to the "Exam Preparation Tasks" section for review. If you are in doubt, read the entire chapter. Table 6-1 outlines the major headings in this chapter and the corresponding "Do I Know This Already?" quiz questions. You can find the answers in Appendix A, "Answers to the 'Do I Know This Already?' Quizzes and Review Questions."

Table 6-1 "Do I Know This Already?" Foundation Topics Section-to-Question Mapping

Foundation Topics Section	Questions Covered in This Section
Working with Input/Output Streams	1
Pipes	2
Executing Multiple Commands	3
Splitting and Processing Streams	4

Foundation Topics Section	Questions Covered in This Section
Filters	5
Formatting Commands	6
Using Regular Expressions and grep	7

1. Which of the following is the file descriptor that matches stdout?

    a. /proc/self/fd/0

    b. /proc/self/fd/1

    c. /proc/self/fd/2

    d. /proc/self/fd/3

2. What is the result of the following command?

    ```
    $ find / -iname "*.txt" | file > sort
    ```

    a. A file named "file" in the current directory

    b. An error message that the files could not be found

    c. A file named "sort" in the current directory

    d. An endless loop on the system

    e. None of the above

3. While creating a script to perform backups from one server to another, you want to ensure that if the first command isn't successful a second command will run. Which of the following when inserted between the two commands accomplishes this?

    a. &

    b. >>

    c. ||

    d. ;

    e. @

4. As the sysadmin of a financial organization, you receive a real-time feed of information that your web team uses to display financial data to customers. You must keep a log of the data you receive as well as send that data on for further processing.

    Which of the following commands would you use to accomplish this?

a. tac

b. split

c. tee

d. branch

e. culvert

5. You are trying to display a formatted text file in a uniform manner as output on the console, but some of the columns don't line up properly. What command could you use to filter this file so that any tabs are replaced with spaces when it's output to the console?

a. convert

b. expand

c. detab

d. spacer

6. You want to replace the words "Linux Tarballs" with "Linus Torvalds" in a given text file. Which of the following commands would you most likely use to execute a search and replace on these words?

a. ex

b. ed

c. edlin

d. tr

e. sed

7. You are using a series of command line tools to display output that is useful, but what you would rather see as output is the exact opposite of what is being shown. Which of the following commands with option shows the reverse or inverse of the normal output?

a. grep -v

b. sort –r

c. find -x

d. indent -u

e. None of the above

Foundation Topics

Working with Input/Output Streams

Linux supports separate streams to handle data on the shell command line. These are called file descriptors and are used primarily to send data to and from programs and files and to handle errors.

Table 6-2 lists the three file descriptors and their associated files.

Table 6-2 Linux File Descriptors

Name	fd Number	Associated File
/dev/stdin	0	/proc/self/fd/0
/dev/stdout	1	/proc/self/fd/1
/dev/stderr	2	/proc/self/fd/2

Standard In

Standard in, or stdin, is what all programs accept, or it's assumed they will accept. Most programs accept stdin either from a redirected file argument or using the file as an argument to the program:

```
program < file
```

or

```
program file
```

For most programs, these examples are identical. We cover several commands that don't handle arguments properly, such as the **tr** command.

> **NOTE** Often, the stdin of a program is the stdout of another program, connected by a pipe symbol.

Standard Out

Standard out, or stdout, is the text or data that's produced by a command and shows up on the screen or console. By default, all text-mode commands produce stdout and send it to the console unless it's redirected. To understand this, run the following command:

```
cat /etc/fstab
```

The text shown onscreen is a perfect example of the **stdout** stream. It's considered elegant to run commands first to see what they produce before redirecting the output to a file, particularly because you might get errors.

Standard Error

Standard error, or stderr, is a parallel stream to the **stdout**, and by default it shows up mixed into the **stdout** stream as the errors occur.

> **NOTE** To visualize this, think of two pitchers of water. One is stdout and the other stderr. If you pour them out and mix the streams of water together, they may be different, but they both go to the same place.

It's hard to produce errors on purpose; however, we can always use the **find** command to produce some access denied or permission errors to experiment with.

As a normal user, run the following command:

```
find / -iname "*.txt"
```

Right away you see errors that indicate the user can't access certain directory trees to find certain items. Notice that useful output (**stdout**) is mixed directly with error messages (**stderr**), making it potentially hard to separate the streams and use the good data for anything constructive.

> **NOTE** The life of a sysadmin is defined by the search for producing good data and properly discarding or storing the errors produced. Good data can be sent on to another program, while errors are usually dumped at the earliest possible moment to use the processor and resources to produce good data more efficiently.

To clean up the good data and get rid of the bad data, we need to use redirection operators. To see this work, use the up arrow and rerun the previous command, as shown here:

```
find / -iname *.txt 2> /dev/null | more
```

This produces output similar to

```
./.kde/share/apps/kdeprint/printerdb_cups.txt
./1.txt
./2.txt
./3.txt
```

Notice that you get only good data (**stdout**) after using a **2>** redirection symbol to dump the bad data (**stderr**) to the system's black hole, or garbage disposal—in other words, a pseudo-device designed to be a place to discard data securely.

You learn more about this in the "Redirecting Standard Error" section.

Redirection of Streams

In the quest for good data, being able to *redirect* or change the destination of **stdout** and **stderr**, and to some degree **stdin**, is essential to your tasks.

Redirection symbols include

- **<**—Redirects a file's contents into a command's **stdin** stream. The file descriptor for the < input redirection symbol is **0**, so it's possible to see <0 used.

- **>**—Redirects the **stdout** stream to the file target to the right of the symbol. The file descriptor for the > output redirection character is 1, which is implied, except in certain instances.

- **>>**—Redirects **stdout** to a file, *appending* the current stream to the end of the file, rather than overwriting the file contents. This is a modifier of the > output redirection descriptor.

- **2>>**—Redirects **stderr** to a file, appending the current stream to the end of the file, rather than overwriting the file contents. This is a modifier of the > or 2> output redirection descriptor.

NOTE If using the > redirection symbol to write to a file, that file is overwritten unless the **noclobber** bash shell option is set. With that option set, you cannot overwrite the file; it produces an error and file. The only way to get data into that file is to use the >> redirection append symbols. This can be configured by running the Set –o noclobber command.

Redirecting Standard Input

Redirecting **stdin** consists of sending a file's contents to a program's **stdin** stream. An example of this is **sort < file1.**

Although it might seem odd to have a couple of ways to do the same thing, the previous command is essentially the same as the **cat file1 | sort** command.

Redirecting Standard Output

Redirecting **stdout** consists of either a single redirection symbol (**>**) or two (**>>**) for appending. The main difference is that the use of a single redirection descriptor overwrites a file, whereas using double redirection descriptors appends to the end of a file, like so:

```
cat file1 > file2
```

This overwrites the contents of **file2** or, if it doesn't exist, creates it.

The following command appends the data from **file1** to **file2** or, if it doesn't exist, creates **file2**:

```
cat file1 >> file2
```

As an alternative example, say you run the **find** command and it produces errors and found files to the screen. You can capture the good data to a file and let the errors show on the console with the command shown here:

```
find / -iname *.txt > foundfiles
```

When you are redirecting **stdout**, the numeral or file descriptor **1** doesn't need to be used for most cases. (In other words, you can just use > and not have to use 1>; the 1 is implied and not necessary.) Redirection of **stdout** is so common that a single **>** symbol suffices.

Redirecting Standard Error

Redirecting **stderr** consists of understanding that, by default, **stderr** shows up on the same target as the **stdout**, mixed right in but separable.

To continue the previous example but capture the **stderr** and let the good data show on the default target (console), you would change the command to

```
find / -iname *.txt 2> errors
```

The **2> errors** section of the command redirects the **stderr** and puts it into the file **errors**, leaving the **stdout** stream free to show on the default target (console) or even get written to another file.

The key to understanding what happens when using **stdout** and **stderr** is to visualize them as shown in Figure 6-1.

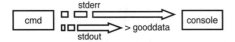

Figure 6-1 Path of data streams

As you can see, the **>** character grabs the **stdout** stream and puts that data into the file **gooddata**, whereas the **stderr** stream is unaffected and is sent to the console for display.

Grabbing both streams and putting them into different files is as simple as adding a redirection symbol preceded with the **stderr** numeral:

```
find / -iname *.txt > gooddata 2> baddata
```

This grabs both streams and puts them into their proper files, with nothing displayed to the console.

Redirection Redux

Sometimes all the possible output from a particular command must be trapped because it will cause problems, such as when a command is run as a background job and you're using vi or some other console-based program. Having **stderr** show up onscreen during an editing session is disconcerting at the least, and if you're configuring important files, it's downright dangerous.

 To trap all output from a command and send it to the **/dev/null** or black hole of the system, you use the following:

```
find / -iname *.txt > /dev/null 2>&1
```

You will see items like the previous as exam topics, and it's important that you've done the task yourself, multiple times if possible. Take a few minutes to experiment with the examples shown in this text. Getting this set of symbols right in a fill-in-the-blank question is difficult if you've not typed it a number of times.

NOTE Don't be confused by the use of the /dev/null device; its sole purpose is to be a catch-all fake device that you can use to discard output of any kind.

Pipes

A *pipe* (|) is used for chaining two or more programs' output together, typically filtering and changing the output with each successive program the data is sent through.

Quite possibly the simplest usage of a pipe is to take the output of a particular command and use a pipe to send it to one of the pagers, such as **more** or **less**. Pagers are called that because, especially with the **more** command, you are shown the output not in a running stream down the console but as if it had been cut up into **pages** that fit your screen. For example, in Figure 6-2 the **ls** command's standard output is sent to the **less** command as that command's standard input.

```
ls -l | less
```

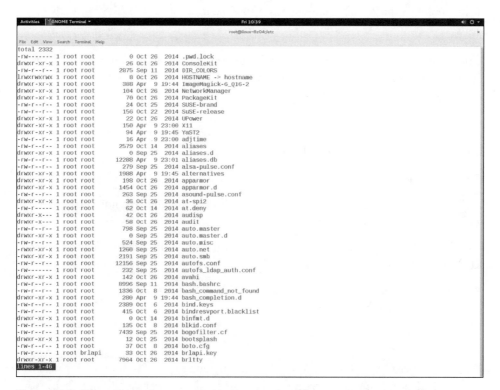

Figure 6-2 The output of a command being piped to **less**

The **less** command offers a lot of great functionality for viewing output. You can search forward for something by entering the **/** character followed by the string you want to find, for example:

```
/somestring
```

Also while in **less,** you can use most of the typical navigation commands used in other programs such as **vi** or **vim** (covered in later chapters), such as **1G** to go to the first character of the first line of the file or **G** to go to the end of the file. The page up and page down keys work as well as the traditional cursor movement (hjkl) and arrow keys to navigate around the file.

Further or more complex use of pipes includes chaining together several commands that each add to the output of the first command to produce something useful.

NOTE It is important to remember that commands pipe output to other commands until the output is finally sent to the screen/console or it's committed to a file with an output redirect, such as the **>** or **>>** characters. Standard error is not being redirected or trapped unless the **2>** designator sends it to a file location or the **/dev/null** device.

For example, to print a code sample with numbered lines (**nl**) and printer formatting (**pr**), you use the following command string:

```
cat codesamp.c | nl | pr | lpr
```

It's essential that you know the difference between a redirection symbol and a pipe. Say you are shown a similar command such as

```
cat file1 | nl > pr
```

This command produces a file in the current directory named **pr,** not output that has been filtered through both **nl** and **pr.**

Ross's Rule: Redirection always comes from or goes to a file, whereas piping always comes from or goes to a program.

Good examples of using pipes to produce usable data include

```
sort < names | nl
```

NOTE Remember that you usually don't have to include the < or input redirect when specifying a file argument to a program such as sort, but we include this here because you may see this on an exam at some point.

This sorts and then numbers the file **names.**

Another example is

```
who | wc -l
```

This counts the users attached to the system and shows just the total number.

Here's one more example:

```
lsof /mnt/cdrom | mail root -s"CD-ROM Users"
```

The previous command is designed to show you who is currently accessing or has opened files on the CD-ROM of the server, so you know who to tell to log off when it's needed.

Executing Multiple Commands

There are several methods for executing multiple commands with a single Enter key. You can use special characters to just have it execute multiple commands or get fancy with if/then types of multiple-command execution.

Multiple Command Operators

When compiling software, scheduling backup jobs, or doing any other task that requires a particular program's exit status to be a particular value, you need to use these operators:

> **NOTE** It's important to remember that each of the commands has its own set of stdin, stdout, and stderr descriptors. They flow into and out of each of the commands in between the operators.

- ;—The semicolon causes all listed commands to be executed independently of each other. The following example echoes back when a long compile is done:

  ```
  make modules ; echo DO MAKE MODULES_INSTALL NEXT
  ```

  The commands are independently executed and neither command fails nor succeeds based on the other's exit status.

- &&—The double ampersand causes the second command to be executed if the first command has an exit status of 0 (success). If an exit status of nonzero (fails) is returned, the second command is not attempted. If you're a sysadmin and want to have a second program do something if the first succeeds, use the double ampersand like this:

  ```
  longcompile && mail root -s "compile complete"
  ```

  This set of commands starts a long compile; if it succeeds, you get an email stating compile complete in the subject line.

- | |—The double pipe causes the second command to not be attempted if the first command has an exit status of 0 (success). If the first command has an exit status of nonzero (fails), the second command is attempted. What if you want to have a second command let you know whether a particular process failed without having to dig through the log files every morning? You could use the following:

```
tar -czvf /dev/st0 / || mail root -s "doh, backup failed"
```

As you can probably guess, this command set attempts a full system backup to a SCSI tape device. Only if it fails does the root user get an email with the subject line indicating it failed.

Command Substitution

In some instances, you need to take the output of a command and place it into a variable, usually for scripting purposes. Substituting the output of a command for the command itself is accomplished by bracketing the command with the backtick (`), aka the unshifted tilde (~) key, like so:

```
'somecmd'
```

An example of this is inserting the output of the **date** command into a variable, possibly for use in a script, such as in this example:

```
export DATETIME='date'
echo $DATETIME
Tue Jan 13 17:18:35 PST 2004
```

The **export** command is used to create a variable named **DATETIME** that is being populated by the `date` command. When this is executed, the backticks around the **date** command cause the output for that command to be inserted into the **DATE-TIME** variable as a value.

Another facet of substituting commands is to enclose the command itself between parentheses and declare it as a variable, as in this example:

```
file $(grep -irl crud /usr/src/linux-2.4)
```

The main reason to use a command substitution like this is it allows you to nest commands within commands. Rather than having to use wildcards, you just use the right substitution.

Another fun example of using command substitution is looking at a given binary and seeing what libraries it requires without knowing where that binary is actually located.

```
ldd 'which ls'


        linux-gate.so.1 =>  (0xb778c000)
        libselinux.so.1 => /lib/i386-linux-gnu/libselinux.so.1
(0xb774e000)
        libacl.so.1 => /lib/i386-linux-gnu/libacl.so.1 (0xb7745000)
        libc.so.6 => /lib/i386-linux-gnu/libc.so.6 (0xb7595000)
        libpcre.so.3 => /lib/i386-linux-gnu/libpcre.so.3 (0xb7557000)
        libdl.so.2 => /lib/i386-linux-gnu/libdl.so.2 (0xb7552000)
        /lib/ld-linux.so.2 (0xb778d000)
        libattr.so.1 => /lib/i386-linux-gnu/libattr.so.1 (0xb754c000)
```

Splitting and Processing Streams

Two commands that work well with and complement the use of pipes are the **tee** and **xargs** commands.

Splitting Streams with the tee Command

The **tee** command is designed to accept a single **stdin** stream and simultaneously send one set of identical output to a specified file and the other one to be used as stdin to another program via pipe.

You might use **tee** when running a program that must produce output to a file and you want to monitor its progress onscreen at the same time, such as the **find** command. To redirect one stream of output to a single file and also see the same output on the screen, use

```
find / -iname *.txt | tee findit.out
```

This command is designed to log the standard output of a stream to a file and pass another complete stream out to the console. Financial institutions that have to log and simultaneously process data find **tee** useful.

Processing Output with the xargs Command

The **xargs** command is another useful command. It takes a list of returned results from another program (such as the output of the **locate** or **find** commands, essentially a series of path/filenames) and parses them one by one for use by another simpler or less-capable command.

A good example of this is your wanting to have all readme files on the entire system in one large file called **mongofile.txt** in your home directory. This would enable you to search the documentation with a single **less mongofile.txt command**.

To do this, we use the **find** command to find the full path and filename of the readme files on your system; then we use the **cat** command to take the contents and redirect the results to our target file:

```
find / -iname readme | cat > mongofile.txt
```

It would appear from the apparent lack of critical errors that we were able to get the results we wanted—that of all lines from each file being output to the mongofile.txt, one after the other. This turns out not to be the case.

To see what went wrong, issue the **less mongofile.txt** command, which reveals that we didn't get the output we wanted—the **cat** command isn't smart enough to determine that the output from the **find** command is actually discrete lines that can be used individually as if they were arguments. It just echoes the output as it was given it, in one big text blob, not treating the individual lines as lines of usable output for the **cat** command.

> **NOTE** Perhaps an easier way to see what happened is to use the **wc –l** command against mongofile.txt. It comes back with a discrete number of lines in the file for your initial reference. (For reference, I got 679 lines of output from my command.)

Run the command again with the **xargs** command acting as a buffer for the **cat** command. It reads all the output and individually feeds **cat** a single line as an argument until there are no more lines to feed to **cat**, like so:

```
find / -iname readme | xargs cat > mongofile.txt
```

Now use the **less mongofile.txt** command to verify that it worked as we originally intended. We now see that all the files have been enumerated and appended to each other to make one large file.

> **NOTE** Again, the **wc –l** command shows the resulting number of output lines, which after we used **xargs**, will be significantly larger, as the final mongofile.txt represents the catenation of all the output of the files, not just the output of the file listing as in the first command. (For reference, I got 76,097 lines of output from my command.)

Filters

A filter is a command that accepts **stdin** as input and performs an action, alteration, or other process on the input, producing **stdout** and (if necessary) **stderr** from it.

Sorting

The **sort** command is a typical filter. It takes a command as an argument or can have **stdin** sent to it; then it either performs a default sort or accepts a large number of options. A good example of how **sort** can help is to take a file (**file1**) that has the following lines in it:

```
Ross Brunson
Peabody McGillicuddy
Ursula Login
Snuffy Jones
```

Sorting this file with the default sort options produces the following output:

```
$ sort file1
Peabody McGillicuddy
Ross Brunson
Snuffy Jones
Ursula Login
```

The **sort** command uses fields to sort by, and the default field is **0**, or starting at the first column and ending at the first blank space. The typical field separator or delimiter is a space character or sometimes a tab. However, the delimiter can be set to be any nonblank character. This particular file was sorted by the first name of the listed people.

To sort by the last names, use the following command and options:

```
sort -k2 file1
Ross Brunson
Snuffy Jones
Ursula Login
Peabody McGillicuddy
```

Another useful option with **sort** is the **-n** (numeric sort) option. If a file contains numbered lines that start with 1 and go to 30, the standard **sort** would sort them as

```
sort numbers
1
11
12
13
```

NOTE The above output is truncated for readability.

To tell **sort** to read the longest number and pad the lower numbers with leading zeroes internally during the sorting process, you use the command shown here:

```
sort -n numbers
1
2
3
4
```

NOTE This illustrates is the difference between a "human-friendly" sort and a "machine" sort. When humans sort we typically want to see things progress from 1 to whatever eventual number, but this wouldn't make sense if you are doing a literal or machine sort.

Numbering Lines

The **nl** command is useful for numbering either every line in a file or stream of input, or just the lines with data on them. This is helpful when trying to troubleshoot source code or producing a list of numbered items automatically.

To number only the lines in a file that contain data, use this command:

```
nl file1
```

To number every line in a file, regardless of the line having data in it, use this:

```
nl -ba file1
```

Expect to see the **nl** command used with commands such as **pr** and **tac** chained or piped together to produce a particular output. Order matters, so be sure to notice whether the question wants to number all lines or just nonempty lines.

NOTE An actual example of using the **nl** command to number lines of a file occurred early on in the author's career. There was a large programming staff and we used to do printouts of the code base for team review. Until we discovered how to properly put line numbers on all lines of the file, as well as number the pages in an automated fashion, preparing for the meeting took a very long time.

In many situations, being able to determine the number of lines or words in a particular file or output is useful. The **wc** command shows items in any of three counts:

- **-l**—Lines of output

- **-w**—Words of output

- **-c**—Characters (or bytes) of output

For example, a great way to see how many users are on the system at a given time is to use **wc** to count the lines of output from the **who** or **w** commands:

```
who | wc -l
34
w | wc -l
36
```

Both of these commands were done on the same system, one right after the other, with the same number of users.

> **NOTE** The **w** command has two header lines counted by the **wc** program, whereas the **who** command simply outputs a line for each user. Be careful when using **wc** to count items without first viewing the raw output; otherwise, you'll misreport or represent inaccurate information.

Tabs

When output is formatted for the screen, a tab-delimited file can display with oddly placed columns due to the length of the data in each field. The **expand** command helps change tabs to a set number of spaces.

Consider a file that contains the following lines (the line numbers are just for reference):

```
1: steve        johnson
2: guillermo    villalobos
3: bo           regard
4: lawrence     aribacus
5: marge        innovera
```

If tabs were used to separate the data fields, lines 1, 3, and 5 would have two tabs between fields 1 and 2, so the columns would line up. Lines 2 and 4 would have only one tab, due to the length of the first field. **expand** *converts* the tabs to a set number of spaces, making the data display right in most cases.

> **NOTE** Watch out on the exams. You'll be presented with a number of plausible-sounding distractors for the **expand** command, possibly including the **convert** command, which is used to convert graphics file formats between each other.

Cutting Columns

There will be plenty of times when you need to take a file that contains columns of data, regardless of the delimiter or separator, and either extract information on a column-by-column basis or perhaps even reorder the columns to make it more usable. Although the objectives of the Level 1 of LPI's exams don't include the **awk** command (the king of columnar data), they do test you on the **cut** command, which is more than adequate for the task:

```
cut -c 20-40 /etc/passwd | tail -n 5
ar/spool/postfix:/bin
hare/pvm3:/bin/bash
ross brunson:/home/rb
home/snuffy:/bin/bash
:/home/quotaboy:/bin/
```

This displays only from column 20 to column 40 of **/etc/passwd,** excluding all other data on each line.

It can also grab certain fields from a file, such as the **/etc/passwd** file. To grab the username, description, and home directory fields for each user, use the following command:

```
cut -d: -f 1,5,6 /etc/passwd | tail -n 5
postfix::/var/spool/postfix
pvm::/usr/share/pvm3
rbrunson:ross brunson:/home/rbrunson
snuffy::/home/snuffy
quotaboy::/home/quotaboy
```

The **-d** option sets the delimiter, which in this case is the : character. By default, **cut** uses tabs for a delimiter.

Pasting and Joining

Two commands that are similar in function are **paste** and **join**. **paste** doesn't remove any data from the output, but **join** removes redundant key fields from the data.

For example, say you have the following files:

```
file1:
Line one of file1
Line two of file1
file2:
Line one of file2
Line two of file2
```

Using **paste** on these two files produces the output:

```
Line one of file1      Line one of file2
Line two of file1      Line two of file2
```

Notice that nothing is lost from the files. All the data is there, but this can be redundant in the extreme if you want to produce a joint file from two or more files.

The **join** command is more of a database join style than a catenation style (just paste one file's contents after the other on the same line). It takes a file as the first argument and by default treats the first field of that file as a key field. The second and subsequent files are treated in the same fashion. The output is each matching line of the files in order, minus the redundant key fields from any but the first file.

For example, say you have the following files, **users** and **location**:

```
users:
rbrunson:500:
snuffy:501:
quotaboy:502:
```

```
location:
rbrunson        123 anystreet    anytown ID      83858
snuffy          123 circle loop chicago IL       88888
quotaboy        123 some lane     anyburg MT      59023
```

As you can see, the output of these includes only the unique information from each file, leaving out the **location** key field:

```
join users location
rbrunson:500:   123 anystreet    anytown ID      83858
snuffy:501:     123 circle loop chicago IL       88888
quotaboy:502:   123 some lane     anyburg MT      59023
```

Unique Data

There will be times when you need to take a number of disparate files with similar data and produce a "master list" from them, such as when you consolidate servers.

One of the tasks to accomplish may be merging the **/etc/passwd** files. As long as all the users have the same UID/GID settings in each file, merging the files still makes an output file that contains multiple entries for various users.

> **NOTE** You should always sort the contents of a file you are about to use the **uniq** command on, as it will group the nonunique lines together and **uniq** will then remove all but one unique instance of a line.

For example, if you copied all the **/etc/passwd** files from three servers into a single file, running the following command outputs only the unique lines from the entire file:

```
uniq -u /etc/bigpasswd
rbrunson:x:500:500::/home/rbrunson:/bin/bash
snuffy:x:501:501::/home/snuffy:/bin/bash
quotaboy:x:502:502::/home/quotaboy:/bin/bash
```

The **-u** option causes only the unique lines from the file to be output, so the command shown here could be used to redirect the output to a new **/etc/passwd** file by just adding a redirection symbol and the new filename:

```
uniq -u /etc/bigpasswd > /etc/newpasswd
```

To print a single example of each line that is a duplicate in a file, use the following command:

```
uniq -d bigpasswd
```

To print every instance of each repeated line, use this command:

```
uniq -D bigpasswd
```

Heads or Tails?

The **head** command is used primarily (and by default) to see the first 10 lines of a given text file by default. **head** can be made to show a particular number of lines, starting at the top of the file. The **-n** parameter followed by the number of lines to be shown starting from the beginning of the file is used to show more than the default. This parameter is used in the following manner:

```
head -n 5 /etc/fstab
LABEL=/                    /                    ext3    defaults
1 1
none                       /dev/pts             devpts  gid=5,mode=620
```

```
0 0
none                        /proc                proc     defaults
0 0
none                        /dev/shm             tmpfs    defaults
0 0
/dev/hda6                   swap                 swap     defaults
0 0
```

The **head** command can't display ranges of lines, only from the beginning of the file.

The **tail** command is the exact opposite of the **head** command: It displays the last 10 lines of a given file by default and can be configured to show less or more lines, but only from the end of the file. It can't show ranges. Here's an example:

```
tail -n 5 /etc/passwd
netdump:x:34:34:Network Crash Dump user:/var/crash:/bin/bash
quagga:x:92:92:Quagga routing suite:/var/run/quagga:/sbin/nologin
radvd:x:75:75:radvd user:/:/sbin/nologin
rbrunson:x:500:500::/home/rbrunson:/bin/bash
snuffy:x:501:501::/home/snuffy:/bin/bash
```

The **tail** command is also useful for following log files, such as the **/var/log/messages** file to see the latest attempts to log on to the system:

```
tail -f /var/log/messages
```

This returns output similar to what's shown here:

```
Feb 23 21:00:01 localhost sshd(pam_unix)[29358]:
session closed for user root
Feb 23 21:00:04 localhost sshd(pam_unix)[29501]:
session opened for user root by (uid=0)
Feb 23 21:00:13 localhost sshd(pam_unix)[29501]:
session closed for user root
Feb 23 21:00:16 localhost sshd(pam_unix)[29549]:
session opened for user root by (uid=0)
```

When you combine the two commands truly interesting things become possible. For example, say you wanted to view lines 31 to 40 of a 50-line file. Remember that you can't display ranges with either of the commands, but by putting them together, you can display a range of lines from the file **50linefile** with the following command:

```
head -n 40 50linefile | tail
31
32  Both software and hardware watchdog drivers are available in the
```

```
standard
33   kernel. If you are using the software watchdog, you probably also want
34   to use "panic=60" as a boot argument as well.
35
36   The wdt card cannot be safely probed for. Instead you need to pass
37   wdt=ioaddr,irq as a boot parameter - eg "wdt=0x240,11".
38
39   The SA1100 watchdog module can be configured with the "sa1100_margin"
40   commandline argument which specifies timeout value in seconds.
```

Watch for the **head** and **tail** commands on the exam—particularly the **-f** option for following a log file's latest entries.

Splitting Files

The **split** command is useful for taking a large number of records and splitting them into multiple individual files that contain a certain amount of data.

The **split** command's options include (the **#** character represents a number of prefix characters)

- **-a #**—Uses a suffix a specified number of characters long (the default is **xaa**).
- **-b #**—Output files contain the specified number of bytes of data.
- **-c #**—Output files contain the specified number of lines of bytes of data.
- **-l #**—Output files contain the specified number of lines of data.

The **#** value can be b (which is 512 bytes), k (which is 1024 bytes), or m (which is 1024 kilobytes). For example, if you need to split an 8.8MB text file into 1.44MB chunks, you can use this command:

```
split -b1440000 bigtextfile.txt
ls -l x??
-rw-r--r--    1 root     root      1440000 Feb 23 09:25 xaa
-rw-r--r--    1 root     root      1440000 Feb 23 09:25 xab
-rw-r--r--    1 root     root      1440000 Feb 23 09:25 xac
-rw-r--r--    1 root     root      1440000 Feb 23 09:25 xad
-rw-r--r--    1 root     root      1440000 Feb 23 09:25 xae
-rw-r--r--    1 root     root      1440000 Feb 23 09:25 xaf
-rw-r--r--    1 root     root       249587 Feb 23 09:25 xag
```

> **NOTE** When taking the exams, you expected to split a file with a known number of lines into multiple component files, be able to determine the default names for the files, and know how many of them would be produced given the defaults for the **split** command.

When cat Goes Backward

In some cases you want to display a file backward or in reverse order, which is where the **tac** command comes in. You can use it like so:

```
cat file1
```

This produces output similar to the following:

```
1      Watchdog Timer Interfaces For The Linux Operating
2
3      Alan Cox <alan@lxorguk.ukuu.org.uk>
4
5      Custom Linux Driver And Program Development
```

Using **tac** on this file produces the following output:

```
tac file1
```

This produces output similar to

```
5      Custom Linux Driver And Program Development
4
3      Alan Cox <alan@lxorguk.ukuu.org.uk>
2
1      Watchdog Timer Interfaces For The Linux Operating
```

Viewing Binary Files Safely

Many times a sysadmin has accidentally used **cat** to send the contents of a file to the screen, only to have it apparently contain machine code or the Klingon language. Usually you can type **clear** and have the screen come back, and then you have to use something other than **cat** to view the contents of that file.

You would typically use the **od** command to safely view binary or non-ASCII files; otherwise, the display will likely become garbled and the system will beep plaintively as the console attempts to interpret the control codes in the binary file.

od is capable of displaying files in different methods, including

- **-a**—Named

- **-o**—Octal

- **-d**—Decimal

- **-x**—Hexadecimal

- **-f**—Floating point

Most of these formats aren't for daily use, with only the hexadecimal and octal formats displaying output of much interest.

> **NOTE** Watch out for questions about how to view binary files. The **od** command is just about the only possibility for such viewing. If you do have a problem with a garbled console after accidentally viewing a binary file, use the **reset** command. It re-initializes the terminal and makes it readable again. Another fun option is the **strings** command, which shows you the text contained in a binary file, instead of garbling up the screen.

Formatting Commands

The **pr** and **fmt** commands are used to do line wrapping and formatting for the printing of text streams or files and are often used with each other to format a set of text properly for a particular purpose, be it peer review or managers who like to think they can read code.

> **NOTE** We used the following 50linefile earlier and it's been numbered by the **nl** command, so if you are trying this and either don't have a file named 50linefile or yours is not numbered, go back and complete the previous examples where this is done.

The **pr** command is useful in formatting source code and other text files for printing. It adds a date and time block, the filename (if it exists), and page numbers to only the top of each formatted 66-line page, like so:

```
pr 50linefile
```

This produces output similar to what's shown here:

```
2112-02-23 21:19                     50linefile
Page 1


    1              Watchdog Timer Interfaces For The Linux Operating
System
    2
    3                   Alan Cox <alan@lxorguk.ukuu.org.uk>
    4
    5               Custom Linux Driver And Program Development
```

The **pr** command can display columns of data, cutting the columns to fit the number per page, like so:

```
pr --columns=2 50linefile
2004-02-23 21:02                     50linefile                        Page
1


    1              Watchdog Timer Inte     26  and some Berkshire cards.
T
    2                                      27  internal temperature in
deg
    3                   Alan Cox <a        28  giving the temperature.
    4                                      29
    5               Custom Linux D         30  The third interface logs
ke
```

The **fmt** command is useful for formatting text files too, but it's limited to wrapping long lines to fit on smaller pages or within columns that **pr** has set.

The previous example of **pr** columns chops the data off at the columns, losing data on the page. This can be fixed by mixing the commands, as shown here:

```
[root@localhost root]# fmt -35 50linefile | pr --column=2
2004-02-23 21:49                     50linefile
                  Page 1


    1         Watchdog              temperature.  29 30  The third
    Timer Interfaces For The        interface logs kernel messages
    Linux Operating System 2        on additional alert events.
    3               Alan Cox        31 32  Both software and
```

Translating Files

The **tr** command is for changing characters in files or streams, but not whole words or phrases—that's for **sed** to do.

For example, if you have a file that contains a lot of commands from a sample in a book, but some of the commands are dysfunctional because the editor capitalized the first characters of the lines, you can translate the file's uppercase letters to lowercase with the following command:

```
tr 'A-Z' 'a-z' < commands.txt
```

The **tr** command isn't capable of feeding itself, or accepting a file as an argument. It's unfair, but we often say that the **tr** command is less intelligent than **cat**, since **cat** can feed itself. As this is the case, the **<** operator is therefore mandatory when using **tr**; otherwise, the command won't work.

The following command can be used to accomplish the same results:

```
tr [:upper:] [:lower:] < commands.txt
```

> **NOTE** Remember that **tr** is incapable of feeding itself or accepting a file as an argument, so the < redirection symbol is needed to send the input file to the command. Anything else is a broken command and produces a syntax error.

He sed, She sed

The **sed**, or stream editor, command is used to process and perform actions on streams of text, such as the lines found in a text file. **sed** is amazingly powerful, which is a way of saying it can be difficult to use.

A good analogy of the way **sed** works is to imagine that your text file is a long string that stretches from one side of the room to the other. On that string, you can put special transforming beads and slide them down the string, having it perform that particular transformation as it slides along the string or the lines of the file. The neat thing about **sed** is that you can stack the beads or send them one behind the other and make what can appear to be an almost magical transformation of a text file occur with a single command or set of commands.

One of **sed**'s most-used operations is searching and replacing text, including words and complete phrases. Whereas **tr** works only on characters/numerals as individuals, **sed** is capable of complex functions, including multiple operations per line.

sed uses the following syntax for commands:

```
sed -option action/regexp/replacement/flag filename
```

Rather than struggle through an explanation of what happens when certain options are entered, let's see what **sed** does when we use those options. Using **sed** properly includes being able to, ahem, "reuse" **sed** commands from other sysadmins.

To replace the first instance of **bob** with **BOB** on each line in a given file, use this command:

```
sed s/bob/BOB/ file1
```

To replace all instances of **bob** with **BOB** on each line in a given file, use this command:

```
sed s/bob/BOB/g file1
```

sed allows for multiple operations on a given stream's lines, all of which are performed before going on to the next line.

To search for and replace **bob** with **BOB** and then search for **BOB** and replace it with **snuffy** for every line and every instance for a given file, use this:

```
sed 's/bob/BOB/g ; s/BOB/snuffy/g' file1
```

The use of a semicolon character is similar to bash's capability to run several commands independently of each other. However, this whole operation, from the first single quotation mark (') to the last single quotation mark is all performed inside **sed**, not as part of bash.

When **sed** is used for multiple commands, you can either use a semicolon to separate the commands or use multiple instances of **-e** to execute the multiple commands:

```
sed -e s/bob/BOB/g -e s/BOB/snuffy/g file1
```

On the exam, and whenever you might use **sed** with spaces in your patterns, bracket the whole pattern/procedure in single quotation marks, such as

```
sed 's/is not/is too/g' file1
```

This keeps you from getting syntax errors due to the spaces in the strings.

Sooner or later, you'll get tired of typing the same operations for **sed** and want to use a script or some method of automating a recurring task. **sed** has the capability to use a simple script file that contains a set of procedures. An example of the previous set of procedures in a **sed** script file is shown here:

```
s/bob/BOB/g
s/BOB/snuffy/g
```

This script file is used in the following manner:

```
sed -f scriptfile targetfile
```

Many multiple procedures can be performed on a single stream, with the whole set of procedures being performed on each successive line.

Obviously, doing a large number of procedures on a given text stream can take time, but it is usually worth it because you only need to verify that it worked correctly when it's done. It sure beats doing it all by hand in vi!

Another feature of **sed** is its capability to suppress or not have displayed any line that doesn't have changes made to it.

For example, if you want to replace **machine** with **MACHINE** on all lines in a given file but display only the changed lines, use the following command with the **-n** option to make the command suppress normal output:

```
sed -n 's/machine/MACHINE/pg' watchdog.txt
```

The **pg** string at the end prints the matched or changed lines and globally replaces for all instances per line, rather than just the first instance per line.

To do a search and replace on a range of lines, prefix the **s/** string with either a line number or a range separated by a comma, such as

```
sed -n '1,5s/server/SERVER/pg' sedfile
The X SERVER uses this directory to store the compiled version of the
current keymap and/or any scratch keymaps used by clients.  The X
SERVER
time.  The default keymap for any SERVER is usually stored in:
On the exam, the sed questions are all about what will find and
replace strings, with particular attention on global versus single
replaces.
```

Getting a grep

One of the more fun text-processing commands is **grep**. Properly used, it can find almost any string or phrase in a single file, a stream of text via **stdin**, or an entire directory of files (such as the kernel source hierarchy).

grep (global regular expression print) uses the following syntax for its commands:

```
grep -options pattern file
```

The **grep** command has many useful options, including

- **-c**—This option shows only a numeric count of the matches found, no output of filenames or matches.

- **-C #**—This option surrounds the matched string with X number of lines of context.

- **-H**—This option prints the filename for each match; it's useful when you want to then edit that file, as well as being the default option when multiple files are searched.

- **-h**—This option suppresses the filename display for each file and is the default when a single file is searched.

- **-i**—This option searches for the pattern with no case-sensitivity; all matches are shown.

- **-l**—This option shows only the filename of the matching file; no lines of matching output are shown.

- **-L**—This option displays the filename of files that don't have a match for the string.

- **-w**—This option selects only lines that have the string as a whole word, not part of another word.

- **-r**—This option reads and processes all the directories specified, along with all the files in them.

- **-x**—This option causes only exact line matches to be returned; every character on the line must match.

- **-v**—This option shows all the lines in a file that don't match the string; this is the exact opposite of the default behavior.

Examples of Using grep

grep can either use files and directories as the target argument or be fed **stdout** for parsing. An example of using **grep** to parse output follows:

```
who | grep ross
```

This command parses the **who** command's **stdout** for the name **ross** and prints that line if found.

A more complex example of **grep** being used is to combine it with another command, such as **find**:

```
find / -name readme -exec grep -iw kernel {} \;
```

The previous command finds all the files on the system named **readme** and then executes the **grep** command on each file, searching for any instance of the whole word **kernel** regardless of case. A whole word search finds the string *kernel* but not *kernels*.

The key to using the **-exec** option is to know that when the **find** command output is returned, instead of getting output as a series of full path and filenames of the found results, the output is fed to the command following the **-exec** option, represented by the {} character, and each line is then executed upon.

Example of a **find** command:

```
find ./ -iname file*.txt
/home/rossb/test/file.txt
/home/rossb/test/file1.txt
/home/rossb/test/file2.txt
```

Then when you add the **-exec** and **{} \;** string, it effectively is as if you had run each of the lines of output through the command you wanted to execute. The **find -exec** combination continues to execute on lines of output as long as they keep coming, ending when they are finished.

An innovative use of the **grep** command's options for finding strings is to have it show you lines that don't match the string. For example, you might want to check the **/etc/passwd** group periodically for a user that doesn't have a shadowed password:

```
grep -v :x: /etc/passwd
snuffy:$1$30238jrk$WcT15uH7V0EgxdtFTlxkK1:501:501::/home/snuffy:/bin/
bash
```

It looks like **snuffy** has an encrypted password in the **/etc/passwd** file. You should therefore run the **pwconv** command to fix this and make **snuffy** change his password immediately.

In classes, we usually spend a reasonable amount of time searching through man pages and additional documentation, reading the friendly manuals, as it were. Now and then a student sees an amusing phrase or a few words that strike them as funny in the documentation and that's when we take some time to show everyone how to use the **grep** command.

We all have some fun, there are any number of chuckles at what we find, and everyone ends up learning a lot about the use of **grep** and perhaps a few new ways to use its options.

Every attempt has been made to use this section as a learning tool by having the reader use **grep** to search for certain terms, the least disturbing having been chosen carefully. The ability to use **grep** and its options is essential to the exam.

> **NOTE** The use of the **tail** command and its options in the following examples is to limit the number of items of output so that it fits on a typical screen.

To search for the word "fool" in the additional documentation directories, use the following command (see Figure 6-3):

```
grep -ir fool /usr/share/doc | tail -n 15
```

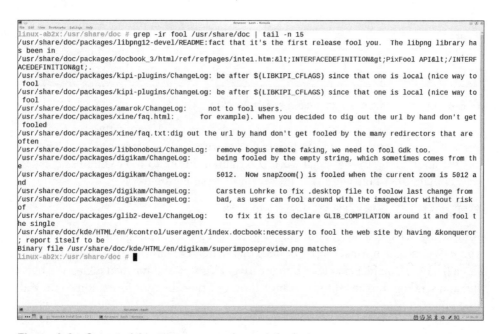

Figure 6-3 Output of the **grep** command search for fool

Notice that you got matches with the pattern "fool" as a whole word and as part of things like "fooled" or "foolish." Hit the "up" arrow and change the word "fool" to "foolish" and execute the command again (see Figure 6-4).

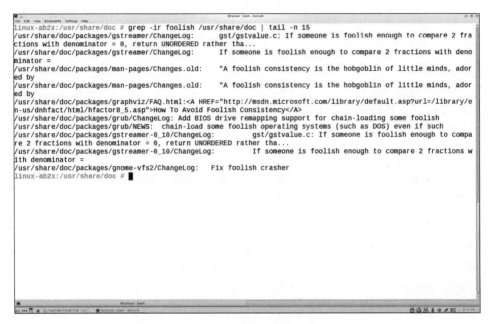

```
linux-ab2x:/usr/share/doc # grep -ir foolish /usr/share/doc | tail -n 15
/usr/share/doc/packages/gstreamer/ChangeLog:        gst/gstvalue.c: If someone is foolish enough to compare 2 fra
ctions with denominator = 0, return UNORDERED rather tha...
/usr/share/doc/packages/gstreamer/ChangeLog:        If someone is foolish enough to compare 2 fractions with deno
minator =
/usr/share/doc/packages/man-pages/Changes.old:    "A foolish consistency is the hobgoblin of little minds, ador
ed by
/usr/share/doc/packages/man-pages/Changes.old:    "A foolish consistency is the hobgoblin of little minds, ador
ed by
/usr/share/doc/packages/graphviz/FAQ.html:<A HREF="http://msdn.microsoft.com/library/default.asp?url=/library/e
n-us/dnhfact/html/hfactor8_5.asp">How To Avoid Foolish Consistency</A>
/usr/share/doc/packages/grub/ChangeLog: Add BIOS drive remapping support for chain-loading some foolish
/usr/share/doc/packages/grub/NEWS:  chain-load some foolish operating systems (such as DOS) even if such
/usr/share/doc/packages/gstreamer-0_10/ChangeLog:        gst/gstvalue.c: If someone is foolish enough to compa
re 2 fractions with denominator = 0, return UNORDERED rather tha...
/usr/share/doc/packages/gstreamer-0_10/ChangeLog:        If someone is foolish enough to compare 2 fractions w
ith denominator =
/usr/share/doc/packages/gnome-vfs2/ChangeLog:  Fix foolish crasher
linux-ab2x:/usr/share/doc # █
```

Figure 6-4 Output of the *grep* command search for "foolish"

Now let's consider that you want to just do a search for the exact word "fool," not any variation of it, just that exact word. To tighten this up to show you lines that only contain the whole word, add the **-w** option (see Figure 6-5):

```
grep -irw fool /usr/share/doc | tail -n 15
```

And finally, let's include a useful option to the **grep** command (**grep -I**) that allows you to see not the normal output of lines that match the item you are searching for, but a listing of the files that match the search. This is useful for then taking the output and sending it to an editor, stream editor, or other file transformation command (see Figure 6-6).

```
File Edit View Bookmarks Settings Help
linux-ab2x:/usr/share/doc # grep -irw fool /usr/share/doc | tail -n 15
/usr/share/doc/packages/librsvg-2-2/ChangeLog:          * acinclude.m4: Change comment so that we won't fool
/usr/share/doc/packages/ncurses/NEWS:    + the panel_window() function was not fool-proof.
/usr/share/doc/packages/libmjpegutils-2_0-0/README.lavpipe:fool proof at the moment. So if you feed matteblend.
flt the wrong number
/usr/share/doc/packages/sane-backends/ChangeLog:          Use MDL string instead of DES as it is mre fool proof
when matching
/usr/share/doc/packages/sane-backends/NEWS:    to scanning to fool the memory management and scanned a full pag
e
/usr/share/doc/packages/libpng16-devel/README:fact that it's the first release fool you.  The libpng library ha
s been in
/usr/share/doc/packages/libpng12-devel/README:fact that it's the first release fool you.  The libpng library ha
s been in
/usr/share/doc/packages/kipi-plugins/ChangeLog: be after $(LIBKIPI_CFLAGS) since that one is local (nice way to
 fool
/usr/share/doc/packages/kipi-plugins/ChangeLog: be after $(LIBKIPI_CFLAGS) since that one is local (nice way to
 fool
/usr/share/doc/packages/amarok/ChangeLog:    not to fool users.
/usr/share/doc/packages/libbonoboui/ChangeLog:  remove bogus remote faking, we need to fool Gdk too.
/usr/share/doc/packages/digikam/ChangeLog:     bad, as user can fool around with the imageeditor without risk
of
/usr/share/doc/packages/glib2-devel/ChangeLog:    to fix it is to declare GLIB_COMPILATION around it and fool t
he single
/usr/share/doc/kde/HTML/en/kcontrol/useragent/index.docbook:necessary to fool the web site by having &konqueror
; report itself to be
Binary file /usr/share/doc/kde/HTML/en/digikam/superimposepreview.png matches
linux-ab2x:/usr/share/doc # █
```

Figure 6-5   Output of the **grep** command search for "fool" as a whole word

```
File Edit View Bookmarks Settings Help
linux-ab2x:/usr/share/doc # grep -irwl fool /usr/share/doc | tail -n 15
/usr/share/doc/packages/gnutls/NEWS
/usr/share/doc/packages/librsvg-2-2/ChangeLog
/usr/share/doc/packages/ncurses/NEWS
/usr/share/doc/packages/libmjpegutils-2_0-0/README.lavpipe
/usr/share/doc/packages/sane-backends/ChangeLog
/usr/share/doc/packages/sane-backends/NEWS
/usr/share/doc/packages/libpng16-devel/README
/usr/share/doc/packages/libpng12-devel/README
/usr/share/doc/packages/kipi-plugins/ChangeLog
/usr/share/doc/packages/amarok/ChangeLog
/usr/share/doc/packages/libbonoboui/ChangeLog
/usr/share/doc/packages/digikam/ChangeLog
/usr/share/doc/packages/glib2-devel/ChangeLog
/usr/share/doc/kde/HTML/en/kcontrol/useragent/index.docbook
/usr/share/doc/kde/HTML/en/digikam/superimposepreview.png
linux-ab2x:/usr/share/doc # █
```

Figure 6-6   Output of the **grep** command search with options to show only path/files

The **grep** command is versatile. You can discover more of its useful options via the man page or other documentation. The discussion in this section is more than enough to be useful and covers the items typically on the exam.

> **NOTE** As a final recommendation, try adding the **-n** option to show the line number of found items within that file, and also the **-v** option for showing you not lines that match your query, but those lines that do not match your query. This is useful when you know what you don't want but don't quite know what you want.

Expanding grep with egrep and fgrep

The most important thing to know about **egrep** and **fgrep** is that they exist as commands primarily so you do not have to use **grep -E** and **grep -F**. Historically, there have been separate binaries, and indeed there are separate binaries on both the RPM-based distribution and the DPKG-based distribution we typically use.

The **egrep** command has many uses, but the main one we need to focus on is the ability to use **egrep** or **grep -E** to process search terms that feature operators, such as OR. For example, you may want to find lines in a very large /etc/passwd file that start with the letter "r" and the next letter is either "p" or "t" followed by any other letters. You can try the following:

```
egrep '^r(p|t)' /etc/passwd
```

This search finds the following lines, if they exist on your learning system:

```
rpc:x:490:65534:user for rpcbind:/var/lib/empty:/sbin/nologin
 rtkit:x:492:490:RealtimeKit:/proc:/bin/false
```

You can also search using **egrep** or **grep -E** for any line in the /etc/passwd file that contains "false" or "nologin" with the command:

```
egrep '(false|nologin)' /etc/passwd
```

This command should return a number of output lines, all of which have either "false" or "nologin" somewhere in the line.

The **fgrep** command is similar in execution, but it's essentially for using a file that contains a set of terms to be searched for, instead of having to specify them all separated by pipes. First create a file named **filetosearch.txt** and make it match the following output:

```
one
two
```

```
three
four
five
six
seven
eight
nine
ten
```

Then create a file named **searchterms.txt** and make it match the following output:

```
one
three
eight
```

Then run the following commands, which should produce the same output.

```
egrep '(one|three|eight)' filetosearch.txt
fgrep -f searchterms.txt filetosearch.txt
```

Essentially, it's easy to use **fgrep** to refer to a file for the discrete search terms you want to use; it is a much more elegant method than packing an **egrep** command line with a dozen or so search terms.

Don't forget that you can use [] ranges, globs (*) of text and several other special characters to help you display what you want using the **egrep** and **fgrep** commands.

Using Regular Expressions and grep

Using **grep** to find particular words and phrases can be difficult unless you use regular expressions. A regular expression has the capability to search for something that you don't know exactly, either through partial strings or using the following special characters:

- **.**—A period matches any single character and enforces that the character must exist (a.v is a three-letter regular expression).

- **?**—A question mark matches an optional item and is matched only once.

- *****—An asterisk matches from zero to many characters (**a*v** finds av, a2v, andv, and so on).

- **+**—A plus sign means that the item must be matched once and can be matched many times.

- **{n}**—A curly-bracketed number means that the item is matched n times.

- **{n,}**—A curly-bracketed number followed by a comma means the item is matched n or more times.

- **{n,m}**—A curly-bracketed pair of numbers separated by a comma matches from n to m times.

What's the use for all of this? Try finding just the word "Kernel" in the source tree with the following command:

```
grep -rl Kernel /usr/share/doc | wc -l
   138
```

The command finds 138 files that contain at least one match for Kernel. Now try finding just the word "Kernel" as a whole word with this command:

```
grep -rlw Kernel /usr/share/doc | wc -l
   131
```

Now try the same command again, but modify it so that the word "Kernel" is searched for, but only followed by a period:

```
grep -rwl Kernel\. /usr/share/doc | wc -l
   27
```

Now, let's search for the word "silly" as the search pattern:

```
grep -rwl silly /usr/share/doc | wc -l
   93
```

Run the command again with the context number set to 2 lines to get more information about what is being commented on:

```
grep -rwn -C2 silly /usr/share/doc
```

The output you see varies on different systems, but essentially you see consecutive lines preceded with the same filename and the number of the lines shown, so you see that there are two lines of context being shown above and below each found search term. This can be useful when trying to find a particular instance of a search term based on the lines around it.

You need to be familiar with how to use regular expressions on the exam, particularly how to find strings that start and end with a particular letter or letters but contain other text in between.

Another example of regular expressions in action is searching for a particular phrase or word, but not another that is similar.

The following file is **watch.txt** and contains the following lines:

```
01 The first sentence contains broad
```

```
02 The second contains bring
03 The third contains brush
04 The fourth has BRIDGE as the last word: bridge
broad 05 The fifth begins with BROAD
06 The sixth contains none of the four
07 This contains bringing, broadened, brushed
```

To find all the words that begin with "br" but exclude any that have the third letter as "i," use the following command:

```
grep "\<br[^i]" watch.txt
01 The first sentence contains broad
03 The third contains brush
broad 05 The fifth begins with BROAD
```

The **\<** string just means that the word begins with those letters. The use of the **[^i]** characters is to find all but the letter "i" in that position. If you use a **^** in front of a search term inside a program such as **vi**, it searches at the front of a line, but using the **^** symbol inside a set of square brackets is to exclude that character from being found.

To find a set of words that ends with a certain set, use this command:

```
grep "ad\>" watch.txt
01 The first sentence contains broad
broad 05 The fifth begins with BROAD
```

As with the previous example, using the **\>** characters on the end of a search looks for words that end in that string.

Search strings that **grep** allows include

- **broad**—Searches for exactly "broad," but as part of other words (such as "broadway" or "broadening") unless you use **-w** to cause broad to be searched for as a standalone word

- **^broad**—Searches for the word "broad" at the beginning of any line

- **broad$**—Searches for the word "broad" at the end of the line

- **[bB]road**—Searches for the words "broad" and "Broad."

- **br[iou]ng**—Searches for "bring," "brong," and "brung"

- **br[^i]ng**—Searches for and returns all but "bring"

- **^......$**—Searches for any line that contains exactly six characters

- **[bB][rR]in[gG]**—Searches for "Bring," "BRing," "BRinG," or any combination thereof

Summary

In this chapter you learned about input and output streams, how to pipe data between programs, and how to write data from programs output into a file. We also covered the filtering of information that comes from programs, how to format that information to make it more useful, and how to use the various versions of **grep** and regular expressions to further separate out and find data.

Exam Preparation Tasks

As mentioned in the section "How to Use This Book" in the Introduction, you have a few choices for exam preparation: the exercises here, Chapter 21, "Final Preparation," and the practice exams on the DVD.

Review All Key Topics

Review the most important topics in this chapter, noted with the Key Topics icon in the outer margin of the page. Table 6-3 lists a reference of these key topics and the page numbers on which each is found.

Table 6-3   Key Topics for Chapter 6

Key Topic Element	Description	Page Number
Table 6-2	Linux file descriptors	154
Paragraph	**stderr** and **stdout**	155
Paragraph	Changing the destination of **stderr**, **stdout**, and **stdin**	156
Figure 6-1	Path of data streams	158
Paragraph	Trapping output of a command and sending it to **/dev/null**	158
Paragraph	Using pipe (I)	159
Note	Exceptions for pipe (I)	160
List	Operators ;, &&, I I	161
Paragraph	Using the backtick (`)	162
Paragraph	The **export** command	162
Paragraph	The **tee** command	163
Paragraph	The **xargs** command	163
Paragraph	The numeric set (**-n**) option	165

Key Topic Element	Description	Page Number
Paragraph	The **nl** command	166
Paragraph	The **expand** command	167
Output	Grabbing the username, description, and home directory fields for each user	168
Paragraph	The **join** command	169
Paragraph	The **–u** option	170
Paragraph	The **head** command	171
Paragraph	The **od** command	173
Paragraph	The **pr** and **fmt** commands	174
Paragraph	Using the **sed** command to search and replace text	176
Paragraph	The **-exec** option	180
Paragraph	The **egrep** and **fgrep** commands	184
Section	Using regular expressions and **grep**	185

Define Key Terms

Define the following key terms from this chapter and check your answers in the glossary:

pipe, redirect, convert, standard in, standard out, standard error, catenate, append

Review Questions

The answers to these review questions are in Appendix A.

1. When executing a command, you want the output, both standard error and standard out to not be displayed on the console. Which of the following accomplishes this? (Choose two.)

   a. **command1 1> /dev/null 2> /dev/null**

   b. **command1 1+2> /dev/null**

   c. **command1 12>> /dev/null**

   d. **command1 stdout> /dev/null +stderr**

   e. **command1 > /dev/null 2>&1**

2. You want to add a log entry in a file named output.txt. This entry includes the output of a particular command that includes a timestamp and unique and critical data each time it is run. You don't want to overwrite the current contents of the output.txt file. Which of the following operators causes the proper result to happen?

   a. !<

   b. >>

   c. <>

   d. >

   e. <<

3. As the sysadmin of a financial organization, you receive a real-time feed of information that your web team uses to display financial data to customers. You must keep a log of the data you receive as well as send that data on for further processing.

   Which of the following commands would you use to accomplish this?

   a. tac

   b. split

   c. tee

   d. branch

   e. culvert

4. While sorting a file that has numbers at the beginning of the lines, you notice that **sort** seems to oddly order the lines, as follows:

   1

   11

   12

   20

   What option to the **sort** command could you use to get a more human-friendly sorting of the file?

   a. -n

   b. -k

   c. -t

   d. -h

5. You are using vi or another text editor to write a technical article for your organization's website, and the instructions from the site's editor are to keep the word count to 500 and the character count to less than 2,000.

Which utility would you typically use to see these statistics for a given text file?

    a. count

    b. num

    c. wc

    d. pr

    e. ed

This chapter covers the following topics:

- Managing Processes
- Sending Signals to Processes
- Job Control
- Managing Process Priorities
- Leaving Programs Running after Logout

This chapter covers the following objectives:

- Create, monitor, and kill processes: 103.5
- Modify process execution priorities: 103.6

## CHAPTER 7

Process Management

Processes and process management are key to a sysadmin's daily work, in that almost everything that runs on your system can be viewed as a process, a hierarchy of related processes, or interrelated processes that depend on each other to be present, working, and responsive.

"Do I Know This Already?" Quiz

The "Do I Know This Already?" quiz enables you to assess whether you should read this entire chapter or simply jump to the "Exam Preparation Tasks" section for review. If you are in doubt, read the entire chapter. Table 7-1 outlines the major headings in this chapter and the corresponding "Do I Know This Already?" quiz questions. You can find the answers in Appendix A, "Answers to the 'Do I Know This Already?' Quizzes."

Table 7-1 "Do I Know This Already?" Foundation Topics Section-to-Question Mapping

Foundation Topics Section	Questions Covered in This Section
Managing Processes	1
Sending Signals to Processes	2
Job Control	3
Managing Process Priorities	4
Leaving Programs Running after Logout	5

1. Which of the following commands can show you a treelike hierarchy of processes and information about them? (Choose all that apply.)

   a. procheir

   b. lsproc

   c. ps

   d. pstree

   e. gvfs-tree

2. Which of the following sets of keystrokes pause or stop a program's execution and allow you to run job control on it?

   a. Ctrl-c

   b. Ctrl-z

   c. Ctrl-p

   d. Ctrl-q

   e. Ctrl-f

3. When you run the **jobs** command, you see the following output:

   ```
           linux-8z04:~ # jobs
   [1]-   Stopped                 top
   [2]+   Stopped                 vim
   [3]    Running                 strace top &
   ```

   If you were to run the **fg** command at this time, what would happen?

   a. The **top** command would be brought to the foreground.

   b. The **strace** command would be brought to the foreground.

   c. Nothing.

   d. The **vim** command would be brought to the foreground.

4. As the sysadmin of a system, you notice in the **top** command output that a particular command is using an inordinate amount of system resources. Which of the following keystrokes or commands would alter the process priority for the unruly command? (Choose two.)

   a. nice

   b. renice

   c. ps -nice

   d. r

   e. kill -nice

5. You are tasked with running a large set of automated reports that have been scripted to be run as the root user. From experience, you know that these reports often take longer than the 8-hour workday, and you're on salary now so you're uninterested in pulling an all-nighter.

Which of the following commands would let you run your script unattended, even after you log out for the evening? (Choose all that apply.)

   a. nohup

   b. exec

   c. screen

   d. unattend

   e. control

Foundation Topics

Managing Processes

Managing programs and processes is essential to running a Linux machine. Various utilities can help you manage those processes. Let's begin with viewing processes and then move on to removing processes. Finally, we affect process priorities.

Viewing Processes

When you need to see what's running on your machine, regardless of any GUI tools or programs, you can use the **ps** command. The **ps** command is used to display process information and has switches to format the output.

For example, to show the processes started by this user and the user's shell, just type the **ps** command, like so:

```
ps
 PID TTY          TIME CMD
19856 pts/0    00:00:00 bash
20057 pts/0    00:00:00 ps
```

This is the simplest view of your system's processes, but it leaves out a lot of back-grounded or nonterminal-associated processes. The **-a** option shows essentially any process that the current user has started besides the actual bash shell. Use the following to show progressively more information:

```
ps -a
  PID TTY          TIME CMD
 1497 tty1     00:00:00 startx
 1510 tty1     00:00:00 xinit
 1523 tty1     00:00:00 gnome-session
 1528 tty1     00:00:00 xinitrc <defunct>
15075 pts/1    00:00:00 ps
... output truncated for readability.
```

Obviously, you got more information because a switch is used for showing all processes that are terminal-bound. That means if another user is on the system, you can see her processes listed too.

Now type the following:

```
ps -a | wc -l
    66
```

The important number is the one reported by the **wc** command: It's the number of lines in the output. Each one represents a running process. This machine has 66 processes found by the **ps** command.

More **ps** command switches to know are as follows:

- **a**—Shows all processes for all users
- **u**—Shows user information for processes
- **x**—Shows processes without a controlling tty

What's the Diff?

There's a lot of confusion among junior sysadmins about why you use **ps aux** sometimes and **ps -aux** at other times.

The man page isn't very helpful either, but it does tell you why the dash is used and why it's not. Linux's version of the **ps** command is a latecomer. There are two main parents to this version: BSD and POSIX, offering differing but similar ways of doing commands and options.

The BSD style of using options with the **ps** command is that you can group them, aka "aux," but they must not use a preceding dash. The POSIX or UNIX method is that you can group them, again "aux," but they must be preceded with a dash, as in **ps -aux**.

In short, the two methods are similar, and Linux's version of **ps** allows for either method.

Use the **pstree** command to show the hierarchical nature of the processes on the system, such as the following example:

```
init-+-apmd
     |-atd
     |-bdflush
     |-bonobo-activati
     |-crond
     |-cupsd
     |-dhcpcd
     |-evolution-alarm
     |-gconfd-2
     |-gnome-cups-mana
     |-gnome-name-serv
     |-gnome-panel
     |-gnome-settings-
```

```
|-gnome-smproxy
|-gnome-terminal-+-bash
|                        `-mgt-pty-helper
```

> **NOTE**   The **ps** and **pstree** commands have many options. It's good to be aware of as many as possible, especially for when you take the exam. Both commands have the capability of showing the system's running processes in a treelike or hierarchical fashion.

Attention, older or seasoned Unix users: There will likely be questions that test how well you know the **ps** command, including what Linux uses as the equivalent of the command:

```
ps -ef
```

Verify how similar **ps –ef** is to **ps aux** with the following:

```
ps -ef > psef
ps -aux > psaux
vimdiff psef psaux
```

You find a number of similarities between the two output streams. The **ps aux** command is from Linux, whereas **ps –ef** originates from Unix.

The free Command

The **free** command is used to determine the amount of free memory on the system, not just by displaying the amount of unused system RAM, but also by giving you more detailed information about how much free and in-use physical memory you have, how much swap space or disk-based fake memory is in use, and finally how much of the used system RAM is being taken up by buffers and caches.

There is a moment in every class we teach where the student/attendee looks at the output of the **free** command and gets a quizzical look on her face, because she can't reconcile the actual amount of RAM in use on the system with the current load. We always take the time to explain that system RAM on a lightly utilized system is like a bus that is only half full of passengers. Everyone has room in the seat next to them for magazines, snacks, and drinks and ample room to stretch out a bit.

We then make the correlation between the passenger and a running process, and the room the passenger has allocated to her is similar to the working set (everything needed to run) for a process. The key here is that when lightly loaded, the system can allocate otherwise unused system RAM to handy and useful items such as cache and buffers, and the processes can stretch out a bit and have fully loaded working sets for efficient running of that process.

Blocks and Buffers

Key to the running of processes and the speed of processing on the system are blocks and buffers. Block devices such as disks have an addressable unit called a *block*. This is typically (not always, but often) 512 bytes in size. System software also uses a construct called a block, but it's typically much larger than the physical size of a block on a hard disk or other block device.

When a disk block is read into system memory, it's stored in what is called a "buffer." Buffers are associated with one and only one block, and that buffer is how the data contained in that block is addressed while in memory.

Pages, Slabs, and Caches

Pages are how the kernel manages memory on your system. The processor can address very small units of memory, aka a "word" or "byte," but the memory management unit uses pages and only addresses memory in page-sized chunks. The kernel addresses every single page of the memory in the struct_page table and includes information critical to managing that page in each page's entry there.

Pages are frequently populated with the same data, read from buffers and written back to *caches* for later reading. The system manages its own structure and marks pages as being used, free, or a number of other flags or parameters entirely secondary to our purpose here.

Caches are made up of *slabs*, which are one or more contiguous pages, although most of the time a slab is only one page. To illustrate the relationship between a cache and a slab, we can say the cache is a city, the slab is a neighborhood, and the page is a block in that neighborhood.

To sum this all up, blocks are a data location on disk, buffers are what blocks are read into when a file or set of files is requested from disk, and then when those buffers are read into a page in memory, that page is a part of a slab or set of slabs that make up a cache.

To continue the bus and passenger analogy, remember that a lightly loaded system shows a large utilization of RAM but also a correspondingly hefty use of cache and buffers, while a heavily loaded system, one with many processes running, shows a lot of RAM in use but relatively low cache and buffers. Effectively, as you load up the system with more processes, all the passengers/processes have to tighten up their working sets, put their magazines, snacks, extra luggage, and drinks in the overhead rack or under the seat and be respectful of their fellow passengers/processes.

Interpreting Displayed Information from free

free has a number of options, but before showing you execution examples, it's important to discuss and define the columns of output you see.

```
total  Total installed memory (MemTotal and SwapTotal in /proc/
meminfo)
used   memory (calculated as total - free)
free   Unused memory (MemFree and SwapFree in /proc/meminfo)
shared   Memory  used  (mostly) by tmpfs (Shmem in /proc/
meminfo, available on kernels 2.6.32, displayed as zero if not
available)
buffers   Memory used by kernel buffers (Buffers in /proc/
meminfo)
cached   Memory used by the page cache (Cached in /proc/
meminfo)
```

These definitions are from the **free** man page, and as you look at the following, remember that all this information is available in raw formats in the **/proc/meminfo** directory in the various files mentioned. All the **free** command does is read that data and display it in a more organized and configurable manner for your viewing pleasure.

> **NOTE**   The **free** command is like a number of other system utilities. It allows you to display its counts or data in a couple of modes, the first being "here's a huge number in bytes, good luck converting that to something mere humans can understand." Or you can just use the -h option; it converts the numeric values into bytes, kilobytes, megabytes, gigabytes, and even terabytes, as shown in Figure 7-1. You may see this referenced on an exam item, so pay close attention to the examples.

```
rbrunson@linux-ab2x:~> free -h
              total        used        free      shared     buffers      cached
Mem:           2.0G        1.2G        802M         20M        876K        744M
-/+ buffers/cache:         458M        1.5G
Swap:          2.0G          0B        2.0G
rbrunson@linux-ab2x:~> █
```

Figure 7-1   Running the free command with the **-h** option

Look at the total column in Figure 7-1. That's the total RAM on the virtual machine we are running the **free** command on. The next two columns, used and free, tell you exactly how much RAM is being used and what remains not in use.

The buffers and cached columns are the amount of RAM currently being used to store the cache and buffers, and these will likely change over time and with differing amounts of loads. If you want to see some of these items change, in particular the cached column, execute the **find / -iname ".txt"** command to find every text file on your system you have access to, and you'll see the cached column expand as it predictively loads a lot of files that the system now assumes you might read or use another utility upon.

Then run the **free** command again to see the changes made to the numbers, particularly the cached column, as many files were found and predictively cached in case you might need to read them, and that read would be from memory, not from disk.

Additionally, you can use the **--lohi** long option to get a more detailed summary of the information. It's helpful to also include the **-h** option to get the summary information in **kb/mb/gb etc** (see Figure 7-2).

```
rbrunson@linux-ab2x:~> free --lohi -h
              total       used       free     shared    buffers     cached
Mem:           2.0G       1.2G       801M        20M       876K       745M
Low:           2.0G       1.2G       801M
High:            0B         0B         0B
-/+ buffers/cache:        458M       1.5G
Swap:          2.0G         0B       2.0G
rbrunson@linux-ab2x:~> 
```

Figure 7-2 Running the **free** command with the **--lohi** option

System Uptime

The obvious usage for the **uptime** command is to determine how long the system has been "up" or running since reboot.

What's not obvious but is handy information is the number of users currently on the system and the average number of *jobs* in the run *queue* for the processor(s) over the last 1/5/15 minutes.

The jobs in the run queue information can be helpful in determining why a system might be slow, or seem sluggish. Too many jobs in the queue means that either the system is heavily overloaded or undergoing a lot of wait time for data to be read from disk, rather than from caches in memory, as per the previous section.

A possible fix for this is to start monitoring the number of processes and how much swap space is being used. A higher number of processes and an active amount of swap in use, not allocated but actually in use, indicates the system is overloaded.

A lightly loaded system returns uptime output similar to the following:

```
14:22pm  up 3 days  3:34,  3 users,  load average:  0.00,  0.02,  0.05
```

> **NOTE** I know some sysadmins who have a cron job that runs **top** and **uptime** once every 30 minutes, and sends the output to them as an email, just so they can periodically see what is happening without constantly monitoring the system. This is a quick and easy way to get important information.

Sending Signals to Processes

Traditionally, when learning about *signals* and processes, you're introduced to a list of signals, with the explanations to the right of the signal, and then taught about the **kill** and **killall** commands. If you're lucky and your teacher likes to use **pgrep** or **pkill**, you learn a bit about those as well.

Table 7-2 shows the commonly used signal names, their numeric equivalents, and what the signal does to a process.

Table 7-2 List of Common Linux Signals

SIGINT	2	Interrupt a process (used by **Ctrl-C**)
SIGHUP	1	Hang up or shut down and restart process
SIGKILL	9	Kill the process (cannot be ignored or caught elsewhere)
SIGTERM	15	Terminate signal, (can be ignored or caught)
SIGTSTP	20	Stop the terminal (used by **Ctrl-z**)
SIGSTOP	19	Stop execution (cannot be caught or ignored)

The most common way to send a signal to a given process is by pressing the **Ctrl-C** keys while the command or script is processing and not interrupting the process unnecessarily. If you wait a reasonable amount of time and nothing happens, or the process seems locked up, by all means interrupt the process; just be aware you might lose a small bit of data or suffer other unintended consequences.

> **NOTE** Obviously, if you are running a data-generating command, interruption might be of consequence, but merely interrupting a long file search or output command is relatively risk free.

Another common method of sending a signal to a running process is to use the **Ctrl-z** keystrokes to send the process a SIGTSTP or 20 signal, effectively pausing the process, which will most often then be backgrounded by the **bg** command, as in job control. This is covered in the "Job Control" section later in the chapter.

Killing Processes by PID

The normal method for stopping a process is to use either the **kill** or **killall** utility to send a polite kill to it. When you encounter a process that can't be removed from memory, because it's not receiving signals or perhaps due to sheer orneriness, you need to kill the process and remove it from memory.

Remember, the **kill** and **killall** commands simply send a signal to the process—they don't actually remove the processes themselves.

The default kill signal is number 15, and the signal name is SIGTERM. This politely requests the process to end, allowing it to clean up its memory. If you type the **kill** command and the process ID (*PID*) of a program, the 15 or SIGTERM signal is sent to that program.

The SIGHUP, HUP, or 1 signal is a special case. It's what we could call a bounce signal, where the process isn't just killed but instead is signaled to end and then restart itself. The most frequently used reason for doing this is to have a process such as a server daemon stop, reread its configuration files, and then start back up. You can specify this signal by either -1 or -hup.

```
kill -1 PID or kill -HUP PID(bounces or restarts processes)
```

> **NOTE** Many a server admin has had to "bounce" a service on a server, either to reread a configuration file or to get the service working again after it mysteriously stopped working. Exam-takers will likely see this; it's a commonly missed section of this topic.

The SIGKILL or 9 signal is the ultimate kill signal. Even if a process is a zombie (can't be killed by any other means), a **kill -9 PID** command usually kills the process and removes it from memory. The process being SIGKILLed has no opportunity to save data or do anything else.

```
        kill -9 PID or kill -KILL PID (puts a bullet in the process,
no saves)
```

Killing Processes by Other Criteria

Sometimes you can't kill a process by the PID—either it's unavailable or you can't find it in the process table using the **ps** command and so on. Other times, there may be so many similarly named processes that you don't want to take the considerable time it would entail to kill them all by PID, or you don't really care which process it is; you want to clean house of that particular sort of named or similar process and reexecute the command.

The most common way to kill multiple similarly named processes is the **killall** command. I used to joke that the command was created by an insanely frustrated Netscape Communicator user who had programming skills, so he could clear off all the "netscape" processes on his machine and restart the browser, but this might not be completely true. (Although, from my experience, it should be.) You might experience this problem with Google's Chrome browser, so if you prefer, use Chrome in your **killall** commands.

Using **killall** is simple. You can run **ps aux** and find out the name(s) of the processes you want to kill and then use the **killall** command followed by the name, such as:

```
killall  processname
```

On a more elegant or complex level, you can use the **pkill** or **process kill** command, which isn't just limited to the use of the process's command name but can find and send signals to processes based on numerous criteria, including

- Process name
- Process ID
- Username
- Process or session ID
- Terminal

Usage of **pkill** is not that complex, but if you use multiple criteria, such as username and controlling terminal, all the criteria must match, or the signal won't be sent. The **pkill** command has a companion app, **pgrep**, which is most often used to test out your desired **pkill** command before figuratively pulling the trigger on it.

Another great and useful feature of **pgrep** is that you can use it to find processes and then feed them to another command, such as **renice**. As an example, to find all running Chrome browser processes and change the *priority* level on them, you could use the following command:

```
renice +5  'pgrep chrome'
```

This finds all the "chrome" named processes in the process table and executes the **renice +5** command on them, effectively dropping their priority from the default.

When using **pkill**, you typically use the same command and options used with **pgrep**, only **pkill** goes ahead and executes the signal pass on the process, instead of sending the output to stdout or the *console*, like **pgrep** usually does.

> **NOTE**   A quick warning about using **killall** or **pkill** as the root user: If you do run the command as root, it kills all the processes on the system that match the criteria, regardless of the owner, which may not be what you wanted. It also introduces you to all your users, as they call to ask what happened on the server. The safest way to run these commands are as a normal user or very carefully as the root user.

Job Control

Job control was invented when users had access to only a single terminal and getting more work done usually required another terminal. Job control allows the user to run multiple commands in a background mode while working in the foreground application.

When using the shell, a program can be run, suspended, and then put into the background, or the command can be invoked and put into the background in one step.

> **NOTE**   When you are putting commands into the background, you use the & character at the end of the command line, separated by a space, such as **command1 -option &**. This will background the command at execution time.

The following steps show how to use job control:

1. Start a task such as an editor.

2. Suspend the program by pressing Ctrl+Z.

3. Execute the **jobs** command to see the status:

```
jobs
[1]+ Stopped                vim
```

4. Send job # 1 to the background by typing **bg** and pressing Enter:

```
bg
[1]+ vim &
```

5. Now start another program such as top in the background with the following:

```
top &
```

6. Run the **jobs** command to see which jobs are there and how they are numbered:

```
jobs
[1]- Stopped          vim
[2]+ Stopped          top
```

When looking at the **jobs** command output, there are three designations a job can have:

- A plus sign (+) next to it indicates the current job, and any commands such as **fg** or **bg** act on that job by default.

- A minus sign (-) next to it indicates the previous job or the next-to-last job to be operated on.

- Lack of a character indicates it's just a regular job, and no actions are taken on it unless specified by job number.

7. Put the default job into foreground mode with the **fg** command.

8. The **top** command should come to the foreground.

9. Quit the **top** command by pressing Q.

10. Run the jobs command again and notice that the vim job is now the current job again.

11. Kill the vim job by typing its ID with the **kill** command:

```
kill %1
Vim: Caught deadly signal TERM
Vim: Finished.
```

12. Run the jobs command again; you see the results of your action as reported by the Job Control function. In this case, job # 1 is terminated.

NOTE   Be prepared to answer a question on the exam about what command or characters might put a process into the background or foreground a process listed in the **jobs** command output. You should also know what the **jobs** command + symbol indicates.

Managing Process Priorities

Linux uses a combination of priority and scheduling to run multiple processes in what appears to be multitasking on a single processor. On multiple processors, this makes for actual multitasking.

Strangely enough, the process priorities are backward, like a lot of other things, and they stretch from the highest (-20) to the lowest (19) (see Figure 7-3).

Figure 7-3 Linux process priorities

A process's default priority is normally 0 when started, unless the programmer needs to set the starting priority higher. Although users can start a process with a lower (from 0 to 19) priority, only the root user can start a process with a higher (0 to -20) priority.

Many a sysadmin has discovered too late what it means to have multiple programs running at too high a priority. Too many processes with high priorities can slow a machine drastically, cause it to become unresponsive, and even cause crashes.

There are two main methods to specify or alter a process's priority: at program start and while it's running.

To start a program with a lower priority (the default), use the **nice** command, such as

```
nice kitty.sh
```

This causes the kitty.sh script to run at a priority of 10. The **nice** utility makes programs play nice with others, relieving some of the stress of running multiple processor or I/O-intensive programs.

You can also specify a priority using the **-n** option followed by the increment you want to alter the default priority by, such as

```
nice -n 10 kitty.sh
```

To change a process's priority while it's running, you use the **renice** program, such as shown here:

```
ps aux | grep mybigcompile
rbrunson  14729  19.2  0.6  1656  524/pts/0  R  01:30  mybigcompile
renice +5 14729
```

This command string causes the process mybigcompile (process ID 14729) to run at an altered priority of +5. When using the **renice** utility, there isn't a default priority—one must be specified.

NOTE   A regular user can only change an existing process to a lower priority, that is, a higher number. Only the root user can change a process's priority to any value.

The other option for altering a running program's priority is a feature of the **top** command. The **top** command shows a refreshing screen of processes with the highest CPU usage, configurable to show only active processes or a specific number of processes (see Figure 7-4).

```
 rbrunson@localhost:~                                                    _ □ X

 File   Edit   Settings   Help

  1:39am  up 35 min,  3 users,   load average: 0.60, 1.33, 1.77
 65 processes: 60 sleeping, 4 running, 1 zombie, 0 stopped
 CPU states:  9.5% user, 58.3% system,  0.0% nice, 32.0% idle
 Mem:     78096K av,   76932K used,    1164K free,      OK shrd,      3104K buff
 Swap:   771112K av,   25000K used,   746112K free                   47112K cached

   PID USER      PRI  NI  SIZE  RSS SHARE STAT %CPU %MEM    TIME COMMAND
 14811 root       25   0  2056 1996  1480 R    56.6  2.5   1:11 sshd
  1511 root       15   0 26092 5896  4088 S     5.1  7.5   0:35 X
 14862 root       15   0  1068 1068   652 S     2.1  1.3   0:03 sftp-server
  1704 rbrunson   15   0  9900 6516  5680 R     0.9  8.3   1:04 rhn-applet
  3831 rbrunson   15   0  2076 1612  1144 S     0.3  2.0   0:13 vmware-toolbox
 14887 rbrunson   15   0  1040 1040   836 R     0.3  1.3   0:00 top
  1325 root       15   0   432  416   368 S     0.1  0.5   0:05 vmware-guestd
  1628 rbrunson   15   0  2984 2748  2664 S     0.1  3.5   0:03 magicdev
  1632 rbrunson   15   0 12072  11M  8512 S     0.1 14.5   0:05 nautilus
     1 root       15   0   472  428   420 S     0.0  0.5   0:05 init
     2 root       15   0     0    0     0 SW    0.0  0.0   0:00 keventd
     3 root       15   0     0    0     0 SW    0.0  0.0   0:00 kapmd
     4 root       34  19     0    0     0 SWN   0.0  0.0   0:00 ksoftirqd_CPU0
     5 root       15   0     0    0     0 SW    0.0  0.0   0:10 kswapd
     6 root       15   0     0    0     0 SW    0.0  0.0   0:04 bdflush
     7 root       15   0     0    0     0 SW    0.0  0.0   0:00 kupdated
     8 root       25   0     0    0     0 SW    0.0  0.0   0:00 mdrecoveryd
    16 root       15   0     0    0     0 SW    0.0  0.0   0:03 kjournald
   136 root       15   0     0    0     0 SW    0.0  0.0   0:00 kjournald
   518 root       16   0   616  548   548 S     0.0  0.7   0:00 dhcpcd
   592 root       15   0   552  504   476 S     0.0  0.6   0:00 syslogd
   598 root       15   0   444  428   420 S     0.0  0.5   0:00 klogd
   618 rpc        15   0   544  512   464 S     0.0  0.6   0:00 portmap
   646 rpcuser    15   0   692  600   600 S     0.0  0.7   0:00 rpc.statd
   774 root       15   0   464  412   412 S     0.0  0.5   0:00 apmd
```

Figure 7-4   The **top** command

top reads its configuration from /etc/toprc or .toprc, where it can be restricted for use by users, removing some of the dangerous features. **top** runs interactively by default, refreshing every 5 seconds.

To make **top** do some fun things, try these:

- **top d 1**—Runs and refreshes every 1 sec.

- **top i**—Shows only active processes, may be toggled on and off

Some of the interactive (inside **top**) options you can use are

- **space**—Updates the display immediately.
- **h**—Provides help for **top**.
- **k**—Kills a process; a prompt appears for the PID.
- **i**—Either displays or ignores zombie/idle processes.
- **n**—Is prompted for the number of processes to display.
- **r**—Prompts for the PID to affect and then provides the new priority.

> **NOTE** You can sort the output of the **top** command by pressing the R key to sort the PIDs from high to low, a reverse sort. You can also invoke **top** with the **-o** option and specify a sort field to show sorted on that field immediately.

Finally, you can use the **top** command as a "fire and forget" command to send the current **top** output to you via email using the following command:

```
top -b -n 1 | mail root@yourserver.xxx -s "Top output from Server 1"
```

This command runs **top** in its batch mode (**-b**) one iteration or time (**-n 1**) and sends the output not to the console, but to the email address indicated with the subject line (**-s**) indicated. Try this on your local system and then check system mail by running **mail**. You'll see the subject line for the email and you can read the output.

Leaving Programs Running after Logout

A common problem exists when you are a systems administrator who runs commands on the command line on servers that don't have a GUI desktop or component: How do you log out and leave for a minute/hour/day and let a command or utility continue to run?

Related and similar is the question: How can you leave a command line *session* and go get a cup of coffee or tea or otherwise use the facilities without leaving your root user session hanging out and vulnerable?

There is a utility that shares a name, or part of a name, with the SIGHUP signal. It's the **nohup** command, and it's designed to be used in front of a command that you want to continue running even after the controlling tty or console has been exited. Think of it as setting a balloon free into a hangar or warehouse. The balloon represents the process to set free, and the building represents your machine's memory space.

Using this utility lets you run the command and then log out, as follows.

```
nohup somecommand
```

Alternatively, you can (and should!) use the screen utility, described in the next section.

Using screen for Multiple Console Sessions

I first began to use **screen** many years ago. I was a lab manager and was building a set of test systems. Part of the process was to download an entire repository consisting of a number of Gigabytes of packages for use in my lab, and it was taking all day. By 6:00 p.m. it was only three-fourths of the way done. I happened to have an important commitment that wouldn't let me stay late and wait for the download process to finish, and I had heard about this command. I spent about half an hour learning about it, stopped the download, began the download all over again using the **screen command/utility**, and by the next morning, everything was downloaded and working.

The **screen** command is a text-based *window* or session manager that runs multiple shell sessions independently of each other, all within a simple-to-use text interface with minimal indication that it's running on screen normally.

screen enables a number of handy features for the busy sysadmin:

- Multiple independent sessions
- Ability to use those windows/sessions for local or remote systems
- Cut and paste of text between all the running windows/sessions
- Ability to detach or "abandon" a window (complete with running program[s]), so you can log out, lock the screen, or otherwise go home
- Scrollback history buffer on a per window/session basis
- Automatic output logging for sessions that run and for which you want to see forensics on the output later

Without a utility such as **screen**, you would either have to stay around, use a graphical window manager and lock the screen, or leave the session open on a system that's unattended, none of which is an elegant or safe solution.

NOTE   The **screen** command is typically installed on systems, but if it's not available, just add it either through your RPM installation or **apt-get** installation routine.

Once installed, invoking **screen** is as simple as typing its name, but **screen** provides a lot of interesting options and capabilities, so let's hit the highlights in the next section.

Taking Control-a of screen Windows

Just about everything in **screen** begins with the pressing of the keys **Ctrl** and **a**. There are numerous options, which you can see on the help screen, reached by pressing **Ctrl+a** then **?**, as shown in Figure 7-5.

```
                    Screen key bindings, page 1 of 2.

                    Command key:  ^A   Literal ^A:  a

   break      ^B b      history    { }      other        ^A        split      S
   clear      C         info       i        pow_break    B         suspend    ^Z z
   colon      :         kill       ^K k     pow_detach   D         time       ^T t
   copy       ^[ [      lastmsg    ^M m     prev         ^H ^P p ^?  title     A
   detach     ^D d      license    ,        quit         ^\        vbell      ^G
   digraph    ^V        lockscreen ^X x     readbuf      <         version    v
   displays   *         log        H        redisplay    ^L l      width      W
   dumptermcap .        login      L        remove       X         windows    ^W w
   fit        F         meta       a        removebuf    =         wrap       ^R r
   flow       ^F f      monitor    M        reset        Z         writebuf   >
   focus      ^I        next       ^@ ^N sp n  screen     ^C c      xoff       ^S s
   hardcopy   h         number     N        select       '         xon        ^Q q
   help       ?         only       Q        silence      _

^]  paste .
"   windowlist -b
-   select -
0   select 0
1   select 1
2   select 2
3   select 3
4   select 4
5   select 5
6   select 6
7   select 7
8   select 8

                    [Press Space for next page; Return to end.]
```

Figure 7-5   **screen** help options

Creating Windows in screen

A new "window" is really a new instance of a console in **screen**, so when you create a window, you are just opening up another session of the shell, and you can then do whatever you want in that session: type commands, run programs, or anything else that the shell allows you to do.

To create a window in **screen**, press **Ctrl+a** and then press **c**, and you'll suddenly be in a new session/window at a shell prompt.

Once in that session/window, start the **top** command for something that shows movement and stays running when you are off in other windows, such as

```
top
```

> **NOTE**   Exam-takers should know the basic commands for **screen**, especially how to create a new window/session and run a command in it automatically, aka **screen someprogram**.

Now switch back to your previous or initial session/window by pressing **Ctrl+a** and then **p**, although since you only have two windows open, **n** or **p** in this instance takes you to the other window.

Now start a new session/window by typing **Ctrl+a** and then **c** and run **strace top**, which shows an ongoing trace of the system calls that this particular instance of the **top** command is conducting and keeps displaying output for you until you cancel the command.

At this point, you should have three sessions/windows to switch to and from, so practice using **Ctrl+a, n** or **Ctrl+a, p** to move forward and backward among the sessions/windows.

You can see a listing of the available windows by pressing **Ctrl+a** and then ", or the double quotation mark. For example, this would return the following listing on your screen, and you could type the number of the window session you wanted, such as "0" or "1" or "2" and be taken directly there.

Detaching and Reattaching from screen

Opening up local instances of the console via **screen** is a common usage pattern, but **screen** really shines when you realize that you can detach a session from **screen** as a new process and it will keep running even if you log out.

To detach a process, you can either perform the detaching on a running process in an existing window or start a window/process in detached mode.

Detaching a current window/process is done by changing to that window/session and pressing **Ctrl-a** and then **d**, which shows output similar to

```
System1:~ rossb$ screen localbash
[detached]
```

You can see the sessions that are currently detached and running by using the **screen –ls** command, which shows you output similar to the following:

There are screens on:

```
....................78229.Localbash (Detached)
....................78520.bashshell (Attached)
2 Sockets in /var/folders/d7/mgwnjgpx1wd6y7pg0jwzytx40000gr/T/.screen.
```

You then can directly and immediately reattach the (sole) detached session by typing:

```
screen -r
```

The window/session is back in the foreground now, the program running as if it never went away or was detached, and it has indeed been running properly all this time.

If there are multiple detached sessions, you can most easily reattach the session you want by specifying its PID, such as

```
screen -r  88229
```

> **NOTE**   Knowing the main operations for the **screen** command is helpful both on the exam and in real life. You should know how to do what we've covered without any documentation, from doing it many times. For those who work in a production environment with systems that only support shell or nongraphical sessions (which is a vast majority), the **screen** command is helpful and should be a part of your working-day toolkit.

Locking Your Console via screen

Locking the **screen** sessions is the last item we need cover, and that's pretty simple to do. Whenever you are signed on to the system and running **screen** and have a window/session active, you can simply press **Ctrl+a** then **x** to lock the screen.

If you have set a password in the ~/.screenrc file, it is the one that you have to enter to restore access to the window/session; otherwise, the lock mechanism prompts you for a key or password. You have to enter that twice and then it reports that it's locked.

Summary

In this chapter we cover a lot of ground, showing you how to manage processes, send signals to properly kill and remove those processes, and force a system service to reread its configuration files. We also show the basics of controlling your system's jobs, managing the priorities of those jobs while they are running, and how to display and understand many pieces of information on the system.

Finally, we cover how to leave programs running after you log out or how to lock your system and leave processes running even if it's a text-only system.

Exam Preparation Tasks

As mentioned in the section "How to Use This Book" in the Introduction, you have a few choices for exam preparation: the exercises here, Chapter 21, "Final Preparation," and the practice exams on the DVD.

Review All Key Topics

Review the most important topics in this chapter, noted with the Key Topics icon in the outer margin of the page. Table 7-3 lists a reference of these key topics and the page numbers on which each is found.

Table 7-3 Key Topics for Chapter 7

Key Topic Element	Description	Page Number
Section	Viewing processes	196
Paragraph	**ps** command switches	197
Paragraph	**ps** command equivalents	198
Section	The **free** command	198
Paragraph	Output columns of **free**	200
Paragraph	Using **–lohi** and **-h**	201
Paragraph	Monitoring the run queue	201
Table 7-2	List of common Linux signals	202
Paragraph	Kill signal and **kill** command	203
Paragraph	**SIGKILL** and **kill -9 PID**	203
Paragraph	**killall** command	204
Paragraph	**pkill** and **pgrep**	204
Paragraph	**renice** and **pgrep**	204
Note	**&** to put commands in the background	205
Note	Exam question tip	206
Paragraph	Setting process priority	207
Note	Who can change process priority	208
Paragraph	**nohup** command	210
Paragraph	**screen** command	210

Key Topic Element	Description	Page Number
Section	Taking Control-a of screen windows	211
Paragraph	Detaching a process	212
Paragraph	Setting a password in the ~.screenrc file	213

Define Key Terms

Define the following key terms from this chapter and check your answers in the glossary:

process, job, PID, priority, signal, page, slab, block, cache, queue, session, console, window

Review Questions

The answers to these review questions are in Appendix A.

1. Which command shows you a frequently updated screen display of the running processes on your system?

    a. threads

    b. procinfo

    c. mem

    d. free

    e. top

2. You execute a command that is supposed to end the execution of a process, and it is not successful. Which signal should you use with the **kill** command to guarantee the termination of the process?

    a. 15

    b. 23

    c. 9

    d. 18

    e. 27

3. As the sysadmin of a heavily used terminal server, you suddenly notice that the same user is logged on to many different terminals executing similarly named processes and the count of these processes keeps rising rapidly.

Which command would allow you to both find all the problem processes and kill them based on the user, controlling the terminal as well as the process name?

   a. pkill

   b. pgrep

   c. pgmnorm

   d. pkmon

   e. pkexec

4. The **jobs** command can only be used on systems that run in text mode or via the **ssh** command. It cannot be used in graphical terminal sessions such as gnome-terminal or xterm. True or False?

   a. True

   b. False

5. You have just executed the **screen** command and are at a bash prompt. After creating three new window sessions, you want to see a list of the available screen sessions. Which keystroke set would you use to show the list?

   a. Ctrl+a show all

   b. Ctrl+a "

   c. Ctrl+a ls

   d. Ctrl+a c

   e. Ctrl+c r

This chapter covers the following topics:

- Editing with vi
- The vi Command mode
- Searching and replacing in vi
- Advanced vi usage
- The Message Line
- Editing in vi
- Searching in vi
- Options in vi
- Advanced vi

This chapter covers the following exam sections:

- Perform basic file editing operations using vi: 103.8

## CHAPTER 8

Editing Text

Much of your time as a Linux administrator will be spent reading and editing text files. Gaining familiarity with the tools available is essential to saving time and reducing mistakes. The LPI exams focus on vi as the default editor for Linux as it is installed on every Linux machine. No matter how much you think emacs rocks, or that pico/nano is much easier to use with the onscreen menus, it's essential that you have basic vi skills.

vi was originally created in 1976 and was focused on making text editing efficient over slow network connections. In the early 1990s a new project was struck to make a more modern version of vi. Appropriately named vim for "vi Improved," the project took the ideas behind vi and added features such as multiple windows, a scripting language, and graphical interfaces.

NOTE vi and vim refer to different pieces of software, but in casual usage they can be used interchangeably. Throughout this chapter we refer to the editor as "vim."

"Do I Know This Already?" Quiz

The "Do I Know This Already?" quiz enables you to assess whether you should read this entire chapter or simply jump to the "Exam Preparation Tasks" section for review. If you are in doubt, read the entire chapter. Table 8-1 outlines the major headings in this chapter and the corresponding "Do I Know This Already?" quiz questions. You can find the answers in Appendix A, "Answers to the 'Do I Know This Already?' Quizzes and Review Questions."

Table 8-1 "Do I Know This Already?" Foundation Topics Section-to-Question Mapping

Foundation Topics Section	Questions Covered in This Section
Editing in vi	1-4
Named and Unnamed Buffers	5
Searching in vi	6
Options in vi	7
Advanced vi	8-9

1. From vim's Command mode you type the letter "i". What does this do?

    a. Begins editing the text at the end of the line

    b. Begins editing the text at the beginning of the line

    c. Begins editing the text at the current cursor position

    d. Inverts the case of the character at the current cursor position

2. Instead of using the up and down arrows, you can use

    a. k for up and j for down

    b. j for up and k for down

    c. Ctrl+d for down and Ctrl+u for up

    d. j for up and h for down

3. If you wanted to start a new line above the current cursor position, from Command mode, you would type:

    a. **I** (capital i)

    b. **i** (lowercase i)

    c. **A** (capital a)

    d. **O** (capital o)

4. Which command deletes from the current cursor position to the end of the line?

    a. **d$**

    b. **DD**

    c. **YP**

    d. **cW**

5. You want to copy 10 lines of text into a named buffer for later use. How do you do this?

    a. "A10yy

    b. 10Y'a

    c. 10Y"a

    d. "a10yy

6. You want to find the previous instance of the string:

```
ls a*
```

but only if it appears at the beginning of the line. Which command will do this?

   a. /^ls a*

   b. ?^ls a*

   c. /$ls a*

   d. ?ls a*

7. You entered:

```
:set number?
```

Into vim and received

```
nonumber
```

In response. What just happened?

   a. You asked vim if you were in number mode and it responded no.

   b. You turned number mode off.

   c. You turned number mode on.

   d. You turned number mode on and also made it permanent.

8. In your vim editor you entered

```
10J
```

What did you just do?

   a. Moved 10 characters down

   b. Moved 10 words to the right

   c. Joined the next 10 lines together

   d. Jumped down 10 screens

9. You are editing a shell script and want to look at a configuration file at the same time. Which vim command opens up /etc/group in a window to the right of your currently open script?

   a. :rsplit /etc/group

   b. You have to quit vim to do this.

   c. :split /etc/group

   d. :vsplit /etc/group

Foundation Topics

A Tour of the vim Editor

One of the most confusing things about vim is the presence of modes, or states, in the editor. The three modes are

- Command

- Insert

- LastLine, also called "ex" mode

Each of these modes is used for different purposes. The Command mode is used for moving the cursor around and doing operations on text. Insert mode is for adding text to your document. LastLine mode is used to invoke more complicated modes such as search and replace or to manipulate split window panes.

The Message Line

The bottom of the vim screen should contain a number of pieces of information that can help you, varying to suit the situation and actions just completed. This section details some of the messages that can appear.

If you've just entered vim file1, when the editor opens the file, the message line should contain something similar to the following:

```
"/home/rbrunson/file1" 57L, 1756C              18,1   Top
```

The numbers 18,1 on the right side of the message line are the current line and column numbers, and the Top text is the current position of the cursor. This changes to Bot if you entered the last half of the file. The other value possible is All, which simply means that all the contents of the file are currently on the screen.

A new file (one invoked with vim file1) would show the line:

```
"file1" [New File]                              0,0   All
```

If you are in Insert mode the message line shows:

```
-- INSERT -
```

Editing in vi

vim always starts in Command mode, unless you specify differently. True editing (you type a character; that character appears on the screen) takes place in what's known as Insert mode. The keys you commonly use to invoke Insert mode from Command mode are

- **i**—The most common method of moving into Insert mode is to press the **i** key, leaving the cursor at the current position. All typing from that point pushes existing text to the right. Think of this as "insert here."

- **I**—The uppercase **I** key moves to the beginning of the current line and from there acts like the **i** key. Think of this as "Insert at the beginning of the line."

- **a**—The second most common method is to press the **a** key, moving the cursor one character to the right, essentially behaving like an **i** key after that. Think of this as "append after current position."

- **A**—The uppercase **A** moves to the end of the current line and from there acts like an **a** key. Think of this as "Append to the end of the line."

- **o**—Use this key to open a new line under the present line. For example, if you're on line 3 in Command mode, pressing **o** drops line 4 down to become 5 and opens a new line 4 that's empty. Remember this with "open a new line below."

- **O**—The uppercase **O** opens a new line at the current line. For example, if you're on line 3, pressing **O** drops line 3 down to become line 4 and opens a new empty line 3 for editing. Remember this with "open a new line above."

Getting back to Command mode is easy: Press the Esc key at least once; many people double-press it just to make sure they're really there. At any time you can return to Command mode from Insert mode by pressing the Esc key.

Opening a File for Editing

To create a new file in the current subdirectory, you type **vi filename**.

To create a new file in a particular directory, use the full path: **vi /full/path/to/file**.

Sometimes you will want vim to open a file with a search string and put the cursor on the first found instance of that string. To accomplish this, enter **vi +/string filename**.

Other times you'll want to edit a file and have the cursor jump to a particular line when the file is opened, such as the **initdefault** line in the

```
/etc/inittab
```

You would enter **vi +18 /etc/inittab**.

> **TIP**   Expect questions about opening files with particular options, searching a file upon opening it, and other ways to start the vim editor. The + command line option tells vim to run that particular command once the file is open.

Navigating Within a File

The vim editor uses the following keystrokes to move left, right, up, and down, but if you have cursor keys, you can use them, too. Here are some useful keystrokes:

- **h**—This is the left arrow; it's easy to remember because it's the leftmost key in the four-key set.

- **j**—Use this for the down arrow.

- **k**—Use this for the up arrow.

- **l**—Use this for the right arrow.

Figure 8-1 illustrates how these keys work.

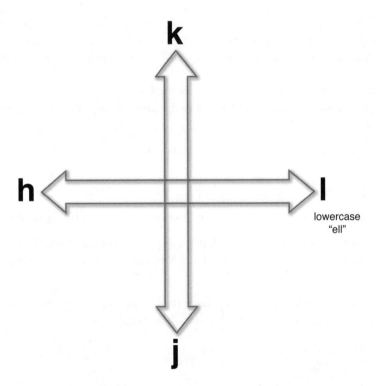

Figure 8-1   Cursor key directions

As you can see in Figure 8-1, one of the ways to remember the keyboard cursor keys is to just look down at the home row and remember that **h** is the leftmost, **j** goes jown (down), **k** goes kup (up), and **l** is on the right. Makes perfect sense, right?

TIP   You'll see questions about the movement keys on the exam. The arrow keys are a favorite topic, whereas the **Ctrl** keys don't get much love. Know those arrow (**h, j, k, l**) movement keys!

Other keystrokes move you around in vim using the **Ctrl** key and a letter:

- **Ctrl+f**—Moves forward a page
- **Ctrl+b**—Moves backward a page
- **Ctrl+d**—Moves forward a half-page
- **Ctrl+u**—Moves backward a half-page
- **G**—Moves to a particular line, such as 12G to go to line 12. Without a number, it goes to the end of the file.

Force Multipliers

Just about any keystroke or action can be done X number of times by prefixing it with a number.

For example, from Command mode to move down 5 lines you would type **5j**. Moving 12 words to the right is accomplished with **12W**.

A lot of editing, inserting, and escaping back can sometimes leave the message line without some pertinent information showing, such as the name of the file being edited. When you get confused as to where you are or under which filename you saved this iteration of the file, pressing **Ctrl+G** while in Command mode shows the filename, total number of lines, and current position expressed as a percentage of the total lines in the file.

Undo Operations

A useful and largely unknown set of options are the undo operations. You press **u** in Command mode to undo a single operation or the latest in a series of changes. If you opened a file, made 30 changes, and then pressed the **u** key 30 times, you would end up with the exact same file you originally opened.

Don't bother trying **U** to undo all changes—that's not what it's for. Instead, use the **:e!** keystroke combination to undo all changes since the last disk write to the file. The **:** takes you to LastLine mode, and the **e!** command reloads the current file, discarding all unsaved changes.

Saving Files

The most straightforward way to save a file in vim is to enter **:w** in Command mode. You save the file and can continue to edit it. To remember the **w**, think of "write".

Quitting vi

When you've made changes to a document, vim won't let you quit normally, such as with **:q**. One of the most frustrating situations every vim user faces is the dreaded "E37: no write since last change (add ! to override)" message. This error can be fixed only by using the correct additional **!** character. To exit a file that is read-only or that you don't want to save the changes to, you must use the keystrokes **:q!**. This is known as qbang or "quit dammit."

> **NOTE**   If the authors had a dollar (US or Canadian) for each time a student got stuck in vim and had to use the above option (**:q!**) to get out of the session, we would be very rich.

Saving and quitting a given file is simple, too. In Command mode you enter **:wq**. Think of "write, quit" to remember this command. If you are editing a file as the root user, such as a configuration file, it is common that this file may lack the write permission. This would result in a **:wq** command to fail. Entering **:wq!** forces the file to be written, as long as the only barrier is a missing write permission.

Two additional methods of saving and quitting a file are available. The first entails entering **:x** to save and exit. The second is to press **ZZ** (hold down the Shift key and press the Z key twice); this is my personal favorite and is easy to remember. As **:x** starts with a colon, the **x** is a LastLine command (as is **wq**). ZZ is a Command mode command. The **x** LastLine command has the added benefit that it won't save a file that's already been saved, which makes exiting that much faster on large files.

TIP   Read questions carefully when asked about saving and/or exiting the vim editor. Many test-takers have mentioned that the question's syntax is critical to getting it right. For example, the question, "Which of the following saves and exits a file in vi?" is very different from the question, "Which of the following can be used to save or exit a file in vi?"

Changing or Replacing Text

The following are incredibly useful when you're altering an existing file and need to change a character, a line, a sentence, or just a word. For example, the **c** command changes text, and you can add additional modifiers after the command to indicate to vim how much text to change.

- **cw**—Changes a single word from the current cursor position. To change a whole word, you put the cursor on the first character of it.

- **c$**—Changes from the current cursor position to the end of the line, even if that line is wrapped to appear as another line on the screen.

- **r**—Replaces the character under the cursor.

- **R**—Replaces text on the same line as you type until Esc is pressed, but it doesn't change text on the next line.

NOTE   Remember to use the force multipliers in the appropriate places. You can easily change multiple words by using **5cw** or replace 10 characters with **10r**. Some commands don't accept the force multipliers, such as **R**, and some behave differently than you might expect. For example, **10O** will accept text and then repeat it 9 more times.

Deleting Text and Lines

A useful feature of vim is to remove or delete characters, words, or even lines. Be careful to check your deletions and changes, or press the **u** key to get things back to normal and try it again.

- **x**—Deletes a single character under the cursor

- **X**—Deletes a single character before the cursor

- **dw**—Deletes a single word that's currently under the cursor, from the cursor position onward

- **dd**—Deletes the current line entirely, regardless of the cursor position in the line

- **D**—Deletes all text from the current cursor position to the end of the line

- **dL**—Deletes all text from the cursor to the end of the screen

- **dG**—Deletes all text from the cursor to the EOF

- **d^**—Deletes all text from the beginning of the line to the cursor

NOTE In the lexicon of computer software verbiage, delete in vim stores the cut or deleted string of text in the unnamed buffer for future use. This buffer's contents will be overwritten by any further cuts or deletions.

TIP How you delete is important on the exam. If asked to delete from the current position to the end of the line, don't pick or type the keys that delete the whole line—there are no partial credits on the exam!

The Cut, Copy, and Paste Commands

The process of moving text around in vim is a little complex, so practice on a scratch file first. The following keystrokes are used to cut, copy, and paste text in a vim session:

- **yy**—Copies a line of text to the unnamed buffer

- **3yy**—Copies three lines of text to the unnamed buffer

- **yw**—Copies from the current cursor to the end of the word to the unnamed buffer

- **3yw**—Copies three words to the unnamed buffer

- **p**—Pastes the contents of the unnamed buffer to the right of the cursor

- **P**—Pastes the contents of the unnamed buffer to the left of the cursor

Yanking (or copying) lines (the **y** key) and pasting (the **p** key) them back in are done on a whole-line basis, whereas yanking a word or several words is done solely on a word basis. Pasting data back in happens to the right of the current cursor position, so take care to put the cursor directly to the left of the desired insertion point. Pasting puts lines as a new entry directly below the current cursor line.

NOTE   A common use of the cut, copy, and paste commands is in the **/etc/fstab** file when you've added another filesystem or disk. Open the file, find a line similar to the desired new one, and press **yy**; then move the cursor to the line above the position you want for the line and then press **p**. The yanked line appears under the current cursor line.

Named and Unnamed Buffers

The vim editor has a total of 27 buffers: 26 named buffers (a–z) and 1 unnamed buffer that is overwritten by each new operation.

Unless you have specified a named buffer, all operations use the unnamed buffer, and two operations right after each other have the second operation overwrite the data from the first operation.

Named buffer operations are always preceded by the double quotation mark ("), which tells the machine that a named buffer operation is to follow.

When you perform named buffer operations, the buffers must be referred to in the command as either a lowercase or uppercase letter of the alphabet (which is part of the command and not sent to the buffer):

- **Lowercase buffer letter**—Overwrites the buffer
- **Uppercase buffer letter**—Appends to buffer

For example, the following string, when entered in Command mode with the cursor in column 1, causes line 1 to copy the next three lines to the named buffer (a), overwriting any contents of that named buffer:

```
"a3yy
```

The Message Line echoes the number of lines and the operation, such as

```
3 lines yanked
```

The syntax for the editing commands remains the same; just remember to precede the operation with a double quotation mark, a lower- or uppercase character, and then whatever operation you want to perform with that named buffer.

Other examples include

- **"ayy**—Yanks a line to the named buffer (a), overwriting the current contents
- **"Ayy**—Appends the current line to the a buffer
- **"A3yy**—Yanks three lines from the current cursor position and appends the lines to the A buffer
- **"ap**—Pastes the a buffer to the right of the cursor (The case of the buffer letter is meaningless in paste operations.)

NOTE   Performing single-line operations with named buffers usually doesn't echo anything to the Message Line, but anything involving more than one line of data echoes the number of lines affected. Word operations are usually not noted in the Message Line either.

Searching in vi

Searching for text in Linux utilities typically follows a common convention. In the **less**, **more**, and **vim** commands, a forward slash followed by a search term searches forward in the file from the current cursor position or the top of the file, highlighting found strings. Initiating a backward search from the cursor position is done with a question mark followed by the string to search for, such as **?sometext.**

NOTE   Searches are performed only in Command mode, so remember to press the Esc key to get back there.

Finding the next occurrence (whether a forward or backward search) is usually accomplished by pressing the unshifted **N** key to search in the same direction as the original search. You press **Shift+N** for a search in the opposite direction of the original search.

Searching and Replacing

Searching a document for a given string or character to replace it is commonly performed either in vim while editing a given file or by the **sed** command on a large set of data. Both vim and the **sed** command share a common search-and-replace syntax, with small differences that won't confuse you if you use both. Indeed, learning to search and replace in one will teach you how to use it in the other.

The search-and-replace syntax is as follows:

```
action/tofind/replacewith/modifier
```

For example, the following string in vim replaces just the first instance of the string bob in the current line with the string BOB:

```
:s/bob/BOB/
```

To replace all instances of the string bob with BOB in the current line, you would use this line:

```
:s/bob/BOB/g
```

The **g** stands for global or doing the action on every found instance of the string.

To replace all instances of bob with BOB in the entire file, no matter how many exist or how many changes are made to each line, you would use this:

```
:%s/bob/BOB/g
```

> **TIP**   It's critical that you read the exam question and all its answers (except for a fill-in-the-blank) to see exactly what is being asked for. A percent symbol (%) in front of the search-and-replace string causes vim to search the entire file, and not just the current line.

Regular Expression Searches

Finding matches using regular expression searches in vim is a good thing to know about. A regular expression search is a fuzzy search: You find something you only know a part of.

For example, if you wanted to find all the instances of the word "The" at the beginning of a line, you could use this search:

```
/^The
```

To find all the instances of the word "kernel" at the end of a line, you could use this search:

```
/kernel$
```

In some instances, you need to find a literal instance of a character that otherwise has special meaning, otherwise known as a metacharacter. For example the asterisk (*) means "zero or more of the preceding character," but you need to search for an asterisk within a string. In this case, escape the metacharacter by prefixing it with a backslash (\). You could use something like this:

```
/The \* character
```

Another example might be finding the text "kernel.", with the period being treated only as a period rather than the metacharacter meaning of "any single character." Otherwise, you would find kernels, kernel?, kernel!, and so on. To find just kernel., you would use the following:

```
/kernel\.
```

Finally, matching a range of characters is helpful, such as trying to find all instances of the version number string v2.1 through v2.9. You either have to perform several searches or use something like this:

```
/v2.[1-9]
```

The square brackets tell vim to match a single instance of the given range, stretching from the first character to the one after the dash. If you wanted instead to find all versions of the word "the," including "THE," "THe," and "tHE," you would use the following:

```
/[tT][hH][eE]
```

However the \c modifier exists to make the search case-insensitive:

```
/\cthe
```

Options in vi

You have three methods of specifying options with the vim editor. All have their place, but if you find yourself frequently having to set options manually, try putting them in the **~/.vimrc** file. An example is shown here:

```
set number
set tabstop=5
set nohlsearch
```

The previous code should be placed in the **.vimrc** file, one option per line, the file being a simple text file in the user's home directory.

Both **/etc/vimrc** and **~/.vimrc** are read when vim starts up. These files allow users to retain custom settings, with **/etc/vimrc** applying to all users and **~/.vimrc** to only the user.

> **TIP**   If you want all users to have the exact same vim options, edit the **/etc/vimrc** file to set the options.

To set options on-the-fly, enter them at the : prompt, such as **:set number**, **:set no-errorbell**, and **set tabstop=5**. These last only for the current session and have to be repeatedly reset in future sessions.

Your final option for setting an option with vim is on the command line that started **vim**. For example, to start vim with nonprinting line numbers onscreen, you would use

```
vim +"set number" file1
```

The reason for the double quotation marks is the space between **set** and **number**; otherwise, you would get a syntax error.

Many options are available in the vim editor. You can view them easily by typing **:set all** in the editor, or to see which options are currently set for your session, type **:set** while in the editor. Finally, you can type **:set optionname?** to find out about that particular option's status.

> **NOTE**   For some reason, LPI really wants you to know the options for setting numbers, including the shortcuts for how options are set. Examples of how you could set the numbers option on and off include
>
> - **:set number**—Turns on line numbers (screen only).
> - **:set nonumber**—Turns the number option off.
> - **:se nu**—This is the shortest string that turns this option on, and putting no in front of the option turns that option off.

Advanced vi

Several tasks are part of vim that don't fit in any other section. Most of these are advanced, such as running external commands, joining lines, and splitting windows. This section covers these in detail.

Running External Commands in vi

A frequent question on the exams is how to run an external command inside **vi,** such as seeing an **ls –l** listing of the current directory so you can remember a filename:

```
:! ls -l
```

In this, the command **ls –l** executes, with the command's output displaying on-screen, and you need only press Enter or enter a command to return to the vim session. If the output scrolls more than one screen, it's piped to the **more** command and all the normal movement keystrokes will apply.

Joining Lines

It's irritating in vim to be at the front of a line and want to use the Backspace key to move that line to the end of the previous line. The Backspace key works only on the current line. If you need a line to be joined to the previous line, you can position the cursor anywhere on the first line and press **J** to cause the second line to be appended to the end of the current line.

Say you have a file named **file1** that contains the following text:

```
This is line 1
This is a longer line 2
This is an even longer line 3
```

You want to join line 1 and line 2, so you position your cursor somewhere on line 1 and press the **J** key. The file then looks like the following:

```
This is line 1 This is a longer line 2
This is an even longer line 3
```

Putting the cursor on line 2 and pressing **J** joins line 2 and line 3 in a similar fashion.

Split Windows

Last, but not least, is splitting windows in vim (not available in the original vi editor). When you're editing a particular file and want to see either another section of that same file or even another file altogether, you can use the following:

- **:split**—This splits the window horizontally, with the same file and lines shown in both windows.

- **:vsplit**—This splits the window on the same file vertically, with the same document shown in both the left and right panes.

Moving between the panes is somewhat counterintuitive because you must press **Ctrl+w** to wake up the "window" mode followed by a directional key. Pressing **Ctrl+w** twice in rapid succession simply moves between the available windows in a sequential manner. Pressing **Ctrl+w** and then an arrow (cursor) key moves the focus to the window located in that direction, as does using the more traditional directional keys such as **h**, **j**, **k**, or **l**.

To open a second file instead of a copy of the current file, simply add a filename to the **split** command, **:split file2**.

To set the height of the newly split window from the split, you could enter:**10split / etc/fstab**. This command splits the top 10 lines of the screen and displays the contents of the **/etc/fstab** file therein.

If you wanted to close the split window, you would focus on it by pressing **Ctrl+W** and then entering **:close**.

Better yet, after comparing something or getting a filename straight, you can close all the other split windows and just have the current window open by entering **:only**.

> **NOTE**   Many times I've opened a couple of split windows to see the difference between two files or used the **diff** command. The easiest way to compare two files and make edits to them is to use the **vimdiff** command, such as **:vimdiff file1 file2**.

> **NOTE**   This loads the two files into a vertically split vim session and uses color and other symbols to show you what is similar or different between the two files. This is useful for comparing a log file before and after a problem or two configuration files to see why one doesn't work.

You can also manage splits from the command line. To open vim with two files in separate windows, you can use **vim –o file1 file2**. These will be horizontally stacked, one with file1 above file2. If you would prefer to open two files in a vertically stacked manner, you would type **vim –O file1 file2**, with file2 appearing to the right of file1 in the interface.

Exam Preparation Tasks

As mentioned in the section "How to Use This Book" in the Introduction, you have a couple of choices for exam preparation: the exercises here, Chapter 21, "Final Preparation," and the practice exams on the DVD.

Review All Key Topics

Review the most important topics in this chapter, noted with the Key Topics icon in the outer margin of the page. Table 8-2 lists a reference of these key topics and the page numbers on which each is found.

Table 8-2   Key Topics for Chapter 8

Key Topic Element	Description	Page Number
List	Three different modes: Command, Insert, LastLine	222
List	Ways to enter Insert mode	222
Paragraph	How to open a file for editing with a search string	223
Figure 8-1	Cursor key directions	224
Paragraph	Saving files in one command	226
List	Deleting text and lines	227
Paragraph	Global search and replace	231
Note	Setting options	233
Paragraph	Splitting windows in vim	234

Review Questions

The answers to these review questions are in Appendix A.

1. What is the default editor for Linux systems?

    a. emacs

    b. joe

    c. vi

    d. nano

2. Which of the following saves and exits a file you are editing in vi? (Choose all that apply.)

    a. :x

    b. :q!

    c. ZZ

    d. zz

    e. :wq

3. After opening a file with **vi**, you want to navigate to the end of the file as quickly as possible. Which of the following, when performed in Command mode, accomplishes this?

    a. **Ctrl+PgDn**

    b. **G**

    c. **Meta+End**

    d. **Shift+End**

4. Which vim command would open the file mytestfile.txt and cause nonprinting line numbers to appear to the left of all file contents? (Choose all that apply.)

    a. **vim +"set number" mytestfile.txt**

    b. **vim --numbers mytestfile.txt**

    c. **vim --setnumber mytestfile.txt**

    d. **vim –o number mytestfile.txt**

5. While editing a file with **vi**, you press **Esc** to enter Command mode and then use the keystrokes **3+j+4+l**. What is the result?

    a. Three columns left and four lines down

    b. Three columns right and four lines up

    c. Three lines up and four columns left

    d. Three lines down and four columns right

6. You are editing a configuration file and realize you've made a big mistake. Luckily, you haven't saved. Which command, from Command mode, will reload the file from disk and leave you in the editor?

   a. :x!

   b. :e!

   c. u

   d. e!

7. You want to edit a file with vim and have the word **string1** highlighted if found. Which of the following accomplishes this in one command?

   a. vi +/"string1" file

   b. vi /string1 file

   c. vi +/string1 file

   d. vi --find string1 file

8. While editing a file in **vi**, you need to display the permissions for the normal files in the current directory. Which command accomplishes this from Command mode?

   a. :x "ls –l"

   b. :e! ls -l

   c. Shift+L+S+-+L

   d. :! ls -l

9. You have made several customizations to your vim editor and want to keep using them every time you use vim. Where is the best place to store your customizations?

   a. /etc/vimrc

   b. ~/.vimrc

   c. .virc

   d. /etc/editorrc

10. While in vi, you need to search and replace all instances of the string snark with FARKLE in the current file. Which statement would include everything necessary to accomplish this from Command mode?

    a. :%s/snark/FARKLE/g

    b. :%s/snark/FARKLE/

    c. :s/snark/FARKLE/

    d. :s/FARKLE/snark/

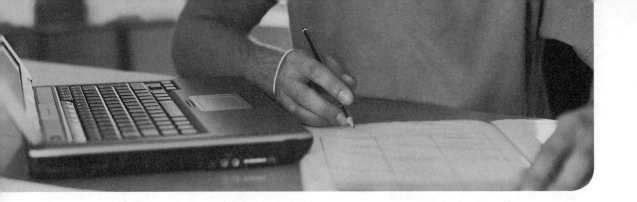

This chapter covers the following topics:

- Creating Partitions
- Filesystems
- Space Utilization

This chapter covers the following exam objectives:

- Create partitions and filesystems: 104.1
- Maintain the integrity of filesystems: 104.2
- Control mounting and unmounting of filesystems: 104.3
- Manage disk quotas: 104.4

## CHAPTER 9

Partitions and Filesystems

So far you've had an overview of the Linux File System Hierarchy Standard, learned a bit about how Linux treats filesystems, and seen how to manipulate files. It's time to dig into the details of the filesystems: the different kinds, how to set them up, use their unique features, fix them when they break, and enforce quotas.

"Do I Know This Already?" Quiz

The "Do I Know This Already?" quiz enables you to assess whether you should read this entire chapter or simply jump to the "Exam Preparation Tasks" section for review. If you are in doubt, read the entire chapter. Table 9-1 outlines the major headings in this chapter and the corresponding "Do I Know This Already?" quiz questions. You can find the answers in Appendix A, "Answers to the 'Do I Know This Already?' Quizzes and Review Questions."

Table 9-1 "Do I Know This Already?" Foundation Topics Section-to-Question Mapping

Foundation Topics Section	Questions Covered in This Section
Creating Partitions	1-3
Filesystems	4-6
Space Utilization	7-8

1. To modify a GUID partition table you would use (choose two):

    a. **fdisk**

    b. **gdisk**

    c. **genguid**

    d. **parted**

2. You are looking at a Linux partition table and the filesystem id is set to 83. What type of partition is this?

   a. LVM

   b. Swap

   c. RAID

   d. Linux

3. Which partition table allows you to have the largest number of primary partitions?

   a. Master boot record

   b. GUID partition table

   c. Logical partition

   d. Primary partition

4. Which of the following is not stored in the file's inode?

   a. Filename

   b. File size

   c. Owner

   d. Location on disk

5. You are creating a file and are using an inode ratio of 4096. What does this mean?

   a. 4096 inodes will be created per megabyte of disk space.

   b. 1/4096 of the disk will be filled with inodes.

   c. Inodes will be created in groups of 4096.

   d. One inode will be created per 4096 bytes of disk space.

6. Your server will not complete booting because one of the filesystems won't mount because of errors. Which command will help you the most?

   a. **fsck**

   b. **df**

   c. **du**

   d. **mkfs**

7. You are trying to figure out how much space David has used in his home directory: /home/david. Which command is most appropriate?

    a. repquota –u david

    b. du /home/david

    c. df /home/david

    d. find /home/david –ls

8. You want to make sure that a particular user never uses more than 1GB of disk space. What do you need to configure?

    a. repquota

    b. Soft limit

    c. Grace period

    d. Hard limit

Foundation Topics

Creating Partitions

Before a disk can be used by users to store their information, the systems administrator must perform a few tasks:

1. Install the device.

2. Partition it.

3. Make a filesystem on the partition(s).

4. Make or choose a mount point (directory).

5. Mount the filesystem

6. Configure the filesystem to be mounted on boot.

7. Set the permissions.

Linux devices are associated with a device file in the /dev directory. There are many preexisting files in this directory. As you saw in Chapter 1, "Installing Linux," a hard drive has a corresponding device file similar to /dev/sda. The device is partitioned into one or more partitions such as /dev/sda1. A filesystem is applied to the partition, and then the device is grafted on to the rest of the filesystem to make the storage usable. Finally, the permissions are configured to allow the necessary people to access it.

Partitions

Disks on PCs can have up to four primary partitions per disk, and in cases when you need more than four, one of the primary partition slots can be exchanged for an extended partition. The extended partition can then be divided further into more partitions called logical partitions.

There is allowance for only one extended partition per disk. The extended partition can hold an unlimited number of logical partitions, although warnings abound to hold the number down to 12 or so.

The logical partitions inside an extended partition are virtually identical to a primary partition; they just happen to live only inside an extended partition. No perceivable difference exists between a primary and logical partition except in the numbering, position on disk, and the fact that the boot files for a Linux machine should exist on a primary partition.

Logical partitions exist to get around the four partition limitation in the master boot record.

Swap

Swap is used as a way to make the system pretend it has more RAM than it does. If the kernel needs to allocate more memory but has already allocated everything, it may copy some memory that hasn't been used in a while to disk. The kernel can copy that information back to RAM if it's ever needed without the applications knowing.

The cost for this is steep. A read- or write-to disk is order of magnitudes slower than the same operation in RAM. If you get some temporary memory pressure, swap can save you from a crash. In extreme cases the demand for memory greatly exceeds the available memory and the resulting swapping makes the system too slow to be usable.

Swap is normally configured as a separate partition on Linux systems. Swap files can be created on demand to satisfy a momentary need but won't perform as well as if they were on a dedicated partition due to having to be accessed via the filesystem.

How much swap space should you have? It depends on your workload. In some server environments you may choose to run without swap if you would rather have the process crash than run slowly. On a workstation you may have swap that is one to two times the physical RAM, especially if you have a laptop that can hibernate by storing RAM to swap before powering off.

Older versions of Linux used to have limitations on how big swap could be or how many partitions were usable. Current limitations depend on the architecture of the computer but are practically bigger than you'll ever need.

Disk Partitioning Tools

The canonical disk tool is the **fdisk** utility. Nearly every system has a copy of **fdisk** that can be used to create or alter the partition table. Having said that, various other tools can be used, and distribution vendors have come up with others that make the partitioning stage easier and clearer, or provide data migration along with partitioning. The three tools that must be discussed are

- **fdisk**—Included on nearly every system that runs Linux

- **gdisk**—Specifically for managing the gdisk partition tables discussed later in this chapter

- **parted**—More features than the others, including reorganizing existing data

fdisk

fdisk is a handy command line tool for managing the master boot record (MBR). If you're trying to get a basic partition set up, you can't do it any faster than with **fdisk**.

fdisk's interface is line-based and has constantly disappearing lines of screen output, making it sometimes hard to remember where you are or what happened unless you have a scrollback buffer set in your terminal.

A key concept with **fdisk** is that your changes are not written to disk until you tell it to save. You can manipulate your partition table at will without fear of making any permanent changes until you're ready.

Starting the **fdisk** tool to partition a drive is easy—just remember to specify the device file that contains the partition table you want to edit, such as

```
fdisk /dev/sda
```

The following steps show you how to create a quick layout of three partitions on a new disk with **fdisk**, including setting the swap and viewing your handiwork afterward:

1. Start the **fdisk** program, passing the name of the device. In this case, it's **sdb**:

   ```
   # fdisk /dev/sdb

   Welcome to fdisk (util-linux 2.25.2).
   Changes will remain in memory only, until you decide to write
   them.
   Be careful before using the write command.


   Device does not contain a recognized partition table.
   Created a new DOS disklabel with disk identifier 0x25fd25d2.
   ```

2. There are no partitions per the previous message. But press **p** anyway to view the device details:

   ```
   Command (m for help): p
   Disk /dev/sdb: 8 GiB, 8589934592 bytes, 16777216 sectors
   Units: sectors of 1 * 512 = 512 bytes
   Sector size (logical/physical): 512 bytes / 512 bytes
   I/O size (minimum/optimal): 512 bytes / 512 bytes
   Disklabel type: dos
   Disk identifier: 0x25fd25d2
   ```

3. This is a good time to verify you're using the right disk. The message says it's an 8GB drive, which is what's expected here. If there were partitions, you could clear them out with the **d** command. You're not deleting the data on the

disk, just the part of the disk that points to the data. Think of data in this situation as lost instead of deleted.

4. Create a new partition by pressing the **n** key and then press the **p** key to make it a primary partition. After that, specify it's the first partition:

```
Command (m for help): n
Partition type
    p    primary (0 primary, 0 extended, 4 free)
    e    extended (container for logical partitions)
Select (default p): p
Partition number (1-4, default 1): 1
```

5. You are then prompted to lay the partition out on disk in terms of the starting and ending sector. It's best to accept the defaults for the starting sector, which here is 2048. You can then enter a value like **+1G** to indicate you want the partition to be one gigabyte. It may seem strange that the partition doesn't start at the beginning of the disk, but **fdisk** is trying to align your partitions on disk in such a way that they start on 1MB boundaries. 2048 sectors at 512 bytes a piece is 1MB, and the first 1MB block contains your partition table so the new partition can't overlap with it. This helps makes things faster as disks and operating systems expect these large blocks.

```
First sector (2048-16777215, default 2048): 2048
Last sector, +sectors or +size{K,M,G,T,P} (2048-16777215, default
16777215): +1G
Created a new partition 1 of type 'Linux' and of size 1 GiB.
```

6. Press **p** to verify that the partition was created, as shown in Example 9-1.

Example 9-1   Verify the Partition Was Created

```
Command (m for help): p
Disk /dev/sdb: 8 GiB, 8589934592 bytes, 16777216 sectors
Units: sectors of 1 * 512 = 512 bytes
Sector size (logical/physical): 512 bytes / 512 bytes
I/O size (minimum/optimal): 512 bytes / 512 bytes
Disklabel type: dos
Disk identifier: 0x2178bc7b


Device      Boot Start      End Sectors Size Id Type
/dev/sdb1        2048 2099199 2097152    1G 83 Linux
```

7. Create another partition for primary partition number 2 the same way you did the first, as shown in Example 9-2.

Example 9-2   Create Partition for Primary Partition Number 2

```
Command (m for help): n
Partition type
    p    primary (1 primary, 0 extended, 3 free)
    e    extended (container for logical partitions)
Select (default p): p
Partition number (2-4, default 2): 2
First sector (2099200-16777215, default 2099200):
Last sector, +sectors or +size{K,M,G,T,P} (2099200-16777215, default
16777215): +2G

Created a new partition 2 of type 'Linux' and of size 2 GiB.


Command (m for help): p
Disk /dev/sdb: 8 GiB, 8589934592 bytes, 16777216 sectors
Units: sectors of 1 * 512 = 512 bytes
Sector size (logical/physical): 512 bytes / 512 bytes
I/O size (minimum/optimal): 512 bytes / 512 bytes
Disklabel type: dos
Disk identifier: 0x2178bc7b


Device      Boot    Start     End Sectors Size Id Type
/dev/sdb1            2048 2099199 2097152   1G 83 Linux
/dev/sdb2         2099200 6293503 4194304   2G 83 Linux
```

8. Allocate the rest of the disk to primary partition 3. The last part of the print command will look as follows:

```
Device      Boot    Start      End   Sectors Size Id Type
/dev/sdb1            2048  2099199   2097152   1G 83 Linux
/dev/sdb2         2099200  6293503   4194304   2G 83 Linux
/dev/sdb3         6293504 16777215 10483712   5G 83 Linux
```

9. The final two columns, Id and Type, are worth noting. Id 83 is for a regular Linux partition. If you want to use swap or LVM, you need to explicitly set the partition type with the **t** command. Set the second partition to swap, which is ID 82:

```
Command (m for help): t
Partition number (1-3, default 3): 2
Hex code (type L to list all codes): 82
Changed type of partition 'Linux' to 'Linux swap / Solaris'.
```

10. The third partition should be used as an LVM physical volume, which is id 8e (the number is in hexadecimal):

```
Command (m for help): t
Partition number (1-3, default 3): 3
Hex code (type L to list all codes): 8e


Changed type of partition 'Linux' to 'Linux LVM'.
```

11. Double check your work with the **p** command:

```
Device    Boot  Start      End  Sectors Size Id Type
/dev/sdb1          2048  2099199  2097152   1G 83 Linux
/dev/sdb2       2099200  6293503  4194304   2G 82 Linux swap / Solaris
/dev/sdb3       6293504 16777215 10483712   5G 8e Linux LVM
```

12. Finally, write your changes by pressing the **w** key and press Enter.

CAUTION   This operation is destructive, so take time to make sure you're configuring the correct disk!

```
Command (m for help): w
The partition table has been altered.
Calling ioctl() to re-read partition table.
Syncing disks.
```

13. Confirming that you correctly partitioned the disk layout after a system is running or viewing the partition tables is easy. You can run the following command:

```
fdisk -l
```

NOTE   The exams test your basic knowledge about **fdisk**, which letter commands are used to accomplish which tasks, the types of partitions used by default, and so on.

For the real world, mail a copy of this output to your sysadmin's account with this command:

```
# fdisk -l | mail me@example.com -s "Fdisk params for server X"
```

This sends an email to your external account with the subject shown in quotation marks, so you can find it if you mess up the partition table of the system.

Tools such as **dd** or **sfdisk** also back up your partition table just in case you mess things up beyond repair. Repair is also easy, just use the same tool to put the partition table back. No matter which way you go about it, the partition table is an important piece of your backup strategy.

gdisk

The MBR partition table format is long in the tooth. There are a few limitations:

- 2Tb limit on a partition size
- Only four partitions (extended partitions are a hack to get around this)
- No checksums, so a single bit error can render a disk useless

For these reasons, and more, the Unified Extensible Firmware Interface (UEFI) specified that MBRs were to be replaced with GUID Partition Tables (GPT), which overcome these limitations. In particular, the maximum partition size is measured in zettabytes (billions of terabytes), and it supports up to 128 partitions.

Key Topic

The GPT is a different format than the MBR, but for compatibility reasons the MBR is stored on the first logical block and the GPT is stored on the second block. When present, the MBR uses a special filesystem id of **0xee**, so that tools that expect an MBR see an unknown operating system and don't attempt to claim the disk as their own.

You must be running a particular configuration to boot off a GPT disk. Either you need an EIFI compatible motherboard (instead of a legacy BIOS), or your bootloader must know about GPT. Later versions of GRUB understand this format, so most Linux distributions work fine.

As **fdisk** initially only worked with MBR partitions, **gdisk** was created to work with GPT. It behaves a lot like **fdisk**; you can run **gdisk -l** to view a disk's partition information, as shown in Example 9-3.

Example 9-3   Using **gdisk –l** to View Partition Information

```
# gdisk -l /dev/sda
GPT fdisk (gdisk) version 0.8.10

Partition table scan:
  MBR: MBR only
  BSD: not present
  APM: not present
  GPT: not present


***************************************************************
Found invalid GPT and valid MBR; converting MBR to GPT format
in memory.
***************************************************************

Disk /dev/sda: 33554432 sectors, 16.0 GiB
Logical sector size: 512 bytes
Disk identifier (GUID): F2A2194A-E316-4A76-9AE4-986527922687
Partition table holds up to 128 entries
First usable sector is 34, last usable sector is 33554398
Partitions will be aligned on 2048-sector boundaries
Total free space is 6077 sectors (3.0 MiB)

Number  Start (sector)    End (sector)  Size      Code  Name
   1             2048         1026047    500.0 MiB  8300  Linux filesystem
   2          1026048        33550335     15.5 GiB  8E00  Linux LVM
```

The preceding command gives a list of the partitions on a disk. **gdisk** points out that the disk only has an MBR partition and gives some details about it. The warnings about converting the table in memory can be ignored because the command is running in read-only mode.

NOTE   Not only do you need to rework your partitions and bootloader to boot from a GPT system on an existing MBR style disk, but you need to make some space at the end of your disk. GPT partition layouts store a duplicate copy of the partition table at the end of the disk for redundancy.

While it is possible to convert an existing MBR partition table to GPT, booting off it is more difficult as you need to create a partition for GRUB and this is not a great job for **gdisk**. For a new disk, **gdisk** behaves almost identically to **fdisk**. Begin by invoking the command on the disk, as shown in Example 9-4.

Example 9-4 Using **gdisk** to Convert an Existing MBR Partition Table to GPT

```
# gdisk /dev/sdb
GPT fdisk (gdisk) version 0.8.10

Partition table scan:
  MBR: not present
  BSD: not present
  APM: not present
  GPT: not present

Creating new GPT entries.
```

The output shows that there are no tables. **gdisk** creates the GUID partition table for you. This is all done in memory, just like **fdisk**, so at this point you can still back out without causing damage.

Listing the partitions shows the new GPT is empty, as shown in Example 9-5.

Example 9-5 List the Partitions

```
Command (? for help): p
Disk /dev/sdb: 16777216 sectors, 8.0 GiB
Logical sector size: 512 bytes
Disk identifier (GUID): CC47CA6B-6C9F-4C83-91CC-2FEC81254B39
Partition table holds up to 128 entries
First usable sector is 34, last usable sector is 16777182
Partitions will be aligned on 2048-sector boundaries
Total free space is 16777149 sectors (8.0 GiB)

Number  Start (sector)    End (sector)  Size       Code  Name
```

Again, just like **fdisk**, the **n** command creates a partition, as shown in Example 9-6. The differences from **fdisk** are that you are prompted for the partition type, and the type is now a four-digit hexadecimal number instead of 2.

Example 9-6   Using **n** to Create a Partition

```
Command (? for help): n
Partition number (1-128, default 1): 1
First sector (34-16777182, default = 2048) or {+-}size{KMGTP}: 2048
Last sector (2048-16777182, default = 16777182) or {+-}size{KMGTP}: +7G
Current type is 'Linux filesystem'
Hex code or GUID (L to show codes, Enter = 8300): 8e00
Changed type of partition to 'Linux LVM'

Command (? for help): n
Partition number (2-128, default 2): 2
First sector (34-16777182, default = 14682112) or {+-}size{KMGTP}:
14682112
Last sector (14682112-16777182, default = 16777182) or {+-}size{KMGTP}:
16777182
Current type is 'Linux filesystem'
Hex code or GUID (L to show codes, Enter = 8300): 8200
Changed type of partition to 'Linux swap'
```

The partition types are mostly the same as before (see Example 9-7) with a trailing **00**. You can then see your handiwork before saving it.

Example 9-7   Partition Verification

```
Command (? for help): p
Disk /dev/sdb: 16777216 sectors, 8.0 GiB
Logical sector size: 512 bytes
Disk identifier (GUID): CC47CA6B-6C9F-4C83-91CC-2FEC81254B39
Partition table holds up to 128 entries
First usable sector is 34, last usable sector is 16777182
Partitions will be aligned on 2048-sector boundaries
Total free space is 2014 sectors (1007.0 KiB)

Number  Start (sector)    End (sector)  Size        Code  Name
   1            2048         14682111    7.0 GiB     8E00  Linux LVM
   2        14682112         16777182    1023.0 MiB  8200  Linux swap

Command (? for help): w

Final checks complete. About to write GPT data. THIS WILL OVERWRITE
EXISTING
PARTITIONS!!
```

```
Do you want to proceed? (Y/N): y
OK; writing new GUID partition table (GPT) to /dev/sdb.
The operation has completed successfully.
```

Parted

Parted is the Swiss army knife of disk partitioning tools. It can manage partition tables in both GPT and MBR formats and modify partition flags and sizes. Truth be told, the other utilities you've seen so far can do much the same thing but **parted** has a much nicer syntax. This is no excuse to forget about **fdisk** though: **fdisk** is on every system and in a crisis it might be all you have access to.

Be careful when resizing partitions, especially when shrinking. You need to shrink the underlying filesystem before the partition itself. When growing the partition, you need to expand the filesystem after expanding the partition. There exists a graphical partition manager, **gparted**, that resizes both the filesystem and the partition for you. Otherwise, you can use the command line tools like **resizefs**, which is covered in detail later.

Start **parted** just like the others, by passing the device on the command line:

```
# parted /dev/sdb
GNU Parted 3.2
Using /dev/sdb
Welcome to GNU Parted! Type 'help' to view a list of commands.
```

 The command to create a partition is **mkpart**, and you can specify all the parameters on one line. Here you create a partition with the label "MyData" going from the beginning of the drive to the 7 Gigabyte marker, as shown in Example 9-8.

Example 9-8   Create a Partition with the Label "MyData" Going from the Beginning of the Drive to 7GB

```
(parted) mkpart MyData 0.0 7G
Warning: The resulting partition is not properly aligned for best
performance.
Ignore/Cancel? ignore
(parted) p
Model: ATA VBOX HARDDISK (scsi)
Disk /dev/sdb: 8590MB
Sector size (logical/physical): 512B/512B
Partition Table: gpt
```

```
Disk Flags:

Number  Start   End     Size    File system  Name     Flags
 1      17.4kB  7000MB                        MyData
```

Curiously, one thing that **parted** doesn't do is set the filesystem type. As it turns out, Linux doesn't care much about those ids—you can overwrite an LVM partition with swap and Linux won't complain. Set it correctly when you have the option and you'll spare someone, or some application, confusion later on.

Filesystems

Once you have the space on disk carved out into a partition, you need to tell Linux how to use that space. You might want to store files on it, either directly or indirectly through LVM. You may want to use it for swap.

A *filesystem* is an organizing construct that acts like a database or hierarchical structure that contains directories and files in a partition. The filesystem is what helps Linux lay out the files into their blocks on disk and to find those blocks later.

Think of everything on a Linux system as a file, starting with the filesystem itself. Typically inodes, or index nodes, store information about the file such as the owner, permissions, timestamps, and where the blocks making up the contents of the file are stored. *Directory entries* relate a filename to an inode, and a directory itself is just a list of directory entries for the files and subdirectories.

Filesystem Types

Linux supports different filesystems, which allows the administrator to choose the one that best suits the needs of the data. The more popular filesystems supported are

- **ext2**—The Linux extended filesystem, which was the default for a long time.
- **ext3**—Essentially ext2 with journaling (logging) to help recover faster after a crash.
- **ext4**—Performance improvements made on top of ext3.
- **iso9660**—The CD-ROM filesystem.
- **udf**—The DVD filesystem.
- **vfat**—A 32-bit filesystem readable by Windows (FAT32).

- **nfs**—The Network Filesystem by Sun Microsystems, which is the default network file sharing protocol for all of Unix/Linux.

- **smb**—The Samba filesystem is Microsoft's default file sharing protocol for network shares. It's otherwise known as CIFS (Common Internet File System).

- **xfs**—The extent filesystem, adopted from Silicon Graphics (SGI) is a higher performance filesystem with many features.

- **ReiserFS**—At the time of its introduction ReiserFS had many novel features that have since been added to other filesystems. In particular it was first to introduce journaling and online resizing.

- **btrfs**—A filesystem still in development (but stable) that builds on ideas from ReiserFS and focuses on the administrative and performance needs of systems with huge amounts of storage.

There are more filesystems that can be used on block devices, plus there are all the pseudofilesystems such as **procfs**.

Each filesystem has advantages and disadvantages. They are mostly incompatible except for the ext2, ext3, and ext4 filesystems, which are mostly evolutions of the original ext standard.

Superblocks

Most filesystems have a *superblock*. The superblock contains information about the filesystem, such as filesystem size, inode statistics, and when the filesystem was last checked by a utility like the **fsck** command. It is usually stored in the first sector of the filesystem and is replicated multiple times, making it much easier to recover from errors. The first available backup superblock in the ext filesystems is usually stored at the 8,193rd block.

Inodes and Files

The files are laid out on disk in individual blocks, which may or may not be together. Each file has a corresponding inode, which contains information about the file (but not the name!) along with the list of blocks comprising the files.

It's easy to see the inode of a file with the **ls -i** command:

```
$ ls -i .bashrc
15272747 .bashrc
```

From this command you can see that the .bashrc file is referenced by inode 15272747. You can get more information about what's in the inode with **stat**:

```
$ stat .bashrc
  File: '.bashrc'
  Size: 966              Blocks: 8          IO Block: 4096    regular
file
Device: fd00h/64768d      Inode: 15272747    Links: 1
Access: (0644/-rw-r--r--)  Uid: (  500/    sean)   Gid: (  500/
sean)
Access: 2014-10-07 09:17:48.000000000 -0500
Modify: 2014-10-07 09:17:48.000000000 -0500
Change: 2014-10-07 09:17:48.000000000 -0500
 Birth: -
```

On the exam it's important to know that everything descriptive about the file except the actual filename is stored in the inode. The file's data is kept in the disk block, which is shown in the inode's **stat** output. The total amount of inodes is set only at the filesystem creation, and their number cannot be changed without re-creating the filesystem.

The **stat** output tells you the various timestamps of the file, its ownership and permissions, and where it's stored. Even though the file is less than 1k long, it takes up eight 512-byte blocks because the minimum block allocation is 4096 bytes.

The **debugfs** command lets you dig into the gory details of disk allocation, as shown in Example 9-9.

Example 9-9   debugfs Command

```
# debugfs /dev/mapper/VolGroup00-LogVol00
debugfs 1.41.14 (22-Dec-2010)
debugfs:  cd /home/sean
debugfs:  stat .bashrc
Inode: 15272747   Type: regular    Mode:  0644    Flags: 0x0
Generation: 873527854    Version: 0x00000000
User:   500   Group:   500   Size: 966
File ACL: 0    Directory ACL: 0
Links: 1   Blockcount: 8
Fragment:  Address: 0    Number: 0    Size: 0
ctime: 0x5433f60c -- Tue Oct  7 09:17:48 2014
atime: 0x5433f60c -- Tue Oct  7 09:17:48 2014
mtime: 0x5433f60c -- Tue Oct  7 09:17:48 2014
BLOCKS:
(0):15291419
TOTAL: 1
```

This information is virtually identical to what the command line **stat** showed, except that you can see that the file is stored on block 15291419. If you were to look at the filesystem at that location—15291419 blocks * 4096 bytes per block—you would see the start of the file.

Inodes and Directories

Directories have inodes too! Instead of pointing to the contents of the file, the disk blocks contain a list of files in the directory, along with the inodes that describe the file.

Figure 9-1 shows the relationship between inodes, files, and directories:

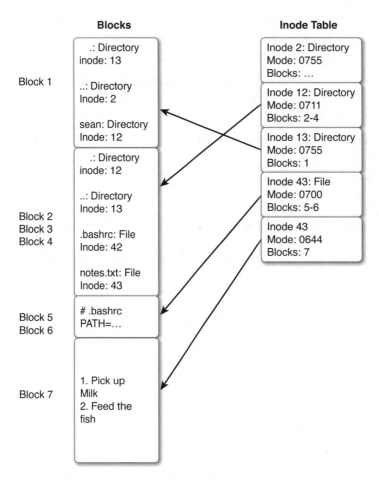

Figure 9-1   How inodes are used in directories

The filesystem has two structures on it. The first is the data blocks that contain the files and directories; the second is the inode table that has all the file metadata.

The first block is pointed to by inode 13. In that block are three directories: . is the directory itself, .. is the parent, and sean is a subdirectory at inode 12. Looking at inode 12 you can see that it is a directory with permissions 711 with information stored in blocks 2-4. Inside those blocks is a list of subdirectories and files. The . and .. directories are there along with two files. Following the inode chain for those files gets you the contents.

An important thing to take from Figure 9-1 is that the name of a directory is always found in its parent. Thus, being able to walk the list of inodes and directory blocks is important. The other thing to note is that there's nothing magical about directories: They're just a list of pointers to inodes.

This diagram also helps reinforce the difference between hard and soft links. A hard link adds a new directory entry to the inode, increasing the link count.

Inodes and Disk Space

Each file and directory needs an inode. Most filesystems are created with a fixed number of inodes, so if it runs out no more files can be stored even if there is free space.

The number of inodes, by default, is calculated as a ratio of bytes per inode, so a lower value gives you more inodes. If you would rather specify the exact number of inodes there is an option for that, which is seen shortly.

If a filesystem is to contain a lot of little files, such as many HTML or cache files, it should be formatted to contain many inodes so that more files can be stored. This is done using the smallest ratio available, effectively creating more inodes to handle the possible number of files. Practically, this would mean setting the bytes per inode to the same as the disk block size.

This topic is largely for the benefit of the exam. These days disks are so large that you get an incredible number of inodes. It's rare to exhaust your inodes even at the default settings. The most common problem is that an application goes berserk and creates a lot of zero byte files without cleaning them up.

If you're expecting to fill your disk with files smaller than 16K, the inode ratio may be an issue. Otherwise, you're going to run out of disk space first.

The real danger of having a large block size and relatively few inodes (such as for a database server) is that you might run out of available inodes and still have disk space left over. A system can run completely out of inodes and still have available disk space, a situation that often requires extensive troubleshooting and work to remedy.

The inodes themselves take up 128 bytes of space each, or about 8,000 per megabyte of space. You must strike a balance between the number of files on disk and the size of the files. Too many inodes and you're wasting space with inodes that never get used. Not enough and you'll run out before the disk is full.

The **df -i** command shows inode utilization.

```
$ df -i
Filesystem          Inodes    IUsed    IFree IUse% Mounted on
/dev/mapper/VolGroup00-LogVol00
                  60686336 1500786 59185550   3% /
```

Here you can see that the root filesystem has about 60 million inodes and is using 3% of them.

Creating Filesystems

You wipe out any existing files on the partition when you create a filesystem, so it always pays to think twice about your filesystem related commands before you press that Enter key!

The mkfs Command

Even though you have your choice of many different filesystems, the commands to create them are fairly consistent. The **mkfs** command is a front end for these individual programs that create filesystems. The **mkfs** command, when used with the **-t fstype** option, calls the **mkfs.fstype** program to make the actual filesystem. Here's an example:

```
mkfs -t ext4 /dev/sdb1
```

This command executes the **mkfs** program, supplying the type of ext4, which in turn executes the **mkfs.ext4** program against the target partition, creating an Ext4 filesystem.

The long commands, (called filesystem builders) can be invoked directly, saving some time and confusion, as shown here:

```
mkfs.ext4 /dev/sda5
```

The DOS and ext2 filesystem builders have additional shortcuts of **mkdosfs** and **mke2fs**, respectively.

Other filesystem creation mk tools are available on the system. Here is a sample list of the important ones:

- **mkisofs**—Creates ISO filesystems and is used for CD creation

- **mknod**—Creates special files (dev files, named pipes, and so on)

- **mkraid**—Creates RAID sets from separate disks

- **mkswap**—Makes a partition or file into swap space for use as part of virtual memory

Filesystem Creation Options

Creating filesystems can either be quick and easy or take some time and involve many options. Several examples of quick and easy were given in the previous section, so let's dive into the long and involved ones.

Creating a specific filesystem such as ext3 is accomplished with one of three methods:

```
mkfs -t ext3 device
mkfs.ext3 device
mke2fs -j device
```

The first two options are synonyms. The third variant uses the **-j** option to create an ext filesystem with a journal, which turns out to be ext3. The contents of /etc/mke2fs.conf also have an impact on these commands.

Setting other options for the filesystem is accomplished with either a specific option or the general-purpose **-O** option (which allows you to specify multiple options after **-O**).

In Example 9-10, the command creates an ext3 filesystem on the **/dev/sdb1** partition with a 4,096 block size, a reserved block percentage of 2%, a volume label of **data**, and the **sparse_super** option for fewer superblock copies for the disk:

Example 9-10   mkfs and Options

```
# mkfs.ext3 -b 4096 -m 2 -L data -O sparse_super /dev/sdb1
mke2fs 1.42.11 (09-Jul-2014)
/dev/sdb1 contains a ext4 file system
        created on Thu Feb 19 00:27:24 2015
Proceed anyway? (y,n) y
Creating filesystem with 1708980 4k blocks and 427392 inodes
Filesystem UUID: 2d6fa418-77f9-47f3-b6ad-e36026cda3a9
Superblock backups stored on blocks:
        32768, 98304, 163840, 229376, 294912, 819200, 884736, 1605632
```

```
Allocating group tables: done
Writing inode tables: done
Creating journal (32768 blocks): done
Writing superblocks and filesystem accounting information: done
```

NOTE On the exam, you need to know exactly what the options do and how to format them properly. The previous examples should serve as a firm foundation. Practice making all the various types of filesystems with the more common options.

The filesystem parameters can be checked with the **dumpe2fs** command, as shown in Example 9-11.

Example 9-11 dumpe2fs

```
# dumpe2fs -h /dev/sdb1
dumpe2fs 1.42.11 (09-Jul-2014)
Filesystem volume name:    data
Last mounted on:           <not available>
Filesystem UUID:           5b5a4a07-57e6-417c-8f1c-7d32e6c1bfeb
Filesystem magic number:   0xEF53
Filesystem revision #:     1 (dynamic)
Filesystem features:       has_journal ext_attr resize_inode dir_index
filetype sparse_super large_file
Filesystem flags:          signed_directory_hash
Default mount options:     user_xattr acl
Filesystem state:          clean
Errors behavior:           Continue
Filesystem OS type:        Linux
Inode count:               427392
Block count:               1708980
Reserved block count:      34179
Free blocks:               1645584
Free inodes:               427381
First block:               0
Block size:                4096
Fragment size:             4096
Reserved GDT blocks:       417
Blocks per group:          32768
Fragments per group:       32768
```

```
Inodes per group:        8064
Inode blocks per group:  504
Filesystem created:      Sun Feb 22 13:31:36 2015
Last mount time:         n/a
Last write time:         Sun Feb 22 13:31:36 2015
Mount count:             0
Maximum mount count:     -1
Last checked:            Sun Feb 22 13:31:36 2015
Check interval:          0 (<none>)
Reserved blocks uid:     0 (user root)
Reserved blocks gid:     0 (group root)
First inode:             11
Inode size:              256
Required extra isize:    28
Desired extra isize:     28
Journal inode:           8
Default directory hash:  half_md4
Directory Hash Seed:     60f8ddfe-961e-40af-8770-381bc895e28b
Journal backup:          inode blocks
Journal features:        (none)
Journal size:            128M
Journal length:          32768
Journal sequence:        0x00000001
Journal start:           0
```

The use of the **-h** option keeps the group information from showing up, which is usually unnecessary unless an error occurs on the filesystem.

Advanced Filesystem Commands

The filesystems on your machines are relatively robust but need some care and attention now and then. Different tools can be used to check the filesystems, configure settings that affect their performance, and debug their operations.

Filesystem Checker

When a filesystem is broken or has errors, an **fsck** (filesystem check) is in order. The mount count and maximum mount count are how the system knows when to check the filesystem structure and data health (see the section "Tuning Filesystems" for more on mount counts and using **tune2fs**). On a filesystem such as **ext4**, this is important because a periodic check can save you hours of heartache and trouble-shooting (repairing the filesystem after a crash) when the data is most needed.

When you run **fsck**, it's really delegating the work to the appropriate filesystem check tool. These commands are

- **e2fsck**—Shortcut for checking the **ext** filesystems

- **dosfsck**—Used for all varieties of the DOS/FAT filesystem

- **reiserfsck**—Used for the ReiserFS filesystem

fsck does not do anything for XFS filesystems, so you must use **xfs_repair** on its own.

The **fsck** tool uses the **/etc/fstab** file to automatically check filesystems at system start. If a filesystem is marked unclean for reasons that include a power outage, un-expected system stoppage, or other event that didn't let the system finish writing to disk properly, a lengthy check of the filesystem is probably required.

The worst scenario is filesystem damage, usually noticed when restarting a system that crashed or was turned off abruptly. The system attempts to run a quick **fsck** session on the filesystems noted in **/etc/fstab**, beginning with those that have a **1** in the sixth column, and continuing on numerically until finished. The **fsck** program skips any that have a **0** (zero) in the sixth column. The fstab file looks like this:

```
UUID=6489f3c4-13fd-449e-8648-918b58a948f5 /                        ext3
noatime         1 1
```

All filesystems that have a 1 in the column are checked first in parallel, then any that have a 2 in the column in parallel, and so on. In this example, the filesystem will be checked on the first pass because the final column is 1.

If the filesystem was shut down cleanly, such as through the **shutdown** or **halt** commands, then **fsck** doesn't need to check anything. It is rare to have a mounted filesystem with corruption. When a filesystem is properly unmounted anything cached in memory is flushed to disk and **fsck** doesn't need to check anything. If the computer was shut down abruptly, it's possible that some of this cache is lost and what is on disk may be missing something. It is the job of **fsck** to fix any damage caused by this missing data.

If the damage is too great to fix automatically, the system presents you with a message stating "Ctrl-d to continue, otherwise enter the root password to perform a filesystem check." Entering the root password displays the shell prompt and prints a helpful message that tells you the filesystem that needs checking. **fsck** options that can help the busy sysadmin include

- **–A**—Moves through **/etc/fstab** checking all filesystems in one long pass

- **–C**—Percentage or hash mark progress bars for any operations that support their display

- **–N**—Performs a dry run (makes no changes), showing what would be done; doesn't change anything (good for seeing how bad it is)

- **–V**—Produces verbose output for everything, including commands that are being executed by **fsck**

- **–a**—Doesn't ask questions and noninteractively repairs the filesystem

fsck makes five passes or types of changes to the filesystem, shown here:

- **Pass 1**—Checking inodes, blocks, and sizes
- **Pass 2**—Checking directory structure
- **Pass 3**—Checking directory connectivity
- **Pass 4**—Checking reference counts
- **Pass 5**—Checking group summary information

When **fsck** finds serious errors such as blocks claimed by multiple files (cross-linked), blocks claimed outside the filesystem, too few link counts (the number of directories linked to an inode), or unaccounted blocks or directories that correspond to unallocated inodes, it displays an error message and asks to be run manually.

NOTE   Always only run **fsck** on unmounted or read-only mounted filesystems. This is mandatory; otherwise, **fsck** might perform an operation on a file a user has open, causing corruption. If it's the root filesystem, you should either do it in single-user mode or use the rescue CD-ROM to ensure that the root is mounted read-only.

Example 9-12 shows a sample of a check on a filesystem.

Example 9-12   Sample Check on a Filesystem

```
# fsck -v /dev/sda1
fsck from util-linux 2.25.2
e2fsck 1.42.11 (09-Jul-2014)
/dev/sda1 is mounted.
e2fsck: Cannot continue, aborting.
# umount /dev/sda1
# fsck -v /dev/sda1
fsck from util-linux 2.25.2
e2fsck 1.42.11 (09-Jul-2014)
/dev/sda1: clean, 430/128016 files, 182615/512000 blocks
```

The system would not run **fsck** on a mounted filesystem, so it failed with an error. When it did finally run, **fsck** reports the system as clean, so there was no need to run the checks. Running it again with the **-f** option forces a check, as shown in Example 9-13.

Example 9-13   –f Forces a Check

```
# fsck -v -f /dev/sda1
fsck from util-linux 2.25.2
e2fsck 1.42.11 (09-Jul-2014)
Pass 1: Checking inodes, blocks, and sizes
Pass 2: Checking directory structure
Pass 3: Checking directory connectivity
Pass 4: Checking reference counts
Pass 5: Checking group summary information

        430 inodes used (0.34%, out of 128016)
          4 non-contiguous files (0.9%)
          2 non-contiguous directories (0.5%)
            # of inodes with ind/dind/tind blocks: 0/0/0
            Extent depth histogram: 420/1
     182615 blocks used (35.67%, out of 512000)
          0 bad blocks
          0 large files

        403 regular files
         17 directories
          0 character device files
          0 block device files
          0 fifos
          0 links
          1 symbolic link (1 fast symbolic link)
          0 sockets
------------
        421 files
```

Tuning Filesystems

The **tune2fs** command is used to set parameters after the filesystem is created. For example, the maximum mount count dictates how many times a filesystem can be mounted before an **fsck** is forced on it. This number is set to **20** by default unless you set it at filesystem creation or change it afterward with **tune2fs**. An example of setting the mount count to **0** (zero) for an **ext3** journaling filesystem is shown here:

```
tune2fs -c 0 /dev/sda1
```

When an application writes to disk, the kernel can cache that write in memory to make the application faster. If the computer reboots before the memory is flushed to disk, the data is lost and corruption of the disk has happened. With a journaling filesystem the write is always logged to a journal, which can be done quickly. The **fsck** that happens on boot can then replay that journal and get the filesystem back to a known good state with no data loss.

By using the journal there is almost no chance at corruption, so there is no need for periodic filesystem checks. Journaling writes to a disk are therefore a good thing to have in a filesystem.

In addition to the mount count, error checking can be altered with **tune2fs -e** so the system does one of three things when a filesystem error is detected by the kernel:

- **Continue**—Continues normally

- **remount-ro**—Remounts the filesystem read-only, ready to **fsck**

- **Panic**—Causes the kernel to panic, which stops the system (not recommended unless you're a system tester)

The reserved percentage (space available only to the root user) associated with the root user can also be associated with a system group with the **-g** option, such as

```
tune2fs -g admins /dev/sdb1
```

XFS Commands

The ext filesystems may get most of the attention, but you shouldn't ignore xfs. It is now the default filesystem for some enterprise Linux systems because it has high performance for large files and has advanced journaling and online backup features.

Making the filesystem is just like ext4, as shown in Example 9-14.

Example 9-14 Making the Filesystem with **xfs**

```
# mkfs -t xfs -f /dev/sdb1
meta-data=/dev/sdb1                 isize=256     agcount=4, agsize=427245
blks
         =                          sectsz=512    attr=2, projid32bit=1
         =                          crc=0         finobt=0
```

```
data        =                      bsize=4096   blocks=1708980,
imaxpct=25
            =                      sunit=0      swidth=0 blks
naming      =version 2            bsize=4096   ascii-ci=0 ftype=0
log         =internal log         bsize=4096   blocks=2560, version=2
            =                      sectsz=512   sunit=0 blks, lazy-
count=1
realtime =none                    extsz=4096   blocks=0, rtextents=0
```

Many of the parameters are best left at defaults. One parameter to note is the **log**, which says where the journal will go. By default it goes on the same device as the filesystem, but you can choose to place it on a dedicated device if it is needed for performance.

You can also see these same details with the **xfs_info** command.

Some advanced commands are different between ext4 and xfs. Instead of using **fsck** to look for and fix problems, you use **xfs_check** to look for problems and fix the problems with **xfs_repair**. If the repair fails you may need to use **xfs_metadump** if you call a vendor for support. This command puts debugging information into a file that helps the vendor diagnose the problem.

An interesting thing about xfs is that you can grow the filesystem with **xfs_growfs**, but you can't shrink it. This is not because of technical reasons but because the project hasn't implemented it! It's a lot of work to implement that could be better spent on other features, and as it turns out, people rarely need to use it.

A final feature of xfs—it supports online defragmentation (called reorganization in xfs lingo) through the **xfs_fsr** command. Over time the blocks comprising a single file might be placed in different parts of the disk, which means it's fragmented and will have lower performance because the disk heads need to seek more. Reorganizing, or defragmenting, the file copies it to a new spot where it's in a contiguous series of blocks.

Debugging Filesystems

The **debugfs** command is useful for debugging and fiddling with the filesystems on your machine, which is needed if you need to recover from an errant deletion or corruption. It's also possible to delete or corrupt a portion or all of the filesystem, so extreme caution is recommended. Fortunately it's run in read-only mode by default for your own safety, and you have to go out of your way to make changes. You've been warned.

The **debugfs** tool is interactive, with a command-line shell environment you can get help with by typing **?** and pressing Enter.

For example, you can enter the tool simply by typing

```
debugfs /dev/sdb5
```

Then type **?** and press Enter to see a menu of commands available to you. Interesting and informative commands include

- **open**—Opens a filesystem for debugging
- **features**—Shows the filesystem's feature set
- **stats**—Shows the statistics for the filesystem and is similar to the **dumpe2fs –h** output
- **ls**—Shows the directory, which by default is the root (/)
- **pwd**—Shows the working directory
- **undelete**—Undeletes a file (used immediately after the deletion in successful cases)
- **logdump**—Shows the contents of the journal (if in a journal-led filesystem)
- **quit**—Quits the tool

Mounting and Unmounting

Filesystems must be mounted to be used. Mounting a filesystem places it in the directory tree where users can access it.

Unmounting is equally important as Linux keeps some information in memory and only writes it to disk when it is advantageous to do so. This keeps things fast but can lead to unclean filesystems if the power were to be suddenly turned off. Unclean filesystems lead to long nights watching **fsck** run and the possibility of data corruption. Data corruption leads to uncomfortable discussions with your manager. So shut down your servers cleanly!

When you are mounting a filesystem you need to be able to tell Linux how to find that device. There are different ways to do this. The first is to refer to the device, such as /dev/sda1. This works on a small scale, but if you add or remove hardware the device names can change.

To get around this unpredictable naming, information can be stored inside the superblock of the filesystem to identify that particular filesystem. The two elements used are the filesystem label and the universally unique identifier (UUID). The label is a human generated name that should be unique across all disks, while the UUID is generated when the filesystem is made and should always be unique.

You can see your label and UUIDs with the **blkid** command:

```
# blkid
/dev/sda1: UUID="4d2b8b91-9666-49cc-a23a-1a183ccd2150" TYPE="ext4"
/dev/sda3: LABEL="flubbers" UUID="bab04315-389d-42bf-9efa-
b25c2f39b7a0" TYPE="ext4"
/dev/sda4: UUID="18d6e8bc-14a0-44a0-b82b-e69b4469b0ad" TYPE="ext4"
```

Here, you can see that each filesystem has a UUID to identify it, and the second one was also assigned a label of "flubbers".

The Filesystem Table

The filesystem table, **/etc/fstab**, is a configuration file that tells the system which mounts it should know about. While the administrator can always mount a filesystem manually, having the mount described in **fstab** ensures that it happens when the system boots and that the correct options are used every time.

An added bonus of using **fstab** is that when you provide only the mount point or device when manually mounting, the fstab file is consulted to determine the rest of the information, including mount options.

Filesystems should be set up in **/etc/fstab**, one per line. Any mounted filesystem, whether or not it is in fstab is also reflected in **/etc/mtab** automatically by the system. This information (or most of it) is also in the **/proc/mounts** file.

Type the **mount** command to see the current list of filesystems. Here's an example:

```
$ mount
/dev/sda1 on / type ext4 (rw,errors=remount-ro)
proc on /proc type proc (rw,noexec,nosuid,nodev)
sysfs on /sys type sysfs (rw,noexec,nosuid,nodev)
udev on /dev type devtmpfs (rw,mode=0755)
devpts on /dev/pts type devpts (rw,noexec,nosuid,gid=5,mode=0620)
tmpfs on /run type tmpfs (rw,noexec,nosuid,size=10%,mode=0755)
/dev/sda3 on /mnt/data type ext4 (rw)
/dev/sda4 on /mnt/timemachine type ext4 (rw)
```

Compare this to the contents of **/etc/mtab**:

```
$ cat /etc/mtab
/dev/sda1 / ext4 rw,errors=remount-ro 0 0
proc /proc proc rw,noexec,nosuid,nodev 0 0
sysfs /sys sysfs rw,noexec,nosuid,nodev 0 0
```

```
udev /dev devtmpfs rw,mode=0755 0 0
devpts /dev/pts devpts rw,noexec,nosuid,gid=5,mode=0620 0 0
tmpfs /run tmpfs rw,noexec,nosuid,size=10%,mode=0755 0 0
/dev/sda3 /mnt/data ext4 rw 0 0
/dev/sda4 /mnt/timemachine ext4 rw 0 0
```

And the same view of the mounted disks, but through **/proc/mounts**:

```
$ cat /proc/mounts
rootfs / rootfs rw 0 0
sysfs /sys sysfs rw,nosuid,nodev,noexec,relatime 0 0
proc /proc rw,nosuid,nodev,noexec,relatime 0 0
udev /dev devtmpfs rw,relatime,size=1980172k,nr_inodes=495043,mode=755
0 0
devpts /dev/pts devpts rw,nosuid,noexec,relatime,gid=5,mode=620,ptmxm
ode=000 0 0
tmpfs /run tmpfs rw,nosuid,noexec,relatime,size=404804k,mode=755 0 0
/dev/disk/by-uuid/309b3416-5a59-4954-b4a6-f2c105d9aac5 / ext4
rw,relatime,errors=remount-ro,data=ordered 0 0
/dev/sda3 /mnt/data ext4 rw,relatime,data=ordered 0 0
/dev/sda4 /mnt/timemachine ext4 rw,relatime,data=ordered 0 0
```

All three outputs show roughly the same information except that the information in **/proc/mounts** is the most detailed. The first two examples omit any default options, but **/proc/mounts** shows all mount options whether they're default or provided.

The filesystem table should consist of one line per filesystem, with a device, a mount point, a filesystem type, options, and dump/check orders. This file should be modifiable only by the root user; otherwise, any user could put a removable device or disk in the system and mount it, potentially replacing system tools with their own.

Here's an example of a live **/etc/fstab** file:

```
LABEL=/          /              ext3     defaults        1 1
LABEL=/boot      /boot          ext3     defaults        1 2
LABEL=/data      /data          ext3     defaults        1 2
none             /proc          proc     defaults        0 0
none             /dev/shm       tmpfs    defaults        0 0
/dev/sr0         /cdroms        ext2     defaults        0 0
/dev/sda3        swap           swap     defaults        0 0
/dev/sdb1        /mnt/media     auto     noauto,user     0 0
/dev/cdrom       /mnt/cdrom     iso9660  noauto,users,ro 0 0
```

The column contents (from left to right) are as follows:

- **Device**—This is any device; local dev files, NFS shares, or partition labels.

- **Mount point**—This is any directory where the device's filesystem will be attached. It should initially be empty.

- **Filesystem type**—This is a valid filesystem type.

- **Options**—Options are separated by a comma. The **defaults** option is made up of **rw**, **suid**, **dev**, **exec**, **auto**, **nouser**, and **async**, or any filesystem specific options.

- **Dump**—If this value is 0 (zero), the **dump** command doesn't act on it; otherwise, a **1** indicates that the filesystem should be dumped on demand.

- **fsck**—This causes the filesystem with a 1 to be checked first and then those with a 2 and so on to be checked next.

The columns closely match the order in which you specify the manual **mount** command. Add a **-t** before the type, an **-o** before the options, and drop the last two columns and you have a **mount** command. The **fstab** format also lets you mount filesystems by label or UUID instead of device, which are separate options to **mount**.

The **auto** option in the filesystem column for the sdb1 removable media disk probes the superblock for the device to attempt identification of the filesystem type. This works for nearly any other filesystem type, including ext2, ext3, iso9660, udf, and ntfs to name a few.

Notice also the mutually exclusive **user** and **users** options in the USB and CD-ROM entries' options column. These enable either exclusive or nonexclusive mounting for users on that device.

For example, if the **user** option is present for the system's CD-ROM and the daytime user Sally mounts her favorite Taylor Swift release into the drive and plays it, only user Sally (and the root user) can unmount that CD-ROM.

This is unacceptable to Steven the night shift operator, who simply must have his Dust Rhinos CD-ROM to help the night pass. Steven should request that the root user switch that option with the **users** option, which allows any user to mount the device and any other user to unmount it.

Manually Mounting Filesystems

If a filesystem isn't configured in the **/etc/fstab** file, it can be mounted manually following this convention:

```
mount -t type -o option device mountpoint
```

The following example of a manual mount includes the type, the option, the device, and a mount point:

```
mount -t iso9660 -o exec /dev/cdrom /mnt/cdrom
```

With this **mount** command, the system's CD-ROM is mounted, allowing users access to the contents. The **exec** option also means that files on the disk can be executed, such as if the CD-ROM included a software installation file.

Important mounting options include

- **-a**—Mounts all filesystems listed in **/etc/fstab**
- **-f**—Fakes the mounting of filesystems
- **-r**—Mounts the filesystem read-only
- **-w**—Mounts the filesystem in write mode
- **-n**—Mounts without updating **/etc/mtab**
- **-L**—Mounts a filesystem with a given **label**, instead of using the device filename

Automatically Mounting Filesystems

All filesystems in the **/etc/fstab** and don't have the **noauto** option set are mounted when the system is booted. This is equivalent to issuing a **mount -a** command as the root user.

The **noauto** option is necessary for removable USB drives and CD-ROMs because access errors would occur if an empty removable media drive were to be affected by the mount system call. This option is also useful for rarely needed or user-specific filesystems, allowing a script or user to invoke the mount as desired.

Unmounting Filesystems

The unmounting command name is **umount**, and it works similarly to the **mount** command, acting on the label, mount point, or device listed in the **/etc/fstab** entry.

For example, to unmount the **/mnt/cdrom**, use either of the following:

```
umount /mnt/cdrom
umount /dev/cdrom
```

The most important fact about the **umount** command is that it doesn't let you unmount any device currently in use, including a device that has a user accessing it via a file manager, a shell session, or a file in use on that device. If you don't know who is using the filesystem, the **fuser** command is there to help:

```
# fuser -m /mnt/data/
/mnt/data:          1929c
```

The **-m** option denotes a mounted filesystem and returns a list of all processes with an open file on that device. In this case /mnt/data is being used by process 1929 and the c denotes that the process is using it as its current directory. The process needs to be killed, or the user needs to get out of the directory, before the device can be unmounted.

Space Utilization

There are several methods of determining the space used by data on your system. It's important to know when to use which command because each acts differently and displays different information.

> **NOTE**   The LPI exams test whether you can parse the question and whether you know what the various utilities produce as output. If you've not used the options for the **du** and **df** commands, some questions will be unanswerable.

Using du

To see the space used by a set of files or a file tree, you use the **du** command. This command is configurable to show file and directory sizes, including summarization and human-readable output (KB, MB, and GB).

To summarize the disk usage, in blocks, for each file and directory, use the following command:

```
# du *
8     a_directory
4     go
4     sharing
```

This command descends into directories, such as the first line in the preceding example. The value reported next to the name of the directory or file is the number of blocks in the file, or in all the files underneath that directory.

To see the current directory and all below with KB/MB/GB human-readable output, use the following command:

```
# du -h
24K      ./.gconfd
8.0K     ./.gstreamer
8.0K     ./.gconf/desktop/gnome/applications/window_manager
12K      ./.gconf/desktop/gnome/applications
8.0K     ./.gconf/desktop/gnome/file_views
24K      ./.gconf/desktop/gnome
28K      ./.gconf/desktop
... Output removed
```

To view the space used by all files on a given directory tree, such as the **/home** user's tree, use this command:

```
du -sh /home
```

Typical output would look like this:

```
404 MB     /home
```

It's important when using **du** to not traverse NFS systems across the network, causing extra traffic and annoying other users. To restrict your query to the local system only, use the following:

```
du -shx /home
22M      /home
```

Without the **x** option, (which restricts **du** to the local system) a remotely mounted user's home directory or attached separate disk drive is shown in the output. Therefore, you should know from which drive and system the data is shown.

Using df

The **df** command is different from the **du** command: It operates on filesystems rather than files.

The **df** command displays used and available disk space for all mounted filesystems, on a per-filesystem basis (shown here with the **-h** human readable output option) such as

```
# df -h
Filesystem          Size  Used Avail Use% Mounted on
/dev/sda2           5.5G  1.8G  3.5G  34% /
/dev/sda1            99M  9.3M   85M  10% /boot
none                 62M     0   62M   0% /dev/shm
/dev/sdb8           966M   38M  909M   4% /data
```

Notice that **df** works only on mounted filesystems, and that the output includes

- The size of the partition
- The size used in MB or GB
- The size available in MB or GB
- The percent used
- Where the device is mounted

To view disk-free statistics on local-only filesystems, (excluding NFS and other re-mote mounts) use the following command:

df -l

To see the disk utilization statistics expressed in KB, use this command:

```
# df -k
Filesystem          1K-blocks       Used Available Use% Mounted on
/dev/sda2            5708320     1794004   3624344  34% /
/dev/sda1             101089        9426     86444  10% /boot
none                   62996           0     62996   0% /dev/shm
/dev/sdb8             988212       38180    929952   4% /home/data
```

Finally, to see the amount of the disk's free and used inodes expressed in disk utiliza-tion statistics, use the following command:

```
# df -i
Filesystem          Inodes   IUsed   IFree IUse% Mounted on
/dev/sda2           725760  104049  621711  15% /
/dev/sda1            26104      41   26063   1% /boot
none                 15749       1   15748   1% /dev/shm
/dev/sdb8           125696     889  124807   1% /home/data
```

Notice that the number of inodes total, used, free, and percent used is shown on a filesystem-by-filesystem basis. This option is incredibly useful for busy sysadmins who are worried about running out of space or inodes.

The **du** and **df** commands are prominently featured on the exams, particularly ques-tions about the output of each and what is shown for various options. Expect to see questions that have the keywords disk utilization and amount of free space or words to that effect.

Using Disk Quotas

Most sysadmins have had a server system partition fill up due to one thing or another, usually followed closely by a system crash or kernel panic (and sysadmin panic). A package on nearly every Unix/Linux system, called **quota**, lets you limit disk usage on a per-user and per-filesystem basis.

One important limitation is that quotas are on a filesystem, not a directory tree. If you have two directory trees (**/home** and **/var/www**, for example) that need to have conflicting or different quotas, these directory trees must be on separate filesystems, which means separate partitions.

Quota Commands and Files

The quota system is designed to limit users to a certain amount of disk space per filesystem. The **quota** command allows a user to view the quotas that are in place for her account.

The commands, settings, and files that are used for quotas are as follows:

- **quotaon**—Turns on quotas
- **quotaoff**—Turns off quotas
- **quotacheck**—Verifies each user's usage is correct and updates the stored values if necessary
- **edquota**—Used for editing the user's quota amounts
- **quota**—Used by users to see quota limits/space
- **aquota.user**—The binary file that contains user quota information
- **aquota.group**—The binary file that contains group quota information
- **usrquota**—The **/etc/fstab** option for user quotas
- **grpquota**—The **/etc/fstab** option for group quotas

Quota Concepts

The following are terms you need to understand to configure quotas:

- **Soft limit**—This is a limit that can be exceeded, with resulting warnings up until the grace period is met.
- **Hard limit**—This is usually set higher than the soft limit and cannot be exceeded.

- **Grace period**—The soft limit can be exceeded up to the hard limit until the grace period value is met. Then, to save more data, the amount used must be brought below the soft limit.

Configuring Quotas

To set up quotas, you need to choose a filesystem. It's not recommended to set quotas on the root (/) filesystem, but instead to set quotas on the filesystems that have the most active sets of users and data.

For example, this next exercise was done on a system that has a partition on the device **/dev/sdb5** mounted to the mount point **/data**. An entry in the **/etc/fstab** mounts this partition on system boot. The permissions for the **/data** filesystem allow users who are in the **users** group to create objects in it. There are already files from various users in that directory.

To set up quotas on the **/data** filesystem, do the following:

1. Ensure the **/data** partition is mounted by issuing the **mount** command and inspecting the output.

2. Edit the **/etc/fstab** file and add **usrquota** and **grpquota**, as shown here, to enable both user and group quotas:

   ```
   /dev/sdb5  /data  ext3  defaults,usrquota,grpquota  0 0
   ```

3. Remount the **/data** filesystem with the following command. This enables the quota options you added previously without taking the filesystem offline.

   ```
   mount -o remount,rw /data
   ```

4. Check that it has the correct options (shows **usrquota** and **grpquota**) with this command:

```
# mount | grep usrquota
/dev/sdb5 on /data type ext3 (rw,noexec,nosuid,nodev,usrquota,grpquota)
```

5. Add a normal user to test quotas with the following:

   ```
   useradd -m quotaboy
   passwd quotaboy
   ```

6. Now update the **aquota.*** files with the command shown in Example 9-15.

Example 9-15   Updating **aquota.** * with **quotacheck -avugc**

```
# quotacheck -avugc
quotacheck: Your kernel probably supports journaled quota but you are
not using it. Consider switching to journaled quota to avoid running
quotacheck after an unclean shutdown.
quotacheck: Scanning /dev/sdb5 [/data] done
quotacheck: Cannot stat old user quota file /data/aquota.user: No such
file or directory. Usage will not be subtracted.
quotacheck: Cannot stat old group quota file /data/aquota.group: No
such file or directory. Usage will not be subtracted.
quotacheck: Cannot stat old user quota file /data/aquota.user: No such
file or directory. Usage will not be subtracted.
quotacheck: Cannot stat old group quota file /data/aquota.group: No
such file or directory. Usage will not be subtracted.
quotacheck: Checked 2 directories and 1 files
quotacheck: Old file not found.
quotacheck: Old file not found.
```

The errors you see are just the **quotacheck** command letting you know the quota files don't contain data yet, but it will update them with the right information. However, options are available for a journaled quota in the mount man page.

7. Edit the quota settings for this user with this command:

```
edquota -u quotaboy
```

8. You see the user's quota information in **vi**, so you can edit the amounts, like so:

```
Disk quotas for user quotaboy (uid 1001):
Filesystem    blocks    soft    hard    inodes    soft    hard
/dev/sdb5        0        0       0        0        0       0
```

9. Set **quotaboy**'s block quotas to match the following:

```
Filesystem    blocks    soft    hard    inodes    soft    hard
/dev/sdb5        0       5000    6000       0        0       0
```

10. Save and exit the file; it will be loaded properly by the quota system.

11. Sign on as, or use the **su -** command to **become, quotaboy**:

```
su - quotaboy
```

12. Create a new file in the **/data** directory as **quotaboy**:

```
touch /data/file1.quotaboy
```

13. As the **root** user, check to see that **quotaboy** has a quota listed:

```
# quota quotaboy
Filesystem  blocks    quota  limit  grace  files  quota  limit    grace
 /dev/sdb5       0     5000   6000               1      0      0
```

14. Turn on the quota system for the **/data** filesystem. Prior to this, the system is tracking quotas but not enforcing them.

```
quotaon /data
```

15. Log in as **quotaboy** or **su** over to his account:

```
su - quotaboy
```

16. Run the **quota** command to see what **quotaboy**'s usage is presently:

```
$ quota
Disk quotas for user quotaboy (uid 1001):
Filesystem  blocks    quota  limit  grace  files  quota  limit    grace
 /dev/sdb5       0     5000   6000             0      0      0
```

17. As the **quotaboy** user, copy all the regular files in the **/etc** directory to the **/data** directory:

```
$ cp /etc/* /data
```

18. Run the **quota** command to see how many blocks are used and free:

```
Disk quotas for user quotaboy (uid 1001):
Filesystem  blocks    quota  limit  grace  files  quota  limit    grace
 /dev/sdb5    2524     5000   6000           152      0      0
```

19. Fill up your quota by copying the entire **/etc/** tree to the **/data** directory, observing the multiple errors about the disk quota being exceeded:

```
cp -r /etc /data
```

20. Be sure to clean up the mess on your test system and try it again until you're comfortable with configuring quotas.

Your distribution should take care of enabling quotas at boot, which you can test by rebooting and checking for quotas. If not, you need to add **/sbin/quotaon** to your startup scripts.

Hard and Soft Limits

Dissecting the **edquota –u quotaboy** editor session is important because several items will be on the exam. Let's look at each section of the output:

```
Filesystem    blocks    soft    hard    inodes    soft      hard
/dev/sdb5          0       0       0         0       0         0
```

The sections are described here:

- **Filesystem**—This is the filesystem on which the user has a quota.

- **blocks**—This is the number of blocks presently used by the user on the filesystem in question.

- **soft**—This is the soft limit, which can be exceeded for the grace period.

- **hard**—This is the hard limit, which cannot be exceeded.

- **inodes**—This is the number of inodes presently in use.

- **soft**—If set, this is the number of inodes for which you want to set a soft limit (if you can't think why, don't use it).

- **hard**—This is the hard limit for inodes, which, if met, keeps the user from creating more files.

The editable fields are the soft and hard settings for both blocks and inodes. Editing any of the other values does not do anything.

Setting the Grace Period

Use **edquota –t** to set the grace period for users; it's configurable in **days, hours, minutes**, or **seconds**. You're a pretty tough sysadmin if you configure a grace period that's less than a day. Here's the syntax for it:

```
edquota -t
```

To establish a grace period before enforcing soft limits for users, use the following format, where time units can be **days, hours, minutes**, or **seconds**:

```
Filesystem                  Block grace period      Inode grace period
/dev/sdb5                        7days                   7days
```

Getting Quota Information

Run the **quota** command as a normal user to get just that user's quota information (as seen in the previous exercise). If there are no quotas for that user, the output states there are none.

The **root** user has the ability to get quota statistical data on all users, like so:

```
# repquota -a
*** Report for user quotas on device /dev/sdb5
```

```
Block grace time: 7days; Inode grace time: 7days
                        Block limits              File limits
User              used   soft   hard  grace    used  soft  hard  grace
---------------------------------------------------------------------
root        --   32844      0      0               5     0     0
snuffy      --       0      0      0               1     0     0
quotaboy    +-    6000   5000   6000  6days     1464     0     0
```

Summary

In this chapter you learned how to work with filesystems. The **mkfs** command creates a filesystem on a partition, and it delegates its work to a filesystem builder such as **mkfs.ext4**. The filesystem is mounted with the **mount** command, and unmounted with **umount**. Should the computer restart without the unmount step, such as after a power outage, the filesystem will be unclean and need to be checked. The filesystem check tool, **fsck**, itself delegates its work to tools such as **fsck.ext4**, except in the case of XFS filesystems where you need to use **xfs_check** and **xfs_repair** to do the same work.

Linux provides a variety of tools to investigate disk space usage, the most popular being **du** to show disk usage of a series of files and directories, and **df**, which shows your disk free statistics. A filesystem's free space is expressed in terms of the number of free bytes of space, along with the number of free inodes it has with which to store files.

Users can also be restricted to a certain amount of disk usage on a particular partition through use of the quota tools. First you must mount the filesystem with the **usrquota** and **grpquota** options and then you create the quota databases with **quotacheck**. Edit a user's quota with **edquota** to allocate the number of files or bytes to allow. The system needs to have quota enforcement on through **quotaon**.

Exam Preparation Tasks

As mentioned in the section "How to Use This Book" in the Introduction, you have a couple of choices for exam preparation: the exercises here, Chapter 21, "Final Preparation," and the practice exams on the DVD.

Review All Key Topics

Review the most important topics in this chapter, noted with the Key Topics icon in the outer margin of the page. Table 9-2 lists a reference of these key topics and the page numbers on which each is found.

Table 9-2 Key Topics for Chapter 9

Key Topic Element	Description	Page Number
List	List of disk partitioning tools	245
Paragraph	**fdisk** commands are not immediately written to disk	246
Step	Creating a new partition with **fdisk**	247
Step	Viewing and setting the filesystem type	248
Paragraph	GUID partition table placement	250
Paragraph	Creating a new partition with **gdisk**	252
Paragraph	Creating a new partition with **parted**	254
Paragraph	Superblock facts	256
Paragraph	Finding a file's inode	256
Paragraph	The inode does not contain the filename	257
Paragraph	How inodes work with directories	259
Paragraph	Specifying the number of inodes	259
Paragraph	Showing a filesystem's inode capacity	260
Paragraph	Creating an ext3 filesystem	261
Note	Need to know options	262
Example 9-11	**dumpe2fs**	262
Paragraph	About **fsck**	263
Paragraph	/etc/fstab fsck order	264
Paragraph	There is no xfs **fsck**	268
Paragraph	The fstab file	270
Paragraph	Mounting with the **user** and **users** option	272
Paragraph	You can't unmount a filesystem in use	273
Paragraph	**du** is not **df**	276
Paragraph	Quotas apply to filesystems, not directories	277
Step list	Setting up quotas	278
Paragraph	Viewing quotas	280

Define Key Terms

Define the following key terms from this chapter and check your answers in the glossary:

swap, filesystem, directory entries, superblock

Review Questions

The answers to these review questions are in Appendix A.

1. You are configuring your **/etc/fstab** file and want to have a filesystem mountable by non-root users. Which option in which column would you use to accomplish this?

   a. **owner** in the third column

   b. **owner** in the fifth column

   c. **noauto** in the fourth column

   d. **user** in the fourth column

2. You are troubleshooting your Linux machine after an unexplained crash. The automated filesystem check fails with a message to perform a check manually. What's the most important thing to make certain of for the affected filesystem before initiating the manual check?

   a. It should be unmounted.

   b. It should be mounted read-write.

   c. It should be in noauto mode.

   d. The **user=root** option should be set.

3. You are installing a Linux server that will primarily hold users' data. If you could place two directory trees on a separate drive, which would be the most effective choice? (Choose two.)

   a. **/tmp**

   b. **/var**

   c. **/home**

   d. **/data**

4. You require your system to check a particular filesystem every 50 times the filesystem is mounted. Which command would you use to make this change?

   a. **debugfs**

   b. **dumpe2fs**

   c. **tune2fs**

   d. **setfs**

5. A user reports that one of his fellow users is hogging all the disk space on their shared server. Which command would you use to show that system's disk statistics for its mounted filesystems?

   a. **dir**

   b. **df**

   c. **du**

   d. **ls**

6. Which portion of a file's information is not stored in the inode or data blocks?

   a. Link count

   b. Link permissions

   c. Filename

   d. Owner

7. Which command is used to alter the maximum mount count so an **ext3** filesystem isn't checked every 20 mounts by default?

   a. **fsck**

   b. **mkfs.ext3**

   c. **hdparm**

   d. **tune2fs**

8. When upgrading a system that has multiple data partitions of the **ext2** filesystem type, which of the following would represent the least disruptive journaling filesystem to upgrade them with?

   a. ext3

   b. ReiserFS

   c. JFS

   d. XFS

9. Which utility on your system can display the number of free and used inodes as a total and percentage?

   a. ls -li

   b. du -sh

   c. df -i

   d. find -inum

10. You are configuring your server after a system crash due to a full disk. When configuring a user quota for the **/home** directory of 1GB and a user quota for the **/var/ftp** directory of 200MB, what must be true about those directory trees for quotas to work?

    a. They can exist only on an **ext2** filesystem.

    b. They must have the **sparse_super** option set.

    c. They must be mounted with the **usrquota** option.

    d. They must exist on different partitions or drives.

11. While setting up quotas you run **repquota** and see that a particular user is well over her hard disk quota. Which of the following are possible reasons? (Choose two.)

    a. The user created the files prior to quotas being enabled.

    b. You didn't mount the filesystem with the right options.

    c. You didn't run **quotaon**.

    d. This is expected, as the user can exceed her hard disk quota for the duration of the grace period.

This chapter covers the following topics:

- Working with Permissions
- Manipulating Permissions
- Special File Permissions
- Finding Files by Permission
- Default Permissions
- Changing User Ownership
- Changing Group Ownership

This chapter covers the following objectives:

- Manage file permissions and ownership: 104.5

## CHAPTER 10

Permissions and Ownership

Both regular users and administrators should understand the importance of object permissions and object ownership. Ensuring that your files and directories are secure is critical. This chapter explores the concepts of object permissions, special permission sets, default permission, and object ownership.

> **NOTE** We use the term "object" to denote something that is either a file or directory.

"Do I Know This Already?" Quiz

The "Do I Know This Already?" quiz enables you to assess whether you should read this entire chapter or simply jump to the "Exam Preparation Tasks" section for review. If you are in doubt, read the entire chapter. Table 10-1 outlines the major headings in this chapter and the corresponding "Do I Know This Already?" quiz questions. You can find the answers in Appendix A, "Answers to the 'Do I Know This Already?' Quizzes and Review Questions."

Table 10-1   "Do I Know This Already?" Foundation Topics Section-to-Question Mapping

Foundation Topics Section	Questions Covered in This Section
Working with Permissions	2
Manipulating Permissions	3
Special File Permissions	4
Finding Files by Permission	5
Default Permissions	1
Changing User Ownership	6
Changing Group Ownership	7

1. Which command lets you alter the default permissions in a shell?

   a. **chmod**

   b. **chgrp**

   c. **chown**

   d. **umask**

2. Consider the following **ls –l** output:

   ```
   -rwxr-xr-- 2 fred     users   0 Jan 26 13:08 22   sample.mp3
   ```

   What are the permissions for the user fred on the sample.mp3?

   a. Read, write, and execute

   b. Read and execute

   c. Read and write

   d. Only read

3. Which command adds execute permission to all permission sets (owner, group, and others)?

   a. **chmod u+x file**

   b. **chmod u=x file**

   c. **chmod a+x file**

   d. **chmod g+x file**

4. Which command sets the sticky bit permission on the /dir directory?

   a. **chown +t /dir**

   b. **chmod o+t /dir**

   c. **chmod u+t /dir**

   d. **chmod g+t /dir**

5. You have been asked to find all the SUID files on the system. Which of the following commands completes this task?

   a. **find / -perm -6000**

   b. **find / -permission -6000**

   c. **find / -mode -6000**

   d. **find / -umask -6000**

6. Consider the following command

```
chown bob:bin file.txt
```

Which of the following statements are true? (Choose two.)

   a. This changes the user owner of file.txt to bin.

   b. This changes the user owner of file.txt to bob.

   c. This changes the group owner of file.txt to bin.

   d. This changes the group owner of file.txt to bob.

7. The user nick owns the file.txt file. He is a member of the payroll and sales group, with the payroll group being his primary group. He executes the following command:

```
chgrp sales file.txt
```

Which of the following statements is true?

   a. This command fails because nobody but the root user can change the group ownership of a file.

   b. This command fails because a user can only change the group ownership of a file to his primary group.

   c. This command fails because the order of the arguments is wrong.

   d. This command works and changes the group owner of the file to sales.

Foundation Topics

Working with Permissions

Permissions determine how users can access resources on the system. System security is configured by the user's UID (user ID), her GIDs (group ID—both primary and secondary), and the permissions on the object she is attempting to access.

Permission Trio Bits

Figure 10-1 shows the 10 positions (1 type bit and 3 trios of permission bits) that make up the permissions section of a file.

```
T    User        Group       Other
y
p   r  w  x   r  w  x   r  w  x
e
    4  2  1   4  2  1   4  2  1
```

Figure 10-1 Permission trios

The first bit of the 10 shown is the type of object:

- **.**—Indicates that this is a normal file

- **l**—Indicates that this is a symlink (symbolic link), which is a file that points to another object

- **b**—Indicates that this is a block device file

- **c**—Indicates that this is a character device file

- **d**—Indicates that this is a directory

The next nine bits are what I call the *permission trios*. Each of the trios affects a certain set of users (user owner, group owner, or other). To determine which permissions a user has to a given object, begin from the left and as soon as a match is made, that trio alone is the permissions in effect for that user and object. Here are the three trios:

- **User owner**—If the user is the user owner, this is the permission trio in effect.

- **Group owner**—If the user's primary or secondary groups are this group, but only if that user is not the user owner, this is the permission trio in effect.

- **Other**—If the user is neither the user owner nor a member of the group owner, this is the permission trio in effect.

NOTE On some modern Linux systems, you see another character right after the permission set. This could either be a "." character, which is related to SELinux, or a "+" character, which is related to access control lists (ACLs). Both of these topics are not testable on the LPIC-1 exams. Do not mix up the Windows environment and Linux in your mind. There is no such thing as "effective permissions" for a Linux object; that is entirely a Windows concept. For example, a user who matches the user owner and is also a member of the group owner does not have the greater permissions of the two trios slapped together; he is restricted only to the user owner trio's permissions.

The trios are made up of 3 bits (symbolized by the values of 4, 2, 1). The bits work like light switches: If the bit is on, then the value counts; if off, the value doesn't count. That value is used with the **chmod** command as well as with other commands.

The bit values equate to the following permissions for files:

- **4**—Read, which is the ability to view the file's contents.

- **2**—Write, which is the ability to change the file's contents.

- **1**—Execute; the file can be executed. (The read is also needed for a script, but binaries can execute with only the execute permission.)

These permissions have similar, but slightly different, meanings for directories:

- **4**—Read, which is the ability to view the directory's contents (using the **ls** command). However, to see file attributes (such as with the **–l** option to the **ls** command), execute permission on the directory is also required.

- **2**—Write, which is the ability to add and delete files in the directory. This is a powerful permission for directories as a user can delete every file in a directory, even files that she doesn't own, if she has the write permission on the directory. Caveat: For write permission to be valid, the user also must have execute permission.

- **1**—Execute; the user can use the **cd** command to get into the directory or use the directory in a pathname. For example, if the user attempts to execute **cd /home/bob**, the user needs execute permission on the **/** directory, the **home** directory, and the **bob** directory.

To better understand directory permissions, think of the directory as a room. If you want to see what is in the room, you need a window. Think of the read permission as the window. If this permission is set, you can see into the directory (room). If you want to get into the room, you need a door. Think of the execute permission as the door. This concept makes the caveat for the write permission make more sense: To remove something from a room, you first need to be able to get into the room!

If you execute the **ls –l** command on an object and its permission trios are 666 (or rw-rw-rw-), the only way that number could be arrived at with the possible bit values is for the 4 and 2 bits to be on, or rw- (read and write, but not execute). If you see a file that is set to 666, that equates to all three trios having the same permissions—read and write, but not execute.

NOTE Watch for questions that try to trick you with a user who is both the user owner and a member of the group owner, but the correct permissions for executing or changing the file aren't in a single trio. You can't mix the trios, even if your user account encompasses several of the trios.

For example, say a user named fred is the user owner of the file object /home/fred/22AcaciaAvenue.mp3 and is also a member of the group owner of that object. The file's listing has the following permissions set:

```
-rw-r-xr-x    2 fred     users   0 Jan 26 13:08 22  AcaciaAvenue.mp3
```

The fred user's permissions might seem to span the various trios, but because fred is the user owner, he matches the first trio and stops there. In other words, the user fred has read and write permission, but not execute, even though fred is a member of the users group and members of that group do have execute permission on this file.

Manipulating Permissions

The **chmod** command is used when modifying or altering an object's permission trio bits. Only the root and object's owner can alter permissions.

The two modes of manipulating the permissions for an object are numeric and symbolic. Both modes have their place; the numeric method is better for changing all permissions while the symbolic method is better for changing one or two permissions.

Numeric Mode

Numeric permissions are the most often used, and they appear on the exam with greater frequency than the symbolic style. As a rule, I recommend using the *numeric mode* to set or force permissions on an object, as opposed to making small changes to permissions.

The numeric method uses the same bits to describe what you want your permissions to be (4=read, 2=write, 1=execute). For example, if you are told that the current permissions for an object are 644 and you are asked to ensure that all users have read and write access to that object, execute the following command:

```
chmod 666 file1
```

The **chmod** command works great on groups of files, too:

```
chmod 644 /home/lukec/*.txt
```

It even works on directories and their contents. For example, say the user bertrandr has a directory that he wants to set all the files to the permission of 640 to make the files more secure. He could use the following command:

```
chmod -R 640 /home/bertrandr/data/*
```

Take a moment to understand why this command works the way it does. The **chmod** command has an **-R** option that affects the object named and all its child objects. The user bertrandr doesn't want to change the permission of the data directory itself, but just the contents, which is why the slash and asterisk characters are on the end of the target. This command acts on the entire contents of the **/home/ bertandr/data** directory but doesn't modify the directory's permissions. However, if there were any directories within the **/home/bertandr/data** directory, all those directories would have the permissions changed (as well as all files and directories beneath them)!

The **chmod** command has a few useful options:

- **-c**—Reports only which files were changed
- **-v**—Reports all files
- **-h**—Changes symbolic links, not the original file
- **-f**—Suppresses error messages
- **-R**—Operates recursively through directories

The **chmod** command's recursive option is an uppercase "R," not a lowercase "r" as in some other commands. Familiarize yourself with the case of the various command options, and you will be fine on the exam.

NOTE When using the numeric method, you should always specify three values (owner, group, and others). If you only specify one value, it uses that value for the others permission set and assumes a value of 0 for the owner and group permissions. This is never a good idea!

Symbolic Mode

When using the **chmod** command with symbolic values, keep in mind that you can change all the permissions like the numeric mode, but this requires a much longer command. The primary reason to use *symbolic mode* is to affect, or alter, smaller sets of permissions rather than to overwrite them all.

The symbolic mode uses a letter to identify the trios:

- User owner = u, group owner = g, other = o, and all = a
- A qualifier (+ to add, - to remove, or = to assign)
- The permissions being set (r = read, w = write, and x = execute)

To use the symbolic values to set permissions, you can change them all at once, like the following command demonstrates:

```
chmod a=rwx file
```

This produces permission trios that are set to -rwxrwxrwx.

Or you can use each one of the identifiers with its qualifier and permissions separated by commas:

```
chmod u=rw,g=rx,a= file
```

This produces a file that has its permissions set to –rw-r-x---.

This method of using the symbolic mode is viewed as unwieldy and somewhat inelegant for constant use. Use symbolic mode when you want to fine-tune the permissions, not set all the permissions.

For example to change just the user owner's permissions to rwx, use the following command:

```
chmod u=rwx mystuff
```

To change the group owner's permissions to r-x, use the following command:

```
chmod g=rx mystuff
```

To change the other or everyone else's permissions to r, use this command:

```
chmod o=r mystuff
```

Keep in mind, when using the symbolic mode, the permissions that you are not specifying stay as they were before executing the **chmod** command.

Setting a file to be executable without knowing its other permissions can be done several ways. For example, if you know a file exists but don't know the permissions and you are told to make sure it's executable by all permission trios, use the following command:

```
chmod a+x file1
```

Alternatively, you can leave the "a" off and get all the trios by default:

```
chmod +x file1
```

Remember: When changing permissions you can always use either the numeric method or the symbolic method. The numeric method is normally easier when changing all the permissions, while the symbolic method is normally easier when changing one or just a few permissions.

Special File Permissions

Several facts about how the Linux and Unix file systems are constructed can cause problems for administrators. For example, only a single group can be the group owner for a given object. Whoever wants access to that object needs to be a member of the group that owns the file (unless you, as the owner of the file, want to give permission to all others). For example, consider the following **ls –l** output:

```
-rw-r----- 1  bob   staff  0 Jan 26 13:08 22   data.txt
```

To be able to see the contents of this file, you either need to be the bob user or a member of the staff group.

Trying to configure many groups and users to have access to the right files can be difficult. Every user has a primary group, and they could be a member of additional groups (secondary groups). This poses problems when sharing files between members who are in "shared" secondary groups. Consider the following scenario:

The bob user (primary group: staff, secondary group: project), the sue user (primary group: payroll, secondary group: project), and the steve user (primary group: acct, secondary group: project) are working on a joint project and sharing files in the **/home/project** directory. The bob user creates a file that ends up looking like the following when listed with the **ls –l** command:

```
-rw-r----- 1  bob   staff  0 Jan 26 13:08 22    data_for_sue_and_
steve.txt
```

Unfortunately, even though all users are in the same group (the project group), the sue and steve users can't view the contents of this file. They are not members of the staff group, so their permission set is "others" for this file.

As we see later, the bob user can change the group ownership of the file to the project group, but this relies on users performing this action every time they create a file. It is unreasonable to assume that all users will remember to do this all of the time (and as an administrator you don't want to have to teach every user to perform this action on their files).

There's a way out of this situation: You can set an additional or special bit on the shared directory, which causes all users who have access to inherit the group owner of the directory on all objects that they create in that directory. This permission set, called *SGID*, is covered in detail later in this chapter.

> **NOTE** There are now access control lists (ACLs) on some Linux distributions, which allow for much more fine-tuning of permissions. However, ACLs are not on the exam, so be careful when answering exam questions related to special bit and group ownership.

Special Bit Permissions

The following special bits are available for Linux file system use:

- **SUID**—The *Set User ID (SUID)* permission allows users to run a program as if they were the user owner of the program; in most cases the user owner is the root user. The numeric value of this permission set is 4XXX (where "XXX" is replaced by the numeric values for the trio sets mentioned previously).

- **SGID**—When set on a directory, the Set Group ID (SGID) permission automatically gives group ownership of all new files created in the directory to the group owner of the directory (numeric = 2XXX). When set on a file, the SGID allows users to run a program as if they were the group owner of the file.

- **Sticky bit**—This permission set is used to keep "nonowners" from deleting files in a common directory (numeric = 1XXX). In a *sticky bit* directory, only the owner of the file or the owner of the directory can delete the file (root always can delete files as well).

Remember that these special permissions are used only when necessary, which isn't often; the SUID and SGID permission sets on an executable file pose a security risk, even when properly used. Avoid providing write permission to SUID and SGID executables. This permission gives a regular user the ability to replace the code within the file, providing a security hole on the system.

Special permissions can be set either of two ways—numeric or symbolic, just like setting other permissions with the **chmod** command.

The use of the characters XXX in the following examples indicates that permissions exist and need to be included but removes the focus from the permissions. In other words, these are the regular permissions that we previously discussed, and I substituted the XXX characters to focus on the special bits instead.

The first way to set these special permissions is to use the numeric mode when executing the **chmod** command. All permissions must be overwritten when using numeric mode; the following sets the SUID permission on the file:

```
chmod 4XXX /some/program
```

Several bits can be changed or set simultaneously; the following command sets both the SUID and SGID bits for the program (which is somewhat rare, but permitted):

```
chmod 6XXX /some/program
```

The second way to set special permissions is to use the symbolic mode. For example, to add SUID on a file:

```
chmod u+s /some/program
```

Again, you can set several special bits at once even with the symbolic mode, although the syntax is a bit more complex:

```
chmod u+s,g+s /some/program
```

Setting the SUID Bit on Files

A good example of the SUID bit is an existing command: **chsh**. The **chsh** command allows a regular user to change her login shell. Note the current permissions for this command:

```
-rws--x-- 1 root root 15432 Apr 29  2013 /usr/bin/chsh
```

The s in place of the user owner's execute permission indicates this is an SUID command. When this command executes, it modifies the contents of the **/etc/passwd** file. The **/etc/passwd** file is not normally something that can be modified by non-root users; as you can see, normally only the root user has this ability:

```
-rw-r--r-- 1 root root 2036 Mar  8 18:39 /etc/passwd
```

However, with the SUID permission set, the **chsh** program is able to access files as either the person who runs the command or as the owner of the **chsh** program (which, in this case, is root).

What if you, as the administrator, do not want users to change their login shells? Just execute the following command as root:

```
chmod u-s /usr/bin/chsh
```

Example 10-1 shows a live example.

Example 10-1   Demonstration of SUID

```
[root@localhost ~]# ls -l /usr/bin/chsh
-rws--x--x. 1 root root 15432 Apr 29  2013 /usr/bin/chsh
[root@localhost ~]# su - student
[student@localhost ~]$ chsh
Changing shell for student.
Password:
New shell [/bin/bash]: /bin/csh
Shell changed.
[student@localhost ~]$ exit
logout
[root@localhost ~]# chmod u-s /usr/bin/chsh
[root@localhost ~]# su - student
[student@localhost ~]$ chsh
Changing shell for student.
Password:
New shell [/bin/csh]: /bin/bash
setpwnam: Permission denied
Shell *NOT* changed.  Try again later.
```

NOTE While the user can "try again later" as the last line of output suggests, until the root user resets the SUID permission set, no regular user will be able to change his login shell.

Setting the SGID Bit on Files

The SGID permission is rarely set on files. Consider the following program with the SGID bit set:

```
-r-xr-sr-x 1 root tty 10996 Jul 19  2011 /usr/bin/wall
```

The s in place of the group owner's execute permission indicates this is an SGID command. The **wall** command allows users to send messages to the terminal windows of all users logged in. Normally this would be a security issue; you don't want a user to interfere with another user's terminal window. Having a message pop up in a terminal where a user is working can be distracting.

The reason why users can use the **wall** command in this way is because it is an SGID program. When this program executes, it accesses files as if the person executing the command were a member of the tty group. This, in turn, allows the **wall** program to have write access to the terminal device files group owned by the tty group:

```
[root@localhost ~]# ls -l /dev/tty1
crw--w---- 1 root tty  4, 1 Jun  2 17:13 /dev/tty1
```

Having problems with users abusing the **wall** command? Take away the SGID access:

```
chmod 0555 /usr/bin/wall
```

NOTE The **wall** program can be used to communicate with others users, but since maturity levels vary among humanity and definitely among computer users, you may have users harassing others, or inappropriately sending broadcast messages, so by restricting the user's access to this command, you improve all system user's productivity.

Setting the SGID Bit on Directories

Consider the previously discussed scenario:

The bob user (primary group: staff, secondary group: project), the sue user (primary group: payroll, secondary group: project), and the steve user (primary group: acct, secondary group: project) are working on a joint project and sharing files in the **/home/project** directory. The bob user creates a file that ends up looking like the following when listed with the **ls –l** command:

```
-rw-r----- 1  bob  staff  0 Jan 26 13:08 22  data_for_sue_and_
steve.txt
```

Recall that this results in a problem: Even though bob, sue, and steve all have a common group, sue and steve can't access this file. If bob were to change the group ownership to the project group, then sue and steve would be able to view the contents of this file. However, expecting users to do this every time they create a file isn't reasonable.

The solution is to add SGID permission to the **/home/project** directory:

```
chmod g+s /home/project
```

As the preceding command changes the group ownership to be the projects group, this means all new files created in the **/home/project** directory are automatically group owned by the group owner of the directory (which would have to be set to the project group, of course). Note: This doesn't solve the problem of the existing file, only for new files.

Setting the Sticky Bit

The sticky bit is used mostly for ensuring that users in a shared directory can't delete anyone else's files. A good example of this is the **/tmp** directory:

```
drwxrwxrwt 29 root 4096 Jun  2 17:27 /tmp
```

The t in place of the others execute permission indicates this is a sticky bit directory. The **/tmp** directory is a location where all users must be able to create files. Unfortunately, the permission that allows users to create files also allows them to delete files—all files—in that directory.

By adding the sticky bit permission, the write permission for directories changes meaning. Instead of meaning "add and delete all files in the directory," the only users who can now delete files in this directory are

- The owner of the file or

- The owner of the directory (which is normally the root user) or

- The root user

Anyone can still add a file into this directory, as long as it doesn't result in overwriting another user's file.

Finding Files by Permission

Attackers who breach your system often attempt to set certain files to have the SUID or SGID bit set, allowing their otherwise normal account to perform all sorts of unauthorized tasks.

The **find** command has an operator that makes finding your vulnerable files easy. The **-perm** operator is usually followed by a three- or four-digit set of permissions, such as the example shown here:

```
find /usr/bin -perm 777
```

This example searches for any object in the **/usr/bin** directory and all subdirectories that has the exact permissions of rwxrwxrwx. This is fine, but it doesn't help find security risks caused by the SUID and SGID bits. This next command does, however:

```
find / -perm -4000
```

At first glance, this might look as if we're searching for all files that have the SUID bits and then blank permissions from that point on. It really searches the entire system for all files that have the SUID bit set, regardless of the other permissions.

You should install the system and then run a **find** command that reports any file that has an SUID bit set, like so:

```
find / -perm -4000 -ls
```

Redirect this output to a file and keep that file on a disk or in some safe place off the system (like on a USB drive). Every so often (especially after installing new software or when you think your system has been exploited), you should run the same **find** command and then compare the results to the original with the **diff** command, such as:

```
diff /root/latestfindperm /mnt/usb/findperm.orig
```

Investigate any differences!

Default Permissions

Consider the following situation: You create a new file and it has the permissions of rw-rw-rw- on it. You realize that this is much too "open," so you execute the following command to place the permissions that you want on this file:

```
chmod 640 file
```

Ten minutes later you create another file, and it also has the permissions of rw-rw-rw- on it. Again you execute the **chmod** command to set the permissions of 640 on the file. You begin to realize that you are going to be executing the **chmod** command a lot. Fortunately, there is a better way.

If your system is a typical Linux system, a value is set in either the **/etc/bashrc** or **~/. bashrc** file that governs the default permissions any created object has. This value is known as the umask, and this single value is used to determine default permissions for both directories and files. This umask only applies when you create a new file or directory.

The maximum default permissions for directories and files are different, which means the *umask value* results in different default permissions for files than it does for directories. The default permissions with no umask value set are

- For files: rw-rw-rw- (or 666)
- For directories: rwxrwxrwx (or 777)

View the umask for your current shell by executing the following command:

```
umask
0022
```

This just means that of the four possible positions to mask out (special permissions, user owner permissions, group owner permissions, and other permissions), the last two have the write permission masked out or not used. Note: The first position never has any effect as the special permissions are never set by default. As a result, the umask value of 0022 is really the same as 022.

If you create a file when the umask is set to 022, the file's permissions is as follows:

```
-rw-r--r--    1 root    root        881 Feb 17 09:11 file1
```

If you create a directory with the same umask set, the directory's permissions are as follows:

```
drwxr-xr-x    2 root    root       4096 Feb 17 14:47 dir1
```

To understand why these permission sets are different, think about the process of how the umask is applied. To begin with, recall the default permissions:

```
                  For Files              For Directories
Maximum           rw-rw-rw-              rwxrwxrwx
```

Now, consider a umask value of 022. This means you are "masking out" or removing the write permissions for the group owner and others (represented by the M values here):

```
                  For Files              For Directories
Maximum           rw-rw-rw-              rwxrwxrwx
MASK              ----M--M-              ----M--M-
```

When those permissions are masked out, you end up getting the following permissions on new files and directories:

```
                  For Files              For Directories
Maximum           rw-rw-rw-              rwxrwxrwx
MASK              ----M--M-              ----M--M-
Result            rw-r--r--              rw-r--r--
```

As you can see, the umask value changes the default permissions of a created object based on the following formula:

```
Maximum default value - umask value = create value
```

You can change the umask value to a more restrictive one with the **umask 027** command.

Now, you can create another file and the permissions should be

```
-rw-r-----    1 root    root        881 Feb 17 09:22 file2
```

Create another directory with the umask value of 027 and the permissions should be

```
drwxr-x---    2 root    root       4096 Feb 17 14:48 dir2
```

Notice that in the previous example the umask has a value greater than the default value of the file being created. The umask values go from 000 to 777 because a directory object has a maximum default value of 777; however, files have a maximum default value of 666. The umask value must encompass both sets of possible values, so if you have a 7 in a umask value, it would affect the file default permission as if it were a 6. In other words, in this case 6 – 7 = 0.

The umask value will show up on the exam. For example, you might see a question that provides a file permission listing and be asked to provide the umask value that resulted in those permissions. To become familiar with how umask values work, try different scenarios to determine what the result would be. Use the following chart and plug in different values for your umask value for practice:

```
                   For Files              For Directories
Default            rw-rw-rw-              rwxrwxrwx
MASK
Result
```

Finally, it is important to note that while each of your shells initially has the same umask value, you can change this value in one shell and it does not affect the umask value in other shells. Recall that this value is initially set via an initialization file (typically either the **/etc/bashrc** or **~/.bashrc** file).

Changing User Ownership

The **chown** command is used to set the user owner, group owner, or a combination of the two with one command. The format for the **chown** command is

```
chown -options user:group object
```

The **chown** command accepts both of the following commands as valid (the owner/group separator can be either a ":" or a "." character):

```
chown snuffy:users file1
chown snuffy.users file1
```

In addition, you can use the following syntax with **chown**:

- **owner**—Changes only the user owner
- **owner:group**—Changes both the user owner and group owner

- **owner:**—Changes the user owner and sets the group owner to the primary group of the current user

- **:group**—Changes only the group owner and leaves the user owner unaffected

Let's say that the user snuffy's primary group is called users and the account is a secondary group member of the accounting group. By default, every object snuffy creates on the system has snuffy as the user owner and users as the group owner. This can cause problems in shared directories.

If snuffy visits a shared directory whose group ownership is set to the accounting group and creates a file named snuffysexpenses.txt, that file is inaccessible to any of the other users who share that directory unless they are also members of the group users.

Say the user martha does expenses and needs to have ownership of the file and you, as the administrator, want to change the group ownership of this file to the accounting group. To accomplish this task, use this command:

```
chown martha:accounting snuffysexpenses.txt
```

Let's say that now the file needs to be owned by another user who cuts the checks, fluchre; you can change just the user owner without having to bother with the group owner:

```
chown fluchre snuffysexpenses.txt
```

If for some reason you decide that an entire directory tree of files needs to have its ownership changed, you can change them all with the following command:

```
chown -R root:accounting /accounting
```

Important note: The only user on the system who can change the user ownership of an object is the root user. Even the owner of the file can't "give ownership" to another user. However, a regular user can change the group ownership of an object as long as the user is a member of the group that she is changing ownership to.

Changing Group Ownership

When just the group owner needs to be changed, the simplest method is to use the **chgrp** command. The syntax of the command is straightforward:

```
chgrp staff file1
```

Changing a large set of files to another group owner requires the use of the **-R** (recursive) option:

```
chgrp -R staff /data/*
```

The previous command changes the contents of the **/data** directory (and all its sub-directories) to the group owner staff but leaves the user owner alone.

Options for the **chgrp** command include

- **-c**—Shows a line of output only for changed objects

- **-h**—Changes symbolic links, not the original file

- **-R**—Recursively affects the target and all children

- **-v**—Shows a line of output for every object, regardless of the actions performed on the object

NOTE Although it is not an exam objective, the **newgrp** command can be handy when it comes to group ownership. A regular user can execute the command **newgrp groupname** if he is a member of groupname. This opens a new shell in which the primary group is groupname. This is useful when creating a bunch of files that need to be group owned by a secondary group. To close this new shell, simply execute the **exit** command.

Summary

In this chapter you learned the concept of basic permissions, including how to set them and how to specify the default permissions for objects. You also learned how special permissions work and how they are important for securing the system.

Exam Preparation Tasks

As mentioned in the section "How to Use This Book" in the Introduction, you have a few choices for exam preparation: the exercises here, Chapter 21, "Final Preparation," and the practice exams on the DVD.

Review All Key Topics

Review the most important topics in this chapter, noted with the Key Topics icon in the outer margin of the page. Table 10-2 lists a reference of these key topics and the page numbers on which each is found.

Table 10-2   Key Topics for Chapter 10

Key Topic Element	Description	Page Number
Paragraph	Permission trio bits	292
Paragraph	The bit values equate to the following permissions for files	293
Paragraph	These permissions have similar but slightly different meaning for directories	293
Paragraph	Numeric permissions are the most often used	294
Paragraph	When to use the **chmod** command	296
Paragraph	Special bit permissions	298
Paragraph	Special bit permissions are used only when necessary	298
Paragraph	A good example of the SUID bit	299
Paragraph	Sticky bit use	302
Paragraph	**find** command operator	302
Paragraph	Default permissions for a typical Linux system	303
Paragraph	The umask value	305
Paragraph	The **chown** command	305
Paragraph	The only user who can change some permissions	306
Paragraph	Changing group ownership	306

Define Key Terms

Define the following key terms from this chapter and check your answers in the glossary:

permission trios, numeric mode, symbolic mode, SUID, SGID, sticky bit, umask value

Review Questions

The answers to these review questions are in Appendix A.

1. The execute permission for directories provides what access?

   a. The ability to list file names in a directory

   b. The ability to add files to the directory

   c. The ability to remove files from the directory

   d. The ability to change into the directory

2. Consider the following output of the **ls –l** command:

```
-rw-rwxr-x    2 fred     users   0 Jan 26 13:08 22   test.mp3
```

Which of the following statements is true?

  a. The user fred has only read permission on test.mp3.

  b. The user fred has only read and write permission on test.mp3.

  c. The user fred has read, write and execute permission on test.mp3.

  d. The user fred has no permission on test.mp3.

3. Which of the following is the equivalent to the command **chmod 644 file.txt**?

  a. chmod a+r,ug+w file.txt

  b. chmod u+rw,g+r,o+r file.txt

  c. chmod u=rw,go=r file.txt

  d. chmod ugo+r,u+w file.txt

4. Which of the following commands sets the SUID permission? (Choose two.)

  a. chmod u+s file

  b. chmod g+s file

  c. chmod 2755 file

  d. chmod 4755 file

5. Consider the following command:

```
umask 077
```

Assuming this command was executed in the current shell, which of the following are true? (Choose two.)

  a. A new directory created in this shell would have the permissions of rw------.

  b. A new directory created in this shell would have the permissions of rwx-----.

  c. A new file created in this shell would have the permissions of rw-------.

  d. A new file created in this shell would have the permissions of rwx------.

This chapter covers the following topics:

- Working Within the Shell
- Extending the Shell
- Localization and Internationalization

This chapter covers the following exam topics:

- Customize and use the shell environment: 105.1
- Localization and Internationalization: 107.3

## CHAPTER 11

Customizing Shell Environments

The shell lets you wield amazing power over your systems. You can perform simple tasks, such as copying files and running programs. You can combine many tasks into one, perform repetitive tasks with a few keystrokes, and even offload simple decision making to the shell. At first glance it's an imposing interface. With a bit of knowledge you can start using these advanced features.

"Do I Know This Already?" Quiz

The "Do I Know This Already?" quiz enables you to assess whether you should read this entire chapter or simply jump to the "Exam Preparation Tasks" section for review. If you are in doubt, read the entire chapter. Table 11-1 outlines the major headings in this chapter and the corresponding "Do I Know This Already?" quiz questions. You can find the answers in Appendix A, "Answers to the 'Do I Know This Already?' Quizzes and Review Questions."

Table 11-1 "Do I Know This Already?" Foundation Topics Section-to-Question Mapping

Foundation Topics Section	Questions Covered in This Section
Working Within the shell	1-2
Extending the Shell	3-4
Localization and Internationalization	5-6

1. Which are proper ways of assigning the value bar to the environment variable FOO? (Choose two.)

   a. set FOO=bar

   b. export FOO=bar

   c. FOO=bar

   d. export FOO bar

2. Consider the following script:

```
#!/bin/bash
echo You are $AGE years old.
```

You run the following:

```
$ AGE=42
$ ./script
You are years old.
```

Why did the script not display the age?

    a. **AGE** should be in lowercase.

    b. The script should have been run as . ./**script**.

    c. The script was not marked as executable.

    d. You should have set age with the **set** keyword.

3. Which of the following scripts are sourced when you have a non-login session?

    a. ~/.bashrc

    b. ~/.bash_profile

    c. ~/.profile

    d. /etc/profile

4. Which of the following are true about Bash alias and functions? (Choose two.)

    a. Both can save you typing.

    b. Both can accept parameters.

    c. Functions can span multiple lines while aliases can't.

    d. Functions must be exported.

5. You're about to call a friend in Thunder Bay but you don't know what time zone they are in. How could you tell what time it is in Thunder Bay?

    a. **tzselect**

    b. **TZ=America/Thunder_Bay date**

    c. **LC_TIME=America/Thunder_Bay date**

    d. **date --timezone=America/Thunder_Bay**

6. One of your coworkers in the Asia-Pacific office sent you a file containing instructions on how to set up the new application he is working on. When you look at the file in your editor, it's a mess. You run **file** on the message and see:

```
message: Big-endian UTF-16 Unicode text
```

How can you decode this file?

    a. It's impossible to decode; the coworker must send it in ISO-8859.

    b. LANGUAGE=en_US.UTF-16 cat message

    c. tr -d UTF-16 < message

    d. iconv -f UTF-16 -t ASCII message

Foundation Topics

Working Within the Shell

The shell is the desktop of the text interface. The shell takes the commands you enter, sends them to the operating system, and displays the results back to you. Along the way the shell implements features such as globbing, which matches files with wildcards, which makes smaller commands more powerful. You can also add your own commands to the shell to further cut down on your work.

So far in this book you've seen many shell commands such as those to manipulate files. Here's where you learn how to customize the shell environment to make what you've learned so far more powerful.

Unless you change the defaults, the Linux shell is normally the **bash** shell. Of course, many other shells exist. A partial list is shown in Table 11-2.

Table 11-2   A Sampling of Linux Shells

	ash	Bourne Again Shell	C-shell	Korn	T C-shell	zsh
Executable	ash	bash	csh	ksh	tcsh	zsh
Job Control	N	Y	Y	Y	Y	Y
Aliases	N	Y	Y	Y	Y	Y
Functions	Y	Y	N	Y	N	Y
Redirection	Y	Y	Y	Y	Y	Y
History	N	Y	Y	Y	Y	Y
Completion	N	Y	Y	Y	Y	Y
Editing	N	Y	Y	Y	Y	Y

Among other pieces of information, the user's default shell is specified in the **/etc/passwd** entry for that user. If the shell specified does not exist, the user gets the **bash** shell by default.

Special shells can be specified, such as **/bin/false** (which returns a nonzero error code, effectively blocking access by a user attempting to log in) or **/sbin/nologin** (which also blocks logins but gives a polite message).

Choosing a shell is a personal matter. Most shells are related to one another somehow. **bash**, the Bourne Again Shell, is an improvement on the Bourne shell, which itself is an improvement on the original Thompson shell from Unix. The Korn shell is derived from Bourne but implements some of the good stuff from the C-shell.

This book will describe the use of **bash**. The concepts can be applied to all other shells.

Environment Variables

A *variable* is a bucket that stores information. If you need to store the process ID of that web server you just launched, put it in a variable called **WEBSERVER_PID** and it'll be there when you need it next, as shown in Example 11-1.

Example 11-1   Example of a Variable

```
$ WEBSERVER_PID=29565

$ echo $WEBSERVER_PID
29565
$ ps -ef | grep $WEBSERVER_PID
nginx    14747 29565  0 Apr10 ?        00:04:09 nginx: worker process

root     29565     1  0 Mar27 ?        00:00:00 nginx: master process
```

The first line assigns the value 29565 to the variable called WEBSERVER_PID. Prefixing the variable name with a dollar sign tells the shell that it is to substitute the value of the variable at that spot. The next two commands in the preceding example use the variable by first displaying it with the **echo** command and then looking for processes containing that number with **ps** and **grep**.

Remember: Use the variable name by itself for assignment. Prepend a dollar sign to use the value inside the variable. It's also important that there are no spaces around the equals sign.

A variable name can be upper- or lowercase and contain letters, numbers, and the underscore (_). By convention, anything you set in the shell is in uppercase. Variables within a script are lowercase or mixed case.

Variables can have meaning to you, or they can have meaning to the shell. **$HOME** is set automatically by the shell to the current user's home directory, so that first command above was redundant!

If you have spaces in the right side of the assignment, you need to escape the space or quote it. These two commands have the same effect:

```
$ GREETING="Hello World"
$ GREETING=Hello\ World
```

Variable Scope

A confusing property of environment variables is that setting them in one shell applies only to that shell and not parents, children, or other shells. For example, if you had a program that looked at an environment variable called WORK_FAC-TOR to see how much work it could do, this wouldn't work:

```
$ WORK_FACTOR=3
$ ./my_command
```

This is because running **./my_command** starts a child process with a new environment. Variables you set aren't passed to children. You need to export that variable:

```
$ WORK_FACTOR=3
$ export WORK_FACTOR
$ ./my_command
```

The **export** command marks the variable as something that gets passed to children. There are less verbose ways of accomplishing this: **$ export WORK_FACTOR=3**.

The **export** keyword can be used on the same line as the assignment. Alternatively, if you just want to pass the variable to the child and not set it in the current environment, you can set it on the same line as the command:

```
$ WORK_FACTOR=3 ./my_command
$ echo $WORK_FACTOR

$
```

The **echo** shows that even though you set WORK_FACTOR to 3 for the child, the current process didn't keep it around.

By itself, **export** prints a list of variables currently exported to child environments.

Setting Variables from a Child

A common pattern is to put the assignments in a separate configuration file and use that file in a script or the command line. This adds consistency and makes commands easier to type. However the variables would be set in the child environment, which is thrown away when the process exits.

Given a configuration file called **config** containing an assignment;
WORK_FACTOR=3.

If you were to run that, your current shell wouldn't know about the variable:

```
$ ./config
$ echo $WORK_FACTOR

$
```

What you need is to make the assignments in the current environment. This is the job of **source**:

```
$ source ./config
$ echo $WORK_FACTOR
3
```

 Sourcing a file executes it in the current shell environment instead of creating a separate child environment. Thus variables set in the script are available in the current environment. If the script didn't **export** the variable, it will not be available to child processes later on.

There is an alternate way to source a file, which is to replace the word **source** with a period:

```
$ . ./config
```

Setting and Unsetting Variables

Bash has two built-in commands, **set** and **unset**, that are related in some sense but in another sense are just confusing.

The easy one is **unset**. Example 11-2 shows how to use this to destroy a variable.

Example 11-2   Using **unset** to Destroy a Variable

```
$ FOO=bar
$ echo $FOO
bar
$ unset FOO
$ echo $FOO
```

Note that when you're unsetting, refer to the variable name without the dollar sign.

set is a multitalented command. By itself it shows all variables and functions in the environment. Contrast this to **export**, which only shows exported variables.

The next use of **set** is to enable or disable features in the shell. For example, **set -x** tells the shell to print each command as it is executed. At the shell this isn't that useful, but you can use this in a shell script for debugging. To revert the behavior, use **set +x**. The alternate way to set this is with **set -o xtrace**.

A useful option is called **noclobber**, which is enabled with **set -C** or **set -o noclobber**, as shown in Example 11-3. This tells the shell not to overwrite existing files with redirects.

Example 11-3   Using **noclobber**

```
$ echo hi > test
$ echo hi > test
$ set -o noclobber
$ echo hi > test
-bash: test: cannot overwrite existing file
```

The first command in the preceding example puts the string **hi** into a file named **test**. It's done once more to show that the shell will let you overwrite a file. The **noclobber** option is enabled and the same test is run, which results in an error. To disable **noclobber** run **set +o noclobber**.

The final use of **set** is to assign *positional parameters*. Within the shell are reserved variable names. Among those are **$1** and other numbered variables, which are used to pass information to scripts from the command line and other functions. Anything not passed to **set** and recognized as an option is assigned to one of these positional parameters:

```
$ set a b c d e f g h i j k l m
$ echo $1
a
$ echo ${10}
j
```

Note the curly braces when trying to expand **$10**. Without them the shell thinks you're trying to expand $1 and then appending a zero, so you would end up with **a0**.

Subshells

You've already seen how parent and child shells interact with respect to environment variables. There are times when you may want to temporarily use child shells to ensure you have a clean slate or to temporarily set some variables without changing your current shell.

The easiest way to get a subshell is to enclose the commands in parentheses. Copy Example 11-4 into a file called **test.sh** and run it.

Example 11-4 A Shell Script to Demonstrate Subshells

```
echo "In parent $BASH_SUBSHELL pid $$"
FOO=bar
echo $FOO
(FOO=baz; echo -n "In subshell $BASH_SUBSHELL "; echo $$)
echo $FOO
```

The first thing the script does is write some information to the console. The two variables are built in to Bash: **$BASH_SUBSHELL** gives the current subshell level and **$$** gives the process id of the current process.

After that the script sets a variable **FOO** and prints it to the screen.

Following that is the script again inside a subshell. **FOO** is assigned a new value and the current values of **BASH_SUBSHELL** and the `pid` are printed. A subshell can span multiple lines, but for compactness the commands are separated with semico-lons (`;`).

Finally, the script prints the contents of **FOO**. Running the script produces the output shown in Example 11-5.

Example 11-5 A Script to Demonstrate BASH_SUBSHELL Levels

```
$ sh test.sh
In parent 0 pid 11966
bar
In subshell 1 11966
bar
```

The value of FOO hasn't changed in the parent shell because it was only changed in the subshell. Also, the subshell didn't spawn a new process.

The env Wrapper

The subshell is a method to make sure some work doesn't pollute your current environment. Sometimes you want to do some work in a known environment, which is where **env** comes in.

You've already seen an example of this need with the **WORK_FACTOR=3 ./ my_command** example.

The **env** command, and note that it's a command not built into the shell, allows you to modify the environment prior to running a command. By itself it displays all environment variables.

The most common use of **env** is at the beginning of a shell script. A script usually starts with the **shebang** line that tells Linux which interpreter to use: **#!/usr/bin/ruby.**

Coming from the first two characters, hash (**#**) and bang (**!**), the interpreter that follows the two characters is used to run the script. In this case it's **/usr/bin/ruby**. But what if **ruby** is somewhere other than **/usr/bin**? Using **#!/bin/env ruby** gets the shell to search for Ruby in the **PATH** (more on this later).

Another use is to wipe out the current environment before continuing. For example, to ensure a predictable PATH you can wipe out the environment and then run a new shell:

```
$ env -i sh -c 'echo $PATH'
/usr/local/bin:/bin:/usr/bin
```

The current environment is kept if **-i** is not used:

```
$ env sh -c 'echo $PATH'
/usr/local/bin:/bin:/usr/bin:/usr/local/sbin:/usr/sbin:/sbin:/home/
sean/bin
```

As running **env** by itself prints the whole environment, you can verify that **env –i** wipes the environment first:

```
$ env -i env
$
```

Extending the Shell

The shell is customizable. If you want to change the way certain commands operate, such as to always request confirmation when the root user deletes a file, you can do that. If you don't like the way the prompt looks you can change it. If you have a few commands you use repeatedly, you can reduce them down to a single word.

Global and User Settings

When users log in to the system, either from a remote shell session or via the console, a series of scripts are run that can modify the environment. Some of the scripts are global to all users on the system and some exist only for a single user. These scripts are all sourced so that they can make changes to the user's environment.

The scripts that get run depend on how the shell was invoked.

A Login Shell Session

A *login shell* is one that is executed when logging in to the system.

The **/etc/profile** script is the global configuration file that affects all users' environments if they use the **bash** shell. It's sourced (read) every time a user performs a login shell. This file is a script and is executed right before the user's profile script. After this, any files inside of **/etc/profile.d** are sourced.

The user's **~/.bash_profile** script, if it exists, is the next script sourced. This file contains variables, code, and settings that directly affect that user's—and only that user's—environment. If **.bash_profile** doesn't exist, the shell looks for **.bash_login** or **.profile**, stopping once a match has been found.

The **.bash_profile**, or alternative script if found, sources **.bashrc**. Note that this isn't behavior in the shell; it's a convention that makes everything easier later.

When the user logs out, the shell sources the **.bash_logout** file. This file is used to issue the **clear** command, so text from any previous command is not left on the user's screen after he logs out. It can also clean up anything that may have been launched as part of the session.

Be careful on the exam because a lot of test-takers do not pick the **.bash_logout** file as part of the user's login session. It's definitely one of the more missed elements in the shell section.

An example of the user's login session might be the following:

1. The user logs in with a username and password.

2. The **/etc/profile** is sourced.

3. Files under **/etc/profile.d** are sourced.

4. The user's **~/.bash_profile** is sourced.

5. The user's **~/.bashrc** is sourced from within the **~/.bash_profile**.

6. The user conducts her business.

7. The user initiates a logout with the **logout** or **exit** command or by pressing **Ctrl+D**.

8. The user's **.bash_logout** script is sourced.

A Non-Login Shell Session

Non-login shell sessions are typically the root user using the **su** command to temporarily become another user or a sysadmin using **su** to become the root user without loading the entire environment of the root or other user. Non-login shells are also started when you open new terminals from within a graphical session.

> **NOTE**   The **su** command creates a non-login shell. If you need a login shell, place a dash after the **su** command, for example, **su - sean**.

When a user executes a non-login session, the only file sourced is the target account's **~/.bashrc** file. (On Red Hat machines, the first action in the **~/.bashrc** is to source the **/etc/bashrc** file if it exists. Other distributions have different files that they run.)

Upon exiting that shell, no logout files or scripts are sourced, nor are the source account's scripts run again.

The PATH

When you run a command the shell looks through the directories in the **PATH** variable to find the program to run. This lets you run **/usr/local/bin/firefox** just by typing `firefox`. Without the path you would always have to qualify your commands, such as to run **./firefox**, **/usr/local/bin/firefox**, or **../bin/firefox** depending on which directory you were in.

The path is a series of directories separated by colons (:) and is stored in an environment variable called **PATH**.

```
$ echo $PATH
/usr/local/bin:/bin:/usr/bin:/usr/local/sbin:/usr/sbin:/sbin:/home/
sean/bin:/home/sean/cxoffice/bin:/opt/IBMJava2-142/jre/bin/
```

The shell looks through each directory in turn, stopping with the first match, or gives you a command not found error if none of the directories contain a match. If you give a relative or fully qualified path name the path is ignored.

Your system will have a default path set, so usually you want to add to it instead of replacing it. In your **.bash_profile** or **.bashrc** add **export PATH=$HOME/bin:$PATH**.

As **$HOME** expands to be your home directory, and **$PATH** expands to be the current path. This example prepends the **bin** directory underneath your home directory to the search path.

There is no implicit check for the current directory in your path. You must explicitly run **./program**, **/full/path/to/program**, or add **.** to your path to run programs from your current directory. Make the shell check the current directory last with **export PATH=$PATH:.**

Again, **$PATH** expands to the current path, and then you're appending the current directory.

Putting the current directory in the path can open up security holes. The thinking is that if someone has an evil program called **ls** in his home directory or maybe in **/tmp** and the root user is in that directory and runs **ls**, the evil program could run instead of **/bin/ls**.

Aliases and Functions

Aliases and functions are two related features that let you run more complicated commands with fewer keystrokes.

An *alias* replaces part of your command with something else. If you wanted to save a few keystrokes on **ls -l** you could make an alias: **alias ll="ls –l"**.

Any time you type **ll** by itself it will be expanded to **ls -l**. For example **ll**, **ll -h**, or **ll *.doc** are all good uses, giving you a long listing, a long listing with human readable sizes, and a long listing of all the **.doc** files, respectively. Typing **all** will not trigger the alias because aliases only operate on distinct words.

Aliases take priority over searching the path so you can make sure you always include options when running a command by redefining the command: **alias rm="rm –I"**.

This redefines the **rm** command to always run **rm -i**, which prompts the user to delete instead of doing it silently.

You can defeat the alias temporarily by either fully qualifying your command (**/bin/rm**) or escaping it (**\rm**). It's assumed that if you're smart enough to override an alias, you're smart enough to know the consequences of what you're doing!

Functions

Functions are invoked just like aliases except that they run Bash code instead of a simple substitution. If you wanted to take a complicated directory copy command like **tar -cf - * | (cd somedir && tar -xf -)** and vary the name of **somedir**, an alias won't do it.

The form of a function is **function name() { commands }**. The commands can span multiple lines. So the function to copy a directory using the **tar** command is

```
function dircp () {
    tar -cf - * | ( cd $1 && tar -xf - )
}
```

The special variable, **$1**, is expanded to the first option passed to the function. **$2** is the second, and so forth. You can refer to all the **parameters** at once with **$***.

You then call the function as if it were a command, such as with **dircp /tmp/**.

Unlike aliases the function must appear at the beginning of the command, and the rest of the command up until any redirections or semicolons is passed as arguments. You're creating a mini program instead of a simple substitution.

PS1

If you're going to spend a lot of time at a shell you might as well enjoy it, right? You can embed information into your command prompt to give you context. Do you work on multiple servers throughout the day? Put the name of the server in the command prompt and never face the embarrassment of running the right command on the wrong server!

The command prompt is stored in an environment variable called **PS1**.

```
$ PS1="Your wish master? "
Your wish master?
```

While that command prompt is sure to stroke your ego it is not that informative. Bash implements several special macros that are expanded each time the prompt is rendered.

```
$ PS1="\h:\w\$ "
bob:~/tmp$
```

In the preceding example the **\h** is expanded to the short name of the host, the **\w** becomes the current directory, and the **\$** is **$** for regular users and **#** for root.

The list of possible macros are as follows:

Code	Displays
• \a	An ASCII bell character (07).
• \d	The date in weekday, month, day format (for example, Tue May 26).
• \e	An ASCII escape character (033).
• \h	The hostname up to the first ..
• \H	The hostname.
• \j	The number of jobs currently managed by the shell.
• \l	The base name of the shell's terminal device name.
• \n	New line.
• \r	Carriage return.
• \s	The name of the shell.

Code	Displays
• \t	The current time in 24-hour HH:MM:SS format.
• \T	The current time in 12-hour HH:MM:SS format.
• \@	The current time in 12-hour a.m./p.m. format.
• \A	The current time in 24-hour HH:MM format.
• \u	The username of the current user.
• \v	The version of bash (for example, 2.00).
• \V	The release of bash, in the format version + patch level (for example, 2.00.0).
• \w	The current working directory.
• \W	The base name of the current working directory.
• \!	The history number of this command.
• \#	The command number of this command.
• \$	If the effective UID is 0, it's a #; otherwise, it's a $.
• \nnn	The character corresponding to the octal number nnn.
• \\	A backslash.
• \[	Begin a sequence of nonprinting characters, which could be used to embed a terminal control sequence into the prompt.
• \]	End a sequence of nonprinting characters.

NOTE   It's unreasonable to need to memorize all these options for an exam, so this list is for reference. You will want to know how to construct a **PS1** command line and know that the macros begin with a backslash.

Adding More Dynamic Content

Is what you want not there? You can run commands or functions in your prompt, as shown in Example 11-6.

Example 11-6   Running Commands and Functions in Your Prompt

```
$ function logged_in_users() {
> w_lines=$(w | wc -l)
> echo -n $(( $w_lines - 2))
> }
$ PS1='$(id) $(logged_in_users) users logged in\$ '
uid=500(sean) gid=500(sean) 2 users logged in$
```

It's important to use single quotes in this case; otherwise, the command will be run before the variable is set and it will always show the same value. The **$()** operator runs the command inside the parentheses and is discussed more in Chapter 12, "Shell Scripting."

It should go without saying to be careful when running commands in your shell prompt. There are many good situations in which to use this feature, but it can also slow you down as it runs commands on each showing of the prompt. You cannot assume you know which directory you're in, so any paths should be fully qualified.

PS2

PS2 is another prompt you can change in your shell. Its contents are displayed when you type a command that spans more than one line.

```
$ PS2="more? "
$ ls |
more?
```

This one is not used as much as **PS1** but can be helpful for novice users for which > is not a good indication that the shell is waiting for more input.

Creating New Users (skeleton)

Now that you have some helpful and cool additions to your Bash startup scripts you may want to share them with users. There are two ways to do this: Move the code into the systemwide /etc/profile or copy the files over when you create a user.

The first option is possible but would make it difficult for users to override what you did if they have something that suits them better. You also don't want to make big changes on existing users.

That leaves making the changes part of the new user setup. One of the things that the **useradd** tool does when it creates a user is to copy the **skeleton directory** over to the new user's home directory. By default this is **/etc/skel**, as shown in Example 11-7, though you can override this in **/etc/default/useradd**.

Example 11-7   Using **/etc/skel**

```
# ls -la /etc/skel/    .
total 64
drwxr-xr-x.   4 root root  4096 Mar 19  2012 .
drwxr-xr-x. 197 root root 20480 Mar  5 07:47 ..
-rw-r--r--   1 root root    18 Jun 22  2011 .bash_logout
```

```
-rw-r--r--      1 root root    193 Jun 22  2011 .bash_profile
-rw-r--r--      1 root root    124 Jun 22  2011 .bashrc
-rw-r--r--      1 root root    201 Feb 23  2012 .kshrc
```

The default skeleton directory includes sample bash logout, profile, and rc files, and a `ksh` default script. This varies from distribution to distribution, however.

Any changes you make to these files are copied over when you create a new user. You can also add new files or get rid of items.

Localization and Internationalization

You'll have particular ways of writing numbers, currency, and time wherever you live. In the United States it's convention to write the date with the month first. Travel north to Canada, and you'll see the month in different spots. North America is standardized on commas to group the thousands in a number and the period separates the integers from the decimals. Fly over to France and they use commas to separate the integers from the decimals. And everyone has their own currency!

Internationalization and *localization* are two concepts that allow a computer to store information one way but display it in a way that suits the conventions of the user. Internationalization is the feature that allows a system to display information in different ways, and localization is the process that bundles up all the regional changes for a single location into a *locale*.

Time Zones

The most readily visible localization features have to do with time. Every location on the planet belongs to a *time zone*. A time zone is defined as an offset from Universal Coordinated Time (UTC). UTC+0 is also known as *Greenwich Mean Time (GMT)* because it's centered around Greenwich, London.

Many of those locations observe some form of *daylight saving time (DST)*. DST is a system where clocks move ahead an hour in the summer to take advantage of longer nights. Each DST zone sets the dates when the hour is added and removed.

A Linux machine may be physically located in one time zone, but the users may connect remotely from other time zones. Unix has a simple solution to this problem: All timestamps are stored in UTC, and each user is free to set the time zone of her choosing. The system then adds or removes the time zone offset before displaying the value to the user.

Unix stores time as seconds since midnight UTC of January 1, 1970. This special date is known as the *epoch*, or the birthday of Unix. As of early 2015 the current Unix timestamp was over 1.4 billion.

Displaying Time

A date and time must include the time zone to have enough meaning to be compared with other dates and times. The **date** command shows the current date and time.

```
$ date
Sun Mar  8 21:15:01 CDT 2015
```

The time zone is displayed as CDT, Central Daylight Time, which is UTC-5. You can specify different formats with the plus sign (+) and percent encodings:

```
$ date  +"%Y-%m-%dT%H:%M:%z"
2015-03-08T21:19:-0500
```

Instead of the time zone as a word, this date format uses the offset itself in a format known as ISO8601. With **date -u** the time is displayed in UTC, which is written as +0000 or sometimes Z, short for Zulu, a way of referring to UTC in military and aviation circles.

The percent encodings in the date commands each have special meaning:

- **%Y**—Four-digit year
- **%m**—Two-digit month
- **%d**—Two-digit day
- **%H**—Two-digit hour in 24-hour time
- **%M**—Two-digit minute
- **%z**—Time zone offset

Other characters, such as the T, colon, and dashes, are displayed as is. Run **man date** to get a full list of encodings.

Setting Time Zones

The configuration for each time zone, and by extension any daylight savings time, is stored in the zoneinfo files under **/usr/share/zoneinfo**. For example, **/usr/share/zoneinfo/America/Winnipeg** has all the configuration for the city of Winnipeg. Unlike most configuration files in Linux, these files contain binary data and can't be directly viewed.

The system time zone is stored in a file called **/etc/localtime**. It is either a copy of the appropriate zoneinfo or a symlink to the appropriate file, depending on the distribution. Symlinks are typically used so that it's clear which time zone is in use. For example you could set your current time zone to Winnipeg with:

```
ln -sf /usr/share/zoneinfo/America/Winnipeg /etc/localtime
```

 Users who don't have a time zone set get this zone as their default. They can override the setting through the **TZ** environment variable.

```
# date +%z
-0500
# TZ=Asia/Hong_Kong date +%z
+0800
```

In the preceding example the system time zone is UTC-5 in the first command but is overridden just for that command to the Hong Kong time zone in the second. The user could just as easily set TZ in her **.bash_profile** file to make the changes persistent.

 Your distribution includes tools to set the time zone from a menu. Depending on the distribution, this may be **tzselect**, **tzconfig**, or **dpkg-reconfigure tzdata**. The **tzselect** command merely helps you find the name of the time zone you want and leaves the work of making it permanent up to you. The other two commands make the changes to the **/etc/localtime** file for you.

Additionally, your distribution may store the time zone as a word in other files. Two such examples are **/etc/timezone** for Debian and **/etc/sysconfig/clock** for Red Hat.

Character Encoding

Once upon a time computers used *ASCII*, the American Standard Code for Information Interchange. ASCII encodes characters into 7 bits, which gives 128 possible characters. This would be fine if all you ever used was English, but eventually the need for accented characters in different languages filled up the possible characters.

Most systems store information in at least 8 bits so computers started using the previously ignored bit to store special characters, giving 128 new spots for a character.

Vendors then started making their own character sets in the spots not already used by the English characters and punctuation, calling them *code pages*. ASCII character 200 might be an accented N in one code page and a Greek letter in another code page. If you wanted to use different characters, you had to switch to a different code page.

Some of these code pages were codified in the *ISO-8859 standard*, which defines the standard code pages. ISO-8859-1 is the Latin alphabet with English characters, ISO-8859-9 is the Latin alphabet with Turkish characters. Confusingly, ISO-8859-3 has some of the Turkish characters along with some other languages.

In the early 1990s it was clear that this was a mess and people got together to come up with a new standard that could handle everything. Thus Unicode, a universal encoding, was born.

Unicode defines each possible character as a *code point*, which is a number. The original ASCII set is mapped into the first 127 values for compatibility. Originally Unicode characters were encoded into 2 bytes giving 16,000 or so possible characters. This encoding, called *UCS-2* (2-byte universal character set), ended up not being able to hold the number of characters needed when you look at all the languages and symbols on the planet. *UTF-16* (16-bit Unicode Transformation Format) fixed this by allowing anything over 16K to be represented with a second pair of bytes.

Around the same time *UTF-8* was being developed. The 2 bytes per character minimum is not compatible with existing ASCII files. The UTF-8 encoding type allows from 1 to 6 bytes to be used to encode a character, with the length of the character cleverly encoded in the high order bits of the number. UTF-8 is fully compatible with the original 127 characters but can still represent any Unicode code point.

UTF is by and large the dominant encoding type.

Representing Locales

Each locale is represented in terms of two or three variables:

- Language code (ISO 639)
- Country code (ISO 3166)
- Encoding (optional)

It may seem odd to have both a language and a country but consider that multiple languages may be spoken in a country and that two countries sharing a common language may speak different dialects. Just ask anyone from France what they think about how French is spoken in Quebec, Canada!

Thus, the language and country are different. ISO 639 describes language names, such as en for English, de for German, or es for Spanish. ISO 3166 is for the country. While Germany happens to be DE for both language and country, that's not always the case. The United States and Canada who both speak English are US and CA, respectively.

The encoding further describes how the characters are stored in the locale file. A particular locale file may use the old ISO-8859 encoding or the more robust Unicode, and even within Unicode there are multiple variants such as UTF-8, UTF-16, or UTF-32.

American English is in the en_US.UTF-8 locale, and Spanish is in es_ES.utf8. See what locales are installed on your system with the **locale -a** command, as shown in Example 11-8.

Example 11-8 Using the **locale –a** Command to See the Locales Installed on Your System

```
# locale -a
C
C.UTF-8
en_AG
en_AG.utf8
en_AU.utf8
en_BW.utf8
en_CA.utf8
en_DK.utf8
en_GB.utf8
... output omitted ...
es_ES.utf8
es_GT.utf8
es_HN.utf8
es_MX.utf8
es_NI.utf8
POSIX
```

Fallback Locales

Sometimes you don't want to deal with locales especially if you're writing a script that deals with output of other programs, which could change based on the user's locale. In this case you can temporarily use the **C** locale. **C**, which can also be called **POSIX**, is a generic 8-bit ASCII locale.

Contents of a Locale

Each locale file contains instructions on how to display or translate a variety of items:

- **Addresses**—Ordering of various parts, zip code format
- **Collation**—How to sort, such as the ordering of accented characters or if capitalized words are grouped together or separately from lowercase

- **Measurement**—Display of various units
- **Messages**—Translations for system messages and errors
- **Monetary**—How currency symbols are displayed and named
- **Names**—Conventions for displaying people's names
- **Numeric**—How to display numbers such as the thousands and decimal separators
- **Paper**—Paper sizes used in the country
- **Telephone**—How telephone numbers are displayed
- **Time**—Date and time formats such as the ordering of year, month, and date, or 24-hour clock versus using AM and PM

These locale files are usually distributed with the operating system as separate packages to save on space. If you don't need the translations, you can generate the rest of the items without installing any packages with **locale-gen** on systems that support it, as shown in Example 11-9.

Example 11-9 Using **locale-gen**

```
# locale-gen fr_FR.UTF-8
Generating locales...
  fr_FR.UTF-8... done
Generation complete.
# locale -a | grep FR
fr_FR.utf8
```

How Linux Uses the Locale

Internationalization in Linux is handled with the GNU **gettext** library. If programmers write their applications with that library and annotate their messages correctly, the user can change the behavior with environment variables.

As multiple things that can be localized, such as numbers and messages, **gettext** has a series of environment variables that it checks to see which locale is appropriate. In order, these are

- **LANGUAGE**
- **LC_ALL**
- **LC_XXX**
- **LANG**

The **LANGUAGE** variable is only consulted when printing messages. It is ignored for formatting. Also, the colon (:) gives the system a list of locales to try in order when trying to display a system message. **LC_ALL** is a way to force the locale even if some of the other variables are set.

LC_XXX gives the administrator the power to override a locale for a particular element. For example, if **LANG** were set to en_US.UTF-8 the user could override currency display by setting **LC_MONETARY**. The **locale** command displays the current settings, as shown in Example 11-10.

Example 11-10   Using **locale**

```
# locale
LANG=en_CA.UTF-8
LANGUAGE=en_CA:en
LC_CTYPE="en_CA.UTF-8"
LC_NUMERIC="en_CA.UTF-8"
LC_TIME="en_CA.UTF-8"
LC_COLLATE="en_CA.UTF-8"
LC_MONETARY="en_CA.UTF-8"
LC_MESSAGES="en_CA.UTF-8"
LC_PAPER="en_CA.UTF-8"
LC_NAME="en_CA.UTF-8"
LC_ADDRESS="en_CA.UTF-8"
LC_TELEPHONE="en_CA.UTF-8"
LC_MEASUREMENT="en_CA.UTF-8"
LC_IDENTIFICATION="en_CA.UTF-8"
LC_ALL=
This example is from a typical English system. You can override just
parts of it:
# LC_TIME=fr_FR.UTF8 date
samedi 7 mars 2015, 23:11:23 (UTC-0600)
# LC_MESSAGES=fr_FR.UTF8 man
What manual page do you want?
# LANGUAGE='' LC_MESSAGES=fr_FR.UTF8 man
Quelle page de manuel voulez-vous ?
```

In the preceding example, the time setting is switched to the French locale and the date is displayed in French. The second command sets the messages setting to French, but the English variant is used because the higher priority **LANGUAGE** is set. A French error message is used once **LANGUAGE** is set to nothing.

Converting Files Between Encodings

Sometimes you get a file encoded with an encoding you are not expecting, and that causes errors with your scripts. The **iconv** tool manipulates files. For example, if you get an ASCII file that contains funny characters you can convert the file into a UTF-8 file with those characters stripped out.

```
iconv -c -f ASCII -t UTF-8 datafile.txt > datafile.utf8.txt
```

In order, the options are

- **-c**—Clear any unknown characters
- **-f ASCII**—From ASCII
- **-t UTF-8**—To UTF-8
- **iconv -l**—Returns a list of all the available encodings

Exam Preparation Tasks

As mentioned in the section "How to Use This Book" in the Introduction, you have a couple of choices for exam preparation: the exercises here, Chapter 21, "Final Preparation," and the practice exams on the DVD.

Review All Key Topics

Review the most important topics in this chapter, noted with the Key Topics icon in the outer margin of the page. Table 11-3 lists a reference of these key topics and the page numbers on which each is found.

Table 11-3   Key Topics for Chapter 11

Key Topic Element	Description	Page Number
Paragraph	Shells to prevent a user from logging in	314
Paragraph	The **export** command	316
Paragraph	Sourcing files	317
Paragraph	**noclobber** option	318
Paragraph	Creating subshells	318
Paragraph	Clearing out the environment	320
Paragraph	The /etc/profile script	321

Key Topic Element	Description	Page Number
Paragraph	.bash_logout is part of the session	321
Paragraph	Non-login shells run ~/.bashrc	322
Paragraph	Running programs out of the current directory	322
Paragraph	Forcing options with aliases	323
Paragraph	Skipping alias processing	323
Paragraph	Format of a Bash function	323
Paragraph	PS1 environment variable	324
Paragraph	The skeleton directory	326
Paragraph	The epoch	328
Paragraph	**/etc/localtime** points to the time zone file	329
Paragraph	Overriding system time zone with TZ	329
Paragraph	Distribution tools to set the time zone	329
Paragraph	ISO-8859 standard	330
Paragraph	Unicode code points	330
Paragraph	UTF-8 encoding	330
Example 11-8	The **locale** command	331
List	Order of **locale** environment variables	332

Define Key Terms

Define the following key terms from this chapter and check your answers in the glossary:

variable, sourcing, positional parameters, login shell, non-login shell, alias, function, localization, internationalization, locale, time zone, Greenwich Mean Time, daylight saving time, epoch, ASCII, code pages, ISO-8859 standard, code point, UCS-2, UTF-16, UTF-8

Review Questions

The answers to these review questions are in Appendix A.

1. On a default Linux system, if a new user is created with user-related commands, what is the default shell?

   a. vsh

   b. ksh

   c. bash

   d. sh

2. Which file if present is sourced from the user's **~/.bash_profile** file during a normal default user's login session?

   a. /etc/profile

   b. ~/.bashrc

   c. /etc/bashrc

   d. ~/.bash_logout

   e. ~/.exrc

3. You want a particular variable that was just declared to be available to all sub-shells. Which command would you use to ensure this?

   a. set

   b. export

   c. bash

   d. source

4. You are in the user named user1's home directory, which is not in the system's path. You want to run an executable named **tarfoo** in the current directory. It won't run when you type just the command. Which of the following executes the program? (Choose all that apply.)

   a. ../.tarfoo

   b. ./tarfoo

   c. ~tarfoo

   d. /home/user1/tarfoo

5. You are the sysadmin for a mid-sized company and have a particular user who consistently overwrites important files with meaningless content. The files cannot be set read-only because they are written to by the shell and its functions. Which of the following options, when used with the **set** command, fixes this problem?

   a. append-only

   b. noclobber

   c. hashall

   d. monitor

6. Tired of missing dot files such as .bash_profile when running a directory listing, you decide you want to always include the **-a** flag when running **ls**. Which
   command will be most helpful?

   a. **export LS_OPTS="-a"**

   b. **LS_OPTS="-a"**

   c. **alias ls="ls –a"**

   d. **alias ls=" –a"**

7. You're vacationing in Hawaii. Ignoring why you chose to bring your work
   computer on vacation, how will you change the time zone for everything on
   your system?

   a. export TZ=US/Hawaii

   b. ln -sf /usr/share/zoneinfo/US/Hawaii /etc/localtime

   c. ln -sf /usr/share/zoneinfo/US/Hawaii /etc/timezone

   d. echo "US/Hawaii" > /etc/profile

8. For a particular server you want to make sure all users have **/usr/local/cad/bin**
   in their search paths. Where is the best place to put this?

   a. /etc/profile

   b. ~/.bashrc

   c. /etc/path

   d. /usr/local/bin

9. Consider this output:

```
# locale
LANG=en_US.UTF-8
LC_TIME="es_ES.UTF-8"
LC_MESSAGES="en_CA.UTF-8"
LC_ALL="de_DE.UTF-8"
```

   If you were to run the **date** command, which locale would be used for the
   formatting?

   a. American (US) English

   b. Spanish (ES)

   c. Canadian (CA) English

   d. German (DE)

This chapter covers the following topics:

- Basics of Scripting
- Shell Script Commands

This chapter covers the following exam objectives:

- Customize or write shell scripts: 105.2

## CHAPTER 12

Shell Scripting

Shell scripting is about writing your own tools to automate some of your routine work. Is there a procedure you have that involves a handful of commands? A shell script can turn it into one command. The time you invest in learning to script will pay for itself many times over with the time you save.

You don't have to be a programmer to be a good scripter. You already know how to work with the Linux command line and all scripting starts from there.

"Do I Know This Already?" Quiz

The "Do I Know This Already?" quiz enables you to assess whether you should read this entire chapter or simply jump to the "Exam Preparation Tasks" section for review. If you are in doubt, read the entire chapter. Table 12-1 outlines the major headings in this chapter and the corresponding "Do I Know This Already?" quiz questions. You can find the answers in Appendix A, "Answers to the 'Do I Know This Already?' Quizzes and Review Questions."

Table 12-1 "Do I Know This Already?" Foundation Topics Section-to-Question Mapping

Foundation Topics Section	Questions Covered in This Section
Basics of Scripting	1-2
Shell Script Commands	3-7

1. A Bash comment starts with which character?

    a. "

    b. !

    c. #

    d. --

2. You have written a Perl script to send emails to users who leave processes that abuse the CPU. Rather than **perl cpu_report.pl**, you want to run it as **./cpu_report.pl**. Which two steps are needed?

   a. Put **#!/usr/bin/perl** on the first line of the script.

   b. **chmod +x cpu_report.pl**.

   c. **chown root cpu_report.pl; chmod +s cpu_report.pl**.

   d. Put **#!perl** on the first line of the script.

   e. Put the script **in /usr/bin** along with **perl**.

3. Reviewing a shell script you found, you see this:

```
if [[ -x /etc/zoid ]]; then
  . /etc/zoid
elif [[ -x $HOME/.zoid ]]; then
  . $HOME/.zoid
fi
```

   Which of the following is true?

   a. /usr/bin/elif needs to be present for this to work.

   b. The script will run **/etc/zoid** and **$HOME/.zoid** if they exist.

   c. If **/etc/zoid** is marked as executable, it will be executed.

   d. **$HOME/.zoid** takes priority over **/etc/zoid**.

4. Consider the following transcript:

```
$ ./report.pl
$ echo $?
1
```

   What can be said about what just happened?

   a. The command completed successfully.

   b. One argument was passed to **report.pl** through the environment.

   c. The script ran for 1 second.

   d. An error happened during the script.

5. During a script's execution, what is stored in **$1**?

   a. The first argument to the script

   b. The shell that called the script

   c. The name of the script

   d. The process ID of the script

6. You are using the scripting statement **case** in a script and keep getting a message such as the following:

```
script1: line 10: syntax error: unexpected end of file
```

   What is the likely cause of the error?

   a. You didn't have a default condition set.

   b. You forgot to close the **case** with **esac**.

   c. You were using the old [ ] bash style instead of [[ ]].

   d. You were comparing an integer when you should have been comparing a string.

7. Given a directory full of files, how could you rename everything to have a **.bak** extension?

   a. **mv * *.bak**

   b. **for i in ls; do mv $i $i.bak; done**

   c. **for i in ls; do mv i i.bak; done**

   d. **for i in *; do mv $i $i.bak; done**

Foundation Topics

Basics of Scripting

A shell script is just a text file containing some commands. The following is a typical script used to deploy new software:

```
#!/bin/bash
# Deploy the application. Run as deploy foo-1.2.war
cp $1 /usr/local/tomcat/webapps/application.war
service tomcat restart
echo "Deployed $1" | mail group@example.com
```

Line by line, this script works as follows:

- **Line 1**—Known as the *shebang* line after the hash or sharp (#) bang (!) that starts it, this tells the kernel that the script should be interpreted by /bin/bash instead of run as a binary.

- **Line 2**—Comments begin with a # and are to help humans understand the program. Computers just ignore the # and everything after it on that line.

- **Line 3**—$1 is the first argument passed to the script on the command line. This line copies that file to the destination directory.

- **Line 4**—Runs a script to restart the service.

- **Line 5**—Sends an email.

Other than the **$1** and shebang line, this script is identical to what you would do at the command line. With only three commands you might wonder what the value of putting it into a shell script would be:

- Even if it takes a minute to run the manual way, it's a distraction because it consumes your attention for the whole procedure.

- You may make mistakes.

- It may be three commands today, but it's sure to grow over time.

- You can't take vacation without writing down the procedure and training your coworkers.

All these problems can be solved with scripting. Scripts do the same thing every time. You can run it in a window and get back to what you were doing. You can add commands to the script over time. Instead of complicated documentation and training, you just need to teach people how to run your script.

Running a Script

There are two ways to run a script. The first is the same as if it were a binary application:

```
$ ./test.sh
Hello, world
```

This format requires the shebang line as the first line in order to work and that the script be marked as executable. The shell tells the kernel to run the script. The kernel sees the special line and knows it's supposed to get that interpreter to run the script.

Try it out yourself and you might find that it works without the shebang line. That's the shell being smart. You should always have the **#!/bin/bash** there because you don't always know how the script will be executed or whether the user might be using a different shell.

The second way is to pass the script as an argument to a new shell:

```
$ bash test.sh
Hello, world
```

This has fewer requirements than the other method. The script doesn't have to be marked as executable. The shebang line is treated as a comment in this case. There's no question about which interpreter should run the script—you said to use **bash** on the command line.

Good Design

Before you start writing shell scripts you should think about what makes a good shell script. At a high level you're not writing the script for yourself, you're writing it for your coworker who may have to use it at 2:00 o'clock in the morning. A good script:

- Does one thing, and does it well.
- Prints descriptive error and success messages.
- Is written in a simple manner and uses comments to make steps obvious to someone looking at the source.
- Has a name that communicates its intent. **deploy_website.sh** is good. The name of your favorite football team is not.
- Has a file extension that indicates how it's to be run, such as .sh.

Follow these guidelines and your scripts will be maintainable long after you wrote them, and you won't have to explain things over and over to coworkers.

Managing Your Scripts

You should try to keep your scripts in a predictable place. There's nothing like spending time automating something and then forgetting where you put your scripts!

The location of the scripts depends on your environment. If you have coworkers to share with, or many computers, you will want your scripts in a more public location. **/usr/local/** may be mounted on all your computers, so placing your scripts in **/usr/local/bin** makes it as widely available as possible.

Another option is to keep your code in **$HOME/bin** and find a way to share with other people. A *version control system (VCS)* such as git or svn is a good choice. Not only does a VCS make it easy to share with people, but it tracks the history of your changes.

Either way the script should be marked as executable and have the shebang header. This allows people to run it directly if they want. The executable flag also signals to other people that the script is intended to be run as opposed to being a text file.

You learned earlier that setting the setuid bit on an executable file allows it to run with the owner's permissions instead of the person who ran it. That is, a file that was owned by root and has setuid enabled would run as root even if a nonprivileged user ran it.

The Linux kernel does not honor the setuid bit on script files. If you need to give elevated privileges within a script you must use something like **sudo**.

Shell Script Commands

Any command from the command line is fair game within a script. The shell itself provides some built-in commands that make shell scripting more powerful.

Use the Output of Another Command

You will frequently need to run a command and capture the output in a variable for later use. For example, you can find the process IDs of your web server:

```
$ ps -ef | grep nginx
root      4846     1  0 Mar11 ?        00:00:00 nginx: master process
/usr/sbin/nginx -c /etc/nginx/nginx.conf
nginx     6732  4846  0 Mar11 ?        00:00:12 nginx: worker process
nginx    19617  2655  0 18:54 ?        00:00:01 php-fpm: pool www
nginx    19807  2655  0 19:01 ?        00:00:00 php-fpm: pool www
nginx    19823  2655  0 19:03 ?        00:00:00 php-fpm: pool www
sean     20007 19931  0 19:07 pts/0    00:00:00 grep nginx
```

And from there you can pick out just the master process by fine-tuning your **grep** statement:

```
$ ps -ef | grep "nginx: master process"
root      4846     1  0 Mar11 ?        00:00:00 nginx: master process
/usr/sbin/nginx -c /etc/nginx/nginx.conf
sean     20038 19931  0 19:09 pts/0    00:00:00 grep nginx: master
process
```

You can weed out the **grep** line, which is the **grep** you ran to find the process, by using a regular expression that matches the **nginx** process but not the **grep** command line.

```
$ ps -ef | grep "[n]ginx: master process"
root      4846     1  0 Mar11 ?        00:00:00 nginx: master process
/usr/sbin/nginx -c /etc/nginx/nginx.conf
```

And finally, extract column 2, which is the process ID.

```
$ ps -ef | grep "[n]ginx: master process" | awk '{ print $2 }'
4846
```

Enclosing the last command in backticks within your script gets you the output in a variable, which is known as *command substitution*:

```
PID=`ps -ef | grep "[n]ginx: master process" | awk '{ print $2 }'`
echo nginx is running at $PID
```

Another way you might see this written is in the **$()** style:

```
PID=$(ps -ef | grep "[n]ginx: master process" | awk '{ print $2 }')
echo nginx is running at $PID
```

Both methods do the same thing. Parentheses are easier to match up when debugging problems, which makes the second method better to use.

You can then use the PID variable to kill the process or restart it:

```
echo Telling nginx to reopen logs using pid $PID
kill -USR1 $PID
```

Do Math

When your teachers told you that you will need math to do work, they were right. There are many cases where being able to do some easy math in a shell script helps.

If you want to know the number of processes on a system, you can run **ps -ef | wc -l**. **ps -ef** gives you the process list; **wc -l** returns the number of lines. That gives you one more than the number you are looking for because **ps** includes a header line.

The shell can do math by enclosing the expression inside **$(())**.

```
PROCS=$(ps -ef | wc -l)
PROCS=$(($PROCS-1))
```

Or on one line:

```
PROCS=$(( $(ps -ef | wc -l) - 1 ))
```

That is starting to get unreadable, so backticks might be better:

```
PROCS=$(( `ps -ef | wc -l` - 1 ))
```

Earlier you were told to assign variables using the name of the variable, such as **FOO=bar**, and to use their values with the dollar sign prefix such as **$FOO**. The **$(())** syntax works with either.

Bash only works with integers, so if you need decimal places you need a tool like **bc**.

```
RADIUS=3
echo "3.14 * $RADIUS ^ 2" | bc
```

bc accepts an arithmetic expression on the input and returns the calculation on the output. Therefore you must **echo** a string into the tool. The quotes are necessary to prevent the shell from interpreting elements as a file glob, as the asterisk was intended for **bc** and not to match a file.

Conditions

Scripts don't have to run start to finish and always do the same thing. Scripts can use *conditionals* to test for certain cases and do different things depending on the output of the test.

```
if ps -ef | grep -q [n]agios; then
  echo Nagios is running
fi
```

The if statement executes some statements and if the condition is true, the code between the **then** and the **fi** is run. In the previous example the code is **ps -ef | grep -q [n]agios**, which looks for **nagios** in the process listing using the regular expression to exclude the **grep** command itself. The **-q** argument tells **grep** not to print anything (to be quiet) because all you care about is the return value, which is stored in the **$?** variable.

```
$ ps -ef | grep -q [n]agios
$ echo $?
0
$ ps -ef | grep -q [d]oesNotExist
```

```
$ echo $?
1
```

$? holds the return code of the last command executed, which is the **grep**. The return code is 0 when the string is matched and 1 when it isn't. Anything greater than 1 indicates some kind of error, so it's generally better to test for either 0 or any positive integer.

NOTE In most computer situations 1 is true and 0 is false. With Bash programming it's the opposite.

If you want to test for the absence of a condition, you can negate the test statement with an exclamation point:

```
if ! ps -ef | grep -q [n]agios; then
  echo Nagios is NOT running
fi
```

Often you want to do one thing if the condition holds true and another thing when it's false, which is where **else** comes in.

```
if ps -ef | grep -q [n]agios; then
  echo Nagios is running
else
  echo Nagios is not running. Starting
  service nagios start
fi
```

Here, if the **grep** condition is true the script just prints a statement to the screen. If it is false it prints a statement and starts the service.

Perhaps you have three possibilities, in which case you need **elif**, which is short for "else if."

```
if ps -ef | grep -q [h]ttpd; then
  echo Apache is running
elif ps -ef | grep -q [n]ginx; then
  echo Nginx is running
else
  echo No web servers are running
fi
```

Testing Files

There is a range of common cases where writing a shell command to test for a condition would be awkward so the **test** command was introduced. With **test** you can perform a series of checks on files, strings, and numbers.

```
if test -f /etc/passwd; then
  echo "password file exists"
fi
```

The **test** command reads a series of options up until the semicolon or end of line and returns a value depending on the results of the test. The **-f** test checks for the existence of a file; in the previous case it is **/etc/passwd**. If the file exists, the **echo** will be run.

There are many other tests. Some accept one filename and others only test one file.

- **FILE1 -ef FILE2**—FILE1 and FILE2 have the same device and inode numbers.

- **FILE1 -nt FILE2**—FILE1 is newer (modification date) than FILE2.

- **FILE1 -ot FILE2**—FILE1 is older than FILE2.

- **-d FILE**—FILE exists and is a directory.

- **-e FILE**—FILE exists.

- **-f FILE**—FILE exists and is a regular file.

- **-h FILE**—FILE exists and is a symbolic link.

- **-r FILE**—FILE exists and the user can read it.

- **-s FILE**—FILE exists and has a size greater than zero.

- **-w FILE**—FILE exists and the user can write to it.

- **-x FILE**—FILE exists and the user has the execute bit set.

There are even more options than that; the **test** man page has more details.

An Easier Test Syntax

The **test** command is used so much that Bash has the "square brackets" [ ] shortcut.

```
if [ conditions ]; then
```

Anything between the square brackets is considered a test. The test to see whether **/usr/bin/nginx** is executable would then be

```
if [ -x /usr/bin/nginx ]; then
```

```
    echo nginx is executable
fi
```

Newer versions of Bash can also use two square brackets:

```
if [[ -x /usr/bin/nginx ]]; then
  echo nginx is executable
fi
```

The new style is more forgiving of errors, such as if you're using a variable that's unset. An unset variable has not been assigned a value and therefore contains nothing when you try to reference its contents. If you're dealing entirely with Linux systems, it is the safer option to use.

The syntax of this style is important. There must be a space before and after the opening square bracket and a space before the closing square bracket. The space after the closing square bracket is optional because the semicolon or line ending is enough to tell the shell that the test has finished. The shell can't differentiate between the square brackets and the test itself if the spaces are missing. Thus the following commands are invalid:

```
if[[ -x /usr/bin/nginx ]]; # no space before first brackets
if [[-x /usr/bin/nginx ]]; # no space after first brackets
if [[ -x /usr/bin/nginx]]; # no space before final brackets
```

Testing Strings

Words, also known as *strings*, can be easily tested, too.

```
echo -n "Say something: "
read STRING
if [[ -z $STRING ]]; then
  echo "You didn't say anything"
else
  echo Thanks for that
fi
```

The first line prints a prompt to the screen; the **-n** option eliminates the newline at the end. The **read** command stores the data gathered from stdin (typically data typed by the user) and places the input into the variable called **STRING**.

The test uses **-z** to check for a zero length string. If the user didn't enter anything, the first condition is run. Anything else and the second condition is used.

The opposite of **-z** is **-n**, which tests for a nonzero length string.

String equality is tested with a single equals sign:

```
if [[ `hostname` = 'bob.ertw.com' ]]; then
  echo You are on your home machine
else
  echo You must be somewhere else
fi
```

The conditional expression does not have to include a variable. In the preceding example the output of the **hostname** command (using command substitution) is compared to a string.

The opposite of **=** is **!=**.

Testing Integers

Strings and integers are treated differently and as such, need different operators to test. There are six integer operators:

- **X -eq Y**—Tests whether X is equal to Y.

- **X -ne Y**—Tests whether X is not equal to Y.

- **X -gt Y**—Tests whether X is greater than Y.

- **X -ge Y**—Tests whether X is greater than or equal to Y.

- **X -lt Y**—Tests whether X is less than Y.

- **X -le Y**—Tests whether X is less than or equal to Y.

You may want to count processes, files, number of users, or elapsed time.

```
LASTRUN=$(cat lastrun)
NOW=$(date +%s)
ELAPSED=$((NOW - LASTRUN))

if [[ $ELAPSED -ge 60 ]]; then
  echo A minute or more has passed since the last time you ran this
script
  echo $NOW > lastrun
fi
```

In the preceding script the script looks for a file with the name of **lastrun** and reads the contents into memory. It also reads the current timestamp in seconds since epoch and then calculates the difference into a third variable.

The script can then check to see whether a minute or more has elapsed, take an action, and then reset the last run timestamp.

Combining Multiple Tests

All the previous examples addressed the need to run a single test. More complicated tests can be run that consider multiple options. This is the realm of *Boolean logic*:

- **A AND B**—True if both A and B are true.

- **A OR B**—True if either A or B is true.

With **test** and **[condition]**, AND and OR are handled with **-a** and **-o**, respectively. Inside **[[condition]]** blocks, use **&&** and **| |**.

```
if [ -f /etc/passwd -a -x /usr/sbin/adduser ]
if [[ -f /etc/passwd && -x /usr/sbin/adduser ]]
```

Boolean logic assigns a higher precedence to AND than it does OR. It's like BED-MAS in arithmetic: Brackets happen before exponents, then division and multiplication, then addition and subtraction. In Boolean logic the order is

1. Brackets

2. AND

3. OR

Therefore **[[A | | B && C]]** is evaluated as **[[A | | (B && C)]]**. This is a great example of how to make your code more clear for the people reading it. If you can write your tests so that there's no way to be confused by the order of operations, then do it!

Case Statements

if/elif/else statements get bulky if you have more than three possibilities. For those situations you can use **case**, as shown in Example 12-1.

Example 12-1   Using **case** Instead of **if/elif/else**

```
case $1 in
  start)
    echo "Starting the process"
    ;;
  stop)
    echo "Stopping the process"
    ;;
  *)
    echo "I need to hear start or stop"
esac
```

A **case** statement starts with a description of what the value to be tested is in the form **case $variable in**. Then each condition is listed in a specific format:

1. First comes the string to be matched, which is terminated in a closing parenthesis. The * matches anything, which makes it a default.

2. Then comes zero or more statements that are run if this case is matched.

3. The list of statements is terminated by two semicolons (;;).

4. Finally the whole statement is closed with **esac**.

Processing stops after the first match, so if multiple conditions are possible only the first one is run.

The string to be matched can also be matched as if it were a file glob, which is helpful to accept a range of input, as shown in Example 12-2.

Example 12-2   A String Matched as if It Were a File Glob

```
DISKSPACE=$(df -P / | tail -1 | awk '{print $5}' | tr -d '%')
case $DISKSPACE in
  100)
    echo "The disk is full"
    echo "Emergency! Disk is full!" | mail -s "Disk emergency" root@
example.com
    ;;
  [1-7]*|[0-9])
    echo "Lots of space left"
    ;;
  [8-9]*)
    echo "I'm at least 80% full"
    ;;
  *)
    echo "Hmmm. I expected some kind of percentage"
esac
```

In this example the **DISKSPACE** variable contains the percentage of disk space used, which was obtained by command substitution as follows:

- Take the output of **df -P /**, which shows just the disk used for the root filesystem in a single line.

- Pipe it through **tail -1**, which only prints the last line so that the header is removed.

- Print the fifth column, which is the percentage of the disk that's free, by piping through **awk**.

- Remove the percent character with the translate (**tr**) command.

If the disk usage is 100, a message indicating a disk is full and the script even sends an email to root with an appropriate subject line using **-s**. The second test looks for something that begins with the numbers 1 through 7 and optionally anything after, or just a single digit. This corresponds to anything under 80% full. The third test is anything beginning with 8 or 9. The first match wins rule ensures that a disk that is 9% full is caught by the second rule and doesn't pass through to the third.

Finally a default value is caught just in case bad input is passed.

Loops

Loops are the real workhorses of shell scripting. A loop lets you run the same procedure over and over.

Bash offers two types of loops. The **for** loop iterates over a fixed collection. The **while** loop keeps running until a given condition is met.

For Loops

The **for** loop's basic syntax is

```
for variable in collection; do
  # Do something on $variable
done
```

The collection can be fixed:

```
$ for name in Ross Sean Mary-Beth; do
> echo $name
> done
Ross
Sean
Mary-Beth
```

Here the collection is a list of three names, which start after the **in** and go up to the semicolon or the end of the line. Anything that you can do in a shell script can be done directly on the command line! Loops are powerful tools that can save work both inside shell scripts and in ad-hoc commands.

Each time around the loop the variable called **name** holds the current value. For this example the loop executes three times.

Note that the declaration of the variable is just the name of the variable and using the variable requires the dollar sign prefix.

The collection can be a file glob:

```
for file in *.txt; do newname=`echo $file | sed 's/txt$/doc/'`; mv
$file $newname; done
```

This example, all on one line, renames every file ending in **.txt** to **.doc**. It does this by iterating over the ***.txt** wildcard and each time setting the variable **file** to the current file. It assigns a temporary variable, **newname**, to the output of a **sed** command that replaces the extension with the new one. Finally it moves the old name to the new name before moving on to the next file.

Sequences

Loops are just as happy iterating over the output of another command as they are a static list of names or a file glob. The **seq** command is particularly suited to this task. It counts from a starting point to an ending point for you:

```
$ seq 1 5
1
2
3
4
5
```

Or counts by twos when the arguments are start, skip, and end:

```
$ seq 1 2 5
1
3
5
```

Or pads the output with leading zeroes if the number of digits changes through the **-w** flag:

```
$ seq -w 8 10
08
09
10
```

With that in mind, iterating over something 10 times becomes straightforward:

```
for i in $(seq -w 1 10); do
  curl -O http://example.com/downloads/file$i.html
done
```

Here the loop counter is more than just to count the number of iterations. The counter, **i**, forms part of a URL on a remote web server. Also note that the **seq** command included **-w** so that the numbers were all two digits, which is common in remote web files. Ultimately this script downloads 10 files with a predictable name from a remote website using **curl**.

While Loops

Some kinds of loops have to run for an unpredictable period of time. What if you had a script that couldn't run at the same time as another program, so it had to wait until the other program finished?

```
while [[ -f /var/lock/script1 ]] ; do
  echo waiting
  sleep 10
done
```

The command on the **while** line looks for the presence of a lock file and pauses for 10 seconds if it's found. The file is checked each time through the loop and the loop ends only when the file is removed.

If you wanted to, you could also count the same way you did with **for** and **seq**:

```
value=0
last=33
while [ $value -lt $last ]
do
        echo $value
        value=$(($value + 1))
done
```

This counts from 0 to 32. It is 32 instead of 33 because the condition is **-lt**—less than—instead of **-le**, which is less than or equal to.

The opposite of **while** is **until**, which behaves as if the loop condition were written with an exclamation point in front of it. In other words the loop continues while the expression is false and ends the loop once the condition is true. You could use this if you're waiting for another script to drop a file in a certain location:

```
until [ -f /var/tmp/report.done ]; do

  # Waiting until the report is done

  sleep 10

done
```

```
rm /var/tmp/report.done
```

This program waits until a file is present, such as from a report job that is run. It then cleans up the state file and continues on.

Reading from stdin in a Loop

While loops are great for reading input from the console. This script behaves the same as the **cat** command. It echoes anything passed to it as a filter to the output.

```
while read LINE; do
  echo $LINE
done
```

This technique is less efficient than piping the output through a series of other tools, but sometimes you need to perform complicated logic on a line-by-line basis, and this is the easiest way to do that.

read can also be used to accept input from the user:

```
echo -n "What is your name? "
read NAME
echo Hello, $NAME
```

Interacting with Other Programs

A shell script is expected to run other programs to do its job. If you use **cp**, **awk**, **sed**, **grep**, or any other Unix utility, you are running another program.

Programs you run might produce output that you want to ignore. You already saw that command substitution lets you capture the output, but if you don't want to see the output you need to use redirection.

The **grep** command can produce warnings if it reads a binary file or can't read a file because of missing permissions. If you're fine with these errors happening, you can eliminate them by redirecting the output to **/dev/null** and also redirecting the error stream to the regular output stream:

```
grep -r foo /etc > /dev/null 2>&1
```

You can still test the return status of this command by looking at **$?** or the usual **if/while/test** commands. The only difference is the output has been thrown away.

Returning an Error Code

You've seen how testing the return value of another program can let you branch and do different things based on the output. It's possible to make your own scripts return a success or error condition to whoever is calling it.

You can use the **exit** keyword anywhere within your program. By itself it returns 0, the success value. If you write **exit 42**, it returns 42. The caller sees this number in **$?**.

Be careful to return something that makes sense. The shell expects that successful execution returns an exit code of 0. If you are going to return anything other than the typical 0 for success and 1 for error, you should describe that in comments at the top of your code.

Accepting Arguments

Your script can be run with arguments:

```
./deploy foo.war production
```

Each of the arguments is stored in **$1**, **$2**, **$3**, and so forth. **$0** is the name of the script itself.

The special bash variable **$#** contains the number of arguments passed to the script. You can use this to provide some basic error checking of the input.

```
if [[ $# -lt 2 ]]; then
   echo Usage: $0 deployable environment
   exit 1 # return an error to the caller
fi
```

Perhaps you're dealing with an unknown number of arguments. The **shift** keyword moves **$2** to **$1**, **$3** to **$2**, and so forth. Shifting at the end of the loop means that $1 is always your current argument, as shown in Example 12-3.

Example 12-3 Using the **shift** Keyword

```
while [[ $# -gt 0 ]]; do
  echo Processing $1
  shift
  echo There are $# to go
done
$ ./test.sh one two three
Processing one
There are 2 to go
Processing two
```

```
There are 1 to go
Processing three
There are 0 to go
```

Using **shift** is helpful when you are processing an unknown list of options, such as filenames.

Transferring Control to Another Program

A bit more esoteric way of calling a program is to use the **exec** command. Normally when you call a program the shell creates a new process and runs the program you called. However, it's possible to replace your currently running program with a new one.

If you want to know the dirty details of how a program is run, it's actually a combination of both methods. A subprocess is started by forking the existing process into two: the parent (original) and child (new). The two processes are identical at this point. The child program then executes the intended program.

For example, when you type **ls** into your bash prompt, bash forks itself into two. The child is an identical copy of your shell. That child then executes the **ls** command, replacing itself with **ls**. The parent waits until the **ls** exits, and returns a shell prompt.

If you call **exec** on a program from within a script, or even from the shell, your session is replaced. When the file you call has finished running, control returns to whatever called the original script, not your script.

For example:

```
echo Hi
exec sleep 1
echo There
```

This simple program prints a line of text, execs a 1 second pause, and then prints another line. When you run it, however:

```
$ sh test.sh
Hi
$
```

Processing stopped after the **sleep**! The shell script was replaced, in memory, by a **sleep**. Control was returned to the shell that called **test.sh**, and not the line following the **exec**.

This technique is used when a shell script's job is to launch another program and it doesn't matter what happens after the program exits. The new program has access to all the variables and context even if they haven't been exported.

Exam Preparation Tasks

As mentioned in the section "How to Use This Book" in the Introduction, you have a couple of choices for exam preparation: the exercises here, Chapter 21, "Final Preparation," and the practice exams on the DVD.

Review All Key Topics

Review the most important topics in this chapter, noted with the Key Topics icon in the outer margin of the page. Table 12-2 lists a reference of these key topics and the page numbers on which each is found.

Table 12-2 Key Topics for Chapter 12

Key Topic Element	Description	Page Number
Paragraph	Ways to run a script	343
Paragraph	Command substitution	345
Paragraph	Arithmetic within the shell	346
Paragraph	The **if** statement	346
Paragraph	**$?** Holds the return code of the last program	347
Paragraph	**if/elif/else/fi**	347
List	File tests	348
Paragraph	Square bracket methods for testing conditions	348
Paragraph	String equality	350
Paragraph	Integer operators	350
Paragraph	**AND** and **OR** operators	351
Paragraph	Loop mechanics	353
Paragraph	How **while** works	355
Paragraph	**read** accepts values from the user	356
Paragraph	Redirecting output	356
Paragraph	The **exit** keyword	357
Paragraph	**$n** special variables	357

Define Key Terms

Define the following key terms from this chapter and check your answers in the glossary:

shebang, version control system, command substitution, conditionals, strings, Boolean logic

Review Questions

The answers to these review questions are in Appendix A.

1. On a Linux system installed with the default shell, you need to execute a shell script that contains variables, aliases, and functions by simply entering its name on the command line. What should be the first line of the script? (Choose all that apply.)

    a. Nothing

    b. `#/bin/csh`

    c. `#!/bin/bash`

    d. `exec=/bin/bash`

2. If **ps -ef | grep nginx | awk '{print $2}'** returns a list of process ids for nginx, how would you kill them all in one line?

    a. kill "ps -ef | grep nginx | awk '{print $2}'"

    b. PIDS="ps -ef | grep nginx | awk '{print $2}'"; kill PIDS

    c. kill $(ps -ef | grep nginx | awk '{print $2}')

    d. kill $((ps -ef | grep nginx | awk '{print $2}'))

3. Your script automates the creation of a virtual machine and you have read the desired size of memory, in gigabytes, into a variable called **MEM**. The tool you are using inside your script to create the virtual machine expects this value in megabytes. How can you convert **MEM** to megabytes?

    a. MEM=$((MEM * 1024))

    b. MEM=$MEM*1024

    c. MEM=`$MEM * 1024`

    d. MEM=eval($MEM*1024)

4. You are writing a shell script that calls another program called **/bin/foo**. If the program does not return successfully, you should print an error to the screen. How can you test for an error condition?

    a. if [-e **/bin/foo**]

    b. if [$? -gt 0]

    c. if [$? -eq 0]

    d. until [**/bin/foo**]

5. You are looking at an old script you wrote and see this line:

```
if [ -x /bin/ps -a -f /etc/app.conf ]
```

In plain English, what does it say?

    a. if **/bin/ps** is excluded from **/etc/app.conf**

    b. if the output of **/bin/ps** contains all the strings from file **/etc/app.conf**

    c. if **/bin/ps** is executable and **/etc/app.conf** exists

    d. if either /bin/ps or /etc/app.conf exists

6. Looking inside a script, you see this line:

```
if [[ `hostname` = 'bob' ]];
```

What is it doing?

    a. Nothing. It is trying to perform an integer comparison on a string.

    b. Checking to see whether the **hostname** command was successful.

    c. Changing the hostname to bob and checking to see whether that was successful.

    d. Checking to see whether the hostname is **bob**.

7. If you had an operation you wanted to perform on every process currently running, the most appropriate loop construct would be

    a. seq

    b. while

    c. for

    d. until

8. You are writing a shell script that accepts parameters on the command line. How can you check to make sure you've received exactly three parameters?

   a. if [[$# -ge 3]]

   b. if [[$ARGV = 3]]

   c. if [[$? = 3]]

   d. if [[3 -eq $#]]

9. When writing a bash script, you find yourself needing to exit early because of an error condition. Which of the following commands should be used?

   a. die

   b. exit 1

   c. raise

   d. exit

10. Consider the following program, which is run as **./script a b c d**.

```
shift
echo $0 $1
```

   What will it print?

   a. b c

   b. a b

   c. /script b

   d. /script a

This chapter covers the following topics:

- Database Basics
- Learning SQL

This chapter covers the following objectives:

- SQL data management: 105.3

Basic SQL Management

Data is usually stored in some kind of database and the most popular databases are queried with a language called Structured Query Language.

As an administrator you'll be responsible for maintaining the servers and often will be called to troubleshoot connection problems or help people use the database.

Additionally, many open source projects use a database to store their data, so learning how to query the database lets you get information out of the application that the developers didn't anticipate.

"Do I Know This Already?" Quiz

The "Do I Know This Already?" quiz enables you to assess whether you should read this entire chapter or simply jump to the "Exam Preparation Tasks" section for review. If you are in doubt, read the entire chapter. Table 13-1 outlines the major headings in this chapter and the corresponding "Do I Know This Already?" quiz questions. You can find the answers in Appendix A, "Answers to the 'Do I Know This Already?' Quizzes and Review Questions."

Table 13-1 "Do I Know This Already?" Foundation Topics Section-to-Question Mapping

Foundation Topics Section	Questions Covered in This Section
Database Basics	1-2
Learning SQL	3-8

1. Which of the following is incorrect about relational databases?

    a. Tables are arranged in rows and columns.

    b. New data elements can be added to a row without changing the schema.

    c. SQL is used to query the data.

    d. Rows are given unique identifiers.

2. What do databases use to look up data quickly?

   a. Binary object

   b. Client-server

   c. Embedded database

   d. Index

3. Which of the following are case sensitive when writing SQL queries?

   a. Names of tables

   b. Keywords such as **SELECT** and **INSERT**

   c. Logic operators such as **AND** and **OR**

   d. Names of database servers

4. Which of the following queries will successfully return people from the **employee** table who are at least 30 years old?

   a. SELECT * FROM Employee WHERE age >= 30;

   b. SELECT * WHERE age >= 30

   c. SELECT * FROM employee WHERE age >= 30;

   d. SELECT * WHERE age >=30 FROM employee;

5. Given two tables representing cars and their owners:

```
cars: id, model, owner_id
owners: id, name
```

How would you display a list of all cars and their owners, including cars that don't have owners?

   a. SELECT * FROM owners LEFT JOIN cars ON owners.id = cars.owner_id;

   b. SELECT * FROM cars, owners WHERE cars.owner_id = owners.id;

   c. SELECT * FROM cars JOIN owners ON owners.id = cars.owner_id;

   d. SELECT * FROM cars LEFT JOIN owners ON owners.id = cars.owner_id;

6. Given a table of cars and a table recalled models, which of the following uses a subselect correctly to find cars where the model has been recalled since January 1, 2010?

```
cars: id, model, owner_name
recalls: id, model, recall_date
```

   a. SELECT * FROM cars LEFT JOIN recalls ON (recalls.model=cars.model) WHERE (recall_date >= '2010-01-01');

   b. SELECT * FROM cars WHERE model IN (SELECT * FROM recalls WHERE recall_date >= '2010-01-01');

   c. SELECT * FROM cars WHERE model IN (SELECT model FROM recalls WHERE recall_date >= '2010-01-01');

   d. SELECT * FROM cars WHERE model IN (SELECT model FROM recalls) WHERE recall_date >= '2010-01-01';

7. Your employee table has a column for last name and office location. How would you produce a report of people sorted first by office and then by last name?

   a. SELECT * FROM employee ORDER BY office_location, last_name;

   b. SELECT * FROM employee ORDER BY last_name GROUP BY office_location;

   c. SELECT * FROM employee ORDER BY last_name, office_location;

   d. SELECT * FROM employee ORDER BY office_location GROUP BY last_name;

8. Your employee table has a column called **years_of_service** that tracks how many years each employee has worked with the company. It is year end and you've been asked to increase this number by one for every employee. Which command does this?

   a. INSERT INTO employee SET years_of_service=years_of_service+1;

   b. UPDATE employee SET years_of_service=years_of_service+1;

   c. UPDATE years_of_service SET years_of_service+1;

   d. UPDATE employee(years_of_service) += 1;

Foundation Topics

Database Basics

Most databases follow a client-server model where an application, called the client, connects over the network to a database server that stores the data. The client issues requests to the server and reads the response back over the network. Sometimes the client and the server are on the same machine but are separate entities and must still talk over some kind of connection.

Sometimes the client is an application, such as something graphical running on a user's desktop. Other times a web server issues the requests when a browser asks and renders web pages based on the data returned from the database. Another possibility is that a user connects to the database and issues queries directly, perhaps importing into a spreadsheet or other analytical tool.

Types of Databases

Data differs based on the application, so no one database solution fits all. However, most databases fall into one of three camps: key-value, relational, and schemaless.

Key-Value Databases

A key-value database acts much like a dictionary. The keys are the words and the values are the definitions. If you know the key you can quickly find the value associated with it. Figure 13-1 shows what a key-value database could look like. The values can be simple words, a data structure that the client can understand, or a binary object like a picture.

DatabaseFile1

Key	Value
author1	joe:joe@ex...
author2	sarah:ssmi...
photo1	...binary...
admin	admin@ex...

Figure 13-1   A key-value database

Key-value databases can be so simple that they don't even need to have a server running. They can be simple files on disk that a local client opens and reads. Tools like **rpm** and **apt** store their data in key-value databases because there is no overhead in running a server, and the application benefits from the speed of looking up keys and *indexes* that can make searches of the values themselves fast.

An index helps a database find content quickly. If you wanted to search a key-value database by value, you would have to visit every key-value pair to find what you want, which is time consuming. An index provides a quick lookup of keys that contain a certain value. There is a performance penalty when writing to the database because each index must be updated, but the speed gain when querying usually makes up for this.

Examples of key-value databases that operate on local files are Berkeley DB and the original Unix DBM, which is the database manager. Network-aware servers that operate in a key-value format include Redis, Dynamo, and Riak.

Relational Databases

Relational databases are given their name because they deal with both data and the relationships between the data. A table stores information about a single entity such as a book with multiple columns storing different pieces of information such as the title, price, and date of first print. The database manages relationships between tables such as between a book and its authors. The database also provides a way to piece the tables together and perform queries, which is almost always the Structured Query Language (SQL).

Figure 13-2 shows a sample set of tables and their relationships.

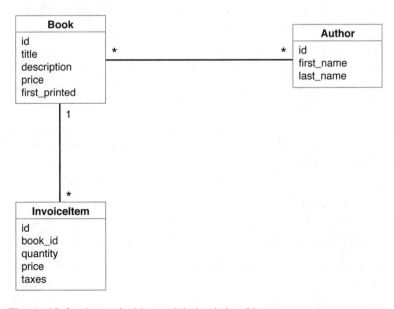

Figure 13-2   A set of tables and their relationships

In Figure 13-2 a book contains columns such as the title, description, price, and first print date. The table also has an identifier. Each book forms a row in the table much like rows in a spreadsheet. Each row is uniquely identified by the ID, though the database is free to search for rows by column such as all books costing between $30 and $40.

Figure 13-2 also shows a table for invoice items, which would represent a sale of a particular book to a particular person. Each invoice item holds a reference to the book so that the database can look up which book was sold by relating the invoice item's book_id to the book's id. If a book were to be sold five times, the database would hold one row in the book table and five rows in the invoice items table. This is called a *many-to-one relationship*.

The author table is related to the book table with a *many-to-many relationship*. A book might have been written by several authors, and any author may have written multiple books.

SQL lets you run complicated reports on your data. A bookstore would be able to produce inventory reports, or to figure out which categories contribute the most to sales.

MySQL, PostgreSQL, Oracle, and SQLite are examples of relational databases. SQLite is notable in that it is an example of an *embedded database*: a SQL compliant database that runs as part of the application that uses it instead of connecting over a network to a server.

Schemaless Databases

The *database schema* is the description of all the tables in the database including the makeup of the columns and any relationships between the objects.

If you need to make a change to the schema, such as to add a middle name to the *author* table or track a different tax in a sale table, you need to modify every row even if they don't need the tax or a middle name. In some databases, this involves downtime to lock the tables against change while the update is running.

A schemaless database does away with the notion of database enforced relationships and moves to document storage. A document is a free-form description of the entity. If an author doesn't have a middle name, it doesn't need one. If you want to track a new piece of data, you just start using it and the new documents will have it.

There are tradeoffs to all design decisions. Schemaless databases are not good for transactional data where you are tracking contents of bank accounts or sales receipts. They are good at huge databases, such as if you were running a large social network.

Schemaless databases are also called NoSQL databases because they typically don't use the SQL language.

Examples of schemaless databases are MongoDB, ElasticSearch, and Couchbase.

Learning SQL

The Structured Query Language, SQL, is a language designed to work with relational databases. In SQL you have commands to create your database, query data, and insert, update, and remove data.

SQL is a standardized language, though each implementation tries to differentiate itself in some way. This book uses only standard commands that work on a variety of databases.

As a Linux systems administrator you may be called on to help people with their queries. Some companies employ a special role called a database administrator (DBA) to do this, but people are often afraid to talk to the DBA. Knowing a bit of SQL can come in handy when the DBA is not available or your company doesn't have one.

Almost every web-based monitoring tool uses a database in the backend, and a bit of SQL knowledge helps you work with these applications and even be able to run custom reports on your own data.

If you have a SQL database installed, such as MySQL, you can use it for these exercises. Otherwise, we suggest you install SQLite.

Using SQLite

SQLite is an embedded database rather than a network-aware database. It's designed to give applications a way to build in a SQL database without the overhead of running a separate server. SQLite is used on everything from Android phones to most web browsers.

Check to see whether your system has the **sqlite3** command by typing **which sqlite3**. If you get back a path to the binary, you have it. If not, install it with **apt-get install sqlite3** for Debian and Ubuntu systems or **yum install sqlite** on Red Hat and Fedora.

A SQLite database is a single file. Any SQLite client can open this file and manipulate it by either using the shared libraries or the command line client.

Run **sqlite3** with the path to a database file to get started. If the file doesn't exist, it is created.

```
$ sqlite3 newdatabase
SQLite version 3.7.13 2012-07-17 17:46:21
Enter ".help" for instructions
Enter SQL statements terminated with a ";"
sqlite>
```

The database used for this book can be found in the downloads section at the book's home page: http://www.pearsonitcertification.com/title/9780789754554. You can download this file and have some sample data to play with.

SQL Basics

SQL is a programming language and it is therefore important to be precise when writing code to get the results you want. It is unlike other programming languages in that you rarely use loops and iterators. Instead you are writing expressions to filter and manipulate data and then looking at that data.

A semicolon (;) terminates each statement in SQL. Commands may span multiple lines and often do for the sake of readability. If you forget to terminate your command, the interpreter thinks you're going to type in some more commands.

Comments start with two dashes (--) and can appear anywhere on a line except within quotes. The following two examples show comments in both styles:

```
SELECT *      -- I want all the columns
FROM t1;      -- t1 holds sales data
```

And

```
-- t1 holds sales data and it's important to get all columns
SELECT *
FROM t1;
```

The SQL commands themselves are case-insensitive, but table names and data strings are case-sensitive. Therefore the following statements are all the same:

```
INSERT INTO name VALUES('Sean');
insert into name values('Sean');
InSeRt INto name VALues('Sean');
```

However, values and data are case sensitive, so these are all different:

```
insert into name values('SEAN'); -- The name will be stored all in
capitals
insert into name values('sean'); -- The name will be stored in
lowercase
insert into NAME values('Sean'); -- The table is called name, not NAME
```

Keywords Versus Data

In Bash a line often starts with some kind of command and is then followed by some data, which is either a string or a variable or both. SQL commands start with a keyword that is followed by a series of clauses to modify that keyword. For example, you might have a keyword to indicate that you want to read data from the database, and then some clauses to filter and sort the data before displaying it. While SQL does have variables they're not used as often, and the keywords and data are mixed together.

A SQL command might look like this:

```
SELECT age
FROM person
WHERE name='Sean' AND age > 20
LIMIT 15
```

In this example the capitalized words are all SQL keywords. The word **age** refers to a column name and **person** is the name of a table. SQL has some particular rules about when to use double and single quotes. Single quotes are for user-entered data, and double quotes are for table and column names. Unless the table or column name contains spaces or symbols, the double quotes are optional.

In the preceding example **age**, **person**, and **name** are database artifacts and are either left bare or double quoted. The string being searched for in the **name** column is single quoted because it's user-entered data.

The numbers are also left bare because they're integers. The query is asking for ages greater than 20 and limiting the results to 15 rows.

Note that the word **Sean** is single quoted, indicating it's a user-entered string. If it were not quoted, it would be referring to a column. **WHERE last_name = maiden_name** is an example of a filter that matches rows where the values of the **last_name** and **maiden_name** columns are identical.

If you have some database experience, you may have come across situations where different quoting rules work. Many databases exhibit nonstandard behavior that can be surprising as you move between systems. In particular, MySQL and SQLite allow you to use double and single quotes for strings interchangeably, where a stricter database such as PostegreSQL would flag the use of double quotes for strings as an error. Just remember: Double quotes or nothing at all for column and table names, and single quotes for data you enter.

Selecting Data

The **SELECT** statement is the command you use to extract information from your database. The simplest way to use it is to ask for a single string:

```
sqlite> SELECT 'Hello, world!';
Hello, world!
```

You can also run expressions:

```
sqlite> SELECT 1 + 1;
2
```

It would be far more interesting to get information out of a table. This requires the **FROM** keyword to indicate the name of the table. The **FROM** clause happens after the **SELECT** clause.

```
sqlite> SELECT * FROM book;
id          title                                 year         author_id
----------  ------------------------------------  ----------   --------
--
1           LPIC 1 Exam Cram 2                    2004         2
2           Linux and Windows 2000 Integration    2001         2
3           Wireless All In One For Dummies       2009         1
4           Check Point CCSA Exam Cram 2          2005         1
```

SELECT * asks for all the available columns, and **FROM book** indicates that the database should search the book table. In the preceding example, the table has two rows with identifiers of 1 and 2, respectively.

Naming things is hard. Should the table be called **book** or **books**? Tables are usually named after the singular version of the entity they contain. In this case each row is a book; therefore, the table is called book. If you're working in a database that already uses the plural form, then stay with that.

You can get more specific columns by asking for them individually:

```
sqlite> SELECT title, year FROM book;
title                               year
----------------------------------  ----------
LPIC 1 Exam Cram 2                  2004
Linux and Windows 2000 Integration  2001
Wireless All In One For Dummies     2009
Check Point CCSA Exam Cram 2        2005
```

Here the query was only for two columns: title and year.

Being Choosy

Tables may have thousands or millions of records and looking at them all would become impossible. A **WHERE** clause lets you filter results based on one or more conditions. This clause comes after the **FROM** clause.

```
sqlite> SELECT year, title FROM book WHERE year >= 2005;
year        title
```

```
----------      ------------------------------------
2009            Wireless All In One For Dummies
2005            Check Point CCSA Exam Cram 2
```

Here the **WHERE** clause asks for anything where the year column is greater than or equal to 2005. Two books are returned. The book written in 2005 is included because the query uses **>=**, which means greater than or equal to. A **>** by itself would mean greater than 2005 and would have only included the one row.

As the year is a bare word, it is referring to a column name. If it were single quoted, it would be referring to the literal string **year**. No column satisfies the condition that the word **year** is the same as the number **2005**, so no rows would be returned.

Suppose that the book **table** also tracked the year the book was started in a column called **written**. A query could check for books started in the year before they were published by looking for rows where **written** is not the same as the published year.

```
sqlite> SELECT title, year, written FROM book WHERE year <> written;
title                               year        written
---------------------------------   ----------  ----------
Linux and Windows 2000 Integration  2001        2000
Check Point CCSA Exam Cram 2        2005        2004
```

In this example, the WHERE clause compares two columns and only returns those where they are not equal using the **<>** operator.

The basic numeric comparison operators are

> **=** - equals
>
> **<>** - not equals
>
> **<** - less than
>
> **<=** - less than or equal to
>
> **>** - greater than
>
> **>=** - greater than or equal to

Searching ranges is possible through the **BETWEEN** operator, which takes two numbers and matches values between the two:

```
sqlite> SELECT title, year FROM book WHERE year BETWEEN 2004 AND 2005;
title                               year
---------------------------------   ----------
LPIC 1 Exam Cram 2                  2004
Check Point CCSA Exam Cram 2        2005
```

You can also search for specific numbers in a set, such as to find books published in 2001 or 2005 using the **IN** keyword. This keyword expects a list of values to check, enclosed in parentheses.

```
sqlite> SELECT title, year FROM book WHERE year IN (2001, 2005);
title                               year
----------------------------------- ----------
Linux and Windows 2000 Integration  2001
Check Point CCSA Exam Cram 2        2005
```

Finally you can perform a substring match on a column with the **LIKE** operator. While the equality operator, **=**, only matches exact strings, **LIKE** lets you look for strings within the column by using one of two metacharacters:

- _ matches a single character.
- % matches zero or more characters.

LIKE behaves the same as **=** if there are no metacharacters. The following two statements have the same output:

```
SELECT * FROM author WHERE first_name = "Sean";
SELECT * FROM author WHERE first_name LIKE "Sean";
```

The statements are the same because they both only find rows where the **first_name** column contains **Sean** and nothing else.

To find all the *Exam Cram 2* books you can ask the database for anything ending in Exam Cram 2.

```
sqlite> SELECT title FROM book WHERE title LIKE '% Exam Cram 2';
title
-----------------------------------
LPIC 1 Exam Cram 2
Check Point CCSA Exam Cram 2
```

Multiple Conditions

You're not limited to one question in your **WHERE** clause. Conditions may be put together with **AND** and **OR**. An AND requires that both conditions are true, an OR requires that only one is true. So you can find all the *Exam Cram 2* books published in 2005 or later, or any book where the writing started in 2000:

```
sqlite> SELECT title, year
FROM book WHERE (title LIKE '%Exam Cram 2' AND year >= 2005)
  OR written = 2000;
title                               year
```

```
------------------------------------  ----------
Linux and Windows 2000 Integration    2001
Check Point CCSA Exam Cram 2          2005
```

If the precedence of ANDs and ORs is confusing, use parentheses to group the conditions. In the preceding case, since AND has higher precedence than OR, the parentheses are unnecessary but do add clarity.

Sorting

Sorting your results helps you to make more sense of the report. Rows normally come back in an indeterminate manner as the query gets more complicated. The **ORDER BY** clause comes toward the end of the query.

ORDER BY typically expects a column name, or set of column names, on which to sort:

```
sqlite> SELECT * FROM book ORDER BY written, year;
id      title                                 year  author_id  written
-----   ------------------------------------  ----  ---------  -------
2       Linux and Windows 2000 Integration    2001      2         2000
1       LPIC 1 Exam Cram 2                    2004      2         2004
4       Check Point CCSA Exam Cram 2          2005      1         2004
3       Wireless All In One For Dummies       2009      1         2009
```

In the previous example, the query first sorts by the year of writing, with the publishing year column used for a tie breaker. Sorts are performed in ascending order by default, which can be overridden with the ASC and DESC keywords:

```
sqlite> SELECT title from book ORDER by title DESC;
title
------------------------------------
Wireless All In One For Dummies
LPIC 1 Exam Cram 2
Linux and Windows 2000 Integration
Check Point CCSA Exam Cram 2
```

The preceding result set was sorted by title in descending order, so the Wireless book is displayed before the Linux books.

Another form of **ORDER BY** refers to the column number rather than the name:

```
sqlite> SELECT title, year from book ORDER by 2 DESC;
title                                 year
```

```
------------------------------------  ----
Wireless All In One For Dummies     2009
Check Point CCSA Exam Cram 2        2005
LPIC 1 Exam Cram 2                  2004
Linux and Windows 2000 Integration  2001
```

Rather than **ORDER BY year DESC** the command orders by column 2, which is the publishing year.

Limiting Results

Even with a **WHERE** clause you may end up with more results than you need. You could be trying to find the top 10 most sold computer books. A **WHERE** clause would restrict your search to only computer books, and an **ORDER BY sales DESC** puts the highest seller at the top, but you're still getting all the results.

LIMIT returns a shortened list of results. **LIMIT** is the last clause in a query, so it comes after **ORDER BY**.

The last two books in the database to be published are found with this query:

```
sqlite> SELECT title, year from book ORDER by 2 DESC LIMIT 2;
title                 year
----------------------------------- ----
Wireless All In One For Dummies     2009
Check Point CCSA Exam Cram 2        2005
```

If you're trying to perform some kind of pagination, where you show a certain number of results on one page and more on the next, the **LIMIT** keyword optionally takes an offset that goes before the number of results you want:

```
sqlite> SELECT title, year from book ORDER by 2 DESC LIMIT 2, 2;
title                               year
------------------------------------  ----
LPIC 1 Exam Cram 2                  2004
Linux and Windows 2000 Integration  2001
```

Here, **LIMIT 2, 2** asks for the database to skip two results and then show two results. For those of us who can't remember whether the offset comes before the number of results or the other way around, the same clause can be written as **LIMIT 2 OFFSET 2**.

Working with Multiple Tables

All the commands so far have operated on a single table. A database has many tables because of a concept called *normalization*.

Consider the books we've been looking at so far. A book has a title, author, and a few other elements. But an author may write more than one book, and a book may have more than one author. (We conveniently ignore the book with multiple authors scenario.)

If the row containing the book also contains the author information, we have duplicated data:

ID	Title	Author
3	Check Point CCSA Exam Cram 2	Sean Walberg
4	Wireless All In One For Dummies	Sean Walberg

This is inefficient especially when you have to track other items about the book and author. If the author changes his address, you need to update each book. What if there are two authors with the same name? How much information would you need to uniquely identify them?

The solution is to split up books and authors into separate tables and link the two of them.

Authors

id	Name
1	Sean Walberg

Books

id	Title	author_id
1	Check Point CCSA Exam Cram 2	1
2	Wireless All In One For Dummies	1

Each book has a link to the author through the identifier column. Picking book ID 2, *Wireless All In One For Dummies*, the author_id is 1. ID 1 in the author table is Sean Walberg.

Writing Queries with Joins

A join is part of a query that tells the database how to match rows between two tables. Tables that are joined are also available to the other clauses such as **WHERE**, **ORDER BY**, and **SELECT**.

A join is performed with the **JOIN** keyword, which comes after the **FROM** clause. The query is built from left to right, so you need to join something onto the table you specified in the FROM clause.

In the simple book database you can obtain a list of books and their authors:

```
sqlite> SELECT * FROM author JOIN book ON book.author_id = author.id;
id first_name last_name id title                 year author_id written
-- ---------- --------- -- -------------------- ---- --------- -------

2  Ross       Brunson   1  LPIC 1 Exam Cram 2   2004 2         2004
2  Ross       Brunson   2  Linux and Windows 20 2001 2         2000
1  Sean       Walberg   3  Wireless All In One  2009 1         2009
1  Sean       Walberg   4  Check Point CCSA Exa 2005 1         2004
```

The key here is the **JOIN book ON book.author_id = author.id**. The query already has **author** through the FROM clause and this joins in **book** based on the condition that the book's **author_id** is the same as the author's **id**.

The condition specified after the **ON** keyword is important. Think of the two tables as sitting next to each other and you've asked the database to join them together. The database goes down the rows of one table and tries to make any matches it can to the other table.

The database doesn't know how to match up the rows if you don't give it conditions. It will match up every row on the left with every row on the right:

```
sqlite> select * from author join book;
id first_name last_name id title                 year author_id written
-- ---------- --------- -- -------------------- ---- --------- -------

1  Sean       Walberg   1  LPIC 1 Exam Cram 2   2004 2         2004
1  Sean       Walberg   2  Linux and Windows 20 2001 2         2000
1  Sean       Walberg   3  Wireless All In One  2009 1         2009
1  Sean       Walberg   4  Check Point CCSA Exa 2005 1         2004
2  Ross       Brunson   1  LPIC 1 Exam Cram 2   2004 2         2004
2  Ross       Brunson   2  Linux and Windows 20 2001 2         2000
2  Ross       Brunson   3  Wireless All In One  2009 1         2009
2  Ross       Brunson   4  Check Point CCSA Exa 2005 1         2004
```

There are eight rows in the result, including rows indicating the wrong author wrote the book. Eight rows comes from two authors times four books for eight different author-book combinations. The ON clause helps the database to match up the rows so that an author is linked to all his books and not someone else's.

Cleaning Up the Query

Looking carefully at the headers of the preceding results you can see that there are two columns called **id**. This is because the joined table contains an **id** column from both **author** and **book**.

The join clause used in the preceding example always mentions the name of the table when talking about the column. **book.author_id = author.id** means the **author_id** from book and the **id** from author. If we forget the names of the tables, the database has problems figuring out where the id column comes from, as there are two:

```
sqlite> SELECT * FROM author JOIN book ON author_id=id;
Error: ambiguous column name: id
```

Typing in column names can be exhausting, so SQL lets you alias tables within the query with the **AS** keyword. The **AS** is used right after the first mention of the table name and is directly followed by the alias.

The query used so far can be rewritten as follows:

```
sqlite> SELECT * FROM author AS a JOIN book AS b ON b.author_id = a.id;
id first_name last_name id title                year  author_id written
-- ---------- --------- -- -------------------- ----  --------- -------
2  Ross       Brunson   1  LPIC 1 Exam Cram 2   2004  2         2004
2  Ross       Brunson   2  Linux and Windows 2000 In 2001  2    2000
1  Sean       Walberg   3  Wireless All In One For D 2009  1    2009
1  Sean       Walberg   4  Check Point CCSA Exam Cra 2005  1    2004
```

Here the **author** table was renamed to **a**, the **book** table was renamed to **b**, and the **JOIN** was able to make use of the shorter names. The output is otherwise identical.

The AS is optional, so the query can be shortened even further:

```
SELECT * FROM author a JOIN book b ON b.author_id = a.id;
```

Be careful when aliasing columns to give it a name that makes sense. Also, as you alias column names you have to use that name for the rest of the query so it will also appear in any **WHERE** or **GROUP BY** clauses.

Advanced Joins

The data earlier was ideal: Every book had an author and every author had a book. But the real world is not so ideal. A book may have no sales, or the author isn't in the system.

The query used in the previous section is called an inner join. It requires that each result row have a row from both the left and right tables; otherwise, the row doesn't make it to the result.

Consider a new author table where there's an author who hasn't written any books:

```
sqlite> SELECT * FROM author;
id   first_name  last_name
---  ----------  ----------
1    Sean        Walberg
2    Ross        Brunson
3    Ada         Lovelace
sqlite> SELECT * FROM book WHERE author_id = 3;
sqlite>
```

The report on books and authors doesn't even mention Ms. Lovelace!

```
sqlite> SELECT first_name, last_name, title FROM author
JOIN book ON author_id=author.id;
first_name  last_name       title
----------  --------------  ----------------------------------
Ross        Brunson         LPIC 1 Exam Cram 2
Ross        Brunson         Linux and Windows 2000 Integration
Sean        Walberg         Wireless All In One For Dummies
Sean        Walberg         Check Point CCSA Exam Cram 2
```

This is because the properties of an inner join require rows to match on both the left and right for something to appear in the result.

In terms of a Venn diagram, see Figure 13-3.

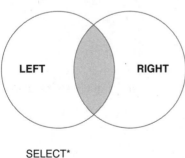

```
SELECT*
FROM left
JOIN right ON left.id = right.id
```

Figure 13-3 A Venn diagram of an INNER JOIN

The result is the intersection of the left and right sides.

Getting all the authors even if they haven't written any books requires a left join. Expressed as a Venn diagram, the left join and its partner the **right join** look like that shown in Figure 13-4.

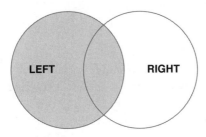

SELECT*
FROM left
LEFT JOIN right ON left.id = right.id

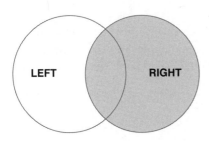

SELECT*
FROM left
RIGHT JOIN right ON left.id = right.id

Figure 13-4   A Venn diagram of a LEFT JOIN and RIGHT JOIN

The left join includes all elements from the left and anything from the right where there's a match. If there's no match on the right, the missing data is filled in with a special *NULL value.*

```
sqlite> SELECT first_name, last_name, title
FROM author
LEFT JOIN book ON author_id=author.id;
first_name  last_name        title
----------  ---------------  -----------------------------------
Sean        Walberg          Check Point CCSA Exam Cram 2
Sean        Walberg          Wireless All In One For Dummies
```

```
Ross          Brunson          LPIC 1 Exam Cram 2
Ross          Brunson          Linux and Windows 2000 Integration
Ada           Lovelace
```

The output is the same as before except that Ada Lovelace has an empty title next to her name.

Left Versus Right Joins

It is difficult to know when to use a left or right join. First you should visualize your query. Which rows have already been added to the query through the **FROM** clause and any previous **JOIN**s, and which are you joining on? That's the left and the right, respectively. Next, which side do you want all the rows included?

Most of the time the answer is going to be a left join only because that's the way queries are often constructed. In the preceding example, the query started from the author table not the book table.

Null

When you query for authors and books and get back an author who hasn't written a book, the database needs to fill in that blank spot somehow. Similarly, a field that has no value, such as the publication date of an unpublished book, needs some kind of placeholder. This placeholder is called a **NULL**.

```
sqlite> SELECT first_name, last_name, title
FROM author
LEFT JOIN book ON author_id=author.id
WHERE author.id = 3;
first_name  last_name        title
----------  ---------------  -----------------------------------
Ada         Lovelace
```

The **NULL** in the preceding example is in the title column. Some database systems explicitly write the word NULL and some leave a blank.

NULL is more than an empty value. NULL means "information is missing." Therefore you can't compare anything to NULL:

```
sqlite> SELECT 1=1;
1=1
----------
1
sqlite> SELECT NULL=NULL;
```

```
NULL=NULL
----------
```

If you can't compare null to anything, how can you write queries like one to find the authors with no books? It would be reasonable to think that this would work:

```
sqlite> SELECT first_name, last_name, title
FROM author
LEFT JOIN book ON author_id=author.id
WHERE title = NULL;
```

However, this won't work because even if the title were NULL it can't be compared to NULL. SQL implements a keyword named **IS NULL** for this case, with a corresponding **IS NOT NULL** to look for values that are not **NULL**.

```
sqlite> SELECT first_name, last_name, title
FROM author
LEFT JOIN book ON author_id=author.id
WHERE title IS NULL;
first_name  last_name       title
----------  --------------  -----------------------------------
Ada         Lovelace
```

When writing queries, especially with joins, take care to make sure you're handling **NULL** correctly.

Subselects

Subselects are another form of join. Instead of one large query, you're inserting the results of a second query, called the child query, into the original, or parent query. This is similar to the command substitution in shell scripts you learned about in Chapter 12, "Shell Scripting."

As a simple example, one can retrieve the author IDs where the author's name is Sean with a simple query:

```
sqlite> SELECT id FROM author WHERE first_name = "Sean";
id
-----------------------------------
1
```

Those results can be injected into another query, such as to find all the books written by that author:

```
sqlite> SELECT title FROM book
WHERE author_id
   IN (SELECT id FROM author WHERE first_name = "Sean");
```

```
title
-----------------------------------
Wireless All In One For Dummies
Check Point CCSA Exam Cram 2
```

The subselects are enclosed in parentheses and usually given as an argument to a **WHERE column IN** clause. The subselect must return only one column; otherwise, you might get an error like this:

```
Error: only a single result allowed for a SELECT that is part of an
expression
```

Grouping Data

So far you've seen how to manipulate several tables into one larger table, and to sort and filter the resulting data. The SQL **GROUP BY** command lets you roll up rows based on similar columns and to perform calculations.

GROUP BY expects a comma-separated list of columns. Rows that have the same values in those columns are rolled up and counted by *aggregate functions* in the **SELECT** clause. This query provides a list of authors and the number of books in the database:

```
sqlite> SELECT first_name, last_name, COUNT(title) AS books
FROM author
LEFT JOIN book ON author_id=author.id
GROUP BY first_name, last_name;
first_name  last_name        books
----------  ---------------  -----
Ada         Lovelace         0
Ross        Brunson          2
Sean        Walberg          2
```

The elements from the previous queries in this chapter are still there. The query selects some columns from **author** and joins in **book** with a left join. The difference is the **GROUP BY** clause and the **COUNT(title)**.

The grouping is what rolls up all rows with similar authors into one. COUNT(title) is an aggregate function that asks the database for the number of non-NULL titles in each grouping.

There are more aggregate functions, depending on your database:

- **AVG(column)**—Returns the average of the column (NULLs are removed.)

- **COUNT(column)**—Counts the number of non-NULL instances of column, or total rows if * is used instead of a column name

- **MIN(column)**—Returns the minimum non-NULL value in the column

- **MAX(column)**—Returns the maximum non-NULL value in the column

- **SUM(column)**—Adds up all the non-NULL values in the column

Inserting Data

The **INSERT** command is the primary way to get new rows into your tables. The format of the INSERT command is

```
INSERT INTO tablename (columns) VALUES (values);
```

So to insert a new book:

```
sqlite> INSERT INTO book (title, year, author_id)
 VALUES ('Sketch of the Analytical Engine', 1842, 3);
sqlite> SELECT * FROM book WHERE author_id = 3;
id     title                                year   author_id  written
-----  ---------------------------------    -----  ---------  --------
5      Sketch of the Analytical Engine  1842   3
```

In the preceding example, the command is telling the database to expect three pieces of data, which will go into the **title, year**, and **author_id** columns of the **book** table.

Notice that the **id** was set to 5 even though the value wasn't specified. This is because that column is the *primary key* of the table and is filled in by the database automatically if it's not provided.

The **written** column was unspecified, so it's left as **NULL** to indicate the value is unknown.

An alternate form of **INSERT** is to specify values for all the columns, which eliminates the need to tell the database which columns you will use.

```
sqlite> INSERT INTO book VALUES (NULL, "LPIC-1/CompTIA Linux+ Cert
Guide", NULL, 3, 2015);
```

As there are two unknown columns, the primary key and the publication year, those are entered in as **NULL**. The database adds its own primary key.

If you have many rows to insert you can add them all in one command:

```
INSERT INTO book (title) VALUES ('title1'), ('title2');
```

Updating Data

Once data is in your database you may need to make changes to existing rows. People change their names, books change their prices, and relationships between different entities change.

The **UPDATE** command changes existing rows. The format of the command is

```
UPDATE table SET column1=value1, column2=value2 WHERE conditions.
```

To set a publication year for the book entered in the last section:

```
sqlite> UPDATE book SET year=2015 WHERE id=6;
```

It's also possible to set a value based on another column, such as if you want to set the year the book was written to the same as the publication year if it's unspecified:

```
sqlite> UPDATE book SET written=year WHERE written IS NULL;
```

This works because of the quoting rules discussed earlier. **Year** is a bare word; therefore, it refers to a column name. If it were single quoted, it would try to set the value of the column to the word **year**. This would fail because the column is set to only accept integers.

It's important to get the command right on the first try, especially the **WHERE** clause. There's no undo button!

Deleting Data

Deleting data is similar to querying data as you're deleting the results of a query:

```
sqlite> DELETE FROM book WHERE author_id IS NULL;
```

This query deletes any book where the **author_id** is missing.

Just like the **UPDATE**, be careful! If you forget the **WHERE** clause, all your rows will be deleted.

Creating Tables

Unless you're a developer, there's a good chance you'll never have to create a table. However, for completeness, tables are created with the **CREATE TABLE** command. The general form of this command is

```
CREATE TABLE tablename (
ColumnName1 type1 options1,
ColumnName2 type2 options2
);
```

Where the ColumnNames are the names you give the column, the type describes what is stored in the column, and the options are some optional adjustments to what is stored in the table.

Common data types are

- **int**—An integer
- **smallint, mediumint, bigint**—Integer types with various limits
- **character, varchar**—Character strings, which require a length to be passed such as varchar(255)
- **text**—A longer string or document that is larger than a database dependent limitation
- **blob**—A binary object such as a picture
- **float**—A floating point number
- **decimal**—A number with a decimal place stored in fixed precision format
- **Boolean**—A true or false value
- **Date and datetime**—Either a date or a date with a timestamp

The options give some more context to the column and allow for better data consistency:

- **NOT NULL**—Do not allow NULL values to be stored.
- **PRIMARY KEY**—This column is a primary key that is indexed and must be unique for each row.
- **UNIQUE**—This column is not the primary key but is not allowed to have any duplicates.

The statements used to create the tables for this book are (with formatting added for clarity):

```
sqlite> .schema
CREATE TABLE author (
id integer primary key,
first_name varchar(255),
last_name varchar(255));
CREATE TABLE book (
id integer primary key,
title varchar(255),
year integer,
author_id integer,
written integer);
```

Summary

Databases are used to store information for easier retrieval and reporting. A relational database is one where various entities are stored in separate tables, and the database provides the Structured Query Language (SQL) with which to query and change the data.

SQL involves a keyword, such as SELECT, INSERT, UPDATE, or DELETE, followed by a series of clauses to provide additional information. For example, you might SELECT some data and filter it with a WHERE clause and aggregate it with GROUP BY.

Exam Preparation Tasks

As mentioned in the section "How to Use This Book" in the Introduction, you have a couple of choices for exam preparation: the exercises here, Chapter 21, "Final Preparation," and the practice exams on the DVD.

Review All Key Topics

Review the most important topics in this chapter, noted with the Key Topics icon in the outer margin of the page. Table 13-2 lists a reference of these key topics and the page numbers on which each is found.

Table 13-2   Key Topics for Chapter 13

Key Topic Element	Description	Page Number
Paragraph	Indexes help the database find information quickly	369
Paragraph	A table in a relational database has rows and columns	370
Paragraph	Semicolons terminate SQL statements	372
Paragraph	SQL comments start with --	372
Paragraph	SQL commands are not case sensitive, but the data is	372
Paragraph	Strings of words are single quoted	373
Paragraph	SELECT * FROM table returns all rows and columns from table	374
Paragraph	Numeric comparison operators	375
Paragraph	The IN keyword matches items in a set	376
Paragraph	AND has higher precedence than OR	377

Key Topic Element	Description	Page Number
Paragraph	Sorts default to ascending order; the DESC keyword specifies descending	377
Paragraph	LIMIT n returns the first N results and goes after any ORDER BY	378
Paragraph	JOIN table comes after FROM and joins table to what's already been specified	380
Paragraph	The database matches all rows on the left to all rows on the right without an ON clause	380
Paragraph	AS lets you define a table alias	381
Paragraph	Inner joins require a match on the left and right to show in the results	382
Paragraph	Left joins include all the rows on the left plus any rows that match up from the right	383
Paragraph	NULL means "missing value"	384
Paragraph	Subselects must return one column and are enclosed in parentheses	386
Paragraph	GROUP BY rolls up the specified columns to be counted by aggregate functions	386
List	A list of aggregate functions	386
Paragraph	How to insert data without naming columns	387
Paragraph	The format of the UPDATE command	388

Define Key Terms

Define the following key terms from this chapter and check your answers in the glossary:

client-server, key-value database, indexes, relational database, many-to-one relationship, many-to-many relationship, embedded database, database schema, normalization, inner join, left join, null value, aggregate function, primary key, table, Structured Query Language

Review Questions

The answers to these review questions are in Appendix A.

1. A table with rows and columns can be found in a(n):

   a. Flat file database

   b. Key-value database

   c. Relational database

   d. Schemaless database

2. Statements in SQL are separated by:

   a. ;

   b. A blank line

   c. A new line

   d. .

3. You have a table containing employee data, and one of the fields is years_of_service. How would you find everyone who has worked for at least 5 years, but no more than 20?

   a. SELECT * FROM employee WHERE years_of_service > 5 AND years_of_service < 20;

   b. SELECT * FROM employee where years_of_service BETWEEN 5, 20;

   c. SELECT * FROM employee where years_of_service BETWEEN 5 AND 21;

   d. SELECT * FROM employee where years_of_service BETWEEN 5 AND 20;

4. Given a table for managers and employees, how would you produce a report of the managers with their employees, ignoring managers with no employees?

   a. SELECT * FROM managers, employees;

   b. SELECT * FROM managers AS m JOIN employees AS ee ON (ee.manager_id = m.id);

   c. SELECT * FROM managers AS m LEFT JOIN employees AS ee ON (ee.manager_id = m.id);

   d. SELECT * FROM managers JOIN employees(id=manager_id);

Chapter 13: Basic SQL Management   393

5. Consider this query:

```
SELECT *
FROM products
LEFT JOIN sales on products.name = sales.product_name
```

Which of the following are true? (Choose two.)

    a. All products will be included even if they have no sales.

    b. All sales will be included even if the product is not missing.

    c. The **sales** table contains the product's name in the **product_name** column.

    d. This query will calculate total sales per product.

6. Which of the following queries properly use table aliases?

    a. SELECT * FROM employee WHERE employee AS ee.hire_date > '2010-01-01' AND ee.status IS NOT NULL.

    b. SELECT * FROM employee WHERE employee.hire_date > '2010-01-01' AND ee.status IS NOT NULL.

    c. SELECT * FROM employee AS ee WHERE ee.hire_date > '2010-01-01' AND employee.status IS NOT NULL.

    d. SELECT * FROM employee ee WHERE ee.hire_date > '2010-01-01' AND ee.status IS NOT NULL.

7. A NULL in a column means:

    a. The value is missing.

    b. It is the same as zero.

    c. It is the same as a blank string.

    d. The column will match anything.

8. You have an employee table that includes a job description and a salary column. How do you calculate the average salary per position using SQL?

    a. SELECT *, SUM(salary) FROM employee GROUP BY description;

    b. SELECT description, SUM(salary) FROM employee;

    c. SELECT description, SUM(salary) FROM employee GROUP BY description;

    d. SELECT description, SUM(salary) FROM employee GROUP BY salary;

9. Which of the following statements is correct about the following SQL statement:

```
INSERT INTO employee (name, age) VALUES ('Alice', 30), ('Bob', 32);
```

   a. The values have the rows and columns mixed; it should be ('Alice', 'Bob'), (30, 22);.

   b. The statement needs to specify all the columns in employee.

   c. The statement needs to be split into two.

   d. The statement inserts two rows.

10. Your employee table tracks years of service, but there are many employees where the years are not known and have a NULL in that column. How could you change everyone in this situation to have 20 years of experience?

   a. UPDATE employee SET years_of_service = 20 WHERE years_of_service = NULL;

   b. UPDATE employee SET years_of_service = 20 WHERE years_of_service IS NULL;

   c. UPDATE employee SET years_of_service = 20;

   d. UPDATE employee.years_of_service = 20 WHERE years_of_service IS NULL;

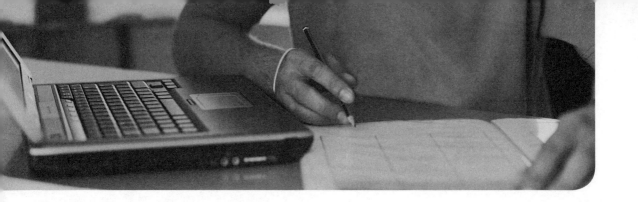

This chapter covers the following topics:

- Quick Overview of X
- The Xorg System
- X Display Managers
- Into and Out of X
- Accessibility Options
- Remote Clients

This chapter covers the following objectives:

- Install and configure X11: 106.1
- Set up a display manager: 106.2
- Accessibility: 106.3

## CHAPTER 14

Configuring User Interfaces and Desktops

Although it may not be a routine task, at times you need to be able to configure the *graphical user interface (GUI)*. Before making such changes, it is important to understand the components of the GUI, including the X Window Server, display managers, and desktops.

This chapter focuses on these components while also addressing the issues regarding GUI security and accessibility.

"Do I Know This Already?" Quiz

The "Do I Know This Already?" quiz enables you to assess whether you should read this entire chapter or simply jump to the "Exam Preparation Tasks" section for review. If you are in doubt, read the entire chapter. Table 14-1 outlines the major headings in this chapter and the corresponding "Do I Know This Already?" quiz questions. You can find the answers in Appendix A, "Answers to the 'Do I Know This Already?' Quizzes and Review Questions."

Table 14-1 "Do I Know This Already?" Foundation Topics Section-to-Question Mapping

Foundation Topics Section	Questions Covered in This Section
Quick Overview of X	1-2
The Xorg System	3-4
X Display Managers	5
Into and Out of X	6
Accessibility Options	7
Remote Clients	8

1. A primary function of a display manager is to?

    a. Manage hardware, such as the mouse and keyboard

    b. Allow X clients to connect to the X server

    c. Facilitate the login process

    d. None of the above

2. Which of the following is most likely to provide a program like a file manager:

   a. The X server

   b. A display manager

   c. A window manager

   d. A desktop

3. Where is the location of the Xorg server configuration file?

   a. /etc/xorg.conf

   b. /etc/X11/xorg.conf

   c. /etc/x11/config/xorg.conf

   d. /etc/xconfig/xorg.xonf

4. Which section of the Xorg configuration file is used to define the fonts location?

   a. Module

   b. Screen

   c. Files

   d. Fonts

5. Which of the following display managers is a part of the Xorg software set?

   a. lightdm

   b. kdm

   c. gdm

   d. xdm

6. To go from the GUI to virtual terminal 3 (/dev/tty3), which keystroke combination would you use?

   a. Ctrl+Alt+F3

   b. Ctrl+F3

   c. Alt+F3

   d. F3

7. Which accessibility feature plays a sound when a user presses a modifier key, like the Ctrl key?

   a. Slow Keys

   b. Toggle Keys

   c. Repeat Keys

   d. Bounce Keys

8. Which command allows users from other systems to access your X server?

   a. **xdisplay**

   b. **xsecure**

   c. **xserver**

   d. **xhost**

Foundation Topics

Quick Overview of X

The X Window System (or simply X) is a set of software that provides the basis for a graphical user interface (GUI). To understand the function of X, it is helpful to provide a list of what X does as well as what it does not do:

- X provides basic window features, such as drawing graphical programs, moving graphical programs, and resizing graphical programs.

- X provides the means to interface with hardware, such as the mouse, video card, and monitor.

- X does not provide a means to log in to the system graphically. This is handled by another software tool called a *display manager*.

- X does not provide "desktop" features such as background images, window-based menus (to launch applications), or right-click menus. These features are provided by software tools called *desktops*.

- X does not provide the standard functionality that you have come to expect from GUI programs. For example, you expect each program to have a title bar, a close box, and scrollbars. This functionality is provided by a software tool called a *window manager*, not by X.

The best way to conceptualize X is to consider what you would see on your screen if you were to start only the X server. This can be accomplished by executing the **X** command. The screen would appear blank with the exception of a large X icon that represents your mouse location. No login screen would be provided, and no graphical programs would be running. To launch graphical programs you would have to switch to a command line environment and execute the program from there.

While X is a key component to a GUI environment, it is only one piece of the puzzle.

 How X Works

The X system uses a client/server model; each system has an X server that interacts with and handles access to the system's hardware. The X server makes it possible for an X client (a GUI program) to display data or graphics on the screen. The X client requests an action, and the X server performs the action.

Server, in this case, is defined as the computer that provides needed functionality for clients requesting services.

Another interesting feature of this model is the capability for an X server to handle X clients from either local or remote sources. In short, an X client executed from the local system displays along with X clients that have been invoked and run on a remote system and displays locally. Figure 14-1 shows the local workstation displaying both local and remote applications.

This flexibility opens up immense opportunities for centralizing your application code on a single server or set of servers and having clients attach and run the applications. Disadvantages include network bandwidth usage and troubleshooting the connections.

NOTE Although the X environment allows for many lovely graphical utilities to be run, such as complex and colorful screensavers, you might find that these drag down the performance of your X server dramatically. Run with caution.

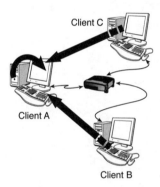

Figure 14-1   Displaying remote and local X clients

Window Managers

It might seem odd to mention and work with window managers before desktops such as *KDE* and *GNOME*, but you need a window manager, while a desktop is not mandatory.

X window managers have one main purpose: When the X server draws a window on the screen, the window manager puts the scrollbars, minimize and maximize buttons, and all the garnish on that X client window. Some window managers are more full-featured than others and can provide the previous features plus virtual desktops, toolbars, wallpaper options, menus, and so on.

> **NOTE** Knowledge of window managers is not required for the LPIC certification exam.

Linux Desktops

KDE was the first Linux desktop environment, and GNOME was primarily invented because its author wasn't happy with the licensing of the libraries used for the KDE desktop.

It doesn't really matter which one you use, but many people feel that KDE is more aesthetically pleasing, whereas GNOME does things from an architecturally correct perspective. Both get the job done.

 A desktop environment can be defined by the following common criteria (to name a few):

- File manager
- Control Panel/Center
- Window manager
- Common look and feel
- Integrated office suite
- Media players

The Xorg System

Although the X Window System was developed at MIT, the Linux version of X is a freely redistributable open-source version of the original and is maintained by the X.org Foundation.

The *Xorg* implementation of the X Window System is similar in function to the original and provides an abstraction layer that allows applications to be either run and displayed locally or run remotely and displayed locally.

 ### The Xorg Configuration File

Although you'll probably never have to construct an X configuration file by hand, you do need to know the overall structure, sections, and some of the entries for the exam. The configuration file for Xorg is **/etc/X11/xorg.conf**; a partial output is shown in Example 14-1.

Example 14-1   Example Xorg Configuration File

```
Section "Files"


    ModulePath    "/usr/lib/xorg/modules"
    FontPath      "catalogue:/etc/X11/fontpath.d"
    FontPath      "built-ins"
EndSection


Section "Module"
    Load  "glx"
EndSection
Section "InputDevice"
    Identifier  "Keyboard0"
    Driver      "kbd"
EndSection


Section "InputDevice"
    Identifier  "Mouse0"
    Driver      "mouse"
    Option          "Protocol" "auto"
    Option          "Device" "/dev/input/mice"
    Option          "ZAxisMapping" "4 5 6 7"
EndSection


Section "Monitor"
    Identifier   "Monitor0"
    VendorName   "Monitor Vendor"
    ModelName    "Monitor Model"
EndSection
Section "Screen"
    Identifier "Screen0"
    Device     "Card0"
    Monitor    "Monitor0"
    SubSection "Display"
        Viewport   0 0
        Depth     1
    EndSubSection
    SubSection "Display"
        Viewport   0 0
        Depth     4
    EndSubSection
```

```
        SubSection "Display"
             Viewport   0 0
             Depth      8
        EndSubSection
        SubSection "Display"
             Viewport   0 0
             Depth      15
        EndSubSection
        SubSection "Display"
             Viewport   0 0
             Depth      16
        EndSubSection
        SubSection "Display"
             Viewport   0 0
             Depth      24
        EndSubSection
EndSection
```

A detailed understanding of these sections is not required for the LPIC certification exam. However, you should understand what is stored in each section:

- **Files**—This section provides information about files used by the X server. For example, fonts are stored in files and need to be accessed by the X server.

- **Module**—This section associates devices (such as your keyboard) with module files. A module file is like a device driver.

- **InputDevice**—This section defines your input devices, such as your mouse and keyboard.

- **Monitor**—This section is used to describe the monitor.

- **Screen**—This describes the features of the screen, including the color depth permitted.

On modern Linux distributions, you rarely need to modify the **/etc/X11/xorg.conf** file. In fact, on some distributions the Xorg server runs without a configuration file. Instead of relying on a configuration file, these servers probe hardware and auto-configure themselves.

If you do need to create a **/etc/X11/xorg.conf** file, make sure you are in a command-line environment and execute the **X –configure** command.

> **NOTE** Keep in mind that different distributions may include additional utilities to accomplish the creation of an xorg.conf file. If the previous command doesn't work, you may also try **Xorg -configure**.

Fonts in X

X comes complete with a set of fonts referenced in the **/etc/X11/xorg.conf** file's Files section, under FontPath. On machines that don't use the X font server (called **xfs**), the font path is configured either as a set of directories and remote paths or as an entry that indicates a local path. The following entries for the FontPath are parsed in memory and put together to form a single font path for the system:

```
FontPath "/usr/X11R6/lib/X11/fonts/100dpi"
FontPath "/usr/X11R6/lib/X11/fonts/75dpi"
FontPath "tcp/somepc.example.com:7100"
```

On some newer systems, a single font directory that contains links to other fonts may be used:

```
FontPath     "catalogue:/etc/X11/fontpath.d"
```

This directory should contain symbolic links to additional fonts:

```
ls -l /etc/X11/fontpath.d
total 0
lrwxrwxrwx. 1 root root 36 Jul  7  2012 default-ghostscript -> /usr/
share/fonts/default/ghostscript
lrwxrwxrwx. 1 root root 30 Jul  7  2012 fonts-default -> /usr/share/
fonts/default/Type1
lrwxrwxrwx. 1 root root 27 Jul  7  2012 liberation-fonts -> /usr/
share/fonts/liberation
lrwxrwxrwx. 1 root root 27 Jul  7  2012 xorg-x11-fonts-
100dpi:unscaled:pri=30 -> /usr/share/X11/fonts/100dpi
lrwxrwxrwx. 1 root root 25 Jul  7  2012 xorg-x11-fonts-
misc:unscaled:pri=10 -> /usr/share/X11/fonts/misc
lrwxrwxrwx. 1 root root 26 Jul  7  2012 xorg-x11-fonts-Type1 -> /usr/
share/X11/fonts/Type1
```

Be aware that some systems use a font server called **xfs**. An advantage of **xfs** is speed when rendering fonts because large sets of complex fonts can make the system freeze up while rendering. **xfs** is multithreaded, so it can handle simultaneous requests, whereas the X server doesn't handle multiple requests well.

If you choose to use the X font server, you have to start it before running X or have it started in the system runlevels; otherwise, X won't start.

Using the **xfs** server (locally, pointing to local files) requires the following line in the **/etc/X11/xorg.conf**:

```
FontPath "unix/:7100" [or "unix/:-1")
```

> **NOTE** The exam requires an awareness of the xfs server but does not require you to have a detailed understanding of this server.

Tuning X

Several programs exist to help you get the most out of your display and monitor with X. These are typically included with X or are a package closely related to X.

For example, some monitors don't display the screen correctly, with part of the output being cut off or off-center. To fix some of these problems, you can use the **xvidtune** command. Running **xvidtune** from within X shows the interface in Figure 14-2.

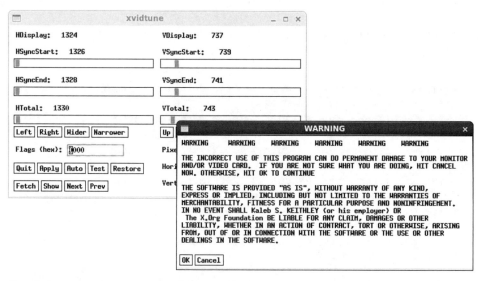

Figure 14-2   The **xvidtune** program

This program comes with some dire warnings, and with good reason. You can damage your monitor, and when the tube goes, you will see (and smell) the "magic blue smoke" from the ruined tube. The best thing about the **xvidtune** program is that it tells you the display resolution and lets you adjust the image on your monitor to stretch properly from edge to edge and be centered properly.

> **NOTE** The **xvidtune** program should only be used on CRT (traditional monitors) as it will not function properly on LED or LCD screens.

Another interesting program is the **xwininfo** tool for querying a window and getting a listing of its geometry and, particularly, the color depth.

Running the **xwininfo** command causes little to happen onscreen; the mouse pointer changes to a plus sign (+) and a message tells you to select the window you want to get information about.

The output shown in Example 14-2 is typical of the tool.

Example 14-2   Example of **xwininfo** Output

```
xwininfo: Window id: 0x260000a "xeyes"
  Absolute upper-left X:   1046
  Absolute upper-left Y:   108
  Relative upper-left X:   2
  Relative upper-left Y:   26
  Width: 150
  Height: 100
  Depth: 24
  Visual: 0x21
  Visual Class: TrueColor
  Border width: 0
  Class: InputOutput
  Colormap: 0x20 (installed)
  Bit Gravity State: NorthWestGravity
  Window Gravity State: NorthWestGravity
  Backing Store State: NotUseful
  Save Under State: no
  Map State: IsViewable
  Override Redirect State: no
  Corners:  +1046+108   -128+108   -128-529   +1046-529
  -geometry 150x100+1044+82
```

The exam tests your knowledge of particular tools, such as what shows the current color depth, what can be used to adjust a screen's video image, and so on.

X Display Managers

The X display managers are for managing logins and sessions on an X server. Their design is such that remote and local logins are handled equally well. The user enters her username and password; then the session is started, transferring control from the display manager to the user's session manager.

For the exam you should be aware of the following display managers:

- **XDM**—This display manager is part of the Xorg software collection. Its executable is **/usr/bin/xdm**, and its configuration files are stored in the **/etc/X11/xdm** directory. Typically this display manager is not used except on servers where full desktops are not installed. On such machines, only a basic X server is installed, and the GUI is only started for specific purposes.

- **KDM**—This display manager is part of the KDE software suite. Its executable is **/usr/bin/kdm**, and its configuration files are stored in the **/etc/kde/kdm** directory. If you install the KDE software suite, the default display manager will likely be KDM.

- **GDM**—This display manager is part of the Gnome software suite. Its executable is **/usr/sbin/gdm**, and its configuration files are stored in the **/etc/gdm** directory. If you install the Gnome software suite, the default display manager will likely be Gnome.

In addition to these display managers, you should be aware of the Lightdm. This display manager is designed to be a replacement for the KDM (and, to some extent, the GDM). To configure this display manager, modify the configuration files located in the **/etc/lightdm** directory. Note: Often the default installation of Lightdm does not include a configuration file in the **/etc/lightdm** directory. While there is no man page for **lightdm.conf**, there is a sample file in the **/usr/share/doc/lightdm** directory.

Regardless of which display manager you choose to use on your system, you should be aware of the following:

- One of the primary functions of the display manager is to provide a means for users to log in.

- A display manager should be able to log a user into any desktop. In other words, KDM provides an option for users to log in to a Gnome desktop, while GDM provides an option for users to log in to a KDE desktop (provided, of course, the appropriate software is installed).

- Many configuration options are available for display managers, including the ability to start multiple display managers (allowing for multiple desktops). Another commonly changed configuration option is the ability to create a custom "greeter" message. This is the message that appears to users when they see the login window.

- Which display manager your system uses by default depends on which distribution you are using. Additionally, how you specify the display manager on the system can vary depending on your distribution.

Into and Out of X

One of the topics that crops up now and then on the exam, and often enough in real life, is how to fix a frozen X display or do anything if X freezes up.

Let's review: Linux configures, by default, the keys **F1–F6** as virtual consoles, mapped to **/dev/tty1** through **/dev/tty6**. You can switch back and forth among these virtual consoles using the **Alt** and **F** keys, each one being an entirely different login session. Typically **F7** represents the GUI (although on some systems, such as Red Hat, **F1** may be the GUI and **F2-F6** the virtual consoles).

Sometimes you need to get from the GUI to the text mode consoles. The **Alt** and **F** keys are mapped inside X, so an additional keystroke is required to escape the surly bonds of a broken X environment. For example, if you're in X, you would press **Ctrl+Alt+F2** to reach a login screen that would drop you to the shell prompt in **/dev/tty2**.

After you're out of X, you can use the **Alt+F** key combinations to switch to any configured virtual console. Most sysadmins just save energy by using the Ctrl key all the time when switching virtual consoles—it doesn't hurt anything.

Let's say you've fixed the problem, killed a program, and freed up X. To get back into X, you press **Alt+F7** or **Ctrl+Alt+F7** to return to /dev/tty7, which is configured for X by default.

Remember that, while you're in text mode

- **Alt+F1–F6** switches text terminals.

- **Alt+F7** switches to X if running.

While you're in an X session

- **Ctrl+Alt+F1–F6** switches to that session.

- **Alt+F7** or **Ctrl+Alt+F7** switches back to X.

Another useful key combination is **Ctrl+Alt+<Backspace>**. This restarts the X server.

 Accessibility Options

Many features are available on desktops that allow users to have a richer experience. These features cater to many individuals who would benefit from such *accessibility options*. The following sections describe the most common of these features/utilities.

Sticky/Repeat Keys

Sticky Keys is a feature that allows the user to perform keyboard combinations, such as **Ctrl+c**, without having to hold down the modifier button while pressing the combination. For example, instead of holding down the **Ctrl** button while pressing the **c** key, the user can press the **Ctrl** button once and then press the **c** key.

Repeat Keys is a feature that continuously inserts a key value when a user holds down a key on the keyboard. For example, if you hold down the key **a** while in a word processing program, you continue to see a's inputted on the screen. In Figure 14-3, the Repeat Keys feature of Gnome's Assistive Technologies program is displayed.

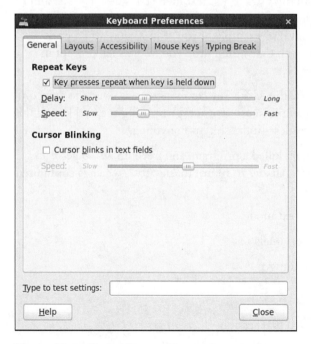

Figure 14-3   Repeat Keys settings

Slow/Bounce/Toggle Keys

Slow Keys are a feature for people who have "heavy hands" when typing on a keyboard. Often they find that extra (unwanted) keys appear when they move their hands from one key to another and accidently press another key. With Slow Keys, a key only results in a displayed character if the key is held down for a short period of time.

If a user has "shaky hands" and accidentally types keys repeatedly, Bounce Keys prevents this from happening. This does make it more difficult to type words like "difficult" because of the repeating **f** keys.

The Toggle Keys feature is used to provide a sound when modifier keys, such as the Shift key, are pressed. This makes it easier for users to know whether they have pressed a modifier key.

Mouse Keys

When Mouse Keys are enabled, the user can move the mouse cursor by using keys on the keyboard. On the number pad, keys **2-4** and **8-6** represent directions to move the mouse. Pressing on the **5** key represents clicking the mouse once. Double pressing **5** represents double-clicking. For this to work, the **Num Lock** feature must be turned off. In Figure 14-4, the Mouse Keys feature of Gnome's Assistive Technologies program is displayed.

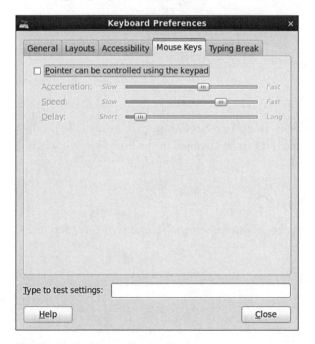

Figure 14-4   Mouse Keys settings

High Contrast/Large Print Desktop Themes

Most desktops provide different themes that allow for easier viewing. A High Contrast theme provides solid colors (typically black and white) to make the display more distinctive. In Figure 14-5, the Theme tab of Gnome's Appearance program is displayed.

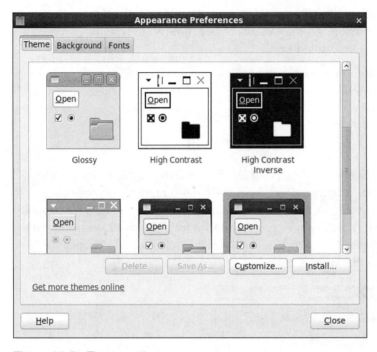

Figure 14-5   Theme settings

Large Print themes are used to display fonts in a larger font than normal. Typically this doesn't require an actual theme but can be changed in the Fonts section of the Desktop settings.

Screen Reader

A screen reader verbalizes the text shown on the screen. Several screen readers are available, including

- Orca
- emacspeak
- espeak
- festival

Braille Display

A Braille Display is a "monitor" that provides Braille output.

Screen Magnifier

A screen magnifier allows the user to better see the screen by magnifying a portion of the screen. An example of a screen magnifier is Kmagnifier, a program available on KDE desktops.

Onscreen Keyboard

An onscreen keyboard provides the user with the ability to "type" using a mouse with a virtual keyboard or on a touch-enabled screen. An example of an onscreen keyboard is Gnome's GOK.

NOTE Although the LPI Exam Objectives list a weight of 1 for the entire Accessibility section, it will seem like you spend an inordinate amount of time on this topic. When budgeting your mental resources, keep in mind that you only get a single question on the exam regarding this topic.

Remote Clients

Remotely displaying X client applications is a strength of X, making a centralized application server with multiple thin or slim clients a possibility. If all the client machine does is boot and connect to run applications, it can be replaced in short order, reducing user downtime significantly.

Allowing remote machines to connect to your X server indiscriminately isn't a good security plan, so configuring the hosts access is accomplished with the **xhost** command.

The **xhost** command has three modes:

- **xhost**—Shows the current state.
- **xhost -** —Enables security; only those that are authorized can connect.
- **xhost +**—Disables security; anyone can connect.

First, run the **xhost** command to determine the state of the security mechanism, like so:

```
xhost
access control enabled, only authorized hosts can connect
```

You now know the machine isn't accepting connections from just anyone, but you have a decision to make; do you want to block everyone and allow a few, or do you want to allow everyone and block just a few?

To leave the system in a secure state and allow just two hosts to connect and run applications, run the following command:

```
xhost +host1 host2
host1 being added to the access control list
host2 being added to the access control list
```

Now these hosts can connect via Telnet (unsecure) or ssh (secure). When they execute an X client, the display output is sent over the network to the client machine's X display. This requires the correct setting of the $HOST variable. For example, if you connect to the host1 system and try to run an X client, the command may fail unless the $HOST variable is set to the machine that you just connected from:

```
setenv HOST "server1:0.0"
```

Say another system doesn't have much on it, but you don't want to spend time messing with the security. Your users are technically literate and it's not a problem to have an open X server, so you run the command shown here:

```
xhost +
access control disabled, clients can connect from any host
```

The machine is wide open. If, at this point, you discover a couple of users who are being ridiculous with the open system, you can block just their systems with this command:

```
xhost -host3 host4
```

The exam focuses on scenarios for X security, including how to disable, enable, and display the status, and how to configure the access list.

Summary

In this chapter you learned about GUI-based components including the Xorg server, desktops and display managers. You also learned about basic Xorg and display manager configuration. Finally, you learned about tools associated with GUI-based components, including commands that display information, allow access from remote hosts, and provide accessibility features.

Exam Preparation Tasks

As mentioned in the section "How to Use This Book" in the Introduction, you have a few choices for exam preparation: the exercises here, Chapter 21, "Final Preparation," and the practice exams on the DVD.

Review All Key Topics

Review the most important topics in this chapter, noted with the Key Topics icon in the outer margin of the page. Table 14-2 lists a reference of these key topics and the page numbers on which each is found.

Table 14-2   Key Topics for Chapter 14

Key Topic Element	Description	Page Number
Paragraph	Working with window managers	401
Section	The Xorg configuration file	402
Paragraph	xvidtune and displaying screens correctly	406
Paragraph	Using xwininfo to query a window's details	407
Paragraph	Awareness of display managers	408
Paragraph	Awareness of the lightdm display manager	408
Section	Accessibility Options	410
Paragraph	Allowing remote machines to connect	413

Define Key Terms

Define the following key terms from this chapter and check your answers in the glossary:

graphical user interface, display manager, desktop, window manager, GNOME, KDE, Xorg, accessibility options

Review Questions

The answers to these review questions are in Appendix A.

1. You installed a new default Linux workstation, and the mouse works in text mode. When X is started, the mouse won't work. Which section of the /etc/X11/xorg.conf file would you look at as part of the process to solve this problem?

   a. Protocol

   b. Mode

   c. Device

   d. Mapping

   e. Emulation

2. When updating an older X system, you decide to install and use the xfs X font server. Which of the following entries should be included in the Files section of the Xorg file to have X use xfs?

   a. Fontpath "/usr/X11R6/bin/xfs"

   b. FontPath "unix/:7100"

   c. FontServer "xfs"

   d. export FSERVER=/usr/sbin/xfs

3. You want to sign on to a remote system via ssh, have an application execute on the remote machine, and be shown on your local system's screen. Which command switches can you use to accomplish this? (Choose two.)

   a. -X

   b. -Y

   c. -R

   d. -T

4. There is a program that provides scrollbars, widgets, menus, background wallpaper, and virtual desktops for the X environment. Which phrase best describes this program?

   a. Desktop

   b. X server

   c. Window manager

   d. X client

5. The _____ command controls access to the local X server's resources. Fill in the blank with just the program name:

   _____

6. You need to modify a feature of the lightdm display manager. In which directory would you store this custom configuration file?

   a. /etc/dm

   b. /etc/X11/lightdm

   c. /etc/lightdm

   d. /etc/lightdm-config

7. Which of the following accessibility features is used to verbally read text displayed on the screen?

   a. Speaknow

   b. Orca

   c. Speakit

   d. text-to-speech

8. Which accessibility program allows you to move your mouse cursor with keyboard keys?

   a. Toggle Keys

   b. Keyboard Keys

   c. Mouse Keys

   d. Slow Keys

9. A theme that provides a distinctive display by using solid colors (typically black and white) is called a _____ theme?

   _____

10. Which of the following programs is a valid onscreen keyboard program?

    a. OSK

    b. on-screen-keyboard

    c. GOK

    d. oc-key

This chapter covers the following topics:

- User Account Fundamentals
- Group Accounts
- Adding Users and Groups
- Modifying Users and Groups
- Removing Users and Groups
- The Shadow Suite
- Changing Accounts

This chapter covers the following objectives:

- Manage user and group accounts and related system files: 107.1

## CHAPTER 15

Managing Users and Groups

The importance of user and group administration cannot be emphasized enough. Your system is a target, and users are the bullets in the gun. All an attacker has to do is get a user to give the attacker his username or password and she can attempt penetration.

This chapter covers some interesting areas of system administration—supporting users and groups, enabling access, setting their default profiles and home directories, and putting the whack on them when they misbehave.

"Do I Know This Already?" Quiz

The "Do I Know This Already?" quiz enables you to assess whether you should read this entire chapter or simply jump to the "Exam Preparation Tasks" section for review. If you are in doubt, read the entire chapter. Table 15-1 outlines the major headings in this chapter and the corresponding "Do I Know This Already?" quiz questions. You can find the answers in Appendix A, "Answers to the 'Do I Know This Already?' Quizzes and Review Questions."

Table 15-1 "Do I Know This Already?" Foundation Topics Section-to-Question Mapping

Foundation Topics Section	Questions Covered in This Section
User Account Fundamentals	1-2
Group Accounts	3
Adding Users and Groups	4-5
Modifying Users and Groups	6
Removing Users and Groups	7
The Shadow Suite	8
Changing Accounts	9

1. Which UID denotes the root account?

   a. 0

   b. 1

   c. 99

   d. 100

2. Which account denotes the nobody account?

   a. 0

   b. 1

   c. 99

   d. 100

3. Based on the following entry from the /etc/group file, who is a secondary member of this group:

   `tim:x:599:nick`

   a. tim

   b. x

   c. 599

   d. nick

4. Which **useradd** option specifies the user's login shell?

   a. -m

   b. -d

   c. -k

   d. -s

5. Which option displays the defaults used by the **useradd** command?

   a. -e

   b. -D

   c. -c

   d. -b

6. Which command can be used to add a user to a group as a secondary group member?

    a. chage

    b. ulimit

    c. groupmod

    d. usermod

7. When removing a user with the **userdel** command, which option also removes the user's home directory?

    a. -r

    b. -d

    c. -m

    d. -f

8. On modern Linux systems, which file stores the user account passwords?

    a. /etc/passwd

    b. /etc/password

    c. /etc/shadow/password

    d. /etc/shadow

9. Which commands allow you to change password aging for a user account? (Choose all that apply.)

    a. usermod

    b. chage

    c. passwd

    d. chpasswd

Foundation Topics

User Account Fundamentals

User and group accounts are not known to the kernel by the name we use and see, but by the *user ID (UID)* and *group ID (GID)* associated with the name. Early versions of the kernel supported two tables of static numbers representing up to 65,536 users and 65,536 groups, but at the 2.6 kernel version mark there were made available 4,294,967,296 possible users and groups.

The only association between the username and the UID are entries in the **/etc/passwd** file that defines users. The only association between the group name and the GID are entries in the **/etc/group** file that defines groups.

Users must have a username entry in the **/etc/passwd** file to log in to the system. Users cannot log in using their UID; only the username is accepted.

What Accounts Are What?

The **/etc/passwd** file contains a number of system accounts, all of which are assigned UIDs that range from 0 to 499. Some of the more interesting (and exam-worthy) are shown here:

- **0**—The root user on the system.

- **1**—The bin user, which is responsible for some system binaries and nonlogin accounts.

- **48**—The apache user, which the HTTPD daemon runs as.

- **99**—The nobody account, which is used for many things, particularly for anonymous access on FTP and HTTP servers. But it also maps to root accounts that attempt NFS access to shares that have been configured to deny access to the root user.

> **NOTE** I normally assign my junior sysadmin and server operator accounts UIDs in the 500–1000 range, just to differentiate them from the other users and to make keeping track of them easier. Users with UIDs between 500–1000 don't automatically gain special privileges. However, these are the accounts that I will set up to have extra access by using the **sudo** command.

Normal User Accounts

Typical users are assigned UIDs ranging from 500 to 65,000. This is fine for a single system, but it can cause problems in larger environments.

If you have the need to allow for both local user accounts and network accounts (for the purpose of using NFS and NIS), it is a good idea to assign network accounts UIDs that start at the five-digit UID mark—in other words, with UIDs from 10,000 to 65,000. Local user accounts would be assigned values from 500 to 9,999. This allows for more structure in your UID numbering system.

NOTE If you can, force the use of a standardized UID and GID structure across all your enterprise systems. If you have more than 100 users, consider using LDAP for managing how users log on to their systems. The now deprecated NIS and the newer LDAP methods are outside the scope of this discussion and not on the LPI Level 1 objectives but are great ways to centralize account and password management across all machines in your environment.

If you are working on a system that has both network and local accounts, displaying user account information can be tricky. Local user account data is stored in local files, such as the **/etc/passwd** and **/etc/shadow** file. Network account information is stored in databases located on a server. One command can be used to search both local and network sources for account information: the **getent** command. For example:

```
getent passwd bob
```

The previous command searches both local and network sources in an order determined by the **/etc/nsswitch.conf** file:

```
passwd:     files nis
shadow:     files nis
```

The value of **files nis** means "search local files first and then search the database for the specified value."

User Entries in /etc/passwd

The user's entry in the **/etc/passwd** file consists of the following:

```
ross:x:500:100:Ross Brunson:/home/ross:/bin/bash
```

The entries in the **/etc/passwd** file are

- **ross**—The username; this must be eight or fewer characters and should be lowercase.

- **x**—Passwords used to be stored in this file. The "x" value tells the system that the password for this account is now stored in the **/etc/shadow** file. For security reasons, the password should never be in the **/etc/passwd** file on modern Linux systems.

- **500**—The user's UID.

- **100**—The user's *primary group*. This group is used as the group owner of all the file objects created by this user account, except in situations where ownership inheritance has been set.

- **Ross Brunson**—This field is a description field (also known as the *GE Common Operating System*, or *GECOS*, for historical purposes). It can be blank or have a comment or full name in it.

- **/home/ross**—The home directory field is used to define the complete path to the user's home directory.

- **/bin/bash**—This field defines the login shell for the user.

> **NOTE** The GECOS field is normally just used for simple comments. However, historically it was used to specify more complex dates, including useful information like the user's name, office location, and phone number. This information (and other user information) could be displayed with the **finger** command.

Special Login Files

Several files affect the user's login experience and define when a user can log in and from where.

These files are as follows:

- **/bin/false**—If the user's shell is set to **/bin/false**, the user cannot log in. This is best used for system accounts that should never be logged in to.

- **/etc/nologin**—When used as a login shell for a user's account, this program displays a message that the account is unavailable and exits with a nonzero exit code. If the **/etc/nologin.txt** file exists, the contents of that file are shown instead of the standard message.

- **/etc/motd**—After a successful login, the **/etc/motd** file contents are displayed, right before the user's shell is executed. This is a great place for warning and legal messages to be displayed.

- **.hushlogin**—This file, if created in the user's home directory, changes the login process so it does not perform a mail check and does not display the last login information or the message of the day to the user.

- **/etc/login.defs**—This file defines the defaults for when users are created by the **useradd** command. These defaults include entries for mail, password complexity and limitations, UID and GID minimum and maximum values, and whether the user's home directory is created by default.

- **/etc/securetty**—This file specifies from where the root user is allowed to log in. If it does not exist, root can log in from any location.

- **/etc/usertty**—This file is used to set the parameters for login locations, days, times, and systems the user can connect from. The **/etc/usertty** file is used only on systems that don't have *PAM (pluggable authentication modules)*.

Watch for questions about the files listed here. Questions focus on what happens when a file exists, whether it's assigned as a login shell, or what shows on a user's screen when she logs in to the system.

> **NOTE** Modern Linux systems utilize a feature called PAM (pluggable authentication modules). PAM provides a rich collection of modules that allow the administrator a great deal of flexibility regarding the manner in which users are granted access to the system. While PAM is not included in the exam objectives, you should consider exploring this useful feature. Start learning about PAM by executing the command **man pam**.

Group Accounts

Groups come in only one type—a grouping of users. No nesting of groups is possible in Linux or Unix. Users are associated with groups using two methods:

- **Primary**—A GID appears in the **/etc/passwd** file entry in the fourth field; this group is made the group owner of all created objects (files, directories, and so on) for this user. The primary group for a user is special; if a user is assigned a primary group in the **/etc/passwd**, she does not have to be listed as a member in the **/etc/group** file because the GID in the **/etc/passwd** entry complements the secondary group membership defined in the **/etc/group** file.

- **Secondary**—If a user's name appears in the **/etc/group** entry for a group, the user is a member of that group, and she gets access to the objects that group is the group owner of. The last field of each entry of the **/etc/group** file stores the secondary member list.

Groups are assigned numbers, just as user accounts are. The group numbers are called GIDs (Group IDs). A few important GIDs:

- **0**—The root group; anyone who is a member of this group has access to resources restricted to the root account.

- **1**—The bin group is similar to the bin user account.

- **100**—The users group is where you can place regular users and then give them access to resources by assigning that group ownership of things that all users should have access to.

> **NOTE** On BSD-related systems (recall BSD is a Unix flavor), a user cannot use the **su** command unless her account is a member of the wheel group, even if she knows the root password. This wheel group feature is not implemented by default on Linux systems, but the group is there for compatibility. Many administrators use the wheel group on Linux to create an "administrator group," providing special access to commands via the **sudo** command.

A special situation exists primarily on Red Hat-based systems, when a user account is created without a specific primary group assigned. In this case, the system creates and assigns a group whose GID should match the number of the user's UID (if that GID is not available, the next incremented number available would be used) and whose group name should be the same as the user account name. This system is called *user private group (UPG)*.

UPG is a security feature. If you have created a user and haven't assigned her a primary group, the system might assign her the users group as a primary group. This is a security risk because this user might be a contractor or an auditor and by default should not have access to the users group's resources.

However, UPG can also cause security issues. Because the user is the only member of this private group, this makes it difficult for the user to share file objects with others. Users are forced to share their files with everyone (the others permission set) to be able to share files with one other person.

Debian-based systems are different in that they don't use UPG, but rather assign new accounts to the users (100) group by default.

In reality, both systems pose security issues. The best solution is to create groups for people who need to share files and place the appropriate users in the correct groups. This requires more work for the administrator but leads to better security.

Group Entries in /etc/group

The entries in the **/etc/group** file are much simpler and shorter than the ones in the password file. Group files consist of the following fields:

```
users:x:100:ross,snuffy
```

The entries in a group file are

- **users**—The name of the group, which should be eight or fewer characters and lowercase.

- **x**—Like user passwords, the group passwords are kept in a different file. The group passwords are in **/etc/gshadow**. Note: while understanding this file can be useful, it is not an exam objective and is not be covered in this book.

- **GID**—This is the system's number for this group and is resolved (translated) to the group name for user viewing convenience.

- **ross,snuffy**—Users in the group are listed one after the other separated with a comma (,); no spaces should occur. This defines secondary group membership.

Group Passwords

Users can have only a single primary group; if they need to create an object that has to be assigned to another group, the user can use the **chgrp** command. For a single file, this is easy, but if the user wants to create a bunch of files owned by a different group, this technique can be tedious.

Another option is for users to temporarily change their primary group with the **newgrp** command. For example:

```
newgrp users
```

The **newgrp** command doesn't alter the **/etc/passwd** file or the **/etc/group** file; it opens a new shell with a different primary group. By default, a user can use the **newgrp** command to temporarily change her primary group to any group she is a member of. After creating the necessary files, the user can return to the shell that has the default primary group by executing the **exit** command. Note that users can change only to groups that they are a secondary member of.

A password can be assigned to the group with the **gpasswd** command, but there is only one password and you have to give it to every user who needs to use this functionality. Once a group is assigned a password, users need to use the password to execute the **newgrp** command, even if the user is a member of that group.

Adding Users and Groups

Although you can edit the **/etc/passwd** and **/etc/group** files directly, this can lead to serious problems if you make any errors in these files. It is much safer to use the commands provided.

Adding Users with **useradd**

The **useradd** command is used to create new user accounts. To add a user with the default values (default primary GID, default home directory, and so on), execute the following command:

```
useradd snuffy
```

Currently, on a Red Hat machine, this command performs several operations including

- Creates the user snuffy with the next available UID (typically next available above 500)

- Creates a group with the same group name and GID as the username and UID

- Sets the user's primary GID to the newly created group

- Creates a home directory for the user under the **/home** directory and with the same name as the username **(/home/snuffy** in this case)

- Copies the contents of the **/etc/skel** directory into the new user's home directory and gives the new user ownership of the copied files and directories

Currently, on a Debian machine, the command **useradd snuffy** creates the user snuffy with the next available UID, the GID set to the users (GID = 100) group, and no home directory is created.

To set up the user on the Debian system with a specified home directory, you have to specify the **-m** and **–d** options. To copy the contents of the **/etc/skel** directory into the user's home directory, use the **–k** option. To specify the primary group, use the **–g** option. The **–u** option can be used to specify the UID for the new user. Note that all these options can also be used on a Red Hat system, but often they are omitted in favor of default values. For example:

```
useradd -m -d /home/snuffy -k /etc/skel -g 100 -u 1025 snuffy
```

This creates the user with all the specified information. On a Red Hat machine the **/bin/bash** shell is auto-supplied, whereas on a Debian machine the shell is blank by default, causing the system to assume the **/bin/sh** shell (which is a symbolic link to **/bin/bash**). On both systems this value can be defined with the **-s** option.

Other important **useradd** options are as follows:

- **-D**—Executing the **useradd** command with this option displays the defaults defined in the **/etc/default/useradd** file. This option can also be used to modify the defaults.

- **-e**—This sets an expiration date on the account; after that date the account is disabled.

- **-G**—This sets secondary group membership at the account creation, something that is often done after creating the account by using the **usermod** command.

- **-f**—This is the number of days after the password has reached its maximum life that the user can still log in (if the user changes his password during the login process). Setting the maximum and minimum password values is discussed in a later section.

- **-o**—This allows the creation of a user with a nonunique UID. This is very dangerous and not recommended.

- **-s**—The full path and filename of the user's login shell must follow the **-s** option.

The useradd Defaults

On Red Hat-based systems, the **useradd** defaults are defined in the **/etc/default/ useradd** file and can be altered with the use of the **-D** option for the **useradd** command. For example, to change the default shell from **/bin/bash** to **/bin/tcsh**, execute the following command:

```
useradd -D -s /bin/tcsh
```

Debian-based systems also use this file. For example, executing the **useradd -D -g 10** command sets the default group to be the wheel group (GID=10) when you add a user on Debian.

```
skel Templates
```

When you use the **useradd** command and the **-m** and **–d** options, a home directory is created for the user. By default, the new home directory is a copy of the **/etc/skel** directory and its contents.

For example, **useradd –m –d /home/snuffy snuffy** creates the home directory **/home/snuffy**. This home directory is copied by default from the **/etc/skel** directory, and the ownership is changed to match the new user (as demonstrated in Example 15-1).

Example 15-1   Demonstration of /etc/skel

```
[root@server1 ~]# ls -la /etc/skel
total 24
drwxr-xr-x.   3 root root   74 May  9 18:15 .
drwxr-xr-x. 154 root root 8192 May 28 20:18 ..
-rw-r--r--.   1 root root   18 Mar  5 14:06 .bash_logout
-rw-r--r--.   1 root root  193 Mar  5 14:06 .bash_profile
-rw-r--r--.   1 root root  231 Mar  5 14:06 .bashrc
drwxr-xr-x.   4 root root   37 May  9 18:15 .mozilla
[root@server1 ~]# useradd -m tim
[root@server1 ~]# ls -la /home/tim
total 12
drwx------.  3 tim  tim   74 May 28 21:25 .
drwxr-xr-x.  4 root root  30 May 28 21:25 ..
-rw-r--r--.  1 tim  tim   18 Mar  5 14:06 .bash_logout
-rw-r--r--.  1 tim  tim  193 Mar  5 14:06 .bash_profile
-rw-r--r--.  1 tim  tim  231 Mar  5 14:06 .bashrc
drwxr-xr-x.  4 tim  tim   37 May  9 18:15 .mozilla
```

You can put just about anything in a new user's home directory by placing files or directories in the **/etc/skel** directory. It's even more elegant to create a set of **/etc/skel_XXX** directories to make creating certain groups of users easier. For example, to have a special home directory structure for users in the payroll department, you might use the following steps:

1. Copy the **/etc/skel** directory to a new directory named **/etc/skel_payroll_staff**.

2. Populate the **/etc/skel_payroll_staff** with the files and directories that you want users who are in the payroll department to have.

3. Next time you create a user from the payroll department, use the following syntax to specify a the correct *skel template* directory:

```
useradd -k /etc/skel_payroll_staff bob
```

Adding Groups with **groupadd**

The **groupadd** command is much simpler than the **useradd** command, with fewer options and shorter command lines. To add a group named somegroup with the defaults for new groups, type the following:

```
groupadd somegroup
```

The previous command creates a group with a GID determined by using the "next available" number above 500. The result should be an entry like the following in the **/etc/group** file:

```
somegroup:x:516:
```

Note that no users are added to the group (the last field is empty). The **usermod** command discussed in the next section is used to add users to existing groups.

To add a group with a particular GID, execute a command like the following:

```
groupadd -g 1492 somegroup
```

Modifying Users and Groups

Creating users and groups is one thing, but being able to make them fit a changing system environment is another. Typically, you add and remove users from secondary groups, locking and unlocking accounts, and even changing a password expiration now and then.

Modifying User Accounts with **usermod**

To modify a user account with the **usermod** command, you need to decide which of the following options is needed:

- **-c**—The new description for the user; this modifies the GECOS field in the **/etc/passwd** file.

- **-d**—Changes the user's new home directory. If there are files in this new home directory, you need to also change the user ownership of these files.

- **-e**—Changes the date the user account expires and is disabled.

- **-f**—Changes the number of inactive days. When a user account is locked out because the maximum password time frame has been exceeded, the user can have a grace period in which she can still log in as long as she changes her password during the login process. More discussion on this occurs when maximum and minimum password aging is discussed.

- **-g**—Changes the primary group for the user; either GID or group name can be specified. Warning: This changes which file objects the user has access to.

- **-G**—Changes the user's secondary groups. This is a single value or a list of comma-separated values of groups the user is to be a secondary member of. Important note: Be sure to include all groups, including groups that the user is already a secondary member of. This command replaces all secondary group memberships with the argument provided to the **–G** option.

- **-s**—Changes the path to the user's login shell.

- **-u**—Changes the user's UID. Warning: While this changes the UID ownership of files in the user's home directory to match the new UID, other files on the system will not automatically be changed!

- **-L**—This locks a user's account by altering the **/etc/shadow** file and prefixing the current encrypted password with an exclamation point (!).

- **-U**—This removes the lock on the user's account by removing the exclamation point (!) from the front of the encrypted password in the **/etc/shadow** file.

NOTE Another way to lock and unlock the user's account is to use the **passwd** command and its **-l** and **-u** options to accomplish the locking and unlocking.

Modifying Groups with groupmod

The **groupmod** command has fewer options than the **usermod** command, and there are only a few reasons to use the command. It's primarily for altering the group's name and GID. To modify a group's GID, execute the following command:

```
groupmod -g 101 users
```

Think twice before altering the GID of a group because you could orphan a lot of important files if you do. Remember: Files and directories are not owned by usernames and group names, but rather UIDs and GIDs. If you modify a group's GID, files previously owned by that GID now no longer have a group name associated with the file, as demonstrated in Example 15-2.

Example 15-2 Demonstration of Changing GID

```
[root@server1 tmp]# ls -l sample
-rw-r--r--. 1 root test 0 May 28 20:17 sample
[root@server1 tmp]# grep test /etc/group
test:x:1001:
[root@server1 tmp]# groupmod -g 2000 test
[root@server1 tmp]# grep test /etc/group
test:x:2000:
[root@server1 tmp]# ls -l sample
-rw-r--r--. 1 root 1001 0 May 28 20:17 sample
```

You should also look in the **/etc/passwd** file to see which users' primary groups will be affected when you change a group. Do not attempt to change the GID of a group that has a user member currently logged in. Finally, be aware that on some systems, removing or orphaning the primary group of a user defaults to the staff (50) group.

Removing Users and Groups

Removing users and groups isn't difficult, but several options need attention. Removing accounts from the system isn't like on a Windows machine, which uses SIDs or security IDs, which are numerically unique and cannot be re-created easily. Linux accounts can be re-created easily (unless you delete the user's home directory, which could only be recovered from a backup). Remember that Linux uses tables of static UIDs and GIDs, not SIDs.

Removing Users

If a user leaves the company, you are faced with either deleting the user account and leaving the user's home directory on the system (perhaps for his replacement) or purging the system of the user by removing his account and home directory in one step.

Removing a user without affecting his home directory is accomplished by executing the following command:

```
userdel snuffy
```

To remove the user along with his home directory (the one configured in the **/etc/passwd** entry), you execute the following command:

```
userdel -r snuffy
```

> **NOTE** If the user also has mail on this system, the **userdel –r** command also deletes the user's mail file. However, other files on the system owned by this user will not be deleted. Those files will be owned by just the UID, not the name, of this user. Additionally, if you create a new user with the same UID as the old user, the new user would be the owner of these files.

You cannot delete a currently logged-in user, so you must find out why he is still logged on. On some Linux systems, if the user is logged in and you attempt to delete that account, you receive an error message like the following:

```
userdel: user tim is currently used by process 17098
```

If you don't receive this sort of message, you can execute the **ps** command to determine the login shell's PID. Before you kill this user's login shell, use the **usermod -L** command to lock the account; then use **kill -9 PID** to log the user off the system. For example, to log off the tim user and delete the account, execute the following commands:

```
usermod -L tim
kill -9 17098
userdel -r
```

One reason you shouldn't just remove a user's home directory is that usually either important files or important evidence (perhaps of wrongdoing on the user's part) exists in that directory. If you are planning to replace the user, consider keeping the directory and just delete the user account. This leaves the home directory and its contents with only a UID where the username was:

```
drwxr-sr-x    2 1002      staff        4096 Mar 18 07:17 snuffy
```

This is actually not a bad thing to see because it is a visual clue to you that the user who owned this home directory was deleted. However, because the home directory still belongs to the UID 1002 and the old user's login name was set as the directory name, you have everything you need to re-create the user or set up a new user. For example, the following uses snuffy's old home directory for the new sarah account:

```
mv /home/snuffy /home/sarah
useradd -u 1002 -d /home/sarah sarah
```

Removing Groups

Before you delete a group, consider checking the following:

- Confirm that the group has no secondary members.
- Confirm that the group isn't a primary group for any user account.

- Use the **find** command to find all files owned by the group. After you find them all, change the group ownership of all these files to another group.

To delete a group, type the following:

```
groupdel grpname
```

> **NOTE** The majority of the questions on the exam focus on the **useradd**, **usermod**, and **userdel** commands. There isn't much to ask about the group commands, but there might be a couple of questions about them in the fill-in-the-blank questions just to see whether you're paying attention.

The Shadow Suite

Another important piece of your Linux machine with regard to security is the *Shadow Suite*. The Shadow Suite is a set of authentication tools and utilities that insinuates itself into the mix of the **/etc/passwd** file and user accounts. Without the use of the shadow tools, your encrypted passwords would be exposed to anyone who wants to see them because they would be in the world-readable **/etc/passwd** file in field #2. The Shadow Suite also provides password aging properties that don't exist without this Suite. All this is accomplished by storing this data in another file: the **/etc/shadow** file.

Encrypted Passwords and Shadow Fields

The following is an example of an entry from the **/etc/passwd** file on a system that doesn't use the Shadow Suite:

```
snuffy:$1$vEEOvj1b$GlzLuD9F..DjlQr/WXcJv1:501:10::/home/snuffy:/bin/sh
```

As you can see, an encrypted string appears in the second field. Unfortunately, all users can view this file, making this a potential security risk. In the next example, the **/etc/passwd** entry is shown on a system with the Shadow Suite enabled; note that the encrypted string is replaced with an "x":

```
snuffy:x:501:10::/home/snuffy:/bin/sh
```

When the Shadow Suite is installed, the system stores encrypted passwords in the **/etc/shadow** file for user accounts and the **/etc/gshadow** file for group accounts. The fields in the **/etc/shadow** file contain the user's account password and password aging information. The following is an example of a shadow file entry:

```
snuffy:$1$vEEOvj1b$GlzLuD9F..DjlQr/WXcJv1:16263:0:99999:7:30:17000:
```

The fields in the **/etc/shadow** file are

- **snuffy**—Login name: The user's login name

- **1vEEOvj1b$GlzLuD9F..DjlQr/WXcJv1**—Password: The user's encrypted password

- **16263**—Last Change: The days since January 1, 1970, that have elapsed since the password was last changed

- **0**—Minimum: The days that must elapse before the password can be changed (0 effectively always allows immediate changes)

- **99999**—Maximum: The days before the password must be changed (99999 effectively disables the need to change the password as this is over 273 years)

- **7**—Warning: The number of days before the password expires due to the Maximum field when the user will be warned

- **30**—Inactive: The number of days after the account expires due to the Maximum field in which the user could still log in if the password is changed during login

- **17000**—Expiration date: The number of days from January 1, 1970, and the day the account will expire on

NOTE The last field in the file is reserved for future use and is not tested or much talked about.

Some of the fields of the **/etc/shadow** file are tricky. Consider the following:

```
julia:$1$vEEOvj1b$GlzLuD9F..DjlQr/WXcJv1:16263:5:90:7:30::
```

The julia account does not have an expiration date (Expiration field is empty); however this user is required to change her password every 90 days (Maximum field is 90). Seven days before the 90-day time frame is up, the user will receive a warning when she logs in (Warning field is 7). If she does not heed this warning, her account will be locked out on day 91. She can still log in for up to 30 days after her account is locked (Inactive field is 30), provided that she creates a new password during the login process. Finally, after changing her password, she cannot change her password again for at least 5 days (Minimum field is 5) to prevent her from just switching back to her original password.

> **NOTE** The password aging provided by the Shadow Suite is far from perfect. Pluggable authentication modules (PAM) provide much richer and more powerful password aging features.

shadow File Permissions

The permissions on the **/etc/shadow** file are important and may appear on the exam. Because the **/etc/shadow** file isn't world-readable, and only the system updates it, your passwords are much safer than without shadow installed.

The **/etc/shadow** file permissions are prominently featured on the exam, as are the permissions for the **/etc/passwd** file. Here is a listing of the files and permissions on both Red Hat and Debian:

```
/etc/passwd"
Red Hat = -rw-r--r--  (644)
Debian   = -rw-r--r--  (644)
/etc/shadow"
Red Hat = -r--------  (400)
Debian   = rw-r-----  (640)
```

As mentioned, these files and their permissions appear on the exams. It's important that you remember that Red Hat has a stricter permission setup than Debian.

> **NOTE** Take note of the security permissions on the shadow file of your various test systems. You'll find small but important variations. Some systems use ------- and some use r------; make sure to note which is which. The /etc/passwd file is essentially open and readable by anyone, even those not on the system. The important and private encrypted passwords are in the /etc/shadow file. The **/etc/gshadow** file mentioned previously is also part of the Shadow Suite. However, this file is not an exam objective.

Changing Accounts

Users' passwords are typically initially set to some easily remembered value by the root user when the account is created and then the user is told to change her password immediately.

To change the root password, execute the following command when you are logged in as the root user:

```
passwd
```

This prompts you for a password that must be entered twice for verification. If you are executing this command as a normal user, the user's current password is required before the new password will be accepted. This is to avoid a situation where you walk away from your system and someone quickly tries to change your password.

If you're changing another user's password, like the snuffy user, you would execute the following when you are logged in as the root user:

```
passwd snuffy
```

NOTE It's important to remember who you are logged in as and what you type on the command line when changing a password. I've seen many a sysadmin change her own password instead of a user's because she was in a big hurry!

Aging Passwords

Users' passwords need to be changed frequently enough so that attackers don't have enough time to guess them. Most users want to come to work, get paid, and go home; system security is of much lower importance than convenience.

To age the passwords properly, use the **chage** command. The syntax for the **chage** command is

```
chage -option value username
```

The command acts on fields in the **/etc/shadow** file, with the following options:

- **-m**—Changes the Minimum value, or how long after a password is changed that the user must wait until it can be changed again.

- **-M**—Changes the Maximum value, which is the maximum number of days that can go by before the user must change the password.

- **-d**—Changes the Last Change value, which is the number of days since January 1, 1970, that the password was last changed. This is rarely modified directly; when a password is changed with the **passwd** command, this value is automatically updated.

- **-E**—Changes the Expiration value, which is the number of days since January 1, 1970, that represents the day the user's account will be disabled. The format used is YYYY-MM-DD.

- **-I**—Changes the Inactive value, or the number of days of inactivity (no logins) after the account has reached the Maximum limit before the user account is locked, requiring root attention to reenable. Setting this to 0 disables the feature.

- **-W**—Changes the Warning value, or the number of days before the user must change her password. This warning is only provided when the user logs in to the system.

Thankfully, you don't have to memorize these values, except for potential exam questions. Just execute the **chage username** command as the root user and the command prompts you interactively for each value that can be configured for the specified user.

Users can use the **-l** option to view their own information, or the root user can view another user's information with this option:

```
chage -l snuffy
```

This produces the following output:

```
Minimum:          0
Maximum:          99999
Warning:          7
Inactive:         -1
Last Change:             Mar 19, 2014
Password Expires:        Never
Password Inactive:       Never
Account Expires:         Never
```

The **passwd** utility includes some of the previous options, such as these:

- **-d**—Disables a user account by removing its password

- **-n**—Sets the minimum password lifetime in days

- **-x**—Sets the maximum password lifetime in days

- **-w**—Sets the warning number of days before the password expires

- **-i**—Sets the number of days an account with an expired password can be inactive before it's locked

- **-S**—Shows the user password information, such as what encryption is used and whether a password is set

User Variables

Next, you learn how to place certain limitations on a user's account. If you want a user to be unable to create objects over a certain size or use too many system resources, you could configure the *ulimit* settings for that user. The **ulimit** command accepts many options, including the following:

- **-c**—Limits the size of core (crash dump) files

- **-d**—Limits the size of the user's process data

- **-f**—Limits the maximum size of files created in the shell

- **-n**—Limits the number of open file descriptors or open files allowed

- **-t**—Limits the amount of CPU time allowed to the user (expressed in seconds)

- **-u**—Limits the number of processes that a given user can run

- **-v**—Limits the maximum amount of virtual memory available to the shell

To check a user's **ulimit** settings, use this command:

```
ulimit -a
```

> **NOTE** Remember that making these limits more permanent requires editing one of the user's configuration files (**.bashrc** or **.profile**) or the systemwide configuration files (**/etc/bashrc** or **/etc/profile**).

Summary

In this chapter you learned the concept of user and group accounts. You learned in which files account information is stored as well as how to create, modify, and delete accounts.

As mentioned in the section "How to Use This Book" in the Introduction, you have a few choices for exam preparation: the exercises here, Chapter 21, "Final Preparation," and the practice exams on the DVD.

Review All Key Topics

Review the most important topics in this chapter, noted with the Key Topics icon in the outer margin of the page. Table 15-2 lists a reference of these key topics and the page numbers on which each is found.

Table 15-2 Key Topics for Chapter 15

Key Topic Element	Description	Page Number
Paragraph	System accounts in the **/etc/passwd** file	422
Paragraph	Working with local and network accounts	423
Paragraph	The user's entry in the **/etc/passwd** file	423
Paragraph	Several files affect the user's login experience and define when a user can log in and from where	424
Paragraph	Primary—A GID appears in the **/etc/passwd** file entry	425
Paragraph	Situations particular to Red Hat systems	426
Paragraph	Entries in the **/etc/group** file	427
Paragraph	The **useradd** command is used to create new user accounts	428
Paragraph	Where the **useradd** defaults are defined	429
Paragraph	Using the **useradd** command	429
Paragraph	Using the **groupadd** command	431
Paragraph	Modifying accounts with the **usermod** command	431
Paragraph	Use **groupmod**, it has fewer options	432
Paragraph	Removing a user without affecting his home directory	433
Paragraph	Considerations before deleting a group	434
Paragraph	What the Shadow Suite causes	435
Paragraph	The **/etc/shadow** file permissions	437
Paragraph	Changing the root password	437
Paragraph	Using the passwd utility	438
Paragraph	Placing limitations on objects	439

Define Key Terms

Define the following key terms from this chapter and check your answers in the glossary:

UID, GID, GECOS, PAM, primary group, secondary group, UPG, user private group, skel template, Shadow Suite, ulimit

Review Questions

The answers to these review questions are in Appendix A.

1. Which field in the **/etc/shadow** file sets the number of warning days before the user's password expires? Fill in just the numeral of this field in the blank below:

   _____

2. If you saw the following output of the **ls -l** command, what would it indicate?

   ```
   drwxr-sr-x    2 1002      staff      4096 Mar 18 07:17 snuffy
   ```

   a. The account was deleted, but not the user's home directory.

   b. The file is not owned by any account.

   c. The **/etc/passwd** file is corrupt.

   d. The user's group is incorrect.

3. If you created 10 accounts beginning with the UID of 501 and then deleted 501 and 504, what would the UID of the next user you create be by default? Write your answer in the blank below:

   _____

4. Which directory is copied by default to a newly created user's home directory when the **-m** and **–d** options are used with the **useradd** command? Fill in the full path and name of the directory in the blank below:

   _____

5. Which command is used to set the password expiration, warning, and other **/etc/shadow** file field information interactively?

   a. **passwd**

   b. **chpass**

   c. **vipw**

   d. **chage**

6. Which command allows a user to open a shell with a different primary group? Fill in the blank below with just the name of the command:

   _____

7. What are the default permissions for the Debian and Red Hat /etc/passwd files? Fill in the blank below with the three numerals that represent the octal value for the permissions:

   _____

8. Which command can be used by regular users to display settings for features like the maximum allowable size of files allowed for the user's account?

   a. umask

   b. dmesg

   c. ulimit

   d. perms

This chapter covers the following topics:

- The Cron System
- Anacron
- Running Ad-hoc Jobs

This chapter covers the following exam topics:

- Automate system administration tasks by scheduling jobs: 107.2

## CHAPTER 16

Schedule and Automate Tasks

Running one server, or a fleet of servers, involves some periodic cleanup tasks. Temporary files need deleting, logs need rotating, caches need expiring, reports need running, and much more. You can either spend every working day with an ever-growing checklist of things to do, or learn how Linux can schedule jobs to be run in the wee hours when you're sleeping.

"Do I Know This Already?" Quiz

The "Do I Know This Already?" quiz enables you to assess whether you should read this entire chapter or simply jump to the "Exam Preparation Tasks" section for review. If you are in doubt, read the entire chapter. Table 16-1 outlines the major headings in this chapter and the corresponding "Do I Know This Already?" quiz questions. You can find the answers in Appendix A, "Answers to the 'Do I Know This Already?' Quizzes and Review Questions."

Table 16-1 "Do I Know This Already?" Foundation Topics Section-to-Question Mapping

Foundation Topics Section	Questions Covered in This Section
The Cron System	1-3
Anacron	4-5
Running Ad-hoc Jobs	6

1. Consider the following cron entry and choose the correct statement.

   ```
   0 10 12 * * /usr/local/bin/backup.sh
   ```

   a. backup.sh will run at 10 minutes after midnight on the 12th day of the month.

   b. backup.sh will run at 10am on the 12th day of the month.

   c. backup.sh will run at 10 minutes after 12 noon every day of the year.

   d. backup.sh will run as 12 minutes after 10 every day of the year.

2. Consider the following cron entry and choose the correct statement.

```
* */2 * * 1 /usr/local/bin/ping.sh
```

   a. ping.sh will run every 2 hours on Mondays.

   b. ping.sh will run every half hour on the first of the month.

   c. ping.sh will run every half hour on Mondays.

   d. ping.sh will run every 2 hours on the first of the month.

3. You are trying to explain how to set up a cron to a user, but the user tells you that she is getting an error:

```
$ crontab -e
You (sean) are not allowed to use this program (crontab)
See crontab(1) for more information
```

   You look, and there is no file called **/etc/cron.deny**. What could be the problem?

   a. sean is not in the sudoers file.

   b. -sean needs to be in **/etc/cron.deny**.

   c. sean needs to be in **/etc/cron.allow**.

   d. The crontab program is not setuid root.

4. Which of the following are not true regarding cron and anacron? (Choose two.)

   a. Both run periodic jobs.

   b. Only root can use anacron.

   c. **Anacron** can run jobs more frequently than cron.

   d. Both guarantee jobs will be run.

5. Which of the following would be valid lines in the **anacrontab** file?

   a. 7 25 weekly.backup root /usr/local/bin/backup.sh

   b. 0 0 7 25 weekly.backup /usr/local/bin/backup.sh

   c. 7 25 weekly.backup /usr/local/bin/backup.sh

   d. 7 25 root weekly.backup /usr/local/bin/backup.sh

6. How does **at** differ from cron?

   a. **at** can only schedule to the nearest day.

   b. **at** is for ad-hoc jobs that are manually created.

   c. **at** is for periodic jobs that need to be run at a certain time every day.

   d. **at** runs jobs when system load is low.

Foundation Topics

Linux has two ways of scheduling jobs based on whether they're regularly occurring. The cron system runs jobs on a schedule that can be monthly, weekly, daily, hourly, or even per minute. The **at** system is used for one-off jobs, such as to run a job over the weekend.

A third system, called anacron, is closely related to cron. It's for running periodic jobs on a system that may not always be on like laptops.

The Cron System

Cron is the main job scheduler in Linux. Named after the Greek word for time, *chronos*, cron runs a job for you on a fixed schedule. Jobs can be anything that can be run on the command line including calling another shell script.

People typically schedule intensive jobs at times when the system is expected to be underused such as overnight. By separating the interactive user sessions from the heavy batch work, both classes get better performance. Your Linux system almost certainly has a handful of jobs set to run overnight or at least on a daily basis.

Cron has several moving parts. A daemon called **crond** runs in the background and executes tasks on behalf of all users. Jobs are configured through **crontab**, which is a utility that manipulates the individual user cron tables. Finally, a series of configuration files under **/etc** can also contain jobs and control which users are allowed to add jobs using **crontab**.

Configuring crontabs

The cron system has evolved over time. The utilities themselves have improved to allow more configuration options. Distributions have also added more default settings to make common tasks easier. This chapter walks you through the various options available and makes it clear which is a distribution configuration and which is a cron option.

The **crontab**, or cron table, is both a thing that stores a list of jobs for a user and the utility to manage the table.

Using the crontab Command

The simplest way to use **crontab** is to run it with the **-e** flag, which means you want to edit the current user's crontab. You are placed into an editor showing the current crontab. After you make changes and save, your input is checked to make sure it's a valid crontab. If the validation check fails, you are given an option to go back so that you don't lose your changes.

> **NOTE**   The editor used to make changes to the crontab is set through the EDITOR environment variable, with **vi** being the default. If you'd rather use **nano**, for instance, make sure that export **EDITOR=/bin/nano** is in your **.bash_profile**.

If you are root, the **-u** option allows you to supply a username so that you can view or edit that user. To edit sean's crontab, run **crontab -e -u sean**.

The **-l** flag displays the crontab rather than editing it:

```
# crontab -l -u sean
PATH=/usr/local/bin:/bin:/usr/bin:/usr/local/sbin:/usr/sbin:/sbin:/
home/sean/bin
MAILTO=sean@example.com
25 * * * * /usr/bin/php /home/sean/fof/update-quiet.php > /dev/null
2>&1
0 2 * * * /home/sean/bin/database_backup 2>&1
```

Matching Times

The crontab itself has undergone some improvements in formatting, and most are built around the idea that there are five columns to specify when the job is run and then the rest of the line contains the text to be executed.

The columns, in order, are

1. Minute (0-59)

2. Hour in 24 hour time (0-23)

3. Day of month (1-31)

4. Month (1-12)

5. Day of week (0-7 with 0 and 7 being Sunday)

Each column must be filled in. If you want to match all values for a column, use an asterisk (*). Some examples illustrate how the schedules work:

0 12 * * *—The minute is 0, the hour is 12, and it is to run on all months and days. This runs at 12:00 noon every day.

0 0 1 1 *—The minute and hour are both 0 so, this means midnight. The day of the month and month are both 1, which is January 1. This job runs at midnight on New Year's day.

* * * * *—Runs every minute.

30 5 * * 1—Runs at 5:30 a.m. every Monday.

All columns must match for the job to run. One interesting exception is that if you specify both the day of the month and the day of the week (columns 3 and 5), the job will run with either match. Otherwise all columns must match up for the job to run. So **30 5 1 * 1** runs at 5:30 on the first of the month *and* every Monday.

Spelling Out Month and Day Names

The syntax shown previously uses a number for the month and day of week—1 is January, 2 is February, and so forth.

You can spell out the month and day of week names by using the first three letters. Not only is this easier to remember, but it helps make more sense of the columns.

0 0 * jan sun runs at midnight on every Sunday in January. The whole file doesn't have to be consistent, so you can use numbers or names at your convenience.

Making Multiple Matches

The syntax you've seen so far does not allow for the same job to run at multiple times. If you wanted to run the same job at midnight and noon, you would need two separate lines. Fortunately cron's syntax has evolved to allow this.

The first way to specify multiple times is to separate the items with a comma. For example, use the following syntax to run a job at midnight and noon:

```
0 0,12 * * *
```

The first column is still 0 to indicate that the job runs when the minute is zero. The hour column is now **0,12**, which means the job will run when the hour is either 0 or 12, which is midnight and noon, respectively.

This also works when using the names of the months. A job can be run twice a day during June, July, and August with this:

```
0 0,12 * jun,jul,aug *
```

The second way to run a job at multiple time periods is to give a range of values. Rather than **jun,jul,aug**, the previous example could have been written with **jun-aug**. Or to run a job on the hour from 9:00 a.m. to 5:00 p.m.:

```
0 9-17 * * *
```

This runs the first job at 9:00 a.m. and the last job at 5:00 p.m.

Both these methods can be combined, such as **8-10,16-18**.

Step Values

The next optimization is to provide an easy way to run a job by stepping over certain periods, such as to run a job every 2 hours. You could do this with **0,2,4,6,8,10,12,14,16,18,20,22**, but that's messy!

Instead, run a job every 2 hours, on the hour with

```
0 */2 * * *
```

Or perhaps every 30 minutes:

```
*/30 * * * *
```

Or on odd numbered hours:

```
0 1-23/2 * * *
```

Think of this operator as saying "skip this number."

Putting the crontab Together

So far you've looked at the first five columns, which collectively describe the time that the job will run. Any remaining text on the line runs as a command at the appointed time. A line such as

```
0 0 * * * /usr/local/bin/backup.sh
```

runs the **/usr/local/bin/backup.sh** program every day at midnight.

The command you run can be any valid shell code:

```
0 0 * * * if [[ ! -f /var/lock/maintenance ]]; then /usr/local/bin/
backup.sh; fi
```

only runs the backup script at midnight if **/var/lock/maintenance** doesn't exist.

Issues About Path

Scripts that work fine when run at the command line but don't work when run from cron are a common problem. The environment is different because cron doesn't run your **.bash_profile** and **.bashrc** scripts. Therefore, you can expect a minimal environment, including a basic PATH.

See it for yourself by adding a cron entry such as:

```
* * * * * env > /tmp/env
```

That job runs every minute and dumps the environment to **/tmp/env**:

```
SHELL=/bin/sh
USER=sean
PATH=/usr/bin:/bin
PWD=/home/sean
LANG=en_US.UTF-8
SHLVL=1
HOME=/home/sean
LOGNAME=sean
_=/usr/bin/env
```

The environment for a cron job is fairly sparse: The path only has /usr/bin and /bin. It is also missing any additions that you are used to at your own shell, such as in **.bash_profile**.

While the scripts run out of cron are free to set their own variables internally, cron lets you set environment variables in the usual format:

```
PATH=/usr/bin:/bin:/usr/local/bin:/home/sean/bin
0 0 * * * /usr/local/bin/backup.sh
```

The backup script then is run with the extended path set on the first line.

You aren't limited to just setting the path. Any variable will work. Some variable names are special:

- **MAILTO**—Anything that a job prints to the screen is mailed to this address.

- **SHELL**—Run the job with a different shell. /bin/bash is used by default.

- **CRON_TZ**—Use an alternate time zone for the crontab; otherwise, use system time.

Dealing with Output

A script often prints something to the screen, either for debugging, status updates, or to log an error. Anything that a job prints to the screen is sent in an email to the current user, which can be overridden with the **MAILTO** variable inside the crontab.

There are three ways of dealing with this:

- Just accept the emails. This often makes for a boring morning as you wade through all the night's emails.

- Write the scripts so that they only generate output when there's a legitimate error.

- Within the crontab, redirect output to **/dev/null**.

Each has its advantages and disadvantages. If a script failing to run is a problem, you should have some way of knowing this, either from an email with the output or an external monitoring system. Too many emails usually means you end up ignoring them all. The option you choose depends on each job.

For a job that is chatty and the output doesn't matter, it's easy to redirect the output to the bit bucket:

```
25 * * * * /usr/bin/php /home/sean/fof/update-quiet.php > /dev/null
2>&1
```

At 25 minutes after the hour, a PHP script is executed. The output is redirected to /dev/null and the error stream is redirected to the standard out stream with **2>&1**.

Recall that all programs have a standard output stream and an error stream, with normal redirects only working on the latter. The **2>&1** ensures that errors are redirected, too. Without this the regular output would be redirected but not the errors, resulting in an email. This may be desirable in some cases.

Nicknames

Most distributions include a version of cron that includes the nicknames extension. This extension provides aliases to commonly used schedules.

- **@reboot**—Run once after reboot.
- **@yearly**—Run once a year at midnight on January 1.
- **@annually**—Same as @yearly.
- **@monthly**—Run at midnight on the first of the month.
- **@weekly**—Run once a week on Sunday at midnight.
- **@daily**—Run once a day at midnight.
- **@hourly**—Run once an hour, on the hour.

Therefore, the following two crontabs are the same:

```
0 0 * * * /usr/local/bin/backup.sh
@daily /usr/local/bin/backup.sh
```

Other Files

As cron has grown over the years, so has the number of files that can be used to run jobs.

The crontabs edited with the **crontab** command are stored in **/var/spool/cron**.

```
# ls -l /var/spool/cron/
total 4
-rw------- 1 root root   0 Nov 17 19:54 root
-rw------- 1 sean sean 559 Mar 29 12:16 sean
```

From this output you can see that there are two crontabs: one for root and one for sean. The root crontab is empty. The files themselves are just text files.

Even though as the root user you can edit the files in /var/spool/cron yourself, you should always use the **crontab** command so that you have syntax checking. Regular users are prohibited from editing these files directly because they are not able to access the **/var/spool/cron** directory.

System crontabs

Some software packages need to bundle periodic tasks. For example, the **sysstat** package includes a valuable tool called the system activity reporter, or **sar**. A cron job fires every 10 minutes to collect some stats, and another job fires around midnight to archive the day's statistics.

If the utility were to manipulate root's crontab, it could accidentally get removed if the root user didn't understand why the entry was there. Removing the entry after the package is removed also becomes a problem.

Therefore there is a second set of crontabs meant to be manipulated only by the root user. There is a shared file called **/etc/crontab** and a directory containing individual tables in **/etc/cron.d**. The file is usually used by the distribution itself to list any default jobs, or for the administrator to list any manually entered jobs. The directory is most helpful for integrating with package management, where a package that needs its own cron to place a file in **/etc/cron.d**. When the package is removed or upgraded, the cron can be removed or changed without accidentally affecting other cron entries.

These system crontabs have one important difference: They contain a sixth column that goes in between the schedule and the command to be run. This column indicates which user should be used to execute the job.

An example of a system crontab such as this looks like the following:

```
# Run system wide raid-check once a week on Sunday at 1am by default
0 1 * * Sun root /usr/sbin/raid-check
```

The first five columns schedule a job for Sunday at 1:00 a.m. Column 6 says the root user will run it. The command is **/usr/sbin/raid-check**.

Convenience crontabs

One problem with scheduling jobs by a specific time is that they all run at the same time. Often you don't care about the specific time a job runs, you just want it to run hourly, daily, weekly, or monthly. Cron is installed with a configuration that has a directory for each of these time periods and will run the jobs in each directory consecutively when the scheduled time comes up.

These directories are

- **/etc/cron.hourly**—Jobs here are run once an hour.

- **/etc/cron.daily**—Jobs here are run once a day.

- **/etc/cron.weekly**—Jobs here are run once a week.

- **/etc/cron.monthly**—Jobs here are run once a month.

We look into the reasons why later this chapter, but these convenience jobs don't necessarily run on a predictable schedule. The system guarantees that monthly jobs are run once every month, but you can't say for sure that it'll happen exactly on the first of the month at midnight.

The files that go in these directories are just scripts. You do not include any schedule columns or user columns. Most of these are placed there by installation scripts. For example, the logrotate package needs to run daily to maintain system logs (see Chapter 18, "Logging and Time Services," for more on logrotate), so it places a script in /etc/cron.daily that runs the script. The periodic updating of the database that the **locate** command uses is also run from **cron.daily**.

Restricting Access

Sometimes you don't want everyone to be able to use cron jobs. Two files, **/etc/cron.allow** and **/etc/cron.deny**, implement a whitelist and blacklist policy, respectively.

You should only have one of these files present; otherwise, the behavior gets hard to understand. Cron's decision process for allowing a user access to edit her crontab is as follows:

1. If **/etc/cron.allow** exists, only users in this file and the root user can use **crontab**.

2. If **/etc/cron.allow** does not exist but **/etc/cron.deny** does, anyone in the latter file is denied access.

3. If neither file exists, only root can manage crons.

Most systems ship with an empty **/etc/cron.deny** file so that anyone can access their crontab. It should be noted that any existing crontabs will continue to run and that the root user can still manage a denied user's crontab. The **cron.allow** and **cron. deny** files only control who can edit their own crontab.

Anacron

Anacron is a simplified cron that complements the existing cron system. It is made to handle jobs that run daily or less frequently and jobs for which the precise time doesn't matter.

Anacron's chief advantage over cron is that it runs jobs that were scheduled to go when the computer was off. Rather than worry about specific times, anacron focuses on when the last time a particular job was run. If the computer was off when the job was supposed to run, anacron simply runs it the next time the computer is on.

Anacron also differs from cron in a few important ways:

- There is no command to manage the jobs. Everything is specified in **/etc/anacrontab**.

- Everything is run as the root user.

- The maximum granularity with which you can specify a schedule is 1 day, as opposed to 1 minute with cron.

- Jobs are run consecutively.

- While anacron can run as a daemon, it's typically run from cron itself to see whether if there are any jobs outstanding, and once processing is done, anacron exits.

The format of the **anacrontab** file is still based around columns. The columns are

1. Period, in days, between runs of this job. Some of the @nicknames are available.

2. Delay, in minutes, that anacron will wait before executing the job.

3. A tag, called a job identifier, for the job that is unique across all jobs. Anacron uses this to track the last time the job was run.

4. The command to run.

Environment variables are specified the same way they are in crontabs. Just put the **key=value** statement on its own line.

The default **anacrontab** on a Red Hat system is

```
#period in days    delay in minutes    job-identifier    command
1          5        cron.daily         nice run-parts    /etc/cron.daily
7          25       cron.weekly        nice run-parts    /etc/cron.weekly
@monthly 45         cron.monthly       nice run-parts    /etc/cron.monthly
```

These three jobs run daily, weekly, and monthly, respectively. The jobs all run **nice run-parts** followed by one of the convenience cron directories you learned about in the previous section.

The **nice** command runs the command at a lower priority. **run-parts** is a tool that comes with cron that runs each file in the given directory one after another.

Thus, the three default anacron jobs run the daily, weekly, and monthly cron tasks, respectively. **cron.hourly** is still handled by cron because anacron can only schedule jobs on a daily basis, not hourly.

As anacron is used for the daily, weekly, and monthly jobs, these jobs eventually run even if the system is off overnight. They just run at a low priority when the system comes on again.

Between cron and anacron you have many options available for running periodic jobs. There is overlap between the two tools and you will run into situations where either will work. Your decision on which to use comes down to a few key points:

- Does your job need to run more than once a day or at a specific time? If so, you need to use crontab.

- Is the timing of the job flexible and you're more interested in making sure it's always run, even if it's late? If so, you should use anacron.

- Is this job on a system that is not always on? As long as the timing constraints work for you, anacron is a good choice.

Running Ad-hoc Jobs

The final class of jobs that can be scheduled are ad-hoc jobs. Cron and anacron run jobs on a periodic basis—you want to run your log rotation every night. There are times when you want to run a job once, just not now. This is the job of the **at** command and its friend, **batch**.

The at Command

The **at** command is designed to run a task once at a specific time. The **at** command's tasks or jobs are queued up in the **/var/spool/at** directory, with a single file representing each job.

A typical **at** job is intended to take care of the one-off or very infrequent jobs that take place at odd times. For example, many sysadmins remind themselves of meetings or to perform some task with **at**:

```
$ at 2pm today
at> xmessage "take a break"
at> <EOT>
job 1 at 2004-04-02 14:00
```

You type the first line of the previous code block (**at 2pm today**) at the command line, causing the **at>** prompt to appear. Then you type the command you want to execute, press Enter, and press Ctrl+D to end the task. Ending the task shows the **<EOT>** notice, followed by a line that echoes the job's scheduling information.

Alternatively, you can pass the job you want to run over the standard input:

```
$ echo '/usr/local/bin/backup.sh' | at 20:00 today
job 10 at Sun Mar 29 20:00:00 2015
```

The **at** command uses a variety of time specifiers, some complex and some simple:

- **midnight**—Runs the task at 00:00 on the current day.

- **noon**—Runs the task at 12:00 on the current day.

- **teatime**—Runs the task at 16:00 (**at**'s British roots are evident).

- **time-of-day**—Such as 2:00 p.m. or 5:00 a.m.

- **date**—You can specify a time on a specific day, such as **2pm jul 23** or **4am 121504**.

- **now + time**—You can specify any number of minutes, hours, days, and weeks from the current time, such as **now + 30 minutes**.

The **at** command just starts the jobs. A couple of commands can help you manage the **at** jobs on the system, including these:

- **atq**—This shows the summary of jobs in the **at** queue with the job number, date and time, and executing user (this also can be seen with **at -l**). It does not show the contents of the job itself; for that the root user needs to look at the file in **/var/spool/at**.

- **atrm**—This deletes **at** jobs by job number, which is determined by using the previous command and the syntax **atrm #** (where **#** is the job number). **at -d** is a synonym for this.

at has a set of security files, **/etc/at.allow** and **/etc/at.deny**, which allow users to or prevent users from queuing up **at** jobs. These behave the same way as the cron restrictions. If the **at.allow** file exists and contains usernames, only those users and the root user are allowed to use **at**. If the **at.deny** file exists and contains usernames, those users are denied and all others are allowed. If neither file exists, only the root user is allowed to submit **at** jobs.

The batch Command

Using the **batch** command is relatively simple; it's somewhat of an extension of the **at** command and shares the same man page. The **batch** command is used to run tasks or jobs at no specific time, but at a particular threshold of system utilization. As you can imagine, some systems are busy and you need to determine which jobs might need to be run with another scheduling utility if they are time-sensitive.

The metric used by **batch** and **at** to know whether the system has capacity to run a job is the *load average*. The load average of the system is seen in the three numbers that shows up when you run the **w** (who) command:

```
$ w
 16:04:34 up 135 days, 17:40,  2 users,  load average: 0.54, 0.60,
 0.51
```

These numbers, 0.54, 0.60, and 0.51, represent the average number of processes waiting to be run when sampled over the last minute, 5 minutes, and 15 minutes, respectively. A load average of 0.60 over 5 minutes means that over the last 5 minutes, when sampled, there was a process waiting to be run 60% of the time.

You can expect that a system with two CPUs is busy when the load average is 2. By looking at the load average over the three different time intervals you can tell whether the load is temporary, in which case the 1 minute measurement will be high and the other two will be low, or if it's sustained by having all three high. Or, if the 15 minute measurement is high and the others are low, you know you had some high load but have recovered.

By default, **batch** runs jobs once at a future time when the system 1 minute load average is less than or equal to 0.8. This can be configured by specifying the desired utilization average with the **atrun** command, such as

```
atrun -l 1.6
```

This sets the threshold that **batch** will watch to 1.6, and if load average drops below that value, the **batch** job is run. A value of 1.8, would be good for a system with two processors. For a system with N processors you want this value to be slightly less than N, such as 80% of N.

Submitting **batch** jobs is similar to **at**, and it even uses the **at** prompt and interface. To submit a compile job that runs when the system threshold is reached, you would use the following:

```
$ echo bigcompile | batch
job 11 at Sun Mar 29 14:36:00 2015
```

You can create a job with **at** or **batch** and then **cat** the file by using a command such as

```
cat /var/spool/at/a000030112ea5c
```

at's spooled jobs use a prefix of the letter a, whereas **batch** jobs use the letter b as a prefix. When you view the file, notice all the environment settings stored in the job, including a line that exports the username used to submit the job. Only the root user can look at these files.

Remember that **at** and **batch** both export a lot of information when the job is run, which goes away after that shell is closed. **at** and **batch** jobs are run in a replica of the environment that existed at the time the job was submitted, which means all variables, aliases, and functions in the shell are available to the job that was started in that shell.

Summary

Periodic tasks can be run through cron or anacron so that the systems administrator doesn't need to run the jobs manually. Cron entries are managed with the **crontab** command, and the entries themselves have a specific format that includes the minute, hour, day of month, month, and day of week, along with the command itself. A user's ability to edit her own crontab is managed with **/etc/cron.allow** and **/etc/cron.deny**, with the root user always being able to edit crontabs.

If a computer is off when a scheduled cron job was to run, the job won't be executed. Anacron solves this problem by running the job when the computer is turned on. The tradeoff is that the minimum time between jobs is one day and that you don't have exact control over when the job runs.

The **at** facility lets you run ad-hoc jobs at a particular future time.

Exam Preparation Tasks

As mentioned in the section "How to Use This Book" in the Introduction, you have a couple of choices for exam preparation: the exercises here, Chapter 21, "Final Preparation," and the practice exams on the DVD.

Review All Key Topics

Review the most important topics in this chapter, noted with the Key Topics icon in the outer margin of the page. Table 16-2 lists a reference of these key topics and the page numbers on which each is found.

Table 16-2   Key Topics for Chapter 16

Key Topic Element	Description	Page Number
Paragraph	Editing a crontab	447
List	The meaning of each column in the crontab	448
Paragraph	Spelling out days and months in the crontab	449
Paragraph	Specifying multiple values in the crontab	449
Paragraph	Specifying a range of values in the crontab	449
Paragraph	Running a job with a step counter	450
Paragraph	Cron environments	451
List	Special environment variables for cron	451
Paragraph	Location of user crontabs	452
Paragraph	Location of system crontabs	453
List	Directories to run hourly/daily/weekly/monthly jobs	454
List	Crontab access	454
List	Anacrontab file format	455
Paragraph	Basic **at** usage	457
List	**at** time specifiers	457
List	Other **at** commands	457

Define Key Terms

Define the following key terms from this chapter and check your answers in the glossary:

cron, anacron, load average

Review Questions

The answers to these review questions are in Appendix A.

1. You want to run a task on the hour, every other hour starting at 1:00 a.m., with no other restrictions. Which crontab accomplishes this?

    a. */120 * * *

    b. 1/2 * * * *

    c. 0 */2 * * *

    d. 0 1-23/2 * * *

2. You have configured a job to run with the **batch** command, but apparently system utilization never drops as low as the default value. Which of the following commands can be used to set a custom value for the **batch** command?

    a. batchavg

    b. atconfig

    c. atrun

    d. crontab

3. You are trying to set up a job to run every night, but the script keeps aborting with errors that the command was not found. Which of the following in your crontab might help?

    a. PATH=/usr/local/bin:/sbin:/usr/sbin:/usr/bin:/bin

    b. SHELL=/bin/sh

    c. MAILTO=you@yourdomain.com

    d. ABORT_ON_ERROR=false

4. User crontabs are stored in:

    a. /var/spool/cron

    b. $HOME/.cron

    c. /var/cron

    d. /usr/local/cron

5. If both cron.allow and cron.deny exist, the behavior is to

    a. Only deny users in cron.deny to use crontab

    b. Only allow users in cron.allow to use crontab

    c. Only allow the root user to use crontab

    d. First check cron.deny and then check cron.allow

6. If a script is in /etc/anacrontab and the computer is off overnight, the script will be run after the computer has booted.

   a. True

   b. False

7. What is the primary purpose of the job identifier in the anacrontab file?

   a. It is used to track the last time the job was run.

   b. It is the way anacron sorts the jobs to be run.

   c. It is what shows up in the process listing when the job is running.

   d. It identifies the owner of the job.

8. Which of the following directories allows you to place crontabs that specify the user under which cron will run the job?

   a. /etc/crontab

   b. /var/spool/cron

   c. /etc/cron.daily

   d. /etc/cron.d

9. You have created a job with the **at** command but later realize you don't want the command to run. How do you delete the job?

   a. **at -q** to find the job, then **at -d** to delete it

   b. **rm /var/spool/at/***

   c. **at -l** to find the job, then **atrm** to delete it.

   d. **atq** to find the job, then **at -r** to delete it

10. If you wanted to run a job when the system load was low, the best command to use would be

    a. **batch**

    b. **at**

    c. **crontab**

    d. **anacron**

This chapter covers the following topics:

- Managing Printers and Printing
- Mail Transfer Agent Basics

This chapter covers the following exam topics:

- Manage printers and printing: 108.4
- Mail Transfer Agent (MTA) basics: 108.3

## CHAPTER 17

Configuring Print and Email Services

Linux systems are often deployed as print and email servers. Both the printing and email servers are lightweight and easy to use. This makes them great candidates for small environments with limited resources, but they also find their way into larger environments where Linux-savvy people just want to get work done.

"Do I Know This Already?" Quiz

The "Do I Know This Already?" quiz enables you to assess whether you should read this entire chapter or simply jump to the "Exam Preparation Tasks" section for review. If you are in doubt, read the entire chapter. Table 17-1 outlines the major headings in this chapter and the corresponding "Do I Know This Already?" quiz questions. You can find the answers in Appendix A, "Answers to the 'Do I Know This Already?' Quizzes and Review Questions."

Table 17-1 "Do I Know This Already?" Foundation Topics Section-to-Question Mapping

Foundation Topics Section	Questions Covered in This Section
Managing Printers and Printing	1-3
Mail Transfer Agent Basics	4-6

1. Your printer, named JonathansDesk, had an error printing a document, and now CUPS has stopped the printer. How do you get jobs printing again?

    a. **cupsenable JonathansDesk**

    b. **lpq -P JonathansDesk**

    c. **cupsaccept JonathansDesk**

    d. **cupsaccept -P JonathansDesk**

2. Which of the following commands prints a file called resume.pdf to a printer called Main?

    a. lpr -d Main resume.pdf

    b. lp -P Main resume.pdf

    c. lp -d Main resume.pdf

    d. lpr resume.pdf

3. Where are CUPS configuration files stored?

    a. /etc/cupsd

    b. /etc/cups

    c. /var/lib/cupsd

    d. /var/etc/cups

4. The component of an email system that is responsible for mail delivery from one computer to another is called:

    a. Mail User Agent (MUA)

    b. Mail Relay Agent (MRA)

    c. Mail Transfer Agent (MTA)

    d. Mail Delivery Agent (MDA)

5. You configured an alias for your helpdesk, so that help@example.com goes to jonathan@example.com, isaac@example.com, and david@example.com.

After trying it out, however, the message bounces. What is the likely cause?

    a. You didn't restart your MTA.

    b. You already have a help@example.com user.

    c. One of the users has a **.forward** file that is overriding the alias.

    d. You didn't run **newaliases**.

6. Which of the following is not a typical Linux Mail Transfer Agent?

    a. Exchange

    b. Sendmail

    c. Qmail

    d. Postfix

Managing Printers and Printing

Despite promises of a paperless office we still live in a world that needs to print. Hooking up a printer to a computer is simple in principle, but the situation gets more complicated once you want other people printing to a shared printer.

The Linux printing system is incredibly extensible, to the point where it can detect the type of file being printed and emulate other network printing systems.

The Print Spooler

Printers have been around for a long time, as has the need to print to them over a network. When you have multiple people submitting work, called print jobs, to the same printer, you find that one person submits a print job while another job is printing. Something needs to control access to the printer so that one print job finishes before the next one starts. This is the job of a *print spooler*.

A spooler is also helpful in receiving the entire job from the remote computer and spoon feeding it to the printer. Without the spooler, each remote computer would be responsible for parceling out data over a relatively fast network to a much slower printer. The spooler lets the computer send the print job across the network and then forget about it.

The print spooler can manage multiple printers. Each printer has one or more *print queues* where the jobs are stacked up to be sent to the printer.

Network Printing Protocols

The first printing protocol to hit Unix was the line printer daemon protocol (also known as *line printer remote*, or LPR). This protocol is simple; a conversation between a client and a server involves a quick handshake and then the job itself. It is so simple that printers often implement the protocol themselves.

The BSD Unixes included the `lpr` set of tools and SysV Unixes included a similar program called `lp`. Both are functionally the same and vary in their command line options.

Network printing stayed the same for several years until an open source project called LPRng (Next generation of LPR) tried to improve on BSD printing. LPRng was compatible with all the BSD commands but added in new features such as an improved security model and better monitoring.

LPR is simple, but it lacked features that were becoming more important in a world where the Internet was taking hold. The *Internet Printing Protocol (IPP)* came out of a collaboration between Novell, Xerox, Microsoft, and Lexmark. IPP is built on top of HTTP, which is what powers the Web, so problems like authentication, encryption, and the protocol definition are already solved.

An independent developer, in parallel, started working on a better printing system for Unix. This project, called the *Common Unix Printing System (CUPS)* uses IPP and makes the job of managing printers much easier. CUPS was picked up quickly by Linux distributions, and the author was later hired by Apple, who also bought the rights to CUPS and continued to support its development. Fifteen years later, CUPS is the dominant printing system in Linux and Apple OSX systems.

The CUPS Daemon

The Common Unix Printing System is built around a daemon that listens for requests both from clients to print and from humans to manage the printers and queues. Data transfer is done through the Internet Printing Protocol, which is built on top of HTTP so the same daemon can do both jobs.

Print requests that come in to CUPS go through a series of conversions and filters until they land on a CUPS backend, which is akin to a printer driver. This pipeline of filters and conversions allows CUPS to accept data in different formats and print correctly on a variety of printers. For example, you can send an image file directly to CUPS, which detects it as an image and then translates it to something the printer understands. In another printing system, sending an image to the printer would end up with page after page of strange characters. You would need each application to do the translation into something the local system supports.

The CUPS Pipeline

If you can understand the way that a print job flows through CUPS, you will be in a better position to fix problems when they happen. The CUPS pipeline used to process print jobs is shown in Figure 17-1.

The top of the pipeline is where jobs are received either through LPR or IPP. If the job is received as an LPR job, a small daemon is spawned to handle the connection and translate it to IPP.

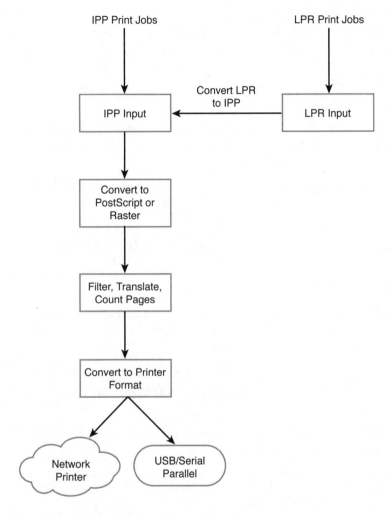

Figure 17-1   How CUPS processes a print job

The print job is received and queued for processing. Images are generally kept in their raster formats, and other file types are converted to PostScript (or kept as PS if it started out there).

Other filters are applied once the job is in either PostScript or raster. Pages can be counted for statistics or accounting purposes; pages can be resized to fit the output or shrunk to be able to fit multiple pages on a single piece of paper.

The final processing step converts the PostScript or raster file into an output suitable for the destination printer. Not all printers support PostScript, so this is where the file gets transformed into Hewlett Packard's Printer Control Language (HP PCL) or a proprietary format.

The software in this step performs a similar role as that of a printer driver, except that most printers don't ship with Linux drivers. Several projects have sprung up to support different printers, either by duplicating the functionality or by allowing you to upload files from the native driver. The two main projects here are Foomatic and Gutenprint. Both provide drivers for common printers, and it is likely that your printer is supported by both projects.

Finally the output is sent to the printer by whichever means is needed. The printer may be connected by USB, Serial, Parallel, or a network connection, and the *CUPS backend* takes care of sending it to the printer.

The final destination does not need to be a printer. The destination could be another IPP queue or a file that lets you print to a local PDF file.

This modular approach to printing lets each step handle the job it is best at. Filters do not need to know about the printer as those details are handled by another step.

Configuring CUPS

CUPS is likely installed on your system, but you can check your package manager for the **cups** package to see whether it's installed. For Debian distributions that's **dpkg -s cups** and for Red Hat it's **rpm -q cups**.

Even though CUPS is ultimately configured with configuration files on disk, most configuration is done from within a web browser. The CUPS daemon can talk to both printers and web browsers.

Begin configuring your printer by pointing your browser to http://localhost:631. You see the welcome screen shown in Figure 17-2.

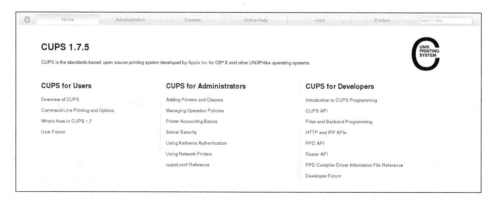

Figure 17-2 The CUPS welcome screen

From the welcome screen, select the **Administration** option to get the administration screen, shown in Figure 17-3.

Figure 17-3   The CUPS administration screen

This administration screen is the main place to perform CUPS configuration, such as adding and removing printers, deleting jobs, and managing who and what can print.

From the administration screen, select **Add Printer** from the top left of the screen. CUPS tries to detect any printers by listening to the network and checking the USB peripherals. Figure 17-4 shows a list of discovered printers, along with generic options to add nondiscovered printers.

If you are prompted to provide information in an Authentication Required pop up, provide the user name of Root and the password for the root user. Changes to CUPS require privileges not available to regular users.

Figure 17-4   List of discovered printers

Modern network-enabled printers implement a protocol called Bonjour that helps computers discover printers and other devices. The printer periodically broadcasts its availability over the network and applications such as CUPS listen for these broadcasts.

If you have a USB printer, CUPS is also able to discover it, and it will be shown alongside other discovered printers. Recall from Chapter 1, "Installing Linux," that the **lsusb** command shows what USB devices are attached to the computer by looking at the **/proc** filesystem. This same method is used to find USB printers.

Not all network printers are discoverable. If you have such a printer, the printer's status page should give enough details to complete the remaining steps using one of the **Other Network Printers** options. You are prompted for those details on the next screen.

In this example, it is the discovered network printer that is of interest. Don't worry if you see the same printer multiple times.

Click on the Continue button to see the details about connecting to the printer, which are shown in Figure 17-5.

Figure 17-5   Viewing the printer connection settings

The Add Printer dialog shown in Figure 17-5 shows the connection settings for the printer. You can provide several pieces of information to organize your printers, most of which are already filled out for you:

- The name of the printer, which is the name of the queue.

- A description that helps people identify the printer when browsing for it.

- The location of the printer, which is further descriptive information for people browsing.

- The connection string, which CUPS does not let you edit for discovered printers. This tells CUPS how to connect to the printer over the network or a local port.

- Whether or not to share the printer to other computers.

Other than the name of the printer, you can change any of the details later.

Click the Continue button to proceed to the next step of choosing the make and model of your printer.

Figure 17-6 gives you a chance to review the settings you just entered and to choose the make, or manufacturer, of your printer.

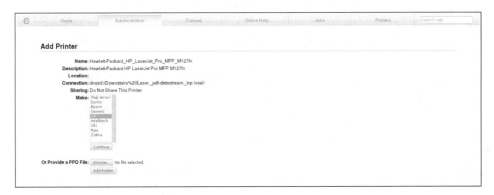

Figure 17-6 Choosing the make of the printer

If your printer happens to include a PostScript Printer Description (PPD) file, you can upload it from this page rather than choosing the make and model by clicking the Browse button to find the file on your local computer and then choose Add Printer to continue. The PPD file would be on the manufacturer's web site or on a disk that came with the printer.

If you don't have the PPD file, which is the more likely scenario, pick your printer manufacturer from the list and click Continue.

The next step is to choose the model of your printer, shown in Figure 17-7.

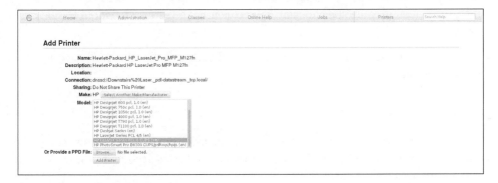

Figure 17-7 Choosing the model of the printer

Select the option associated with your printer, or choose a generic option. For example, HP printers tend to understand the Printer Control Language (PCL), so the HP LaserJet Series PCL 6 option is chosen in Figure 17-7.

If your printer is not listed, you can experiment with the generic option, or check your distribution's package system to see whether drivers are available. For example, for an Epson printer you could run **yum search Epson** or look for packages with Gutenprint or Foomatic with **apt-cache search gutenprint** and **apt-cache search foomatic**.

Finally, click Add Printer and you are taken to the final step, shown in Figure 17-8.

Figure 17-8   Setting the printer's default options

This last step, shown in Figure 17-8, allows you to set the default options for people using the printer. You can choose the Query Printer for Default Options button or choose your own options at the bottom, and then choose the Set Default Options button.

The default options set properties like the paper size and resolution. Depending on the printer, you may also be choosing a paper source or features like double-sided printing.

Select the Administration menu to get back to the main menu. You now have a printer configured.

CUPS Maintenance

The basic administration of a printer can be done from the printer's status screen. From Administration, click on Manage Printers, and then select your printer. You can see an example in Figure 17-9.

Figure 17-9   Viewing the printer status

The key parts of this status screen are

- The title, which also gives the status of the printer and the queue such as Processing, Accepting Jobs, Not Shared

- The Maintenance and Administration pull-downs that let you manage the printer

- The Jobs list, which shows any print jobs being printed or awaiting printing

Printer State

The state of the printer is tracked in two ways. First, the queue itself is either accepting or rejecting jobs. This refers to CUPS receiving a request to print and taking responsibility for that request. CUPS can accept a job even if the printer is off, as it will be spooled to disk in **/var/spool/cups**. The job prints when the printer is ready.

Next, the printer itself can be in one of a few states:

- **Idle**—The printer is not printing anything and is awaiting work.

- **Processing**—CUPS is currently sending data to the printer.

- **Stopped**—An error happened with a print job, so CUPS stopped further printing to the printer.

- **Paused**—The administrator has temporarily suspended printing to this printer.

In normal operation, a printer will be either idle or processing.

Maintenance and Administration Pull-downs

The maintenance and administration pull-downs give you several options that either perform actions or change the state of the printer.

From the maintenance menu you can

- Print a test page.

- Clean print heads, which is only helpful on an inkjet printer.

- Print a self-test page, such as the printer's status page.

- Pause or resume the printer.

- Accept or reject further jobs from the queue.

- Move all jobs to another queue.

- Cancel all jobs in the queue.

The difference between pause/resume and accept/reject is an important one. The queue is either in accept or reject mode. A remote client trying to print to a queue in reject mode will get an error. If the queue is in accept mode but the printer is paused, the job will be accepted but will not print until the printer itself is resumed.

The latter two options are helpful when dealing with a malfunctioning printer. There will usually be several jobs backed up, and if they're not going to print soon you should move them to another printer or get rid of them so you can troubleshoot properly.

Administration Menu

The Administration menu offers some options relating to the configuration of the printer:

- **Modify Printer**—Takes you back through the setup steps you did earlier so you can change the address or enable sharing

- **Delete Printer**—Removes the printer from the system

- **Set Default Options**—Performs just the last step of printer creation, which is to determine the default settings such as paper size

- **Set as Server Default**—Make this the default queue for jobs not assigned a queue

- **Set Allowed Users**—If authentication is set up you can restrict who can print to the queue or to prevent certain people from printing

Jobs List

The Jobs List shows you the list of jobs, in order, that are awaiting printing. The Show All Jobs button switches the view to include jobs that have already been printed; otherwise, you only see jobs awaiting printing.

Each job has three control buttons:

- **Hold**—Prevents printing of the job without removing it from the queue. Release the job by pressing the button again.

- **Cancel**—Removes the job from the queue.

- **Move Job**—Moves the job to another queue.

Command Line Tools

CUPS has several command line tools. Some are specific to CUPS and some are for compatibility with the old lpr/lpd printing systems. Furthermore, the configuration for CUPS is held in human readable text files that can be edited instead of using the web interface.

> **NOTE** The exam focuses on the command line tools. Reviewing the web configuration is important to get an understanding of CUPS but is not on the exam. If you don't have a printer to practice with, you can create a fake printer with a command like **lpadmin –p FakePrinter –E –v /dev/null –m raw**, or select the Virtual PDF printer option when creating a new printer. The command creates a printer called FakePrinter where all output is discarded; the second option generates PDFs of the output for you.

Legacy Tools

CUPS provides an interface compatible with the legacy **lp** printing system. It is used to print from the command line and to view print queues. As some applications still print through the legacy printing system, this interface is important.

Even though these legacy compatibility commands were originally used with the LPR protocol, the versions implemented by CUPS support IPP.

lp/lpr

The **lp** and **lpr** commands print whatever they receive on the input stream, or any files passed on the command line. Example 17-1 shows a simple way to print:

Example 17-1   Printing from the Command Line

```
# echo "testing" | lp
request id is Hewlett-Packard_HP_LaserJet_Pro_MFP_M127fn-6 (0 file(s))
# lp memo.ps
request id is Hewlett-Packard_HP_LaserJet_Pro_MFP_M127fn-7 (1 file(s))
```

The response to this command is a message indicating whether the job was accepted. If you use the **lpr** command in the same fashion, it does not return any output.

If you are not printing to the default printer, you need to tell **lp** which destination queue to print to with the **-d** option, such as with **lp -d Hewlett-Packard_HP_ LaserJet_Pro_MFP_M127fn.**

lp and **lpr** differ in some of their options, as each is a compatible implementation of its BSD and SYSV predecessor, respectively. The biggest difference is that **lp** expects the name of the printer to be specified with **-d** (destination), while **lpr** expects the **-P** option.

To print multiple copies, such as 2, use **lp -n 2** or **lpr -#2**.

lpstat

lpstat provides status information about your printers and jobs. It shows the list of jobs you have queued when it is run with no arguments.

A good use of **lpstat** is to see all the print queues and their status through the **-a** (all) option. Example 17-2 shows this in action:

Example 17-2   Showing the Status of All Printers

```
# lpstat -a
Hewlett-Packard_HP_LaserJet_Pro_MFP_M127fn
    accepting requests since Sat 02 May 2015 09:47:31 PM CDT
```

lpstat is primarily concerned with the queue rather than the printer itself. The printer is paused in Example 17-2, but the queue itself is accepting requests. The fact that the printer is paused is not reflected in the output.

Some other uses of **lpstat** are

- **lpstat -d**—Displays the name of the default printer

- **lpstat -r**—Indicates whether CUPS is running

- **lpstat -s**—Provides a status summary of how the system is configured

- **lpstat -t**—Provides a more detailed summary of how the system is configured

Without any options, **lpstat** shows a list of jobs queued by the current user to the default printer. You can also pass the name of a printer to see jobs queued by the current user to that printer.

lpq

lpq queries the print queue for the status of the printer and any jobs. The description of each job includes helpful information such as the owner and an identifier for the job that can be used with other commands. Example 17-3 shows such a query:

Example 17-3   Querying the Printer for Status

```
# lpq
Hewlett-Packard_HP_LaserJet_Pro_MFP_M127fn is not ready
Rank    Owner   Job     File(s)                 Total Size
1st     root    3       Test Page               1024 bytes
```

Example 17-3 shows that the printer is not ready, which is the same as the printer being paused in the web interface. It does not say anything about the status of the queue itself. You can also see that a job with job ID 3 is in the queue.

By default you only see the default printer. Use the **-a** option to see all printers on the system, or **-P** to specify an individual printer. **lpq** is slightly different from **lpstat** in that **lpstat** without any options shows you all jobs queued by the current user, while **lpq** shows all users.

lprm

lprm removes jobs from the queue, just like the **rm** command removes files from the filesystem. Example 17-4 shows a print job being removed.

Example 17-4 Removing a Print Job

```
# lprm 3
# lpq
Hewlett-Packard_HP_LaserJet_Pro_MFP_M127fn is not ready
no entries
```

The **lprm** command prints nothing if it succeeds; otherwise, it tries to print a helpful message such as to indicate that the job doesn't exist or the user doesn't have permissions.

Like other commands, you can specify a printer with **-P**. Running **lprm** with no job ID removes the top ranked job on the given queue. Use **lprm -a** to remove all print jobs in the queue.

An alternative way of cancelling a job is with the **cancel** command. This command works similarly to **lpq**. Cancel job 13 with **cancel 13**. If you want to cancel a job from a queue other than the default queue, use the name of the queue and the job number, separated with a dash:

```
$ lpstat
Hewlett-Packard_HP_LaserJet_Pro_MFP_M127fn-9 sean                3072
Sun 03 May 2015 10:19:24 AM CDT
$ cancel Hewlett-Packard_HP_LaserJet_Pro_MFP_M127fn-9
```

Both methods work equally well, and you should know both for the exam.

CUPS Tools

CUPS provides a small number of tools for interacting with the printing system from the command line.

cupsaccept/cupsreject

These two commands control the status of the given queue. Unlike the **lp** series of commands, the names of the printers are specified without a separate option.

cupsreject tells CUPS to reject all jobs sent to the queue, and **cupsaccept** reenables the queue. Example 17-5 shows such an example.

Example 17-5   Rejecting Jobs

```
# cupsreject Hewlett-Packard_HP_LaserJet_Pro_MFP_M127fn
# echo hi | lp
lp: Destination "Hewlett-Packard_HP_LaserJet_Pro_MFP_M127fn" is not
accepting jobs.
# lpstat -a
Hewlett-Packard_HP_LaserJet_Pro_MFP_M127fn not accepting requests since
Sat 02 May 2015 09:47:31 PM CDT -
```

Example 17-5 shows that after the queue has been rejected, any attempt to print to it shows an error that the queue is not accepting jobs. This status can be verified with the **lpstat** command.

cupsenable/cupsdisable

These two commands enable and disable the printer itself, rather than the queue. Just like **cupsaccept** and **cupsreject**, give the name of the print queue on the command line.

If the printer is in a stopped state because of an error, you can use the **cupsenable** command to reenable it. If you need to take down the printer for some maintenance, you can disable printing, while still accepting jobs, with **cupsdisable**. Once you reenable the printer, the jobs begin printing again.

cupsctl

cupsctl is a tool to manage the configuration of the CUPS daemon. Run it by itself to get a list of the current configuration options.

By default, the CUPS web interface only listens to requests from the machine that it's running on. If you want to enable remote administration, run **cupsctl --remote-admin**. You disable remote administration with **cupsctl --no-remote-admin**.

Shared printers usually only accept requests from machines on the local network. In larger networks this can be a problem because two machines that are talking to each other may be on different networks, connected with a router. In this case, run **cupsctl --remote-any** to allow anyone that can connect to the computer to print to it. Disable this with **cupsctl --no-remote-any**.

If you are in a more informal setting where you trust users to delete jobs even if they don't own them, **cupsctl -- user-cancel-any** allows anyone to cancel jobs.

Configuration Files

CUPS has a variety of files in **/etc/cups**. Most of the options you will ever want to change can be done in the web interface. The Server panel in the Administration screen gives you an opportunity to set some global options and to edit one of the configuration files from within the web interface.

Some of the interesting files in the configuration directory are

- **classes.conf**—Contains the classes, which can also be created in the web interface. A class is a group of printers, and printing to a class queues the job to the first available printer.

- **cupsd.conf**—The main configuration file, which can also be edited in the web interface. This contains default settings such as timeouts, rules about what can be done by different people, and logging settings.

- **cupsd.conf.default**—A default configuration file that you can use if you really break your production cupsd.conf. Editing the configuration file on the Web also gives you an option to revert to the default file.

- **printers.conf**—Configuration for each printer that you configured on the system.

- **ppd**—A directory containing the PPD files for each configured printer.

Troubleshooting Printing

Printing seems to be the most tedious area of system administration to troubleshoot. You have users involved, software applications generating output, queues on servers, and mechanical components that have to operate with tight tolerances. Printing is a real-time process built as a series of components playing a big game of hot potato; one component is trying to hand off work to the next component as fast as possible.

Troubleshooting printing means understanding the flow of a print job and the tools necessary to investigate each step of the flow.

Problems tend to fall into one of two categories: Either nothing at all was printed, or something printed but it didn't work correctly.

Try Printing from the Command Line

If nothing at all is printing, especially from within an application, try printing from the command line to see whether this is a problem with the application or with CUPS. Run something like **echo "test" | lp -d PRINTERNAME** and see whether anything prints.

If it works from the command line but not the application, it is likely a configuration problem with the application or a permissions problem. Reconfigure the application, paying special attention to the name and type of the printer.

Was the Job Queued?

If you print something and nothing comes out of the printer, you should check to see whether the job was queued. This can be done from the CUPS web interface by looking under the Printers tab, or with the **lpq** command.

If the job was not queued, you should check to see whether CUPS is running. You should also verify the name of the queues, and that the queue is accepting jobs either through the web interface or the **lpstat -a** command. Reenable the queue with **cupsaccept** or through the web interface.

Can CUPS Send the Job to the Printer?

At this point you've verified that clients can submit jobs to the queue, but the queue is not being processed by the printer.

The first check should be to see whether the printer is either in the Stopped or Paused states. If so, reenable it through the web interface or use the **cupsenable** command.

If the printer is in the stopped state, that means a previous job had a problem. Clearing this job from the queue with **lprm** or the web interface may get jobs flowing again.

At this point it's a good idea to check the printer itself to make sure it's on and properly connected to the network. Chapter 19, "Networking Fundamentals," discusses methods of testing network connectivity to devices.

The printer itself may be jammed or otherwise display an error. If so, take care of those problems.

Turn On Debugging

If nothing up until has solved the problem, you should enable extra logging within CUPS and check those logs. This can be done from the Administration screen in the Server pane:

- Check Save Debugging Information for Troubleshooting and then click Change Settings.
- Try the previous troubleshooting steps.
- Click View Error Log.

The error logs guide the rest of your troubleshooting.

Mail Transfer Agent Basics

Email is as old as the Internet itself, having existed in various formats since the early 1970s. What we now recognize as email evolved from simple beginnings to support images, rich text, and attachments.

You may recognize an email address, such as sean@example.com. The @ separates the user, in this case sean, from the domain, which is example.com. When you send an email to sean@example.com, a detailed set of steps are followed by many machines across the Internet to get your email delivered.

How Email Flows

Getting email to work properly involves several different components. Each of these components must do a particular job and then hand off the email being delivered to the next component in the chain.

Sometimes a single server or application handles multiple components. Even when this is the case, troubleshooting is more effective when you continue to think of the system in terms of components. We look at each component in turn.

Mail User Agent

The *Mail User Agent*, or MUA for short, is the technical term for an email client. You use your MUA to send and receive email. Many things can do the job of the MUA such as a dedicated program, a web page, a smartphone, or even an application that sends out alerts.

The MUA's job is to capture the email in some format, including the recipient, and send it to the next link in the email chain—the *Mail Transfer Agent (MTA)*.

The MUA is free to communicate to the MTA in whatever protocol makes sense. Where the email system is a proprietary one such as Microsoft Exchange using Microsoft Outlook as the MUA, the communication is done in some kind of application-specific protocol. The MUA might be an application running inside a browser, so the communication there might be called to a remote web server. Other times the communication is done in the protocol used to transfer mail over the Internet itself: the *Simple Mail Transfer Protocol (SMTP)*.

Mail Transfer Agent

The MTA's job is to receive an email from an MUA or other MTA and get it one step closer to the final destination. The process of getting an email between two parties might take several MTAs. It is common for organizations to *relay* email from MTAs in the field to a smaller set of outbound MTAs. Relaying happens when an MTA forwards a message on behalf of another MTA.

This relaying step is also where a great deal of spam email comes from. Any server that is relaying should take care to make sure that the email being relayed is either from a known source or going to a known source. Without this check, someone could anonymously funnel the latest request for help from the fake prince of a small nation through your server and you would forward the email for him.

Locking down your MTA to prevent spam is a weighty topic, but fortunately Linux distributions come minimally configured to prevent this, and the detailed configuration of an MTA is not in scope for the exam.

The Language of Email

Email exchange over the Internet is done through the Simple Mail Transfer Protocol. This is a text-based communications protocol that lets different email systems talk to each other even if they would normally talk with proprietary protocols.

Example 17-6 shows what an SMTP conversation looks like.

Example 17-6   An SMTP Conversation Between Two MTAs

```
220 www.ertw.com ESMTP Postfix
HELO www.ertw.com250 www.ertw.com
MAIL FROM: sean@ertw.com
250 2.1.0 Ok
RCPT TO: swalberg@gmail.com
250 2.1.5 Ok
DATA
354 End data with <CR><LF>.<CR><LF>
Subject: Testing

Hi Sean, just testing
.
250 2.0.0 Ok: queued as 8E720731A
QUIT
221 2.0.0 Bye
```

In Example 17-6 you can see that the conversation is all readable instead of being some kind of binary protocol. The server prefixes all its responses with a number indicating a status code. The wording that follows the number is actually for humans, not other computers!

Understanding SMTP is not necessary for the exam, but for real world troubleshooting it's valuable to know the kind of information carried inside the protocol, and what's in the email itself. For example, SMTP doesn't care about the subject line. It just needs to know who sent the email, where it's going, and the contents of the email. The final system is the one that cares about the contents.

Linux MTAs

Linux has a variety of MTAs. Each one still speaks SMTP, but what differs is how the software is configured and what extra features it can have. There are four MTAs relevant to the exam.

- *Sendmail* was once the most popular MTA on the Internet. It can speak a variety of protocols order to connect different email systems. Sendmail is less of an MTA than it is a system for building an MTA out of a language called M4, and is therefore incredibly complicated. This author, not fondly, remembers having a large book on his shelf that was needed to explain how to configure Sendmail. Other than the complexity, Sendmail's main criticisms are that it puts too many responsibilities in a single process and has a history of security problems.

- *Postfix* is an MTA that came out of IBM Research and is still actively developed by the open source community. Postfix has extensive policy configuration to prevent spam and separates concerns into separate processes for security. Even though programs like sendmail had support for external filters such as Anti-Virus scanners bolted on, this external filtering functionality is a first-class citizen in the Postfix world.

- *Qmail* was written as a secure replacement to Sendmail. Like Postfix, the concerns are compartmentalized to prevent a successful compromise of one component from gaining access to other components. The configuration is fairly simple, perhaps even more so than Postfix. The source is now in the public domain, so the development seems to have fragmented and slowed down.

- *Exim* is another monolithic MTA, like Sendmail, but has a better security record. Exim is highly configurable without needing to devolve into the madness that is sendmail's M4. At one point Exim was the default MTA in Debian, but the project has since switched to not offering an MTA in a standard installation.

Despite the variety of MTAs with their own configurations, there are some commonalities when it comes to some basic commands and functionality. Part of these commonalities are on the part of the MTA itself, and some are through work done by most distributions to ease the transition between MTAs.

Domain Name System

The domain name system (DNS) is what translates between hostnames, such as www.example.com, and IP addresses, such as 127.0.0.1. The DNS plays an integral role in delivering email.

Your MTA needs to know where to deliver email. This information might be statically configured to send everything to a centralized mail server, but at some point an MTA needs to look up this information in the DNS if the destination is outside your organization.

First, the MTA extracts the domain from the email address. For joe@example.com, the domain is **example.com**. Next, the MTA queries the DNS for the Mail Exchange (MX) record. It may get back the names of one or more MTAs. For example, Google's public mail servers are listed in Example 17-7.

Example 17-7   Querying a Domain's MX Records

```
$ host -t mx google.com
google.com mail is handled by 20 alt1.aspmx.l.google.com.
google.com mail is handled by 10 aspmx.l.google.com.
google.com mail is handled by 40 alt3.aspmx.l.google.com.
google.com mail is handled by 30 alt2.aspmx.l.google.com.
google.com mail is handled by 50 alt4.aspmx.l.google.com.
```

Google lists five mail servers, each with a different priority level: 10, 20, 30, 40, and 50 (while the records may display in any order, the priority number dictates the order in which they should be tried). The lowest value has the highest priority, so a remote MTA would first try delivering to aspmx.l.google.com. If that fails, it is free to try the next one in the list. However, by advertising five MTAs, Google is promising that any one of them is valid to deliver mail for people at google.com.

If a domain does not publish any MX records in the DNS, an MTA can try to resolve the domain name to an address and deliver mail there. If that fails, the domain likely doesn't accept email and the message should *bounce*. In email terminology, a bounce happens when an email is rejected at some point in the chain. Most of the time a user can expect to receive an email in return indicating that the email was not delivered. Some systems will not return bounce messages for users that don't exist because spammers who try and make up usernames will generate an excessive amount of bounces.

Mail Delivery Agent

The *Mail Delivery Agent (MDA)* receives email through SMTP like an MTA and delivers it to a local mailbox in whichever format is used at the destination site. Sometimes it is writing the email to a flat file unique to the user; sometimes it is writing it to a database for performance reasons.

The MDA, in its capacity as an MTA, also has the opportunity to perform *aliasing* and *forwarding*. Aliasing happens when a user wants to receive email with a different name. For example, instead of creating an account for sales@example.com, you can create an alias pointing sales to one or more existing accounts. Thus you can make your sales address public but send all the email to a particular user's account. This lets you switch the destination without needing to make the change public and also means that people only need to check one mailbox.

Forwarding is similar to aliasing except that the redirect is to different email system. joe@example.com might want to send all his email to his mobile phone that has its own email address. Some organizations prohibit this to maintain control over email, or may have policies on where emails can be forwarded. Some MDAs also allow users to create their own forwarding rules.

The MDA is usually a function of the MTA. The MTA might deliver the mail itself or pass the email to an external command should it determine that the email should be delivered locally.

Once the MDA has processed the message and delivered it to a mailbox, the email is considered to be delivered. It's up to the recipient to read the email.

Mail Server

The final piece of the puzzle is the mail server that reads the user's mailbox and allows the recipient to read the email. Usually the user reads the email in the same MUA she uses to send email. This MUA can connect to the mail server with the same proprietary protocol used to send messages. If emails are sent with SMTP, something else needs to be used, as SMTP is only for sending messages, not reading them.

The Post Office Protocol (POP) or Internet Message Access Protocol (IMAP) are used by the MUA to read emails off the mail server. POP is primarily used to download emails to the local computer and delete them off the computer, and IMAP usually leaves the email on the server and reads the email over the network.

POP is simple as it was designed to transfer email to the client and then delete it off the server. IMAP was designed to mirror features on the client so that more work could be performed server-side; therefore it supports folders and searching.

The MDA and mail server are closely linked in that the MDA must write email in a place and format that the mail server can read, but they don't necessarily need to be the same software.

Creating Aliases and Forwarding Email

When the MTA decides that the email it received is to be delivered to a local account it hands off the email to the MDA. The MDA can then deliver the email to a local account's email box, which is usually a file in /var/spool/mail. Before delivery, the MDA first checks to see whether there are additional instructions on how to handle the email, which is called an alias.

Mail aliases are systemwide and stored in a file called **/etc/aliases**. They are system-wide because an alias does not belong to a user. The email comes in, the MDA sees there is an alias for that name, and the MDA delivers the email to the user specified in the alias.

The format of **/etc/aliases** is simple:

```
alias: recipient
```

An alias can have multiple recipients, in which case they are separated by a comma:

```
alias: recipient1,recipient2
```

An alias name may or may not exist as a local user account. For example, it is common to send root's email to a named user:

```
root: sean
```

Comments are allowed with the hash mark:

```
# Send root's mail to sean
root: sean
```

Even though the root account exists, any mail that was to be delivered to root goes to sean instead.

Committing Changes

Your changes to **/etc/aliases** do not go into effect immediately. Your MDA actually reads a database file called **/etc/aliases.db**, which is optimized for reading. Making your email software read the file every time would put a damper on performance, so you need to compile the text file into something that can perform lookups quickly.

The **newaliases** command updates the **aliases.db** file for you so that your changes to **aliases** take effect. This command must be run as root because the permissions of the files should not allow users to modify it.

If there are no problems, the **newaliases** command returns nothing. If there is a formatting problem you get an error:

```
# newaliases
postalias: warning: /etc/aliases, line 96: need name:value pair
```

The server usually lets you know if you forgot to run **newaliases** with a message in the mail log, usually **/var/log/messages**.

```
warning: database /etc/aliases.db is older than source file /etc/
aliases
```

This indicates that you haven't run the **newaliases** command since last changing **/etc/aliases**.

Other Types of Aliases

You have seen how to alias a single address to other local accounts, such as to give Rebecca all the emails going to the human resources alias. There are more things you can do to the email other than deliver it to a local account.

The aliases file also accepts fully qualified email addresses. If you were to have a line in your **aliases** file like:

```
isaac: i.smith@example.com
```

any email destined to the isaac account would be sent back to the MTA to be directed to i.smith@example.com.

The destination of the alias could also be a file:

```
support: /var/log/support.please.ignore
```

would redirect all email to the support account to a file in **/var/log**. Imagine how much easier an administrator's job would be if she didn't have to deal with those pesky users!

The destination can also be a script if the name of the file is prefixed with the pipe (|) operator:

```
support: | /usr/local/bin/new_ticket.sh
```

In this case, the email would be passed to a script that would presumably ingest the email into a new support ticket.

Don't forget, you need to run **newaliases** after making any changes!

User-Defined Forwarding

Users can define their own forwarding rules by placing a file called **.forward** (note the leading period) in their home directory, containing the forward instructions.

The instructions in the **~/.forward** file are the same as those in the **/etc/aliases** file. The only difference in the format is that there is no need to specify the aliased user, as it is the owner of the **~/.forward** file. Thus, if user **Isaac** had a **~/.forward** file containing i.smith@example.com, all his email would be redirected to the external address.

One thing to keep in mind is that an alias can refer to other aliases. If Isaac wanted to redirect his mail offsite and keep a copy locally, he would need to escape the local alias to prevent it from being reprocessed as an external redirect:

```
\isaac
i.smith@example.com
```

Managing Queues

An MTA receives a message and stores it in a queue for later processing. A queue allows the MTA to process an email later if the destination MTA isn't listening, or sends an error indicating your MTA should retry the connection later. The **mailq** (mail queue) command shows the queue, shown in Example 17-8.

Example 17-8   A Mail Queue

```
# mailq
-Queue ID-   --Size--   ----Arrival Time---- -Sender/Recipient-------
AC1687363*    3229   Tue Apr 14 05:48:57    MAILER-DAEMON
                                            cfvxfvrsi@example.com


451817349     651 Sat Apr 11 13:06:09  nginx@www.noreply.com
       (connect to example.org[172.16.33.111]:25: Connection timed out)
                                     jermainewillilams@example.org
```

This command looks at the mail queue files in **/var/spool/mqueue** and displays them on the screen. You can see from Example 17-8 that there are two messages in the queue. It is normal to see mail there as typos and spam cause delivery to all sorts of incorrectly configured servers.

If you are looking into problems with delivery to a particular destination, the mail queue is a good place to look, as you'll see the emails waiting to go out there. The logs, usually **/var/log/maillog**, are also a good place to look for a historical accounting of each email.

mailq is actually a command from sendmail, but due to the compatibility layer most distributions put in place, it runs the appropriate command depending on your MTA of choice. For example, Postfix uses **postqueue -p**, exim uses **exim -bp**, and qmail uses **qmail-qread**.

Even **newaliases** is a sendmail compatibility command!

Summary

Printing involves a series of discrete steps that get a print job from an application to the final printer. CUPS, the Common Unix Printing System, uses the Internet Printing Protocol (IPP) for communication, as opposed to the older Line Printer Remote (LPR) based commands.

A series of command line tools allow you to enable and disable both printers and queues, and to query and modify the jobs being processed.

Email is much like printing in that there are several discrete steps. The Mail Transfer Agent does the bulk of the work in moving email closer to its destination, relying on the Mail Delivery Agent to do the final work of delivering the email to the user's mailbox.

Email aliases are used to redirect email from one user to another, even if that first user doesn't exist. Users can also set up their own forwarding rules, such as to send email to another account or pass it through a filter.

Exam Preparation Tasks

As mentioned in the section "How to Use This Book" in the Introduction, you have a few choices for exam preparation: the exercises here, Chapter 21, "Final Preparation," and the practice exams on the DVD.

Review All Key Topics

Review the most important topics in this chapter, noted with the Key Topics icon in the outer margin of the page. Table 17-2 lists a reference of these key topics and the page numbers on which each is found.

Table 17-2 Key Topics for Chapter 17

Key Topic Element	Description	Page Number
Paragraph	Configuration page is at http://localhost:631	470
List	The various printer states	475
Paragraph	**lp** and **lpr** commands are used to print	478
Paragraph	Printing multiple copies with **lp -n** or **lpr -#**	478
Paragraph	**lpstat** views the status of a queue	479
Paragraph	**lp** commands operate on the default printer; **-P** selects a different printer	479
Paragraph	**lprm** with no **job id** removes the first job	480
Paragraph	**cups** commands take the name of the queue directly	480
Paragraph	**cupsenable** reenables a stopped printer	481
Paragraph	The CUPS web interface doesn't respond to other hosts by default	481
List	A list of key configuration files	482
List	Current Linux MTAs	486
Paragraph	Mail aliases are in **/etc/aliases**	489
Paragraph	Aliases changes must be followed by **newaliases**	490
Paragraph	Users can forward email with commands in the **.forward** file	491
Paragraph	**mailq** shows the status of the mail queue and must be run as root	491
Paragraph	**mailq** is a compatibility command, as is **newaliases**	492

Define Key Terms

Define the following key terms from this chapter and check your answers in the glossary:

print spooler, print queue, line printer remote, Internet Printing Protocol, Common Unix Printing System, CUPS backend, Mail User Agent, Mail Transfer Agent, Simple Mail Transfer Protocol, relay, Sendmail, Postfix, Qmail, Exim, bounce, Mail Delivery Agent, aliasing, forwarding

Review Questions

The answers to these review questions are in Appendix A.

1. What is the proper URL to access the CUPS administrative interface running on the same machine as the web browser?

   a. http://localhost

   b. https://localhost

   c. http://localhost:631

   d. http://localhost:389

2. Which of the following printer states would indicate that something went wrong with the printer and that some administrative action is necessary?

   a. Idle

   b. Processing

   c. Stopped

   d. Paused

3. How would you determine the default printer that print jobs go to? Type the command and all arguments.

4. A user calls you in panic and says he printed something to a printer called OfficePrinter and it's sending out page after page of junk. You turn to your command line and check the queue:

```
OfficePrinter is printing
Rank    Owner   Job    File(s)                    Total Size
1st     john    3      randomjunk             8765309 bytes
```

   How do you stop the job?

   a. **lprm -P OfficePrinter**

   b. **lprm -P OfficePrinter 1**

   c. **lpq -P OfficePrinter --delete-all**

   d. Turn off the printer.

5. One of your printers, CentralArea, has a broken paper feeding mechanism and won't be fixed for a few days. Rather than queue jobs until it's fixed, how can you make things so that people trying to print to it get an immediate error, without needing to delete the printer?

   a. **lpstat --disable -P CentralArea**

   b. **cupsreject -P CentralArea**

   c. **lpadmin -x CentralArea**

   d. **cupsreject CentralArea**

6. What are two example of Mail Transfer Agents that operate as a series of daemons with separated responsibilities?

    a. Sendmail

    b. Qmail

    c. Exim

    d. Postfix

7. You have been asked to send all emails to hr@yourcompany.com to rebecca@yourcompany.com and edward@yourcompany.com. What's the name of the file that you will be editing? Use the full path to the file.

8. After adding an email alias to the appropriate file, what command should you run?

    a. **mailq**

    b. **update-aliases**

    c. **postmap**

    d. **newaliases**

9. A user comes to you and asks how she can send all her email to her second account, j.smith@example.com, instead of reading it locally. What are the instructions you would give her?

    a. Run **sendmail -f j.smith@example.com**.

    b. Add **j.smith@example.com** to **~/.forward**.

    c. Add j.smith@example.com to /etc/aliases.

    d. Add **j.smith@example.com** to **~/.aliases**.

This chapter covers the following topics:

- Maintain System Time
- System Logging
- Rotating Logs

This chapter covers the following exam topics:

- Maintain system time: 108.1
- System logging: 108.2

## CHAPTER 18

Logging and Time Services

When confronted with a problem you will usually want to look at the system logs to try and piece together what happened so that you can work on a solution. Linux has a built-in logging facility that provides a way for each application to write a log message that will live on disk or on another system. By piecing together your logs you can start to understand your problems and find problems that have yet to become user complaints.

Your Linux machine also has a clock that should be correct. Just like a watch that has the wrong time, a server with a bad clock is annoying and can lead to incorrect information. It is difficult to understand logs because the log entries won't line up with reality. Some protocols rely on strict clock synchronization such that a clock that is wrong by more than a few minutes might not allow people to log in.

"Do I Know This Already?" Quiz

The "Do I Know This Already?" quiz enables you to assess whether you should read this entire chapter or simply jump to the "Exam Preparation Tasks" section for review. If you are in doubt, read the entire chapter. Table 18-1 outlines the major headings in this chapter and the corresponding "Do I Know This Already?" quiz questions. You can find the answers in Appendix A, "Answers to the 'Do I Know This Already?' Quizzes and Review Questions."

Table 18-1   "Do I Know This Already?" Foundation Topics Section-to-Question Mapping

Foundation Topics Section	Questions Covered in This Section
Maintain System Time	1-3
System Logging	4-6
Rotating Logs	7-8

1. The source of the Linux system clock is

   a. The motherboard's real-time clock

   b. The Network Time Protocol daemon

   c. The Linux kernel

   d. A GPS clock

2. If you ran **date "+%Y %m %d %H %M"** on April 26, 2015 at 8:19 p.m., which of the following would you see?

   a. 2015 04 26 20 19

   b. 2015-04-26 8:19

   c. 1430097577

   d. Sun Apr 26 8:19:45pm CDT 2015

3. If you ran **hwclock -w**, what would happen?

   a. The hardware clock's time would be displayed in the local time zone.

   b. The software clock time would be copied to the hardware clock.

   c. The hardware clock time would be copied to the software clock.

   d. The hardware clock's time would be displayed in UTC.

4. If your syslog.conf file contained a line such as

   ```
   *.notice;mail.none   /var/log/foo
   ```

   which of the following messages would make it into /var/log/foo? (Choose two.)

   a. kernel.warning

   b. cron.info

   c. mail.err

   d. cron.err

5. Which command will log a message to syslog from the command line?

   a. logger This is a message

   b. log This is a message

   c. syslog "This is a message"

   d. echo "This is a message" | syslogd

6. How do you watch the systemd journal logs in real time?

    a. **tail -f /var/log/journal/***

    b. **journalctl | tail -f**

    c. **journalctl -f**

    d. **journalctl --continuous**

7. You have configured logrotate to rotate your custom application's log file, but the logs do not seem to be written to the new file—they are still going to the timestamped file. What could be needed? (Choose two.)

    a. The application is not a candidate for **logrotate**.

    b. logrotate is not running.

    c. You need the **copytruncate** option.

    d. You need to restart your **logrotate** daemon.

8. Log rotation is triggered:

    a. From the log rotation daemon

    b. From cron or anacron

    c. By the kernel

    d. Manually

Foundation Topics

Maintain System Time

Your computer has a clock that is used for many reasons, including

- Setting timestamps on files

- Determining when scheduled jobs are to run

- Annotating log entries with the time they were received

- Showing the current time to the user

- Cryptographic operations that rely on a timestamp to expire tokens

If the clock on one computer is different from another computer, problems can arise. It is difficult to correlate logs between systems. Jobs may run at the wrong time. Tokens may arrive already expired. You might miss lunch.

A time difference of even a few seconds can be troublesome. If you are looking at logs between two computers, you may misinterpret the order in which things happened, or miss matching up logs.

Not One, But Two Clocks

Your Linux machine actually has two clocks. The *hardware clock* is on the motherboard of your computer and is implemented as a separate chip. This chip is called the *real-time clock* because it is separate from other functions on the motherboard. It continues running even when your computer is off so that when you boot your computer you have a way of knowing the current date and time.

The other clock is the *system clock* and it is a part of the Linux kernel. When you are asking the kernel for the time, such as to write a timestamp to a log entry, you are getting the system clock time.

The hardware and system clocks do differ from each other and from the real time, in a process known as *drift*. A clock drifts because it runs slightly faster or slower, and therefore needs periodic synchronization.

Working with the System Clock

You can check the current time with the **date** command:

```
$ date
Wed Apr 15 14:36:05 CDT 2015
```

The default output shows the date and time, including the time zone, according to your current locale. For a discussion about locales and internationalization see Chapter 11, "Customizing Shell Environments." You can quickly display the time in Universal Coordinated Time with the **-u** flag.

```
$ date -u
Wed Apr 15 19:36:05 UTC 2015
```

The system time is kept as the number of seconds since January 1, 1970, which is also known as the Unix epoch:

```
$ date +%s
1429126571
```

At the time of writing it has been some 1.4 billion seconds since the Unix epoch. There are roughly 31.5 million seconds in a year.

You can also change the date and time, if you are running as the root user, by passing the new time to the **date** command. The format of the setting is complicated, described by the man page as **[MMDDhhmm[[CC]YY][.ss]]**.

Items in square brackets indicate optional arguments so you can pass nothing, which doesn't set the clock at all. The minimum amount of information is the month, day, hour, and minute (MMDDhhmm); each is two digits. You can optionally specify the year by appending it to the minute. The year can either be two digits or four digits. The command returns the value, in words, that you set it to. Thus the samples in Example 18-1 are almost all identical.

Example 18-1   Setting the Time in Various Formats

```
# date 041514492015.35
Wed Apr 15 14:49:35 CDT 2015
# date 04151449
Wed Apr 15 14:49:00 CDT 2015
# date 0415144915
Wed Apr 15 14:49:00 CDT 2015
# date 041514492015
Wed Apr 15 14:49:00 CDT 2015
```

In Example 18-1 the commands all set the date to 2:49 in the afternoon of April 15, 2015. Where the year isn't specified, such as the second example, **date** assumes the year hasn't changed. If no seconds are given, that value is assumed to be 0, so the first example is the only one to set a seconds value.

The **date** command can display the time in a variety of formats, which lends itself well to using in shell scripts. Tell **date** to display the time in a different format with a plus sign (**+**) and then a format string. Common format strings are listed in Table 18-2.

Table 18-2   Common Format Strings for the **date** Command

Format String	Value
%Y	The four-digit year, such as 2015
%m	The two-digit month, such as 01
%d	The two-digit day, such as 13
%H	The current hour in 24-hour time, such as 15
%M	The current minute, such as 09
%S	The current second, such as 59
%s	The current time since epoch, such as 1429373522
%%	A literal %

If you need a timestamp, the current time since epoch is an easy candidate:

```
$ date +%s
1429373851
```

Or perhaps you need something more user friendly, such as the date and time components concatenated:

```
$ date +%Y%m%d%H%M%S
20150418111854
```

In a shell script you might capture this in a temporary variable and use it for later, such as shown in Example 18-2.

Example 18-2   Using **date** in a Shell Script

```
#!/bin/bash
NOW=$(date +%Y%m%d%H%M%S)
cp -r /var/www/html/ /var/backup/website.$NOW
echo "Backed up site into /var/backup/website.$NOW" | mail root
```

Example 18-2 saves the current timestamp into a variable and then uses it in two places: First for the unique name of a directory containing backups, and then to tell the root user where the files were stored. If the script were to calculate the current timestamp each time it was needed, it would change as the script ran.

Another advantage of using a timestamp in a file is that it sorts nicely and is easy to pick out particular periods with **grep**.

You are not limited to just using the format strings shown previously; you can add arbitrary strings that will be echoed back to you. For example, the script in Example 18-2 could eliminate some duplication by having **date** calculate the whole file path:

```
$ date +/var/backup/website.%Y%m%d%H%M%S
/var/backup/website.20150418112516
```

You can also quote the whole format string to get more complicated output that includes spaces:

```
$ date +"Today is %A"
Today is Saturday
```

Working with the Hardware Clock

Your computer has a real-time clock (RTC) ticking away on the motherboard. It's usually only used when the computer boots so that Linux has something from which to set the system clock. Keeping the hardware clock relatively accurate means that your boot logs will have the correct time.

Some computers don't have a hardware clock. In particular, some virtualization technologies don't expose the clock to the underlying virtual machine. Here, a larger server called a *virtual machine host* is emulating many smaller servers called *virtual machine guests*. The host controls the guest's system clock so there is no need for an RTC in the guest. You'll know you don't have a hardware clock if the commands in this section give you an error.

The **hwclock** Command

The **hwclock** command manipulates the hardware clock by talking to the motherboard. You need to be root to run the command.

```
# hwclock
Sat 18 Apr 2015 12:12:11 PM CDT   -0.189472 seconds
```

The output of **hwclock** is much like that of **date**. The difference is that there is an extra value at the end, expressed in seconds. This value calculates how long it was between the time the command was started and the clock was read, which is used inside the **hwclock** command to help correct for drift. When viewing the current hardware clock time this should be ignored.

The hardware clock is simple and has no notion of time zones. You are given the choice of running your hardware clock in UTC or local time when you install your system. You can see which mode you are in by looking at **/etc/adjtime**, shown in Example 18-3.

Example 18-3   /etc/adjtime

```
31.307682 1429376895 0.000000
429376895
LOCAL
```

The first two lines track any calibration that has been done on the hardware clock. The last line is either **LOCAL** or **UTC** to indicate the hardware clock is in UTC or local time.

Some systems don't have the **adjtime** file, which means they've never had the clocks synchronized, and the time is in UTC.

If your hardware clock uses UTC, you should check the hardware clock using the **-u** flag.

```
# hwclock -u
Sat 18 Apr 2015 12:40:40 PM CDT  -0.906883 seconds
```

Synchronizing Time Between Clocks

The two clocks should be synchronized; otherwise, drift between them will make troubleshooting difficult. The **hwclock** command has two functions to do this:

```
hwclock -w or hwclock --systohc writes the time in the system clock to
the hardware clock.
hwclock -s or hwclock --hctosys sets the system clock using the hard-
ware clock's time
```

Usually you will want to use your system clock as the canonical source of time; otherwise, the time on your system will seem to jump frequently as the time is reset.

If you are using something to keep the system clock in time with another time source, such as the Network Time Protocol described in the next section, it will likely set a kernel flag that automatically writes the system clock to the hardware clock every 11 minutes.

Network Time Protocol

Fortunately it is easy to keep your clock in sync without manually fiddling with the clock. The *Network Time Protocol (NTP)* is a protocol that enables a computer to get its time from a remote server and to be accurate within milliseconds even if the network is unreliable. Coupled with NTP is a globally distributed network of freely usable servers that participate in the protocol.

Throughout the world are various clock sources, such as government agencies broadcasting the time over radio, high-quality cesium clocks, or devices that read the current time from satellites. These clocks are called *reference clocks* in the NTP system.

NTP servers that get their time directly from a reference clock are called *stratum 1 servers*. These servers are considered to have the most accurate time in the NTP hierarchy. Even with this accuracy, there is no guarantee that all the servers have the same time!

An NTP server that gets its time from a stratum 1 server is called a stratum 2 server, and a server that gets its time from that is called a stratum 3 server, and so on.

Generally your server will be at stratum 3 or 4, which means it is getting its time from a stratum 2 or 3 server. If you have more than a dozen computers you probably want to have a small pool of servers at stratum 2 and have the other servers configured to point to that pool, making them stratum 3. This reduces load on your network and makes for more consistent time across your machines. Four time servers are enough for most environments, and they can run alongside existing applications.

Setting the Time from the Command Line

The simplest way to use NTP is to set the clock with the **ntpdate** command. You need to be root because you are setting the system clock. This asks the provided remote for the time and sets your local time to that value:

```
# ntpdate ntp1.torix.ca
18 Apr 15:19:54 ntpdate[11559]: adjust time server 206.108.0.131
offset 0.003552 sec
```

Here the name of the remote server is ntp1.torix.ca, and the local clock was only 3/1000 of a second out of sync with the remote server. If the local server was further out of sync, even if it was hours ahead or behind, the time would be abruptly changed to the new value.

The pool.ntp.org Servers

At one point you needed to know the names of a few publicly available NTP servers to use NTP, and you would get this from a web page that changed frequently. The pool.ntp.org project hides that complexity by pooling all the public servers behind a DNS alias. The servers themselves are run by individuals like you who have contributed their time servers to the greater good.

pool.ntp.org gives you access to the global list of NTP servers. You also have four aliases to use:

- 0.pool.ntp.org
- 1.pool.ntp.org
- 2.pool.ntp.org
- 3.pool.ntp.org

Each one of these resolves to a list of servers geographically close to your server. Depending on your distribution your aliases might be slightly different, such as X.debian.pool.ntp.org, but they are all the same set of servers.

There are four different names for the same set of servers because some systems expect to connect to multiple servers by different names, and the number in front of the name is an easy way to accomplish that.

Configuring ntpd

The **ntpd** daemon is a long-running daemon that continually adjusts the local clock, as opposed to **ntpdate**'s one-off behavior. **ntpd** runs in the background and continually queries remote servers for their time while learning about how network conditions are affecting the communications and compensating for local time drift. Thus, a server running **ntpd** always has the correct time with no need for a periodic job to reset the clock.

The configuration file for **ntpd** is **/etc/ntp.conf**. Your distribution should include a more complicated file that restricts queries and sets up cryptographic keys, but a simple file is shown in Example 18-4.

Example 18-4   An Example **ntp.conf**

```
driftfile /var/lib/ntp/drift


server 0.fedora.pool.ntp.org iburst
server 1.fedora.pool.ntp.org iburst
server 2.fedora.pool.ntp.org iburst
server 3.fedora.pool.ntp.org iburst
```

Example 18-4 shows two directives. The first is the **driftfile** that tracks local clock drift over time, and allows ntpd to compensate. The second directive is a set of one or more servers from which the local server attempts to synchronize. Having more than one server results in more accurate clock setting and redundancy should one server go out of service or become unreliable.

If the clock is out of sync, ntpd gradually brings it back into alignment by speeding up the local clock or slowing it down as necessary. If the time difference is too great, which is defined as 1,000 seconds by default, ntpd will exit and you will need to set the clock with **ntpdate** before continuing.

ntpd also enables a mode in the Linux kernel where the hardware clock is set every 11 minutes. Thus a system running **ntpd** has both clocks in sync.

Monitoring ntpd

The **ntpq** command is used to query an NTP server for its statistics and connects to the local host by default. The two commands that are most helpful are **peers** and **associations**, as shown in Example 18-5.

Example 18-5   Querying an NTP Server's Peers

```
ntpq> peers
     remote          refid         st t when poll reach delay offset jitter
==============================================================================
+174.137.63.116   206.108.0.131   2 u   47   64    1  44.521  -3.491  0.485
-ntp3.tranzeo.co  206.108.0.132   2 u   46   64    1  49.107  -5.770  4.501
*ntp1.torix.ca    .PPS.           1 u   45   64    1  83.315   0.505  0.634
+c1110364-13198.  132.163.4.103   2 u   44   64    1  49.312   1.754  4.643
ntpq> associations

ind assid status  conf reach auth condition  last_event cnt
==========================================================
  1 10782  943a   yes   yes  none candidate    sys_peer  3
  2 10783  9324   yes   yes  none   outlyer   reachable  2
  3 10784  963a   yes   yes  none  sys.peer    sys_peer  3
  4 10785  9424   yes   yes  none candidate   reachable  2
```

The **peers** command gives details about each of the servers defined with the **server** keyword in the configuration. The **association** command gives more details on each server, including how well the remote server is performing.

In Example 18-5 there are four servers. The first column shows the name of the re-mote server but is prefixed by a special character. If that character is a *, that server is the currently active peer. If the character is a +, the server is a good time source but not the main server. Anything else and the server is not considered to be good for time synchronization and will be monitored.

The second column shows the name of the remote server from where your machine is getting its time. The third column shows which stratum that server is, and the re-maining columns are statistics used by **ntpd**.

The **associations** command gives even greater detail about each server in the same order that they appear in the **peers** command. The most interesting column is the condition column, which explains the state of the server. The **peers** command showed that the second server was not being used because the name of the server was prefixed with a minus sign (-), and the condition of that server is **outlyer**. This means that the time on that server was too different from the others to be trusted.

Other than the condition, you can see that the servers are all reachable.

System Logging

Logs tell you what was happening while you weren't looking. The kernel and run-ning applications emit logs when events happen. These logs might be informational, such as a web request, or they might be errors such as the ntpd daemon exiting be-cause the time difference was too large.

Most applications in Linux log in some form or another. Linux provides a central-ized logging facility that applications can use. This means that an application can use a standard interface to log and doesn't have to worry about configuring file loca-tions. This also means that the administrator can split up logs according to function, or to ignore unimportant logs and email errors directly to themselves.

Some applications, such as web servers, choose to do their own logging. Usually this is needed to get the performance or customization that the application needs, or sometimes it's because the application was designed to work on many different sys-tems, some that don't have syslog. As a systems administrator you will have to deal with all kinds of logs.

systemd and syslog

Linux has two different logging systems: syslog and systemd's journal. syslog is a standardized system that can receive messages from local applications or remote servers and write them to disk or send to another server. It is ubiquitous such that many network enabled appliances generate syslog messages. The systemd journal is a newer form of logging for distributions that have moved to systemd. Fortunately, it is backward compatible so that applications that can log to syslog can also log to systemd, and it can also forward messages to a syslog server for centralized logging.

Applications that use systemd's version of logging can also log the additional metadata tracked by the journal. For example, the name of the method and the line number are logged alongside the message, which allows for additional statistics to be gathered.

syslog

syslog is a simple protocol, which has led to its adoption across many different systems and applications.

A message can be logged in several ways:

- From within an application using the **syslog** library call
- From the command line using the **logger** command
- Remotely by connecting to a syslog server over the network

A message is logged with a severity and a facility, and the **syslog daemon** takes care of processing the message. The severities are listed in Table 18-3.

Table 18-3 Syslog Severities

Level	Tag	Meaning
0	emerg	Emergency: The system is unusable.
1	alert	Alert: Immediate action is needed to prevent a failure.
2	crit	Critical: The system has reached a critical level, such as disk space almost running out.
3	err	Error: Some part of the system encountered an error.
4	warn warning	Warning: Something happened that may have been processed incorrectly.
5	notice	Notice: Not an error condition, but may need special handling.
6	info	Informational: A normal log entry about a routine event that happened successfully.
7	debug	Debug: A message about internal state that is for debugging problems.

When you log at a particular level, you're saying that you're only capturing logs at that level or with a lower priority level and throwing away anything else. For example, most systems log at the informational level (6). This would ignore debug logs (7) and capture anything else. You may decide to log at the warning level (4) to ignore reports of normal operation at levels 5, 6, and 7 and only concern yourself with level 4 warnings and more severe items at levels 1, 2, and 3.

For the exam, it is important to remember the seven log levels and their order.

Each log is also tied to a facility that describes what generated the log. The combination of facility and level gives you control over what is stored. You may choose to log the email system at the informational level, which gives you reports of each email that goes through the system, but logs cron at warning, so you only hear about things that go wrong.

Table 18-4 lists the available facilities.

Table 18-4   Log Facilities

Tag	Type of Messages
kern	Kernel messages
user	Random user level messages
mail	Email server
daemon	Other system daemons
auth	Security logs that can be public
syslog	Internal messages for syslog
lpr	Printing
cron	Scheduled jobs such as cron and at
authpriv	Security logs that need to be private
local0-7	Eight different user-definable facilities

The syslog daemon is responsible for the collection and distribution of log messages. You can think of it as a pipeline that takes messages from various sources and directs them to the appropriate destination. Figure 18-1 shows a typical syslog configuration in graphical form.

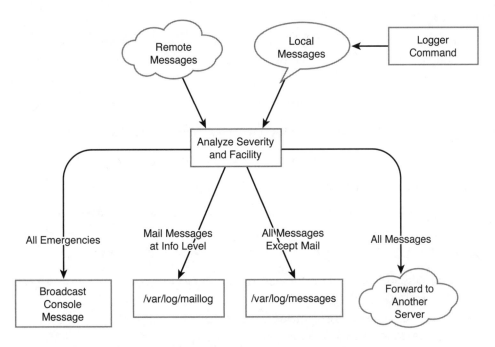

Figure 18-1   The flow of logging information

In Figure 18-1 the logs come in from one of two places: remotely, over the network, or from the local system. Locally, the **logger** command acts as an application and takes messages from the command and turns them into local syslog messages.

The middle box analyzes the messages and, based on the severity and facility, decides where to send them. Starting from the left, anything with an emergency severity is displayed to the system console. This is partially to capture the attention of anyone who happens to be watching the console, but also to ensure a trace is left. If the log is truly about an emergency, it's possible that it's related to the disks or the system is in the process of crashing. Next, all mail messages logged with a severity of at least info are stored in **/var/log/maillog**. All messages except for mail messages go to **/var/log/messages**. Finally, all messages are sent to a remote syslog server.

A single message may be sent to multiple outputs, or none. An emergency mail message would go to the console, **/var/log/maillog**, and the remote syslog server. A mail related debugging message would only go to the remote server.

Figure 18-1 only shows a sample. Your needs may be different and call for a different configuration.

The logger Command

The **logger** command is helpful for both testing your logging configuration and for logging within scripts. The easiest way to use it is just to pass the log message on the command line:

```
$ logger Starting script processing
```

Looking in the logs, such as **/var/log/messages**, you see something like

```
Apr 20 19:55:02 bob sean: Starting script processing
```

The log entry contains both the hostname (bob) and the user (sean).

For additional information you can pass the process ID with the **-i** flag.

```
$ logger -i Starting script processing
Apr 20 19:55:57 bob sean[8969]: Starting script processing
```

The default destination of the message is the user facility at the notice level, which can be overridden with the **-p** flag:

```
$ logger -i -p mail.info Checking user quotas
Apr 20 19:57:28 bob sean[9054]: Checking user quotas
```

Configuring syslogd

Linux has several syslog daemons that can be used, but the simplest is part of the sysklogd package. The name is an amalgamation of **syslog** and **klogd**. **syslogd** is the component that handles the logging of messages as described in Figure 18-1. **klogd** listens specifically for kernel logs and forwards them to **syslogd**. **klogd** can also do processing on the message before sending it along, such as to translate memory addresses into names that would be helpful to kernel developers.

klogd has very little to configure, so the interesting parts are found in **syslogd**.

syslogd's configuration file is in **/etc/syslog.conf**. This file defines a set of rules, one per line. Each rule is evaluated, and if the log matches that rule, the log is sent to the destination specified in the rule.

Example 18-6 shows a simple **syslog.conf**.

Example 18-6   A Sample **/etc/syslog.conf**

```
# This is a comment
authpriv.*                                      /var/log/secure
*.info;mail.none;authpriv.none;cron.none        /var/log/messages
mail.*                                          -/var/log/maillog
```

```
cron.*                                  /var/log/cron
*.emerg                                 *
local7.*                                /var/log/boot.log
local4.*                                /var/log/slapd.log
```

Comments start with a hash sign and are ignored by **syslogd**. The rules in Example 18-6 are split into a selector and a destination, separated by whitespace. Each selector is made up of one or more patterns, and each pattern is a facility and a severity separated by a period (.).

Most of the patterns in Example 18-6 have a single facility and a selector of *, which means any severity will match. This could also have been written with a severity of **debug**, as that is the lowest severity possible. Thus, **authpriv.** matches all the private authentication messages. If the destination part of the rule is a filename, the logs go to that file.

The line associated with the mail facility has a dash (-) in front of the destination. This tells syslogd that it shouldn't commit each log entry to disk as it's logged but to let the kernel write to disk when it has time, as the mail facility can log heavily and this improves performance at a cost of potential lost data after a crash.

The second selector has more than one pattern; each is separated by a semicolon (;). The first pattern matches any facility at info level or greater, and the remaining three use the special **none** severity to ignore any log coming from mail, authpriv, or cron. This is because those logs have their own files and this eliminates duplication.

The ***.emerg** selector matches any log at the emergency level and sends it to a special destination of *, which means to send a message to the console of anyone logged in to the system.

While individuals are free to place logs wherever they want, several conventions have emerged to make logs easier to find as you move from system to system (see Table 18-5).

Table 18-5 Common Logs and Their Location

Log File	Purpose
/var/log/messages	General purpose log messages that aren't in one of the other files
/var/log/secure	Security logs, such as records of connection attempts and failures
/var/log/maillog	All logs relating to email
/var/log/cron	Logs of schedule job activity
/var/log/xferlog	Logs of local File Transfer Protocol (FTP) server activity

Splitting each major application into its own log files makes it easier to find what you want and doesn't mingle logs between two applications when you are reviewing them. A common pattern is to watch a log in real time, also called "following a log." To follow a log, run **tail -f logfile**, such as **tail -f /var/log/secure** to watch for people logging in.

Once you have more than a few servers, especially if more than one do the same role, you'll get tired of accessing different servers to read logs. One solution is to have the various syslogds on your servers to forward all their messages to a single server. With that in place you can read all your logs on a single server.

Centralizing your syslogging requires two things. First, the centralized syslog server must be started with the **-r** flag, which tells it that it can receive remote messages.

Next you need a rule that forwards the desirable messages to the remote server by supplying a destination hostname prefixed with an **@**. For example,

```
*.info      @logserver.example.com
```

sends all info messages and above to logserver.example.com for central analysis.

Other syslog Implementations

The ksyslogd package isn't the only syslog implementation available for Linux systems. There are two prominent alternatives: rsyslogd and syslog-ng.

rsyslogd is meant to be a "rocket-fast" implementation of a syslog daemon with support for plugins, alternate storage mechanisms, and more flexible rules processing. With rsyslogd you can store your logs in a database, filter the logs based on keywords, and keep statistics. One advantage of rsyslogd is that the basic ksyslogd configuration is also a valid rsyslogd configuration, which gives you an easy transition mechanism.

syslog-ng is a next generation syslog server that offers both open source and commercial versions. It has many of the same features as rsyslogd, but the configuration syntax has been reworked. This means that complicated filters are easier to write than with rsyslogd.

systemd Logging

The systemd set of tools is being rapidly adopted by major Linux distributions. For better or worse, systemd has its own logging system called the systemd journal or journald.

The journal's main difference from syslogd is that it logs to a binary file and annotates each log entry with metadata rather than using a text format. This gives you several advantages over syslogd:

- Looking at the logs is the same no matter which distribution you are using.

- You can query on metadata such as the level, facility, or message, and by date and time.

- You have access to more metadata than possible in a text file, such as the full command line, process id, binary, and security privileges of the process.

- You can annotate the logs with your own metadata, such as source file, line number, or customer id.

Additionally, systemd integrates the journal with the rest of systemd such that anything a daemon writes to the console is saved as a proper log entry. In the current init system, each daemon is responsible for its own logging. The daemon's startup script is supposed to capture any logs that the daemon prints to the console. In the system model, this is all logged into the journal without any extra work needed by the startup script.

Querying the Log

The journal's log is stored in a binary format under **/var/log/journal**, so you need special tools to read the log.

You access the journal using the **journalctl** command. By default you see the entire contents of the journal file on your screen. Depending on your configuration, such as the contents of the **PAGER** environment variable, the output might be paginated. Example 18-7 shows a typical, unfiltered, log.

Example 18-7   Viewing the Unfiltered Log with **journalctl**

```
# journalctl
-- Logs begin at Mon 2014-12-15 22:40:24 CST, end at Sun 2015-04-26
12:56:07 CDT. --
Dec 15 22:40:24 localhost.localdomain systemd-journal[439]: Runtime
journal is using 8.0M (max allowed 100.0M, trying to leave 150.1M free
of 992.8M available → current limit 100.0M).
Dec 15 22:40:24 localhost.localdomain systemd-journal[439]: Runtime
journal is using 8.0M (max allowed 100.0M, trying to leave 150.1M free
of 992.8M available → current limit 100.0M).
Dec 15 22:40:24 localhost.localdomain systemd-journald[86]: Received
SIGTERM from PID 1 (systemd).
```

```
Dec 15 22:40:24 localhost.localdomain kernel: audit: type=1404
audit(1418704824.175:2): enforcing=1 old_enforcing=0 auid=4294967295
ses=4294967295

Dec 15 22:40:24 localhost.localdomain kernel: SELinux: 2048 avtab hash
slots, 111331 rules.

Dec 15 22:40:24 localhost.localdomain kernel: SELinux: 2048 avtab hash
slots, 111331 rules.

Dec 15 22:40:24 localhost.localdomain kernel: SELinux:  8 users, 103
roles, 4980 types, 295 bools, 1 sens, 1024 cats

Dec 15 22:40:24 localhost.localdomain kernel: SELinux:  83 classes,
111331 rules

Output truncated...
```

Example 18-7 shows all the logs held within systemd's journal. Rather than unbounded text files like syslog, the journal keeps a rolling log that expires old entries as the log file hits its size limit. By default the journal uses up to 10% of the file system for logs.

The system that Example 18-7 was run on did not have many logs, so the first log shown is of the first boot. You can see that the journal is documenting its size usage, followed by the system booting up.

As a systems administrator you're often interested in keeping a watch on the logs, so you would want to see the last logs to come in. For that you can either use the **-e** flag to view the end of the log, or the **-r** flag to view the logs in reverse order.

A common pattern with syslog is to monitor a log with the **tail** command in follow mode, such as **tail -f /var/log/messages**, so that new log entries are shown as they are written. With **journalctl** you can follow the new logs being added to the journal with **journalctl -f**.

syslog had an advantage in that logs were separated into appropriate topic files. Your mail logs went into one file, general system logs into another, and cron logs into yet another. systemd does not do this. Instead, you create ad-hoc filters that match log entries according to their metadata.

You can still run commands like **journalctl | grep sshd** to look for log entries containing the phrase sshd. The new, preferred way is to use a filter. Example 18-8 shows a query for sshd related logs.

Example 18-8 Querying the Journal for sshd Logs

```
# journalctl SYSLOG_IDENTIFIER=sshd | tail -5
-- Reboot --
Apr 18 17:01:14 localhost.localdomain sshd[790]: Server listening on
0.0.0.0 port 22.
```

```
Apr 18 17:01:14 localhost.localdomain sshd[790]: Server listening on ::
port 22.
Apr 26 12:56:07 localhost.localdomain sshd[6986]: Accepted password for
root from 192.168.1.171 port 51888 ssh2
Apr 26 12:56:07 localhost.localdomain sshd[6986]: pam_
unix(sshd:session): session opened for user root by (uid=0)
```

Example 18-8 shows the journal entries where the SYSLOG_IDENTIFIER field is sshd and only shows the last five of those. This shows sshd's last four log entries.

systemd tracks logs according to the service that started it, so you can just as easily ask for any logs originating from the sshd.service service, as in Example 18-9.

Example 18-9 *Querying All the Service's Logs*

```
# journalctl -u sshd.service | tail -5
Apr 12 16:15:03 localhost.localdomain sshd[5328]: Server listening on
:: port 22.
-- Reboot --
Apr 18 17:01:14 localhost.localdomain sshd[790]: Server listening on
0.0.0.0 port 22.
Apr 18 17:01:14 localhost.localdomain sshd[790]: Server listening on ::
port 22.
Apr 26 12:56:07 localhost.localdomain sshd[6986]: Accepted password for
root from 192.168.1.171 port 51888 ssh2
```

The **-u** option, used in Example 18-9, restricts the display to only those generated by the given systemd unit. It is interesting to note that the "session opened" log from Example 18-8 does not show up in Example 18-9! To find out why, more details about the logs are needed.

View the output in verbose mode with **-o verbose** so that you see all the log fields, as shown in Example 18-10.

Example 18-10 *Looking at the Logs Verbosely*

```
# journalctl SYSLOG_IDENTIFIER=sshd -o verbose
... Output omitted ...
Sun 2015-04-26 12:56:07.623479 CDT [s=d2a5e6cac56c4ed6a50d8eaa85db3e76;
i=270c;b=464f14b29d3c4fdea5b70fd65b150323;m=73242431c;t=514a4580761a8;x
=a69a5419382c0e40]
    PRIORITY=6
    _UID=0
    _GID=0
```

```
    _SYSTEMD_SLICE=system.slice
    _MACHINE_ID=bc31f38de2ee4e2cab0ad674986cee12
    _HOSTNAME=localhost.localdomain
    _CAP_EFFECTIVE=3fffffffff
    _TRANSPORT=syslog
    SYSLOG_FACILITY=10
    SYSLOG_IDENTIFIER=sshd
    _COMM=sshd
    _EXE=/usr/sbin/sshd
    _SYSTEMD_CGROUP=/system.slice/sshd.service
    _SYSTEMD_UNIT=sshd.service
    _SELINUX_CONTEXT=system_u:system_r:sshd_t:s0-s0:c0.c1023
    _BOOT_ID=464f14b29d3c4fdea5b70fd65b150323
    SYSLOG_PID=6986
    MESSAGE=Accepted password for root from 192.168.1.171 port 51888
ssh2
    _PID=6986
    _CMDLINE=sshd: root [priv]
    _SOURCE_REALTIME_TIMESTAMP=1430070967623479
Sun 2015-04-26 12:56:07.788532 CDT [s=d2a5e6cac56c4ed6a50d8eaa85db3e76;
i=271b;b=464f14b29d3c4fdea5b70fd65b150323;m=73244c83b;t=514a45809e6c7;x
=bd3026565414c9e5]
    PRIORITY=6
    _UID=0
    _GID=0
    _MACHINE_ID=bc31f38de2ee4e2cab0ad674986cee12
    _HOSTNAME=localhost.localdomain
    _CAP_EFFECTIVE=3fffffffff
    _TRANSPORT=syslog
    SYSLOG_FACILITY=10
    SYSLOG_IDENTIFIER=sshd
    _COMM=sshd
    _EXE=/usr/sbin/sshd
    _SELINUX_CONTEXT=system_u:system_r:sshd_t:s0-s0:c0.c1023
    _SYSTEMD_OWNER_UID=0
    _SYSTEMD_SLICE=user-0.slice
    _AUDIT_LOGINUID=0
    _AUDIT_SESSION=9
    _SYSTEMD_CGROUP=/user.slice/user-0.slice/session-9.scope
    _SYSTEMD_SESSION=9
    _SYSTEMD_UNIT=session-9.scope
    _BOOT_ID=464f14b29d3c4fdea5b70fd65b150323
```

```
    SYSLOG_PID=6986
    _PID=6986
    _CMDLINE=sshd: root [priv]
    MESSAGE=pam_unix(sshd:session): session opened for user root by
(uid=0)
    _SOURCE_REALTIME_TIMESTAMP=1430070967788532
```

This verbose listing in Example 18-10 shows all the metadata fields in the log entries. Both logs come from the same SYSLOG_IDENTIFIER, but the _SYSTEMD_UNIT is different. As the **-u** option queries on _SYSTEMD_UNIT, the session open notification is not shown in Example 18-9. The difference in units, even though it is the same process, is because sshd undergoes a change as the user logs in. The process first starts out as a system daemon and then changes context to that of the user. The _SYSTEMD_CGROUP has also changed to reflect this change in context.

You can filter your journal on any of the fields listed in Example 18-10.

An alternative search filter is to ask for any logs generated from a certain binary, such as **journalctl /usr/sbin/sshd**. This would give output identical to Example 18-8.

Configuring journald

The systemd journal's configuration file is **/etc/systemd/journald.conf**. It is a series of key-value assignments with a header. Example 18-11 shows a simple **journald.conf**.

Example 18-11   An Example **journald.conf**

```
[Journal]
ForwardToSyslog=yes
SystemMaxFileSize=200M
```

Example 18-11 starts with the header indicating that the configuration is for the journal. Next are two directives. The first enables forwarding of messages to syslog, which means that any message received by systemd will also be sent to syslog. By default messages aren't sent to syslog because that will duplicate all the messages. However, the feature is there for people who are transitioning off syslog or who use syslog for centralized log collection.

The second directive sets the maximum log file size as 200 Megabytes instead of the default of 10% of disk size.

The entire list of options is in the man page for journald.conf, which you can see by typing **man journald.conf**. Restart journald with **systemctl restart systemd-journald** after making any changes.

Rotating Logs

Your systems will generate log files. Even if you use systemd's journal, there will still be daemons such as web servers that have their own logging frameworks built in.

Log files that grow without any limits have some problems:

- They can fill the disk.

- It is difficult to find what you want in a large log file.

- Large files are unwieldy to copy.

- You can't compress an active log file.

Log rotation is a process that solves these problems by periodically archiving the current log file and starting a new one. With log rotation, you can

- Start a new log file on a schedule, such as daily, weekly, or monthly.

- Compress old log files to save disk space.

- Prune old archives so that you only keep a certain number of old logs.

- Rename old log files with a date stamp so you know where to look for older logs.

- Run commands before or after a set of logs is rotated.

Configuring Log Rotation

Linux distributions use the logrotate package to do all of this. logrotate's configuration files are **/etc/logrotate.conf**, along with any files in **/etc/logrotate.d**. The main logrotate.conf file specifies any default settings and system files to be rotated, and each file in **logrotate.d** is used to add additional settings or override the default settings for specific files. A package manager usually manages the configuration files in logrotate.d, thus a package can also include its own log rotation strategy by including the configuration file. You can also add your own configurations to this directory or to the main configuration file.

Example 18-12 shows an example of a set of log files to be rotated:

Example 18-12   A logrotate Configuration

```
/var/log/httpd/*log {
    weekly
    rotate 4
    missingok
    notifempty
    sharedscripts
    delaycompress
    postrotate
        /bin/systemctl reload httpd.service > /dev/null 2>/dev/null ||
true
    endscript
}
```

A logrotate configuration is defined by a file glob that matches the log files, followed by a series of instructions enclosed inside curly braces. In the case of Example 18-12 the logs that are rotated are the Apache web server logs, which is anything in **/var/log/httpd** with a name ending in **log**.

The configuration for the Apache logs are

- **weekly**—Rotates the log files once a week.

- **rotate 4**—Rotates a given log four times before deleting it, so this keeps four weeks of logs online.

- **missingok**—Don't raise an error if the log is missing.

- **notifempty**—Don't rotate the log if it has nothing in it.

- **sharedscripts**—If the wildcard matches several files, run any scripts once for all files.

- **delaycompress**—Don't compress the file until it has already been rotated. This is to prevent corruption if the daemon doesn't close the log file immediately.

- **postrotate**—Run the commands that follow, up until the endscript keyword, after the logs were rotated. In this example the script tells Apache to restart itself.

If an option isn't specified in the stanza attached to the name of the log file, the top level option from **/etc/logrotate.conf** takes priority. If **logrotate.conf** is contained the line **rotate 5**, any individual configuration that didn't specify a **rotate** value would default to 5.

logrotate is run from cron or anacron as a daily job. Each time it is run it looks to see whether any logs need to be rotated, which is calculated from the presence of the daily, weekly, monthly, or yearly keywords. If logrotate sees that the current log is due to be rotated, it rotates the log. Thus running logrotate from the command line may result in no logs being modified.

Dealing with Open Files

The most troublesome part of log rotation involves handling an application that keeps a log file open while it runs. If logrotate is told to rotate **/tmp/log**, it moves **/tmp/log** to **/tmp/log-XXXX** where **XXXX** is the current timestamp. However, if an application still has the file open it continues writing to the timestamped file.

There are three common solutions, in order of decreasing desirability:

- Move the log files and then send the application a signal to close its logs and reopen them. This is ideal, but the application must support doing this.

- Restart the application after moving the files over and it should start logging in a new file. The **create** keyword can also be used to create the new file after rotation if special permissions are needed or the application doesn't do it itself. This is good as long as restarting the application doesn't impact service.

- Copy the logs instead of moving them and then truncate the old file in place, using the **copytruncate** keyword. This involves a lot more disk operations than the other two options and may lose log entries written after the copy operation started.

Summary

Your Linux machine has two clocks: a hardware clock on the motherboard and a software clock that Linux maintains. You can set and view the software clock with the **date** command, and the hardware clock with the **hwclock** command. The use of the Network Time Protocol means that your clock is always synchronized.

Linux systems produce a number of logs that help in troubleshooting problems, both during the problem and after the fact. The syslog daemon is responsible for receiving the logs and sending them to the appropriate destination, such as a local file or remote machine. Most modern distributions have moved to systemd, which has its own syslog replacement called the journal.

Logs stored on disk should be rotated so they don't fill up the disk and become too unwieldy to read. The logrotate system reads a set of instructions pertaining to sets of log files and renames them on a schedule, including deleting old logs.

Exam Preparation Tasks

As mentioned in the section "How to Use This Book" in the Introduction, you have a few choices for exam preparation: the exercises here, Chapter 21, "Final Preparation," and the practice exams on the DVD.

Review All Key Topics

Review the most important topics in this chapter, noted with the Key Topics icon in the outer margin of the page. Table 18-6 lists a reference of these key topics and the page numbers on which each is found.

Table 18-6   Key Topics for Chapter 18

Key Topic Element	Description	Page Number
Paragraph	A Linux machine has two clocks	500
Paragraph	The system time is in seconds since January 1, 1970	501
Paragraph	Setting the current time	501
Table 18-2	Common format strings for the **date** command	502
Section	The **hwclock** command	503
List	Synchronizing the hardware clock to the system clock and back	504
Paragraph	Stratum 1 versus stratum 2 servers	505
Paragraph	Setting the clock with **ntpdate**	505
List	The **pool.ntp.org** service	506
Paragraph	**ntpd** keeps clocks in sync over time	506
Example 18-4	An example **ntp.conf**	506
Paragraph	The **ntpq peers** and **associations** commands	507
List	Ways to log a message	509
Table 18-3	Syslog severities	509
Table 18-4	Syslog facilities	510
Paragraph	Using **logger** to send a message to a given severity and facility	512
Paragraph	klogd forwards kernel messages to syslogd	512
Paragraph	Centralizing syslogs	514
Paragraph	rsyslogd and syslog-ng are alternative syslogd implementations	514

Key Topic Element	Description	Page Number
Paragraph	Difference between syslogd and journald	515
Paragraph	Using **journalctl**	516
Paragraph	Using **journalctl** in follow mode	516
Paragraph	Filtering the journal by the source of the log	517
Example 18-11	An example **journald.conf**	519
Paragraph	**logrotate** configuration	520
List	How to deal with rotating an open file	522

Define Key Terms

Define the following key terms from this chapter and check your answers in the glossary:

hardware clock, real-time clock, system clock, drift, virtual machine host, virtual machine guest, Network Time Protocol, reference clock, stratum 1 server, log rotation

Review Questions

The answers to these review questions are in Appendix A.

1. A Linux computer typically maintains two clocks. What are they? (Choose two.)

   a. Hardware clock

   b. System clock

   c. NTP clock

   d. cron clock

2. Which of the following sets the clock to 6:30 p.m. on January 21, 2016, if the current year is 2015?

   a. **date 012120161830**

   b. **date 201601211830**

   c. **date +201601211830**

   d. **date 012118302016**

3. You are about to reboot your computer but want to make sure that the computer boots with the correct time. How do you set the hardware clock using the value of the system clock? (Choose two.)

 a. hwclock --hctosys

 b. hwclock --systohc

 c. hwclock -w

 d. hwclock -r

4. Which command is most helpful in troubleshooting NTP problems?

 a. ntp --debug

 b. date

 c. ntptool

 d. ntpq

5. Your server's clock is badly out of sync. How could you set the clock from a remote time source?

 a. ntpdate pool.ntpd.com

 b. ntpdate pool.ntp.com

 c. ntpdate 0.pool.ntpd.org

 d. ntpdate pool.ntp.org

6. Type the full path to the directory where systemd stores its log files:

 _____

7. Which of the following is an alternative syslog implementation?

 a. syslog-ng

 b. rsyslog-ng

 c. syslog++

 d. journald

8. Which of the following syslog severities are more severe than notice? (Choose two.)

 a. debug

 b. warning

 c. info

 d. alert

9. Which of the following syslog configuration rules ignores anything from the mail facility but captures info messages from other places?

   a. *.debug;mail.none

   b. *.alert;mail.*

   c. *.notice;mail.none

   d. *.info;-mail.*

10. You find out that your server is a stratum 2 NTP server. What does this mean?

   a. There are two levels of servers getting time from your server.

   b. It is getting its time from two different servers and averaging the results.

   c. The time is within two standard deviations of normal.

   d. The server that it is getting its time from has a reference clock.

This chapter covers the following topics:

- Conceptual Overview of Networking
- Managing Interfaces
- Network Configuration Utilities

This chapter covers the following objectives:

- Fundamentals of Internet protocols: 109.1
- Basic network configuration: 109.2
- Basic network troubleshooting: 109.3
- Configure client side DNS: 109.4

## CHAPTER 19

Networking Fundamentals

Without network connectivity, the modern Linux systems will seem about as useful as a doorstop (and your users are likely to use them for just that). As an administrator you are tasked with configuring systems to connect not only to the local network, but to the Internet. This requires understanding things like IP addresses, subnetting, and gateways.

In this chapter you learn the basic concepts of networking, how to display networking information, how to configure network access for a Linux system, and how to perform basic networking troubleshooting.

"Do I Know This Already?" Quiz

The "Do I Know This Already?" quiz enables you to assess whether you should read this entire chapter or simply jump to the "Exam Preparation Tasks" section for review. If you are in doubt, read the entire chapter. Table 19-1 outlines the major headings in this chapter and the corresponding "Do I Know This Already?" quiz questions. You can find the answers in Appendix A, "Answers to the 'Do I Know This Already?' Quizzes and Review Questions."

Table 19-1 "Do I Know This Already?" Foundation Topics Section-to-Question Mapping

Foundation Topics Section	Questions Covered in This Section
Conceptual Overview of Networking	1-4
Managing Interfaces	5-7
Network Configuration Utilities	8-9

1. For a class B IP address of 130.88.101.75, what is the network part of the IP address?

   a. 130

   b. 130.88

   c. 130.88.101

   d. 101.75

2. Consider the following: 10.122.189.77/255.0.0.0. Which of the following is the equivalent?

   a. 10.122.189.77/32

   b. 10.122.189.77/24

   c. 10.122.189.77/16

   d. 10.122.189.77/8

3. Consider the following: 192.168.10.0/255.255.255.0. What is the broadcast address?

   a. 192.168.10.0

   b. 192.168.10.1

   c. 192.168.10.100

   d. 192.168.10.255

4. Which protocol offers reliable data package transfer?

   a. TCP

   b. UDP

   c. IGMP

   d. ICMP

5. Which of the following commands display your IP address information? (Choose two.)

   a. **ifconfig**

   b. **route**

   c. **ifup**

   d. **ip**

6. Which command displays your default gateway?

   a. **ifconfig**

   b. **route**

   c. **ifup**

   d. **ip**

7. Consider the following entry in the /etc/nsswitch.conf file:

```
hosts: files dns nis ldap
```

When the command **ping test.com** executes, which location will be searched first for hostname resolution?

    a. The DNS server

    b. The NIS server

    c. The LDAP server

    d. A local file

8. Which command allow you to request an IP address as a DHCP client? (Choose all that apply.)

    a. dhcpcd

    b. dhcpclient

    c. pump

    d. dhcpd

9. Which command allows you to perform a direct DNS query on a specific DNS server?

    a. ping

    b. traceroute

    c. dig

    d. getent

Conceptual Overview of Networking

An *Internet Protocol (IP)* is a unique address or locator for a host on a network or on the Internet. All machines and internetworking devices that communicate via *Transmission Control Protocol/Internet Protocol (TCP/IP)* have an *IP address* they are known by and communicated through.

To understand how all this works, think of the Internet, which is a large network made up of many interconnected smaller networks. The smallest building block of a network is the host, or any machine that has an IP address and could respond to a ping.

Hosts are considered standalone unless they are connected to a network, and a logical grouping of hosts on a network is usually known as a subnet.

The difference between a subnet and a segment is that a subnet is a logical grouping of hosts, based on their addressing, whereas a segment is usually a physical grouping of hosts attached to the same wire, hub, or switch.

When trying to understand the concepts of networks and hosts, think of a network as a street that has houses on it that represent hosts. If you wanted to find a particular house, you could very well go to that street and begin looking up and down it at the house numbers. Figure 19-1 illustrates a network as a street and hosts as houses.

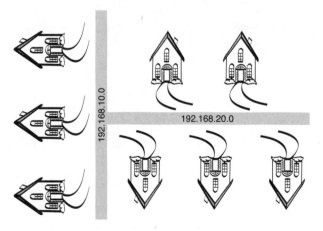

Figure 19-1 Networks and hosts

Following the analogy of networks being streets and hosts on those networks being houses on the streets, an intersection between two streets would be similar to a router or *gateway* between networks.

In this day of subnet calculators, the temptation is to skip some of this information. None of this is blue-sky knowledge; it's all applicable to the exam and in most cases to real-life work on a daily basis for a network sysadmin.

Necessary Configuration Information

To participate in more than a single subnet or network, a host needs to have three things:

- **IP address**—Assigned either statically or dynamically, the address must be valid to work.

- **Network mask**—Each logical network or subnet has a particular *network mask* that helps define where one section of addresses ends and another begins. This is also known as the subnet mask, particularly in a Microsoft environment.

- **Gateway address**—Like a door leading out of a room, a gateway address is the local IP associated with a network card or interface on a gateway or router device. Hosts configured with this address as the default gateway send traffic to this address when they need to access remote hosts.

IP Addresses

An *IPv4* IP address consists of 32 bits grouped in four *octets* of 8 bits, with each octet separated by a dot. This is also known as a *dotted quad notation*. A particular IP, such as 192.168.10.100, would be expressed as the bit values shown here:

```
11000000.10101000.00001010.01100100
```

Bits in an octet have a specific value, and each octet's bits have the values shown in Figure 19-2.

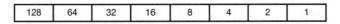

Figure 19-2 Bit values in an octet

When a bit in an octet is turned on, that value is added to any other bit values that are turned on to make a decimal number. With the way the bits are arranged, there is only one bit pattern to make any given number.

It might help to visualize these bits as a bank of light switches, each representing a particular value of watts. For example, if you had a bank of light switches with corresponding wattage, you would turn on the switches for 64, 32, and 4 to produce 100 watts of light. Figure 19-3 shows how this would look.

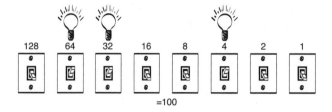

Figure 19-3   The light switch analogy

Typically, you'll work with IP addresses that have been assigned by a higher authority— either your IT department or corporate headquarters, or even an Internet service provider (ISP).

Networks and Hosts

The basic tenet of all networking with IP addresses is that there will be two portions to any given address that are assigned. Using the previous "streets = networks" and "houses = hosts" analogy, you could look at a host's address, such as 192.168.1.200, as being broken up into two parts: the street or network address (192.168.1) and the house or host address (.200).

Just as houses on the same street use that street as part of their addresses, a host address is treated as belonging to the network address it shares with the other hosts that belong to that network. To communicate with another system on a shared physical network, both systems must have the same numbers in their network part of their IP address. What determines the network part of the IP is the combination of classes and a feature called *subnetting*.

Address Class Ranges

Five address class ranges are defined by a Request For Comment (RFC 1918). An *address class range* is defined by the bit pattern of the first two or three bits in the first octet. This is important because the address class determines the number of hosts possible by default for each of the resulting networks.

A *Request For Comment (RFC)* documents specifications for Internet standards. As a draft for a particular specification is evaluated, it goes through a process that ends with it becoming an RFC, which is similar to a standard but is often treated as a firm suggestion.

The five address classes are as follows:

- **A**—From 1 to 126; each of these permits up to 16,777,214 host addresses. (minus 2! ID and Broadcast).

- **B**—From 128 to 191; each of these permits up to 65,534 host addresses. (minus 2! ID and Broadcast).

- **C**—From 192 to 223; each of these permits up to 254 host addresses. There can be 2,097,150 Class C networks.

- **D**—From 224 to 239. This range is reserved for such activities as multicast and is not usually available for host addresses.

- **E**—From 240 to 254; this range is reserved for future use.

For those who are asking where the 127 range is, the designers saw fit to leave the entire 127 range for loopback or local host networking only. Yes, that's 16,777,216 addresses all so someone can **ping** his local host to see whether IP is working!

Remember that when looking at the massive expanse of IPs available for Class A and Class B address ranges, those are typically broken up into many smaller networks by the use of custom subnet masks, which are covered later in the chapter.

Using the Bits to Determine Class

If you look at the bit pattern for the first octet of an address that's a Class A, you see the first bit must always be off because no Class A address is above a 126 in the first octet:

```
Low:      1= 00000001
High:     126 = 01111110
```

Similarly, a Class B address must have the first bit in the first octet on. All Class B addresses range from 128 and higher:

```
Low:      128 = 10000000
High:     191 = 10111111
```

By the same token, no Class C address can exist without the first two bits in the first octet set to on. All Class C addresses range from 192 and higher:

```
Low:      192 = 11000000
High:     223 = 11011111
```

Network Masks

I've long said that one way to understand IP addresses and their partner network (or subnet) masks is to think of every IP address as consisting of two pieces: a network section and a host section. The network mask sets where network bits end and host-assignable bits begin.

For each class, the point at which a network mask stops is where the network portion of an address ends and the host-assignable portion begins. For example, if you take the address 192.168.1.200 and a default subnet mask, the first three octets represent the network and the last octet is where hosts can be assigned.

Address class ranges come with their own built-in default subnet mask; only one can be the default per range:

- **A**—255.0.0.0 or /8 for the number of bits that represent the network mask

- **B**—255.255.0.0 or /16 for the number of bits that represent the network mask

- **C**—255.255.255.0 or /24 for the number of bits that represent the network mask

LPI follows the industry in its use of either fully spelled-out network masks (255.255.255.0) or using abbreviated notation (/24) to represent any network mask assigned to a host or set of hosts. The number 24 relates to the number of bits used for the subnet mask. This technique that uses the number of bits for the subnet mask is referred to as the Classless Inter-Domain Routing (CIDR) notation.

Be prepared to solve questions that use either method of expressing the network mask.

Using Default Network Masks

As previously mentioned, the place where the network portion of an address ends is where the subnet mask bits stop. If you have a network address such as 192.168.10.0 and a default subnet mask of 255.255.255.0 or /24, a single network (192.168.10.0) exists and the remaining 8 bits outside the network portion are available for assignment to hosts.

It might help to express the network address and then the network mask as a set of bits, like so:

```
11000000.10101000.00001010.00001010     (The IP)
11111111.11111111.11111111.00000000     (The Subnet Mask)
```

The boxes highlight the network partition of the IP address. Because the network mask is a /24, or default Class C network mask, you can easily see where the network ends and what's usable for host addresses. The boundary in this example is the last dot, leaving 8 bits worth of addresses for this single network assignable to hosts.

Gateway Addresses, or "Do I Dial with the Area Code?"

Gateway addresses were previously mentioned as an important part of the host's networking configuration. If a host needs to communicate on a different network, it must have a portal or door to the network, typically known as a gateway (also known as a router).

> **NOTE** The term "gateway" is one that doesn't have a firm definition in the IT industry. Some IT experts insist that gateway really means "default gateway." Essentially your system can be connected to multiple networks, each connectable via a router. The *default gateway* is the router that your system sends network traffic to by default instead of a specific router. However, many IT experts feel the terms "gateway" and "router" are synonymous and that the term "default gateway" distinguishes this router from all others. For this book, we use this definition (gateway = router).

When a host wants to communicate with another host on a network, it inspects the other host's network address to determine whether that host is on the local network or on another network. If the host exists on the local network, it can be contacted directly; otherwise, a gateway must be used.

Effectively, it's as if you need to make a phone call to another person and need to find out whether she is in the same area code (local, just dial it) or outside the area code (other network, dial area code first and then the number).

The host uses its network mask to determine whether it needs to send traffic targeted to a remote host via the router for further delivery or whether it can just communicate on the local network to deliver the traffic to the target host.

For example, if you have an IP of 192.168.10.10 and your target host has an IP of 192.168.11.10 (and both use the /24 default network mask), your machine will look at your IP/mask as such:

```
11000000.10101000.00001010.00001010
11111111.11111111.11111111.00000000
```

It then applies the same network logic to the target host, such as

```
11000000.10101000.00001011.00001010
11111111.11111111.11111111.00000000
```

The network mask is expressed by the digits in the first three octets. If there is even a single bit of difference inside the bits that make up the network mask, the host has to "dial the area code," or send the traffic to the gateway to have it further delivered. In this case, the networks are different (see the shaded portions), so the gateway is needed.

Broadcast Addresses

All IP networks use the concept of a broadcast to send traffic designed to impact all hosts on that network. For example, if you have a small Class C network represented by the address 192.168.10.0 and a default subnet mask of 255.255.255.0, the network address is 192.168.10.0 but the broadcast address for every host on that network is 192.168.10.255. No matter how small or large, all networks include the concept of the *broadcast address*, which is not assignable to any host.

Custom Network Masks

The art of custom subnetting is fading, but you have to know how to do at least a Class C custom subnetting problem in your head to determine whether a host has a bad gateway address or how many hosts are possible on a particular network, given the defaults and a custom network mask.

Determining a Custom Network Mask

We discuss two scenarios. In one, you create the subnet map and determine the custom network (subnet) map, and in the other, you solve how many hosts can fit on the network you are assigned.

Scenario 1: Custom Subnetting from Scratch

You are the sysadmin of a small company, and your boss wants to plan a set of networks for your main office and a few other locations. He arranges to rent a Class C network from your network reseller and tells you that you need to have six networks with as many hosts as possible on those networks.

> **NOTE** In the example provided, a private IP class is used to avoid any potential problems in a "real world" implementation. 192.168.0.0/16 represents a private network that cannot be directly routable on the Internet.

Your task is to define a new network mask that will be applied to every host on the entire network. All subnets must have a network address, broadcast address, and gateway address, plus as many hosts as possible from the remaining addresses.

Because you know that you are dealing with a Class C network, you can assume that your default network mask that covers 24 bits will allow you to do your custom subnetting in the last 8 bits left over.

Typically, you would be doing host addressing in the last octet, but because you're breaking up a single network into multiple smaller networks, bits from the last octet are "stolen" or used from the highest value end (128), leaving fewer bits for hosts per resulting subnet.

You know that your network address information is as follows:

Class C address	=	192.168.33.0
Network mask	=	Default (255.255.255.0)
Subnets needed	=	6
Hosts needed	=	As many as possible

Here are the steps you need to perform:

1. Convert the number of networks (6) to binary = 00000110.

2. Turn all the bits after the 4 bit to on = 00000111.

3. Flip the entire octet from end to end = 11100000.

4. Add the bits together to get the new custom network mask:

   ```
   128 + 64 + 32 = 224 (the new subnet mask)
   ```

5. Start at 0 and use the LSB (least significant bit) or 32 as the increment for the networks (keep in mind that a network's 0 and 224 might be network and broadcast addresses and thus invalid for use).

   The network addresses (0, 32, 64, and so on) are not assignable as host addresses. The first odd-numbered address (1, 33, 65, and so on) on each of these new networks is the first possible host address.

Network	Address Range	Broadcast
0	192.168.33.1–192.168.33.30	31
32	192.168.33.33–192.168.33.62	63
64	192.168.33.65–192.168.33.94	95

Network	Address Range	Broadcast
96	192.168.33.97–192.168.33.126	127
128	192.168.33.129–192.168.33.158	159
160	192.168.33.161–192.168.33.190	191
192	192.168.33.193–192.168.33.222	223
224	192.168.33.224–192.168.33.254	255

6. You can now assign these ranges to the networks that you build, with each representing 30 host addresses, a network address, and a broadcast address.

The previously listed network numbers represent the subnet or network to which you are assigning hosts. The network address, such as 192.168.33.32, is not assignable to a host. It isn't even assigned anywhere—it's agreed upon by the hosts on the network and the custom network mask.

Additionally, the first and last networks (192.168.33.0 and 192.168.33.224) are traditionally not seen as valid for assigning hosts to, unless the networking equipment supports it. Because I can't predict the hardware capabilities, we use the most common and compatible method.

The address range represents the numbers assignable to hosts, with one exception: The last or odd number on each range is the broadcast address and is not assignable to a host. It's used to address all hosts when broadcasts are sent over the network.

Scenario 2: How Many Hosts on a Network?

Another situation that might occur is that you are a new consultant for a small company and part of the initiation ritual seems to be setting you down in a cube with a workstation and a slip of paper that has your IP and an abbreviated notation network mask on it and having you discover your default gateway and other IP information.

The IP information you've been given is 10.30.200.120/26, and your gateway is supposed to be the last host-assignable IP on your network.

You can convert the /26 into a standard subnet mask by dividing 26 by 8; each 8 becomes a 255 and the remainder of 2 becomes a .192. In other words, convert the 26 into the number of bits in a subnet mask starting from the leftmost bit and moving right.

To solve this, you should do a quick subnetting problem, such as

1. The 10.30.200.180 address is a Class A address, but the network mask of 26 translates into a 255.255.255.192, or a small chunk of the original 10.0.0.0 network.

2. Turn the 192 into the bit values = 1100000.

3. The smallest bit is 64, so the subnets increment by 64, starting at 0.

Network	Address Range	Broadcast
0	10.30.200.1–10.30.200.62	63
64	10.30.200.65–10.30.200.126	127
128	10.30.200.129–10.30.200.190	191

4. After you have your network (180 falls in the 129–191 network) you can stop, unless you just have to finish the networks.

Your network address is 10.30.200.128, the first addressable host IP is 10.30.200.129, the last addressable host IP is 10.30.200.190, and the broadcast address is 10.30.200.191. There are 62 host IP addresses on your subnet.

Be prepared to reread questions to see whether they want to know all IPs on a network or whether you leave out the router and broadcast address. If you're asked for the number of IPs that could be assigned to hosts, it's always an even number; if you are to disregard or leave out the router/gateway address, it has to be an odd number.

Additional Protocols

There are many networking protocols, but just four are critical to know for the exam. Recall that a protocol is a set of rules that define communication between two devices. You should be familiar with the following protocols:

- **IP (Internet Protocol)**—The Internet Protocol handles the addressing and communication between devices on a network. It defines IP addresses, subnetting, and routing.

- **TCP (Transmission Control Protocol)**—TCP is designed to be a complement protocol to the Internet Protocol. Often the two protocols are described as the TCP/IP suite. While IP focuses on the addressing of systems, TCP focuses on the transport of data packages. It is often contrasted with the *User Datagram Protocol (UDP)* as they both perform similar functions. TCP differs from UDP in that the data packages are considered "reliable" because TCP performs error checking to make sure all data packages arrive at the destination. While this results in additional overhead, it is necessary for situations when the data must get through without errors.

- **UDP (User Datagram Protocol)**—Designed to be a complement protocol to the Internet Protocol. Often the two protocols are described as the UDP/IP suite. While IP focuses on the addressing of systems, UDP focuses on the transport of data packages. It is often contrasted with TCP as they both perform similar functions. UDP differs from TCP in that the data packages are sent connectionless, so no error checking is performed.

- **ICMP (Internet Control Message Protocol)**—The primary focus of this protocol is to allow networking devices, such as routers, the capability to send error messages. An example would be when a router is unreachable. ICMP also provides the capability to perform queries, such as when an administrator uses the **ping** command to determine whether a remote system is reachable.

Common Ports

For the exam you are expected to know what a network *port* is and be familiar with common network ports. To understand ports, consider the following: You decide to connect to a remote system via SSH. The remote system has many network-based services (FTP, SSH, mail server, and so on) running. How does the SSH server on the remote system know that you are trying to connect via SSH rather than the other network-based services?

The answer is that the SSH server listens to a port. A port is a numeric value assigned to a service. Remember the analogy of how an IP address is like a house address? In fact, it is more like an apartment address with the port numbers being the apartment number that you are trying to access.

How a service determines which port to listen to is complex. Traditionally, the service was supposed to look at the entries in the **/etc/services** file. Example 19-1 shows a small portion of this file:

Example 19-1 An Example of the **/etc/services** File

```
# The latest IANA port assignments can be gotten from
#        http://www.iana.org/assignments/port-numbers
# The Well Known Ports are those from 0 through 1023.
# The Registered Ports are those from 1024 through 49151
# The Dynamic and/or Private Ports are those from 49152 through 65535
#
# Each line describes one service, and is of the form:
```

```
#
# service-name    port/protocol   [aliases ...]    [# comment]

tcpmux            1/tcp                             # TCP port service
multiplexer
tcpmux            1/udp                             # TCP port service
multiplexer
rje               5/tcp                             # Remote Job Entry
rje               5/udp                             # Remote Job Entry
```

Based on this output, the tcpmux (TCP port service multiplexer) service is to use TCP and UDP port #1.

The reality is that few services actually look at this file. Most of them have settings in their configuration files to specify which port to listen to (although most services use a default that matches the entry in the **/etc/services** file).

Port numbers 0-1023 are designated as well-known ports. These ports are supposed to be assigned to commonly used network services (sometimes referred to as legacy services). Ports 1024-49151 are called registered ports. These ports are assigned by the Internet Assigned Numbers Authority (IANA) to provide some sort of standardization of ports. The last range of port numbers, 49152-65535, are called dynamic (or private or ephemeral) ports. These cannot be "reserved" and can be used for any purpose.

For the exam, you should be aware of the following port numbers and the services that commonly utilize the ports:

- **20 & 21**—FTP
- **22**—SSH
- **23**—Telnet
- **25**—SMTP
- **53**—DNS
- **80**—HTTP
- **110**—POP3
- **123**—NTP
- **139**—NETBIOS
- **143**—IMAP

- **161** and **162**—SNMP

- **389**—LDAP

- **443**—HTTPS

- **465**—SMTPS

- **514**—SYSLOG

- **636**—LDAPS

- **993**—IMAPS

- **995**—POP3S

IPv6

The Internet Protocol discussed previously in this chapter was actually IPv4 (Internet Protocol, version 4). This IP has been widely used on both local networks and the Internet for decades (since 1982). A newer version of this protocol was introduced in the mid-1990s: *IPv6*. The two protocols have many differences, and IPv6 is considered a great improvement over IPv4. However, implementing this newer protocol in the huge network called the Internet has proved difficult.

NOTE Google has a graph that shows how many of its users have some form of IPv6 connectivity. As of mid-2015, this number is at about 7%, up 5% from 2013, but still a low percentage.

For the LPIC-1 exam, you should know some of the difference between IPv6 as well as some of the basic commands. While most examples throughout this chapter focus on IPv4, there are some IPv6 examples as well.

The major differences between IPv4 and IPv6 include

- **Address scheme**—IPv4 uses a 32-bit number for addressing (Dotted Decimal Notation: 192.168.1.1). IPv6 uses a 128-bit number for addressing (Hexadecimal Notation: 3FFE:F200:0134:AB00:0143:1111:8901:AAAA). IPv4 is limited to about 4.2 billion addresses (much less when you consider IP addresses lost to subnetting), while IPv6 has a considerably higher limit (2128 or 340,282,3 66,920,938,463,463,374,607,431,768,211,456). This difference is considered the "big one" by many because with so many devices connecting to the Internet (think computers, cell phones, tablets, routers, cable boxes, etc.), 4.2 billion unique addresses is inadequate.

NOTE A feature in IPv4 addresses the limited number of Internet-connectable addresses: NAT (Network Address Translation). With this technology, a private network can use nonroutable IP addresses and funnel all Internet connections via a router that "translates" the private IP addresses into a single public IP address. With this technology you could connect hundreds of devices to the Internet with a single public IP address. This technology is considered by some to be the reason why IPv6 hasn't really taken hold quickly.

- **Routing**—Routing in IPv6 is considered more efficient.

- **Security**—IPv6 has security built in. For IPv4, security is implemented as a separate feature and is not as strong as IPv6.

- **Autoconfigure**—With IPv4, addresses are either assigned statically (via a configuration file) or dynamically (via a *DHCP* server). With IPv6, both of these techniques are available, but the IPv6 protocol also allows for *autoconfiguration*, making administration much easier.

- **Header**—The beginning part of a network package is called the header. The header for IPv6 packages is much more robust and requires less processing overhead.

Managing Interfaces

A Linux machine has a default interface called the loopback or local interface. The device appears as **lo** (that's a lowercase L, not a number one) and can be configured like other interfaces, with the main difference being that the loopback is never going to connect to a network. The loopback interface is only there so your machine can have IP bound to an interface even if it's not otherwise configured to use a network card.

Real life, bosses, and the exam will require you to be able to set your IP via the interface configuration files or even statically configure the interface from the command line.

Viewing IP Information

The primary tool for viewing your IP information is the **ifconfig** command. By default, **ifconfig** shows all active interfaces, including the loopback. To display the interfaces on a Linux machine, you would enter the **ifconfig** command.

This produces output similar to that shown in Example 19-2.

Example 19-2 Example of an **ifconfig** Command's Output

```
eth0    flags=4163<UP,BROADCAST,RUNNING,MULTICAST>  mtu 1500
        inet 192.168.1.21  netmask 255.255.255.0  broadcast
192.168.1.255
        inet6 fe80::a00:27ff:fe52:2878  prefixlen 64  scopeid
0x20<link>
        ether 08:00:27:52:28:78  txqueuelen 1000  (Ethernet)
        RX packets 310881  bytes 279637701 (266.6 MiB)
        RX errors 0  dropped 0  overruns 0  frame 0
        TX packets 64257  bytes 6386376 (6.0 MiB)
        TX errors 0  dropped 0 overruns 0  carrier 0  collisions 0


lo: flags=73<UP,LOOPBACK,RUNNING>  mtu 65536
        inet 127.0.0.1  netmask 255.0.0.0
        inet6 ::1  prefixlen 128  scopeid 0x10<host>
        loop  txqueuelen 0  (Local Loopback)
        RX packets 751  bytes 126427 (123.4 KiB)
        RX errors 0  dropped 0  overruns 0  frame 0
        TX packets 751  bytes 126427 (123.4 KiB)
        TX errors 0  dropped 0 overruns 0  carrier 0  collisions 0
```

In the previous output, you see a wealth of information; particularly of note is the eth0 interface. Pay attention to the following information:

- **ether**—This displays the hardware address, also known as the Media Access Control (MAC). In any case, it's the 48-bit physical address of the interface hardware.

- **inet**—The address assigned to the interface.

- **broadcast**—The broadcast address for the network this machine is on; it's entirely dependent on the network mask.

- **netmask**—The network mask, or how the system knows the logical network it's on.

Also note the receive (RX) and transmit (TX) statistics and collisions that might exist for a particular interface. I've not mentioned the local interface; it's there but doesn't impact the machine's network presence.

If you see any output from the **ifconfig** command on the exam, inspect it carefully for configuration errors, collisions, and whether the interface state is up or down. LPI doesn't use screen real estate lightly, so that information will be key to the answer to the question, whatever it is.

Be aware of the **ip** command; it is designed to replace many of the commands that you see in this chapter. For example, the **ip** command can also display network configuration data, just like the **ifconfig** command. If you execute the **ip addr show** command, the output looks like that shown in Example 19-3.

Example 19-3   Example of **ip addr show** Command Output

```
1: lo: <LOOPBACK,UP,LOWER_UP> mtu 16436 qdisc noqueue state UNKNOWN
    link/loopback 00:00:00:00:00:00 brd 00:00:00:00:00:00
    inet 127.0.0.1/8 scope host lo
    inet6 ::1/128 scope host
       valid_lft forever preferred_lft forever
2: eth0: <BROADCAST,MULTICAST,UP,LOWER_UP> mtu 1500 qdisc pfifo_fast
state UP qlen 1000
    link/ether 08:00:27:08:ea:ff brd ff:ff:ff:ff:ff:ff
    inet 192.168.1.22/24 brd 192.168.1.255 scope global eth0
    inet6 fe80::a00:27ff:fe08:eaff/64 scope link
       valid_lft forever preferred_lft forever
```

Red Hat Interface Configuration

On a Red Hat machine, the **/etc/sysconfig/network-scripts** directory contains the scripts used to configure and bring up and down the interfaces on the machine.

NOTE There have been recent changes in networking configuration files and utilities on Red Hat-based systems. The following applies to Red Hat Enterprise Linux 6.x (discussion of Red Hat Enterprise 7.x is not included in this section). It is important to note that these specific networking files in this section are not exam testable; they are included to provide you with a basic understanding of how specific distributions are different.

For example, if you have an eth0 interface you need to configure with a static IP and other configuration, you could modify the **/etc/sysconfig/network-scripts/ifcfg-eth0** file. This file can also be modified by a tool called **system-config-network**.

To display the **ifcfg-eth0** file, use

```
cat /etc/sysconfig/network-scripts/ifcfg-eth0
```

With a static configuration for IPv4, you see output similar to the following:

```
DEVICE=eth0
```

```
ONBOOT=yes
BOOTPROTO=static
IPADDR=192.168.1.73
NETMASK=255.255.255.0
GATEWAY=192.168.1.1
```

With a static configuration for IPv6, you see output similar to the following (for autoconfiguration, just specify the first line):

```
IPV6INIT=yes
IPV6ADDR=3FFE:F200:0134:AB00:0143:1111:8901:0002
IPV6_DEFAULTGW=3FFE:F200:0134:AB00:0143:1111:8901:0001
```

If the interface is configured for DHCP, you see output similar to the following for IPv4:

```
DEVICE=eth0
ONBOOT=yes
BOOTPROTO=dhcp
```

If the interface is configured for DHCP, you see output similar to the following for IPv6:

```
IPV6INIT=yes
DHCPV6C=yes
```

Whichever method you decide to use can be implemented by editing this file and setting the parameters you want. The parameters are self-explanatory, with the possible exception of the **BOOTPROTO** parameter. The **BOOTPROTO** parameter, when set to either static or dhcp, tells the network daemon how to configure this interface, either by reading the other parameters in the **ifcfg-eth0** file or by using DHCP to get the address.

After changing these settings, restart networking by executing **service network restart**.

This restarts the networking and brings the interfaces down and back up again.

Debian Interface Configuration

Debian uses a different style of configuring interfaces. Instead of several smaller scripts or configuration files, Debian uses the **/etc/network/interfaces** file for all interfaces. Although Debian doesn't include the **system-config-networking** utility by default, the **netcardconfig** program is included in some Debian distributions and does roughly the same tasks.

NOTE It is important to note that these specific networking files in this section are not exam testable; they are included to provide you with a basic understanding of how specific distributions are different.

To see the contents of this file, use

`cat /etc/network/interfaces`

This produces output similar to that shown in Example 19-4.

Example 19-4   Example of Contents of the /etc/network/interfaces File

```
# /etc/network/interfaces -- configuration file for ifup(8), ifdown(8)
# The loopback interface
# automatically added when upgrading
auto lo eth0
iface lo inet loopback
iface eth0 inet static
        address 192.168.15.5
        netmask 255.255.255.0
        network 192.168.15.0
        broadcast 192.168.15.255
        gateway 192.168.15.2
```

Each interface defined in the interfaces file starts with the keyword **iface**, then the name of the interface, the type of address (inet for IP, ipx for IPX, and inet6 for IPv6), and the method for the interface (either static or dhcp).

After configuring the interfaces file with the correct parameters, it's recommended to restart the network daemon with **/etc/init.d/networking restart**.

This restarts the networking and brings the interfaces down and back up again.

Notice that the Debian interfaces file contains the gateway address but doesn't use uppercase letters like Red Hat does. Nor does Debian use an equal sign (=) between the parameter and the value in the interfaces file. Debian also uses the scripts as an input or source file, whereas Red Hat actually executes its configuration scripts.

It's important to note that, although Debian does primarily use the previous method, an instance of the file **/etc/sysconfig/network-scripts/ifcfg-eth0** is often found on the Debian machine. You need to read the documentation for your distribution or method to determine what relationship exists between the two. You can safely assume that this won't be an issue on the exam as the networking questions on the exam are distribution neutral.

Viewing and Configuring Gateway Addresses

The default gateway is used for sending traffic to an interface that is the doorway or gateway to the rest of your networks, hence the name. A default gateway is necessary because you don't want to have static routes on all your machines for every destination network—that would be unwieldy and quickly become outdated.

Viewing the Default Gateway

To view the default gateway configured on your machine, you can use either the **route** command or the **netstat –r** command.

This displays output similar to the following:

```
Kernel IP routing table
Destination  Gateway      Genmask        Flags  MSS Window  irtt
Iface
192.168.1.0  *            255.255.255.0  U      40  0          0 eth0
127.0.0.0    *            255.0.0.0      U      40  0          0 lo
default      192.168.1.2  0.0.0.0        UG     40  0          0 eth0
```

This is an important set of output. Without a properly configured gateway, your machine is capable of reaching hosts only on your local network.

The line that begins with 192.168.1.0 is the actual network address of your subnet or network. Any network packages sent to a machine on this network are just broadcast on the local network. However, any network packages sent to a machine on a different network are sent to the default gateway of 192.168.1.2.

Beware of any questions or answers on the exam that try to trick you into thinking that the actual IP of the gateway is 0.0.0.0. It's not; that's just the method that IP addressing schemes use to represent the default gateway when you are looking for a destination network for which a route isn't configured.

Configuring a Default Gateway

As you have seen in the configuration files for both Red Hat and Debian, a valid GATEWAY or gateway parameter and a value of an IP can configure a valid gateway for the interface.

On a Red Hat machine, you can edit either the **/etc/sysconfig/network** file or the **/etc/sysconfig/network-scripts/ifcfg-eth0** file and add the GATEWAY entry:

```
GATEWAY=10.0.0.1
```

Debian uses the **/etc/network/interfaces** file to set each individual interface's gateway value.

On both types of systems, you can add a default gateway manually with the following command:

```
route add default gw 10.0.0.1
```

It's important to note the syntax for the previous command:

- **route**—The **route** command, which is used for many things related to establishing, viewing, and removing routes to other networks.

- **add**—Used to add the default gateway. Other options include **del** to delete a particular route.

- **default**—The default gateway is the one used if no other route exists or matches the target address.

- **gw**—Notes that the entry is a gateway to the rest of the networks and traffic should be routed through this interface.

- **10.0.0.1**—Replaced with your gateway address, or the resolvable domain name of the host that provides this functionality.

Expect to troubleshoot, configure, or fill in the blank on a question about a default gateway. This type of question appears several times on the exam, as either fill-in-the-blank or multiple choice (and often both) stated slightly differently.

Local Name Configuration

Local name configuration is a mish-mash of different files, the most notable of which are

- **/etc/hosts**
- **/etc/resolv.conf**
- **/etc/nsswitch.conf**

NOTE These files are distribution neutral and can definitely show up on the exam!

These three files are used to configure how local name resolution occurs. Figure 19-4 shows the relationship between these files and how they use each other to resolve the name for a host to which a client software application needs to connect.

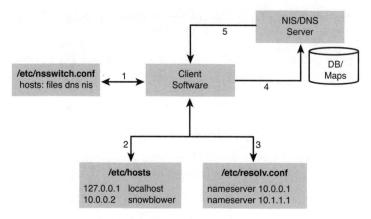

Figure 19-4   Name resolution diagram

The numbered steps in Figure 19-4 represent the steps that would be followed during a normal name resolution. The following examples show how different variations would work on a system with this configuration.

For example, we issue the **ping snowblower** command on a host with the sample configuration shown in Figure 19-4.

When a name is used instead of an IP, the client software asks the system to resolve that name to an IP address. The system follows these steps:

1. The system first refers to the **/etc/nsswitch.conf** file and the hosts: line for the order in which it should look for the name's resolution. In Figure 19-4, the hosts: line is set to first look at the local files, then dns, and then nis:

   ```
   hosts: files dns nis
   ```

2. The system looks in the file **/etc/hosts** for the resolution of the name snowblower to an IP; in this case, it finds a matching entry with an IP address of 10.0.0.2.

3. The system returns the IP address to the client and the name resolution portion of the transaction is complete.

As a more complex example, let's see what happens if we issue the **ping shpdoinkle** command on a host that has the previous configuration.

The system follows the same general set of steps, with an addition:

1. The system first refers to the **/etc/nsswitch.conf** file and the hosts: line for the order of resolution.

2. The **/etc/hosts** file is inspected for a matching entry.

3. When none is found, the **/etc/nsswitch.conf** file is read and the next option for resolution is found to be dns.

4. The system then reads the **/etc/resolv.conf** file for the name server entries, with an upper practical limit of three expected. The **/etc/resolv.conf** file defines the DNS servers used by this system.

5. The system queries the first found name server for the resolution of the name. If the name is resolved, resolution is halted. If the first name server doesn't reply in a reasonable amount of time, it tries the next configured name server until no entries remain; if no resolution is found, it fails.

6. If the name is resolved, the system returns the IP address to the client and the name resolution portion of the transaction is completed.

7. If the DNS queries all fail, then the NIS server is queried because the last entry on the hosts: line is nis. This assumes that an NIS server is configured for this system.

NOTE Just because an entry in the local files resolves a hostname to an IP address doesn't mean that the IP address is the correct one for the target host! A prime troubleshooting topic on the exam is having name resolution problems for hosts right after switching to using *domain name services (DNS)* for name resolution. The host does not query further if a resolution is made.

Other name resolution-related files can be used on a Linux system, but most are, by default, not on the Red Hat or Debian systems you see these days:

- **/etc/hostname**—Used to statically store the fully qualified domain name, such as snowblower.brunson.org. Note that this file is included in the exam objectives while the other two files are not.

- **/etc/networks**—Used to map a network name to an otherwise IP-related network, more often used in Solaris environments than Linux.

- **/etc/host.conf**—Similar in function to the **/etc/nsswitch.conf** file. It sets the order in which resolution sources are searched (this file is overridden by **/etc/nsswitch.conf**).

Network Configuration Utilities

A number of commands are used to view, configure, or troubleshoot your network configuration, including

- **ifconfig**—Used to set and display the host's IP address and network mask.

- **ifup**—Used to bring an interface up.

- **ifdown**—Used to bring an interface down.

- **ip**—Designed to replace the collection of commands (**ifconfig**, **ifup**, **ifdown**, **route**, and so on).

- **route**—Used to set and display the host's routing and gateway information.

- **dhcpcd, dhclient, and pump**—Used (variously) to initiate, release, or renew the client's DHCP-assigned address(es).

- **host, nslookup, and dig**—Used to look up DNS names and return information about the targeted host.

- **hostname**—Used to set or view the host's hostname; other name utilities can create name-related links to this file.

- **netstat**—Used to view information about the networking subsystem, statistics, and attached hosts/ports.

- **ping**—The simplest way to establish that a host is alive and responding; essentially a network "hello."

- **traceroute**—Used to determine the path, names, and statuses of the routing devices that a set of traffic uses to reach a given remote host.

- **tcpdump**—Used to capture and inspect the contents of packets from the network.

NOTE All these utilities are useful; however, not all are included in the exam objectives. Review the objectives carefully when studying for the exam.

Network Utility Examples

Many of the previously listed utilities are complex and robust programs and could be the subject of a much longer book. This section consists of quick examples and relevant exam tips for these utilities.

The **ifconfig** Command

The **ifconfig** command is used primarily to view or set the IPs for a host. You can set everything like the default gateway with this command, including the bringing up or activation of the interface.

To set up the eth0 interface to communicate on the 192.168.33.0 network with an IP of 192.168.33.2 and a network mask of 255.255.255.0 and to activate the interface, use the following command:

```
ifconfig eth0 192.168.33.2 netmask 255.255.255.0 up
```

The **ifconfig** command displays the working or activated interfaces for the system. If any are down or not activated, they can be shown with the **-a** switch—for example:

```
ifconfig -a
```

The **route** Command

The **route** command was featured earlier in this chapter for the purposes of adding default gateways, but it's also used in defending your system from an attack in progress.

When you have a host that is being attacked by a denial-of-service attack, or some sort of denial of service is being attempted, the quickest action you can take is to add a route that causes any responses to the attacker's IP to be routed through the loopback address, effectively causing your system to misroute the traffic to that host.

To stop a particular host from attacking a server, open a shell on the server and enter the following (where 10.1.1.69 is the attacker's IP) command:

```
route add 10.1.1.69 lo
```

Any of the traffic that your host would have sent in return to the attacking host is now sent to the loopback network, where it times out and the attacking host times out and gives up on your poor server.

Obviously, this is not a long-term solution, but try this on your local network with the **ping** command from a host and type the previous command on the host being attacked. You see that the attacking or pinging host suffers a time-out very quickly.

NOTE Although not directly related to the **route** command, if you need to turn on IP forwarding on a host, one of the ways is to echo a "1" into the **/proc/sys/net/ipv4 /ip_forward** file. This effectively turns on the forwarding of traffic between the different interfaces on the machine. For example:

```
echo 1 > /proc/sys/net/ipv4/ip_forward
```

DHCP Client Tools

This section assumes that you know how to use DHCP and that you understand that IPs are leased from the DHCP server by the client for a specified period of time, timing out and expiring unless renewed by the client utilities mentioned later in this section.

Depending on the distribution, to cause an interface to request a DHCP address, one or more of the following DHCP-related programs must be present:

- **dhcpcd**
- **dhclient**
- **pump**

The **dhcpcd** (DHCP Client Daemon) program runs on the client to help configure the client's IP and watch the lease time-out period, requesting a new address lease when needed for the client.

The **/sbin/dhcpcd** daemon is typically invoked from the startup scripts or from the **/sbin/ifup**; this utility executes the commands in the **/etc/sysconfig/network-scripts/ifup** script on a Red Hat machine and the **/etc/network/interfaces** script on a Debian machine.

If you need to immediately renew or refresh your client's address lease, you can restart or "HUP" the **dhcpcd** daemon with the following command:

```
dhcpcd -k
```

This kills and restarts the daemon, causing it to either recontact the DHCP server and get a new lease or reconfirm the old one.

The **dhclient** program is used by some distributions as a method of getting a DHCP lease, using the **dhclient.conf** file for configuration, including its time-out and retry values. The **dhclient** command attempts to obtain a lease for all interfaces set up to use DHCP, keeping the lease information in the **dhclient.leases** file.

Using **dhclient** is simple. If you need a new address, restart the network services and run

```
dhclient
```

The **pump** command is another of the possible variations you can use to obtain a DHCP lease. To obtain a new address with **pump**, use the command as such:

```
pump
```

Of course, after running the available client tool, it's best to confirm that an address was actually obtained or renewed with the **ifconfig** or **ip** command.

The host, getent, and dig Commands

The **host**, **getent**, and **dig** commands are another set of commands used for a particular function—name lookups or troubleshooting of hostname or fully qualified domain names.

The **host** command is simple and has little use other than to return the resolved IP address for a hostname:

```
host brunson.org
```

This returns output like the following:

```
brunson.org has address 192.168.1.1
```

You can use options to gather further information about the targeted host or domain, but these options are not testable on the LPIC-1 exam.

The **host** command is designed specifically to perform DNS lookups. This can pose problems when your system resolves hostnames from both DNS servers and from the local host file (**/etc/hosts**). Conversely, the **getent** command can search both locations (as well as hostname to IP address translation on NIS and LDAP servers).

The **getent** command uses the aforementioned **/etc/nsswitch.conf** file to determine the search order. For example, consider the following entry in this file:

```
hosts:      files dns
```

Based on the previous output, the **getent** command first searches the local hosts file and then, if the lookup isn't found, performs a DNS query. The command is executed like the following:

```
getent hosts brunson.org
```

If you want to perform only DNS queries, the **dig** command is the correct tool. The **dig** command is usable in a command-line mode or batch mode for larger sets of target servers. When you use the **dig** command, follow this syntax:

```
dig server name type
```

The server is the domain or server IP you are querying for information. Typically, you use the server section only if you need to specify a particular one. The name is the actual domain or host you are searching for, such as lpi.org. The type allows you to specify whether you want to see MX, SIG, A, or ANY record types.

Using the **dig** command is relatively simple. To find just the MX records (mail server) for the brunson.org domain, use the **dig brunson.org MX** command, which returns the output shown in Example 19-5.

Example 19-5   Example of **dig** Command Output

```
; <<>> DiG 9.2.4rc2 <<>> brunson.org MX
;; global options:  printcmd
;; Got answer:
;; ->>HEADER<<- opcode: QUERY, status: NOERROR, id: 41375
;; flags: qr rd ra; QUERY: 1, ANSWER: 1, AUTHORITY: 2, ADDITIONAL: 3
;; QUESTION SECTION:
;brunson.org.                    IN      MX
;; ANSWER SECTION:
brunson.org.            3598    IN      MX      0 brunson.org.
;; AUTHORITY SECTION:
brunson.org.            1835    IN      NS      NS3.INDYSERV.NET.
brunson.org.            1835    IN      NS      NS4.INDYSERV.NET.
;; ADDITIONAL SECTION:
brunson.org.            1835    IN      A       207.238.213.12
NS3.INDYSERV.NET.       167293  IN      A       207.238.213.33
NS4.INDYSERV.NET.       167293  IN      A       207.238.213.34
;; Query time: 65 msec
;; SERVER: 192.168.33.2#53(192.168.33.2)
;; WHEN: Wed May 12 11:31:16 2004
;; MSG SIZE  rcvd: 141
```

The output for a **dig** query is structured, consisting of the following:

- **HEADER**—This contains information about the **dig** environment and options.

- **QUESTION**—This section simply echoes back your query.

- **ANSWER**—This section is the reply to your query.

- **AUTHORITY**—This section shows the servers that are the authoritative name servers for the requested target.

- **ADDITIONAL**—This is a catch-all section, typically displaying the name servers for the target.

- **STATISTICS**—This section shows you how much time it took in milliseconds or seconds to answer the query as well as the date and time of the query.

Expect to see **host, getent**, and **dig** on the exam, especially the ability to see a particular type of host with the **dig** command.

Hostname Utilities

The **hostname** command is used to view and set the host and domain names for a system. The system's hostname can be set by this command, or it can be set in the boot process by various scripts depending on the distribution and version.

The **hostname** command is linked to the following commands:

- **domainname**
- **dnsdomainname**
- **nisdomainname**
- **ypdomainname**

You can also use options to the **hostname** command to show information, such as the following command:

```
hostname --fqdn
```

This returns similar output to the following:

```
localhost.localdomain
```

Using netstat

The **netstat** command is useful for determining statistics for network interfaces, connections to and from the local machine, and a lot of other information.

Using **netstat** without any options outputs a list of the open sockets on the system, but the most useful output is produced when you use options or combine them for richer information and troubleshooting.

The **netstat** command has lot of options; the most relevant of the options include the following:

- **-t**—Shows TCP statistics
- **-r**—Shows the routing table
- **-a**—Shows all the sockets on all functioning interfaces
- **-c**—Shows a refreshing (every 1 second) view of statistics for usage
- **-p**—Shows the name and PID of the program related to each socket (very useful!)

To see all the interfaces' usage statistics, use the **netstat -s** command, which returns output similar to

```
(Output truncated for space)
Ip:
    216167 total packets received
    0 forwarded
    0 incoming packets discarded
    216092 incoming packets delivered
    104652 requests sent out
    80 dropped because of missing route
```

The **netstat** command is also used for viewing the routing table for the system:

```
netstat -r
```

This returns output similar to the following:

```
Kernel IP routing table
Destination  Gateway        Genmask          Flags  MSS Window  irtt Iface
192.168.1.0  *              255.255.255.0    U      40  0          0 eth0
127.0.0.0    *              255.0.0.0        U      40  0          0 lo
default      192.168.1.1    0.0.0.0          UG     40  0          0 eth0
```

The final and most exam-related use of the **netstat** command is the detection and troubleshooting of connections to and from your machine. The output from the next command is voluminous, so I've truncated it to a usable portion, while maintaining a reasonable facsimile of what you see on your system.

To see what your system has for connections, use the following command (using the **head** command and line numbering to keep the output manageable):

```
netstat -a | head -n 20
```

This returns output similar to that shown in Example 19-6.

Example 19-6   Example of **netstat** Command Output

```
1   Active Internet connections (servers and established)
2   Proto Recv-Q Send-Q Local Address      Foreign Address _____ State
3   tcp      0      0   *:pop3s            *:*                        LISTEN
4   tcp      0      0   *:netbios-ssn      *:*                        LISTEN
5   tcp      0      0   *:sunrpc           *:*                        LISTEN
6   tcp      0      0   192.168.15.5:domain *:*                       LISTEN
7   tcp      0      0   *:ssh              *:*                        LISTEN
8   tcp      0      0   *:smtp             *:*                        LISTEN
```

```
9   tcp    0    0    *:7741              *:*                      LISTEN
10  tcp    0    1    192.168.15.5:36651  206.235.223.112:smtp     SYN
11  tcp    0    48   192.168.15.5:ssh    192.168.15.1:4417        ESTABL
12  tcp    0    0    192.168.15.5:36619  www.certmag.com:www      ESTABL
13  0           1    192.168.15.5:36657  206.235.223.112:pop3     SYN
14  tcp    0    1    192.168.15.5:36653  206.235.223.112:pop3     SYN
15  tcp    0    0    192.168.15.5:36594  moviesunlim:www          ESTABL
16  tcp    0    0 192.168.15.5:36595  moviesunlim:www            ESTABL
```

The output from the **netstat** command is divided up into a number of columns, including

- **Proto**—The protocol used, typically TCP or UDP.
- **Recv-Q**—The bytes not yet received by the service or client attached to the socket.
- **Send-Q**—The bytes not yet acknowledged by the remote host.
- **Local Address**—This is your machine, the address, and the port number or name of services.
- **Foreign Address**—The address and port number of the remote end of the connection, or the other user's machine.
- **State**—Typically this is set to ESTABLISHED if a connection is or has been recently active; otherwise, it might be TIME_WAIT when it's almost done processing packets and LISTEN when the socket is a service/daemon waiting for a connection.

Key items in the output listed previously are

- **Line 6**—The 192.168.15.5:domain in the Local Address column and a state of LISTEN represent a name server (typically Bind) listening for DNS queries on the local machine.
- **Line 10**—This is the beginning stage of connecting to the remote SMTP server from this machine with an email client, hence the SYN state.
- **Line 11**—The 192.168.15.5:ssh in the Local Address column shows this is the daemon side of an ssh connection, with the foreign address of 192.168.15.1:4417 being the connecting client.
- **Line 12**—This is a web client on the local machine attaching and requesting data from a site on the remote machine, as are Lines 15 and 16.
- **Lines 13 and 14**—These are a POP3 connection from the local machine to the remote machine.

Expect to see **netstat** output and to be asked to pick the client and server sides of the right connections on the exam. This is important for real-life situations, too, because it's always a good idea to know who's connecting to the system you are responsible for!

Use **netstat -c** to show **netstat** output continuously; use **netstat** in cron jobs to keep track of what's happening to a host during off-hours.

The ping Command

The **ping** command uses Internet Control Message Protocol (ICMP) ECHO_REQUEST and ECHO_RESPONSE packets to determine whether a host is functioning, or is at least able to respond to a ping request. The **ping** command is used for many things, including finding whether a host is available, whether a network can be reached, whether a gateway is functioning, and so on.

The **ping** command is the simplest and easiest way to determine whether a host is alive. If you need to determine the route taken by a set of packets, it's more useful and accurate to use the **traceroute** command, covered next.

To determine whether a host is functioning (or at least responding to an ICMP request), use this command:

```
ping 192.168.1.1
```

This returns output similar to

```
PING 192.168.1.1 (192.168.1.1) from 192.168.1.73 : 56(84) bytes of
data.
64 bytes from 192.168.1.1: icmp_seq=1 ttl=150 time=9.23 ms
64 bytes from 192.168.1.1: icmp_seq=2 ttl=150 time=0.774 ms
64 bytes from 192.168.1.1: icmp_seq=3 ttl=150 time=0.715 ms
64 bytes from 192.168.1.1: icmp_seq=4 ttl=150 time=11.3 ms
```

When using the **ping** command, watch the time it takes to return the ECHO_RESPONSE. If you see anything higher than 1000ms, you might be experiencing some congestion between your host and the target. Some latency is to be expected. The best method is to periodically measure the response time; any large variation from the norm might indicate an issue.

When you use **ping**, **traceroute**, and similar utilities that typically accept either a hostname or an IP as the target, it's important to remember that DNS might not be present or configured and that the speediest method is to use the **-n** option to not have it resolve the hostname.

NOTE For the exam you should be aware of the **ping6** command, which performs the same function as the **ping** command, but for IPv6 systems.

Using **traceroute**

The **traceroute** command is used primarily to troubleshoot and view the route taken between two hosts. If you are a sysadmin and your users can reach internal hosts but not Internet destinations, your primary tool to diagnose this problem is the **traceroute** command.

The **traceroute** command uses three UDP packets to map the set of devices between the source and target hosts. The first set of three packets has a time to live (TTL) of 1, which is decremented when the packets reach the first device on the way to the target host.

When a packet's TTL reaches 0, the packet is expired and a message is sent to the originating host to that effect. The host then sends three more packets with a TTL of 2, which make it past the first device and die at the second one. This continues for as many devices as it takes to reach the target host.

The **traceroute** command output is useful for determining the number and status of the devices between your host and a target host.

To see the routers between your host and another (but not show the resolved names for speed), you could use the following command:

```
traceroute -n brunson.org
```

This shows output similar to that shown in Example 19-7.

Example 19-7   Example of **traceroute** Command Output

```
traceroute to brunson.org (207.238.213.12), 30 hops max, 38 byte
packets
 1   66.23.145.1   15.741 ms   15.020 ms   15.200 ms
 2   66.70.95.221   11.532 ms   12.271 ms   15.714 ms
 3   66.66.180.41   58.104 ms   57.294 ms   59.119 ms
 4   66.109.15.109   58.019 ms   57.665 ms   56.713 ms
 5   66.109.3.157   56.701 ms   59.802 ms   57.235 ms
 6   66.109.3.130   60.236 ms   94.471 ms   227.276 ms
 7   206.223.123.33   88.672 ms   126.281 ms   59.622 ms
 8   165.117.200.193   170.647 ms   129.370 ms   123.876 ms
 9   165.117.200.122   51.481 ms   58.137 ms   57.667 ms
```

```
10   165.117.192.26   59.002 ms   57.756 ms   58.730 ms
11   165.117.200.66   63.039 ms   62.622 ms   62.201 ms
12   165.117.192.38   61.137 ms   53.314 ms   115.764 ms
13   165.117.200.45   82.695 ms   93.937 ms   94.976 ms
14   165.117.192.18   93.599 ms   97.354 ms   93.501 ms
15   165.117.200.1   102.788 ms   116.023 ms   110.338 ms
16   165.117.192.2   91.001 ms   116.288 ms   123.706 ms
17   165.117.200.6   127.074 ms   188.887 ms   110.655 ms
18   165.117.175.133   111.660 ms   133.583 ms   129.227 ms
19   165.117.48.182   132.952 ms   110.658 ms   175.021 ms
20   165.117.178.84   130.887 ms   99.306 ms   135.562 ms
21   67.95.172.210   120.904 ms   132.106 ms   203.681 ms
22   207.238.213.12   150.149 ms   132.494 ms   111.996 ms
```

If you see a series of * (asterisks) where a return time should be, that's an indication that the router is either configured to not return ECHO_REQUESTs from the **traceroute** command, or it is too busy, or it is down and can't respond. That is typically the bottleneck or problem that caused you to start troubleshooting in the first place.

When you're troubleshooting a user's access problem, it can be a number of things, the most likely of which are

- **User can't connect to anything**—This is a local IP or network mask problem. If she can't even "ping" someone on her local network, her machine is the likely problem.

- **User can see her network, but not others**—This is a problem with her default gateway. The only path out of her network is misconfigured.

- **User can see internal network, but not Internet**—This is usually a firewall or even DNS problem. If she can "ping" Internet sites by IP address, but not by hostname, it's definitely DNS.

For all these instances, use the **ping** command first. Then, if you can't find the problem or it's outside your area of responsibility, use the **traceroute** command.

The **tracepath** command does essentially the same thing as **traceroute**. However, only the root user can use the **traceroute** command while all users can use the **tracepath** command.

> **NOTE** For the exam you should be aware of the **traceroute6** command, which performs the same function as the **traceroute** command, but for IPv6 systems. The same can be said for the **tracepath** command: Use **tracepath6** for IPv6 systems.

Using **tcpdump**

The **tcpdump** utility is used to capture and display packets from a network. Either you can search the output in real time by redirecting the captured data to grep or the data can be written to a file for later searching.

> **NOTE** The following is not exam testable, but it is useful for troubleshooting networking issues. The command in this section, **tcpdump**, is also not normally installed on Linux systems. You may need to add a software package to execute this command.

The **tcpdump** utility has a dizzying array of options to choose from; the man page for most versions rivals the **bash** man page. A couple of half-hour sessions with a few machines and the **tcpdump** man page will have you past the dangerous stage and able to use **tcpdump** properly for troubleshooting and security assessments.

To use **tcpdump** to capture all the data going across your local network and put that data in a file, use the command shown here:

```
tcpdump -w capturefile.cap
```

This does not display real-time output to the screen but captures the packets on the network to the file named **capturefile.cap**. Take great care not to leave this capture process running for extended periods of time because filling up your system's root partition can crash the machine or make it unavailable.

To view the data contained in the capture file, such as FTP packets, use the following command:

```
tcpdump -r capturefile.cap dst port 21
```

This shows output similar in format to

```
01:42:27.452770 192.168.1.101.2659 > 192.168.1.2.ftp:
S 2841408587:2841408587(0) win 64240 <mss1460,nop,nop,sackOK> (DF)
01:42:27.452935 192.168.1.101.2659 > 192.168.1.2.ftp:
 . ack 2413194434 win 64240 (DF)
01:42:27.567524 192.168.1.101.2659 > 192.168.1.2.ftp:
 . ack 50 win 64191 (DF)
01:42:31.216098 192.168.1.101.2659 > 192.168.1.2.ftp:
 P 0:13(13) ack 50 win 64191 (DF)
```

Summary

In this chapter you learned the concept of networking, including IP addresses, ports, protocols, and subnetting. You learned which files you must modify to configure the network for your system. Additionally, you learned several networking commands that allow you to change your network configuration and perform troubleshooting tasks.

Exam Preparation Tasks

As mentioned in the section "How to Use This Book" in the Introduction, you have a few choices for exam preparation: the exercises here, Chapter 21, "Final Preparation," and the practice exams on the DVD.

Review All Key Topics

Review the most important topics in this chapter, noted with the Key Topics icon in the outer margin of the page. Table 19-2 lists a reference of these key topics and the page numbers on which each is found.

Table 19-2 Key Topics for Chapter 19

Key Topic Element	Description	Page Number
Paragraph	Participating in more than a single subnet or network	533
Paragraph	Five address classes	535
Paragraph	Address class ranges come with their own built-in default subnet mask	536
Paragraph	Communicating with another host on a network	537
Paragraph	All IP networks use the concept	538
Paragraph	There are many networking protocols	541
Paragraph	Port numbers to be aware of	543
Paragraph	Major differences between IPv4 and IPv6	544
Paragraph	Viewing IP information	545
Paragraph	Viewing the default gateway	550
Paragraph	Configuring a default gateway	550
Paragraph	Hostname utilities you can use	556
Paragraph	The **host**, **getent**, and **dig** commands	557

Key Topic Element	Description	Page Number
Paragraph	The **netstat** command	559
Paragraph	How to determine whether a host is functioning	562
Paragraph	Viewing router information	563
Paragraph	Using the **tracepath** command	564

Define Key Terms

Define the following key terms from this chapter and check your answers in the glossary:

IP address, network mask, gateway, IPv4, IPv6, octet, dotted quad notation, subnetting, address class ranges, RFC, broadcast address, IP, TCP, UDP, ICMP, port, autoconfiguration, DHCP, DNS, default gateway

Review Questions

The answers to these review questions are in Appendix A.

1. If your IP is 192.168.33.35 and your network mask is /28, what is the address of your local network?

   a. 192.168.33.16

   b. 192.168.33.32

   c. 192.168.33.0

   d. 192.168.33.64

2. You need to view a user's routing information on his workstation. Which command, with any needed options, would you use to accomplish this?

   _____

3. Your boss wants you to create a subnet scheme that gives your company eight networks with at least 10 hosts per network. Which subnet mask for a Class C leased network address meets those objectives?

   a. 255.255.255.192

   b. 255.255.255.224

   c. 255.255.255.240

   d. 255.255.255.248

4. A user complains that she can't reach a web mail site she frequents, but she can reach other hosts on your networks and on the Internet. Which command would show you where the problem is occurring? Fill in the blank with just the most appropriate command name:

_____

5. You are configuring a system and need to set your eth0 interface to have a default gateway with the address 192.168.33.1. Fill in the blank with the exact command and options to accomplish this from the command line:

_____

6. You want to find the mail servers for a particular domain but not see all the address records. Which of the following commands can accomplish this? (Choose all that apply.)

   a. digger

   b. host

   c. resolver

   d. dig

7. On a Red Hat machine, you need to edit a file that sets the order for how names are resolved. Fill in the blank with the full path and filename for this file:

_____

8. Which of the following is a valid entry for resolution methods on the hosts: line in the **/etc/nsswitch.conf** file? (Choose all that apply.)

   a. files

   b. ylwpage

   c. dns

   d. nis

9. You need to capture data packets from the network for later analysis. Fill in the blank with only the command name that will accomplish this on a default machine:

_____

This chapter covers the following topics:

- Gaining Access to the root Account
- Providing Services on Demand
- Using TCP Wrappers for Securing Services
- Understanding Permissions Problems
- GnuPG Keys
- Secure Shell
- Additional Security Features

This chapter covers the following objectives:

- Perform security administration tasks: 110.1
- Set up host security: 110.2
- Securing data with encryption: 110.3

## CHAPTER 20

System Security

One of the most important tasks that all Linux administrators face is securing each of the systems in the network. Security breaches can occur both locally and remotely, so you need to know how to protect your systems from more than one threat.

In this chapter you learn the basic concepts of securing network services, securing data using encryption techniques, and securing local user accounts.

"Do I Know This Already?" Quiz

The "Do I Know This Already?" quiz enables you to assess whether you should read this entire chapter or simply jump to the "Exam Preparation Tasks" section for review. If you are in doubt, read the entire chapter. Table 20-1 outlines the major headings in this chapter and the corresponding "Do I Know This Already?" quiz questions. You can find the answers in Appendix A, "Answers to the 'Do I Know This Already?' Quizzes and Review Questions."

Table 20-1 "Do I Know This Already?" Foundation Topics Section-to-Question Mapping

Foundation Topics Section	Questions Covered in This Section
Gaining Access to the root Account	1-2
Providing Services on Demand	3
Using TCP Wrappers for Securing Services	4
Understanding Permission Problems	5
GnuPG Keys	6
Secure Shell	7
Additional Security Features	8

1. Which file provides users the ability to execute commands as other users, such as the root user?

   a. /etc/sudo

   b. /etc/su

   c. /etc/suers

   d. /etc/sudoers

2. Which of the following options provide a login shell when using the **su** command? (Choose two.)

   a. -l

   b. -s

   c. --

   d. -

   e. -k

3. Which of the following services can launch other services on demand? (Choose two.)

   a. inetd

   b. xinetd

   c. linetd

   d. dinet

4. Which of the following files are used by TCP wrappers? (Choose two.)

   a. /etc/wrap.allow

   b. /etc/wrap.deny

   c. /etc/hosts.allow

   d. /etc/hosts.deny

5. Which of the following commands can be used to display all the SUID files on the system?

   a. search

   b. locate

   c. ls

   d. find

6. Which option to the **gpg** command generates private and public keys?

    a. --key-gen

    b. --gen-key

    c. --key

    d. --gen

    e. --keygen

7. Which files contains a list of SSH host public keys? (Choose two.)

    a. /etc/ssh/ssh_known_hosts

    b. /etc/ssh_known_hosts

    c. /etc/known_hosts

    d. ~/.ssh/known_hosts

8. Which commands can change the password aging for user accounts? (Choose two.)

    a. fuser

    b. chage

    c. usermod

    d. ulimit

    e. lsof

Foundation Topics

Gaining Access to the root Account

The best security practice is to avoid logging in as the root user unless you need to perform specific administration commands. In most cases you should not log in as the root user directly, but rather gain root access by executing either the **su** command or the **sudo** command.

The su Command

To gain access to another user account with the **su** command, use the following syntax:

```
su account_name
```

For example, to switch to the root account, execute the following command:

```
su root
```

This provides you with a non-login shell for the root user. Typically you want a login shell as this provides you with the full user environment (environment variables, shell customizations, etc.). This can be accomplished by using the **–l** option or just a **–** option:

```
su - root
su -l root
```

To gain access to a regular user account, you must provide the account name. However, if you don't provide an account name, the **su** command assumes you want to switch to the root account. As a result, the following commands are all the same:

```
su - root
su -l root
su -
su -l
```

When switching from the root account to a regular user account, no password is required. This allows the root user to switch to a regular user account to test that account's features (or troubleshoot problems for the user) without having to change that user's password.

To switch from a regular user account to any other account requires knowing the password of the account you are switching to.

NOTE Some distributions' versions of the **su** command allow for the use of X and remote X; simply use the **sux** command instead of the **su** command. This is most notably present on the openSUSE and SUSE Linux Enterprise distributions.

The sudo Command

The problem with the **su** command is that to provide a user with elevated privileges, you would need to provide the user with the root password. This would allow that user full administrative access to the system.

Often you want to allow a regular user to execute some commands as the root user, but not all commands. For example, if a network error occurs on a user's workstation, you want that user to be allowed to restart the networking service. On some systems this can be accomplished by executing the following command:

```
/etc/rc.d/init.d/network restart
```

To execute this command successfully, the user needs to have root privileges. Instead of providing the user with the root password, you can set up the **sudo** command to allow the user to run just the necessary command. To do this, you need to log in as the root user and then execute the following command:

```
visudo
```

This command allows you to edit the **/etc/sudoers** file, the file that allows you to provide root access for specific commands to specific users. The **visudo** command automatically assumes you want to use the **vi** editor to edit this file. To use a different editor, such as the **nano** editor, execute a command like the following:

```
export EDITOR=nano
```

NOTE Why use the **visudo** command instead of editing the **/etc/sudoers** file directly? The **visudo** command performs some error checking when you exit the editor to make sure you didn't make any formatting mistakes.

The **/etc/sudoers** file has many options. For the certification exam you just need to know how to provide a user with the ability to execute commands as the root user. For example, if you want a user account with the name of "ross" to be able to run all commands as the root user, add the following line:

```
ross          ALL=(ALL)      ALL
```

To limit a user to a specific command, such as the **/etc/rc.d/init.d/network** command, add the following line:

```
ross          ALL=(ALL)        /etc/rc.d/init.d/network
```

For a user to execute a command as root, he uses the **sudo** command. The syntax is as follows:

```
sudo /etc/rc.d/init.d/network restart
```

The user then is prompted for his own password (not the root password). If the correct password is given and the access is permitted based on an entry in the **/etc/sudoers** file, the command is executed as the root user. If the user attempts to execute a command that he is not authorized to execute, an error message appears on the screen and the attempt is logged.

Providing Services on Demand

A Linux system provides many services. Therein lies one of its greatest strengths, and for a weak-willed sysadmin, one of its greatest weaknesses. If you configure your server to provide too many services that run constantly, performance suffers.

The three strata of service configuration for a server are

- **Always on**—This level is for services that should be always running because clients expect their presence.

- **On demand**—This level is for periodically used services, those that should be present but not on using RAM and CPU constantly.

- **Off or disabled**—This level represents those services that you're not going to run regardless, such as ISDN services on an Ethernet-connected server and so on.

Although having standard services capable of being started on demand is advantageous, many services require the starting of multiple child processes or the generation of various security keys that make them less likely candidates for being run on demand. Examples of such services include **httpd** (which needs to start several to many child processes), **sshd** (which needs to generate keys and so on), and **ssl** (which can also require the generation of keys when starting).

Using inetd and xinetd

The older of two services, the **inetd** *daemon*, is intended to provide services upon client demand. The idea behind **inetd** is to provide a method to start and run services on demand, particularly to start the service on receipt of a client connection request. The **inetd** configuration file (**/etc/inetd.conf**) contains a line for each service **inetd** controls.

The **xinetd** service is the newer of the two services and provides more atomic control, using a main configuration file (**/etc/xinetd.conf**) to point to a directory (typically **/etc/xinetd.d**) that contains a single text configuration file for each controlled service, such as **/etc/xinetd.d/telnet**.

> **NOTE** Writing about **inetd/xinetd** without switching back and forth in a confusing manner is difficult; therefore, I cover both in one section, splitting into notes and tips when needed or when one deserves more attention. The two services are similar, with the main difference being the layout of the configuration files. Additionally, whenever you see a directory that ends in ".d" you can typically find a directory that contains include files that affect a particular service or set of services.

A number of services are governed by **inetd/xinetd**; the more familiar of these include

- **finger**—Used to provide user login information and is considered to be a security risk.

- **imap**—A daemon that enables users to store their email on a server rather than download it to a client. This is often moved to a full-time service.

- **ktalk/ntalk**—Used to provide chat/instant messenger–type services; they're not needed often.

- **rsh/rexec/rlogin**—The unsecure "r" services; these should be disabled and replaced by **ssh** and **scp**.

- **telnet**—Another unsecure service, but one frequently used for providing a shell session to a remote client.

inetd Configuration Files

The **inetd** server is much older than **xinetd**, and the main difference between the two is the structure of the configuration files.

The **inetd** server uses a single configuration file, typically the **/etc/inetd.conf** file. This file contains comments that begin with # and entries that each define a single service. An example of a couple (many more exist) of typical lines from **/etc/inetd.conf** are

```
ftp      stream  tcp   nowait   root   /usr/sbin/in.ftpd       in.ftpd
telnet   stream  tcp   nowait   root   /usr/sbin/in.telnetd    in.telnetd
```

The lines shown here are broken up into the following fields and definitions:

- **Service name**—This name must match a valid service name entry in the **/etc/services** file.

- **Socket type**—This can be any of the following: stream, dgram, raw, rdm, or seqpacket.

- **Protocol**—This is one of the protocols defined in the **/etc/protocols** file; typically it's either tcp or udp.

- **wait or nowait parameter**—Use the **wait** parameter for single-threaded servers that grab the socket and operate until timeout; use **nowait** for multi-threaded servers that free up the socket when not active.

- **User/group**—The user or group this service should run as, giving you the ability to restrict a risky service to an account that's not root.

- **Server program**—The full path and name to the program that provides the service.

- **Server argument(s)**—Any parameters the service might need to run properly.

xinetd Configuration Files

The **xinetd** daemon initially uses the **/etc/xinetd.conf** file to set a few daemon configuration settings and the defaults that will be picked up by all **xinetd**'s governed services and to specify the include directory. (These defaults are overridden by any settings in the individual service configuration files.)

The "include" directory is typically **/etc/xinetd.d**, which contains a single text file for each governed service. The service configuration files contain the definition of a service and any special settings that need to be set for correct functioning. Figure 20-1 shows the relationships between the components of the xinetd services and files.

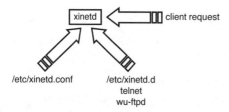

Figure 20-1   How xinetd works

As you can see, **xinetd** reads **/etc/xinetd.conf** and gets its configuration, including the "include" directory location; then it waits for a client request for one of its services. When a client request arrives, **xinetd** looks at the packets and finds the target port/service and looks up that service by name in the **/etc/xinetd.d** directory. This directory contains one file per service, named exactly as the service name appears in the **/etc/services** file.

The **/etc/xinetd.conf** file is simple by nature, as shown in Example 20-1.

Example 20-1   Contents of an **/etc/xinetd.conf** File

```
# Simple configuration file for xinetd
# Some defaults, and include /etc/xinetd.d/
defaults
{
        instances            = 60
        log_type             = SYSLOG authpriv
        log_on_success       = HOST PID
        log_on_failure       = HOST
        cps                  = 25 30
}
includedir /etc/xinetd.d
```

The file contains a few lines that set the default limitations for the services governed by **xinetd**. If an individual service has a conflicting setting in its configuration file, that individual file setting takes precedence.

You're likely to see questions about how to have a service run as a different user, which is accomplished by editing the service's configuration file and changing the user line.

Several of these lines bear defining:

- **instances**—This sets the total number of daemon instances allowed; this daemon is limited to 60 instances.

- **cps**—This limits the number of connections per second allowed through **xinetd**. Any more than the maximum (25) causes the service to be disabled for 30 seconds and then check whether it can accept more connections.

The other settings are log related, logging the host and PID for successful connections and just the host for unsuccessful connections

An individual service configuration file from the **/etc/xinetd.d** directory such as telnet would contain the output shown in Example 20-2.

Example 20-2   Contents of an **/etc/xinetd.d** Service File

```
service telnet
{
        disable = yes
        flags           = REUSE
        socket_type     = stream
        wait            = no
        user            = root
        server          = /usr/sbin/in.telnetd
        log_on_failure  += USERID
        access_times     =  08:00-17:00
        only_from     =   snowblower
}
```

These files contain a number of settings:

- **service**—This keyword must be followed by the service name, such as telnet.

- **disable**—Values include yes (which disables the service and no connections are accepted) and no (which doesn't disable or enables the service for connections).

- **flags**—Many and varied flags exist; the most common is REUSE, which allows the port and service to accept multiple connections.

- **socket type**—This can be stream, dgram, raw, rdm, or seqpacket.

- **wait**—Use the **wait** parameter for single-threaded servers that grab the socket and operate until timeout; use **nowait** for multithreaded servers that free up the socket when not active.

- **user**—The user or group this service should run as, giving you the ability to restrict a risky service to an account that's not root.

- **server**—This is the full path and filename of the server or daemon program run when a client requests a connection.

- **log_on_failure**—This can also be log_on_success, and values include HOST, USERID, and PORT, to name a few options.

- **access_times**—This setting lets you set access timeframes for the service, such as from 8 a.m. to 5 p.m. in the previous file.

- **only_from**—This can be a list of hostnames, IPs, globs of addresses, and defined networks by name from the **/etc/networks** file.

To enable a service governed by **xinetd**, such as the previous telnet service, use the **chkconfig telnet on** command. This changes the previous file to contain the following line:

```
disable = no
```

The service is now enabled and can accept requested connections. Changes to the file for a service don't require any restarting of services or **xinetd**; those changes take place for the next and subsequent instances of the service whose file you changed.

If you edit the **/etc/xinetd.d/telnet** file by hand, the **xinetd** service might have to be restarted for the change to take effect. This is done automatically by the **chkconfig** command.

To disable the service completely from being initiated and governed by **xinetd**, use the **chkconfig telnet off** command.

This disables the service and **xinetd** ignores requests for this service from this point on.

The **inetd** service must be restarted after a new configuration is written to the **/etc/inetd.conf** file, but the **xinetd** service reads the service configuration files in the **/etc/xinetd.d** directory dynamically and requires restarting only if you manually edit **/etc/xinetd.conf** file.

Using TCP Wrappers for Securing Services

If you want to protect your on-demand services, use *TCP wrappers* as one of the layers of protection for seldom-used services.

The common concept of using TCP wrappers is that only services in the **/etc/inetd.conf** file can be wrapped or protected, but that's untrue. The TCP wrappers package includes a library called **libwrap.a** that an increasing number of Linux services reference for security.

inetd and TCP Wrappers

When used with **inetd**, the concept of using TCP wrappers is to place a controlling daemon with instructions as to who's allowed and denied in front of each service that runs on your machine. Most services in the era of widespread **inetd** usage didn't have any built-in protection, so they were configured to be run as parameters of the **tcpd** daemon.

The **tcpd** daemon is set up to refer to the **/etc/hosts.allow** and **/etc/hosts.deny** files for the hosts that are allowed and denied access to services protected by **tcpd**.

xinetd and TCP Wrappers

If you are using **xinetd** or running a current distribution of Linux, many of the services are developed to use the **libwrap.a** library, finally divorcing TCP wrappers from the **/etc/inetd.conf** file.

In the case of current distributions and **xinetd**, any service capable of referencing **libwrap.a** has the potential to benefit from the protection that the **/etc/hosts.allow** and **/etc/hosts.deny** files provide.

Additionally, if you wanted to run a set of services that were both secure and fast, you would use TCP wrappers and a standalone daemon, instead of putting the service under **inetd** or **xinetd** control. Anytime you put services behind **inetd** or **xinetd**, they must be started to function, and that means a small though noticeable delay—often enough that a client request times out.

The hosts.allow and hosts.deny Files

The two tables that affect which clients can connect to which services (provided the service uses **libwrap.a** or is controlled by **inetd/xinetd**) are **/etc/hosts.allow** and **/etc/hosts.deny**.

The format of a typical **hosts.allow** or **hosts.deny** file is as follows:

```
daemons: hosts : option : option
```

Key Topic

Daemons or services can be specified several ways, including

- **ALL**—This means just that, all services.

- **service**—A single service name affects only that service.

- **daemon,daemon**—Multiple daemons affected by an entry should be separated by spaces or commas.

Hosts can be specified by many methods, including

- **hostname**—This affects a single unqualified hostname, typically from the local domain.

- **hostname.example.com**—This affects a resolvable, fully qualified hostname, typically from a remote domain.

- **@group**—This is used by NIS to denote a Net group and is unlikely to appear on the exam.

- **10.1.1.0/255.255.255.0**—This notation affects the hosts 10.1.1.1–10.1.1.255. The /XX notation for bits can be used, too, such as /24 to denote a default Class C subnet mask.

- **/path/filename**—This causes the listed file (full path and filename) to be referred to as the list of hosts that will be affected.

Wrapper Read Order

The following rules are important to understand when using TCP wrappers to protect services:

1. The **/etc/hosts.allow** file is read and parsed first. Any matches in it cause access to be allowed, skipping the **/etc/hosts.deny** file entirely.

2. The TCP wrapper files are read each time a service is requested. Therefore, any changes to the **hosts.deny** and **hosts.allow** files are immediately used.

3. The files are read sequentially. This means that two conflicting entries in the same file cause the first one to be matched, ignoring the second and subsequent entries.

4. The files are read only if they exist. If they don't exist, no rules can be applied, allowing complete access for services as far as TCP wrappers are concerned.

The most important point about how these files are processed is the order in which rules are matched from the files.

Format of hosts.allow and hosts.deny

It's important to choose what you want to deny or allow with the following guidelines:

- **Deny by default**—You deny all host access to all services by inserting an entry that reads ALL: ALL in the **/etc/hosts.deny** file; then you can allow any specific hosts with entries in the **/etc/hosts.allow** file.

- **Allow by default**—If you trust everyone more than not, don't have an allow file and just put the bad hosts or domains in the deny file.

- **Mix and match**—The most complex style, this is when you don't have a clear delineation of good and bad. You should carefully inspect the allow files for lines that invalidate your deny rules.

Sample Configurations

Scenario #1: Deny all access, as shown in Figure 20-2.

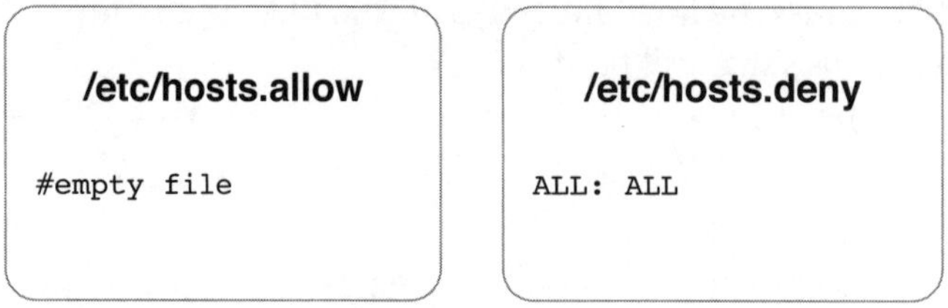

```
/etc/hosts.allow

#empty file
```

```
/etc/hosts.deny

ALL: ALL
```

Figure 20-2 How all access is denied.

In this scenario, all access is denied. The presence of an **/etc/hosts.allow** file in this example is unnecessary because we're denying everyone, so no allow rules are needed.

Scenario #2: Deny all access from a specific domain, with the exception of one machine within the domain, as shown in Figure 20-3.

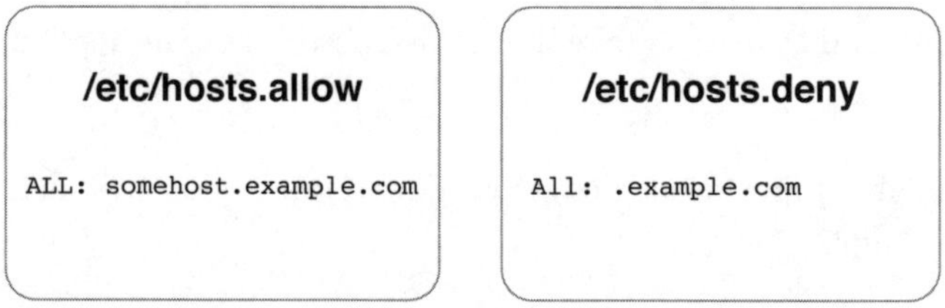

```
/etc/hosts.allow

ALL: somehost.example.com
```

```
/etc/hosts.deny

All: .example.com
```

Figure 20-3 The order in which the allow and deny rules are read.

The rule in the **/etc/hosts.allow** file is read before any rules from the **/etc/hosts.deny** file. As a result, the somehost.example.com machine is permitted access to the local system. All other machines from this domain are denied access based on the rule in the **/etc/hosts.deny** file. If a machine from any other domain attempts to connect to the local system, that machine is granted access since no rule would apply to that situation.

Another way to accomplish the preceding is to not have the **/etc/hosts.allow** file and in the **/etc/hosts.deny** file have the following line:

```
ALL: EXCEPT somehost.example.com
```

Scenario #3: Allow all systems to connect to the named and sendmail servers. Deny access to all other servers, as shown in Figure 20-4.

```
 ┌─────────────────────────┐      ┌─────────────────────────┐
 │                         │      │                         │
 │   /etc/hosts.allow      │      │   /etc/hosts.deny       │
 │                         │      │                         │
 │  named: ALL             │      │  All: ALL               │
 │  sendmail: ALL          │      │                         │
 │                         │      │                         │
 └─────────────────────────┘      └─────────────────────────┘
```

Figure 20-4   Using Service Names to allow access

To have more granular control of who can access services, you can use service names to deny and allow access to just that service. The following **/etc/hosts.deny** file entry allows access to all services but named:

```
named: ALL
```

Using Rule Options

Remember that the **/etc/hosts.allow** and **/etc/hosts.deny** files have the possibility of four configuration fields:

```
daemons: hosts : option : option
```

The real strength of using TCP wrappers comes out when you use the option fields to add characteristics to the entries that control access to services. Options can be a single keyword or take the form of keyword values when using programs or utilities that need arguments.

For example, if you wanted to log the fact that a host had attempted to access one of your services configured to be denied, you might use the following line in the **/etc/hosts.deny** file:

```
service: badhost : severity auth.info
```

This entry not only denies the host access to the service, but also logs to the **auth** facility any messages that are severity level info or higher when the denial occurs.

Two useful keywords in the option fields are **twist** and **spawn**. You use the **twist** keyword when you want to booby-trap what would appear to be a service with another program or action. For example, if you wanted to cause a message to be sent back to an offending host that tries to use your finger daemon, you might employ the following entry in the **/etc/hosts.deny** file:

```
in.fingerd: ALL : twist /bin/echo "421 Buzz off!"
```

This sends a standardized message to the host's console telling it access is denied.

The last keyword we cover is **spawn**. Often you want to allow some host to connect to a service, but at the same time be notified of the access. For example, to be notified via email every time someone accesses telnet so you can in turn email him with an SSH FAQ and scolding note to stop using telnet, you would use the following entry in the access file:

```
in.telnetd: ALL : spawn /bin/echo 'date' from %h | mail root
```

This works for just about any service, as long as it can use the TCP wrappers or can be configured to work from **inetd** or **xinetd**.

If you spawn a command, it runs the command as a child of the current shell, but if you use **twist** to run the command, it replaces the current process with the command you run.

Watch carefully for denial file modifications, such as **twist** and **spawn** statements. Being able to verify which entries are valid or invalid is essential.

Understanding Permission Problems

When you install a distribution, a number of files are set with special bits or permissions, mostly to make it easier for normal users to accomplish mild setup tasks. You should run a **find** command that shows these files right after you install the system and then keep that output in a file in a different location for referral later.

> **NOTE** One of the first changes to your system that a hacker or cracker makes is to set permissions on certain programs to allow an otherwise normal user special or root privileges.

As a reminder, the special bits that can be set for files include

- **SUID**—Represented by the numeral 4, the *Set User ID* special bit allows processes to run with the permissions of the file's owner.

- **SGID**—Represented by the numeral 2, the *Set Group ID* special bit allows processes to run with the permissions of the file's group owner. If it's set on a directory, it forces group ownership inheritance for all objects created in that directory.

- **Sticky bit**—When set on a directory it keeps any nonowners from deleting files in the directory.

It's important to know how to find the files on the system that have special bits set. In particular, the SUID and SGID special bits are used to gain access to elevated levels of capability and could be disastrous if set on utilities such as passwd, shutdown, and useradd.

Finding Files by Permissions

It's important to periodically run a **find** command to see which special bits are set on which files. To find all the files on your entire system that are owned by the root user with any special bit set and mail that list to yourself, use the following command:

```
find / -user root -perm +7000 -exec ls -l {} \; | mail -s "Files with
any special bit set" root
```

This command finds the files that have any sort of special bit set, produces an **ls –l** listing from each, and sends an email that has the entire listing of files to the root user with the subject line in quotation marks.

When you use the **-perm** option with permissions, it matters whether you use a + or a - symbol or don't use one at all. If you are searching for a particular permission setting, such as all the files that have an exact permission setting, use the **find / -perm 4777** command.

This command finds only files whose permission trios and special bit match exactly the permissions specified. If you use the + and - symbols to search for special bits, the - symbol means to look for the exact combination of special bits that match the first numeral, such as 6, which would be 4 and 2—or SUID and SGID. To find any or all of the bits set that match the first numeral, you use the + symbol.

Once a week, run the same report again and then compare the first one with subsequent reports with the **diff** command to see what has changed. I suggest automating this with a script.

You'll probably see questions about the **find** command and the permissions, so be prepared to parse the commands to see which perform the specified tasks.

GnuPG Keys

Sometimes you want to encrypt data. In these cases an option that exists in Linux is *GnuPG (Gnu Privacy Guard)*. This software creates *private* and *public keys* that can be used to encrypt data.

To create these keys, execute the **gpg –gen-key** command.

This tool first prompts you for several bits of information, including which sort of key you want (normally you should choose #1, RSA, and RSA), the size of the RSA keys, and how long the keys will be valid, as shown in Example 20-3.

Example 20-3 Output of the **gpg --gen-key** Command

```
gpg (GnuPG) 1.4.18; Copyright (C) 2014 Free Software Foundation, Inc.
This is free software: you are free to change and redistribute it.
There is NO WARRANTY, to the extent permitted by law.

Please select what kind of key you want:
   (1) RSA and RSA (default)
   (2) DSA and Elgamal
   (3) DSA (sign only)
   (4) RSA (sign only)
Your selection? 1
RSA keys may be between 1024 and 4096 bits long.
What keysize do you want? (2048)
Requested keysize is 2048 bits
Please specify how long the key should be valid.
        0 = key does not expire
     <n>  = key expires in n days
     <n>w = key expires in n weeks
     <n>m = key expires in n months
     <n>y = key expires in n years
Key is valid for? (0)
Key does not expire at all
Is this correct? (y/N) y
```

Next, you are prompted to input data to identify your key, including your real name, email address, and comment field (which can be useful to describe your key). You are also instructed to enter a passphrase (see Example 20-4).

Example 20-4 Output of the **gpg --gen-key** Command

```
You need a user ID to identify your key; the software constructs the
user ID
from the Real Name, Comment and Email Address in this form:
    "Heinrich Heine (Der Dichter) <heinrichh@duesseldorf.de>"

Real name: Steve Smith
```

```
Email address: test@test.com
Comment: Test key
You selected this USER-ID:
    "Steve Smith (Test key) <test@test.com>"

Change (N)ame, (C)omment, (E)mail or (O)kay/(Q)uit? o
You need a Passphrase to protect your secret key.

Enter passphrase:

Repeat passphrase:
```

After entering your passphrase, the utility needs to make use of random data to generate the keys. This may take some time as the following message indicates:

```
We need to generate a lot of random bytes. It is a good idea to
perform
some other action (type on the keyboard, move the mouse, utilize the
disks) during the prime generation; this gives the random number
generator a better chance to gain enough entropy.
```

You could open a terminal window and perform some other work as the random data is generated by your actions and system actions. Once enough random data has been collected, you receive the message shown in Example 20-5.

Example 20-5   Output of the **gpg --gen-key** Command

```
gpg: /home/test/.gnupg/trustdb.gpg: trustdb created
gpg: key 8C85EB9D marked as ultimately trusted
public and secret key created and signed.

gpg: checking the trustdb
gpg: 3 marginal(s) needed, 1 complete(s) needed, PGP trust model
gpg: depth: 0  valid:   1  signed:    0  trust: 0-, 0q, 0n, 0m, 0f, 1u
pub   2048R/8C85EB9D 2015-03-06
      Key fingerprint = 4178 1944 9909 64B2 0A53  5CE8 9417 5E52 8C85
EB9D
uid                  Steve Smith (Test key) <test@test.com>
sub   2048R/83AAAB8C 2015-03-06
```

A key part of the previous output is the public key identifier (8c85EB9D in this case). This can be used to refer to your keys.

Note that these keys are stored in the .gnupg directory within your home directory. Each user has her own GnuPG keys.

To encrypt a file and send to another person, you first should import the recipient public key to a file. By providing this file to someone else, she can decrypt the file that you encrypt with your private key. By default the **gpg** utility generates a binary file with your public key. Use the **–a** option to generate a text-based public key file (which is easier for others to manage):

```
gpg -a -o pub_key_file --export 8c85EB9D
```

To encrypt a file, use the following syntax:

```
gpg -e recipient file
```

The recipient could be something like "bob@test.com." The **gpg** command creates an encrypted file named file.gpg (where "file" is the original filename).

You then need to provide the recipient with the encrypted file and with the public key that you created (the pub_key_file from the previous example). If you directly transfer this public key, the user could import it by executing the **gpg –import pub_key_file** command.

Or you can upload your public key to a key server using the following syntax:

```
gpg --keyserver server_URL --send-keys 8c85EB9D
```

Perform an Internet search to find available key servers and replace "server_URL" with the URL of the key server. If you upload your key to a key server, the recipient can download the key using the following syntax:

```
gpg --recv-keys 950B76C6
```

Note that you can see what keys have been imported to your account by executing the **gpg –list-keys** command.

Once the user has imported your key and has the encrypted file, the file can be decrypted with the **gpg file.gpg** command.

Another use of GnuPG is to digitally sign a file. Software packages are often digitally signed to provide administrators with a means to verify the source of the software package. To verify a package, execute the **gpg –verify pkg_name** command.

Secure Shell

By this time, you are probably aware that the Telnet protocol sends passwords and data in clear-text and shouldn't be trusted for important sessions and tasks. The *Secure Shell (SSH)* suite includes a protocol, a daemon, and client utilities that make your host-to-host shell sessions much more secure—about as secure as being at the physical console.

One of the features that makes SSH desirable as a remote protocol is its end-to-end encryption, which encrypts not only the username and password but also all communications.

The SSH suite replaces **telnet**, as well as **rsh**, **rexec**, **rcp**, and other unsecure utilities. You can use SSH to connect for a shell session, or you can use the **scp** command to remotely transfer files through the secure pipe that SSH builds between the hosts.

SSH Components

SSH includes a number of programs and files:

- **ssh**—Used for remote shell sessions on another host, it replaces the **telnet**, **rsh**, and **rexec** commands.

- **scp**—Used for remote copying operations, it replaces the **rcp** command.

- **sshd**—The SSH daemon.

- **ssh-agent**—Runs as a wrapper to the user's session and provides authentication when requested.

- **ssh-add**—Loads the user's key(s) into the agent.

The SSH package configuration files are somewhat scattered. SSH daemon and global configuration files are kept in the **/etc/ssh** directory, with local or user-specific configuration files being kept in the **~/.ssh** directory for each user.

The global configuration files include

- **/etc/ssh/sshd_config**—The main configuration for the **sshd** daemon.

- **/etc/ssh/ssh_host_[dr]sa_key**—These files, the **ssh_host_dsa_key** file and the **ssh_host_rsa_key** file, are in the same directory and are the private parts of the host's key structure and should be protected from public view. The permissions for these files are 600 or rw for the root user and no permissions for anyone else.

- **/etc/ssh/ssh_host_[dr]sa_key.pub**—These files, the **ssh_host_dsa_key.pub** file and the **ssh_host_rsa_key.pub** file, are in the same directory and are the public parts of the host's key structure. These must be world-readable and write-only by the root user, or set to 644.

■ **/etc/nologin**—This isn't a part of SSH. However, if it's present, no one can log in via SSH except the root. Non-root users see the contents of the **/etc/nologin** file and then are denied access to the system.

A couple of special file pairs affect how SSH works, particularly the **/etc/ssh /ssh_known_hosts** and **~/.ssh/known_hosts** files. The global file (**/etc/ssh /ssh_known_hosts**) is used to check the public key of a host attempting to attach via SSH. The local file (**~/.ssh/known_hosts**) is the file from which the client gets the public key of the remote server. If a new connection is begun to a previously unknown host, the user sees a message informing him that the host is an unknown host and asking whether he wants to store the host's key in his known hosts file. If the user answers in the affirmative, the host's public key is added to the **~/.ssh /known_hosts** file.

The **/etc/ssh/ssh_known_hosts** file should be world-readable and root-writable. The **~/.ssh/known_hosts** file must be owned by and writable for the user.

A file of interest is one that affects only a particular user's environment: the **~/.ssh /authorized_keys** file. This file is used to store the public keys that can be used for logging as this user. These are matched with the keys presented by an **ssh** or **scp** client upon login request.

Using SSH Client Utilities

The SSH client utilities are versatile, with a number of options available to customize the experience. You just need the basics for the exam, but I include a few fun things I've picked up along the way.

The SSH client command is used to replace the RSH and Telnet programs specifically. Its syntax is as follows:

```
ssh -l username remotehost
```

If you don't specify a username with the **-l** option, the **ssh** command assumes you want to use the account name of whom you are locally logged in as. For example, if you are logged in as the user "ross" and you execute the **ssh** command without the **–l** option, the command attempts to log you in as "ross" on the remote system.

For example, I could attach to the host mp3server as the user snuffy with this command:

```
ssh -l snuffy mp3server
```

If I have not connected to this server before, I get a message similar to what's shown here:

```
The authenticity of host 'mp3server (192.168.33.44)' can't be
established.
RSA key fingerprint is 73:4f:fa:b0:42:a4:3a:a8:64:2c:ad:26:1d:b1:21
:e0.
Are you sure you want to continue connecting (yes/no)?
```

If I answer with yes, the host's public key is added to my **~/.ssh/known_hosts** file and looks something like this:

```
192.168.3.44 ssh-rsa AAAAB3NzaC1yc2EAAAABIwAAAIEA1gFIB9VQpF
KWAZUzNM+ac/U81Tk9R8OCFfUkegVJXwj6nqCISPyV2iJwaukcVVaVAQ+JR
3EhvOvh4PhoSg4yzBSUkJ8aUBYoRSGj7PCD+vyWyi1922HGxWbWooMBAO/
Was8I7N0zQ6jxDO9qNOHcrIFeU7qbOCrKjQDM08HQjk0=
```

Rather than work with *RCP* or *FTP*, most of my file transfer work is with SCP. The **scp** command uses the SSH protocol and encrypts the files sent from one host to another host.

For example, if I wanted to transfer file1 from my root user's home directory on my machine to the same location on a host named remotehost, I could use the following command:

```
scp /root/file1 root@remotehost:/root/file1
```

This would prompt me with the RSA key question (as shown in the previous **ssh** example) if I have not connected to this system previously from this account. I would be prompted for the password and then it would transfer the files. The output from a file transfer looks like this:

```
root@192.168.1.73's password:
mypubkey.txt  100% |*********************| 1379  00:00
```

You can copy files from your host to another as shown previously or copy files from a remote host to your system by reversing the source and target specification.

You can even copy files from one remote system to another remote system. For example, the following command recursively copies the **/data** directory and all its contents from the remote1 host to the remote2 host after prompting you for the password for both hosts:

```
scp -r root@remote1:/data root@remote2:/data
```

Another use of the SSH protocol is to log in to a host and use SSH to forward the output from an X client back to your display. This is feature can be specifically invoked with the **-x** option. This feature is referred to as an X11 tunnel.

SSH allows for skipping the password prompt when signing on between computers, which can be convenient if you use the **ssh** or **scp** command frequently and don't mind the possibility that someone could sit down at your accidentally unlocked station and have her way with your network!

> **NOTE** There has been a lot of talk about why it's important to delete **.rhosts** files from user directories. Basically, if you have a user that has a hostname in her **.rhosts** file and that host also has the user's hostname in its **/etc/hosts_equiv** file, that user can log in without a password by using the **rlogin** command! This would be a security risk, so my advice is to delete these files with the following command:
>
> ```
> find /home -iname .rhost -exec rm -f {} \;
> ```

This deletes all **.rhosts** files it finds in users' home directories and does not prompt you for each deletion.

When I need to enable SSH usage without a password, here are the steps I take. In this example I have two machines, fattyre and murphy, both of which are Linux workstations with the necessary SSH software loaded as per the defaults. This demonstration assumes that fattyre and murphy are both in each other's **/etc/hosts** files or resolvable via DNS.

Here's how you can enable SSH usage without passwords:

1. Log in to fattyre as the root user

2. For this example, use a new user named user1. Create it with the **useradd –m user1** command.

3. Set user1's password with the **passwd** command to whatever you want: **passwd user1**.

4. Switch to the user1 user account with the **su – user1** command.

5. Create and set the permissions for the .ssh directory with the **mkdir .ssh ; chmod 700 .ssh** command.

6. Generate an RSA key: **ssh-keygen -b 1024 -t rsa**.

7. When prompted for the location for the file, press Enter to accept the default.

8. When prompted for a passphrase, enter **seatec astronomy**.

9. Reenter the passphrase when prompted.

10. Change into the .ssh directory and set the permissions on the id_rsa.pub file with these commands:

    ```
    cd .ssh ; chmod 644 id_rsa.pub
    ```

11. Copy the id_rsa.pub file to a new file called authorized_keys:

```
cp id_rsa.pub authorized_keys
```

NOTE The next steps take place on the host murphy.

12. Ensure you can contact the host fattyre with a ping:

```
ping fattyre
```

13. Sign on to the host murphy as the root user.

14. Add a user named user2 with the **useradd –m user2** command.

15. Set the password for user2:

```
passwd user2
```

16. Enter the password twice to confirm it.

17. Switch to the user2 account with the **su – user2** command.

18. Make a directory and set its permissions with the following command:

```
mkdir .ssh ; chmod 700 .ssh
```

NOTE The next steps take place on the host fattyre.

19. Connect to the murphy host as user2:

```
ssh -l user2 murphy
```

20. When prompted about the RSA key, answer yes and then enter user2's password.

21. While logged in as user2 on the host murphy via SSH, copy the authorized_keys file from the fattyre host with the following command:

```
scp user1@fattyre:~/.ssh/authorized_keys ~/.ssh
```

The output of the scp program should look similar to this:

```
authorized_keys   100% |************************| 236   00:00
```

22. Exit user2 on the host murphy and return to being user1 on fattyre.

23. On fattyre as user1, invoke the **ssh-agent** as a wrapper to your shell with the **ssh-agent $SHELL** command.

24. Add your key to the agent:

```
ssh-add
```

25. When prompted for the passphrase, enter **no more tears**.

26. You then see output similar to this:

```
Identity added: /home/ssha/.ssh/id_rsa (/home/ssha/.ssh/id_rsa)
```

27. Now try to log in as user2 on murphy, and watch what happens:

```
ssh -l user Murphy
```

28. You shouldn't see any password prompt; you should see only the confirmation of where you last logged in from:

```
Last login: Wed May 26 13:46:55 from fattyre
```

If you do see a prompt for the passphrase, enter **no more tears** as you did before.

That's all it takes to get two accounts and machines set up to use SSH utilities without having to enter anything but the **ssh-agent** command along with the passphrase. Remember that **ssh-agent** resides in memory and wraps a security blanket around your shell session, answering any SSH-related security requests for you. The **ssh-add** utility is for adding your key information into the agent and doesn't have to be run again as long as your key information remains the same.

Additional Security Features

Security is an important matter, so security features have been discussed throughout this book. As a result, some of the certification topics that align to this chapter have been discussed in detail in other chapters of this book. Table 20-2 serves as a reference guide for these topics.

Table 20-2 Additional Security Utilities

Feature/ Command	Details Found	Security Note
find	Chapter 5	Useful to find program with permissions that pose potential security risks, such as setuid and setgid permission.
passwd	Chapter 15	Use to generate a new password for a user. This is important when a user account has been compromised.
fuser	Chapter 20	Displays open files on a filesystem. This data can be used to determine whether there is a breach on the system.
lsof	Chapter 20	Like the **fuser** command, this command displays open files. This data can be used to determine whether there is a breach on the system.

Feature/ Command	Details Found	Security Note
chage	Chapter 6	Used to change password aging policies on a specific account. This is important to ensure users change passwords frequently.
usermod	Chapter 15	Used to change user account features, including password aging. This is important to ensure users change passwords frequently.
ulimit	Chapter 15	Used to change how much system resources specific users can utilize. If a user uses the bulk of system resources, it can make the system unusable for other users and system services.
who	Chapter 6	Used to display users who are currently logged in. Important to determine whether a security breach is in progress.
w	Chapter 6	Like **who**, displays users who are currently logged in, but **w** also outputs what they are doing. Important to determine whether a security breach is in progress.
last	Chapter 12	Used to display users who are currently logged in and users who logged in to the system recently. Important to determine whether a security breach is in progress or whether one has occurred in the past.
/etc/passwd	Chapter 11	Contains user account data. Important for security to determine whether there are specious accounts on the system.
/etc/shadow	Chapter 11	Contains user password data. Important for security to determine whether there are specious accounts on the system.
/etc/inittab	Chapter 2	Used to boot the system to a specific runlevel on some Linux distributions. If set to the wrong runlevel, this could result in security issues.
/etc/init.d	Chapter 2	Directory contains scripts important for system startup and could result in security issues.

Summary

In this chapter you learned how to secure the system using a variety of techniques. You learned how to secure network access to services with inetd, xinetd, and TCP wrappers. You also discovered how to utilize Secure Shell and GnuPG to secure data.

Exam Preparation Tasks

As mentioned in the section "How to Use This Book" in the Introduction, you have a few choices for exam preparation: the exercises here, Chapter 21, "Final Preparation," and the practice exams on the DVD.

Review All Key Topics

Review the most important topics in this chapter, noted with the Key Topics icon in the outer margin of the page. Table 20-3 lists a reference of these key topics and the page numbers on which each is found.

Table 20-3   Key Topics for Chapter 20

Key Topic Element	Description	Page Number
Paragraph	The **su** command and non-login shells	574
Paragraph	Options in the **/etc/sudoers** file	575
Paragraph	Some of the services governed by **xinetd**	577
Paragraph	Lines in the **/etc/xinetd.conf** file	579
Paragraph	Specifying daemons or services in the **host.allow/deny** files	582
Section	Wrapper read order	583
Section	Using rule options	585
Paragraph	Special bit definitions	586
Paragraph	Finding files by their permissions	587
Paragraph	Creating GnuPG keys	587
Paragraph	Other uses of GnuPG	590
Paragraph	Global configuration files	591
Paragraph	The SSH client command	592
Paragraph	Enabling SSH usage	594

Define Key Terms

Define the following key terms from this chapter and check your answers in the glossary:

daemon, TCP wrappers, SUID, SGID, GnuPG, public key, private key, SSH, telnet, RCP, FTP

Review Questions

1. When a user on host1 uses the SSH client to successfully connect to host2 for the first time, which file is updated with SSH-related information?

   a. ~/.ssh/known_hosts on host1

   b. /etc/ssh/known_hosts on host2

   c. ~/.ssh/authorized_keys on host2

   d. /etc/ssh/authorized_keys on host1

2. You are ordered to deny access to the Telnet service on your server for the host snuffypc and to use the TCP wrappers files and utilities to accomplish this. In the blank, write the full path and filename of the file that should contain this entry:

   _____

3. You are the root user on your managed systems. You need to send the /root/file6 file from host1 to host3 in the same location, but you're on host2. Which of the following commands accomplishes the task? (Choose all that apply.)

   a. scp root@host1:~/file6 root@host3

   b. scp root@host1:/root/file6 root@host3

   c. scp root@host1:/root/file6 root@host3:~

   d. scp root@host1:file6 root@host3

4. You just downloaded a new public key and imported it into your GPG key ring. Fill in the blank with the command and any necessary options that show you the contents of your key ring:

   _____

5. One of the systems you manage is acting funny, leading you to believe some files might have special bits set that allow standard users to run important utilities as root. Which of the following search commands shows you all files that have any combination of special bits set?

    a. **find / -perm -7000**

    b. **find / -perm +7000**

    c. **find / -perms 7000**

    d. **locate --permissions=rws**

6. You need to be able to attach, via a shell session, to other hosts over a secure and encrypted connection and to log on to the remote system without entering a password every time. Which of the following is the program or utility that directly makes this possible?

    a. ssh-add

    b. ssh-keygen

    c. ssh-agent

    d. .ssh/authorized_keys

7. A security situation requires you to create a 1K RSA public/private key combination for your currently logged-in account. Fill in the blank with the correct command, with any necessary options and arguments, to accomplish this:

    _____

This chapter covers the following topics:

- How to Prepare for LPI Exams
- How NOT to Prepare for LPI Exams
- LPI Exams and Distributions
- Question Types and Strategies
- How to Be Successful (aka PASS)

## CHAPTER 21

Final Preparation

The LPI exams are computer based and are purposely not easy exams to take. A number of proven strategies will help any candidate be successful, given the person has actually learned the information laid out in the objectives and can perform those actions in the real world.

Foundation Topics

How to Prepare for the LPI Exams

In our many years as sysadmins, managers, and especially instructors on the topic of Linux and Open Source, we have identified a number of key methods and strategies that help any exam-taker be more successful, and in particular here we focus on the LPI exams.

Caveat and Warning

The LPI exams specifically, and exams about computer technology topics in general, are not an end but are a means to an end. In other words, passing the exam isn't everything that you should have mastered to be an awesome sysadmin. You must have mastered or shown proficiency at the actual tasks being measured via an exam.

We can't guarantee that you read every word in this book, or followed our advice and executed all the commands multiple times, or ruined multiple virtual machines getting good at being a sysadmin. That's all up to you; it's your career. Possessing the abilities an employer can depend on to accomplish its corporate goals of providing services via Linux and Open Source systems is the base of the pyramid, but the capstone is being able to prove that you are qualified, and that's where exams come in.

With all that said, this chapter is the distillation of decades of helping exam-takers be prepared and pass their chosen exams, given all the knowledge is there.

Exam Objectives

It always amazes us when we see someone either not studying for an exam, or simply leaving it to chance, especially when the person's career can be affected or she might not be promoted depending on the outcome.

The LPI exams all have a well-laid-out and comprehensive set of objectives, which are an effective listing of what appears on the exam you are studying so hard for! Spending all your time reading books and doing labs and never even looking at the guide from which the exams are developed is not a wise strategy in our opinion.

You can find the LPI exam objectives on the LPI.org website. They have moved around a bit over the years, but typically they are on the Certification tab. Regardless of where they appear, they're easy to find, and no exam-taker should appear at a testing center without a solid understanding of what is on the exam objectives, or how many questions of a given variety they will likely see. Go and look at the exam objectives for the 101 and 102 exams. You see a lot of good information there, and an understanding of what you see will help you a great deal when you are preparing for the exams.

I highly recommend that you create a checklist from the objectives. Place a check mark next to each item in each objective once you feel you understand that item well. Don't take the exam until every item of the exam objective list has a check mark next to it.

Important Exam Facts

The LPI exams on the Professional level—the LPIC-1, LPIC-2, and LPIC-3—are all 60 questions each, and you have 90 minutes to complete the exams. This may sound like a long time, but it's not much for each question. You only have 1.5 minutes per question if you evenly distribute the time, and of course some questions take longer than others, so keep an eye on your watch or the clock.

Right Before Your Exam Starts

We have developed a couple of preparation steps that you can take immediately before you go into the torture, okay, well, the exam chamber.

For years we have recommended that you consume several things immediately before entering the exam room: a banana and a liter of water. Nope, it's not a joke or something we recommend and then laugh about afterward; there are good reasons for this recommendation.

We say to eat the banana because the potassium and other minerals contained are helpful to your mental processes, as well as helping make sure you don't go hypoglycemic sometime during the next 1.5 hours—something we have seen happen too many times to our poor exam-takers.

The liter of water is probably as important or more than the banana, as our brains and nervous systems are essentially big electronic circuits, and nothing conducts electrons better than water or liquid. Drinking a liter of H20 before you go use that big electronic circuit is just good sense. You'll be well-hydrated and things should function at the top of their form.

NOTE The author(s) initially made this recommendation in the previous edition of this book, and we continue to receive photos of students and exam-takers holding bananas and bottles of water! Send us your photos here: LPICBook@brunson.org

How to Look at the Objectives

The objectives are laid out in topics and subtopics. The 101 Exam Objectives are as such:

- 101 – System Architecture

- 102 – Linux Installation and Package Management

- 103 – GNU and Unix Commands

- 104 – Devices, Linux Filesystems, Filesystem Hierarchy Standard

Each of the major topics, such as 101 - System Architecture, is broken up into subtopics, such as the following:

- 101.1 - Determine and configure hardware settings

- 101.2 - Boot the system

- 101.3 - Change runlevels/boot targets and shut down or reboot system

Each of these subtopics has several sections that bear mentioning. Figure 21-1 uses the 103.1 subtopic to show you the important features of a subtopic.

As you can see, the subtopic title, Work on the Command Line, lets you know the overall topic the objective focuses on. This is followed by the weight of the subtopic; in this case it's a weight of 4.

The weight of a subtopic is important information. Not only does the weight indicate the number of actual exam questions that will be drawn from the subtopic, but also the sum of all the subtopic weights equals exactly 60, the number of questions on each exam.

Next in the subtopic is the Key Knowledge Areas section, which is normally a set of bullet points that describe the areas focused on. In this case the focus is clearly on being capable of running single commands and one-line command sequences to accomplish a given task, work with the shell environment and variables, manipulate command history, and run commands in or out of the path.

It's critical that you read each one of these as a statement of intent to test a given set of knowledge. In years past (about a decade ago), these were written as if they were cryptic sentences dropping from the mouth of an oracle on a mountaintop, but they are pretty direct these days.

The next area, the Terms and Utilities section, is directly related to the Key Knowledge Areas, in that these are the commands, concepts, and files that appear as the supporting cast of actors to the stars in the Key Knowledge Areas.

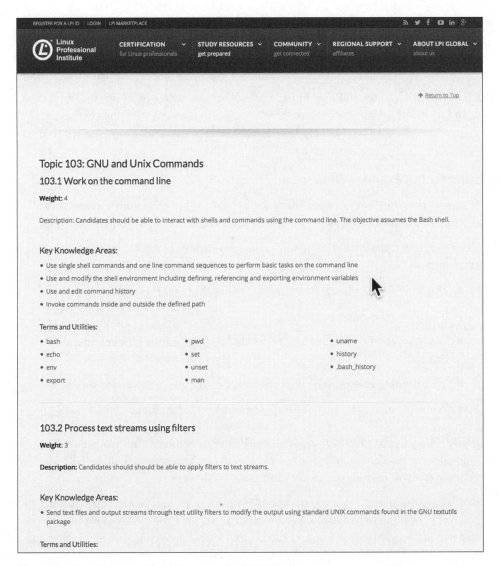

Figure 21-1   LPI Exam Objective subtopic 103.1 Work on the command line

It's critically important that you use the Key Knowledge Areas as statements of what will be tested, and the Terms and Utilities as the commands and files that you typically use to accomplish the tested tasks.

You should try each of the commands, run the man pages for them, look at the Examples section of those man pages, and know by heart the most common options and usages of those commands. Keep going, investigate every file, read every man page, and blow up dozens of virtual machines learning all about everything in a given subtopic.

Preparing this way not only helps you on the exam, but the knowledge also makes you an even more awesome sysadmin.

> **NOTE** We often recommend that those studying for the exams print out the objectives and mark the appropriate items off when you are finished studying them.

Studying for the Exams—What to Do

It's important that you not only study the objectives, but thoroughly investigate all the other options for getting more information about the topic you are studying.

We recommend that you use the following resources to study for every item on the exam objectives:

- Live machine or virtual machines with snapshot and rollback
- Books like this one
- Study guides, documentation from tldp.org (The Linux Documentation Project)
- Man pages, and especially the web-based easily searched versions
- Websites such as Linuxquestions.org and YouTube videos

If you need to, take a class from someone. Plenty of vendors offer instructor-led, online live or on-demand classes, videos, and so on. You can start at the LPI Marketplace (www.lpimarketplace.com) and go from there.

Don't just stop there; get some needed context for what you're reading, studying, and trying out on your machine instances. Read all the Linux-related topics you can find online; good places to go are Linux.com, Opensource.com, and just in general search for "Linux System Administration" on Google.

We did most of our studying and got our certifications before we had our respective children. We know just how hard it is to focus when all the rest of the world seems to be dedicated to distracting you. We highly recommend studying either early in the morning before everyone else is up or late at night when all the rest of the family has gone to bed.

Installing a lock on your office or den door and putting up a "Do Not Disturb - Daddy/Mommy is studying" sign is a good way to get the family to help you out with your goals. We also encourage you to take a weekend day every month or so to just go off somewhere and read as much as you can.

Machines or Virtual Machines?

A quick word about our recommendation for study machines: Go virtual; it's much easier to reload machines when they are completely based in software, and you can have many different distributions loaded up and ready on pause, so you can just use a single hardware machine.

We get a lot of questions about what virtual machine software to use, and while we are partial to VMWare and KVM, you can use just about anything that provides a virtual machine environment.

Possibilities for virtual machine software include the following:

- **VMWare**—Workstation for Windows and Linux, Fusion for Mac. For the cost-conscious, VMWare Player can be used; it's commercial but free (www.vmware.com).

- **Parallels**—For the Mac platform, this software is a competitor to VMWare Fusion. There used to be a Parallels Workstation product that ran on Windows.

- **VirtualBox**—Cross-platform and in use all over the place, this is a great choice and it's Open Source. The parent company that came up with Virtual-Box is now owned by Oracle.

- **KVM or XEN**—Less popular among those studying Linux or just getting into Linux, these are options typically provided by large virtualization vendors, so you might not use these on your local workstation to study and learn Linux.

Studying for the Exams—What Not to Do

Almost as important are the things that you should avoid when studying for exams. Many use the Testking products, and it's probably fair to say that the use of such sources is cheating. If you are caught, disciplinary procedures apply.

There are a number of question dump and brain dump sites out there, and we monitor many of them for what questions are being posted and how accurate the answers are. We can positively state that this also is cheating and dishonest. You should be studying and preparing to be a sysadmin, not someone who memorizes things and spits them back out on the exam. Besides, most of the time, the answers to these are horribly inaccurate. So if you must look at them, just look at the questions, and if you don't know the answer, GO LOOK IT UP.

NOTE Whatever you do, unless you are truly into getting abused and possibly reported as a cheat, don't post actual exam questions on LinkedIn or Facebook and ask people who have worked hard to get their certifications by the proper means to help you cheat and pass those exams without knowing the actual information being tested. At the very least, you'll be ignored, and I have seen some deeply unpleasant flame fests started over such postings.

Don't Believe Everything

There are a lot of credible sources for classes, boot camps, and so on, and then there are some certification mills and places that will be happy to take your money and give you questionable return for it.

If a vendor states it will teach you for a week and you'll be ready to pass seven Linux exams, we propose that they won't be able to do that. The team writing this book has about a combined 40 years of teaching experience, a lot of it in accelerated formats. Avoid vendors that make unrealistic claims. You are better off taking one exam at a time and not trying to force feed yourself.

Don't Worry, Be Happy

With apologies to Bobby McFerrin, this is great advice. We have seen way too many people get so stressed out about the exams that they don't do well, or they give themselves an ulcer over it.

To put this in perspective, these are exams. They are a means to an end; they are not life itself nor something to make yourself miserable or sick over. Many times we take an exam and find we are not properly prepared. Most of the time we can use that as an experience that teaches us something; in this case, it's to go back and study more and be more prepared next time!

LPI Certifications and Distributions

Many years ago, some distributions were noted on the LPI exams, as you had to use something to study the topic, and sometimes it appeared they were based mostly on Red Hat and Debian.

This has changed. You will likely see zero mention of any distributions on the exams. Instead you see mention of the packaging formats in the installing and managing packages section. You must know both DPKG and RPM styles of managing packages, and you might see mention of systems that use the sysvinit or systemd processes for runlevels. But we would be surprised if any remaining questions mention a particular system type.

To be crystal clear, the LPI exams are focused on Linux, not a particular distribution. It's key to know Linux, and the commands and files around the Linux Kernel, not the weird and wonderful stuff that vendors want to encourage you to know about.

You Have to Install Something

With the preceding advice in mind, we are aware that you have to install something, some distribution or several, to study Linux; so here are some recommendations:

1. Install at least one each of an RPM and DPKG distribution.

2. openSUSE and Fedora are key RPM-based choices. Arch is great also.

3. Ubuntu and Linux Mint are excellent DPKG-based choices.

4. Know both the apt-get and zypper/yum systems very well; you'll see them on the exam.

If it's not obvious yet, we are huge fans of using virtual machines to study and prepare for your Linux exams. The benefits of using virtual instances include

- You can mess them up and roll back to a functional version.

- You can have many different instances on a single machine.

- You can vary your distributions given the task, server, or workstation.

- You become more balanced as a sysadmin. You'll be working with virtual machines a lot in your future jobs in the open source world.

Remember, the goal is to know Linux. All the distributions are just an offshoot of the main branch. You can learn whatever you need about a given distribution with not much additional effort, but LEARN LINUX.

LPI Exam Question Types

The LPI exams feature a number of types of questions. Some of them occur often, some not so often, and some make up almost 25% of the exam. A good knowledge of the question types and awareness of key points about those types will help you prepare properly and may even cause you to pass your exam because you know how to deal with certain questions.

NOTE Since the LPI exams are not practical exams or machine-based, they take especial care to introduce question types such as fill-in-the-blank, so as to make the exams as close to being a command terminal as possible.

NOTE LPI questions are typically blunt and short, to the point, and don't fool around. The exam writers are not there to fool you, trick you with silly distractors, or do anything other than test your knowledge. The best answer is always the one that most simply answers the question being asked. Don't get tricky or fancy and try show off your mad terminal skills. Just answer the question and move on to the next; time is rapidly moving on.

The question types are

- Single answer multiple choice

- Choose two/choose three

- Choose all that apply

- Fill in the blank

Let's take them one at a time. We explain the question type, show you an example, and give you some important tips for properly and accurately answering this type of question.

Single Answer Multiple Choice

A slight majority of the questions are of this type. There is a straightforward question, anywhere from four to six possible choices, and you have to choose one single answer.

Example Single Answer Multiple Choice Question

Which of the following commands shows a listing of the current directory that indicates the owner and permissions for the listed files?

A. **ls -h**

B. **ls -1**

C. **ls -l**

D. **ls /**

All you have to do is pick the one that most accurately and closely matches the question. In this case it's C; the **ls -l** command shows you the ownership and permissions for the list files in the current directory. Note that some of the other answers do interesting things, but they don't do exactly what is being asked about.

Choose Two/Choose Three

This question type(s) is slightly harder than the single answer questions. You have to look closely at the answers and pick either two or three answers, all of which must be correct, to get this entire question marked as right.

At times you may be asked to pick the two or three things that do a particular task, or even pick the two or three items that together produce a given result. The key here is getting all the proper answers and just the number asked for. If you think there are four items that answer a choose three question, you're incorrect, and marking all four will cause the entire answer to be wrong. There are no partial credits; each question is either answered properly or it's not. Period.

Example Choose Two/Three Question

Which of the following commands/functions must be performed before a new and uninitialized disk can be used for storing data on your system? (Choose three.)

   A. fdisk

   B. dd

   C. mkfs

   D. mount

   E. fsck

The key to this question is that there are several commands or functions that must be performed on "a new and uninitialized disk" so you can write data to it. You must partition the disk (fdisk), make a file system on it (mkfs), and mount it to your system somewhere (mount); so A, C, and D are the correct three answers to this question. The other two are either not necessary for the answering of the question or something that might be done but is not critical.

Choose All That Apply

This question type is slightly more difficult than even the choose two/three type, in that you don't even know at first glance how many of the answers are being asked for. You have to parse, study, and validate every one of the possible answers before you can choose them.

We highly recommend using your note paper for this type of question. Write down the answer choices and work through them on paper. Then mark what you think is right on the computer, but don't take too much time doing it; time is moving on.

> **NOTE** The key to all these questions, particularly the ones that are actual commands, is "will this produce the result asked for if I executed this on the command line?" If you know it will execute, that's good, but will it do exactly what's being asked for and nothing extra?

Example Choose All That Apply Question

Which of the following commands will create a second file that is identical to the first file?

- **A. cp file1 file2**
- **B. cat file1 | file2**
- **C. cp < file1 > file2**
- **D. dd if=file1 of=file2**
- **E. cat file1 > file2**
- **F. if file1 > file2**

A lot of attendees and exam-takers hate this question type, as all the answers must be parsed and thought through before you can mark it as one of the "all that apply" answers.

The best way to answer this question is to actually have tried this sort of thing on the command line many times and to know about things like dd and if and what they actually do.

This question is a tough one, in that you must know how the <, >, and | work, and how the displayed commands work with them to produce the result. The given result is hopefully no errors and a file named file2 that is an exact copy of file1.

Answer A works; it's a straightforward copy of file1 to file2. Answer B doesn't work; it's an inappropriate use of the | character, which is only used to connect two commands to each other or to "pipe" them. Answer C doesn't work either, and this is the one that most everyone misses. It looks like it ought to work, but **cp** doesn't accept the < character the way it looks like it ought to. Answer D works great; the **dd** command just read in the file1 file and produced the output of it as a file named file2. Answer E works perfectly; it's just taking the contents of file1 and redirecting that output to a new file named file2, but if this had used a >> character set, it might not work. Answer F doesn't work; it produces a prompt for more input.

Fill in the Blank

Easily the most dreaded question type, these are called command line questions, FIBs, and "those damned questions." In reality, they are simple. You just have to type in what is being asked for, and if it both executes and does the function being asked for, you are going to get this question marked correct.

Example Fill-in-the-Blank Question

What command with the appropriate switches queries a .rpm file in the local directory named somefile.rpm and shows you information about the package author, build host, and so on, as well as a listing of the files that would be copied to the system if the package were installed? (Type the answer in the space below.)

_____

The tricky part of this question, and the answer, is not really that you don't know the switches, but that there are several methods of arranging the switches, using long options and short options, and so on, that would actually work, and you can only type in one answer.

Let's answer the question first, and then we give you a tip that will really help you out on the exam.

You of course start with the **RPM** command itself. Then because we're querying you use a **-q** and then the **-i** switch for information about the package and the **-l** switch for listing the files that will be copied to your system.

The final key to answering this question properly is to note that you are being asked about a file, a package file, located on disk. Because we're using the **RPM** command and the package file is on the disk, there must be a **-p** or **--package** switch used in the answer. The **RPM** command normally queries the package database or the database that indicates the set of packages installed on the system. If you're querying a package on disk, you must indicate so with the appropriate switches or it will default to querying the packages in the package database.

The most common way to answer this question might look like this:

```
rpm -qilp somefile.rpm
```

However, it could also look like this:

```
rpm --query --info --list --package somefile.rpm
```

Those of you who have been around systems for a while know that there are many different possible combinations of long and short options as well as the order of those options that could constitute a correct answer to this question. The conundrum is that you're only allowed to type one valid command into the dialog box in the hopes of answering this question.

The answer to the million dollar question here is that there is an actual database behind this question containing a comprehensive list of correct possible answers. The software that makes up the testing engine will use this database to check whether your answer is correct.

All you, the exam-taker, need to do is to type in one of the possible correct answers (typically one that you know will execute because you've typed it a number of times) and then move on to the next question.

> **NOTE** This fact alone is enough to cause you to be able to answer properly with a great reduction in stress; approximately 20% to 25% of the questions on the exam are this question type.

Final Recommendations

Now that we have hopefully demystified the question types as well as giving you some idea of what to do and not to do, let's finish up with a set of recommendations that we think are useful in adequately preparing for, taking, and hopefully passing the LPI exams.

Things to remember:

- Try everything, every command.
- Look at every file's contents.
- Read the man pages for everything you encounter.
- Google and search for additional information on everything.
- Use the Examples section of the man page for starters.
- Get a copy of Unix Power Tools from O'Reilly and Associates; it's awesome.
- Install virtualization software and get used to virtual machines; they're the future.
- Don't whine about the command line; systems don't need X in particular servers.
- Try to know all the commonly used switches to commands; it's just good info.

Summary

We have poured everything we know and can tell you into this book. It's the culmination of decades of being technologists and in particular Linux sysadmins. We want to hear about your successes and any comments you might have, so please look us up online by our names or email us at lpicbook@brunson.org and we authors will get all your emails.

Thanks for giving us the chance to make a difference in your life and career and for taking the time to learn how to become an awesome sysadmin. We need you in the workforce. There is always a place for someone who knows Linux and can support and maintain it and its application services in an enterprise environment.

Good luck on those exams—all of us authors and technical editors are rooting for you!

Answers to the "Do I Know This Already?" Quizzes and Review Questions

Chapter 1

"Do I Know This Already?" Quiz

1. **D.** A is incorrect because IO ports are used to transfer data between the CPU and devices. B is incorrect because DMA allows a device to access memory directly. C is incorrect because IRQs are used by a device to ask for the CPU's attention. D is correct because TCP/IP ports are used to talk to other hosts, not peripherals.

2. **B.** A is not correct because **lspci** gives an overview of just the PCI hardware. B is correct because **lsdev** aggregates many different files under /proc to give you a description of all your hardware. C is not correct because **lsusb** enumerates the USB bus and nothing else. D is not correct because **sysinfo** is not a valid command.

3. **A.** A is correct because sda3 includes both the device and an offset indicating the partition. B is not correct because a flash drive would not have a number. C is not correct because the filesystem goes on the partition. D is not correct because the disk does not have a number in it.

4. **D.** A is not correct because the PV is the disk itself. B is not correct because the VG pools all the PVs but still does not allocate disks to be used. C is not correct because PEs are just a unit of allocation. D is correct because the LV is comprised of multiple PEs allocated from the VG.

5. **A.** A is correct because /sbin holds binaries necessary to manage the system and boot it. B is not correct because /home is often placed on a separate partition to make it easier to share. C is not correct because /usr can be separated to keep system binaries separate, or to make it easier to grow. D is not correct because /tmp is often put on its own partition so that it can have different mount options, or to prevent temporary files from filling the root partition.

6. **D.** A is not correct because the BIOS is used to load the first stage of the boot manager. B is not correct because /boot contains the kernel and later stages. C is not correct because the partition table is just a table pointing

at the locations of the various partitions. D is correct because the MBR is the first place the BIOS looks for a bootable block.

7. **B.** A is not correct because menu.lst is for the Legacy GRUB. B is correct because the new name of the file is grub.cfg. C is not correct because grub.conf is also for the old version of GRUB. D is not correct because that name is not used by any version of GRUB.

Review Questions

1. **B.** B is correct because direct memory access lets the peripheral talk directly to memory. A is incorrect because an interrupt request is a signal from the peripheral to the CPU that it needs attention. C is incorrect because the Transmission Control Protocol is a network concern. D is incorrect because it is not a hardware matter.

2. **D.** D is correct because **lsdev** shows information about system resources including devices, IO ports, and DMA channels.

3. **C.** C is correct because the IRQ is a signal to the processor. A is incorrect because IO ports are used by the CPU to talk to the device. B is not correct because pushing to memory does not involve the CPU. D is incorrect because devices don't execute code out of main memory.

4. **B.** B is correct because /proc exposes files containing information about the system. A is incorrect because /dev contains device files used to talk to devices. C and D are incorrect because they are file storage locations.

5. **D.** D is correct because the udev subsystem monitors for device changes and makes the appropriate changes in /dev. A is incorrect because systemd is used for managing processes, though udevd can be a component of systemd. B is incorrect because init is used for managing processes. C is incorrect because procfs is used for exposing system information to the user.

6. **B.** B is correct because a hotplug device can be inserted or removed at any time. A is incorrect because the device still needs a driver. C is incorrect because the device can be removed without a reboot. D is incorrect because there are more hotplug devices than just hard drives.

7. **C.** C is correct because the memory of the system is not persistent. All the others are persistent block devices.

8. **D.** D is correct because /dev/sda2 refers to the second partition on the first hard drive. A is incorrect because sda would be the name of the hard drive. B is incorrect because sda refers to a physical disk, not a logical volume. C is not correct because network adapters are named differently.

9. **B.** B is correct because a partition contains a filesystem. A is incorrect because you need to partition a hard drive before applying a filesystem. C and D are incorrect because the PV is added to a volume group and then sliced up into logical volumes that contain filesystems.

10. **A.** A is correct because the file would be stored under /usr but not /usr/local.

11. **B.** B is correct because integration is not a core consideration—integrity is, however. The others are primary considerations when laying out hard drive partitions.

12. **D.** D is correct because the hard drives are added as PVs. A is incorrect because the LV is the target of a filesystem and is mounted. B is incorrect because the volume groups are a collection of physical volumes. C is incorrect because the PVs are carved up into PEs.

13. **A.** True. Hot resizing is possible because the makeup of the disk is all logical under LVM.

14. **A.** A is correct because the kernel's virtual memory allows a memory page to be swapped to disk and swapped back later when it's needed. B is incorrect because the memory was promised earlier and can't be discarded. C is incorrect because the VM subsystem doesn't compress memory. D is incorrect because if swap exists, it can be used to make the system appear as if it has more memory than it actually does.

15. **C.** C is correct because the MBR is the first block on the disk where the first stage of the bootloader and the partition tables are located. A and B are incorrect because GRUB is a bootloader that uses the MBR. D is incorrect because the index is a component of the filesystem and is not stored on the MBR.

16. **D.** D is correct because grub.cfg is the new name of the configuration file. A and B are incorrect because they are the name of the configuration for GRUB Legacy. C is incorrect because that file is not used.

Chapter 2

"Do I Know This Already?" Quiz

1. The correct answer is 2. Entering the character 2 at the boot prompt causes the majority of distributions to then subsequently enter Runlevel 2. The same would be true for the various other configured numerals and their corresponding runlevels.

2. **B.** In a GRUB configuration file, the disks are referred to by (hd#,#). The first disk is referred to by (hd0) and the fifth partition, the first logical, is referred to by (hd0,4) as GRUB starts counting from 0.

3. **C. e** is the command used by GRUB at the boot menu to edit the parameters for the entry you want to change.

4. **B.** The **dmesg** command is designed to show to standard output the kernel ring messages generated by the Linux Kernel.

5. **B, C.** If you do a **ls –l** on the shutdown, halt, poweroff, and init commands, you see that halt and poweroff are symlinks that point to the /sbin/reboot command, while shutdown is its own command and not a symlink. The "init 6" command string will simply cause the system to reboot, but it is NOT a symlink to the reboot command.

6. **C, E. journald** is one of the daemons that is a part of the systemd suite, and systemctl is a configuration utility that is also part of the systemd suite. The others are incorrect.

7. **D.** Killing more than one process by name is done via the **killall** command. halt is a command used to bring the system to a halted state, **pskill** doesn't exist, **kill** just kills a single instance of foobar, likely the first one found in the process table, and **pstree** shows the treelike hierarchy of processes and alone does not kill a process.

Review Questions

1. **A, D, E.** Answers A, D, and E are correct because the numeral 1 puts the system into runlevel 1, a troubleshooting mode. The characters "s" and "S" also are used to put the system into a troubleshooting mode where few modules are loaded and mostly you are presented with a shell prompt. The other answers are incorrect because they don't match the criteria or are nonexistent.

2. **A, D.** Answers A and D are correct because these are valid locations for the boot loader code to reside. The other answers are incorrect because they don't match the criteria or are nonexistent.

3. **B.** Answer B is correct because group tags are used by systemd to refer to and allow the loading and removal of groups of processes. The other answers are incorrect because they don't match the criteria or are nonexistent.

4. **B.** Answer B is correct because the **–k** option to **shutdown** is for simulating a system shutdown event, as well as sending a message to the attached users. The other answers are incorrect because **–h** halts the system, **-r** reboots the system, and **–c** cancels a shutdown that has already been issued, if there is sufficient time.

5. **A, D, E.** Answers A, D, and E are correct because they are all valid variations of the SIGHUP signal and will "hang up" or restart the service, rereading the configuration file. The other answers are incorrect because they don't match the criteria and will either politely kill the service (9) or abruptly kill the service (15).

6. **B, D, E.** Answers B, D, and E are correct because they are all three capable of showing just the system's boot messages from the last boot. The other answers are incorrect because they don't match the criteria or are nonexistent.

Chapter 3

"Do I Know This Already?" Quiz

1. **B.** B is correct because the .so moniker indicates a shared library (or literally "shared object"). A is not correct because a static library would be bundled with the binary. C and D are not correct because the file is more likely to be a shared library.

2. **A.** A is correct because the name of the linker is ld.so, sometimes also called ld-linux.so. The configuration file is in /etc/ld.so.conf. The other answers either get the name wrong or the configuration file locations wrong.

3. **C.** C is correct because the **dpkg** tool is used to install local Debian packages. A and B are not correct because **yum** and **rpm** are for RPM-based systems. D is not correct because **apt-get** is for retrieving packages from remote repositories.

4. **D.** A is not correct because the **--info** option is used to examine a local Debian package. B is not correct because **apt-cache** is used to update the cache of remote packages. C is not correct because **rpm** is a tool for RPM-based systems. D is correct because the **--list** option searches the list of locally installed packages.

5. **D.** D is correct because the **apt-get update** command is used to update the list of remote repositories and their contents. A is not correct because **dpkg** does not deal with repositories. B and C are not correct because **apt-cache** is only used for searching the cache.

6. **B.** B is correct because the option tells **dpkg** to install dependency errors. A is incorrect because the default is to stop processing when a dependency error has been found. C is not correct because that overrides an error indicating a package is conflicting, rather than missing a dependency. D is incorrect because that overrides packages that need to be reinstalled.

7. **D.** D is correct because the architecture, such as x86_64, is not part of the package name. The long name contains the name of the package, version, and the distribution version. For example, kernel-3.17.7-300.fc21 is a long name.

8. **A.** A is correct because the **-K** option checks signatures. B is not correct because the query option (**-k**) does not accept a **-k** parameter. C is not correct because there is no **--check-sig** option to **rpm**. D is not correct because there is no **rpm-sig** command.

9. **C.** C is correct because the query (**-q**) checks the installed RPMs. A and B are not correct because there is no **-V** option to **rpm** query. D is not correct because the **-p** makes the operation work on a local file, not the rpm database.

Review Questions

1. **B.** B is correct because the combination of the **-qp** and **--changelog** options shows the changelog or revision history for a package that's on disk. Answer A is incorrect because there is no such thing as a **--revision** option for the **rpm** command. Answer C is incorrect because there isn't a **-p** option to query the package on disk, nor does **-qc** show the required information. Answer D is incorrect because the **-qlp** option shows the files in the package, not the revision history, and there isn't a **--showrev** option to the **rpm** command.

2. **B.** B is correct because that is the name of the cache file generated by ldconfig.

3. **C.** C is correct because the **ldd** program, when used with a program name as the argument, shows the necessary libraries for the program's functionality. Answer A is incorrect because **ldconfig** is used to rebuild links to library files, not **ldd**. Answer B is incorrect because creating a link to a library file is done by the **ldconfig** or **ln** command, not ldd. Answer D is incorrect because the **ldd** command does not read a program's library capabilities; instead it reads its dependencies.

4. **D.** D is correct because the dynamic linker will use the LD_LIBRARY_PATH environment variable to load extra libraries if the variable is present. None of the other options refers to a variable that's in use.

5. **A, B, D.** Answers A, B, and D are correct because they cannot be performed in any way except singly at any given time because the database is locked or because normal users cannot perform the action. Answer C is incorrect because multiple verification commands can be performed simultaneously because the operation is a read, not a read-write.

6. **D.** D is correct because the command is the only one that removes all instances of the package woohoo with a single command. Answer A is incorrect because asterisks do not invoke multiple removals and can be used only in installation situations for multiple packages on disk. Answer B is incorrect because the **-ea** option does not allow for multiple removals and works only in queries. Answer C is incorrect because there is no **--remove** option for the **rpm** command.

7. **A.** A is correct because the **Freshen** command only upgrades packages and won't install new packages. B is incorrect because the **upgrade** command installs new packages. C is incorrect because that queries a package file and does not install it. D is incorrect because the **Freshen** command does not use the **-p** option.

8. **B.** B is correct because the query and requires options together produce a list of what the package needs. A is incorrect because that queries the basic information about the package. C is incorrect because the **--whatrequires** option gives a list of which packages depend on the given package or capability, not the other way around. D is incorrect because it gives a list of all installed packages.

9. **D.** D is correct because the **dpkg --list** command lists installed packages. A is incorrect because that command searches remote repositories for the packages. B is incorrect because **apt-get** does not search local packages. C is not correct because the **--info** command reads a local package and gives information about it.

10. **A.** A is correct because the **install** command both installs and upgrades packages. B is incorrect because **update** resynchronizes the remote package list. C is incorrect because the **upgrade** command upgrades all packages on the system. D is incorrect because there is no **--upgrade** option to **dpkg**, and that command only operates on local files.

Chapter 4

"Do I Know This Already?" Quiz

1. **B.** The bash shell takes the words/commands we type into it and interprets those to make the system take certain actions. The other phrases are not indicative of what is happening in the Bash shell.

2. **D.** None of the files listed are "executed" during the user's login. They are instead "sourced," which loads their settings and variables into the current version of the shell. The files are relatively meaningless to the question, as it is the method of executing versus sourcing that is being tested.

3. **C.** C is the correct answer because it properly uses the ~ character, which represents the path of the currently logged-in user, followed by the /test and /.h directories. The others are incorrect syntax or distractors.

4. **B.** B is correct because when you place double pipe characters between two commands, the shell monitors the exit status for the first command, and if it exits with an error, only then is the second command executed. Double asterisks (a) means any character or none followed by any character or none, the double ampersands (c) means to execute the subsequent command if the first is successful and the not equal (!=) means that the two items on either side of it are not equal to each other.

5. **A.** Typing the **env** command is the simplest and most complete way to see all variables in your current environment.

6. **C, E.** When setting options, you use the set –o option command; when unsetting the option, you either use **unset** option or **set +o** option.

Review Questions

1. **D.** Answer D is correct because the C shell is the only one listed that doesn't offer inline command line editing.

2. **E.** Answer E is correct because none of the others correctly completes the statement. Sourcing is where instead of instantiating a new lower-level shell, the commands and variables in the script are loaded into the current shell's environment.

3. **C.** Answer C is correct because you are using Tab completion to complete the missing characters of the command. The rest are simple characters that do their appropriate actions, but not the one asked for.

4. **B.** Answer B is correct because echoing **$?** displays the exit code for the previously executed program.

5. **A, C, D.** Answers A, C, and D are correct because they are the recognized ways to be transported back to your home directory.

6. **B.** Answer B is correct because the **history** command when piped through the **tail** command shows only the last 10 lines of your command history.

Chapter 5

"Do I Know This Already?" Quiz

1. **D.** D is correct because the /var directory is reserved for data that changes. A is not correct because /usr is for sharable, read-only, data. B is not correct because /proc exposes kernel variables and status through the procfs pseudofilesystem. C is not correct because /root is for the root user's home directory.

2. **B.** B is correct because the path given first descends one directory to /usr, then moves into bin. A is incorrect because the shell would have to descend two levels, not one. C is incorrect because /usr/local/bin is a subdirectory of the current working directory. D is incorrect because the command is valid.

3. **D.** D is correct because items in /sbin are needed to boot the system, and therefore must be on the root partition. All the remaining options can be on their own filesystem because they are not essential to booting.

4. **A.** A is correct because the **file** command uses several heuristics to find out what a file is. B is not correct because that executes the file, which may not work in the case of text or data files and could be dangerous if you don't know what it does. C is incorrect because displaying the contents of the file on your screen does not work for binary files and is cumbersome for large text files. D is not correct because **which** looks for the file in your search path. You happen across a file in a directory called **foo**. What is a good way to find out what the file is or does?

5. **D.** D is correct because the **touch** command updates dates on files. A is not correct because **tar** is for archiving files. B is not correct because **file** is for determining what a file is. C is not correct because that queries and sets the system date.

6. **C.** C is correct because the **-p** option is needed to create the nested structure; otherwise, you get an error because the parent directories don't exist. A is not correct because it takes far more typing than doing it with the correct option. B is incorrect because the command will not create the parent directories. D is not correct because **md** is not a Unix command for making directories.

7. **D.** D is correct because **which** looks at your shell aliases and search path to find which command will be run when you type a particular command. A is not correct because **whereis** returns multiple matches and doesn't tell you which of multiple options will be run. B is not correct because it finds anything with **doit** in the name. C is not correct because **find** searches for any file and the command is not a correct use of **find**.

8. **A.** A is correct because that searches your entire filesystem for a file named backup.tar.gz. B is not correct because the **find** command needs a search predicate such as **-name**. C is not correct because **locate** does not include anything from the current day—the database must be updated on a nightly basis. D is not correct because **whereis** does not search the filesystem extensively.

9. **C.** C is correct because it creates a bzip2 compressed archive in the correct location, using files from /home/fred. A is not correct because **tar** does not accept a list of files as input, and with the **-f** parameter, it expects a filename. B is not correct because **tar** does not write to standard out if a filename is present, and the /home/fred passed will be interpreted as the output filename, not the files to archive. D is not correct because the command is run out of Fred's home directory and will result in all the files being part of the root when extracted. This is less optimal than the previous option.

10. **C.** C is correct because the **-t** option lists what's in the archive, and passing a filename only returns matches. A is not correct because the **-c** option creates an archive. B is not correct because **-r** adds to an archive. D is not correct because extraction is done with **-x**.

11. **A.** A is correct because bzip2 provides the best compression of them all. gzip generally beats compress, and cpio doesn't offer compression.

Review Questions

1. **A, D.** Answers A and D are correct because the FHS states that the /root and /home partitions are optional. Answers B and C are incorrect because the FHS doesn't list them as optional for the root filesystem.

2. **B.** Answer B is correct because the FHS states that sharable programs should be in /usr/local/appname. Answer A is incorrect because the /usr/local/bin directory is for single binaries and is often just a link to some application in /usr/local/appname/bin. Answer C is incorrect because the /usr/share directory contains files for multiple architectures and the question does not state that multiple architectures are involved. Answer D is incorrect because the /opt directory is for locally installed programs only and is not to be shared out for multiple system usage.

3. **A, B, C, D, E.** All of these answers are correct. A filename can contain virtually any character, though in the case of spaces, ampersands, and backslashes, care must be taken to escape the character lest it be interpreted as a command to the shell.

4. **C.** Answer C is correct because the use of a ~ character in front of a string parses the /etc/passwd file for a username of that string. So in this case /home/tarfoo. Answer A is incorrect because functions begin with a left parentheses mark and contain commands. Answer B is incorrect because, for that string to denote a directory named tarfoo in your home directory, it would need to be ~/tarfoo. Answer D is incorrect because the /data directory is not mentioned in the command, nor is it implied by the ~ character.

5. **D.** Answer D is correct because the series of .. and forward slashes that precede the /home12/user3 string correctly navigate to that directory. Answer A is incorrect because the path is not absolute; it's relative and would work only from the root of the system. Answer B is incorrect because the ~/user3 string denotes a subdirectory of the current user's home directory named user3 and would have to be changed to ~user3 to work. Answer C is incorrect because the string does not go back to the root of the system; it only goes back up to the /home1 directory.

6. **B.** Answer B is correct because, to copy the contents of a directory, the source must end with a /*; otherwise, the directory itself is copied as a subdirectory of the target. Answer A is incorrect because there isn't a **--contents** option to the **cp** command. Answer C is incorrect because the **xcopy** command is offered only on DOS and Windows machines. Answer D is incorrect because the source directory doesn't include a /* suffix and therefore copies the source into the target as a subdirectory.

7. **C.** Answer C is correct because this command moves the contents from the source to the target and is the shortest command. Answer A is incorrect because this command doesn't work for copying the contents—*.* is incorrect syntax for the command. Answer B is incorrect because the same condition exists—the string *.* doesn't match all files or directories. Answer D is incorrect because it moves the /ccc directory to be a subdirectory of the /bbb subdirectory.

8. **D.** Answer D is correct because the **-p** option allows **mkdir** and **rmdir** to create and remove parent directories. Answers A, B, and C are incorrect: These options are not available to the **mkdir** and **rmdir** commands.

9. **A.** A is correct because it uses the correct combination of starting directory (/ home) search predicates (modify time is greater than 7 days, name is core) and action (execute the **rm -f** command on the name of the file). B is not correct because the starting directory is the current user's home directory. C is not correct because the **mtime** search predicate is **-7**, indicating "less than 7 days old". D is not correct because there is no **-older** search predicate.

10. **A.** A is correct because the link points to the inode of the file, and that wouldn't work if the file were on a filesystem. D is correct because this is a limitation imposed in Linux to avoid cycles in the directory structure that would break the tree model. The rest of the options are incorrect because the name and type of the file do not matter for the hard link.

11. **C.** C is correct because the **tar** command uses the create option with **bzip2** compression, and the correct ordering of output filename and files to archive. A is incorrect because it uses **gzip** compression, which creates larger archives than does **bzip2**. B is incorrect because it uses a **cpio** style of archiving—**tar** does not accept the list of files over **stdin**. D is incorrect because it uses the extract option instead of the create option.

Chapter 6

"Do I Know This Already?" Quiz

1. **B.** The file descriptors are 0 = stdin, 1 = stdout, 2 = stderr, and 3 is not an existing file descriptor.

2. **C.** The output of the **find** command is sent to the **file** command, which sends its output to be redirected into a file named "sort" in the current directory.

3. **C.** The characters chosen are based on the exit code for the first command. Only the double | |'s will cause the second command to run based on the failure of the first command.

4. **C.** Answer C is correct, as the **tee** command allows you to simultaneously log a stream of output to a file and send the identical stream on to be further processed. The other commands do not accomplish the described task.

5. **B.** The tabs in files combined with the length of the data in each column often display oddly when the file is output to the console. The proper command to temporarily remove tabs and replace them with the appropriate number of spaces is the **expand** command. The other commands are either not correct or don't exist.

6. **E.** All the answers are functional commands, but most are simple editors or— in **edlin**'s case a DOS command—and don't work on Linux. The **tr** command could possibly be used to replace the words specified, but it would take a great deal of work to use it, as **tr** replaces single characters with other characters. Only the **sed** command is designed to easily replace whole words as words.

7. **A.** The **grep** command is well known for being able to show the exact opposite of the current output by the use of the **–v** option. All the other commands are functional commands, but either don't have that option or the option is not for reversing output.

Review Questions

1. **A, E.** Answers A and E are correct because you can use the specific stdout and stderr number descriptors to redirect output or you can use the **2>&1** option to send the stderr to wherever stdout is directed.

2. **B.** Answer B is correct because double redirect symbols catenate the output of the command into the described file properly. The > redirect overwrites the file each time, and the other operators are either input redirects or invalid.

3. **C.** Answer C is correct, as the **tee** command allows you to simultaneously log a stream of output to a file and send the identical stream on to be further processed. The other commands do not accomplish the described task.

4. **A.** The **–n** option performs a nonmachine or human-friendly sort, effectively padding any numbers such as 1 with a leading 0. If the numbers go to multiple positions, such as 1 to 100, then additional leading 0s are added so that all the numbers are sorted in the human-friendly format. These 0s are not input into the file nor displayed, just used in the sort of the file's data.

5. **C.** Answer C is correct because it is the only answer whose command shows a count of lines, words, and characters for a given file.

Chapter 7

"Do I Know This Already?" Quiz

1. **C, D.** C and D both have the capability of listing out the running processes on a system in a hierarchical or treelike format. A is a nonsense command to distract you, B, lsproc shows you a listing of the /proc directory, while E, gvfs-tree is for listing files in a directory structure.

2. **B.** The keystrokes Ctrl-z send a SIGTSTP or 20 signal to the process, pausing or freezing its execution. The logical next step is to use the **bg** command and put that process back to executing in the background. The other Ctrl-? combinations all send signals, but don't perform the function specified.

3. **D.** The **fg** command acts on the last used or last suspended, notated by the + sign after the [2]. The other jobs must be interacted with by their job **#**.

4. **B, D.** Answers B and D are correct. The **r** keystroke within **top** allows you to enter a numeric value that changes the priority of the specified process, and the **renice** command alters the priority of a running process, which the unruly process is, which leaves out the **nice** command, used for starting processes at an altered priority. The other answers have invalid options.

5. **A, C.** The **nohup** command and the **screen** command both allow you to execute something and log out. They both essentially detach the process from the controlling terminal and set it free. The other commands don't do what is being asked.

Review Questions

1. **E.** Answer E is correct because **top** is the only command listed that does what is being asked about.

2. **C.** Answer C is correct because the original signal must have been 15, and the signal guaranteed to terminate the process is the 9 signal.

3. **A.** The **pkill** command allows you to specify a concise set of requirements for killing a process or set of processes. The pgrep command can be used to find those processes, but **pkill** is used to kill them.

4. **False.** The **jobs** command can run and work properly inside any bash shell instance.

5. **B.** Answer B is correct because it's the only possible answer that causes the **screen** command to show you a listing of the available sessions. All the others are variations on the Ctrl-a theme, but either are false or don't work as described.

Chapter 8

"Do I Know This Already?" Quiz

1. **C.** A is incorrect because you edit the text at the end of the line with **A**. B is incorrect because that would be **I** as opposed to **i**. C is correct because the **i** command begins editing at the current place. D is incorrect because the ~ command inverts the case of the character.

2. **A.** A is correct because k and j represent up and down motions. B is incorrect because the keys are inverted from their described functions. C is incorrect because Ctrl+d and Ctrl+u move down and up in terms of half pages, not lines like the arrows. D is incorrect because h moves to the left and j moves down.

3. **D.** A and B are incorrect because the **i** and **I** commands insert on the current line. Similarly, the A command appends on the current line, so C is incorrect. D is correct: The **O** command opens a new line before the current cursor position.

4. **A.** A is correct because the D command deletes and it is applied to the end of the line with the **$**. B is incorrect because a single **D** by itself deletes from the character position to the end of the line, but the second **D** deletes more characters. **YP** is incorrect because it duplicates the current line (Yank, Put). D is incorrect because **cW** changes the current word.

5. **D.** A is incorrect because the capital A appends the yanked text into the named buffer rather than replacing it. B and C are incorrect because they do the same operation 10 times on the same buffer rather than bringing 10 lines into the buffer. D is correct because it first indicates the operation is on a named buffer and then yanks 10 lines.

6. **B.** A is incorrect because the / searches forward, not backward. B is correct because the command searches backward, anchors the search with the ^, and also escapes the splat operator correctly. C is incorrect because it searches forward and doesn't anchor the search to the beginning of the line. D is incorrect because the search isn't anchored nor is the * escaped.

7. **A.** A is correct because a set command ending in a question mark queries the setting. The remaining answers are incorrect because the command queries and doesn't set.

8. **C.** A and b are incorrect because the **j** command joins lines rather than moving the cursor. C is correct because you are running the **join** command 10 times. D is incorrect because that would involve the **Ctrl+F** command.

9. **D.** A is incorrect because **rsplit** is not a vim command. B is incorrect because you can do this within vim. C is incorrect because **:split** opens a window above, not to the right. Only D, the **:vsplit**, works here.

Review Questions

1. **C.** Answer C is correct because vim is in nearly every distribution of Linux that exists. Answer A is incorrect because, even though emacs is very well known, it's considered an add-on to Linux. Answer B is incorrect because joe is a specialized editor and not normally included in a distribution by default. Answer D is incorrect because nano is used only for document-style text editing and is not the default editor.

2. **A, C, E.** Answers A, C, and E are correct because they save and exit a given file in vi. Answer B is incorrect because it forces a nonsaving exit to a modified

buffer or file. Answer D is incorrect because only a shifted pair of **z** characters saves and exits a file properly.

3. **B.** Answer B is correct because it takes the cursor to the end of the file. Answer A is incorrect because Ctrl+PgDn does nothing in **vi**. Answer C is incorrect because it moves to the end of the current line. Answer D is incorrect because it does nothing in **vi**.

4. **A.** A is correct because the + command line option passes a command that vim will run; in this case it sets the number mode to on. B and C are not correct because there are no long options to set the line numbers. D is incorrect because **–o** is used to open split windows.

5. **D.** Answer D is correct because the J key denotes the down arrow and the L character denotes the right arrow. Answers A, B, and C are incorrect because they don't use the correct keystrokes.

6. **B.** Answer B is correct because it enters LastLine mode and reloads the file, discarding changes. A is not correct because that exits the file with no changes. C is not correct because that only goes back one level in the undo history. D is not correct because you need to enter LastLine mode and **e!** is not a valid command within Command mode.

7. **C.** Answer C is correct because it searches for and highlights the string string1 properly. Answer A is incorrect because it has added quotation marks around the search string. Answer B is incorrect because it's missing the necessary plus symbol. Answer D is incorrect because there is no --find option for vi.

8. **D.** Answer D is correct because it starts a subshell and displays the normal files in the current directory. Answer A is incorrect because it exits the file and ignores the **ls** command. Answer B is incorrect because it attempts to edit all the files returned by the **ls** command and errors out. Answer C is incorrect because it just starts displaying the text on the screen in vi.

9. **B.** Answer B is correct because vim looks for user-specific configuration files in a file called .vimrc, located within the user's home directory. Answer A is not correct because the file in /etc applies to all users, and they may not appreciate your customizations. Answer C is incorrect because the file named is a fake. Answer D is incorrect because no such file as /etc/editorrc exists.

10. **A.** Answer A is correct because it specifies that the whole document will be searched (%s), that snark will be replaced by FARKLE (/snark/FARKLE/), and that all matches are to be considered (g). B is not correct because it is missing the g. C and D are incorrect because they are missing the % and g, and so only operate on the first match in the current line. Additionally, D has the search and replace clauses swapped.

Chapter 9

"Do I Know This Already?" Quiz

1. **B, D.** B is correct because gdisk is a command line utility that works on GUID partition tables. D is correct because parted works on all kinds of partition tables. A is not correct because fdisk only works on MBR tables. C is incorrect because it does not exist.

2. **D.** D is correct because code 83 is for Linux partitions—a filesystem will be directly placed on this partition. A is not correct because LVM is type 8e. B is not correct because swap is type 82. C is not correct because RAID is fd.

3. **B.** B is correct because GPTs allow up to 128 partitions. A is not correct because MBRs allow 4 primary partitions. C and D are not correct because they are not partition tables.

4. **A.** A is correct because the name is stored in the directory entry, not the inode. All the remaining options are attributes of the inode.

5. **D.** D is correct because the ratio is otherwise known as the bytes per inode ratio; therefore, one inode will be created for every 4096 bytes of disk space.

6. **A.** A is correct because **fsck** is the filesystem checker, and it will clean the dirty filesystem. B is not correct because **df** is used to determine how much free space each filesystem has. C is not correct because **du** calculates disk usage of a set of files or directories. D is not correct because that creates a filesystem.

7. **B.** B is correct because **du** shows the disk usage for a particular directory. A is not correct because **repquota** shows quota usage across all files on the partition and the command requires you give it a partition or **–a** for all partitions. C is not correct because **df** operates on filesystems not directories. D is not correct because the **find** command shows you individual files.

8. **D.** D is correct because the hard limit is the absolute maximum disk space that can be used. A is not correct because **repquota** is a command to display the quota information. B is not correct because the soft limit can be exceeded. C is not correct because the grace period is the length of time that a soft limit can be exceeded.

Review Questions

1. **D.** Answer D is correct because the fourth column is the options column and the **user** option is the proper one to use. Answers A and B include valid options but are in the wrong column. Answer C is the wrong option in the right column.

2. **A.** Answer A is correct because the filesystem should be unmounted if possible, mounted read-only if not. Answer B is incorrect because mounting it read-write would cause errors in the **fsck** process. Answer C is incorrect because there isn't a noauto mode, although there is a **noauto** option. Answer D is incorrect because the user being set to something in options doesn't affect the **fsck** process.

3. **B, C.** Answers B and C are correct because the highest traffic partitions in the choices are **/home** (users data) and **/var** (log files, print spools, Web, and FTP). Answer A is incorrect because on a user file server **/tmp** isn't as heavily used as it would be on a developer station. Answer D is incorrect because anything at all could be in a directory tree named **/data**, whereas the **/home** directory tree is almost certainly user data.

4. **C.** Answer C is correct because the maximum mount count option can be set with the **tune2fs** command. Answer A is incorrect because the **debugfs** command manipulates the filesystem inodes and contents but not the needed parameter. Answer B is incorrect because the **dumpe2fs** command shows only parameters for the filesystem. Answer D is incorrect because the **setfs** command doesn't exist.

5. **B.** Answer B is correct because the **df** command shows the disk statistics for mounted filesystems. Answer A is incorrect because **dir** is only an alias for the **ls** command. Answer C is incorrect because the **du** command can show the space used by files but not disk statistics like **df** can. Answer D is incorrect because the **ls** command can show file sizes but not disk statistics.

6. **C.** Answer C is correct because the filename is not stored with the inode or in the data location for the file; it occurs only in the directory file that contains the filename entry. Answer A is incorrect because the link count affects only hard links and is shown by the **stat** command. Answer B is incorrect because link permissions affect only a symbolic link, and the symbolic link permissions are kept in the link's inode. Answer D is incorrect because the ownership information is kept in the inode for the file.

7. **D.** Answer D is correct because the **tune2fs -c 0** command changes a filesystem's maximum mount count to not have it checked automatically. Answer A is incorrect because the **fsck** command can't change the maximum mount count. Answer B is incorrect because the **mkfs.*** tools are for creating filesystems, and even though they can set the maximum mount count at filesystem creation, using these tools on existing filesystems would destroy the filesystem. Answer C is incorrect because, although **hdparm** is good for changing parameters, the **tune2fs** command is the best choice for this task.

8. **A.** Answer A is correct because the **ext3** filesystem type does not require any reformatting to upgrade an **ext2** filesystem. Answers B, C, and D are incorrect

because they require backing up the filesystem data, formatting with the new advanced filesystem, and restoring the data.

9. **C.** Answer C is correct because the **df** command has an option to query the number and percentage of inodes used and free for all mounted filesystems. Answer A is incorrect because the **ls -li** command shows only groups of file object inode information, not totals. Answer B is incorrect because the **du -sh** command doesn't show inode percentages, just object sizes and size totals. Answer D is incorrect because **find -inum** searches for a specific inode but does not show totals or percentages.

10. **D.** Answer D is correct because quotas are configurable only on a per-file-system basis. In this case, one or both must be off the root (/) filesystem to have a different quota assigned. Answer A is incorrect because the **ext3** filesystem and others support user quotas. Answer B is incorrect because the **sparse_super** option is used only for creating fewer superblock backups for a filesystem. Answer C is incorrect because these are directories, not filesystems, and the **usrquota** option is entered in the **/etc/fstab** entry for a filesystem, not a directory tree.

11. **A, C.** A is correct because the files existing prior to the quotas being implemented would not retroactively delete any files. C is correct because **quotaon** is the trigger to start enforcing quotas. B is not correct because without the filesystem options, the quota system would not be tracking usage. D is not correct because the grace period applies to the soft limit, not the hard quota.

Chapter 10

"Do I Know This Already?" Quiz

1. **D.** A is not correct as the **chmod** command changes permission on an existing object. Answer B is not correct as the **chgrp** command changes group ownership of an existing object. Answer C is not correct as the **chown** command changes user and/or group ownership of an existing object.

2. **A.** A is correct because the user fred is the owner of the file and the owner's permissions are rwx, which stands for read, write, and execute.

3. **C.** C is correct because the letter "a" in **a+x** stands for "all," the "+" character adds the permission, and the "x" stands for the execute permission.

4. **B.** B is correct because the **chmod** command is used to set permissions. The letter "o" in **o+t** stands for "others," which is where the sticky bit permission is applied in the permission set. The "+" character adds the permission, and the "t" stands for the sticky bit permission.

5. **A.** A is correct because the **–perm** option is used to search for files by permission.

6. **B, C.** The **chown** command can change both user owner and group owner. The user owner is listed first, followed by a ":" character and then the group owner.

7. **D.** A user can change the group ownership of a file owned by that user to any group the user is a member of.

Review Questions

1. **D.** Answer A is incorrect because this is the access provided by the read permission. Answers B and C are incorrect because these are the access provided by the write permission.

2. **B.** The user fred is the owner of the file, so only the owner permission set (rw-) applies. The "r" stands for read and the "w" stands for write.

3. **C.** Answer C is correct because it sets all the permissions equal to 644. The other answers only change some permissions, so it is possible that the execute permission could be still set for user owner, group owner, or others, and the write permissions could still be set for group owner and others.

4. **A, D.** Answers A and D are correct. The SUID permission can be set symbolically by using **u+s** or numerically by using **4XXX** (with XXX being regular permissions). Answers B and C set the SGID permission, not the SUID permission.

5. **B, C.** Answers B and C are correct. The **umask 077** command "masks out" all permissions for group and others. The maximum permissions of directories is normally rwxrwxrwx, so the resulting new permissions would be rwx------. The maximum permissions of directories is normally rw-rw-rw-, so the resulting new permissions would be rw-------.

Chapter 11

"Do I Know This Already?" Quiz

1. **B, C.** B is correct because it assigns the value using the equals sign and also marks it for export. C is also correct for the same reason except that it's not exported. A is not correct because **set** is used for shell options. D is not correct because it is missing an equals sign.

2. **B.** B is correct because it executes the script in the current shell rather than opening a new shell. AGE was not exported; therefore it doesn't exist in the subshell. A is not correct because the capitalization is consistent between the

script and the environment variable. C is not correct because the permissions of the script don't have a bearing on the environment. D is not correct because **set** is used for shell options.

3. A. A is correct because the ~/.bashrc file is sourced in non-login sessions and indirectly from login sessions. The other scripts are only called in login sessions.

4. A, C. A is correct because both aliases and functions can perform larger commands with a shorter command. C is correct because only a function can span multiple lines. B is not correct because only a function can accept parameters. D is not correct because functions can be used without being exported.

5. B. B is correct because the **date** command looks for the **TZ** environment variable. A is not correct because that would change the time zone for the entire system. C is not correct because **LC_TIME** is used for formatting and expects the name of a locale rather than a time zone. D is not correct because **date** doesn't have a **timezone** long option.

6. D. D is correct because it uses **iconv** to go from UTF-16 to ASCII. A is not correct because it's possible to convert a file to plain ASCII. B is not correct because the locale setting won't change how the file is displayed on the screen. C is not correct because it doesn't have options to automatically convert UTF-16.

Review Questions

1. C. Answer C is correct because **bash** is the default Linux shell. Answer A is incorrect because there isn't a **vsh** command. Answer B is incorrect because **ksh** is the default. Answer D is incorrect because **sh** is the Bourne shell, ostensibly the first, but not the default.

2. B. Answer B is correct because it's sourced from the user's **~/.bash_profile** file. Answer A is incorrect because it's the system's profile file. Answer C is incorrect because it's the system's **bash** configuration file and is sourced from the **~/.bashrc** file if needed. Answer D is incorrect because it's the last file that gets run as the user exits the system. Answer E is incorrect because it's the configuration file for the vi editor.

3. B. Answer B is correct because running **export VARNAME** makes that variable available for all subshells. Answer A is incorrect because it is used to set **bash** shell options, not to export variables. Answer C is incorrect because it is the **bash** shell executable. Answer D is incorrect because the **source** command is used to reexecute configuration scripts, not export variables.

4. B, D. Answers B and D are correct because commands not in the path can be specified either via the full path or by prefixing them with ./. Answer A is incorrect because it attempts to execute a file in the **/home** directory named

.tarfoo. Answer C is incorrect because that string would attempt to execute the home directory for the user **tarfoo**.

5. **B.** Answer B is correct because the **noclobber** option allows the user to only append to files, not overwrite their contents. Answer A is incorrect because it doesn't exist as an option in **bash**. Answer C is incorrect because the **hashall** option builds a table of recently used commands. Answer D is incorrect because the **monitor** option has to do with job control and notification of process statuses.

6. **C.** C is correct because it sets a shell alias to replace **ls** with **ls -a**. A and B are not correct because the **LS_OPTS** environment variable is not checked by the **ls** command. D is not correct because it omits the **ls** and would replace the **ls** command with **-a**.

7. **B.** B is correct because the /etc/localtime file should either be a copy of, or point to, the time zone file under /usr/share/zoneinfo. A is not correct because changing the TZ environment variable won't make everything on your system change over. C is not correct because the time zone file is specific to Debian and contains the name of the time zone itself. D is not correct because /etc/profile is a shell script that is executed.

8. **A.** A is correct because /etc/profile is sourced on login by all bash shells. B is not correct because you would have to put that in each user's .bashrc. C is not correct because /etc/path is not sourced on login. D is not correct because /usr/local/bin may be in everyone's PATH already but will not execute files on login.

9. **D.** D is correct because LC_ALL takes priority over the other variables. A is not correct because the LANG variable has the lowest priority. B is not correct because LC_TIME is overridden by LC_ALL. C is not correct because LC_MESSAGES is not used for date formatting.

Chapter 12

"Do I Know This Already?" Quiz

1. **C.** C is correct because comments start with the hash symbol. The other answers are incorrect.

2. **A, B.** A is correct because the shebang line indicates how the script is to be run; in this case it is with /usr/bin/perl. B is correct because the script needs to be executable. C is not correct because that would let the script run as root, and that is unnecessary here. D is not correct because the shebang line needs a fully qualified path to the interpreter. E is not correct because the script being

in /usr/bin won't let you run the script with ./ because that means the current directory and the script still need the executable bit and the shebang line.

3. **C.** C is correct because the script will source **/etc/zoid** if it has the executable bit set. A is incorrect because **elif** is a shell built-in. B is incorrect because only one of the two files can be executed because the second is in an "else if" block. D is incorrect because the priority is the opposite.

4. **D.** D is correct because a result code (**$?**) of a nonzero number indicates an error condition. A is not correct because **$?** would have been 0. B is not correct because there's no way to tell what was passed in the environment from the output. C is not correct because timing information was not included.

5. **A.** A is correct because the $1, $2, and so forth variables contain the arguments passed to the script. B is not correct because that is usually stored in $SHELL. C is not correct because the name of the script is in $0. D is not correct because the PID of the script is in $$.

6. **B.** B is correct because the shell expects an **esac** to close out the **case** and will get to the end of file and throw an error if it's missing. A is not correct because you won't get an error if you don't match any conditions. C is not correct because the test style doesn't matter to a case statement. D is not correct because you will get a message indicating the shell was expecting an integer.

7. **D.** D is correct because it correctly uses a file glob in the **for** clause and moves the file to the same name plus a **.bak**. A is not correct because the **mv** command won't expand the names as expected and returns an error. B and C aren't correct because the **ls** will be treated as a string, not a command substitution. Additionally, C refers to the variable by name and not value (**$i**).

Review Questions

1. **A, C.** Answers A, and C are correct because the features mentioned as being in the script are all related to the bash shell. Either you use answer C to specifically set it or you allow the default of **bash** to be used by not specifying a shell. Answer B is incorrect because the syntax is incorrect for the string and the **csh** shell won't do what the question requires. Answer D is incorrect because the line is incorrect and means nothing in a shell script.

2. **C.** C is correct because it properly substitutes the command for the arguments to the **kill** command. A is not correct because double quoting the command won't make it execute. B is similar to A but with an intermediate variable; therefore, it won't work. D is not correct because the **$(())** is for arithmetic evaluation, not command substitution.

3. **A.** A is correct because it uses the **$(())** syntax to evaluate an arithmetic expression. B is not correct because it will try to run the numbers as a command,

which doesn't exist. C is not correct because it will try to run the numbers as a command and capture the output, which is no more helpful than B. D is not correct because **eval** is for running programs. There is an older style of arithmetic evaluation that uses **expr**, however.

4. **B.** B is correct because it checks the value of **$?**, which stores the exit code of the last program ran, for the value of 1 or greater, which means an error. A is incorrect because it checks for the existence of the program that was just run. C is not correct because it checks for success of the last program. D is not correct because the **until** command loops while the condition is false.

5. **C.** C is correct because the **-x** and **-f** mean "is executable" and "exists," respectively, and the **-a** requires both with a logical AND. A is incorrect because there is no option to look inside a file. B is not correct for the same reasons. D is not correct because the **-x** means that the file is executable; that it exists is not sufficient. Also the **-a** means an AND clause.

6. **D.** D is correct because the script is performing a string equality check on the output of the **hostname** command against the string **bob**. A is not correct because an integer comparison is done with **-eq**. B is not correct because the equality operator means the result is of the check for equality, not the command substitution. C is not correct because the equals sign separates the **hostname** from the string, so nothing is passed to the **hostname** command.

7. **C.** C is correct because the collection is known and a **for** loop can easily iterate over every process. A is not correct because **seq** is for counting. B is not correct because the size of the collection is known and using a **while** loop would be more confusing. D is not correct because **until** loops until a condition is true.

8. **D.** D is correct because it uses the **-eq** integer equality operator to compare 3 to **$#**, which holds the number of arguments. A is not correct because it checks for three or more through the greater than or equal to operator. B is not correct because **ARGV** does not contain the number of arguments. C is not correct because **$?** holds the exit code of the last program to run.

9. **B.** B is correct because it uses the **exit** keyword with a value of 1, which indicates an error. A is not correct because **die** comes from Perl. C is not correct because **raise** is not used in bash. D is not correct because it will exit with a code of 0, which indicates successful completion.

10. **C.** C is correct because after the **shift**, $1 becomes "b" and $0 contains the name of the script. A is not correct because $0 is the name of the program and the arguments are counted starting at $1. B is not correct because the $0 is not shifted. D is not correct because the "b" will have been shifted to the first argument position.

Chapter 13

"Do I Know This Already?" Quiz

1. **B.** B is correct because variable elements are a property of schemaless databases, not relational databases. A is incorrect because a table is a series of columns corresponding to data elements, with each record forming its own row. C is incorrect because SQL is the typical language used to query a relational database. D is not correct because each row has a primary key that identifies it.

2. **D.** D is correct because indexes provide fast lookups to large sections of data. A is not correct because a binary object is some data, such as a picture, that is not text in nature. B is not correct because client-server is a method used to communicate with a database but does not contribute to looking up data quickly. C is not correct because embedding a database reduces the footprint of the application but does not contribute to speed the same way an index would.

3. **A.** A is correct because table names are case sensitive; that is, table is different from Table. B is not correct because SQL keywords can be written in any case. C is not correct because AND and OR are also SQL keywords and are therefore case insensitive. D is not correct because the server name is not part of SQL.

4. **C.** C is correct because it has the proper ordering of clauses: SELECT, FROM, and WHERE. It also uses the correct case for the table. A is not correct because the table name is capitalized in the answer, but the table given in the question is all lowercase. B is not correct because it is missing the FROM clause and does not end with a semicolon. D is not correct because the FROM and WHERE clauses are reversed.

5. **D.** D is correct because it takes all the cars and left joins the owners. A is not correct because it returns all the owners even if they don't have cars, not the other way around. B is not correct because that is doing an inner join, showing only cars that have an owner. C is not correct because it is also doing an inner join.

6. **C.** C is correct because the subselect includes a single column of models, and the query uses the IN clause. A is not correct because it does not use a subselect; it uses a join. B is not correct because the subselect includes all the columns and cannot be executed by the database. D is not correct because the WHERE clause is outside the subselect; cars does not have a recall_date.

7. **A.** A is correct because it uses a single sort with two columns, where office location is before last name. B is not correct because grouping by office location will return one row per office. C is not correct because the sort columns are reversed. D is not correct because of similar reasons to B.

8. **B.** B is correct because it uses the UPDATE command and contains the required elements—a table name and instructions for the SET clause. A is not correct because the problem requires data be updated, not inserted. C is not correct because the word that follows the UPDATE keyword should be a table name. D is not correct because the column to be updated needs to be specified with the SET keyword.

Review Questions

1. **C.** C is correct because relational databases store entities in tables, which are comprised of rows and columns. A is not correct because flat files have no structure. B is not correct because key-value databases have a key and a value rather than a table. D is not correct because schemaless databases store documents and don't have a set of formal rows and columns.

2. **A.** A is correct because the semicolon is the statement delimiter. New lines, blank or not, are ignored. Periods are not special in SQL.

3. **D.** D is correct because it selects people who have between 5 and 20 years of service, inclusive. A is not correct because the conditionals miss people who have been working for 5 or 20 years. B is not correct because the syntax of the BETWEEN keyword requires an AND, not a comma. C is incorrect because the ranges are inclusive, and this includes people with 21 years experience.

4. **B.** B is correct because it performs an inner join so that the managers without employees are excluded. A is not correct because that returns a cross join with all managers and employee combinations. C is not correct because a left join includes managers without employees. D is not correct because the join syntax is invalid.

5. **A, C.** A is correct because the left join of products onto sales ensures all products will be included. C is correct because the join matches the product name to the product_name column in sales. B is not correct because the sales need to match up to the product. D is not correct because there is no aggregate clause like SUM or a GROUP BY clause.

6. **D.** D is correct because it aliases the table name in the FROM clause and then uses the alias throughout the query. A is not correct because the table is not aliased in the FROM clause. B is not correct because the table is not aliased at all, but the WHERE clause includes a use of the alias. C is not correct because the second condition doesn't use the alias.

7. **A.** A is correct because a NULL is a placeholder for a missing value. NULL is not comparable to anything; therefore, it is not zero, a blank string, or able to match anything.

8. **C.** C is correct because it uses the GROUP BY keyword to group on description and sums the salary. A is not correct because columns are rolled up so SELECT * is meaningless. B is not correct because the query is missing a GROUP BY clause. D is not correct because the query needs to group by description, not salary.

9. **D.** D is correct because the statement is a valid INSERT with two data items. A is not correct because each row is enclosed in parentheses. B is not correct because the statement only specifies two columns and that is allowed as long as there are no constraints on missing data. C is not correct because you can insert multiple rows at a time by separating each row with a comma.

10. **B.** B is correct because it uses an UPDATE with an appropriate WHERE clause, remembering that you can't directly compare NULL and need to use IS NULL. A is not correct because it tries to compare directly to NULL. C is not correct because there is no WHERE clause, so everyone will be set to 20 years. D is not correct because the format is not correct: The UPDATE specifies the table name and the SET specifies the column.

Chapter 14

"Do I Know This Already?" Quiz

1. **C.** The display manager is there to ensure that the user is presented with the opportunity to securely log in and access the system. Even when not logged in there may be the option to shut down the system and other tasks. The other choices are incorrect as they do not perform the function of a display manager.

2. **D.** Desktop suites almost all contain a set of additional programs such as an office suite, file manager, and settings or configuration manager. The other answers are components of an X Window System, or part of the desktop suite itself.

3. **B.** This is the correct location of the file; the others are just good distractors.

4. **C.** The Files section is the appropriate section of the Xorg file for the location of system fonts. The other sections do not deal with fonts, they deal with loadable Modules, the Screen dimensions or in the case of Fonts, they are distractors.

5. **D.** The Xorg system includes by default the Xorg Display Manager or xdm. The gdm is associated with the GNOME Desktop, the kdm is associated with the KDE Desktop and lightdm is the display manager that is default in Ubuntu distributions.

6. **A.** When going from the GUI to a text-based virtual terminal, you must use the Ctrl key in front of the standard Alt+F3. You don't need to use Ctrl when

switching back from the text-based terminal to the GUI. The other keystrokes are not able to move you from a GUI to the virtual terminals/tty sessions. They will do whatever they have been mapped to do inside the GUI, but unless Ctrl and Alt plus a Fkey are pressed, you will stay inside the GUI environment.

7. **B.** Toggle Keys is capable of being configured to emit a sound when a key such as the Ctrl key is pressed. Slow Keys governs the duration of a key's press before the system accepts it, Repeat Keys governs how many times a key will be repeated with a single press and Bounce Keys governs how the system will ignore several quick or repeated presses on a key.

8. **D.** The **xhost** command makes it possible for users and systems to access your system. The other answers are either unrelated configuration parameters or distractors.

Review Questions

1. **C.** The other sections do not exist in the /etc/X11/xorg.conf file.

2. **B.** Answer B is correct because this entry enables the xfs X font server if it has been installed. Answer A is incorrect because the FontPath entry doesn't allow an executable as an argument. Answer C is incorrect because there isn't a FontServer entry in the Xorg file. Answer D is incorrect because there isn't an FSERVER variable that affects the font server selection.

3. **A, B.** Answers A and B are correct because both cause programs to execute remotely but allow them to display locally. The difference is that **-Y** is permissive and **-X** uses the inherent X11 Security extension to apply security measures or restrictions to the connection. Answer C is incorrect, it has to do with rekeying the connection and Answer D is incorrect as it is for disabling pseudo-tty connections.

4. **C.** Answer C is correct because the window manager is capable of providing scrollbars, widgets, and so on for the X environment. Answer A is incorrect because a desktop typically has the mentioned features but is better known for providing an integrated environmental look and feel along with an Office suite and other utilities. Answer B is incorrect because the X server just manages the display and paints the output on the screen. Answer D is incorrect because an X client depends on the window manager to provide the mentioned options.

5. The correct answer is **xhost**.

6. **C.** The other directories do not exist on a typical Linux distribution.

7. **B.** The others are not valid software programs.

8. **C.** Answer C is correct because Mouse Keys allow you to use your keyboard keys to move your mouse cursor. Answer A is incorrect because Toggle Keys make a sound when a modifier key is pressed. Answer B is incorrect because there is no such feature called Keyboard Keys. Answer D is incorrect because Slow Keys require a user to hold down a key for a brief period before it is displayed.

9. **C.** The correct answer is High Contrast.

10. **C.** None of the others exist as valid Linux programs.

Chapter 15

"Do I Know This Already?" Quiz

1. **A.** The UID for the root user account is 0. The other UIDs are non-root.

2. **C.** Answer C is correct because the nobody account is typically the UID 99. This account exists to allow a user to be assigned to services that need to run as a user but should not be logged in to. The rest of the UIDs are not associated with the nobody account.

3. **D.** Answer D is correct because the last field of the entry is the member list. The group is named tim, and you can assume that there is a user named tim who has the group assigned as his primary group in the /etc/passwd file. The usernames in the last field are always secondary users of the group; therefore, they do not have that group name in their primary group field in the /etc/passwd. Answer B is the contents of the password field and Answer C is the GID of the group.

4. **D.** Answer D is correct. The **–m** option makes the home directory, so Answer A is incorrect. Answer B is incorrect because the **–d** option specifies the home directory. The **–k** option specifies the skel directory, so Answer C is incorrect.

5. **B.** Answer A is incorrect because the **-e** option specifies the home directory. Answer C is incorrect because **-c** is the option for the Comment field, and Answer D is incorrect because **-b** is the option for the base-dir or default base directory.

6. **D.** The **chage** command changes password aging policies for a user, so Answer A is incorrect. The **ulimit** command doesn't modify group ownership, so Answer B is incorrect. The **groupmod** command does change group information but not group membership, so Answer C is incorrect.

7. **A.** Answers B and C are not valid options. Answer D forces the removal of the account.

8. **D.** Answer A is the file where passwords used to be stored on older Linux systems. Answers B and C are not valid files.

9. **A, B, C.** Answers A, B, and C are correct. Answer D is not a valid command.

Review Questions

1. The correct answer is 6. There are no alternative answers.

2. **A.** Answer A is correct because this output indicates that the user's account associated with UID 1002 was deleted. Answer B is incorrect because all files must be owned by an account. Answer C is incorrect because the /etc/passwd file being corrupted would not cause this output. Answer D is incorrect because the user's group has nothing to do with the output, other than showing what the group owner is currently.

3. The correct answer is 511. There are no alternative answers.

4. The correct answer is **/etc/skel**. There are no alternative answers.

5. **D.** Answer D is correct because using the **chage** username command interactively asks and sets the /etc/shadow options. Answer A is incorrect because the **passwd** command doesn't interactively change the options in the /etc/shadow file. Answer B is incorrect because there is no such thing as a **chpass** command. Answer C is incorrect because the **vipw** command is used to alter the /etc/passwd file.

6. The correct answer is **newgrp**. There are no alternative answers.

7. The correct answer is 644. There are no alternative answers.

8. **C.** Answer C is correct because the **ulimit** command shows account limitations. Answer A is incorrect because the **umask** command shows the altered permissions for created objects. Answer B is incorrect because **dmesg** is for system initialization log file viewing. Answer D is incorrect because there isn't a **perms** command.

Chapter 16

"Do I Know This Already?" Quiz

1. **B.** B is correct because the column order is minute, hour, day of month. A is not correct because that transposes the first two columns. C is not correct because that is reading the day column as an hour. D is not correct because that is reading the day column as minutes.

2. **A.** A is correct because */2 in the hours column means "every 2 hours" and 1 in the fifth column means "Monday." B is not correct because half hour would

be */30 in the first column and the day of the month is the third column. C
and D are not correct for the same reasons.

3. **C.** C is correct because with no cron.deny file, cron.allow dictates who can
    run **crontab**. A is not correct because sudo access is not needed to edit a user's
    own crontab. B is not correct because full usernames go in that file. D is not
    correct because, while crontab eventually will need to have root access, it does
    not give this error.

4. **C, D.** C is correct because cron specifies jobs down to the minute and anacron
    down to the day. D is correct because cron doesn't guarantee jobs will be run.
    If the system is off at the appointed time, the job will be missed. A is not cor-
    rect because both systems run periodic jobs. B is not correct because anacron
    does not know about users and relies on a single configuration file.

5. **C.** C is correct because the anacrontab file has four columns: The period in
    days, the delay in minutes, the job identifier, and the command. A is not cor-
    rect because there is no need to specify a username, as everything runs as root.
    B is not correct because there are only two numbers at the beginning. D is not
    correct because there is no user in the file.

6. **B.** B is correct because **at** is for one-off jobs. A is not correct because that is
    anacron's limitation. C is not correct because **at** jobs are not periodic. D is not
    correct because that is the function of **batch**.

Review Questions

1. **D.** D is correct because it uses the 1-23 range of hours and skips 2 every time.
    A is not correct because a skip of 120 over the span of 60 minutes doesn't
    work. B is not correct because the minutes column is being used and that is an
    invalid use of the skip counter. C is not correct because that will execute on
    even hours instead of odd hours.

2. **C.** Answer C is correct because the **atrun** command can be used to set the load
    average that **batch** uses as its threshold. Answer A is incorrect because there is
    no such command as batchavg. Answer B is incorrect because there is no such
    command as atconfig. Answer D is incorrect because the **crontab** command
    has no such capability.

3. **A.** A is correct because it is likely the search path is not expansive enough. B
    is not correct because the shell is already using bash. C is not correct because
    that just sends out emails of the error, which you already know. D is not cor-
    rect because that environment variable does not exist.

4. **A.** A is correct because the user crontabs are stored in /var/spool/cron. The
    rest of the options are incorrect.

5. **B.** B is correct because the cron.allow file takes priority over cron.deny. A is not correct because the allow file takes priority. C is only correct if the files are empty or nonexistent. D is incorrect because allow takes priority over deny.

6. **True.** A is correct because anacron ensures daily jobs are executed even if the computer was off when the job was supposed to run.

7. **A.** A is correct because anacron holds the timestamp of the last run of that job in a file bearing the name of the job identifier. B is not correct because jobs are sorted by the period and delay. C is not correct because identifying the process in the process list is not the primary purpose of the identifier. It may show up briefly, but this is not the goal. D is not correct because everything in anacron runs as root.

8. **D.** D is correct because /etc/cron.d contains system crontabs in the extended format that includes a user name. A is not correct because /etc/crontab is a file, not a directory. B is not correct because it contains standard crontabs. C is not correct because it does not contain crontabs at all. Instead, /etc/cron.daily contains scripts that are run daily through anacron.

9. **C.** C is correct because at **-l** (also known as atq) lists the jobs and **atrm** (also known as **at -d**) deletes jobs by their id. A is not correct because **-q** is not a valid flag to **at**. B is not correct because that would delete every scheduled job, not just yours. D is not correct because at **-r** is not valid.

10. **A.** A is correct because the **batch** command is used to run jobs when the system load average gets below a certain threshold. B is not correct because **at** is used to schedule jobs for a certain time. C and D are not correct because they are used to schedule regularly occurring jobs for a particular time.

Chapter 17

"Do I Know This Already?" Quiz

1. **A.** A is correct because the printer itself has been stopped, and cupsenable fixes that. B is not correct because lpq shows the status of the printer and does not change it. C is not correct because cupsaccept enables the queue, not the printer, and in this case the queue is accepting jobs. D is not correct for the same reasons as C, with the addition that the name of the printer is passed directly without any options.

2. **C.** C is correct because the **lp** command's **-d** option selects the destination printer, and the command expects a filename to print. A is not correct because **lpr** expects the printer to be selected with **-P**. B is not correct because **lp** selects the printer with **-d**, not **-P**. D is not correct because it will print to the

default printer, if it exists, which is not necessarily Main given the information in the question.

3. **B.** B is correct because that is the location of the CUPS configuration files. Other answers are incorrect.

4. **C.** C is correct because the MTA's job is to transfer mail from one computer to the next, on its way for delivery. A is not correct because the MUA is the piece that the user uses to send and receive email. B is not correct because the Mail Relay Agent is not a typical component of email delivery. D is not correct because the MDA is responsible for the final delivery of email from the final MTA to the user's mailbox.

5. **D.** D is correct because the **newaliases** command must be run after editing the alias file. A is not correct because that will not rebuild the aliases.db file to make your changes take effect. B is not correct because the aliases file still overrides the presence of a local user. C is not correct because a .forward file doesn't override an alias.

6. **A.** A is correct because Exchange is a commercial product made for Microsoft servers. B, C, and D are all open source MTAs that run on Linux.

Review Questions

1. **C.** C is correct because the IPP protocol listens on TCP port 631. A is not correct because that URL points to a local web server. B is not correct because that URL points to a local web server running in secure mode. D is not correct because that points to a non-web port (lightweight directory access protocol).

2. **C.** C is correct because the stopped state is reserved for the case when CUPS stops a queue because there is some kind of error. A is not correct because the idle state means that the printer is online and waiting for work. B is not correct because processing means that CUPS is currently sending something to the printer. D is not correct because paused means that the administrator has disabled the printer.

3. **lpstat -d**

4. **A.** A is correct because the **lprm** command deletes a job from the printer named by the -**P** option. Without a job ID it deletes the first job. B is not correct because it deletes job number 1, but the job has an ID of 3. C is not correct because there is no such option to **lpq**, which is used for querying the printer queue. D is not correct because the job will still be there if the printer is turned off.

5. **D.** D is correct because the **cupsreject** command rejects all jobs to the given queue immediately. A is not correct because there is no such option to **lpstat**, and the command itself is read-only. B is not correct because the **cupsreject**

command expects the name of the queue with no parameters. C is not correct because that actually deletes the queue.

6. **B, D.** B and D are correct because both Qmail and Postfix are implemented as a series of separate components so that a problem with one doesn't compromise functionality of others. Both A and C refer to monoliths that have a single daemon doing all the work.

7. **/etc/aliases**

8. **D.** D is correct because the **newaliases** command updates the /etc/aliases.db file with the contents of /etc/aliases. A is not correct because that displays the contents of the mail queue. B is not a command. C is a command used to update Postfix databases but is incomplete.

9. **B.** B is correct because the user's .forward file tells the mail delivery agent to forward mail to another account instead of delivering locally. A is not correct because that is used to send an email through sendmail. C is not correct because /etc/aliases is not accessible to users, nor does that line specify a source address, which is required. D is not correct because the name of the file should be **~/.forward**.

Chapter 18

"Do I Know This Already?" Quiz

1. **C.** C is correct because the Linux kernel maintains the system clock. A is not correct because the RTC on the motherboard is the source of the hardware clock. B is not correct because the NTP system keeps the clock up to date but is not the source. D is not correct because the GPS clocks are used to calibrate stratum 1 servers.

2. **A.** A is correct because the format string given separates all elements by spaces and specifies year, numeric month, day of month, hour in 24-hour time, and minute. The others are incorrect.

3. **B.** B is correct because the **-w** option writes the current system clock to the hardware clock. A is not correct because that is the default mode of the **hwclock** command. C is not correct because that is done with the **-s** option. D is not correct because that is done with the **-u** option.

4. **A, D.** The rule matches anything of notice priority or more important unless it is mail. A is correct because warning is more important than notice. D is correct because err (error) is more important than notice. B is not correct because info is less important than notice and is excluded here. C is not correct because the mail facility was excluded.

5. **A.** A is correct because the **logger** command takes a message on the command line and sends it to syslog. B is not correct because there is no log command for syslog. C is not correct because there is no syslog command to log messages. D is not correct because **syslogd** doesn't take information from stdin, nor does it log messages to itself from the command line.

6. **C.** C is correct because the **-f** flag puts **journalctl** in follow mode. A is not correct because the files under /var/log/journal are in binary format and can't be read by tail. B is not correct because the output of **journalctl** stops when the end of the file is reached. D is not correct because there is no --continuous option.

7. **C, D.** C is correct because the **copytruncate** option rotates a log file by copying it and truncating the original. This allows you to rotate a log file without touching the process that owns it. D is correct because restarting the daemon gets it to reopen the log files with the nontimestamped names. A is not correct because the log rotation can be handled with one of the options in answers C or D. B is not correct because if logrotate were not running, the log file would not have been renamed.

8. **B.** B is correct because anacron runs the logrotate program, which performs log rotation. A is not correct because the log rotation program is not a daemon. C is not correct because the kernel does not deal with log rotation. D is not correct because even though the program can be run manually, it only provides benefit if run regularly from cron.

Review Questions

1. **A, B.** A is correct because the hardware clock is the real-time clock on the computer's motherboard. B is correct because the system clock is the clock maintained inside the Linux kernel. C is not correct because the NTP is not a clock but a protocol designed to keep a clock updated with the correct time. D is not a clock, as cron reads the system clock to figure out when to trigger a job.

2. **D.** D is correct because it uses the correct format—the year comes last, and the items before it are month, day, hour, and minute. A is not correct because the year is in the wrong spot, as is the case with B. C is not correct because the format is incorrect, but it also uses the **+** option, which means to print the date in the given format.

3. **B, C.** B and C are correct because they are the long and short ways of writing the system clock to the hardware clock. A is not correct because that saves the hardware clock into the system clock. D is not correct because that reads the hardware clock, not writes it.

4. **D.** D is correct because the **ntpq** command is used to query the ntp daemon and find out the status of peers. A is not correct because there is no --debug flag. B is not correct because the **date** command tells you about the system clock and not ntpd. C is not correct because there is no ntptool command.

5. **D.** D is correct because pool.ntp.org is the name of the public NTP pool. All the remaining options are incorrect.

6. **/var/log/journal**

7. **A.** A is correct because syslog-ng, along with rsyslog, are alternative syslog implementations. B and C are not the names of any project. D is not correct because journald is not a syslog implementation; it is a complete replacement for system logging.

8. **B, D.** B and D are correct because the severities, in order of least to most severe, are debug, info, notice, warning, err, crit, alert, emerg. The remaining two come before notice.

9. **A.** A is correct because it captures everything at debug level and greater, which includes info, and removes mail with the mail.none keyword. B is not correct because that would capture anything at alert and higher and all mail messages. C is not correct because it captures everything at notice level and greater, which doesn't include info. D is not correct because the -mail is not a valid configuration.

10. **D.** D is correct because a stratum 2 server gets its time from a stratum 1 server, which must have a reference clock. A is not correct because the stratum of your server is defined by who it gets its time from, not the other way around. B is not correct because the stratum doesn't dictate how the time is calculated locally. C is not correct because the clock skew doesn't define the stratum.

Chapter 19

"Do I Know This Already?" Quiz

1. **B.** The first and second octet of the address are the network part of an address with Class B or 16-bit network mask. The other answers are either not a Class B network or are the wrong range.

2. **D.** The 255.0.0.0 subnet mask is identical to the notation /8 or 8-bit subnet mask. The other answers are incorrect because they don't match properly.

3. **D.** The subnet mask is a /24, indicating that the last octet is a network, the first address or 0 is the network itself, and the last address 255 is the broadcast address. The other answers are incorrect or don't match properly.

4. **A.** The TCP protocol is capable of making network communications much more reliable than its lesser-capable fellow protocol UDP. TCP can detect lost packets, reorder them if delivered out of order, and perform other functions that make network communications more reliable. Answer B is incorrect because UDP is much less reliable and is used for more broadcast-oriented or less-critical network communications. Answer C is incorrect because the IGMP protocol is an add-on to the TCP layer but does not transport actual data, and Answer D is incorrect because the ICMP protocol is typically used to transmit necessary diagnostic information between hosts.

5. **A, D.** The **ifconfig** command is a historical method of viewing your IP address information, whereas the **ip** command is a newer and more commonly supported version that introduces some new and useful functions. Answer B is incorrect because the **route** command is used to view and change the routing table. Answer C is incorrect because the **ifup** command is used to bring an interface "up" or make it active.

6. **B.** The **route** command is used to display and manage the default gateway. The other commands are typically used for manipulating or showing the IP address information.

7. **D.** The order of the query is files first, which means the /etc/hosts file will be consulted. The rest of the servers in the answers would be queried only if a name resolution is not achieved from the local files.

8. **A, B, C.** Answers A, B, and C are correct, as they are all client tools that request an IP address from the DHCP server. Answer D is the DHCP server daemon and not a client utility or command.

9. **C.** The **dig** command is used to gather or query information from the DNS server you are using it upon. The other answers are not related to DNS entries.

Review Questions

1. **B.** Answer B is correct because the network is a Class C; therefore, the network mask of /28 causes the LSB to be 16, and networks are incremented by 16, making the 192.168.33.35 address's network address 192.168.33.3 2. Answer A is incorrect because that is the first valid network but not the one your IP resides on. Answer C is incorrect because 192.168.33.0 is the default network if you were using a /24 network mask. Answer D is incorrect because it's two networks past the one your IP is on.

2. The correct answer is **route**. An alternative is **netstat -r**.

3. **C.** Answer C is correct because, with the number of networks needed, a 240 subnet mask is needed and allows for at least 10 hosts per network. Answer

A is incorrect because a 192 subnet mask allows for only 4 possible networks. Answer B is incorrect because a 224 subnet mask allows for only 8 possible networks, but with the loss of the first and last subnets, a 224 subnet mask really means that 6 networks are usable. Answer D is incorrect because a 248 subnet mask allows for enough networks (32) but not enough hosts per network.

4. The correct answer is **traceroute**. There are no correct alternative answers.

5. The correct answer is **route add default gw 192.168.33.1**. There are no correct alternative answers.

6. **B, D.** Answers B and D are correct because they both can be used to show MX records or the names of the mail servers. Answers A and C are incorrect because these commands don't exist.

7. The correct answer is /etc/nsswitch.conf. There are no correct alternative answers.

8. **A, C, D.** Answers A, C, and D are correct because they all are valid resolution methods on the hosts: line in the /etc/nsswitch.conf file. Answer B is incorrect because there is no method named ylwpage.

9. The correct answer is **tcpdump**. There are no correct alternative answers.

Chapter 20

"Do I Know This Already?" Quiz

1. **D.** The /etc/sudoers file is the configuration file for the **sudo** command. The others are incorrect or don't exist.

2. **A, D.** The -l and just the - symbol both cause the **su** command to execute the login as a login shell, reading and sourcing all the appropriate configuration files, just as if the user had logged in to the console of the system as that user. Answer B is incorrect in that it will run a specific shell that you have to specify. Answer C is incorrect because double dashes is not a part of the options that the su command supports. Answer E is incorrect because there is no –k option to the su command.

3. **A, B.** The inetd and xinetd super servers are start on demand server environments, they receive a request from a client on a configured port and protocol and start an instance of that service to answer the request. The other answers are simply distractors and don't exist.

4. **C, D.** The /etc/hosts.allow and /etc/host.deny files are used by the librwrap and TCP wrappers to protect services. There are no such files as Answer A or Answer B.

5. **D.** You can use the **find** command with the **-perm** option to find SUID files on the system. Answer A is incorrect as there is no search command installed by default on a Linux system. Answer B is incorrect in that locate simply locates files via a database search. Answer C is incorrect because it cannot easily display all SUID files on your system.

6. **B.** The **gpg --gen-key** command and option generate the private and public keys on the system. The other answers are incorrect because they are partially-formed answers based on the correct answer.

7. **A, D**. The /etc/ssh/ssh_known_hosts file is the system location for the SSH public host keys, and the ~/.ssh/known_hosts file is the user-specific location for the SSH public host keys. The other answers are existing files on the system, but they don't contain the list of keys being asked for.

8. **B, C.** The **chage** and **usermod** commands both allow for the changing of the user's password aging information. Answer A is incorrect because the fuser command shows the PID's of processes a user owns, Answer D is incorrect because ulimit has to do with limiting the user's environment and Answer E is incorrect because it shows the files being used by processes on a given filesystem.

Review Questions

1. **A.** Answer A is correct because when a user connects to a host for the first time via SSH, the RSA host key is copied to that user's local .ssh/known_hosts file. Answer B is incorrect because the known_hosts file exists only in user configurations. Answer C is incorrect because the authorized_keys file on host2 has nothing to do with this connection. Answer D is incorrect because authorized_keys files are used only in user configurations.

2. The correct answer is /etc/hosts.deny. There are no alternative correct answers.

3. **A, B, D.** Answers A, B, and D are correct because they all copy the file properly from host1 to host3. Answer C is incorrect because the addition of the :~ to the end of the host3 target causes an error trying to write a file to a directory that can't be resolved.

4. The correct answer is **gpg --list-keys**. There are no alternative correct answers.

5. **B.** Answer B is correct because the +7000 means to look for any combination of special bits that are set when using the **-perm** option for **find**. Answer A is incorrect because it finds only files that have all the special bits set. Answer C is incorrect because it finds only files that have the permissions ---s------. Answer D is incorrect because the **locate** command doesn't have a **--permissions** option.

6. **C.** Answer C is correct because ssh-agent wraps around the current shell and provides requested credentials, enabling you to not enter a password for a connection. Answer A is incorrect because it is used to load the user's key into the ssh-agent, but it doesn't run otherwise. Answer B is incorrect because it's used to generate the user's private and public keys but isn't otherwise used. Answer D is incorrect because the .ssh/authorized_keys file is not a program or utility.

7. The correct answer is **ssh-keygen -b 1024 -t rsa**. There are no alternative correct answers.

Glossary

$PATH—When used as a variable, it contains a list of directories that will be searched for executable files when a user enters a command.

. (period)—Shorthand for the **source** command, a bash shell built-in command that specially runs or loads the content of the file passed as argument in the current shell. See sourcing. Can also refer to the current directory, which can be requested using the **pwd** command.

absolute file name—A file name that is complete and starts with the name of the root directory, including all directories up to the current file or directory.

absolute path—The location of a file or directory that starts from the root of the filesystem, and therefore begins with a slash character (/).

access control list—In Linux permissions, a system that makes it possible to grant permissions to more than one user and more than one group. Access control lists also allow administrators to set default permissions for specific directories.

accessibility options—A feature provided on desktops that makes it easier for individuals (usually the handicapped) to work with the desktop.

address class ranges—The primary subnets of class A, B, C, D, and E networks.

advanced package tool—A package management system for Debian derived systems that wraps lower level tools and provides easy searching of remote package sources, including downloading any needed dependencies.

aggregate function—An SQL function, such as COUNT OR SUM, that provides a summary of rows returned from a query.

alias—A shell feature typically used to shorten a much longer command and which runs that command when the user enters the alias as if it were a command.

aliasing—To assign an alternate name to an email or group of emails. For example, a support alias might send an email to whoever is currently on the support desk.

Anaconda—The system used on RHEL for automatic installations.

anacron—A service that runs background jobs in roughly scheduled intervals. If the computer is off at the scheduled time, Anacron runs these jobs after the computer is turned on again.

AND—A logical construct that can be used in scripts. In an AND construct, the second command is executed only after successful execution of the first command.

application server—In Kerberos, refers to a server that hosts a Kerberized application. This server needs a keytab file so that the application can authenticate with Kerberos.

APT –See Advanced Package Tool.

archiving—A system that ensures that data can be properly backed up.

ASCII—The American Standard for Information Interchange encodes letters, numbers, punctuation, spaces, and other characters into a number between 0 and 255.

at—A service that can be used to schedule future jobs for one time execution.

attribute—A property that can be set to a file or directory and that will be enforced, no matter which user with which access permission accesses the file. For instance, a file that has the immutable attribute set, cannot be deleted, not even by the root user. The root user does have the capabilities though to change the attribute, which would allow him to delete the file anyway.

auditd—A service running by default on some distributions of Linux and that can be configured to log detailed information about what is happening on some distributions of Linux. Auditing is complementary to system logging and can be used for compliancy reasons. On some distributions of Linux, the auditing system takes care of logging SELinux related messages, which makes it a relatively important system.

audit log—The main log file in /var/log/audit/audit.log, which by default contains all messages that are logged by the auditd service.

autoconfiguration—The process of automatically assigning network configuration such as IP address, hostname, gateway, and subnet addresses.

autofs—A service that takes care of automatically mounting network-based file systems at the moment a specific directory is accessed. This service is useful to ensure the automatic mounting of home directories for users in a centralized user management system, as can be implemented by the LDAP service.

automount—The process started by the autofs service. See autofs for more details.

background—A process running on a system without actively occupying a console. Processes can be started in the background by adding an & after the command that starts the process.

backup—A copy of important data that can be recovered if at any point in time the original data gets lost.

bash—The default shell used on most Linux systems.

Basic Input Output System (BIOS)—The first software that is started when a computer starts on older IBM compatible computers. Settings in the BIOS can be changed by using the BIOS setup program.

binary—A numbering scheme based on bit values that can be on or off. Binary numbers are 0 and 1. Because they are difficult to use, on most occasions decimal, hexadecimal, or octal numbers are used.

binary packages—A collection of applications, documentation, libraries, and configuration files that can be downloaded and run without needing to compile from source.

BIOS—See Basic Input Output System.

bonding—In networking, refers to the technology that allows the creation of a network trunk that consists of multiple bundled network interfaces. Bonding is used for redundancy and performance.

boolean logic—Operations such as OR and AND that operate on the true and false primitives that computers understand, rather than numbers that humans understand.

boot manager—A piece of software that runs when the computer first starts up. The boot manager is responsible for loading the operating system kernel.

boot loader—The program called by the BIOS to start a computer and that takes care of loading the operating system kernel and initramfs.

bounce—To return an email after it has been found to be undeliverable.

broadcast address—A network address on an IPv4 network that is used to send network messages to all hosts on the subnet.

btrfs—A general purpose Linux file system expected to become the default file system on some distributions of Linux in a future release.

buffer—In memory management, refers to the area of memory where unstructured data is stored.

bus—A hardware component that allows other components to connect and talk to each other over a single shared connection rather than each component needing a unique connection to every other component.

cache—In memory management, refers to the area of memory where recently used files are stored. Cache is an important mechanism to speed up reads on servers.

capability—A specific task that can be performed on Linux. User root has access to all capabilities; normal users have access to limited sets of capabilities only. See man 7 capabilities for more information.

CentOS—A Linux distribution that uses all Red Hat packages but has removed the Red Hat logo from all these packages to make it possible to distribute the software for free.

certificate—In PKI cryptography, a certificate contains the public key of the issuer of the certificate. This public key is signed with the certificate of a Certificate Authority, which guarantees its reliability.

Certificate Authority—A commonly known organization that can be used to guarantee the reliability of PKI certificates. The Certificate Authority provides a certificate that can be used to sign public key certificates. Instead of using a commonly known organization, self-signed certificates can be used for internal purposes as well.

CGI—See Common Gateway Interface.

chrony—The new service that offers time synchronization services in some distributions of Linux.

chroot—An environment where a part of the file system is presented as if it were the root of the file system. chroot is used as a security feature that hides the parts of the operating system not required by specific services.

CIFS—See Common Internet File System.

client-server—An application architecture where a user-facing client gets information and instructions from a shared backend server.

cloud—A computing platform that allows for flexible usage of hosted computing resources.

code pages—A table that maps characters in a particular set to a number.

code point—An individual mapping of a character in a code page to a number.

coldplug—A hardware device that needs the computer to be turned off and on to be recognized.

column—In relational databases, a column consists of similar fields from different records. Columns can be used to sort data in a database or table.

command substitution—A shell scripting technique where a command is run and then injected into another command.

Common Gateway Interface (CGI)—A standard for generation of dynamic web pages by using some scripting technology. CGI does not define which specific scripting technology has to be used.

Common Internet File System (CIFS)—The standardized version of the Microsoft Server Message Block (SMB) protocol, which is used to provide access to shared printers, files, and directories in a way that is compatible with Windows servers and clients. CIFS has become the de facto standard for file sharing in IT.

Common Unix Printing System (CUPS)—The software responsible for printing on most Linux systems.

compression—A technology used to reduce file sizes, by analyzing redundant patterns and storing them more efficiently. Mainly used to save storage space, reduce network traffic, or increase network transfer rates.

conditional loop—In shell scripting, a set of commands executed only if a specific condition has been met.

conditionals—A piece of shell code that tests for given conditions and executes different code depending on the result of the test.

connection—In configuration of network cards: A set of network configuration parameters associated to a network interface. In network communication: A session between two parties that has been initialized and will exist until the moment that the connection is tiered down.

console—In Linux, the console is the primary terminal where a user works. It is also a specific device with the name /dev/console.

context—In SELinux a context is a label used to define the security attributes of users, processes, ports, and directories. These rules are used in the SELinux policy to define security rules.

context switch—A context switch happens when the CPU switches from executing one task to executing another task.

context type—In SELinux, a context type is used as a label that identifies the SELinux properties of users, processes, and ports.

Create, Read, Update, and Delete (CRUD)—In relational databases (as well as persistent storage), create, read, update, and delete are the four basic operations. In MariaDB databases CRUD is implemented by using the **INSERT**, **SELECT**, **UPDATE**, and **DELETE** commands. CRUD is universal and occurs in other protocols also. In HTTP for example, CRUD is implemented with the **POST**, **GET**, **PUT**, and **DELETE** commands.

credentials file—A file that can be used to mount CIFS file systems automatically from the /etc/fstab file. The credentials file is stored in a secure place, like the home directory of user root, and contains the user name and password that are used to mount the remote file system.

cron—A service that runs background jobs at scheduled times.

CRUD—See Create, Read, Update, and Delete.

cryptography—A technique used to protect data. This often happens by converting information to an unreadable state, where keys are used to decipher the scrambled data. Cryptography is not only used to protect files while in transit, but can be used also to secure the authentication procedure.

CUPS—See Common Unix Printing System.

CUPS backend—A piece of the Common Unix Printing System responsible for sending the processed print job to the printer.

daemon—A process that runs in the background and provides some sort of service, either to the local machine or to remote machines.

database—In relational databases, a collection of tables that all together are used to store data.

database schema—A description of all the tables, columns, and relationships of a relational database.

Daylight Saving Time—The source of frustration for developers and systems administrators alike. In summer months, clocks are moved ahead an hour to take advantage of the longer nights.

decimal—A numbering scheme based on the numbers 0-9. This numbering scheme is easy to use for humans, but not so easy for usage in computer environments, which is why alternatively binary, octal, and hexadecimal numbering schemes are frequently used.

default gateway—The gateway used by default for a host. See also gateway.

default route—The router used by default to forward IP packets that have a destination on an external network.

dependency—General: A situation where one item needs another item. Dependencies occur on multiple levels in Linux. In RPM package management, a dependency is a software package that needs to be present for another package to be installed. In systemd, a dependency is a systemd unit that must be loaded before another unit can be loaded.

dependency hell—Refers to the situation in which, for package installation, other packages are needed, which by themselves could require dependencies as well. The problem of dependency hell has been fixed by the introduction of repository based systems.

desktop—A software program that acts as the interface between users and a GUI environment.

destination—In rsyslog, specifies the destination where log messages should be sent to by the logging system. Destinations are often files but can also be input modules, output modules, users, or hosts.

device—A peripheral attached to a computer to perform a specific task.

device file—A file created in the /dev directory and used to represent and interact with a device.

device mapper—A service used by the Linux kernel to communicate with storage devices. Device mapper is used by LVM, multipath, and other devices, but not by regular hard disks. Device files created by device mapper can be found in the /dev/ mapper directory.

DHCP—See Dynamic Host Configuration Protocol.

directive—Name for a parameter in the Apache configuration.

direct mount—In automount, refers to an automount performed on a directory that already has to exist before the automount can take place. Direct mounts always have /- as the starting point of the mount and can be created by the root user only.

directory—A folder in the file system that can be used to store files in an organized manner.

directory entries—A piece of the filesystem that stores the list of files in a directory and a pointer to the file's inode.

display manager—A software program that provides users with a GUI login.

distribution—A Linux version that comes with its own installation program or that is ready for usage. As Linux is a collection of different tools and other components, the Linux distribution gathers these tools and other components, may or may not enhance them, and distributes them so that users don't have to gather all the different components for themselves.

dmesg—Utility that can be used to read the kernel ring buffer, which contains log messages generated by the Linux kernel.

DNS—See Domain Name System.

DNSSEC—A system used to secure DNS. In DNSSEC keys are used to guarantee the authenticity of a server that is contacted.

DocumentRoot—In Apache, the DocumentRoot defines the location where the Apache web server looks for documents that will be served to the Apache clients.

domain—The Domain Name System, defines a domain hierarchy. In this hierarchy, a domain is a branch object identified by a worldwide unique name such as example. com. Within the domain leaf, objects are typically created to identify resources in a globally unique way.

Domain Name System (DNS)—The system that makes it possible to translate computer names to IP addresses and vice versa. In the Domain Name System, several domain levels are used, resembling a directory structure in a file system.

dotted quad notation—An IPv4 address that consists of four octets.

dracut—A utility used to generate the initramfs, an essential part of the Linux operating system that contains drivers and other vital files required to start a Linux system.

drift—The slowly growing difference between a computer's clock and the actual time.

driver—A piece of software that allows a kernel to understand how to communicate with a particular device or set of devices.

Dynamic Host Configuration Protocol (DHCP)—A protocol often implemented by a server and that takes care of providing an IP address and other related configuration to clients. Using DHCP makes it possible to use systems in a computer network without the need to configure all of them with the required IP address configuration and related parameters.

dynamic linker (ld.so)—The library on a Linux system responsible for finding dynamic libraries and presenting them to the application that needs them.

dynamic linking—The process of sharing library code between applications rather than requiring each application to keep a copy of the library.

dynamic route—A network route managed by an automatic routing protocol.

EFI—See Extensible Firmware Interface.

embedded database—A database, such as SQLite, that does not need to run as a separate daemon.

enforcing—The SELinux mode where SELinux is fully operational and applies all restrictions that have been configured for a specific system.

environment—The collection of settings that users or processes are using to do their work.

epoch time—In Linux, epoch corresponds to midnight of Thursday, January 1, 1970. Linux time is calculated as the number of seconds that have passed since epoch. This number of seconds is referred to as epoch time. Some utilities write epoch time instead of real clock time.

escaping—In a shell environment, escaping ensures that specific characters are not interpreted by the shell. Escaping may be necessary to show specific characters on-screen, or to ensure that regular expression metacharacters are not interpreted by the bash shell first.

exim—A mail transfer agent that is monolithic like sendmail but easier to configure.

export—In NFS, refers to a directory shared on an NFS server to allow access to other servers.

Ext2, Ext3, and Ext4—Three different versions of the Ext file system. As of now Ext4 is the default file system on some distributions of Linux. It is now considered inadequate for modern storage needs, which is why Ext4 in RHEL 7 has been replaced by XFS as the default file system.

Extensible Firmware Interface (EFI)—A replacement of the Basic Input Output System that is used on older IBM compatible computers as the first program that runs when the computer is started. EFI is the layer between the operating system and the computer firmware.

extended partition—On MBR disks, a maximum of four partitions can be stored in the partition table. To make it possible to go beyond that amount, one of these four partitions can be created as an extended partition. Within an extended partition, logical partitions can be created, which perform just like regular partitions, allowing system administrators to create more partitions.

external command—A command that exists as a file on disk (as opposed to a bash internal "shell built-in" command).

Fedora—The free, community Linux distribution sponsored by Red Hat. In Fedora, new features are provided and tested. Some of these features will be included in later releases of enterprise distributions of Linux.

fiber channel—A storage infrastructure that can be used in SAN environments. Its opponent is iSCSI.

field—In relational databases, fields are used to compose records. A field typically is a name-value pair. Records consist of several fields.

file descriptor—A pointer used by a Linux process to refer to files in use by the process.

file system—A logical structure created on a storage device. In a Linux file system, inodes are used for file system administration, and the actual data is written to blocks.

File System Hierarchy (FSH)—A standard that defines which Linux directories should be used for which purpose. Read man 7 hier (the man page for hier in category 7 of the man pages.) for a specification of the FSH.

File Transfer Protocol (FTP)—A software program that allows users to copy files to and from a remote system. Unfortunately, this process sends data in plain text, making it a poor method.

filesystem—Both the single virtual disk presented to the Linux system and the layout of files on the disks.

firewall—A solution that can be used to filter packets on a network. Firewalls are used to ensure that only authorized traffic can reach a system. A firewall can be offered through the Linux kernel Netfilter functionality but often is also offered as an appliance on the network.

firewalld—The modern service used in RHEL 7 to implement firewalling based on the Linux kernel firewalling framework.

flush—In email, mail queues can be flushed. This is useful if a message could not be sent on the first attempt. By default, the email software will try to send the message again, typically once an hour. By flushing the mail queue, the mail server is triggered and tries to immediately send out the stalled messages. In file systems, flushing refers to the direct write of files to the storage media, instead of writing the files to the file system cache first, from which they are synchronized to the disk platters.

folder—Also referred to as a directory, a structure in the file system used to organize files that belong together.

foreground—Linux processes started by users can be started in the foreground or in the background. If a process has been started as a foreground process, no other processes can be started in the same terminal until the process finishes or is moved to the background.

forwarding—Taking an email destined for person A and automatically sending it to person B.

FQDN—See Fully Qualified Domain Name.

FSH—See File System Hierarchy.

fstab—A configuration file used on Linux to mount file systems automatically when the system starts.

FTP—See File Transfer Protocol.

Fully Qualified Domain Name (FQDN)—In DNS, a complete hostname, including the domains and subdomains, that the host is defined in. server1.example.com is an example of an FQDN.

function—A piece of shell code that is reusable and can be called, optionally with arguments, by users and other shell scripts.

gateway—A host used to allow hosts to communicate with other networks. Also known as a router.

GECOS—Originally stood for General Electric Comprehensive Operating System. In Linux it remains as the Gecos field in the /etc/passwd file, a field that can be used to store personal data about a user on the Linux operating system.

GID—See group identification number.

Global Unique ID (GUID)—An identification number that consists of parts that ensure it is globally unique.

GNOME—A common desktop. See desktop.

Gnu Privacy Guard (GnuPG)—A software suite that allows users to encrypt data and digitally sign files.

GnuPG—See Gnu Privacy Guard,

GPT—See GUID partition table.

Grand Unified Boot Loader (GRUB)—The standard Linux boot manager that can boot many different operating systems.

graphical user interface (GUI)—The term used for Windows-based interfaces.

Greenwich Mean Time (GMT)—The reference time zone by which all other time zones calculate their time as an offset from GMT. A time zone is defined as being a certain number of hours and minutes ahead of, or behind, GMT.

group—A collection of items. In user management, groups are used to assign permissions to multiple users simultaneously. In Linux, every user is a member of at least one group.

group identification number (GID)—A unique number assigned to a group account.

group owner—On Linux, every file and directory has a user owner and a group owner. Group ownership is set when files are created and unless configured otherwise is set to the primary group of the user who creates the file.

GRUB—See Grand Unified Boot Loader.

GRUB2—The boot loader installed on most systems that need to start Linux. GRUB2 provides a boot prompt from which different kernel boot options can be entered, which is useful in case the boot procedure needs to be troubleshot.

GUI—See graphical user interface.

GUID—See Global Unique ID.

GUID partition table—A modern solution to store partitions on a hard disk, as opposed to the older MBR partition table. In GUID partitions a total of 128 partitions can be created, and there is no difference between primary, extended, and logical partitions anymore.

hard link—For storing Linux files, inodes are used. An inode contains the complete administration of the file, including the blocks where the file is stored in. A hard link is a name associated to that inode. A file that doesn't have at least one hard link is considered a deleted file. To increase file accessibility, more than one hard link can be created for an inode.

hardware—The physical components of a computer, such as CPU, RAM, disk, network card, and so on.

hardware clock—A clock that is on the computer's motherboard and continues to run when the computer is powered off.

hardware time—The time provided by computer hardware, typically the BIOS clock. When a Linux system boots, it sets the software time based on the hardware time. As hardware time often is inaccurate, most Linux systems use the Network Time Protocol to synchronize the system time with a reliable time source.

HBA—See host bus adapter.

hexadecimal—A 16 based numbering system based on groups of four bytes. Hexadecimal numbers start with the range 0-9, followed by A-F. Because it is much more efficient in computer technology, hexadecimal numbers are frequently used. In IPv6, IP addresses are written as hexadecimal numbers.

host bus adapter (HBA)—An interface card that connects a computer to network and storage devices. Most commonly, a host bus adapter refers to a device that connects the computer to a storage network.

hotplug—A device that can be inserted and recognized while the computer is running.

hypervisor—A piece of computer software, firmware, or hardware that creates and runs virtual machines. In Linux, KVM is used as the common hypervisor software.

ICMP—See Internet Control Message Protocol.

indexes—A database function that stores frequently searched data so that the corresponding row can be quickly found without needing to search the entire table.

indirect mount—In automount, refers to a mount that is effected in a fully automated manner by automount. The directory on which the file system is mounted is created by automount. Indirect mounts can happen completely from user space, which means that no direct kernel interaction or root privileges are required.

inheritance—In permission management, inheritance refers to the situation where new files created in a directory inherit the permission settings from the parent directory.

init—The first process started once the Linux kernel and initramfs have been loaded. From the init process, all other processes are started. In RHEL 7 the init process has been replaced by systemd.

initial RAM disk—A memory backed disk created during the boot phase that contains the computer's drivers, so that the system can be booted off of the current hardware.

initiator—In iSCSI, the initiator is the iSCSI client. It is the system that wants access to shared storage offered by the iSCSI target system.

initramfs—The initial RAM file system. The initramfs contains drivers and other files needed in the first stages of booting a Linux system. On some distributions of Linux, the initramfs is generated during installation and can be manually re-created using the dracut utility.

inner join—Combining two database tables such that the result contains only results where a match between both tables are found.

inode—The administration of a file. Every Linux file has an inode, and the inode contains all properties of the file, but not the file name.

input module—In rsyslog, a module that allows rsyslog to receive log messages from specific sources.

installation server—A server that can be used to make installation of Linux easier. In an RHEL context, it normally consists of a repository, a DHCP server, and a TFTP server, together with a kickstart file that contains instructions on how the automatic installation has to be performed.

integrated peripherals—A piece of hardware that's part of the motherboard rather than being something removable or upgradable.

interface—In Linux networking, the set of configuration parameters that can be activated for a specific device. Several interface configurations can exist for a device, but only one interface can be active at the same time for a device.

internal command—A command that is a part of the shell and does not exist as a file on disk.

internationalization—A software method of allowing an application to change out the language used without needing separate versions of the application.

Internet Control Message Protocol (ICMP)—Focuses on allowing networking devices, such as routers, the capability to send error messages.

Internet Printing Protocol—A modern web-based protocol that allows printers to communicate with computers over a network.

Internet Protocol (IP)—Handles the addressing and communication between devices on a network. It defines IP addresses, subnetting, and routing.

IP—See Internet Protocol.

IP address—An Internet Protocol address, used to direct network traffic to a specific host.

iptables—A solution to create firewall rules on the Linux operating system. iptables interfaces with the netfilter Linux kernel firewalling functionality, and it was the default solution to create software firewalls on previous versions of some distributions of Linux. In some distributions of Linux it has been replaced with firewalld.

IPv4—Internet Protocol, version 4. An older version of IP that uses dotted quad notation for IP addresses.

IPv6—Internet Protocol, version 6. A newer version of IP that uses larger IP addresses and enhanced features.

iSCSI—A storage protocol that encapsulates SCSI storage protocol commands in IP packets. This makes it possible to offer access to SCSI devices over the Internet.

ISO-8859 standard—A series of standards that define standard 8-bit code pages for character encoding.

iteration—In shell scripting, an iteration is one time of many that a conditional loop has been processed until the desired result has been reached.

job—In a Linux shell, a job is a task running in the current terminal. Jobs can be started in the foreground as well as the background. Every job is also visible as a process.

journald—The part of systemd that takes care of logging information about events that have been happening. The introduction of journald ensures that information about all services can be logged, regardless of how the service is configured itself to deal with information to be logged.

KDC—See key distribution center.

KDE—A common desktop. See desktop.

Kerberos—A computer network authentication protocol that works on the basis of tickets to allow nodes and users communicating over a nonsecure network to prove their identity. It provides mutual authentication and on Linux is used for authentication of users as well as services.

kernel—The central component of the operating system. It manages I/O requests from software and translates them into data processing instructions for the hardware in the computer.

kernel ring buffer—A part of memory where messages generated by the kernel are stored. The **dmesg** command can be used to read the contents of the kernel ring buffer.

kernel space—The part of memory reserved for running privileged instructions. Kernel space is typically accessible by the operating system kernel, kernel extensions, and most device drivers. Applications are normally running in user space, which ensures that a faulty application cannot crash the computer system.

kernel virtual machine (KVM)—The Linux kernel module that acts as a hypervisor and makes it possible to run virtual machines directly on top of the Linux kernel.

key-based login—In SSH, uses public/private keys to prove the identity of the user that wants to log in. Key-based login is generally considered more secure than password-based login.

key-value database—A database consisting of a series of keys with corresponding values optimized for fast lookup.

key distribution center (KDC)—The part of the Kerberos configuration that takes care of handing out Kerberos tickets to users who have proven that they are authorized specific services.

keytab—A file used by services in Kerberized environments. The keytab contains the name of the service and the credentials that the server needs for authentication purposes.

kickstart—The system used for automatic installations.

kill—A command that can be used to send a signal to a Linux process. Many signals are defined (see man 7 signal, aka run the "man 7 signal" command to view that man page), but only a few are commonly used, including SIGTERM and SIGKILL, which both are used to stop processes.

KVM—See kernel virtual machine.

label—A name that can be assigned to a file system. Using labels can be a good idea, because once it is assigned, the label never changes, which guarantees that the file system can still be mounted, even if other parameters such as the device name have changed. However, UUIDs are considered safer than labels as the chance of having a duplicate label by accident is much higher than the chance of having a duplicate UUID.

LDAP—See Lightweight Directory Access Protocol.

left join—Combining two database tables, A and B, such that all rows from table A are shown even if there is no match from table B.

libraries—A collection of reusable software components that can be used by multiple applications.

libvirt—An open source API, daemon, and management tool used to manage virtualization. libvirt on RHEL 7 is implemented by libvirtd and used to manage KVMs.

Lightweight Directory Access Protocol (LDAP)—Originally, a protocol used to get information from an X.500 directory (which is a kind of address book). In modern computing environments, LDAP is also the service that provides centralized information that can be used for logging in and other purposes.

line printer remote—An older network printing protocol optimized for less powerful printer hardware.

link—A file, with its own inode, that points to another file.

Linux—A UNIX-like operating system that consists of a kernel that was originally developed by Linus Torvalds (hence the name Linux). A current Linux operating system consists of a kernel, and many open source tools that provide a complete operating system. Linux is packaged in the form of a distribution.

load average—A metric representing the number of processes waiting to be run by the CPU that gives some indication of system load. Load averages are usually given as a weighted average over the past 1, 5, and 15 minutes.

locale—In the context of internationalization and localization, the current language and country being used.

localization—The process of displaying numbers, monetary values, dates, and times in a manner appropriate for the given country and language.

log rotation—A service that ensures that log files cannot grow too big. Log files are monitored according to specific parameters, such as a maximum age or size. Once this parameter is reached, the log file closes and a new log file is opened. Old log files are kept for a limited period and then are removed, often after only a couple of weeks.

logical backup—A backup that consists of the structure of the data but not the actual files containing the data. Logical backups in general are easier to make but require access to the functional program as opposed to a physical backup.

logical extent—The building block used in LVM to create logical volumes. It normally has a size of a few megabytes, which corresponds to the size of the physical extents that are used.

logical partition—A partition created in an extended partition. See extended partition for more details.

logical unit (LUN)—In iSCSI, the item shared through iSCSI. It gives access to the backend storage.

logical volume (LV)—The LVM component that represents a filesystem. A logical volume is comprised of multiple physical extents.

logical volume manager (LVM)—The Linux component that abstracts the layout of filesystems from the actual disks, allowing filesystems to be grown without needing to be contiguous.

login shell—What results when a user signs on to a system as if she were at the console; all appropriate files are read, sourced, and a bash or other shell prompt is presented, and the user is a fully-functional user of the system.

LUN—See logical unit.

LV—See logical volume.

LVM—See logical volume manager.

Mail Delivery Agent—The piece of an email system responsible for final delivery to the recipient of the email.

mail queue—In email, messages that have to be sent are placed in a mail queue. From there the message is picked up by a process that sends out the message. By using mail queues it is possible to handle many messages simultaneously.

Mail Transfer Agent—The piece of an email system responsible for getting the email to a computer that is closer to the final destination.

Mail User Agent—The software used to send and receive emails.

many-to-many relationship—A relationship between two entities that allows each side to have multiple relationships. A parent may have many children, and a child may have many parents.

many-to-one relationship—A relationship between two entities where one side belongs to another. A car has many tires, but a given tire only belongs to one car.

masquerading—In firewalling, the configuration where a computer on the private network uses the public IP address of the router to connect to computers on the Internet. The computer on the Internet sees only the public IP address and therefore cannot connect to the computer on the private network directly. Masquerading makes it possible to share one public IP address between many computers and at the same time is a security feature.

master boot record (MBR)—On a BIOS system, the master boot record is the first 512 bytes on the primary hard disk. It contains a boot loader as well as a partition table that gives access to the different partitions on the hard disk of that computer. It is the first block on disk that is executed on boot to launch the boot manager.

MBR—See master boot record.

MDA—See Message Delivery Agent.

Message Delivery Agent—The part of an email solution that takes care of delivering a message to the right location.

Message Transfer Agent—The part of an email solution that takes care of sending out a message to its intended recipient. On the recipient, the MTA takes care of accepting the message from the sending MTA.

Message User Agent—The part of an email solution used by the user to access and receive messages.

module—A piece of snapin code. Modules are used by several systems on Linux such as the kernel, GRUB2, rsyslog, and more. By using modules, Linux components can be extended easily and adding functionality doesn't require a total rewrite of the software.

Monkeyboy—See Ross.

mount—To access files on a specific storage device, the storage device needs to be mounted on a directory. This sets up the specified directory as the access point to files on the storage device. Mounts are typically organized by the systems administrator and are not visible to end users.

mount points—A directory on disk to which another filesystem is attached.

MTA—See Message Transfer Agent.

MUA—See Message User Agent.

multi-booting—Using multiple operating systems, selectable by the boot manager, on a single system.

multipath—In a SAN environment, it is important that redundancy is provided to access storage devices. The result is that the same storage device may be seen twice, which makes it unclear to the client which storage device it needs to connect to. To fix this problem, a multipath driver can be used. This driver presents one uniform multipath device, and from this device access to the specific backing device is regulated.

name server—In DNS, the server configured with a database that contains resource records used to answer the DNS queries.

NAT—Network Address Translation; also referred to as masquerading. See masquerading for more details.

netfilter—The part of the Linux kernel that implements firewalling.

netmask—See subnet mask.

Network Address Translation (NAT)—See masquerading.

Network File System (NFS)—A common UNIX solution to export physical file systems to other hosts on the network. The other hosts can mount the exported NFS directory in their local file system.

Network Information System (NIS)—A legacy system used to provide centralized databases on Linux to store information about users, groups, hosts, and more.

network mask—A dotted quad notation used to define the network part of the IP address.

network time—Time provided on the network.

Network Time Protocol (NTP)—A service that allows a computer to query time servers for the purpose of keeping accurate time.

NFS—See Network File System.

nice—A method to change the priority of Linux processes. A negative nice value makes the process more aggressive, giving it a higher priority (which is expressed by a lower priority number!); a positive nice value makes a process less eager, so that it gives priority to other processes.

NIS—See Network Information System.

non-login shell—A shell mode where it is not expected that a user is interacting with the shell.

normalization—A database term where entities are split up into various relationships to reduce duplication. For example, a book may be related to an author so that there is less duplication as an author writes more books.

NTP—See Network Time Protocol.

null client—In email, refers to a mail client where an SMTP service such as Postfix is running but is configured only to allow the client to send outgoing messages. For receiving incoming messages additional services are needed.

null value—A value in a database that represents an unknown value.

numeric mode—A method using octal numbers for setting object permissions.

octal—A numbering scheme that uses the numbers 0-7 only. Used when working with Linux permissions using the **umask** or the **chmod** commands.

octet—A portion of an IPv4 address consisting of eight bits (eight values of 0 or 1).

OpenStack—An open source cloud solution that is rapidly becoming the de facto standard in cloud computing and offers infrastructure as a service.

openSUSE—A community distribution sponsored by SUSE Linux GmbH and other companies. It is widely used throughout the world, with thousands of developers. The focus of its development is creating usable open-source tools for software developers and system administrators, while providing a user-friendly desktop, and feature-rich server environment.

OR—A logical operation where the second command is executed only if the first command was not able to execute.

output module—In rsyslog, a module used to send log messages to a specific destination. Output modules make rsyslogd flexible and allow for the usage of log destinations not native to rsyslog.

ownership—In file system permissions, the effective permissions that a user has are based on ownership. Every file has a user owner and a group owner assigned to it.

package—A software bundle used to distribute files such as executables, libraries, and documentation. A package typically contains a compressed archive of files and metadata that includes instructions on how to install those files.

package group—A group of packages that can be installed as such, using the yum **group install** command.

package managers—Systems such as APT and RPM that install software and keep track of what's currently installed.

pager—A program that can be used to browse page by page through a text file. The less utility provides one of the most common Linux pagers.

PAM—See pluggable authentication modules.

parent shell—The environment from which a shell script or program is started. Processes or child scripts inherit settings from the parent shell.

partition—A subdivision of a hard disk on which a file system can be created to mount it into the directory structure.

password—A token used in authentication. The password is a secret word that can be set by individual users and is stored in an encrypted way.

passphrase—Basically a password, but longer and more secure than a password.

path—The complete reference to the location of a file.

PE—See physical extent.

peripherals—Devices, such as printers and monitors, that connect to the computer.

permission trios—The permission sets for the object user owner, group owner, and others.

permissions—Attributes that can be set on files or directories to allow users or groups access to these files or directories.

permissive—A mode in SELinux where nothing is blocked, but everything is logged in the audit log. This mode is typically used for troubleshooting SELinux issues.

physical backup—A backup where the files containing the actual data are written to the backup. Physical backups are more difficult to create than logical backups, but at the same time are more reliable.

physical extent—A component of logical volume management. A physical volume, such as a disk, is split into blocks called physical extents. The physical extents form the basis of logical volumes.

physical volume—The foundation building block of an LVM configuration. The physical volume typically corresponds to a partition or a complete disk device.

PID—See process identification number.

pipe—A structure that can be used to forward the output of one command to be used as input for another command.

pluggable authentication modules (PAM)—A collection of libraries designed to provide the administrator with the means to change how user accounts are authenticated.

policy—See SELinux policy.

port—A number associated with a service. The service listens for incoming network packets assigned to the port number.

Portable Operating System Interface (POSIX)—A standard created to maintain compatibility between operating systems. The standard mainly applies to UNIX and guarantees that different flavors of Linux and UNIX are compatible to one another.

The POSIX standard goes relatively deep and defines how exactly programs should operate to maintain optimal compatibility. Other operating systems are partially POSIX compliant as well, including different Windows versions.

positional parameters—The shell variables, $1, $2, and so forth, that represent the arguments passed to a script or function.

POSIX—See Portable Operating System Interface.

port forwarding—A firewalling technique where traffic coming in on a specific port is forwarded to another port, which may be on the same host as well as on a different host.

portmap—The port mapper is a remote procedure call service that needs to run on systems that provide RPC services. Portmapper uses dynamic ports that do not correspond to specific TCP or UDP ports; the service picks a UDP or TCP port that is used as long as the process is active. When restarted, chances are that different ports are used. They need to be mapped to fixed UDP and TCP ports to make it possible to open the firewall for these ports. Portmapper is still used by components of the NFS service.

portal—In iSCSI, a portal is the IP address and ports on which iSCSI target services are available.

Postfix—A mail transfer agent, originally built by IBM, that is split into separate components to enhance security.

primary group—Every Linux user is a member of a primary group. When creating files, the primary group is assigned as the group owner of the file.

primary key—The main index for a database table.

primary partition—In MBR, one of a maximum of four partitions that can be created in the master boot record. See also extended partition.

principal—In Kerberos, refers to the entity that can be identified and verified using Kerberos credentials.

print queue—A list of print jobs waiting to be printed.

print spooler—The component responsible for taking the next job off the print queue and sending it to the printer.

priority—In rsyslog, used to specify the severity of a logged event. Based on the severity, specific actions can be taken.

In process handling, specifies the importance of a process. Process priority is expressed with a number (which can be modified using nice). Processes with a lower priority number are serviced before processes with a higher priority number.

private key—A key used to decrypt data that has been encrypted with the public keys.

privileged user—See root.

proc—A kernel interface that provides access to kernel information and kernel tunables. This interface is available through the /proc file system.

process—A task running on a Linux machine. Roughly, a process corresponds to a program, although one program can start multiple processes.

process identification number (PID)—A unique number used to identify a process running on a Linux system.

protocol—A set of rules used in computing, for instance, in computer networking to establish communications between two computers.

pseudo root file system—In NFSv4, refers to a solution where multiple shares are exported by an NFS server. Instead of mounting each individual share, the NFS client mounts the root file system on the NFS server, which gives access to all shares he is entitled to.

pseudofilesystem—A directory that looks like a regular filesystem, but is not backed by files but resides in RAM. For example, /proc exposes kernel settings and the process listing as a pseudofilesystem.

public key—A key provided to other users and hosts used to encrypt data. This data, when returned to the original host, can be decrypted by the private key.

PV—See physical volume.

queue—In process management, the queue is used for processes waiting before they can be executed.

Qmail—A mail transfer agent written to be secure and easy to use.

RAID—See Redundant Array of Independent Disks.

RCP—See remote copy.

realm—An authentication domain in Kerberos.

real time clock—A hardware component on the motherboard that keeps time even when the computer is off.

reboot—The procedure of stopping the computer and starting it again.

record—In relational databases, a collection of fields that together are used to store data about one object in the database.

recursion—In DNS, recursion happens when one name server isn't capable of resolving DNS requests and needs to forward the request to another name server. In file systems, recursion refers to including the contents of a subdirectory, as in **ls -R**.

Red Hat Package Manager—The name for the package format used on Red Hat for software packages, as well as for the package management software. RPM has become the standard for package management on many other Linux distributions as well.

Redundant Array of Independent Disks (RAID)—A method of using regular disks to build a larger and more reliable set of disks, such as by mirroring writes to two separate disks.

reference clock—A clock used as a time source in an NTP time configuration. Typically a reference clock is a highly reliable clock on the Internet, but it can be an internal clock on the computer's motherboard as well.

regular expression—A search pattern that allows users to search text patterns in a flexible way. Not to be confused with shell metacharacters.

relational database—A database that models entities as tables and allows you to write queries that join and aggregate multiple tables.

relative path—The location of a file specified as an offset from the current working directory.

relay—A mail system that takes mail from one system and sends it to another, rather than delivering the email to a mailbox.

relay host—In email traffic, a host that messages are forwarded to. Relay hosts are used to prevent all clients from having to send out messages for themselves. The advantage of using relay hosts, is that it is much easier to secure them, as security efforts can be focused on one or a limited number of hosts.

remote copy—A software program that allows users to copy files to and from a remote system. Unfortunately, this process sends data in plain text, making it a poor method.

Remote Procedure Calls (RPC)—A method for interprocess communication that allows a program to execute code in another address space. Remote Procedure Calls is an old protocol and as such is still used in the Network File System.

repository—An installation source that contains installable packages as well as an index that contains information about the installable packages so that the installation program yum can compare the version of packages currently installed with the version of packages available in the repository.

Request For Comments (RFC)—A publication that defines a standard, such as a protocol like IP.

resident memory—Memory pages in use by a program.

resolver—The DNS client part that contains a list of DNS servers to contact to resolve DNS queries.

resource record—An entry in the DNS database. Multiple types of resource records exist, of which the Address (A) resource record takes care of translating names to IP addresses.

RFC—See Request For Comments.

rich rules—Rules in firewalld that allow the usage of a more complicated syntax so that more complex rules can be defined.

root—The privileged user account used for system administration tasks. User root has access to all capabilities, which means that permissions don't apply to the user root, which means that the root user account is virtually unlimited.

root directory—The starting point of the file system hierarchy, noted as /.

root filesystem—The filesystem that contains the root (/) directory.

Ross—See Monkeyboy.

RPC—See Remote Procedure Calls.

RPM—See RedHat Package Manager.

RTC—See real time clock.

runner—In network teaming, refers to the protocol used to send packets over the different interfaces in the network team configuration.

Samba—The name for the Linux service that implements the SMB protocol.

SAN—See Storage Area Network.

scheduler—The part of the Linux kernel that monitors the queue of runnable processes and allocates CPU time to these processes.

Scientific Linux—A Linux distribution based on the Red Hat packages from which the Red Hat logo has been removed. Scientific Linux is primarily used by US government research organizations and is a good choice for people looking for a freely available alternative to Red Hat Enterprise Linux.

secondary group—A group that a user is a member of, but for which membership is not defined in the /etc/passwd file. When creating new files, the secondary group does not automatically become the owner of those files. Users can access files via permissions when using a secondary group.

secure shell—A solution that allows users to open a shell on a remote server, where security is implemented by using public/private key cryptography.

SELinux—A Linux kernel security module that provides a mechanism for supporting access control security policies.

sendmail—One of the original mail transfer agents.

Server Message Blocks (SMB)—An application level protocol used to provide shared access to files, printers, and serial ports, which on Linux is implemented in the Samba server.

ServerRoot—In Apache, refers to the location where server configuration files are expected to be found.

services—In systemd: Processes that need to be started to provide specific functionality. In firewalld: A configuration of firewall settings used to allow access to specific processes.

SetGID—A special permission set in which a command executes using the privileges of the group owner of the command.

SetUID—A special permission set in which a command executes using the privileges of the user owner of the command.

SGID—See SetGID.

Shadow Suite—A system function that allows for the encrypted passwords on the system to be kept in the much more secure /etc/shadow file instead of the less secure and often publicly available /etc/passwd file. Group passwords are also made more secure, being relocated from the public /etc/group file to the more secure /etc/gshadow file.

share—A directory to which remote access is configured using a remote file system protocol such as NFS or CIFS.

shared object—A library used by multiple applications and linked at runtime by the dynamic linker. Shared object files almost always end in .so.

shebang—Used in a script to indicate which shell should be used for executing the code in the shell script. If no shebang is used, the script code is interpreted by the parent shell, which may lead to errors in some cases. A shebang starts with a #, which is followed by a ! and the complete path name of the shell, such as #!/bin/bash.

shell—The environment from which commands can be executed. Bash is the default shell on Linux, but other shells exist as well.

shell metacharacters—Characters such as *, ?, and [a-z] that allow users to refer to characters in file names in a flexible way.

signal—An instruction that can be sent to a process. Common signals exist, such as SIGTERM and SIGKILL, but the Linux kernel allows a total of 32 different signals to be used. To send a signal to a process, the **kill** command can be used.

Simple Mail Transfer Protocol (SMTP)—A text based protocol that allows different mail transfer agents to send mail between themselves.

skel template—A directory used to populate a new user account's home directory with files.

SMB—See Server Message Blocks.

SMTP—See Simple Mail Transfer Protocol.

software time—See system time.

source context—In SELinux, a context is a label that identifies allowed operations. Everything in an SELinux environment has a context. The source context is the context of the processes or users that initiate an action.

source RPM—A package containing source code and the instructions on how to build the source into a binary.

sourcing—Reading in or running a script in the context of the current shell rather than a subshell. Scripts that are sourced can alter the current environment, as opposed to scripts that are executed and affect only a subshell and its environment.

SQL—See Structured Query Language.

SSH—See secure shell.

SSH tunneling—A technique where a secure connection is created using SSH, which can be used to send data in a secured way.

standard error—The default location where a program sends error messages to.

standard input—The default location where a program gets its input from.

standard output—The default location where a program sends its regular output to.

static linking—Taking code from common libraries and making it a part of the runnable application, rather than something brought in from a shared library.

static route—A route defined manually by a network administrator.

STDERR—See standard error.

STDIN—See standard input.

STDOUT—See standard output.

sticky bit—A special permission set that modifies the meaning of the write permission on a directory so that the only user who can delete a file in the directory is the file owner, the directory owner, or the root user. Historically, the sticky bit was used to keep a program resident in memory, not allowing it to be swapped to disk.

Storage Area Network (SAN)—A solution where disk devices are shared at a block level over the network. As such they can be used in the same way as local disk devices on a Linux system. iSCSI and Fiber Channel are the common SAN protocols.

storage backend—In iSCSI, the storage device used on the iSCSI target behind the LUN that provides access to the shared block devices to iSCSI initiators.

stratum 1 server—A network time protocol server that has a reference clock.

strings—A collection of characters, such as "hello," as opposed to a numeric type like an integer or a date.

Structured Query Language (SQL)—A language used to query and manipulate relational databases.

subdomain—In DNS, a subdivision of any domain. In the domain example.com, example is a subdomain of the top level domain .com.

subnet mask—A logical subdivision of an IP network.

subnetting—The process of using a network mask to define the network part of the IP address.

subshell—A shell started from another shell. Typically, by running a shell script a subshell is started.

SUID—See SetUID.

SUSE—SUSE is the original provider of the enterprise Linux distribution and the most interoperable platform for mission-critical computing.

SUSE Linux Enterprise—SUSE Linux Enterprise or SLE refers to the commercial and supported version of SUSE Linux's distributions. The SUSE Linux Enterprise suite of options includes SUSE Linux Cloud based on OpenStack, SUSE Linux Storage, SUSE Linux for SAP and many other options.

superblock—A structure on the filesystem that contains pointers to other important parts on the filesystem, such as directories and inodes.

swap—To take memory and put it on to disk so that the system can offer more memory to applications than actually exists on the computer.

swap partition—A slice of the disk dedicated to swap.

swappiness—The willingness of the Linux kernel to move memory pages from physical RAM to swap. Swappiness is set as a parameter in the /proc/sys/vm directory, which can be modified to tune the swap behavior.

symbolic link—A special type of file that contains a reference to another file or directory in the form of an absolute or relative path.

symbolic mode—A method using symbols for setting object permissions.

sysctl—A service used on system startup to allow kernel tunables to be set automatically, or to set kernel tunables manually and to display the parameters currently in use.

sysfs—The kernel interface mounted on the /sys directory and used to provide access to parameters that can be used for managing hardware settings.

systemd—The service manager on RHEL 7. systemd is the first process that starts after the kernel has loaded, and it takes care of starting all other processes and services on a Linux system.

system clock—The clock that the Linux kernel keeps, as opposed to the hardware clock on the motherboard.

system time—The time maintained by the operating system. When a Linux system boots, system time is set to the current hardware time, and while the operating system is running, it is often synchronized using the Network Time Protocol.

table—A collection of rows and columns for a SQL database.

tainted kernel—A kernel in which unsupported kernel modules have been loaded.

target—In systemd: A collection of unit files that can be loaded all together.

target context—The SELinux context set to a target object, such as a port, file, or directory.

TCP—See Transmission Control Protocol.

TCP wrappers—A library designed to allow the administrator the means to secure network-based services by using the /etc/hosts.allow and /etc/hosts.deny configuration files.

teaming—In networking, refers to a technique that allows multiple network interfaces to be joined in a trunked network interface. Network teaming is used for increased performance, as well as increased redundancy.

Telnet—A software program that allows for connection to remote systems. Unfortunately, this connection is sent in plain text, making it a poor method.

terminal—Originally, the screen used by a user to type commands on. On modern Linux systems, pseudo terminals can be used as a replacement. A pseudo terminal offers a shell window from which users enter the commands that need to be executed.

TFTP—See Trivial File Transfer Protocol.

TGT—See ticket granting ticket.

thrashing—When memory is swapped back and forth from disk too often, the system is slowed down.

thread—A thread can be used as a subdivision of a process. Many processes are single threaded, which means that it is basically one entity that needs to be serviced. On a multicore or multi-CPU computer system, it makes sense working with multithreaded processes. If that is the case, the different cores can be used to handle the different threads, which allows a process to benefit from multicore or multithreaded environments.

ticket granting ticket (TGT)—In a Kerberos environment, a small encrypted identification file that a Kerberos user or service may use to get access to services in a Kerberized environment.

time stamp—An identifier that can be used on files, database records, and other types of data to identify when the last modification has been applied. Many services rely on time stamps. To ensure that time stamped based systems work properly, time synchronization needs to be configured.

time synchronization—A system that ensures that multiple servers are using the exact same time. To accomplish time synchronization, it is common to use an external time server, as defined in the Network Time Protocol (NTP).

time to live (TTL)—In IP traffic, the time to live defines how long a packet must stay alive until it is discarded. Time to live is expressed as the number of routers that can be passed as a maximum. In DNS, time to live refers to the maximum amount of time that DNS information is allowed to be kept in cache before it needs to be requested again.

time zone—A set of locations that share a common time, measured in an offset from the universal coordinated time.

TLS—See Transport Layer Security.

top level domain—In Domain Name System, the top level domain identifies the highest level of DNS domain names. Originally there was a limited amount of top level domains available (such as .com, .org, and .net), but this amount has recently been extended.

Transmission Control Protocol (TCP)—Focuses on the transport of data packages. TCP differs from UDP in that the data packages are considered "reliable" because TCP performs error checking to make sure all data packages arrive at the destination.

Transport Layer Security (TLS)—A cryptographic protocol created to ensure secured communications over a computer network. In TLS public and private keys are used, as well as certificates that authenticate the counterparty.

Trivial File Transfer Protocol (TFTP)—A service used on installation servers and in other environments. The server that needs to be installed will boot from the network card, using PXE boot. The DHCP server is the first to answer to this PXE boot, by providing an IP address. Next, the DHCP server redirects the request to the TFTP server, which provides a boot image.

TTL—See time to live.

TTY—A program that provides a virtual terminal on Linux. Every terminal still has a TTY name, which is either tty1-6 for virtual TTYs, or /dev/pts/0-nn for pseudo terminals.

UCS-2—A format that attempts to define all characters in 2 bytes (65,536 combinations).

Udev—A service that works together with the Linux kernel to initialize hardware.

UDP—See User Datagram Protocol.

UEFI—Unified Extensible Firmware Interface. See Extensible Firmware Interface.

UID—See user identification number.

ulimit—A feature that allows the administrator to limit access to system resources for users and groups.

umask—An octal value that defines the default permissions as a shell property.

umask value—A value applied to the default permissions for files and directories when creating a new file or directory. The umask modifies the permissions placed on the new file or directory.

unbound—The name of the DNS service on RHEL 7 that can be used as a caching only DNS name server.

unit—In systemd, refers to an item managed by systemd. Different types of units exist, including service, path, mount, and target units.

Universal Time Coordinated (UTC)—A time standard that is globally the same, no matter which specific time zone a user is in. Universal Time Coordinated corresponds to Greenwich Mean Time.

Universal Unique ID (UUID)—An identification number that consists of a long random hexadecimal number and is globally unique.

unmount—The process that needs to be performed to decouple a storage device from the directory it is mounted on.

unprivileged user—A regular non-root user account, to which access restrictions as applied by permissions do apply.

Upstart—The system used in RHEL 6 to start services during system initialization. It is similar in features to systemd as an improvement over init.

UPG—See user private group.

user—An entity used on Linux to provide access to specific system resources. Users can be used to represent people, but many services also have a dedicated user account, which allows the service to run with the specific permissions needed for that service.

User Datagram Protocol (UDP)—Focuses on the transport of data packages. It is often contrasted with TCP as they both perform similar functions. UDP differs from TCP in that the data packages are sent "connectionless," so no error checking is performed.

user identification number (UID)—A unique number assigned to a user account.

user private group (UPG)—A technique in which new users are assigned their own private group that matches their user name.

user space—The area of memory accessible by application software that has been started with non-root privileges.

UTC—See Universal Time Coordinated.

UTF-16—A character encoding format that encodes all characters in a variable width using blocks of 16 bits. That is, characters are either 2 or 4 bytes each.

UTF-8—A character encoding format that encodes all characters in a variable width using blocks of 8 bits. That is, characters are from 1-4 bytes long. UTF-8 is also backward compatible to 8 bit ASCII.

UUID—See Universal Unique ID.

variable—A label that corresponds to a location in memory that contains a specific value that can be changed dynamically. In scripting, variables are frequently used to allow the script to be flexible.

version control system—Software that tracks changes to files over time and can be used to see history or revert to older versions of a file.

Vfat—The Linux kernel driver used to access FAT based file systems. FAT is a commonly used file system in Windows environments. The Linux Vfat driver allows usage of this file system.

VG—See volume group.

virsh—A shell interface that allows for management of KVM virtual machines and their environment.

virtual host—In the Apache web server, a collection of configuration settings used to address a web server. What makes it a virtual host is that one installation of the Apache web server can be configured with multiple virtual hosts, which allows administrators to run multiple websites on one Apache server.

virtual machine guest—An emulated computer that runs on a virtual machine host. The guest thinks it is running on real hardware.

virtual machine host—A server that runs multiple guests. The guests don't know other guests are running on the same hardware. Most computers don't run at full capacity so you're getting more use out of a smaller number of servers.

virtual memory—Memory given to a computer but that can be transparently moved to disk by the kernel if needed.

volume group—A collection of physical volumes in a logical volume manager system. You can then split up the volume group into logical volumes on which you make filesystems.

want—An indication for a systemd unit file that it is supposed to be started from a specific systemd target.

Web Server Gateway Interface (WSGI)—A specification for a uniform interface between web servers and web server applications or framework for the Python programming language.

wildcard—The * metacharacter, which in a shell environment is referred to an unlimited amount of any characters.

window manager—A software program that controls the look and feel of a GUI environment.

WSGI—See Web Server Gateway Interface.

XFS—A high-performance 64-bit file system created in 1993 by SGI and is the default file system in some distributions.

xinetd—The Internet Superservice. This is a service that listens for incoming connections on other managed services. These managed services are started by xinetd when their service is needed, and they are be shut down when they are needed no longer.

Xorg—A software program that acts as a server, allowing client programs to display graphically. This program interfaces with hardware devices such as the video card, mouse, and keyboard.

Yellowdog Update Manager (YUM)—The meta package handler that on RHEL 7 is used to install packages from yum repositories.

Yum—See Yellowdog Update Manager.

zone—In firewalld, a collection of one or more network interfaces that specific firewalld rules are associated with.

Index

Numbers

A

D

F

H

I

O

T

X

Y

Z

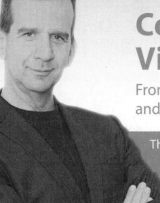

CompTIA Linux+ / LPIC-1 Video Training

SAVE 40%
CODE: LPIC40

From **SANDER VAN VUGT:** Expert author, trainer, and instructor with more than 20 years of experience

These unique products include
- Live trainer discussions
- CLI presentations
- Live demos
- Whiteboard teaching
- Detailed exam explanations

The *Complete Video Course* also includes
- Interactive hands-on exercises
- Multiple-choice quizzes

livelessons◉
video instruction from technology experts

CompTIA
Linux+ / LPIC-1
Complete
Video Course
SBN: 9780789756572

PIC-1 (Exam 101)
LiveLessons:
Linux Professional
nstitute Certification
Covers the LPIC-1
Exam 101) and the
CompTIA Linux+
LX0-103 Exams
SBN: 9780789754547

PIC-1 (Exam 102)
LiveLessons:
Linux Professional
nstitute Certification
Covers the LPIC-1
Exam 102) and the
CompTIA Linux+
LX0-104 Exams
SBN: 9780789754776

Complete Video Course
CompTIA Linux+ / LPIC-1
Sander van Vugt
livelessons◉

livelessons◉
LPIC-1 (Exam 101)
Sander van Vugt
video

livelessons◉
LPIC-1 (Exam 102)
Sander van Vugt
video

- These unique video products provide a solid understanding of all topics that candidates need to master to pass the CompTIA Linux+ / LPIC-1 certifications.

- CompTIA Linux+ / LPIC-1 Complete Video Course offers 28 lessons that cover every objective in the CompTIA Linux+ LX0-103 and LX0-104 and the LPIC-1 101 and 102 exams. You also receive practice exam questions, interactive exercises, and CLI simulations so you can practice your skills and knowledge before taking the exams.

- Each course doesn't just offer a preparation for the exams; they also serve as an introduction for people who want to learn basic Linux administration skills.

- Each video provides thorough coverage of command-line skills that work on multiple distributions and prepares anyone who wants to acquire more in-depth knowledge of common Linux administration tasks.

- The course can be used to study for the newest CompTIA Linux+ LX0-103 and LX0-104 exams, the LPIC-1 (Exam 101) and LPIC-1 (Exam 102) certifications, and the SUSE CLA exams.

SAVE 40%
CODE: LPIC40

COMPTIA LINUX+ / LPIC-1 VIDEO TRAINING
Save 40% – Use coupon code LPIC40
PearsonITcertification.com

AYS LEARNING

PEARSON

To receive your 10% off Exam Voucher, register your product at:

www.pearsonitcertification.com/register

and follow the instructions.